A CRITICAL ANTHOLOGY OF SPANISH VERSE

A CRITICAL ANTHOLOGY *of* SPANISH VERSE

Compiled and Edited

BY

E. ALLISON PEERS

PROFESSOR OF SPANISH IN THE UNIVERSITY OF LIVERPOOL

UNIVERSITY OF CALIFORNIA PRESS

Berkeley and Los Angeles

1950

PREFACE

THE principle which has governed the compilation of this book is the desire to foster, not merely a wider acquaintance with Spanish verse, but a better understanding and a deeper appreciation of it. Almost anyone can throw together the most familiar poems in a language, garnish them with a few biographical notes on their authors, and serve, complete with an index of first lines, in a tasty binding. But no anthology of Spanish verse, so far as I am aware, includes even a brief study of each of the poems selected as well as a survey of the field as a whole.

The length of the general commentary which I have given upon each author is, with a few exceptions, proportionate to his merit, but no rule can be laid down as to the length of the commentary upon each poem. Sometimes the poem has not lent itself to a commentary at all; sometimes several poems by a single author have been so similar in character as to be best treated together. What has all the time been kept in view is the most effective method of stimulating the reader to criticism and appreciation. Except where a clear and close relationship exists between the author's life and work, the commentaries include no biography, which any history of Spanish literature will supply. The emphasis has all the time been laid upon the content of the author's work—it is to be hoped with advantage.

Though the reader is assumed to have a good knowledge of Spanish, he is not envisaged as an erudite, and these pages will be found to contain no discussions on sources or variant readings, which will often be dealt with in the editions enumerated in the Appendix. Such discussions would frequently have touched questions of great interest to the scholar but would have allowed less space for the poems themselves and for concentration upon their intrinsic qualities.

The great problem attending the compilation of the anthology has been one of selection, for so vast and varied a field would require many volumes to do it the barest justice. I have begun by rigidly excluding (with the few exceptions universally admitted and familiar to all students) Spanish-American verse, which demands a separate volume, and also verse in the languages of Portugal, Galicia, Euzkadi, Catalonia and Valencia. Apart from songs, sonnets and other purely lyrical poems which occur in the course of dramas, no dramatic extracts are admitted: these, too, can only be satisfactorily treated in an independent volume. A more difficult aspect of this problem has been the treatment of long poems. Wherever possible, the entire poem has been included, even though this may have meant the exclusion of some other: it has seemed better to print five out of six such poems as they stand and to omit the sixth than to print five-sixths of all of them. On this principle a few outstanding poems have had to be sacrificed, such as Garcilaso's elegies and Quevedo's Epistle to Olivares. Where—as with *Mío Cid*, the *Araucana* and the *Moro expósito*—excerption was unavoidable, the passages included have been made as substantial as possible.

Considerable thought has been expended on the presentation of the extracts from mediaeval poetry, especially as regards spelling and punctuation. In the selections from the *Cantar de Mío Cid*, I follow the best of authorities, Sr. Menéndez Pidal, and after Jorge Manrique I modernize entirely, save for occasional archaisms the preservation of which gives the language colour and in places where modernization would interfere with scansion or rhyme. Between those limits (*i.e.*, from Nos. 6 to 51), I have attempted a partial modernization, deferring on the one hand to the characteristic form of my originals and on the other to the convenience of the reader. Specifically, I have retained the forms *nn* or *n* (using *ñ*, however, in the later mediaeval extracts), *nb*, *np*, *qu* and intervocalic *ss*. Vocalic *v*, *y* are written as *u*, *i*; consonantal *i*, *u*, as *j*, *v*; initial *ff*, *rr*, *ss* as *f*, *r*, *s*; *c* as *ç* before *a*, *o*, *u*, *r*, and as z before *e*, *i*. When not etymological, *h* is suppressed, but it is always written in *he*, *has*, *ha*, etc. Accents are used where necessary to indicate pronunciation, but the termination *ién* is shown as *ien*. Where any of these usages is not observed, the student will generally at once see the reason. The only late author whom I have not attempted to modernize is Herrera. I should add that, not only in the older but also in the more modern authors, the punctuation of standard editions is arbitrary and often meaningless, and I have had to revise it freely.

I am deeply grateful to the contemporary authors, and to their representatives or executors—some of them friends of many years' standing, some complete strangers to me—who have generously allowed me to make use of copyright material. The difficulty experienced, first during the Spanish Civil War and then during the World War, in getting into communication with a few of these, and the obstacles which recent conditions have presented to the publication of a book of this size, will explain why I have apparently been slow in taking advantage of permissions given me some years since. Impediments to contact, too, will, I trust, excuse the possible infringement of copyright in a few cases where my repeated attempts to trace its owners have been fruitless.

E. A. P.

CONTENTS

PAGE

THE ROMANCERO.

I. ROMANCES HISTÓRICOS.

II. ROMANCES DEL CICLO CAROLINGIO.

III. ROMANCES NOVELESCOS Y LÍRICOS.

INTRODUCTION

THERE was a time, long ago, when the fact of Spain's El Dorado—her golden Indies at the other end of the rainbow—seemed stranger and more wonderful than any fiction; when Spain herself was a symbol of vision and adventure—

> of most disastrous chances,
> Of moving accidents by flood and field,
> Of hair-breadth scapes i' the imminent deadly breach.

of

> antres vast and deserts idle,
> Rough quarries, rocks, and hills whose heads touch heaven.

The awestruck foreigner of those days had indeed reason to build his imaginative castles in Spain. It was not long, however, before they became—to use the Spaniard's own phrase—" castles in the wind." To-day the material glory has departed—perhaps for ever. But the vision and the adventurousness of that most fearless race still cling to Spanish poetry, which outshines even the wealth of the Incas and surpasses it in its inexhaustible variety.

I

Like all the art of a country of paradox and surprise, Spanish verse defies generalization and eludes every attempt made to define it.

In part this elusive quality is due to the sharpness of the divisions between the regions of a land so deeply cleft in all directions by mountains. San Ignacio de Loyola as a mystic and a religious organizer; Unamuno as a poet, a philosopher and an essayist; Baroja as a novelist; Zuloaga as a painter—these are not so much " Spaniards " as Basques. Cervantes noticeably, and Santa Teresa and San Juan de la Cruz most markedly, are, despite the universality of their genius, Castilian. Velázquez, though he belongs to the whole world, belongs in a more intimate sense to his native Seville. So, more strongly, does the less universal Murillo; while countless men of letters—such as Herrera, Góngora,

Rivas, Juan Ramón Jiménez and the Álvarez Quinteros—are, if judged by their writings, Andalusians first and Spaniards a long way after. And, strange to say, the last hundred years, during which more rapid communications have brought the regions into easier reach of one another, have seen an intensification of specifically regional art. No earlier writer is more Galician than Valle-Inclán, more Asturian than Palacio Valdés, more Montañés than Pereda, more Levantine than Miró. While Madrid, which has always produced a type of writer *muy suyo*—very much its own—has not been content with such great names as Lope de Vega, Calderón, Larra and Benavente, but has adopted writers of all types from all parts of Spain.

Even if we leave out of account the literatures, mediaeval and modern, created by several of these regions in their own languages—which are quite distinct from the Castilian now generally known as "Spanish"—we shall find an incredible degree of divergence between one region and another. In all essentials, Catalans are more like Gascons, and Kentish men more like Normans, than Aragonese are like Andalusians and men of Valencia like men of Vigo.

In the second place, considering Spain as a whole, or limiting our survey to those Spaniards whose native tongue is Castilian, we find a number of characteristics—some purely literary, some not—which militate against any kind of generalization.

There is, for example, the immense fertility of the Spaniard, his extreme agility of mind, his incredible industry, his resourcefulness in every kind of invention. For actual productiveness, the palm would probably go to Andalusia, home of such prolific nonentities as Fernández y González in the novel and Rodríguez Rubí in drama. But of productiveness and quality combined there are examples all over Spain—most of them found in its *corazón de roble*, the arid but invigorating land of Castile. How can one generalize about Lope de Vega, with his five hundred extant dramas, and his non-dramatic work overflowing into twenty-one volumes? Or about Calderón, who wrote more than five times as many plays as Shakespeare? Or about Zorrilla, with his dramas in two parts and ten acts, his long, rambling narratives in formless verse and his wealth of lyricism? Or about the critic Menéndez y Pelayo, who died at fifty-five, yet whose complete works can barely be contained in sixty large volumes? Even if, as in this sketch, we ignore the vast and growing literatures of Spanish America, we are left with a body of purely Peninsular work so immense that no man can ever read more than the minutest fraction of it. Where totals are unimaginably great, who shall say which of them is greatest? Whatever we look for in Spanish literature, we shall not fail to find, and to find in substantial quantity.

Then, again, generalization is precluded by the Spaniards' dislike of making divisions between the genres and love of breaking down any which tradition has succeeded in establishing. There are modern essayists who in essentials are lyric poets, just as once there were so-called poets who were no more than verse essayists. There are poems which must technically be classed as narrative, since they are built upon a story, but the whole beauty and appeal of which lie in qualities that are pictorial or lyrical. Above all, there is the Spaniard's temperamental tendency to transform everything into drama. A narrative poem, an essay, a novel, a short story, may turn into drama as one turns a page. Much of the appeal of the ballads derives from their being essentially dramatic. The worst plays may owe redeeming, even outstanding, moments to their author's inbred sensitiveness to the dramatic. Therefore it is from the dramatic standpoint that Spanish literature must more often be judged than comes naturally to an Englishman.

But the most elusive—and even mystifying—trait in Spanish literature, which derives from the very heart and core of the Spanish character, is its blending of idealism with realism. Except in Galicia, where it is apt to be unpractical and dreamy, Spanish idealism is the most definite manifestation imaginable of pronounced personality. The Spaniard's goal is always straight ahead, always clear-cut and distinct—sometimes deceptively so. Towards it he will press persistently and confidently; to reach it he will make any sacrifices. And yet, though by comparison he is indifferent to the material amenities which most people demand of life, he never loses his sense of the reality of the world around him. He cares little for abstractions: he is tremendously attracted by the concrete. His children know no "fairy" tales: the touchstone of the child's story is "Did it really happen?" His hero, to use a phrase famous in Spanish, is "the man of flesh and bones." In the history, in the literature and in the painting of Spain, the outstanding things are the figures of men and women. If we are to understand Spanish poetry, we must learn to understand the man whose feet are planted firmly upon the earth while his eyes are no less firmly fixed upon Heaven. We must take equal notice of his stance and of his gaze—and it is so deceptively easy for the critic to concentrate exclusively upon the one or upon the other!

One could say much more about this—it is the surest of all keys to an appreciation of Spanish literature—but its bearing upon our present subject will be sufficiently clear. Not only because Spanish verse is so vast a treasury is it hard to characterize as a whole, not only because it embraces so many types which are so inextricably intertwined, but because it reflects an essential trait in the Spanish character which at first seems incomprehensible but on examination proves to be only of a strange and unfamiliar subtlety. In its most complicated forms it will appear again and again in the poems which follow, but for the moment we shall only observe that it has facilitated the development, to a very high degree, of two types of verse—the lyric, in which the ideal attains its fullest and noblest expression, and the narrative, which gives scope for a love of the concrete, and for the representation, in habit as he lived, of the man of flesh and bones.

II

What do we mean by lyric poetry? Without, at least, some working idea of this we can hardly discuss Spanish lyricism with any degree of intelligibility. Not, following a conventional notion, mere song-poetry. Not, following the French, any kind of poetry whatever which is subjective. Rather a type of verse which gives the fullest possible scope to the essential quality of poetry—to the "substance" that remains after any such accidental elements as the dramatic, the narrative, the didactic, have been distilled away. And that essential quality seems to arise from a creative impulse which releases a spiritual energy, of greater or lesser intensity, communicable to other human beings by means of the literary art. Neither wholly aesthetic, nor wholly objective, nor wholly personal, it is unique of its kind. It implies emotion, though this may often be latent in a whole poem rather than overt and perceptible in any one part of it, or may be veiled from ordinary perceptions by a restraint which adds greatly to the poem's beauty. Obviously this definition is incomplete, as are definitions of heat, light and other forms of energy in the world of matter. In the realms of the spirit exactness is even less possible. The poet Juan Ramón Jiménez has aptly remarked that the best definition of poetry can be found in three lines which were written by a much earlier poet in an attempt to describe something else :

Su origen no lo sé, pues no lo tiene . . . .
Sé que no puede ser cosa tan bella . . . .
Bien sé que suelo en ella no se halla.[1]

Poetry lives—and, if my definition is accurate, lyricism lives—not by mere music, nor by mere emotion, any more than by mere description or mere anecdote, but by a spiritual energy which vouchsafes to us what Jiménez calls " entradas y salidas de lo temporal en lo eterno."[2] If that be so, the Spanish genius, with its blending of the ideal and the real, ought to have a strong propensity to the lyric, and Gil Vicente's apostrophes to *marinero*, *caballero*, and *pastorcico* (p. 158) or San Juan de la Cruz's to *bosques*, *espesuras* and *prado* (p. 260) will be typical, and not exceptional, examples of a fusion of imagination with material reality.

And yet it is generally held, even by persons conversant with Peninsular culture, that Castilian literature is less lyrical than are the literatures of the surrounding regions of Catalonia, Galicia and Portugal. In one sense there is truth in this. A larger proportion of the verse literature of each of the three is non-dramatic and non-narrative. In Galicia and Portugal lyricism sets the tone for the mediaeval poetry of the entire Peninsula. The Portuguese narrative ballad is in essence an importation from Spain. Portuguese drama appears—and forthwith begins to languish ; and some of its greatest exponents, such as Gil Vicente, in the sixteenth century, and Almeida Garrett, in the nineteenth, are not so much dramatists as poets who wrote plays. Camoens, the greatest poet of the Peninsula, left a large body of lyrical verse as well as an epic which is in a high degree lyrical. A great part of contemporary Portuguese literature, and almost the whole of contemporary Galician, consists of lyric poetry ; and Catalan literature, since the Renaixença (which dates from the publication of a lyric poem, in 1833), has consisted predominantly of lyric poetry. The remaining genres

[1] San Juan de la Cruz. See "Poesía y literatura," in *University of Miami Hispanic-American Studies*, No. 2, January 1941, p. 83.

[2] *Ibid.*

need stimuli from France, Italy or Castile—or from Catalonia's own lyricism. Not without reason do Castilians credit every Catalan with being a poet. Iglesias and Guimerá are dramatists; Verdaguer made his name with narrative verse; Rusiñol is an essayist and a story-teller. But the greatest moments in the work of them all, and of most of their contemporaries, are purely lyrical.

Castilian literature can show nothing like the same proportion of lyric poetry to its total output, nor is there, in its verse, such a predominance of those types of emotion—*saudade* in Galician and Portuguese, *enyorança* in Catalan—which have been so largely responsible for giving its neighbours a reputation for undiluted lyricism. But one feels that its verse has no less of genuine lyric energy, and close study reveals at least three qualities of Castilian poetry which give it the greater force. First, there is its considerable diversity of subject. The Castilian finds inspiration, not merely in such time-honoured lyric themes as God and Nature, love and death, but in subjects of all kinds—unemotional, prosaic, even trivial and vulgar. Then there is the great variety of metres used in Castilian, from the long, irregular, bi-partite line of the twelfth-century *Cid* to the long, irregular, "free" line of *vanguardistas* like Rafael Alberti: native Spanish metres, Latin metres, Italian metres, French metres, idiosyncratic metres devised by authors fertile in invention—examples of them all would fill a book. And then there is the restraint which we find in Castilian poetry, corresponding to the *sosiego* of the Castilian temperament. For all its individualism, its passion for freedom and its frequent indifference to, and even aversion from, preoccupation with form, Castilian poetry often develops form to a very high degree. Expansive though it tends to be, it has sonnets ranking with any in European literature—and few forms demand stricter restraint than the sonnet. It has great single lines, notable now for the sharpening of emotion through some literary device:

Que para largo amor no hay breve olvido.[1]

Ya pasó mi dolor, ya sé qué es vida;[2]

now for a blend of melody and pathos:

Verme morir entre memorias tristes;[3]

[1] Lope de Vega: *Porfiar hasta morir*, III, vi.

[2] Herrera: *Elegías*, X.

[3] Garcilaso de la Vega: *Sonetos*, X. Cf. pp. 174-5, below.

now for really remarkable word-economy:

Lleva quien deja y vive el que ha vivido.[1]

Lyricism in Castilian poetry bubbles and springs up everywhere. The critic who once termed it a literary by-product[2] was right. Most of Spain's poets have been novelists, dramatists, essayists as well. Hardly any of them have even been simply and solely men of letters. Garcilaso de la Vega was a soldier and a courtier; Luis de León an Augustinian monk and a University professor; San Juan de la Cruz, a hard-working Carmelite friar. In our own day Unamuno held a Chair at León's University; Antonio Machado was a schoolmaster; Manuel Machado, a municipal librarian; Salinas and Guillén are professors in the United States. And as we go through Spanish libraries we find lyrics—not only, as in other literatures, scattered through novels and plays or embedded in didactic or narrative poetry, but dispersed over arid ascetic or glowing mystical treatises, illumining pictures of life in town or country, breaking into essays, commentaries, critical studies and I know not what besides. And of the reason for this anyone who has lived in Spain and mingled closely with the people is well aware. It is that in Spain lyric poetry is of the people, to be heard every day in streets, fields and workshops; for no lyrics are more rapturous or more poignant than the quatrains known as *coplas*, often familiar only to the regions which gave them birth—the crooning *villancicos*, the dancing *seguidillas*, the *saetas* which seek to cleave the heavens. Some of them have come down from the past, but many of them are but newly born. Lyricism in Spain is no mere accomplishment, or art, practised by erudite professionals—no "clerkly trade," or *mester de clerecía*, to use the mediaeval phrase. It is, of course, that, but it is also a natural, spontaneous uprising, and much of it is as truly popular as were the anonymous songs of the mediaeval minstrels, or *juglares*: a *mester de joglaría*, in short, still kept alive by the nameless many in the midst of a sophisticated age.

None the less, there have been several periods in Spanish history when lyric energy has been unusually active: some idea of the riches which these periods have created will be gained from the pages which follow.

[1] Antonio Machado: "A D. Francisco Giner de los Ríos." Cf. pp. 629-30, below.

[2] Aubrey F. G. Bell: *Castilian Literature*, Oxford, 1938, p. 107.

First, there was a period roughly coincident with the fifteenth century—a period when Berceo's artless songs already belonged to a distant past; when the lyric had not only emerged from anonymity but was becoming self-conscious; when themes grew on every bush and poets had only to pluck them; when graceful, if often slight and conventional, little poems were collected, without much thought as to order and sequence, in song-books (*Cancioneros*), some of which, having come down to us, will serve as evidence of their authors' fertility. This was the period when Villena, Mena and Micer Imperial went to school in ancient Rome and contemporary Italy; when the Marqués de Santillana wrote, not only his italianate sonnets and delicious native hill-songs, but also what is believed to be the first book in Spanish on the theory and history of poetry; above all, the period—approximately speaking—of the earliest of the ballads which were to be collected later in *Romanceros*. As narrative poems, these ballads fall to be considered in the following section; but, though many of them have no lyrical quality at all, others are in essence lyrics, with anecdote, as it were, lying on their surface; and in many others there are gleams and flashes of lyricism here and there.

The brevity, vitality, energy, vividness and dramatic tone of the ballads give full play to lyric emotion. This is often heightened by a few characteristic devices, such as repetition, parallelism and the introduction of a refrain, and by the choice of themes which lend themselves, not only, as do those of the *malcasada* (p. 147) and the *serranilla* (p. 69) to lyrical treatment, in the popular conventional sense, but to the permeation of the poem with really deep emotion. Such themes are patriotism—and at this time, it must be remembered, the Moors still held part of Spain; melancholy, often closely connected with the poignant vicissitudes of the War of Reconquest; love, generally turning on constancy in face of separation or peril; and the supernatural, with its insistence upon the marvellous, sometimes Christian in tone, but not infrequently secular or pagan. Many of the non-historical ballads give the impression of being lyrical, not only in fact, but in conception: that is to say, of being written to communicate a sentiment or an emotion, and not to tell a story at all.

As this period draws to a close, the date of which is marked approximately by Jorge Manrique's monumental elegy on the death of his father, Spain, touched by the spell of the Renaissance, is invaded by a new wave of lyricism. The influence of Italy, already considerable, now becomes a paramount force in Spanish poetry: not only sonnets, but verses of every kind, are "fechos al itálico modo" and the nationalistic movement, represented chiefly by Castillejo, is hard put to it to make a fight against the italianizers. The lesser men of this time, numerous though now forgotten, went even so far as to write in Italian; the greater poets, however, while receiving and absorbing Italian influences, preserved their own individuality; and in two of these, Boscán and Garcilaso de la Vega, Spanish poetry rose to the highest pitch of excellence that it had yet attained.

Though Boscán, a few years the older of the two, has been rated less highly than he merits, by far the greater—as an inspired singer, as a technical artist and as a man—was Garcilaso. Setting aside the artificiality of his style, and the curiously intellectual quality of his passion which detracts from his appeal to our day, one is amazed at the combination of restraint and fervour which this successor of no greater poets than Santillana and Manrique controlled with such apparent ease. The torments of a life of intense and unrequited passion are metamorphosed into a calmly melancholy beauty; and whether he speaks in his own quiet, measured tones, or depicts a poetic Arcadia with green lawns and streams and nymphs and shepherds, he conveys a sense of power such as Spanish readers had not previously dreamed of. He is beyond all doubt the earliest great lyric poet in the language.

The brief glamour of the Spanish Renaissance now fades into the long and splendid Age of Gold, stretching approximately from the death of Boscán in 1542 down to that of Calderón 139 years later. Both in the social and economic life of the nation, and in every form of art, this period saw great changes, and in no sphere of literature were these more marked than in lyric poetry, the development of which finds appropriate symbolical expression in the well-known phraseology of Calderón's sonnet on the rose (pp. 382-3). Wakening to life at the dawn of the Renaissance, opening gradually and displaying all the freshness of the rosebud during the early decades of the Golden Age, Spanish lyricism was clothed by Herrera and Góngora with "pompa y alegría" till it challenged the very rainbow; but in the evening of that glorious day it rapidly faded, and, as the cold night of pseudo-classicism descended upon Spain, vanished altogether.

The earlier years of the Golden Age were perhaps the greatest, because the most genuinely inspired. The nationalist and italianate currents were completely fused in the work of three poets who rank with, and indeed above, Garcilaso de la Vega and represent the summit of Spain's lyrical achievement. The Platonist, Nature-poet and quasi-mystic Luis de León, though his volume of work is slender, appeals to the most fastidious of scholars by his Classical perfection of form and yet plumbs depths of feeling common to all humanity. San Juan de la Cruz, unsurpassed as a mystical poet the world over, wrote even less than León, but went both higher and deeper : in the glowing heat of his descriptions of the intimacy of Lover and Beloved universality fuses with timelessness. Lope de Vega is far more discursive, but also more varied ; and, whether in the lyrics scattered through his numerous plays, in the poems of diverse kinds which appear in his prose writings, or in his highly personal sonnets of sacred and profane love, he typifies the freshness and spontaneity of this glorious morning of Spain's greatest day.

Then, with the " purple style " of Herrera, leader of the so-called " Sevilian school," lyricism enters into full flower. In his magnificent but too little known love-poetry, Herrera is another of Spain's first-rank poets ; what he lacks in depth of emotion (and on occasion he can show that too) he fully makes up in the brilliance of his lights and colours and the sonority and melody of his tone. In the by no means negligible poets who surrounded or succeeded him—Camoens, Medrano, Barahona de Soto, Espinosa, Rioja—the full flower of lyricism tends to become overblown and tendencies creep into the language of poetry which are soon to vaunt themselves as inseparable from it.

Of these the chief were two closely connected but normally distinct and separable manifestations—conceptism and cultism. Conceptism, concerned principally with thought, is characteristic of our own metaphysical poets of the seventeenth century : it has a passion for refinements and subtleties ; discovers in totally dissimilar things unexpected, often imaginary, resemblances ; sacrifices sense, logic and sometimes truth to " conceit " and " wit." At its best, it can be highly effective ; at its worst, it is a sheer vice : " adelgaza los conceptos," as Menéndez y Pelayo puts it, " hasta quebrarlos."[1] Cultism (also known as " culteranism ") chiefly

[1] *Historia de las ideas estéticas en España*, Madrid, 1890-1907, III, 478.

concerns form: it neologizes from Greek and Latin, transfers Latin constructions to Spanish; exaggerates literary devices; metaphorizes metaphors; and, in general terms, strives after an academic and aristocratic obscurity of expression. Beginning by emphasizing and exalting form, and therein undoubtedly enriching the language, it soon began to emphasize and exalt obscurity. Conceptism and cultism may be regarded as two symptoms of the *barroquismo* which increasingly characterizes the latter part of the Golden Age, and they are seen to best advantage, because united with outstanding genius, in the poems of Luis de Argote y Góngora.

This "vivo raro ingenio sin segundo," as Cervantes calls him,[1] was not exclusively addicted to the style which has become known as Gongorism, nor is it even possible to attribute his obscure and academic manner to any one period of his life. Not, for example, until long after he had finished his two super-cultist poems, the *Polifemo* and the *Soledades*, do we find him penning that melodious and simple exercise in Baroque poetry:

Aprended, flores, en mí
lo que va de ayer a hoy (pp. 341-2).

It is in the best of his *romances*, *letrillas* and sonnets that Góngora excels as a lyric poet. The *Polifemo*, and still more the *Soledades*, it is hard to call either lyrical or narrative. Except here and there, the story plays quite an unimportant part in both, while their plastic virtuosity, though involving an energy which undoubtedly falls within the category of genius, has nothing akin to the penetrating, illumining power of lyricism.

Of the contemporaries of Góngora not already treated, none was his equal in inventiveness or imagination, though many left a permanent impress on poetry. The brothers Leonardo de Argensola are typical of a great number. Their inspiration is academic and restrained; poetry is for them no compelling passion but an elegant occupation pressing into service the experience of years spent in courtly and literary circles and the leisurely reflection of cultured minds. Valdivielso has left some striking examples of the combined naïveté and artifice which so often express the religious consciousness of the people of Spain. Arguijo, a late Herreran, is an artist in melody. Caro, by virtue of one poem, is an outstanding elegiast. Villamediana is a gon-

[1] *Galatea*, Book VI, Canto de Caliope.

goristically inclined epigrammatist. Jáuregui now follows Gongorism and now is its determined critic. Quevedo, Jáuregui's contemporary, twenty years younger than Góngora, inclines to conceptism, but under each of a number of categories writes brilliant verse: at heart, however, he is not a singer, but a satirist.

After this, lyric poetry fades away. Calderón, who, despite his Baroque exaggerations, was so often a pure lyricist in his plays, outlived everyone else who in any true sense can be called a poet at all, unless we count the Mexican nun, Sor Juana Inés de la Cruz. Not until late in the eighteenth century does lyricism re-appear. Timidly and uncertainly it re-emerges—in the intermittent passion of Iglesias, in the emotionalism of Cienfuegos, in the patriotic oratory of Quintana and in the somewhat sentimental sensibility of Meléndez Valdés. The last-named made a surprisingly deep impression as a lyric poet upon his own generation and upon that which followed it. Their standards not being high, they thought of him as the "restorer of our poetry" and as the leader of a lyrical renaissance.[1] For the destruction of that illusion some considerable time was necessary and only in the fourth decade of the nineteenth century did lyricism in verse break out anew.

Since then it has hardly once failed, though its quality has fluctuated, and at the beginning, it must be confessed, was far from high. In 1837, appeared Zorrilla, with his exuberance and colour, and, almost exactly at the same time, Espronceda, with his melody, his verve and his power. In 1840, the Romantic movement, which had already declared itself in drama and had attempted somewhat feebly to do so in prose fiction, broke out in lyric poetry with the publication of volumes of Romantic lyrics by Espronceda, Nicomedes Pastor Díaz, García Gutiérrez, Campoamor, Arolas and a host of less known writers. The flood continued during the whole of the decade, and for long afterwards. It must not be supposed, however, that poetry had returned to the level of León, Herrera and Lope de Vega. The new mode was more facile, more pictorial, and, above all, more superficial. It insisted upon attempting an appeal to the many, whereas the greatest poets have always appealed to the few. Not until the Romantic movement, somewhat discredited by the mediocrity of its achievements, had yielded place to an eclecticism which has

[1] *H.R.M.S.*, I, 26, 302.

never wholly passed away did lyric poetry make a re-entry with its former power.

The poet who led this re-entry was Bécquer. Some critics would maintain that there was no Spaniard who can be called a genuine poet—*i.e.* who wrote both with art and out of the depths of his interior life—between San Juan de la Cruz and Bécquer. Certainly no nineteenth-century poet earlier in date than Bécquer, unless it be Espronceda in a very few of his poems, conveys the essential impression of writing poetry rather than, as it were, of writing *around* and *about* poetry. The elusive, ethereal art of the author of the *Rimas* seems to conceal depths of feeling comparable with those plumbed by almost any of his contemporaries.

Another generation was to elapse before Spain saw Bécquer's equal. Campoamor, who had begun as a Romantic, and returned more than once, though in a different spirit, to his early haunts, found his vocation, or at any rate a successful career, in prosaic verse of epigrammatic vigour. The other leading verse-writer of the century, Núñez de Arce, seems to have been prosaic *malgré lui*. It was upon a Spain whose idea of poetry was the turgid oratory of Núñez de Arce and to whom Bécquer was already a receding memory that there broke the revolution associated with the name of Rubén Darío.

Since that revolution, like so many such events in Spain, cannot be dissociated from the man who led it, the reader must turn to the pages which treat of Darío himself for a description of the joint impact upon Spain of a new inspiration and a new art, and for a description of that movement, generally known as Modernism, which he popularized there. Modernism had its success in the years immediately preceding and following the turn of the new century and its vitality is nowhere better seen than in the various movements, groups and tendencies to which, somewhat late in its life, it gave birth. Leaving aside such poets as Unamuno and Antonio Machado, who belong to a not purely literary group—that of 1898 (p. 573)—we may distinguish between such early Modernists as Villaespesa, Marquina and Manuel Machado and the younger writers who trace their immediate descent from Juan Ramón Jiménez, whose great achievement has been to guide poetry into a channel acceptable to poets of to-day. These poets, however they may label themselves or be labelled by the critics, are all in essence seekers after *poesía pura.* For them poetry which paints, which narrates, which describes, which embroiders, is no poetry at all. Their lyricism, which began to make its mark about 1920, and which all the subsequent vicissitudes of their country's tragic history have failed to quench, works exclusively in impressions fundamental to the emotion or sentiment which they are seeking to convey. They attempt to divest their art of everything that prevents it from delving to the very soul of poetry: "ni más nuevo al ir, ni más lejos: más hondo .... La depuración constante de lo mismo."[1] Obscure though they may sometimes prove to all but the very few, excessively though they may have reacted against the vulgarization of the poet's art by the nineteenth century, their faults are but the defects of the most exquisite qualities, and the greatest among them, it may safely be predicted, will rank singularly high in the judgment of generations to come.

III

Narrative verse, in Spain as elsewhere, was the earliest mode of self-expression to be adopted by writers who were striving after art. But in Spain it proved exceptionally persistent: spread as it was over the whole course of her literary history much more evenly than lyricism, it must be adjudged the more characteristic of the two arts if we disregard interpenetration and take every piece of verse at its face value. On the other side, it must be recorded that the lyric element invades narrative verse much more frequently and potently than the narrative element invades lyric verse, and also that, of Spain's non-dramatic poets, the very greatest, almost without exception, excel in the lyric, rather than in the narrative, art. There we have the contrast: narrative the more popular and natural form of expression; lyricism having a higher average degree of perfection, at any rate in verse other than anonymous.

If some of Spain's best anonymous verse, however, as we have seen, is lyric, a great deal more is narrative. *Mío Cid*, that masterpiece of sober mediaeval objectivity and realism, has its lyrical moments, but, fine as they can be, they are no more than moments

[1] Juan Ramón Jiménez: *Diario de un poeta recién casado*, Madrid, 1917 [p. 14].

—quickly gone. Basically, it is the poem's long sweep of narration that attracts us, just as in Nature it is the panorama that we remember, not the sunlit spots in it which have an equal, but a different, beauty. The same is true of the long poems of the *mester de clerecía*—the *Alexandre*, *Fernán González* and *Apolonio*—save that here the patches illumined by lyricism are fewer and the panorama of narrative is drearier and less humane. In the mischievous Juan Ruiz and the satirical López de Ayala, narrative and lyric meet. Then chronicles begin to be written in prose and lyricism in verse outstrips narrative. But with the beginning of the fifteenth century the influence of Vergil and Dante infuses new life into the older genre and the same period sees the development of its most striking phenomenon—the Romancero.

The *romances*, or ballads, of Spain have not only given the country its most popular and ubiquitous metre, together with a complete conspectus in verse of native legend and history, but they have become, as it were, a national habit. True, the finest of the mediaeval ballads have in their own country had no subsequent equals; but in moments of exaltation and at times of crisis the national spirit has invariably found expression in this particular form, which is thus as completely rooted in the soil as the lyrical *copla*. Wherever there is a group of Spaniards, there are *coplas;* wherever there is a Spanish community, even at the Antipodes, there spring up *romances*. "Not only do they continue to be written on new themes, but ancient ballads are being constantly recovered in all parts of the world, ballads which have survived, unknown to scholars, in the recesses of the plains of León, Castile and Catalonia, as well as on Mediterranean shores, at Salonica, Beirut, Oran, Tangier, wherever the exiled Jews carried them, and, finally, throughout the American colonies."[1]

The importance of the Spanish ballad is thus far greater than might be deduced from statistics or from descriptions showing the vastness of its thematic range. Even the sixteenth-century collections known as *Romanceros* show how deeply the ballads are embedded in the popular tradition: they are narrative, reflective, lyrical, elegiac; they are faintly literary, highly literary, purely popular, semi-popular, frankly academic; they are heroic, patriotic, personal, objective, amorous, religious; they are as

[1] Ernest Mérimée and S. Griswold Morley: *A History of Spanish Literature*, New York, 1930, p. 172.

realistic as *Mio Cid* or as idealistic as the *Chanson de Roland ;* they may depend entirely on the supernatural, or they may equally well exclude any suggestion of it.

From the beginning of the sixteenth century down to the present day the flow of *romances* and *romanceros*—now a mere trickle, now a deluge—has scarcely ever ceased. After the *Cancioneros de romances*, the *Silvas*, *Rosas*, *Flores*, *Florestas*, *Tesoros*, *Primaveras* of *romances*, and the less glamorously entitled *Romanceros*, all of the Golden Age, came a lull during the pseudo-Classical eighteenth century. Notwithstanding such eulogies as López de Sedano's of these "most precious treasures,"[1] only occasional ballads were reprinted, the most considerable collection being that of "Ramón Fernández" in 1796. On the other hand, a good many authors wrote ballads of their own. One of these was the gifted Nicolás Fernández de Moratín, who has life and skill, but tends to be too lavish with his colours. Another, rather surprisingly, was the pedant García de la Huerta ; a third, the pre-Romantic, Meléndez Valdés.

Among the earliest manifestations of the Romantic movement was the resuscitation of the Spanish ballads of the fifteenth and sixteenth centuries. First came the collections published by Grimm and Depping in Germany, and by Abel Hugo in France, followed later by Wolf's well-known *Floresta ;* then, collections issued in Spain,[2] the best known of which was Durán's five-volume anthology of *romances* of the most varied types (1828-32), later republished, in enlarged form, as a *Romancero general* (1849-50).[3] A number of authors composed new *Romanceros* of their own[4] : some, soon forgotten ; others, longer-lived ; a few—the collections of Rivas and Zorrilla—of first-class importance. Rivas' *Romances históricos* are in themselves one of his four major works (two of the other three being historical and legendary narrative poems also, though not written in the same metre), to which he prefaced an essay of some length eulogizing the ballad. Zorrilla made considerable use of the freer form employed by Rivas in his collection

[1] *H.R.M.S.*, I, 46.

[2] Such as González del Reguero's early reprint of Escobar ; Hartzenbusch's *Romancero pintoresco ;* and Ochoa's *Tesoro de los Romanceros* (*H.R.M.S.*, I, 158 ; II, 233, 252).

[3] *H.R.M.S.*, I, 94, 124, 161-3.

[4] E.g., Mármol's *Romancero*, Hurtado's *Romancero de Hernán Cortés* and García Gutiérrez's "Romances históricos" in *Luz y tinieblas* (*H.R.M.S.*, I, 308 ; II, 231, 252).

entitled *Leyendas*, though he frequently wrote in the octosyllabic ballad-metre as well.

Throughout the nineteenth century one contemporary event after another found its ballad-chronicler. For the Moorish War of the eighteen-fifties there was the *Romancero de la Guerra de África*, edited by Molíns ; for the Carlist War of the eighteen-seventies there was Ribot y Fontseré's *Romancero del Conde-Duque ;* and so on. And when the full literary history of our own day comes to be written there will fall to be chronicled a *Romancero de la Guerra Civil*—or rather, two : one coming from each of the contending parties.

This digression, which has carried us so rapidly through three centuries, has seemed necessary to convey some idea (for it can do no more) of the significance of the ballad in Spanish life and letters. That single form, however, is far from constituting the sum total of Golden Age narrative poetry. Long poems of religious inspiration, generally hagiographical in type, appeared in great numbers. Lope de Vega's *Isidro*, the ten-canto verse biography of Madrid's patron saint which first brought him into public notice, is among the most famous of them, but there were hundreds of others. More epical in tone is Hojeda's *Cristiada*, which has been called Miltonic. Unless the meaning of the word epic be stretched to include *Mío Cid*—or the *Romancero* itself, which Hugo termed " an Iliad without a Homer "—Spain has had no great poem which is genuinely epical. Yet not only in her religious, but in her historical literature, masses of mediocre collections of epical or quasi-epical type testify that a Spanish Camoens would have found the atmosphere propitious. There are many such poems, selections from which cannot be given for lack of space, and in which, furthermore, the general effect is more significant and striking than any individual passages. Among these are Vecilla Castellanos' *El León de España*, mentioned in *Don Quijote ;* Suárez de Figueroa's Tassoesque *España defendida*, Balbuena's much finer *Bernardo, o Victoria de Roncesvalles*, and three works, of particular interest to English readers, by Lope de Vega : *La Dragontea*, written after the death of Sir Francis Drake ; *Jerusalén conquistada*, on Richard Cœur de Lion and the Second Crusade ; and the polemical *Corona trágica*, on the life and death of Mary, Queen of Scots. Superior to all these is a work which comes near to being a really great epic—Alonso de Ercilla's *Araucana*. The inclusion of an extract from this work alone may possibly convey the incorrect impression that the *Araucana* was the only considerable epic based on the history of the Spanish Empire. Actually, it was one of a vast number which the feats of the *conquistadores* drew from those who stayed at home—or occasionally from those who went with them. Italian influence was also responsible for numerous poems either imitating, continuing or emulating the *Orlando furioso*, one of the best known of which is Barahona de Soto's *Las Lágrimas de Angélica*, another theme treated in a long poem by Lope de Vega. As well as all these quasi-epics there were other groups best termed erudite; others, romantic; others, satirical; and others, jocular or burlesque.

Right through the prosaic eighteenth century narrative verse continued to appear. Even the now dreary and third-rate epics were esteemed so highly that prizes for them were offered by the Royal Spanish Academy. Only a few poems of that century have qualities which save them from oblivion.[1] What is probably its best-known poem, however, if not also its best, "Fiesta de toros en Madrid," is a verse narration by Nicolás Fernández de Moratín, to whose original ballads reference has already been made.

The pre-Romantic Sevilians carried narrative verse from the old century into the new—Reinoso, for example, in his epic *La Inocencia perdida*, and Lista, in some surprisingly good *romances* —but it was not until romanticism came into its own that the genre rose to real heights of success. A much more valuable contribution to the new movement than Rivas' "romantically romantic" drama *Don Álvaro, o La Fuerza del sino*, was his *Moro expósito*, in the preface to which Alcalá Galiano pointed to mediaeval Spanish history as a "most fertile field . . . . greatly neglected by our poets." Even had he not written the later *Romances históricos* and *Leyendas*, Rivas would have been remembered, by this extensive treatment of a mediaeval and national theme, as a pioneer in the re-introduction of the mediaeval spirit into modern literature.

Concurrently with *romances* and *leyendas*, which during the Romantic period were penned by every writer and published by

[1] Such are the *Adonis* of José Antonio Porcel, an official of the notorious Academy of Good Taste, and two works by Alfonso Verdugo y Castilla, who is remembered chiefly by the incipient romanticism of his lyrics—*El Juicio Final* and a fragmentary epic, *El Deucalión*.

every newspaper and magazine with literary interests, appeared other long poems of mediaeval and Romantic inspiration,[1] most of which are now forgotten. But narrative poetry of a more modern kind appeared also. Espronceda's *Estudiante de Salamanca*, notwithstanding its lyric moments, has essentially the qualities of a story, and it is from this fact that it derives one of its most striking and effective traits, the speed which it gathers as it goes. The same author's unfinished poem, *El Diablo Mundo*, reveals new qualities and influences which, had he lived, would undoubtedly have carried him to greater heights. As we have it, however, it is inferior to the *Estudiante* and its purple patches alone redeem it from mediocrity.

Almost to the end of his long life Zorrilla continued to write—and to Zorrilla writing invariably meant verse narrative or drama. Campoamor—rather surprisingly, it might be thought—twice turned aside from the short epigrammatic *doloras* which brought him his fame to produce two unwieldly and somewhat inchoate poems of great length: *Colón* (1853), which in four thousand lines of *octavas* tells the story of the events leading to the discovery of America, and *El Drama universal* (1869), nearly twice its length, which provides the sharpest possible contrast to the *Doloras* with its vague religiosity and symbolism.

On the heels of the *Drama universal* came the *Rimas* of Bécquer, and it might seem as if this re-emergence of "interior" poetry after so long an eclipse had for a time checked the Spanish love of narrative verse. Ballads, and collections of ballads, have continued to appear, and no one has done more for that particular form than the author of *Romancero Gitano*, one of the most modern of Spanish poets, Federico García Lorca. But for the last three-quarters of a century lyric poetry has completely outstripped narrative and it would seem that the day of the "long poem" is, for the time being, over.

IV

All the minor types of verse are found in Spanish; and, because everything that grows in Spain grows so abundantly, they are

[1] E.g., Maury's fantastic *Esvero y Almedora*, Navarro Villoslada's "ensayo épico," *Luchana*, and Ribot y Fontseré's *Solimán y Zaida* (*H.R.M.S.*, II, 238-9, 254).

found in considerable quantity. But in quality they fall far below the two types we have studied and they need not long detain us.

Satire, after the mediaeval pattern, was chiefly represented, in pre-Renaissance verse, by two very different and distinctive characters, Juan Ruiz and Pero López de Ayala. There were satirical romances, too, and satirical *coplas*—both, as a rule, political. Of the latter type the best example is the *Coplas de Mingo Revulgo*. But Spain has never had a Juvenal; and her two greatest satirists—again two very diverse personalities—made their name in prose. One of these is the fifteenth-century Archpriest of Talavera, whose *Corbacho*, in its author's words, "tells of the vices of evil women and of the humours of men"; the other, and the greater of the two, is Francisco de Quevedo, the satire of whose *Sueños* and *Buscón* mingles now with burlesque, now with bitter invective.

Burlesque is another type of which there is no distinguished example in verse: it is characteristic that the best-known poem of this kind is a dull production of the eighteenth century, Gabriel Álvarez de Toledo's *La Burromaquia*. Pure humour, which, though less general than in English, abounds in the novel, from *Lazarillo de Tormes* to Palacio Valdés, is also rare in verse. Góngora's merry cynicisms (p. 318) and the stinging caricatures of Quevedo (pp. 363, 368) are the best things of their kind to be found in first-class writers. High in the second class, however, comes Alcázar, whose pleasant, unassuming manner and good-humoured fancy, applied to reminiscences of domestic incidents, bring us near to the heart of the everyday life of his age.

In every literature much mediaeval verse is, as regards either morals or religion, didactic, so far do Churchmen or Church influences go towards moulding it. Didactic poetry after the Renaissance reached no great heights and the enumeration of a string of authors would probably win none of them a single reader. In the Golden Age, Lope de Vega stands high in the list with his *Triunfos divinos*, which, like Covarrubias' *Emblemas*, is inspired by Italy. Better than these are a number of verse treatises on the art of letters: Juan de la Cueva's *Ejemplar poético*, Vicente Espinel's *Arte poéticá*, and, of course, Lope de Vega's blank-verse *Arte nuevo de hacer comedias*. There is more meat in the last of these than in either the same author's pretentious *Laurel de Apolo* or Cervantes' *Viaje del Parnaso*. In the same way, Iriarte's charming and sprightly eighteenth-century literary fables are worth all the gloomy verse treatises on literature, painting and music which strewed that age.

The epigram, from Alcázar to Campoamor, is more generally cultivated than one would expect of the diffuse and expansive Spaniard. Perhaps his fondness for proverbs, *coplas* and *refranes* has given him a potential talent for conciseness and compression which co-exists with his fertility and fluency in less exacting forms but operates only intermittently.

As has already been implied, the Spaniard's dislike for precise definition leads him to combine these different forms and to blur the distinctions between them till they are no longer recognizable. We shall not wish to be more particular than he. English critics have debated, at considerable length, whether or no the sonnet and the elegy should be considered as coming within the category of "lyric poetry" and have reached their conclusions only after considerable hesitancy. Not so is it in Spain. The greatest of Spanish critics, Menéndez y Pelayo, when embarking on that extraordinary *Antología de poetas líricos castellanos* which, even as he left it, resembles an encyclopaedia, and, had he not died in 1912, might easily be still in progress, decided, with a light-hearted inclusiveness more generous than critical, to include *everything:* "todos los poemas menores—oda, elegía, égloga, sátira, epístola, poemitas descriptivos, didácticos, etc."[1] In this anthology of far more restricted scope, space need not be spent in the dividing of verse into water-tight compartments and the labelling of each in turn. Poems thus treated will soon become too elusive. We shall do better to consider each poem, on its merits, as we come to it.

V

And what may we expect to find in them as a whole? Three things in particular, I think, which are hardly to be found in such great measure in any other modern literature than our own.

1. First, a most remarkable energy. It is strange that this is not generally realized as being one of the traits most highly characteristic of the Spaniard of to-day: because the way he expresses it is not the way we ourselves should choose, we too often fail to apprehend it at all. But he would be an insensitive reader

[1] M.P. *Ant.*, I, xxxix.

indeed who had no perception of the energy that throbs through Spanish poetry. Elsewhere I have drawn attention to the militant ardour of the Spanish mystics as expressed in their metaphors of strife, ascent, wrestling, attack, progress. Their profession was *caballería a lo divino*[1]—"Divine knight-errantry"; they were the discoverers and *conquistadores* of "God's Indies." The same is true of the Spanish poets. From the *Cid* to Unamuno, the key-note of all their writing is activity. They reflect the centuries of reconquest at home, and of discovery, conquest and colonization across the ocean, either in the most literal sense, by composing long epics inspired by imperial adventure, or, more generally, by writing at a length and with an intensity which showed what they could have done had their instrument been not the pen but the sword.

Sometimes this energy is compressed and concentrated into *copla*, epigram or sonnet, but more frequently it is dispersed over works of immense size—a fact which leaves every anthologist with the feeling that when he has done his utmost he has still done nothing at all. The diffusion, which is continuous throughout Spanish literature, no anthology can of course possibly illustrate, though the best of the cultists—and, most clearly of all, Góngora in the *Soledades*—display it in a particular form. The whole of Baroque art in Spain is intensely alive—architecture and sculpture no less notably than literature—and it is often the mental vigour and agility of the conceptists and cultists that provokes an instinctive reaction in the condemnatory critic's sluggish, easy-going brain. "His poetry," it has been said of Góngora, "is full of life and movement, of the will to be alive. It foreshadows the rapid sketches of Goya; its concrete pictures seem to wilt and flicker as the sunshine or rustling wind disturbs them. . . . He soars with flashing wing. . . . The spirit which makes alive runs like a fire through his verse."[2] All—even those who will not concede that his fiery energy took the best direction—must recognize that.

In one sense this energy of Gongorism is diffused rather than concentrated, but there is also much energy in Spanish poetry which is concentrated to a high degree. This is found chiefly in the Renaissance, in the early Golden Age and in the half-century which has elapsed since a new energy was brought over the sea,

[1] *Spanish Mysticism*, London, 1924, p. 44.

[2] A. F. G. Bell: *Castilian Literature*, London, 1938, pp. 169-71.

from the America to which so much had gone, by Rubén Darío. It can be studied in a variety of media—in the sonnets of Garcilaso de la Vega, Herrera and Unamuno; in the *Cántico espiritual* (the poem and the commentary taken in conjunction) of San Juan de la Cruz, in the *Soledades* and *Galerías* of Antonio Machado and in the *creacionistas* of yesterday and to-day. How many pages of concentrated feeling, for example—if feeling could be measured in pages—are telescoped into those four lines of Gerardo Diego:

> Habrá un silencio verde
> todo hecho de guitarras destrenzadas.
>
> La guitarra es un pozo
> con viento en vez de agua.[1]

Equally well this concentration of energy can be studied in the apparent simplicity of the popular *coplas*. The flight of the *saeta* (literally the word means "arrow") is a picture, a symbol, of the highest and most intense of all flights possible to human activity—the flight of the mystic. The two can no more be compared than a man can be compared with the photograph of a man, but there is that in each which is common to both. A *copla* of another type may contain within itself all the elements of a drama: many Spanish dramas, indeed, may well have been built on *coplas*. Or it may express the essential steps in a whole chain of reasoning—and without the reasoning, perhaps given greater vividness and reality by experience, it could not have been written. Or it may seize upon images and symbols, extract their essence and with searing intensity impress it, through them, upon the receptive reader's mind.

If Spanish poetry exercises a hold upon the reader, as the modern poetry of few other countries can, the reason is that, as he delves into it and bathes in it, he goes all the time deeper and deeper. It is of the soul, rather than of the intellect, and the soul has greater and more penetrative power than the intellect—a profounder and a more dynamic energy.

2. Secondly—and this follows from what has just been said—idealism. The vitality which welled up within the Spaniard and demanded a means of expression found it as the arrow finds it when, loosed from the bow, it shoots forward or upward towards a clearly-defined goal. The arrow-image is popular in Spanish

[1] Cf. p. 672, below.

literature because it is the symbol of Spanish idealism. In prose, it may be the realism in the Spanish character that strikes one: the flight from abstractions, the attraction of the concrete, the practical common-sense of the ascetics and mystics, the development of the picaresque, the wealth of prosaic detail in chronicles, the popularity of *costumbrismo*, and so on. But in poetry, though realism and idealism blend, the stress is on idealism: not only on religious idealism—though the sonnet "No me mueve, mi Dios. . . ." (pp. 193-4) can hardly be surpassed in that respect outside the Scriptures—but on idealism of any and every kind. There is the idealization of love, so complete that poems can be found in which it is impossible to say if the beloved is the lady Dulcinea del Toboso or the Blessed Virgin. Nowhere had Platonism a soil more thoroughly prepared than in sixteenth-century Spain; and if, as would naturally be the case in so full-blooded a people, physical love finds ample expression too, there is a quality in the love of Garcilaso and Herrera, and even in that of the less skilful Boscán, which comes as near to divine love as one can well imagine. It is because of this that we can turn and re-turn the pages of the *Cancioneros* without impatience or boredom. Did they contain nothing but courtesies, paradoxes and the skilful masking of a hypothetical emotion they would soon exasperate. Had they nothing but elegant, graceful and even musical language, they would cloy. But while many of their trifles have in fact no more than these, ever and anon one finds something deeper.

There are lesser idealizations too. Of Nature, as continually in Luis de León and San Juan de la Cruz, as here and there in the eighteenth-century pre-Romantics, and as most markedly in the poets of to-day. Of freedom, in the ballads, in the *serranillas*, in the sturdy quatrains of some of Spain's greatest Golden Age dramas, in the turgid but sonorous odes of Quintana and Gallego, in the poets of '98. Of solitude, in the ascetics and mystics, in Bécquer, Antonio Machado, Enrique de Mesa and Juan Ramón Jiménez. And so one might go on. Always these poets are idealists. Always they press onward and upward. Always they are of the soul of Spain.

3. Thirdly, universality. The text-book at this stage would point us to Jorge Manrique's stanzas on the death of his father—and certainly, as will be said later, those stanzas are among the finest examples of commonplaces exquisitely and unforgettably

enshrined in a perfect setting that modern literature can show. But let it not be forgotten that we can find the same characteristic, to almost the same degree, in Jorge's uncle Gómez, in more than one sonnet of Santillana, in Escrivá's *canción* to death—and that without straying beyond the circle of Jorge's immediate contemporaries. There are many other pages of Spanish verse where the words leap at us from the page and say: "That is truth—universal truth: that is what all men have in common." Boscán's sonnet on the desert; San Juan de la Cruz's "Noche oscura"; Quevedo's "Miré los muros . . . ."; some one of the *Rimas* of Bécquer; some one of the *Doloras* of Campoamor; the poets of '98—Antonio Machado, Unamuno . . . . But it is not so much the number of moving and compelling passages of this kind in the works of great geniuses that is significant as the frequency with which, in the seldom-thumbed pages of the anonymous or the third-rate writer, one is brought up against phrases, figures and refrains which catch one's breath, or which draw back the veil of illusion. The verse *coplas*, like the prose proverbs, of Spain are full of these. They are part of Spain.

Why is this? Why have the proverbs of *Don Quijote* been compared with the Proverbs of Solomon? Why has "Recuerde el alma dormida . . . ." been termed "the most celebrated page of the Ecclesiastes" which Spain has "contributed to the living Bible of Europe"?[1] Is it perhaps because in the early centuries of its history the Peninsula's tempting situation made it the most invaded of lands and gave its eventual inhabitants a finer blend of racial qualities than most others? Or is it that centuries of idealism and disillusion produced rich fruits of meditation? Or that a country so keenly divided by high *sierras* predisposes its people to solitude and thought? It may be for any of these reasons, or for all of them combined, but none can deny that "the Spanish genius seems to have a special gift for cutting away the accidental growths and irrelevancies which separate the individual from the universal, the transient from the permanent."[2]

VI

My aim in writing these few simple pages has not been to preface this anthology with an elegant essay, scintillating with

[1] S. de Madariaga *The Genius of Spain*, Oxford, 1923, p. 26.
[2] A. F. G. Bell: *Castilian Literature*, p. x.

either poetry or wit. I am anxious that the extracts should speak for themselves, and this workaday introduction, like the commentaries which precede the poems, has been planned merely to provide the necessary background and to give information which it might be hard to obtain elsewhere. My few remarks made, I commend the reader to the poets, only reminding him that while no anthology can give more than a suggestion of what remains when it has been read, this one leaves even more undiscovered land than is usual. For besides lacking the space to include so much that is worth reading in Castilian, it takes no account of the rich and diverse literatures of Spanish America, and it contains hardly a hint of the literatures of the other Peninsular languages, which can be learned with so little toil by those who already know one of them. With so many literatures to conquer no student of Hispanic culture can ever expect to achieve satiety.

ABBREVIATIONS USED IN THE TEXT

(Where references indicated in the text by *op. cit.*, or *ed. cit.*, are not given below, they will be found in the index to Authors, Works and Editions, pp. 709-23.)

B.A.E.—Biblioteca de Autores Españoles.

B.S.S.—*Bulletin of Spanish Studies.* Liverpool.

C.B.—*Cancionero de Juan Alfonso de Baena* (Siglo XV). Madrid, 1851.

C.C.—Clásicos Castellanos.

C.H.C.—*Cancionero de Hernando del Castillo.* Madrid, 1882, 2 vols.

C.R.F.-D.—*Cancionero castellano del siglo XV*, ed. R. Foulché-Delbosc. Madrid, 1912-15, 2 vols.

D.A.—Dámaso Alonso: *Poesía española.* Antología, I. Madrid, 1935.

Diego.—*Poesía española, 1915-1931.* Madrid, 1932.

Flor.—Juan Valera: *Florilegio de poesías castellanas del siglo XIX.* Madrid, 1902-4, 5 vols.

H.R.M.S.—E. Allison Peers: *A History of the Romantic Movement in Spain.* Cambridge, 1940, 2 vols.

M.P., *Ant.*—Marcelino Menéndez y Pelayo: *Antología de poetas líricos castellanos.* Madrid, 1890-1908, 13 vols. (The 10-vol. "Edición Nacional," Madrid, 1944-5, appeared too late to be used here.)

Mont.—Manuel de Montoliu: *Literatura Castellana.* Barcelona, 1930.

N.B.A.E.—Nueva Biblioteca de Autores Españoles.

N.H.—James Fitzmaurice-Kelly: *A New History of Spanish Literature.* Oxford, 1926.

O.—Federico de Onís: *Antología de la poesía española e hispano-americana.* (1882-1932). Madrid, 1934.

R.H.—*Revue Hispanique.* New York, Paris.

V.P.—Ángel Valbuena Prat: *Historia de la literatura española.* Barcelona, 1937, 2 vols.

CANTAR DE MÍO CID

*c.*1140

ONE of the greatest of the world's epics, the *Cantar de Mío Cid*, which was "discovered" and published by a Madrid librarian at the end of the eighteenth century, is extant in the form of a fourteenth-century manuscript copy, comprising 3,730 lines. It was written, in all probability, less than half a century after the death of its hero, to whose figure it owes its artistic unity, and whose personality, as we see it against the background of the narrative, is amazingly vivid and real. Hardly less attractive is the narrative itself: the long, irregular, assonanced lines tell their chronicle-like story in the most natural possible way, and the dramatic and lyrical passages, written, like the rest of the poem, not for reading but for recitation, have real force. As one would expect of so early a work, simplicity—in language, style, narrative, description and characterization—is an outstanding trait. Another is realism, sometimes manifesting itself in a grim irony and humour, though, as in so much later Spanish literature, this is relieved by flashes of lyrical feeling, usually springing either from a naive piety or from a sympathetic treatment of the Cid's love for his wife and daughters. With the exception of the hero, the personages of the story are sketched only in outline, but revealing phrases continually throw unexpected lights upon them. The artistry of the poem, rudimentary as it is, will repay study, and the detail and accuracy of its topography are quite astonishing. Historically it is less trustworthy: many of the events described, and most of the chief figures, are distorted or romanticized by invention. But, as many centuries were to pass before Spanish literature adopted an even approximately modern conception of historical truth, this will not surprise us.

When the narrative begins, the Cid Campeador, Rodrigo (Ruy) Díaz de Vivar, has just been exiled from Castile by King Alfonso VI, by whose command the city of Burgos is closed to him as he turns southward, with a handful of loyal followers, to carve out a new country for himself by conquests from the Moors. Leaving in the care of some good monks at Cardeña his wife, Doña Ximena, and his daughters, Doña Elvira and Doña Sol, he crosses the Castilian frontier, and, fighting as he goes, brings a successful campaign to its height by besieging and conquering Valencia. The Castilian King, who has been growing increasingly mollified by the news of the Cid's continual victories and by the trophies of his prowess which that wily chieftain has sent him as gifts, receives him back into favour and offers to marry his daughters to two young nobles, Diego and Fernando González, the Infantes of Carrión. These youths, however, prove to be despicable cowards, and, after making themselves ridiculous in the eyes of the Cid and his retinue, ask and receive permission to take their brides home. On the way, they maltreat them in an oak-forest, and then ride away, abandoning them for ever. Complaint about this is made to the King, who sees to it that justice is done, and, after the villains have been defeated and disgraced in single combat, marries Doña Elvira and Doña Sol once more—this time into the royal Houses of Aragon and Navarre.

1. *El Cid entra en Burgos*

This episode of the poem, which in our own day has been retold in a new and no less exquisite form by Manuel Machado (*pp.* 619-20), *tells its own story. A striking interpretation of it has been given by the poet and critic Pedro Salinas* (*p.* 662), *who describes the " niña de nuef años " as " the first feminine character in Spanish literature."*[1]

Mio Çid R*o*y Díaz　　por Burgos entr*ó*v*e*,
en su*e* conpaña　　sessaenta pendones ;
exien lo ve*e*r　　mugieres e varones,
burgeses e burgesas　　por las finiestras son*e*,
plorando de los ojos,　　tanto avien el dolor*e*.
De las sus bocas　　todos dizían una razón*e* :
" ¡ Dios, qué buen vassallo,　　si oviesse buen señor*e* ! "

[1] *Reality and the poet in Spanish poetry*, Baltimore, 1940, pp. 8-9.

Conbidar le ien de grado,   mas ninguno non osava :
el rey don Alfonsso   tanto avie la grand saña.
Antes de la noche   en Burgos dél entró su carta,
con grand recabdo   e fuertemientre se*e*llada :
que a mio Çid R*o*y Díaz,   que nadi nol diessen posada,
e aquel que gela diesse   sopiesse vera palabra
que perderie los averes   e más los ojos de la cara,
e aun demás   los cuerpos e las almas.
Grande duelo avien   las yentes cristianas ;
ascóndense de mio Çid,   ca nol osan dezir nada.

El Campeador   adelinó a su posada ;
así commo llegó a la puorta,   fallóla bien çerrada,
por miedo del rey Alfons,   que assi lo para*ran* :
que si non la quebrantás,   que non gela abriesse*n* por nad*a*.
Los de mio Çid   a altas vozes llaman,
los de dentro   non les querien tornar palabra.
Aguijó mio Çid,   a la puerta se llegaua,
sacó el pie del estribera,   una ferídal dava ;
non se abre la puerta,   ca bien era çerrada.

Una niña de nuef años   a ojo se parava :
" ¡ Ya Campeador,   en buen*a* çinxiestes espada !
El rey lo ha vedado,   anoch dél e*n*tró su carta,
con grant recabdo   e fuertemientre se*e*llada.
Non vos osariemos   abrir nin coger por nada ;
si non, perderiemos   los averes e las casas,
e *aun* demás   los ojos de las caras.
Çid, en el nuestro mal   vos non ganades nada ;
mas el Criador vos vala   con todas sus vertudes santas."
Esto la niña dixo   e tornós pora su casa.

2. *Las Arcas de arena*

Perhaps the most celebrated passage in Mío Cid, *and the first, in chronological order, of a large number of realistic passages which are to be found all over Spanish literature. The Cid, his benchman Martín Antolínez and the two Jews, Raquel and Vidas, are delineated, not only with skill, but with a remarkable verve : were it not for the language, it would be difficult to believe that the poem is eight hundred years old. Vividness of description, trenchant dialogue, humour and irony all delight the reader.*

Fabló mio Çid, el que en buen ora çinxo espada :
" ¡ Martin Antolínez, sodes ardida lança !
si yo bivo, doblar vos he la soldada.
Espeso e el oro e toda la plata,
bien lo veedes que yo no trayo *nada*,
huebos me serié pora toda mi compaña ;
fer lo he amidos, de grado non avrié nada.
Con vuestro consejo bastir quiero dos arcas ;
inchámoslas d'arena, ca bien serán pesadas,
cubiertas de guadalmeçí e bien enclaveadas.

Los guadameçís vermejos e los clavos bien dorados.
Por Raquel e Vidas vayádesme privado :
quando en Burgos me vedaron compra y el rey me a ayrado,
non puedo traer el aver, ca mucho es pesado,
enpeñar gelo he por lo que *fore* guisado ;
de noche lo lieven, que non lo vean cristianos.
Véalo el Criador con todos los sos santos,
yo más non puedo e amidos lo fago."

Martín Antolínez non lo deta*rda*va
passó por Burgos, al castiello entrava,
por Raquel e Vidas apriessa demandava.

Raquel e Vidas en uno estavan amos,
en cuenta de sus averes, de los que avien ganados.
Llegó Martín Antolínez a guisa de menbrado :
" ¿ O sodes, Raquel e Vidas, los mios amigos caros ?
En poridad fablar querría con amos."
Non lo detardan, todos tres se apartaron.
" Raquel e Vidas, amos me dat las manos,
que non me descubrades a moros nin a cristianos ;
por siempre vos faré ricos, que non seades menguados.
El Campeador por las parias *fo* entrado,
grandes averes priso e mucho sobejanos,

retovo dellos   quanto que f*o* algo ;
por en vino a aquesto   por que f*o* acusado.
Tiene dos arcas   llennas de oro esmerado.
Ya lo ve*e*des   que el rey le a ayrado.
Dexado ha heredades   e casas e palaçios.
Aquellas non las puede levar,   sinon, serie ventad*o* ;
el Campeador   dexar las ha en vuestra mano,
e prestalde de aver   lo que sea guisado.
Prended las arcas   e metedlas en vuestro salvo ;
con grand jura   meted i las fe*de*s amos,
que non las catedes   en todo aqueste año."

Raquel e Vidas   seiense consejando :
" Nos huebos avemos   en todo de ganar algo.
Bien lo sabemos   que él algo *a* gañ*ado*,
quando a tierra de moros entró,   que grant aver *a* sac*ado* ;
non duerme sin sospecha   qui aver trae monedado.
Estas arcas   prendámoslas am*o*s,
en logar las metamos   que non sea ventad*o*.

Mas dezidnos del Çid,   de qué será pagado,
o qué ganançia nos dará   por todo aqueste año ? "
Respuso Martín Antolínez   a guisa de menbrado :
" Myo Çid querrá   lo que ssea aguisado ;
pedir vos a poco   por dexar so aver en salvo.
Acógensele omnes   de todas partes me*n*guados,
a menester   seysçientos marcos."
Dixo Raquel e Vidas :   " Dar gelos *hemos* de grado."
—" Ya vedes que entra la noch,   el Çid es pressurado,
huebos avemos   que nos dedes los marcos."
Dixo Raquel e Vidas :   " Non se faze assí el mercado,
sinon primero prendiendo   e después dando."
Dixo Martín Antolínez :   " Yo desso me pago.
Amos tred   al Campeador contado,
e nos vos ayudaremos,   que assí es aguisado,
por aduzir las arcas   e meterlas en vuestro salvo,
que non lo sepan   moros nin cristianos."
Dixo Raquel e Vidas :   " Nos desto nos pagamos.
Las arcas aduchas,   prendet seyesçientos marcos."

Martín Antolínez cavalgó privado
con Raquel e Vidas, de voluntad e de grado.
Non viene a la puent, ca por el agua a passado,
que gelo non ventassen de Burgos omne nado.
Afévoslos a la tienda del Campeador contado;
assí commo entraron, al Çid besáronle las manos.
Sonrrisós mio Çid, estávalos fablando:
" ¡ Ya don Raquel e Vidas, avédesme olbidado!
Ya me exco de tierra, ca del rey so ayrado.
A lo quem semeja, de lo mio avredes algo;
mientra que vivades non seredes menguados."
Raquel e Vidas a mio Çid besáronle las manos.
Martín Antolínez el pleyto a parado,
que sobre aquellas arcas dar le ien seysçientos marcos,
e bien gelas guardarien fasta cabo del año;
ca assil dieran la fe*d* e gelo auien jurado,
que si antes las catassen que f*o*ssen perjurados,
non les diesse mio Çid de ganançia un dinero malo.
Dixo Martín Antolínez: " Carguen las arcas privado.
Levaldas, Raquel e Vidas, ponedlas en vuestro salvo;
yo iré convus*c*o, que adugamos los marcos,
ca a mover a mio Çid ante que cante el gallo."
Al cargar de las arcas veriedes gozo tanto:
Non las podien poner en somo maguer eran esforçados.
Grádanse Raquel e Vidas con averes monedados,
ca mientra que visquiessen refechos eran amos.

Raquel a mio Çid la manol *h*a besa*da*:
" ¡ Ya Canpeador, en buen*a* çinxiestes espada!
De Castiella vos ides pora las yentes estrañas.
Assí es vuestra ventura, grandes son vuestras ganançias;
una piel vermeja morisca e ondrada,
Çid, beso vuestra mano en don que la yo aya."
" Plazme," dixo el Çid, " daquí sea mandada.
Si vos la aduxier dalla; si non, contalda sobre las arcas."

Raquel e Vidas las arcas levavan,
con ellos Martín Antolínez por Burgos entrava.
Con todo recabdo llegan a la posada;
en medio del palaçio tendieron un almoçalla,

sobrella una sávana de rançal e muy blanca.
A tod el primer colpe trezientos marcos de plata,
notólos don Martino, sin peso los tomava ;
los otros trezientos en oro gelos pagavan.
Çinco escuderos tiene don Martino, a todos los cargava.
Quando esto ovo fecho, odredes lo que fablava :
" Ya don Raquel e Vidas, en vuestras manos son las arcas ;
yo, que esto vos gané, bien mereçía calças."

Entre Raquel e Vidas aparte ixieron amos :
" Démosle buen don, ca él no' lo ha buscado.
Martín Antolínez, un Burgalés contado,
vos lo mereçedes, darvos queremos buen dado,
de que fagades calças e rica piel e buen manto.
Dámosvos en don a vos treínta marcos ;
mereçer no' lo hedes, ca esto es aguisado :
atorgar nos hedes esto que avemos parado."
Gradeçiólo don Martino e recibió los marcos ;
gradó exir de la posada e espidiós de amos.
Exido es de Burgos e Arlançón a passado,
vino pora la tienda del que en buen ora nasco.

Reçibiólo el Çid abiertos amos los braços :
" ¿ Venides, Martín Antolínez, el mio fidel vassallo ?
¡ Aun vea el día que de mí ayades algo !
" Vengo, Campeador, con todo buen Recabdo :
vos seysçientos e yo treynta he ganados.
Mandad coger la tienda e vayamos privado . . . "

3. *La Oración de Doña Ximena*

Often the lyrical element in Mío Cid *is to be found in short phrases and single lines rather than in long passages. So it is here. The Cid, with his wife and daughters, is at the Cardeña monastery, about to leave them and set out upon his campaign. Don Rodrigo and Doña Ximena go to church at the hour of Matins, and Doña Ximena, throwing herself on her knees before the altar, utters a long prayer. But in most of it there is little emotion. It begins like a gloss on the Apostles' Creed, next enumerates a variety of incidents from the Old and New Testaments, in anything but chronological order, and ends with a line and a half of real prayer, so touching as almost to be poetry —by mistake. But the whole of this oration to the Almighty has less poetry than the single line on which the extract closes and in which for a moment the chronicler's habitual laconism fails to conceal a wave of emotion :*

assís parten unos d'otros   commo la uña de la carne.

Tañen a matines   a una priessa tan grand*e* ;
mio Çid e su mugier   a la eglesia van*e*.
Echós doña Ximena   en los grados delantel altar*e*,
rogando al Criador   quanto ella mejor sabe,
que a mio Çid el Campeador   que Dios le curiás de mal*e* :
“ Ya señor glorioso,   padre que en çielo estas*e*,
fezist çielo e tierra,   el terçero el mar*e* ;
fezist estrellas e luna   y el sol pora escalentar*e* ;
prisist encarnaçión   en santa María madre,
en Belleem apareçist,   commo f*o* tu veluntad*e* ;
pastores te glorifficaron,   ouieron *t*e a laudare,
tres reyes de Arabia   te vinieron adorar*e*,
Melchior   e *C*aspar e Baltasar*e*,
oro e tus e mirra   te offreçieron *de* veluntad*e* ;
salvest a Jonás,   quand cayó en la mar*e*,
salvest a Daniel   con los leones en la mala cárçel,
salvest dentro en Roma   a señor san Sabastián,
salvest a santa Susanna   del falso criminal ;
por tierra andidiste treynta y dos años,   Señor spirital,
mostrando los miraclos,   por en avemos qué fablar ;
del agua fezist vino   e de la piedra pan,
resuçitest a Lázaro,   ca f*o* tu voluntad ;
a los judios te dexeste prender ;   do dizen monte Calvarie
pusiéronte en cruz   por nombre en Golgotá ;
dos ladrones contigo,   estos dé señas partes,
el uno es en para*d*iso,   ca el otro non entró allá ;
estando en la cruz,   vertud fezist muy grant :
Longinos era çiego,   que nu*n*qua vi*d*o alguandre,
diot con la lança en el costado,   dont yxió la sangre,
corrió por el astil ayuso,   las manos se ovo de untar,
alçólas arriba,   llególas a la faz,

abrió sos ojos, cató a todas partes,
en tí crovo al ora, por end es salvo de mal;
en el monumento *oviste a* resuçit*ar*,
fust a los infiernos, commo f*o* tu voluntad;
*cr*ebanteste las puertas, e saqueste los santos padres.
Tú eres rey de los reyes, e de todel mundo padre,
a tí adoro e cre*do* de toda voluntad,
e ruego a san Peydro que me ayude a rogar
por mio Çid el Campeador, que Dios le curie de mal.
Quando oy nos partimos, en vida nos faz juntar."

La oraçión fecha, la missa acabada la an,
salieron de la eglesia, ya quieren cavalgar.
El Çid a doña Ximena ívala abraçar;
doña Ximena al Çid la manol va besar,
llorando de los ojos, que non sabe qué se far.
E él a las niñas tornólas a catar:
" A Dios vos acomiendo e al Padre spirital;
agora nos partimos, Dios sabe el ajuntar."
Llorando de los ojos, que non vid*ie*stes atal,
assís parten unos d'otros commo la uña de la carne.

4. *Los Infantes de Carrión y el León*

Note how the terseness of the narrative reflects the author's scorn for the cowardly Infantes. He will waste no words in describing the incident in detail—he will merely outline it, neither inveighing against the cowards nor concealing his disgust with them, and pass on. There is enough detail, however (e.g., ll. 15, 20), to make the scene live, and the contrast drawn between the actions of the Infantes and of the Cid is eloquent in its brevity.

En Valençia se*dí* mio Çid con todos *los* sos,
con el*le* amos sos yernos ifantes de Carrión.
Yazies en un escaño, durmie el Campeador,
mala sobrevienta, sabed, que les cuntió:
saliós de la red e desatós el león.
En grant miedo se vieron por medio de la cort;
enbraçan los mantos los del Campeador,
e çercan el escaño, e fincan sobre so señor.

Ferran*t* Gonçál*v*ez ;   *ifant de Carrión*,
non vi*d*o allí dos alçasse,   nin cámara abierta nin torre ;
metiós sol escaño,   tanto ovo el pavor.
Dí*ag* Gonçál*v*ez   por la puerta salió,
diziendo de la boca :   " ¡ Non veré Carrión ! "
Tras una viga lagar   metiós con grant pavor ;
el manto e el brial   todo suzio lo sacó.

En esto despertó   el que en buen ora naçió ;
vi*d*o cercado el escaño   de s*o*s buenos varones :
" ¿ Qués esto, mesnadas,   o qué queredes vos ? "
" Hya señor ondrado,   rebata nos dió el león."
Mio Çid fincó el cobdo,   en pie se levantó,
el manto trae al cuello,   e adelinó pora' león ;
el león quando lo vío,   assí envergonçó,
ante mio Çid la cabeça   premió e el rostro fincó.
Mio Çid don Rodrigo   al cuello lo tomó,
e liévalo adestrando,   en la red le metió.
A maravilla lo han   quantos que i son,
e tornáronse al palaçio   pora la cort.

Mio Çid por sos yernos   demandó e no los falló ;
maguer los están llamando,   ninguno non responde.
Quando los fallaron,   assí vinieron sin color ;
non vi*d*iestes tal juego   commo iva por la cort ;
mandólo vedar   mio Çid el Campeador.
Muchos tovieron por enbaídos   ifantes de Carrión,
fiera cosa les pesa   desto que les cuntió.

5. *La Afrenta de Corpes*

With the story of the Infantes' villainous treatment of their brides we reach the highest point of emotional tension in the whole poem. The introductory description—hyperbolic in l. 2, picturesque in l. 4—itself suggests a change of tone, an impression confirmed by the ejaculation in l. 8 and by the contrast between the dark beast-haunted wood and the " vergel con una linpia fuont," which translates into material terms the contrast between hope and reality. The passage describing the maltreatment of the girls carries realism to a degree seldom found either elsewhere in this poem or elsewhere in mediaeval Spanish verse. Note the exclamatory form used by the author in ll. 45-6 in order to express his indignation and repeated in l. 57. Elsewhere in the passage, too, the device of repetition is used to convey emotion.

Entrados son los ifantes   al robredo de Corpes,
los montes son altos,   las ramas pujan con las nu*o*ves,
elas bestias fieras   que andan aderredor.
Fallaron un vergel   con una linpia fu*o*nt;
mandan fincar la tienda   ifantes de Carrión,
con quantos que ellos traen   i yazen essa noch,
con sus mugieres en braços   demuéstranles amor;
¡ mal gelo cunplieron   quando salie el sol!

Mandaron cargar las azémilas   con averes *a nombre*,
cogida han la tienda   do albergaron de noch,
adelant eran idos   los de criazón:
assí lo mandaron   ifantes de Carrión,
que non i fincás ninguno,   mugier nin varón,
si non amas sus mugieres   doña Elvira e doña Sol:
deportar se quieren con ellas   a todo su sabor.

Todos eran idos,   ellos quatro solos son,
tanto mal comidieron   ifantes de Carrión:
" Bien lo creades   don Elvira e doña Sol,
aquí seredes escarnidas   en estos fieros montes.
Oy nos partiremos,   e daxadas seredes de nos;
non abredes part   en tierras de Carrión.
Hirán aquestos mandados   al Çid Campeador;
nos vengaremos aquesta   por la del león."

Allí les tuellen   los mantos e los pelliçones,
páranlas en cuerpos   y en camisas y en çiclatones.
Espuelas tienen calçadas   los malos traydores,
en mano prenden las çinchas   fuertes e duradores.
Quando esto vieron las dueñas,   fablava doña Sol:
" ¡ Por Dios vos rogamos,   don Dí*a*go e don Ferrando, *nos*!
Dos espadas tenedes   fuertes e tajadores,
al una dizen Colada   e al otra Tizón,
cortandos las cabeças,   mártires seremos nos.

Moros e cristianos departirán desta razón,
que por lo que nos mereçemos no lo prendemos nos.
Atan malos enssienplos non fagades sobre nos :
si nos fuéremos majadas, abiltaredes a vos ;
retraer vos lo an en vistas o en cortes."

Lo que ruegan las dueñas non les ha ningún pro.
Essora les conpieçan a dar ifantes de Carrión ;
con las çinchas corredizas májanlas tan sin sabor ;
con las espuelas agudas, don ellas an mal sabor,
ronpien las camisas e las carnes a ellas amas a dos ;
linpia salie la sangre sobre los çiclatones.
Ya lo sienten ellas en los sos coraçones.
¡ Quál ventura serie esta, si ploguiesse al Criador,
que assomasse essora el Çid Campeador !

Tanto las majaron que sin cosimente son ;
sangrientas en las camisas e todos los çiclatones.
Canssados son de ferir ellos amos a dos,
ensayandos amos quál dará mejores colpes.
Hya non pueden fablar don Elvira e doña Sol,
por muertas las dexaron en el robredo de Corpes.

Leváronles los mantos e las pieles armiñas,
mas déxanlas marridas en briales y en camisas,
e a las aves del monte e a las bestias de la fiera guisa.
Por muertas las dexaron, sabed, que non por bivas.
¡ Quál ventura serie si assomas essora el Çid *Roy Díaz* !

Ifantes de Carrión por muertas las dexaron,
que el una al otra nol torna recabdo.
Por los montes do ivan, ellos ívanse alabando :
" De nuestros casamientos agora somos vengados.
Non las deviemos tomar por varraganas, si non fossemos rogados,
pues nuestras parejas non eran pora en braços.
La desondra del león assís irá vengando."

6. RAZÓN D'AMOR

Early 13th Century

Most early mediaeval lyrics, including the *Cantigas* of one of Spain's foremost poets, Alfonso X, were written, not in Castilian, but in Galician, and hence find no place in this collection. The earliest Castilian lyric poem is generally considered to be the "Razón d'amor," which, followed by a burlesque dispute in verse, in mediaeval fashion, between Water and Wine, is found in a manuscript belonging to the Bibliothèque Nationale, Paris. At the end of the manuscript stands the name of one " Lupus de Morus ", who may have been the author but was more probably a copyist. If we can judge by the author's own words (ll. 5-10: they may, of course, be simply in character) he was a blend of the cosmopolitan, the scholar and the courtier, but, despite much mediaeval artificiality and stylization, the atmosphere of the poem is popular and *juglaresco*. This is particularly true of the opening lines, the direct and personal appeal of which is reinforced by imagery affecting in turn all the senses, even those of touch (e.g., ll. 40-2) and smell (e.g., ll. 49-50). The principal evocations, however, are visual: it is interesting, even so early, to find so much colour—if simple and even crude—and so many references to individual, named flowers. The vivacity and energy of the dialogue are also noteworthy.

Qui triste tiene su coraçón
benga oir esta razón.
Odrá razón acabada,
feita d'amor e bien rimada.
Un escolar la rimó
que siempre duennas amó ;
mas siempre ovo criança
en Alemania y en Francia ;
moró mucho en Lombardía
pora aprender cortesía.

En el mes d'abril, depués yantar,
estava so un olivar.
Entre cimas d'un mançanar
un vaso de plata vi estar.
Pleno erą d'un claro vino
que era vermejo e fino ;
cubierto era de tal mesura
no lo tocás' la calentura.
Una duenna lo í eva puesto,
que era sennora del uerto,
que, quan su amigo viniesse,
d'aquel vino a bever le disse.
Qui de tal vino oviesse
en la manana quan comiesse,
e dello oviesse cada día
nuncas más enfermaría.
Arriba del mançanar
otro vaso vi estar ;
pleno era d'un agua frida
que en el mançanar se nacía.
Beviera d'ela de grado,
mas ovi miedo que era encantado.
Sobre un prado pus' mi tiesta
que no m' fiziesse mal la siesta ;
partí de mí las vistiduras
que nom' fiziés' mal la calentura.
Pleguém' a uña fuente perenal,
nunca fué omne que vies' tal ;
tan grant virtud en sí avía,
que de la fridor que d'í ixía,
cient pasadas a derredor
non sintríades la calor.
Todas yerbas que bien olién
la fuent cerca sí las tenié :
í es la salvia, í son as rosas,
í el lirio e las violas ;
otras tantas yervas í avía,
que sol' nombra no las sabría.
Mas ell olor que d'í ixía
a omne muerto ressucitaría.

Pris' del agua un bocado
e fuí todo esfriado.
En mi mano pris' una flor,
sabet, non toda la peyor,
e quis' cantar de fin amor.
Mas vi venir una doncela,
pues nací non vi tan bella :
blanca era e bermeja,
cabelos cortos sobr'ell oreja,
fruente blanca e loçana,
cara fresca como maçana ;
nariz egual e dreita,
nunca viestes tan bien feita,
ojos negros e ridientes,
boca a razón e blancos dientes,
labros vermejos, non muy delgados,
por verdat bien mesurados ;
por la centura delgada,
bien estant e mesurada ;
el manto e su brial
de xamet era, que non d'al ;
un sombrero tien' en la tiesta
que nol' fiziesse mal la siesta ;
unas luvas tien' en la mano,
sabet, non gelas dió vilano.
De las flores viene tomando,
en alta voz d'amor cantando,
e decía : " ¡ Ay, meu amigo,
si me veré ya más contigo !
Amet sempre e amaré
quanto que biva seré.
Porque eres escolar
quisquiere te devría más amar.
Nunqua odí de homne decir
que tanta bona manera ovo en sí.
Más amaría contigo estar
que toda Espanna mandar.
Mas d'una cosa so cuitada ;
he miedo de seder enganada,
que dizen que otra dona,

cortesa e bela e bona
te quiere tan gran ben,
por ti pierde su sen,
e por eso he pavor
que a ésa quieras mejor.
¡ Mas si io te vies' una vegada,
a plan me queriés por amada ! "

Quant la mia senor esto dizía,
sabet, a mí non vidía ;
pero sé que no me conocía,
que de mí non foiría.
Yo non fiz aquí como vilano ;
levém' e pris' la por la mano.
Junniemos amos en par
e posamos so ell olivar.
Dix' le yo : " Dezit, la mia senor,
si supiestes nunca d'amor."
Diz ella : " A plan, con grant amor ando,
mas non connozco mi amado ;
pero dizem' un su mesajero,
qu'es clérigo e non cavalero,
sabe muito de trobar,
de leyer e de cantar ;
dizem' que es de buenas yentes,
mancebo barvapunnientes."
—" Por Dios, que digades, la mia senor,
¿ qué donas tenedes por la su amor ? "
—" Estas luvas y es' capiello,
est' oral y est' aniello
enbió a mí es' meu amigo,
que por la su amor trayo conmigo."
Yo connocí luego las alfayas
que yo gelas avía enbiadas.
Ela connoció una mi cinta man a mano,
qu'ela la fiziera con la su mano.
Toliós' el manto de los onbros,
besóme la boca e por los ojos ;
tan gran sabor de mí avía,
sol' fablar non me podía.

—" ¡ Dios Senor, a ti loado
quant conozco meu amado !
¡ Agora he tod' bien comigo
quant conozco meo amigo ! "
Una grant pieça alí estando,
de nuestro amor ementando,
ela dixo : " El mio senor,
oram' sería de tornar
si a vos non fuesse en pesar."
Yo l' dix' : " It, la mia senor,
pues que ir queredes,
mas de mi amor pensat, fe que devedes."
Elam dixo : " Bien seguro seit de mi amor,
no vos camiaré por un enperador."
La mia senor se va privado,
dexa a mi desconortado.
Que que la vi fuera del uerto,
por poco non fuí muerto.
Por verdat quisieram' adormir,
mas una palomela vi,
tan blanca era como la niev del puerto,
volando viene por medio del uerto . . .
Un cascavielo dorado
tray al pie atado.
En la fuent quiso entrar ;
quando a mi vido estar
entrós en el vaso del malgranar.
Quando en el vaso fué entrada,
e fué toda bien esfríada,
ela que quiso exir festino,
vertiós' el agua sobr'el vino . . .

GONZALO DE BERCEO

*c.*1180-1250

BERCEO, a monastery-bred priest (but not a monk), is an erudite who affects simplicity, a man who conceals a sense of humour beneath a grave manner and a poet *in posse* who is too often prosaic and even prosy. " Tuvo alma de poeta ", says Menéndez y Pelayo of him[1], which is about as far in that direction as one can go. But he is generally readable, often amusing and now and then surprisingly good. Practically all his poems, long or short, are religious in character—panegyrics of the Virgin Mary, biographies of local saints or thinly disguised treatises on doctrine. One reads them to-day chiefly for their touches of humanity, of feeling for Nature, and more rarely, of lyric emotion : it is noteworthy that in recent years Berceo should have been eulogized and imitated by writers as modern as Antonio and Manuel Machado, Pérez de Ayala and Azorín.

7. *Eya velar*

When he can escape from the bondage of the cuaderna vía *(p. 26), or " fourfold way " (which Rubén Darío once described as a primitive cage imprisoning a divine bird), Berceo is a tuneful song-writer. This* canción de vela, *in the fifty-four lines of which the quaint, plaintive refrain, with the alternating vowels, which has popularized it occurs thirty-two times, has little merit beyond melody ; but it comes as a relief after the " Duelo de la Virgen " of which it forms a part. Here Berceo is labouring (or so it seems) to give life to the* cuaderna vía *by means of such devices as antithesis, repetition and climax. Actually his simplest lines are his best :*

Dia que el sol muere non es complido día,

especially when they are lit by a flash of imagination :

Fijo, que más alumnas que el sol ni la luna.

[1] M.P., *Ant.*, II, xlviii.

At the end of the poem the Jews go to the Holy Sepulchre to watch over the body of Christ. " Eya velar " is introduced by the two following quatrains :

Tornaron al sepulcro vestidos de lorigas,
diciendo de sus bocas muchas sucias nemigas,
controbando cantares que non valían tres figas,
tocando instrumentos, cedras, rotas, e gigas.

Cantaban los trufanes unas controvaduras
que eran a su Madre amargas e muy duras :
" Aljama, nos velemos, andemos en corduras,
si non, farán de nos escarnio e gahurras."

Eya velar, eya velar, ¡ eya velar !

Velat aljama de los judiós,
¡ eya velar !,
que non vos furten el Fijo de Dios.
¡ Eya velar !

Ca furtárvoslo querrán,
¡ eya velar !
Andrés e Peidro et Johan.
¡ Eya velar !

Non sabedes tanto descanto,
¡ eya velar !,
que salgades de so el canto.
¡ Eya velar !

Todos son ladronciellos,
¡ eya velar !
que assechan por los pestiellos.
¡ Eya velar !

Vuestra lengua tan palabrera,
¡ eya velar !,
havos dado mala carrera.
¡ Eya velar !

Todos son omnes plegadizos,
¡ eya velar !,
rioaduchos mescladizos.
¡ Eya velar !

Vuestra lengua sin recabdo,
¡ eya velar !,
por mal cabo vos ha echado.
¡ Eya velar !

Non sabedes tanto de enganno,
¡ eya velar !,
que salgades ende este anno.
¡ Eya velar !

Non sabedes tant razón,
¡ eya velar !,
que salgades de la prisión.
¡ Eya velar !

Tomaseio e Matheo,
¡ eya velar !,
de furtarlo han grant deseo.
¡ Eya velar !

El discípulo lo vendió,
¡ eya velar !,
el Maestro non lo entendió.
¡ Eya velar !

Don Philipo, Simón e Judas,
¡ eya velar !,
por furtar buscan ayudas.
¡ Eya velar !

Si lo quieren acometer,
¡ eya velar !,
¡ oy es día de parescer !
¡ Eya velar !

Eya velar, eya velar, ¡ eya velar !

8. *Milagros de Nuestra Señora*

(*Introduction*)

Nowhere, perhaps, in Berceo, is one more conscious than here of the inhibiting effect upon him of his metrical "cage". He seems to be striving with all his might to express strong lyrical emotion, yet without success. Centuries later San Juan de la Cruz could have taught him (p. 267, ll. 38-40) how to give reality to the line

Yaciendo a la sombra perdí todos cuidados,

and Luis de León (also "tendido . . . . . . a la sombra": p. 209, l. 1) could have shown him how to describe the birds' songs with emotion and delight, not by piling up adjectives and amassing comparisons, but by one simple touch:

Despiértenme las aves
con su cantar sabroso no aprendido (p. 207, ll. 31-2)

Yet, for all their stiffness and prosiness, there is a sense of spring-time about these lines—of the spring-time of Spanish poetry, with its quickening emotion and nascent power; for which reason alone they will be sure of immortality.

Amigos e vasallos de Dios omnipotent,
si vos me escuchássedes por vuestro consiment,
querría vos contar un buen aveniment;
terrédeslo en cabo por bueno verament.

Yo maestro Gonçalvo de Berceo nomnado
yendo en romería caecí en un prado
verde e bien sencido, de flores bien poblado,
logar cobdiciaduero pora omne cansado.

Daban olor sobejo las flores bien olintes,
refrescavan en omne las caras e las mientes,
manavan cada canto fuentes claras corrientes,
en verano bien frías, en ivierno calientes.

Avie í grand abondo de buenas arboledas,
milgranos e figueras, peros e mazanedas,
e muchas otras fructas de diversas monedas;
mas non avie ningunas podridas nin acedas.

La verdura del prado, la olor de las flores,
las sombras de los árbores de temprados sabores
refrescaronme todo, e perdí los sudores:
podrié vevir el omne con aquellos olores.

Nunqua trobé en sieglo logar tan deleitoso,
nin sombra tan temprada, ni olor tan sabroso.
Descargué mi ropiella por yacer más vicioso,
poséme a la sombra de un árbor fermoso.

Yaciendo a la sombra perdí todos cuidados;
odí sonos de aves dulces e modulados.
Nunqua udieron omnes órganos más temprados,
nin que formar pudiessen sones más acordados.

Unas tenien la quinta, e las otras doblavan,
otras tenien el punto, errar no las dexavan;
al posar, al mover todas se esperavan,
aves torpes nin roncas i non se acostavan.

Non serie organista, nin serie violero,
nin giga, nin salterio, nin mano de rotero,
nin estrument, nin lengua, nin tan claro vocero,
cuyo canto valiesse con esto un dinero.

Pero que vos dissiemos todas estas bondades,
non contamos las diezmas, esto bien lo creades:
que avie de noblezas tantas diversidades,
que no las contarien priores ni abbades.

El prado que vos digo avie otra bondat:
por calor nin por frío non perdie su beltat;
siempre estava verde en su entegredat,
non perdie la verdura por nulla tempestat.

Man a mano que fuí en tierra acostado,
de todo el lazerio fuí luego folgado;
oblidé toda cuita, el lazerio passado:
¡qui allí se morasse serié bien venturado!

Los omnes e las aves quantas acaecien,
levaban de las flores quantas levar querien;
mas mengua en el prado niguna non facien:
por una que levaban, tres e quatro nacien.

Semeja esti prado egual de paraíso,
en qui Dios tan grant gracia, tan grant bendición miso:

el que crió tal cosa, maestro fué anviso :
omne que í morasse, nunqua perdrie el viso.

El fructo de los árbores era dulz e sabrido,
si don Adam oviesse de tal fructo comido,
de tan mala manera non serie decibido,
nin tomarien tal danno Eva ni so marido.

Sennores e amigos, lo que dicho avemos,
palabra es oscura, esponerla queremos :
tolgamos la corteza, al meollo entremos,
prendamos lo de dentro, lo de fuera dessemos.

Todos cuantos vevimos que en piedes andamos,
si quiere en presón, o en lecho yagamos,
todos somos romeos que camino andamos :
Sant Peidro lo diz esto, por él vos lo provamos.

Quanto aquí vivimos, en ageno moramos ;
la ficança durable suso la esperamos.
La nuestra romería estonz la acabamos
quando a paraíso las almas enviamos.

En esta romería avemos un buen prado,
en qui trova repaire tot romeo cansado :
la Virgin Gloriosa, Madre del buen criado,
del qual otro ninguno egual non fué trobado.

Esti prado fué siempre verde en onestat,
ca nunca ovo mácula la su virginidat :
post partum et in partu fué Virgin de verdat,
illesa, incorrupta en su entegredat.

Las quatro fuentes claras que del prado manavan,
los quatro evangelios esso significavan,
ca los evangelistas quatro que los dictavan,
cuando los escrivien, con ella se fablavan.

Quanto escrivien ellos, ella lo emendava,
esso era bien firme, lo que ella laudava :
parece que el riego todo della manava,
quando a menos della nada non se guiava.

La sombra de los árbores, buena, dulz e sanía,
en qui ave repaire toda la romería,
sí son las oraciones que faz Santa María,
que por los peccadores ruega noch' e dia.

Quantos que son en mundo justos e peccadores,
coronados e legos, reys e enperadores
allí corremos todos, vassallos e sennores,
todos a la su sombra imos coger las flores.

Los árbores que facen sombra dulz e donosa,
son los santos miraclos que faz la Gloriosa,
ca son mucho más dulzes que azúcar sabrosa,
la que dan al enfermo en la cuita raviosa.

Las aves que organan entre essos fructales,
que han las dulzes vozes, dicen cantos leales,
éstos son Agustínt, Gregorio, otros tales,
quantos que escrivieron los sos fechos reales.

Estos avien con ella amor e atenencia,
en laudar los sos fechos metien toda femencia,
todos fablaban della, cascuno su sentencia ;
pero tenien por todo todos una creencia.

El rosennor que canta por fina maestría,
siquiere la calandria que faz grant melodía,
mucho cantó mejor el varón Isaía,
e los otros prophetas, onrada companía.

Cantaron los apóstolos muedo mui natural,
confessores e mártires facien bien otro tal,
las vírgines siguieron la grand Madre caudal,
cantan delante della canto bien festival.

Por todas las eglesias, esto es cada día,
cantan laudes antella toda la clerecía ;
todos li facen cort a la Virgo María :
estos son rossennoles de grant placentería.

Tornemos ennas flores que conponen el prado,
que lo facen fermoso, apuesto e temprado :
las flores son los nomnes que li da el dictado
a la Virgo María, Madre del buen criado.

La benedicta Virgen es estrella clamada,
estrella de los mares, guiona deseada,
es de los marineros en las cuitas guardada,
ca quando essa veden, es la nave guiada.

Es clamada, e eslo de los cielos, Reína,
tiemplo de Jesu Cristo, estrella matutina,

sennora natural, pïadosa vezina,
de cuerpos e de almas salut e medicina . . . . . .

Non es nomne ninguno que bien derecho venga,
que en alguna guisa a ella non avenga :
non ha tal que raíz en ella no la tenga,
nin Sancho nin Domingo, nin Sancha nin Domenga,

Es dicha vid, es uva, almendra, malgranada
que de granos de gracia está toda calcada ;
oliva, cedro, bálssamo, palma bien ajumada,
piértega en que sovo la serpiente alzada.

El fust de Moises enna mano portava
que confondió los sabios que Faraón preciava,
el que abrió los mares e depues los cerrava
si non a la Gloriosa, al non significava.

Si metieremos mientes en ell otro bastón
que partió la contienda que fué por Aarón,
al non significava, como diz la lección
si non a la Gloriosa, esto bien con razón.

Sennores e amigos, en vano contendemos,
entramos en grand pozo, fondo nol trovaremos ;
más serien los sus nomnes que nos della leemos
que las flores del campo del más grand que savemos.

Desuso lo dissiemos que eran los fructales
en qui facien las aves los cantos generales,
los sus santos miraclos grandes e principales,
los quales organamos ennas fiestas caubdales.

Quiero dexar con tanto las aves cantadores,
las sombras e las aguas, las devant dichas flores :
quiero destos fructales, tan plenos de dulzores,
fer unos poccos viessos, amigos e sennores.

Quiero en estos árbores un ratiello sobir,
e de los sos miraclos algunos escrivir,
la Gloriosa me guíe que lo pueda complir,
ca yo non me trevría en ello a venir.

Terrélo por miráculo que lo faz la Gloriosa
si guiarme quisiere a mí en esta cosa :
¡ Madre plena de gracia, Reína poderosa,
tú me guía en ello, ca eres piadosa !

9. POEMA DE FERNÁN GONZÁLEZ

*c.*1250

THIS is one of several long poems written about the middle of the thirteenth century which use a stanza, composed of four Alexandrine or fourteen-syllabled lines, with one single rhyme, known as the *cuaderna vía* or " fourfold way ". Antonio Machado aptly describes these stanzas as

monótonas hileras
de chopos invernales, en donde nada brilla.

They are, indeed, apt to be monotonous, even where melodious, as in Berceo, and most of all when, as here and in the *Libro de Apolonio*, they go on for nearly three thousand lines, or, as in the *Libro de Alexandre*, for over ten thousand. Fernán González was the famous Count of Castile who early in the tenth century gained Castile her independence of León. Throughout a great part of its course the poem pursues an uninspired and uninspiring narrative : it has purple patches, however, some of which derive their attractiveness from the author's feeling for his " country ". What that last word means to him will be clear from the passage which follows.

Por eso vos digo aqueso, que bien lo entendades,
mejor es d'otras tierras en las que vos morades :
de todo es bien conplida en la que vos estades,
dezir vos he agora quantas ha de vondades.

Tierra es muy tenprada, sin grandes calenturas :
non faze en ivierno destenpradas friuras ;
non es tierra en el mundo que aya tales pasturas,
árvoles pora fruta siquier de mil naturas.

Sobre todas las tierras, mejor es la montanna,
de vacas e de ovejas non hay tierra tamanna,
tantos ha y de puercos que es fiera fazanna:
sírvense muchas tierras de las cosas de Espanna.

Es de lino e lana tierra mucho avastada,
de cera sobre todas vuena tierra provada,
non sería de aceite en todo el mundo tal fallada,
Inglatierra e Francia desto es mucho avondada.

Buena tierra de caça e buena de venados,
de río e de mar, muchos buenos pescados,
quien los quiere recientes, quien los quiere salados:
son d'estas cosas tales pueblos muy abastados.

De panes e de vinos tierra muy comunal,
non fallarían en el mundo otra mejor nin tal,
muchas de buenas fuentes e mucho buen río cabdal,
e otras muchas mas fuertes de que fazen la sal.

Ha y sierras e valles e mucha de buena mata,
todas llenas de grana pora fer escarlata.
Ha y venas de oro, que es de mejor varata,
ha y muchas venas de fierro, muchas de cal e plata.

Por lo que ella más val, aun non vos lo dixemos,
de los buenos cavalleros aun mención non fiziemos:
mejor tierra es de las que quantas nunca viemos,
nunca tales cavalleros en el mundo nunca viemos.

Dexarvos quiero desto, que assaz vos he contado,
non quiero más dezir, que podría ser errado,
pero non olvidemos al apóstol honrado,
fijo del Zebedeo, Santiago llamado.

Fuertemente quiso Dios a Espanna honrar,
quando al santo apóstol quiso aí enbiar,
d' Inglatierra e Francia quísola mejorar,
que sabet que non yaze apóstol en todo aquel logar.

Onróle d'otra guisa el precioso Sennor:
fueron i muchos santos muertos por su sennor,
que de morir a cochillo non ovieron temor,
muchas vírgenes y santas e mucho buen confesor.

Commo ella es mejor de las sus vezindades,
assí sodes mejores quantos aquí morades,
omnes sodes sesudos e mesura heredades,
desto por todo el mundo muy gran precio ganades.

Pero de toda Espanna, Castilla es mejor,
porque fué de los otros el comienço mayor,
guardando e temiendo sienpre a su sennor,
quiso acrecentar assí el Criador.

Aun Castilla Vieja, al mi entendimiento,
mejor es que lo al, porque fué el cimiento,
ca conquirieron mucho, maguer poco conviento :
bien lo podedes ver en el acabamiento.

10. LIBRO DE APOLONIO

*c.*1250

ANOTHER of the mid-thirteenth-century verse narratives in the *cuaderna vía* is this Byzantine romance on a theme made familiar to English readers by Shakespeare's *Pericles.* It is the story of Apollonius of Tyre, whose wife Luciana, while on a voyage, gives birth to a daughter, is thought to be dead and is buried at sea. Her coffin is washed up on a foreign shore, and, recovering from her death-like swoon, she becomes a priestess of Diana, while later her daughter, Tarsiana, is kidnapped and sold as a slave. Eventually, by a series of romantic coincidences, husband, wife and daughter are brought together again and live happily ever after.

The passage here reproduced—a typical specimen of the author's style—refers to Luciana's courtship by Apollonius, who is teaching her music. So intense is her love for him that she falls ill with a malady to which the doctors can give no name. Meanwhile three princes come to woo her. The King, her father, bids them apply for her hand in writing, and it falls to her music-master to deliver her the three letters.

Fué luego Apolonio recabdar el mandado ;
levólas a la duenya como le fué castigado.
Ella, quando lo vió venir atán escalentado,
mesturar non lo quiso lo que havía asmado.

" Maestro ", dixo ella, " quiero te demandar
¿ qué buscas a tal ora, o qué quieres recabtar ?
Que a tal sazón como ésta tú non sueles aquí entrar.
Nunca lición me sueles a tal hora pasar."

Entendió Apolonio la su entención :
" Fija ", dixo, " non vengo por pasarvos lición.
Desto seyet bien segura en vuestro corazón,
mas mentsage vos trayo, porque merecía gran don.

" El rey vuestro padre salióse a deportar,
fasta que fuesse ora de venir a yantar ;
vinieron tres infantes pora vos demandar,
todos muy fermosos, nobles e de prestar.

" Sópoles vuestro padre ricamiente recebir,
mas non sabie atanto que pudiese dezir.
Mandóles sendas cartas a todos escrevir.
Vos veyet qual queredes de todos escogir."

Priso ella las cartas maguer enferma era,
abriólas e católas fasta la vez tercera.
Non vio í el nombre en carta ni en cera,
con cuyo casamiento ella fuese plazentera.

Cató a Apolonio, e dixo con gran sospiro :
" Dígasme, Apolonio, el mio buen Rey de Tiro,
en este casamiento de ti mucho me miro ;
si te plaze, o si non, yo tu voluntat requiro."

Respuso Apolonio e fabló con gran cordura :
" Duenya, si me pesasse faría muy gran locura.
Lo que al Rey ploguiere e fuere vuestra ventura,
yo si lo destajasse faría gran locura.

" Hevos yo bien ensenyada de lo que yo sabía ;
más vos preciaron todos por la mi maestría.
Desaquí si casardes a vuestra mejoría,
avré de vuestra hondra muy grant plazentería."

" Maestro ", dixo ella, " si amor te tocase,
non querries que tu lazerio otrie lograse,
nunqua lo creyería fasta que lo provase,
que del Rey de Tiro desdenyada fincase."

Escrivió una carta, e cerróla con cera ;
dióla a Apolonio que mensajero era,
que la diesse al Rey que estava en la glera.
Sabet que fué aína andada la carrera.

Abrió el Rey la carta, e fízola catar,
la carta dizía esto, sópola bien dictar :
que con el pelegrino quería ella casar,
que con el cuerpo solo estorció de la mar.

Fízose de esta cosa el Rey maravillado,
non podía entender la fuerça del dictado.
Demandó que quál era el infante venturado,
que lidió con las ondas e con el mar irado.

Dixo el uno de ellos, e cuydó seyer artero,
Aguylón le dizen por nombre bien certero:
" Rey, yo fuí esse e fuí verdadero,
ca escape apenas en poco dun madero."

Dixo el uno dellos: " Es mentira provada,
yo lo sé bien que dizes cosa desaguisada;
en uno nos criamos, non traspasso nada,
bien lo se que nunca tu prendiste tal espadada."

Mientre ellos estavan en esta tal entencia,
entendió bien el Rey que dixera fallencia.
Asmó entre su cuer una buena entencia,
ca era de buen seso e de gran sapiencia.

Dió a Apolonio la carta a leyer
si podrie por aventura la cosa entender;
vió el Rey de Tiro qué avía de seyer;
començóle la cara toda a embermejecer.

Fué el Rey metiendo mientes en la razón,
fuésele demudando todo el corazón,
echó a Apolonio mano al cabeçón,
apartóse con él sin otro nuyll varón.

Dixo: " Yo te conjuro, maestro e amigo,
por el amor que yo tengo establecido contigo,
como tú lo entiendes que lo fables comigo;
si non, por tu fazienda non daría un figo."

Respuso Apolonio: " Rey, mucho me embargas,
fuertes paraulas me dizes e mucho me amargas;
creio que de mí traen estas nuevas tan largas,
mas si a ti non plazen son pora mí amargas."

Recudióle el Rey como leyal varón:
" Non te mintré, maestro, que sería traiçón.
Quando ella lo quiere, plázeme de corazón.
Otorgada la ayas sin nulla condición."

Destajaron la fabla, tornaron al concejo.
" Amigos," diz, " non quiero trayervos en trasecho.
Prendet vuestra carrera, buscat otro consejo,
ca yo vo entendiendo dello un poquellejo."

Entraron a la villa, que ya querien comer,
subieron al castiello la enferma veyer.
Ella, quando vido el Rey cerca de sí seyer,
fízose más enferma, començó de tremer.

" Padre ", dixo la duenya con la boz enflaquida,
" ¿ qué buscastes a tal hora ? ¿ Cuál fué vuestra venida ?
De coraçón me pesa, e he rencura sabida,
por qué vos es la yantar a tanto deferida."

" Fija ", dixo el padre, " de mí non vos quexedes :
más cuita es lo vuestro que tan gran mal avedes.
Quiero vos fablar un poco que non vos enojedes,
que verdat me digades quál marido queredes."

" Padre, bien vos lo digo quando vos me lo demandades,
que si de Apolonio en otro me camiades,
non vos miento, desto bien seguro seyades,
en pie non me veredes quantos días bivades."

" Fija ", dixo el rey, " gran placer me ficiestes ;
de Dios vos vino esto que tan bien escogiestes.
Condonado vos seya esto que vos pidiestes,
bien lo queremos todos cuando vos lo quisiestes."

Salió, esto partido, el Rey por el corral,
fallóse con su yerno en medio del portal.
Afirmaron la cosa en recabdo cabdal ;
luego fué abaxando a la duenya el mal.

Fueron las bodas fechas ricas e abondadas ;
fueron muchas de yentes a ellas conbidadas ;
duraron muchos días, que non eran pasadas ;
por esos grandes tienpos non fueron olvidadas.

Entró entre los novios muyt gran dilección ;
el Criador entre ellos metió su bendición ;
nunca varón a fembra, nin fembra a varón
non servió en este mundo de mejor coraçón.

LIBRO DE ALEXANDRE

Mid-13th Century

This huge erudite epic, for long erroneously attributed to Berceo, is now generally believed to have been written by a certain "bon clérigo e ondrado", Juan Lorenzo, a native of Astorga, whose name is given at the end of one of the extant manuscript copies. Prosaic and uninspired though much of it is, it has many fine passages, and a few pages of excerpts are quite inadequate for giving an idea of its varied qualities. Among these are vivid descriptions, digressions testifying to a powerful imagination, vast allegorical ingenuity, a sweep and range which suggested to Mérimée a blend of Dante, Sindbad the Sailor and Jules Verne, and an encyclopaedic knowledge. The poem has been described as the first chivalric romance in Spanish, not only because its hero, Alexander the Great, is the "very perfect gentle knight," but because of its impregnation with the idealistic and "marvellous".

11. "*El omne en su tierra . . . .*"

El omne en su tierra vive más a sabor;
fázenle a la morte los parientes honor;
los ossos e l'alma han folgança maor
quando muchos parientes están aderredor.

Los omnes de la villa al que es estraño
en cabo del fossano lo echan orelano;
danle cuemo a puerco ena fossa de mano;
nunca diz más nadi: "Aquí iaz fulano."

Mas el omne que es de çruda voluntad
cuida que los otros son sen piadat:
cuemo assí él es leno de malvestat,
tien que ennos otros non ha caridat.

Non serien las mugieres tan desvergonçadas
que por dulda del sieglo non fuessen defamadas,
que no lieven a la eglesia candelas e obradas
e non fagan clamores tanner a las vegadas.

Los fijos e las fijas dulces son de veer,
han de su companna los parientes placer:
encara no los puede tanto avorrecer
que descobiertamiente le quieran fallecer.

Amigos, quien quesier creer e ascuchar,
non plantará majuelo en ajeno lugar:
buscará cuemo pueda a su tierra tornar:
crudo es e loco quien su casa quier desamparar.

12. *El Mes de Mayo*

El mes era de mayo, un tiempo glorioso,
quando fazen las aves un solaz deleitoso;
son vestidos los prados de vestido fremoso;
da sospiros la duena, la que non ha esposo.

Tiempo dolce e sabroso por bastir casamientos,
ca lo tempran las flores e los sabrosos vientos;
cantan las donzelletas, son muchas a convientos;
fazen unas a otras buenos pronunciamientos.

Caen en el serano las bonas rociadas;
entran en flor las miesses ca son ya espigadas;
¡ entón casan algunos que pues messan las varvas!
fazen las duenas triscas en camisas delgadas.

Andan moças e viejas cobiertas en amores;
van coger por la siesta a los prados las flores;
dizen unas a otras: "¡ Bonos son los amores!"
Y aquellos plus tiernos tiénense por mejores.

Los días son grandes, los campos reverdidos;
son los passariellos del mal pelo exidos;
los távanos que muerden non son aún venidos;
luchan los monagones en bragas sen vestidos.

13. *La Tienda de Alejandro*

Bien parecie la tienda, quando era alzada :
suso era redonda en derredor quadrada ;
de somo fasta fondo era bien escoriada
qual cosa conteció a omne cual temporada.

Era enna corona el cielo deboxado
todo de creaturas angélicas poblado,
mas el lugar do fuera Lucifer derribado
todo está yermo, pobre e desonrado.

Criava Dios al omne pora enchir es lugar ;
el malo con enbidia óvogelo a furtar ;
por el furto los ángeles ovieron grant pesar ;
fue julgado el omne pora morir e lazdrar.

Cerca estas estorias e cerca un rincón
alzavan los gigantes torre a grant misión ;
mas metió Dios en ellos tan grant confusión
por que avien de ir todos a perdición.

Las ondas del deluvio tanto querien sobir ;
per somo de Tiburio fascas querien salir.
Noe bevie el vino, no lo podie sofrir,
azie desordenado queria lo encobrir.

En un de los fastiales, luego enna entrada,
la natura del anno sedie toda pintada :
los meses con sos días, con su luna contada,
cada uno cual fazienda avie acomendada.

Estava don Janero a todas partes catando,
cercado de cenisa, sus cepos acarreando ;
tenie gruessas gallinas, estávalas assando,
estava de la percha longaniças tirando.

Estava don Fevrero sos manos calentando,
oras fazie sol, oras sarraceando ;
verano e invierno ívalos destremando ;
porque era más chico seiesse querellando.

Marcio avie grant priessa de sus vinnas lavrar,
priessa con podadores, e priessa de cavar ;
los días e las noches fazíelos iguar,
faze aves e bestias en celo entrar.

Abril sacava huestes pora ir guerrear,
ca avie alcaceres grandes ya pora segar;
fazie meter las vinnas pora vino levar,
crecer miesses e yervas, los días alongar.

Sedie el mes de Mayo coronado de flores,
afeitando los campos de diversas colores,
organeando las mayas, e cantando d'amores,
espigando las miesses que sembran lavradores.

Madurava don Junio las miesses e los prados,
tenie redor de sí muchos ordios segados,
de ceresas maduras los ceresos cargados;
eran a mayor siesto los días allegados.

Seía el mes de Julio cogendo segadores,
corríenle por la cara apriessa los sudores,
segudavan las bestias los moscardos mordedores,
fazie tornar los vinos de amargos sabores.

Trillava don Agosto las miesses per las serras,
aventava las parvas, alçava las ceveras:
iva de los agrazes faziendó uvas veras:
estón fazía Outunno sus órdenes primeras.

Setembrio trae varas, sacude las nogueras,
apretava las cubas, podava las vimbreras,
vendimiava las vinnas con fuertes podaderas;
non dexava los pássaros llegar a las figueras.

Estava don Ochubrio sus missiegos faziendo;
iva como de nuevo sus cosas requiriendo;
iva pora sembrar el invierno veniendo,
ensayando los vinos que azen ya ferviendo.

Novenbrio secudía a los puercos las landes,
caera d'un rovre, levávanlo en andes;
compieçan al crisuelo velar los aveçantes,
ca son las noches luengas, los días non tan grandes.

Matava los puercos Decembrio por mannana;
almorçavan los fégados por amatar la gana;
tenie niubla escura siempre por la mannana,
ca es en es(e) tiempo ela muy cotiana.

SEM TOB

Early 14th Century

If there is little poetry in the verses of the Rabbi Sem Tob, there is a great deal both of individuality and of technical skill. His *Proverbios morales*, totalling 2,744 lines, are for the most part aphoristic in style, Oriental in flavour and Biblical in phraseology. They have little feeling for Nature—indeed, they maintain a complete impassivity here—and their images are undeveloped and external. Yet, bare and unadorned though the *Proverbios* are, they often attract the reader by their very conciseness and austerity. Sem Tob maintains a notable economy of words, as might be expected of one who chose to write exclusively in quatrains of which the lines had only seven syllables. The panegyric of reading here reproduced reveals the Rabbi as one of Spain's first "bookmen".

14. *Non hay commo el saber*

En el mundo tal cabdal
non hay commo el saber :
más que heredad val,
nin thesoro, nin aver.
El saber es la gloria
de Dios y donadío :
non se fallará en estoria
tal joya nin averío.
Nin mejor compannía
que el libro, nin tal ;
tomar grande porfía
con él, más que paz val.
Quanto más va tomando
con el libro porfía,
tanto irá ganando
buen saber toda vía.

Los sabios que querría
ver, ahí los fallará
en él, y toda vía
con ellos fablará.
Los sabios, muy loados,
que onbre deseava,
filósofos honrados
que ver los cobdiciava.
Lo que de aquellos sabios
él cobdicia avía,
e de los sus labrios
oír sabiduría ;
allí lo fallará
en el libro signado,
y respuesta averá
dellos por su dictado.
Fallará nueva cosa
de buen saber onesto,
y mucha sotil glosa
que fizieron al testo.
Si quiero, en leer
sus letras y sus versos,
más sé que non por ver
sus carnes y sus huesos.
La su ciencia muy pura
escrita la dexaron,
sin ninguna boltura
corporal la sumaron.
Sin mezcla therrenal
de ningunt elemento :
saber celestial,
claro de entendimiento.
Por esto sólo quier
todo onbre de cordura
a los sabios veer,
non por la su figura.
Por ende tal amigo
non hay commo el libro :
para los sabios, digo,
que con los torpes non libro.

JUAN RUIZ, ARCIPRESTE DE HITA

*c.*1283-*c.*1350

JUAN RUIZ, author of the *Libro de Buen Amor*, is one of the most brilliant Spanish writers of the Middle Ages. Beyond the facts that he was Archpriest of Hita (a town lying between Guadalajara and Sigüenza), and in the latter part of his life was imprisoned by order of the Archbishop of Toledo, nothing is known of him from external sources with any certainty. In his book, however, we find a complete account of his personal appearance, ample proof of his considerable learning and numerous indications that he led a life quite unbefitting a cleric—though of course there is no means of ascertaining if these details are genuinely autobiographical. Ruiz is of the greatest significance both for his artistry and for what lies beneath it. His glorification of the sensuous and the sensual foreshadows Rabelais, while his frequent outbursts of apparently sincere piety remind us that this age of licence was also the age of faith. With his go-between, Trotaconventos, derived from Ovid, Ruiz inaugurates that splendid succession of realistic portraits which adorns Spanish fiction, and of which an outstanding example is Trotaconventos' direct descendant, Celestina. Other of his figures—Don Melón and Doña Endrina, Don Carnal and Doña Cuaresma, and, of course, Don Amor—are also, in their several ways, masterpieces. As a satirist, he lacks indignation, but is trenchant and convincing—and one can never be sure that his satire does not go much deeper than it appears to do, as, for instance, in the book's very title. Many of his digressions, such as that on " little women " reproduced below, are among the most striking of his passages. He rejuvenates the *cuaderna vía* and sometimes transforms it, as well as using all kinds of other metres with consummate skill. He is, in short, an all-round genius.

15. *Enxienplo de la propiedat que'l dinero ha*

In a less robust personality the Archpriest's typically ironical attitude towards life would be called cynical. His acute mind fully apprehends human frailty, inconsistency and injustice, but his artistic faculty prefers to dwell on the engrossing spectacle it presents, and does so with keen gusto. So in these lines he lavishes vivacious detail on the simony, greed and corruption of his age, without passing any moral judgment upon it as a whole.

Mucho faz' el dinero, mucho es de amar :
al torpe faze bueno e ome de prestar.
Faze correr al coxo e al mudo fablar ;
el que non tiene manos, dineros quier' tomar.

Sea un ome nesçio e rudo labrador,
los dineros le fazen fidalgo e sabidor.
Quanto más algo tiene, tanto es de más valor ;
el que non ha dineros, non es de sí señor.

Si tovieres dineros, avrás consolación,
plazer e alegría e del papa ración ;
conprarás paraiso, ganarás salvación :
do son muchos dineros, es mucha bendición.

Yo vi allá en Roma, do es la santidat,
que todos al dinero fazianl' omilidat.
Grand onra le fazían con grand solenidat :
todos a él se omillan como a la magestat.

Fazíe muchos priores, obispos e abbades,
Arçobispos, dotores, patriarcas, potestades.
A muchos clérigos nescios dávales denidades.
Fazíe verdat mentiras e mentiras verdades.

Fazíe muchos clérigos e muchos ordenados,
muchos monges e mongas, religiosos sagrados :
el dinero les dava por bien esaminados ;
a los pobres dezían que non eran letrados.

Dava muchos juizios, mucha mala sentencia :
con malos abogados era su mantenencia ;
en tener malos pleitos e fer mal' abenencia ;
en cabo por dineros avía penitencia.

El dinero quebranta las cadenas dañosas,
tira cepos e grillos, presiones peligrosas ;

al que non da dineros, échanle las esposas:
por todo el mundo faze cosas maravillosas.

Vi fazer maravillas a do él mucho usava:
muchos merescían muerte, que la vida les dava;
otros eran sin culpa, que luego los matava:
muchas almas perdía, muchas almas salvava.

Faze perder al pobre su casa e su viña;
sus muebles e raizes todo lo desaliña;
por todo el mundo cunde su sarna e su tiña;
do el dinero juzga, allí el ojo guiña.

Él faze cavalleros de necios aldeanos,
condes e ricos omes de algunos villanos;
con el dinero andan todos omes loçanos,
quantos son en el mundo, le besan oy las manos.

Vi tener al dinero las mayores moradas,
altas e muy costosas, fermosas e pintadas,
castillos, heredades, villas entorreadas:
al dinero servían e suyas eran conpradas.

Comía munchos manjares de diversas naturas,
vistía nobles paños, doradas vestiduras,
traía joyas preciosas en vycios e folguras,
guarnimientos estraños, nobles cavalgaduras.

Yo vi a muchos monges en sus pedricaciones
denostar al dinero e a sus tenptaciones;
en cabo, por dineros otorgan los perdones,
asuelven los ayunos e fazen oraciones.

Pero que lo denuestan los monges por las plaças,
guárdanlo en convento en vasos e en taças:
con el dinero cunplen sus menguas e sus raças:
más condedijos tiene que tordos nin picaças.

Monges, clérigos e frayres, que aman a Dios servir,
si varruntan que el rico está para morir,
quando oyen sus dineros, que comiençan reteñir,
quál dellos lo levará, comiençan a reñir.

Como quier que los frayres non toman los dineros,
bien les dan de la ceja do son sus parcioneros;
luego los toman prestos sus omes despenseros:
pues que se dizen pobres, ¿ qué quieren thessoreros ?

Allí están esperando qual avrá el rico tuero:
non es muerto e ya dizen *pater noster* ¡ mal agüero!
Como los cuervos al asno, quando le tiran el cuero:
" Cras nos lo levaremos, ca nuestro es por fuero."

Toda mugèr del mundo e dueña de alteza
págase del dinero e de mucha riqueza:
yo nunca vi fermosa, que quisiese pobreza:
do son muchos dineros, y es mucha nobleza.

El dinero es alcalle e juez mucho loado,
este es conssejero e sotil abogado,
aguacil e merino, bien ardit, esforçado:
de todos los oficios es muy apoderado.

En suma te lo digo, tómalo tú mejor:
el dinero, del mundo es grand rebolvedor;
señor faze del siervo e del siervo señor;
toda cosa del siglo se faze por su amor.

16. *De cómo murió Trotaconventos e de cómo el Arcipreste faze su planto*

Here, in an extraordinarily acute form, we meet the clash of ideas characteristic of the Libro de Buen Amor *as a whole—the instinctive paganism, for example, of l. 31 and the traditionally religious reaction, sounding rather like an afterthought, of l. 33. Here, too, Ruiz's mock-pious prayers for the soul of the former accomplice of his irregularities illustrate his grimly fantastic humour.*

Dize un filósofo, en su libro se nota,
que pesar e tristeza el engeño enbota:
e yo con pessar grant non puedo desir gota,
porque Trotaconventos ya non anda nin trota.

Así fué ¡ mal pecado! que mi vieja es muerta:
murió a mí serviendo: ¡ Lo que me desconfuerta!
Non sé cómo lo diga, ca mucha buena puerta
me fué después cerrada, que ante m'era abierta.

¡ Ay Muerte ! ¡ muerta seas, muerta e malandante !
Matásteme mi vieja : ¡ matasses a mí enante !
Enemiga del mundo, que non as semejante :
de tu memoria amarga non sé quien non se espante.

¡ Muerte ! al que tú fieres, liévastelo de belmez.
Al bueno e al malo, al noble e al rehez,
a todos los igualas e lievas por un prez :
por papas e por reyes non das una vil nuez.

Non catas señorío, debdo e amistad,
con todo el mundo tienes continua enamistad ;
non ay en ti mesura, amor nin piadad ;
sinon dolor, tristesa, pena e crueldad.

Non puede foyr ome de ti nin se asconder ;
nunca fué quien contigo podiese bien contender ;
la tu venida triste non se puede entender.
¡ Desque vienes, non quieres al ome atender !

Dexas el cuerpo yermo a gusanos en fuesa ;
al alma, que lo puebla, liévastela de priesa ;
non es el ome cierto de tu carrera aviesa.
¡ De fablar en ti, Muerte, espanto me atraviesa !

* * * *

¡ Ay ! ¡ mi Trotaconventos, mi leal verdadera !
Munchos te seguían biva ; ¡ muertas yases señera !
¿ Dó te me han levado ? ¡ Non sé cosa certera !
Nunca torna con nuevas quien anda esta carrera.

¡ Cierto en paraíso estás tú asentada !
¡ Con los mártires deves estar aconpañada !
¡ Sienpre en el mundo fuste por Dios martiriada !
¿ Quién te me rebató, vieja, por mi lasrada ?

A Dios merced le pido que te dé la su gloria,
que más leal trotera nunca fué en memoria ;
fasert' he un petafio, escrito con estoria :
pues que a ti non viere, veré tu triste estoria.

Faré por ti limosna e faré oración,
faré cantar las misas e faré oblación ;
¡ Dios, mi Trotaconventos, te dé su bendición !
El que salvó el mundo ¡ él te dé salvación !

Dueñas, ¡ non me rebtedes nin me llamedes neçuelo !
Que si a vos serviera, ¡ oviérades della duelo !
¡ Lloraríedes por ella! ¡ por su sotil ansuelo !
¡ Que a quantas seguía, tantas ivan por el suelo !

Alta muger nin baxa, cerrada nin escondida,
non se le detenía, do fasía abatida :
non sé ome nin dueña, que tal ovies' perdida,
que non tomas' tristesa e pesar sin medida.

Yo fisle un petafio pequeño con dolor ;
la tristessa me fiso ser rudo trobador.
Todos los que 'l oyeredes, por Dios nuestro Señor,
la oración digades por la vieja d' amor.

17. *De las propiedades que las dueñas chicas han*

This famous passage, made more familiar to English-reading people by Longfellow, aptly illustrates the transition from primitive crudity to the refined sensuality of the Renaissance. Technically, it should be noted how with his verve and humour Juan Ruiz transforms into something vital the usually conventional and lifeless antitheses of the Middle Ages.

Quiero vos abreviar la predicación,
que siempre me pagué de pequeño sermón,
e de dueña pequeña e de breve razón,
ca lo poco e bien dicho finca en el corazón.

Del que mucho fabla ríen, quien mucho ríe, es loco ;
es en la dueña chica amor grande e non poco ;
dueñas hay muy grandes que por chicas non troco,
e las chicas por las grandes, non se arrepiente del troco.

De las chicas, que bien diga, el amor me fizo ruego,
que diga de sus noblezas, yo quiero las dezir luego :
dirévos de dueñas chicas, que lo avredes por juego :
son frías como la nieve, e arden como el fuego.

Son frías de fuera, con el amor ardientes :
en la cama solaz, trebejo, plazenteras, rientes ;
en casa cuerdas, donosas, sosegadas, bien fazientes.
Mucho al fallaredes, bien parad i mientes.

En pequeña girgonça yaze grand resplandor,
en açúcar muy poco yaze mucho dulçor,
en la dueña pequeña yaze muy grand amor:
pocas palabras cumplen al buen entendedor.

Es pequeño el grano de la buena pemienta,
pero más que la nuez conorta e calienta;
así dueña pequeña, si todo amor consienta,
non ha plazer en el mundo que en ella non sienta.

Como en chica rosa está mucha color,
en oro muy poco grand precio e gran valor,
como en poco blasmo yaze grand buen olor,
ansí en chica dueña yaze muy grand amor.

Como robí pequeño tiene mucha bondad,
color, virtud, e precio, e noble claridad,
ansí dueña pequeña tiene mucha beldad,
fermosura, donaire, amor, e lealtad.

Chica es la calandria, e chico el ruiseñor,
pero más dulce cantan que otra ave mayor;
la muger, por ser chica por eso non es pior;
con doñeo es más dulce que açúcar nin flor.

Son aves pequeñuelas papagayo e orior,
pero cualquier dellas es dulce gritador;
adonada, fermosa, preciada cantador:
bien atal es la dueña pequeña con amor.

De la muger pequeña non hay comparación,
terrenal paraíso es, e consolación,
solaz e alegría, placer e bendición:
mejor es en la prueva que en la salutación.

Siempre quis' muger chica más que grande nin mayor,
non es desaguisado del grand mal ser foidor;
del mal tomar lo menos, dízelo el sabidor:
por ende de las mugeres la mejor es la menor.

PERO LÓPEZ DE AYALA

1332-1407

A PROMINENT political figure in four reigns, ending his life as Chancellor of Castile; a writer of some fecundity, of considerable versatility and of vast learning, López de Ayala is known in literature chiefly as the author of a satire on life at court, the *Rimado de palacio.* He suffers inevitably (and deservedly) by comparison with Juan Ruiz, for he is a somewhat gloomy satirist, and both his moralizings and his devout verses, while they do him the utmost credit, make one sigh for the sunshine of the *Libro de Buen Amor.* The passage here reproduced shows him in one of his livelier moments. The inaccessibility of the great ones of the earth was a common theme in mediaeval literature, but it can seldom have been more convincingly or more dramatically presented than here. Note the blunt, disrespectful language of the irascible *porteros,*

que todo el palacio quieren tener por sí,

so easily exasperated, yet so amenable to the suggestion of a gratuity. Such scenes are still enacted even in the Spain of to-day and some of the moments are still true to life, even down to the very details of the phraseology.

18. *Aquí comiença de los fechos del palacio*

Grant tienpo de mi vida pasé mal despendiendo,
a señores terrenales con grant cura serviendo,
agora ya lo veo e lo vo entendiendo
que quien í más trabaja más irá perdiendo.

Las cortes de los reyes, ¿ quién las podría pensar ?
¡ Quánto mal e trabajo el omne ha de pasar,
perigros en el cuerpo e el alma condenar,
los bienes e el algo siempre lo aventurar !

Si mill años los sirvo e un día fallesco,
dizen que muchos males e penas les meresco;
si por ellos en cuitas e cuidados padesco,
dizen que como nescio por mi culpa peresco.

Si por ir a mi casa licencia les demando,
después, a la tornada, nin sé cómo nin quándo,
fallo mundo rebuelto, trastornado mi vando,
e más frío que nieve en su palacio ando.

Fallo porteros nuevos, que nunca conoscí,
que todo el palacio quieren tener por sí;
si llego a la puerta, dizen: "¿Quién está í?"
"Señores", digo, "yo, que en mal día nascí.

"Grant tienpo ha que cuidaba esta corte saber;
agora me paresce que non sé qué fazer.
Querría, si pudiese, al rey fablar e ver."
Dizen: "Estad allá, ca ya non puede ser.

"Está el rey en consejo sobre fechos granados,
e non están con él si non dos o tres privados,
e a todos mando que non sean osados
de llegar a la puerta, aun que sean onrados."

"Señor", le digo yo, "de ver al rey non curo;
mas acogedme allá, siquiera en eso escuro,
e de mí vos prometo, e por mi fe vos juro,
de vos dar un tabardo, desto vos aseguro."

Dize el portero: "Amigo, non podes entrar,
ca el rey mando agora a todos daqui echar;
esperad allá un poco, podredes después tornar;
allá están otros muchos con quien podedes fablar."

"Señor", le digo yo, "allá están más de ciento:
desde aquí oyo yo el su departimiento:
pues non so yo agora de tan astroso tiento
que allá non esté tan quedo que non me sienta el viento."

"Tiradvos allá", dize el portero tal.
"Paresce que avedes sabor de oír mal.
¡Yo nunca vi tal omne e tan descomunal!:
o vos yo tiraré dende si Dios me val."

" Señor ", le digo yo, " siquier esta vegada
me acojed allá, e id a mi posada,
e darvos he una hopa que tengo empeñada."
Diz : " Entrad agora muy quedo e non fabledes nada."

Entro dentro apretado e asiéntome muy quedo,
que calle e non fable me faze con el dedo.
" ¿ Quién sodes ", diz otro, " que entrastes i tan cedo ? "
" Señor ", le digo, " un omne que vengo de Toledo."

" Salid luego ", diz, " fuera, aquí non estaredes."
Trávame luego del braço, yo apégome a las paredes ;
viene luego el otro, dize : " Vos fincaredes ;
mas lo que me mandastes luego cras lo daredes."

" Sí, señores ", digo luego, " yo lo daré de grado
todo lo que oviere, e más de lo mandado."
Con esta pleitesía finco asosegado,
e estó entre los otros, commo omne asonbrado.

Levántase el consejo e veo al rey estar ;
vo luego espantado por le querer fablar ;
él buelve las espaldas, e manda luego llamar
que vengan reposteros, que quiere ir cenar.

Yo estó en mi comidiendo : " Mesquino, ¿ qué faré ?
Muy grant vergüença tengo, non sé si lo fablaré,
o por ventura cras mejor gelo diré.
Desputando comigo, nunca buen tiento he."

Pero allego a él, así como a morir :
" Señor ", digo yo, " merced, queredme agora oír :
yo so vuestro vasallo, e mandástesme venir
aquí a vuestra guerra, e agora mandástesme ir.

" De sueldo de tres meses non puedo ser pagado,
de la tierra de antaño dos tercios no he cobrado,
he perdido mis bestias, mis armas enpeñado ;
ha dos meses que yago doliente, muy lazrado."

Respóndeme un privado : " Los contadores han carga
de librar los tales fechos, que'l rey nunca se enbarga."
Desque veo mi fecho, que va así a la larga,
levántome muy triste, con boca muy amarga.

Viene luego el portero, quexoso a más andar.
Dize : " Amigo, avedes librado, ca vos vi agora fablar
con el rey ; por tanto, vos vengo a acordar
que me dedes lo mandado, darlo hedes en buen logar."

Dígole : " Señor, non sé en qué está la mi fazienda ;
de todo quanto perdí non puedo haver emienda ;
que aquí moraré, esperando que entienda
él cómo le serví aunque non tengo qué espienda."

Dize el portero : " Amigo, Fulano es muy privado;
esperaldo a la salida, de vos sea compañado.
Id con él a su posada, e dezilde que de grado
le daredes alguna cosa, que seades ayudado.

" Non vos duela a osadas prometer a grant medida,
ca del agua que se vierte la media non es cogida,
e si por él librardes, non fué en balde la venida."
" Señor ", digo, " gracias muchas ; aconsejádesme la vida."

Espero a don Fulano, con él vo a su posada ;
fasta que descavalga, yo nunca le digo nada.
Otro día allí vengo con muy fría madrugada ;
sus moços me dizen luego : " La mula tiene ensellada.

" El rey ha enviado por él quatro mensajeros,
que se vaya a palacio, ca están allá los cavalleros."
Vo con él asaz cuitado, ca non tengo dos dineros
que yo coma aquel día, nin otros mis conpañeros.

Atiéndole todo el día, pintando por las paredes,
en mi cabo apartado, quál estó vos lo entendedes ;
vienen a mí los porteros, dízenme : " Convién que dedes
lo que nos avés mandado, o aquí non estaredes."

" Señores ", digo, " cierto, si Dios me ayuda a librar,
non partiré desta villa sin vos pagados dexar.
Aguardo a don Fulano, que me fuestes vos mostrar,
mas aun con las sus priesas non me quiere escuchar."

Don Fulano del consejo sale bien a medio día,
yo luego so con él, aguardándole todavía,
e yendo por la carrera, dígole : " Señor, querría
que fuese vuestra merced de aver la carga mía."

Cátame muy espantoso e dize : " Andar, andar ;
en la posada podredes comigo mejor fablar."
Dízenme sus escuderos : " ¡ Non le fagades ensañar ! "
Yo finco muy espantado e comiénçome a mesar.

Pero nunca lo desanparo, sienpre le vo aguardando ;
desque so en su posada, dígole : " Señor, yo ¿ quándo
vos mostraré mi fecho, que tomásedes mi vando,
e de lo que aver debo, fuésedes vos trabajando ?

" A mí deven contadores de dineros grant quantía,
non puedo cobrar dinero fasta oy en este día:
Señor, cobradlos vos, e por vuestra cortesía
dadme lo que quisierdes, porque me vaya mi vía."

Luego me faz buena cara e dize : " Tornad a mí
quando non esté aquí ninguno, que bien non vos entendí,
e sed cierto que faré en todo yo por vos í,
quanto yo más pudiere, sin perder maravedí " . . .

DIEGO HURTADO DE MENDOZA

d. 1404

FATHER of Iñigo López de Mendoza, Marqués de Santillana (p. 69), this modest writer of " gentiles decires e canciones "— the description of him is a contemporary one—is remembered chiefly by the *cossante*[1] here given. The title of this poem definitely links it to a form common at the time in Galicia and Portugal—a form comprising two-lined stanzas, each with an invariable single-line refrain, and generally exhibiting parallelisms, repetitions and interlaced phraseology. The subject-matter was, as here, slight, but as again here, the author would contrive to endow an almost static situation, or a single incident, with a remarkable freshness and liveliness. Aubrey Bell aptly describes the *cossantes* as " wild but deliciously scented " flowers[2]: the figure is nowhere more appropriate than here.

19. *Cossante*

A aquel árbol que mueve la foxa
algo se le antoxa.

Aquel árbol del bel mirar
face de maniera flores quiere dar:
algo se le antoxa.

Aquel árbol del bel veyer
face de maniera quiere florecer:
algo se le antoxa.

[1] The derivation of this word is uncertain: it may be an abbreviation for *consonante* (rhyme, rhyming poem), but is more probably from *cosso*, an enclosed place used for dancing. For some examples of the word in Spanish, see Aubrey F. G. Bell: *Portuguese Literature*, Oxford, 1922, p. 23, n.

[2] *Ibid.*

Face de maniera flores quiere dar :
ya se demuestra ; salidlas mirar :
algo se le antoxa.

Face de maniera quiere florecer :
ya se demuestra ; salidlas a ver :
algo se le antoxa.

Ya se demuestra ; salidlas mirar.
Vengan las damas las fructas cortar :
algo se le antoxa.

ALFONSO ÁLVAREZ DE VILLASANDINO

*c.*1350-1420

THIS Galician versifier, whom the aristocratic Pero Niño employed to write his love-songs, was more highly thought of in his own time than he is to-day. Baena said of him : " por gracia infusa que Dios en él puso fué esmalte y luz y espejo y corona de todos los poetas y trovadores que hasta hoy fueron en toda España ", and in his *Cancionero* he gives him over one hundred poems. From these we may gain some knowledge of his life, not all of it edifying. Yet, whether he wrote for pay, for flattery or for his own satisfaction and pleasure, there is no denying the genuineness of the lyric note in his verses. His eulogy of Seville, for example, is said to have brought him substantial monetary compensation ; but even to-day it trembles with the emotion of joy caused by reunion. The *cantiga* to a lady, though more conventional in language, is melodious in the extreme. The curious device should be noted by which the final rhyme of each stanza recalls the *tema.* The change of metre in the last stanza marks the transition from lyric to narration.

20. *A la Ciudad de Sevilla*

Linda sin conparación,
claridat e luz de España,
plazer e consolación,
briossa cibdat extraña,
el mi coraçón se baña,
en ver vestra maravilla,
muy poderosa Sevilla
guarnida de alta compaña.

Paraíso terrenal
es el vestro nonbre puro;
sobre cimiento leal
es fundado vestro muro,
onde bive amor seguro
que será sienpre ensalçado:
si esto me fuer negado
de maldicientes non curo.

Desque de vos me partí
fasta agora que vos veo,
bien vos juro que non vi
vestra egual en asseo:
mientra más miro e oteo
vestras dueñas e donzellas,
resplandor nin luz de estrellas
non es tal, segunt yo creo.

En el mundo non ha par
vestra lindeza e folgura,
nin se podrían fallar
dueñas de tal fermosura:
donzellas de grant mesura
que en vos fueron criadas,
éstas deven ser loadas
en España de apostura.

FIN

Una cossa que non es,
si en vos fuesse, sería
más guarnido vestro arnés
de plazer e de alegría;
que la flor de grant valía
en el mundo ensalçada,
si fiziesse en vos morada,
vestro par non avería . . . . . .

21. *Por amor e loores de una señora*

Visso enamoroso,
duélete de mí,
pues bivo pensoso
desseando a ti.

La tu fermosura
me puso en prisión;
por la cual ventura
del mi coraçón
non parte tristura
en toda sazón:
porén tu figura
me entristece assí.

Todo el mi cuidado
es en te loar,
quel tienpo passado
non posso olvidar:
farás aguissado
de mí te menbrar,
pues sienpre de grado
leal te serví.

Estoy cada día
triste sin plazer;
si tan solo un día
te pudiesse ver,
yo confortar me ía
con tu parescer:
porén cobraría
el bien que perdí.

Razonando en tal figura
las aves fueron bolando;
yo aprés de una verdura
me fallé triste cuidando.
E luego en aquella ora
me menbró gentil señora
a quien noche e día adora
mi coraçon sospirando.

FERNÁN PÉREZ DE GUZMÁN

*c.*1376-*c.*1460

THOUGH best known as a writer of prose, Pérez de Guzmán was also a most prolific rhymester. He carries his historical and moralizing propensities into verse, praising famous men to some effect in *Loores de los claros varones de España*—though this is a collection of rhymed quatrains arranged in pairs, rather than poetry. In the poems, chiefly amatory, to be found in the *Cancionero de Baena* he is better. Of the two of these here reproduced, the first, written in *octavas de arte mayor* (p. 59), betrays some Italian influence; without being more than typical of its kind, it is tuneful and picturesque. The second poem, one of his many panegyrics of Our Lady, halts here and there, but in the main is extraordinarily musical. The sporadic medial rhymes, the alternation of long lines with short and the occasional cutting of the long line with a caesura are all successful devices to that end.

22. *A una Dama*

El gentil niño Narciso
en una fuente engañado,
de sí mesmo enamorado,
muy esquiva muerte priso:
señora de noble riso
e de muy gracioso brío,
a mirar fuente nin río
non se atreva vuestro viso.

Deseando vuestra vida
aun vos dé otro consejo,
que non se mire en espejo
vuestra faz clara e garrida.
¿Quién sabe si la partida
vos será dende tan fuerte,
porque fuese en vos la muerte
de Narciso repetida?

Engañaron sotilmente
por emaginación loca
fermosura e edad poca
al niño bien paresciente:
estrella resplandeciente,
mirad bien estas dos vías,
pues edad e pocos días
cada qual en vos se siente.

¿ Quién, si no los serafines,
vos vencen de fermosura,
de niñez e de frescura,
las flores de los jardines ?
Pues, rosa de los jasmines,
aved la fuente escusada
por aquella que es llamada
estrella de los maitines.

Prados, rosas e flores
otorgo que los miredes,
e plázeme que escuchedes
dulces cantigas de amores;
mas por sol nin por calores
tal codicia non vos ciegue;
vuestra vista siempre niegue
las fuentes e sus dulçores.

Con plazer e gozo e risa
ruego a Dios que resplandezcan
vuestros bienes e florezcan
más que los de Dido Elisa:
vuestra faz muy blanca, lisa,
jamás nunca sienta pena.
¡ Adiós, flor de azuzena,
duélavos de esta pesquisa !

23. *A la Virgen*

O María, luz del día
e resplandor:
¿quién tu virtud loaría
e gran valor?
Señora, pulcra e decora
e mansueta,
de los cielos regidora
muy discreta:
¿quál balada e cancioneta
bastaría
a te loar con perfecta
melodía?
¿Quál prosa tan copïosa
es o será,
que a tu virtud glorïosa
loará?
Quál música cantará,
Virgen María,
tus loores, no podría
nin sabrá.
Virgen santa de quien canta
Salamón,
de cuyo viso se espanta
el dragón:
angélica profesión
e gerarchía,
a loar tu perfección
fallescería.

FIN

Tenplo, divino tenplo,
el tu dulçor
con que aplazes sin enxemplo
al Salvador;
¡o sancta e preciosa flor!
acorre e guía
al tu pobre servidor,
que en ti confía.

FERRÁN SÁNCHEZ CALAVERA

Early 15th Century

SÁNCHEZ CALAVERA (also known as " Talavera ") was a Comendador of the Order of Calatrava who died about 1450 and is remembered chiefly for his *dezir* on the death of the Almirante Ruy Díaz de Mendoza, which is sometimes compared with the famous elegiac *coplas* of Jorge Manrique (p. 98). The poem is written in *octavas* of the anapaestic type termed *de arte mayor*, rhyming *abbaacca*—a scheme commonly associated with the name of Juan de Mena (p. 93). In the last stanza, it will be observed, the dominant ending is *agudo*. The author has much of Manrique's terse eloquence: compare ll. 11-14 with ll. 55-60 (p. 101) of the *coplas*. Both this resemblance, however, and others (e.g., the " ¿ Qué se fizieron . . . . . ? " theme, compared with " ¿ Qué se fizo el rey don Juan . . . . . ? " etc.) may have been partly a matter of convention and too much should not be made of them. In any case Sánchez Calavera can be over-discursive, which Manrique never is, and his effects are sometimes weakened by over-enumeration. His great contributions to literature are the combination of simple thought with profound emotion and a grave eloquence, the deep note of which had thus far been little heard in Spain.

24. *Dezir*

Por Dios, señores, quitemos el velo
que turba e ciega así nuestra vista ;
miremos la muerte qu'el mundo conquista
lançando lo alto e baxo por suelo.
Los nuestros gemidos traspasen el cielo,
a Dios demandando cada uno perdón
de aquellas ofensas que en toda sazón
le fizo el viejo, mancebo, mozuelo.

Ca non es vida la que bevimos,
pues que biviendo se viene llegando
la muerte cruel, esquiva ; e cuando
penssamos bevir, estonce morimos.
Somos bien ciertos dónde nascimos ;
mas non somos ciertos a dónde morremos.
Certidumbre de vida un ora non avemos ;
con llanto venimos, con llanto nos imos.

¿ Qué se fizieron los emperadores,
papas e reyes, grandes perlados,
duques e condes, cavalleros famados,
los ricos, los fuertes e los sabidores,
e quantos servieron lealmente amores
faziendo sus armas en todas las partes,
e los que fallaron ciencias e artes,
doctores, poetas e los trobadores ?

¿ Padres e fijos, hermanos, parientes,
amigos, amigas, que mucho amamos,
con quien comimos, bevimos, folgamos,
muchas garridas e fermosas gentes,
dueñas, doncellas, mancebos valientes
que logran so tierra las sus mancebías,
e otros señores que ha pocos días
que nosotros vimos aquí estar presentes ?

¿ El Duque de Cabra e el Almirante
e otros muy grandes asaz de Castilla,
agora Ruy Díez, que puso manzilla
su muerte a las gentes en tal estante
que la su grant fama fasta en Levante
sonava en proeza e en toda bondat,
que en esta grant corte luzie por verdat
su noble meneo e gentil semblante ?

Todos aquestos que aquí son nonbrados,
los unos son fechos ceniza e nada ;
los otros son huesos, la carne quitada
e son derramados por los fonsados ;

los otros están ya descoyuntados,
cabeças sin cuerpos, sin pies e sin manos ,
los otros comiençan comer los gusanos ;
los otros acaban de ser enterrados.

Pues ¿ dó los imperios, e dó los poderes,
reínos, rentas e los señoríos,
a dó los orgullos, las famas e bríos,
a dó las enpressas, a dó los traheres ?
¿ A dó las cïencias, a dó los saberes
a dó los maestros de la poetría ;
a dó los rimares de grant maestría,
a dó los cantares, a dó los tañeres ?

¿ A dó los thesoros, vasallos, servientes,
a dó los firmalles, pïedras preciosas ;
a dó el aljófar, posadas costossas,
a dó el algalia e aguas olientes ?
¿ A dó paños de oro, cadenas luzientes,
a dó los collares, las jarreteras,
a dó peñas grisses, a dó peñas veras,
a dó las sonajas que van retinientes ?

¿ A dó los conbites, cenas e ayantares,
a dó las justas, a dó los torneos,
a dó nuevos trajes, estraños meneos,
a dó las artes de los dançadores,
a dó los comeres, a dó los manjares,
a dó la franqueza, a dó el espender,
a dó los rissos, a dó el plazer,
a dó menestriles, a dó los juglares ?

Segunt yo creo sin fallecimiento,
conplido es el tiempo que dixo a nos
el profeta Issaias, fijo de Amós :
diz que cessaría todo ordenamiento
e vernie por fedor podrimiento,
e los omnes gentiles de grado morrien,
e a sus puertas que los llorarien,
e sería lo poblado en destruimiento.

Esta tal muerte con grant tribulança
Geremias, profeta lleno de enojos,
con repentimiento llorando sus ojos
e de muchas lágrimas grant abondança,
mostrando sus faltas e muy grant errança.
Quien este escripto muy bien leerá
en este capítulo bien claro verá
que este es el tiempo sin otra dubdança.

Por ende buen sesso era guarnescer
de virtudes las almas que están despojadas,
tirar estas honras del cuerpo juntadas,
pues somos ciertos que se han de perder.
Quien este consejo quisiere fazer
non avrá miedo jamás de morir,
mas traspasará de muerte a bevir
vida por siempre sin le fallescer.

FRANCISCO IMPERIAL

Early 15th Century

A SEVILIAN, but the son of an Italian, "Micer Francisco Imperial", as Santillana calls him in his *Prohemio* (p. 69), was one of the earliest Spanish poets to prepare the way for that Italian influence which became so strong in Spain after the Renaissance. "No . . . . . decidor o trovador, mas poeta", was Santillana's tribute to him, but his *Dezir a las siete virtudes*, imitated from, and closely modelled upon, Dante, will excite little admiration to-day. The extract here given will show him at his best. It describes the garden of the virtues, into which the poet is led by Dante, who in the fiction, as well as in fact, acts as his guide. There is the same evocation of varied sense-impressions as two centuries earlier, in the *Razón d'Amor*. But there is, of course, much more skilful artistry. Among other traits of Imperial's work are few and rich end-rhymes (his *octavas* rhyme *ababbccb*) and medial jingles, either in the shape of imperfect or exact rhymes or of assonances. As to smoothness of rhythm, the poem is somewhat unequal, giving the impression of an inability to decide between the Italian hendecasyllable and the Spanish *arte mayor*.

25. *Dezir a las siete virtudes*

(Extract)

Era cercado todo aquel jardín
de aquel arroyo a guissa de cava,
e por muro muy alto jazmín
que todo a la redonda lo cercava :
el son del agua en dulçor passava
arpa, duçayna, vihuela de arco,
e non me digan que mucho abarco
que non sé si dormía o velava.

En mí dezía : " Mucho me maravillo
que non veo aquí alguna entrada ;
non veo puente, puerta nin portillo."
Esto diziendo, vi una puerta alçada
entre el jazmín, non tabla labrada,
mas de robí más vivo que centella :
commo moví a ir derecho a ella,
non vi de quién, luego fue abaxada.

Muy a vagar passé allén la puente,
oliendo del jardín los dulces olores,
porque de entrar ove mayor talante
e fize entrada entre flores e flores.
Ante que entrase, ove muchos suores.
De que fuí entrado, ¡ oy qué aventura ! :
vi toda blanca la mi vestidura,
e luego conoscí los mis errores.

Desque bolví a man diestra el rostro,
vi por la yerva pissadas de omme,
onde alegre fuíme por rastro
el qual derecho a un rossal llevóme :
e commo quando entre árboles asome
alguno que ante los ramos mesce,
e poco a poco todo assí paresce,
tal vi un omme : muy cortés saluóme.

Era en vista benigno e süave,
e en color era la su vestidura
ceniza o tierra que seca se cave ;
barva e cabello alvo sin mesura :
traía un libro de poca escriptura
escripto todo con oro muy fino,
e començava : " En medio del camino ",
e del laurel corona e centura.

De grant abtoridat avía senblante,
de poeta de grant excelencia,
onde omilde enclinéme delante,
faciéndole devida reverencia,

e díxele con toda obediencia :
" Afectuossamente a vos me ofresco,
e maguer tanto de vos non meresco,
sea mi guía vuestra alta ciencia."

Dióme respuesta en puro latín :
" A mí plaze lo que tú desseas."
E de sí dixo en lengua florentín :
" E porque cierto tú más de mí seas
buelve comigo, e quiero que veas
las siete estrellas que en el cielo relunbran,
e los sus rayos que al mundo alunbran ;
e esto, fijo, ciertamente creas."

Tomóme la mano e bolvió por do vino
e yo siguiendo sienpre sus pisadas,
e los ojos baxos por non perder tino,
non fueran ciento aun bien contadas,
que oí bozes muy asonssegadas,
angelicales, e mussicado canto ;
mas eran lexos de mí aun tanto
que las non entendí a las vegadas.

" Manet in caritate, Deus manet in eo,
et credo in Deum ", allí se respondía,
e a las vezes : " Espera in Deo."
Aquesto entendí en quanto allí oía.
E en otra parte, segunt por ciencia[1],
cantavan manso cantares morales,
e ansí andando por entre rossales,
oí (que) una boz e canto dezía :

" Qualquier qu'el mi nonbre demanda
sepa por cierto que me llamo Lía,
e cojo flores por fazer guirlanda,
commo costumbro al alva del día."
Aquesto oyendo, dixo mi guía :
" Creo que duermes o estás ociosso,
¿ non oyes Lía con canto graciosso
que d'estas flores su guirlanda lía ? "

[1] D.A. reads : ' Segunt parecía '.

Dixe: " Non duermo." "¿ Pues por qué tan mudo
atanto sin falla has ya andado ?
E si non duermes, eres omme rudo.
¿ Non ves que tú eres ya llegado
en medio del rossal en verde prado ?
Mira adelante las siete estrellas."
Onde yo miré e vilas tan bellas
que mi dezir aquí será menguado.

Forma de dueña en cada estrella
se demostrava, e otrossí fazía(n)
en cada rayo forma de doncella :
las tres primeras en triángulo seía(n)
e quadrángulo, segunt me parescía(n),
las otras cuatro non mucho distantes,
ommes avré coronas portantes,
e las donzellas guirlandas traía(n).[1]

Las tres avíen color de llama biva,
e las quatro eran alvas atanto
que la su alvura a alva nieve priva :
las tres continuavan el su cantar santo
e las otras cuatro el su moral canto
con gesto manso de grant onestat,
tal que non puedo mostrar igualdat
ca el nostro a su par sería grant planto.

[1] In *C.B.*, ll. 90, 92, 93 lack the final *n* demanded by form and sense.

ESTEBAN DE ZAFRA

THE verses of this author, of whose life nothing is known, are curious rather than inspiring. Not everyone, for example, will appreciate so flowery a panegyric as this to Our Lady. Its opening conceit, the triteness of its central metaphor, and the often meaningless application of this must all, from a modern standpoint, be regarded as blemishes. And yet the poem cannot be dismissed without comment. It has an individuality which expresses itself metrically in a curious stanzaic scheme and thematically in a piling-up of impressions with the apparent aim of conveying a truth through sheer weight of metaphorical emphasis. One may dislike the poem, but one remembers it.

26. "*Bajo de la peña nace . . . . .*"

Bajo de la peña nace
la rosa que no quema el aire.

Bajo de un pobre portal
está un divino rosal
e una reina angelical
de muy gracioso donaire.

Esta reina tan hermosa
ha producido una rosa
tan colorada y hermosa
qual nunca la vido naide.

Rosa blanca e colorada,
rosa bendita e sagrada,
rosa por qual es quitada
la culpa del primer padre.

Es el rosal que decía
la Virgen Santa María,
la rosa que producía
es su Hijo, Esposo e Padre.

Es rosa de salvación
para nuestra redención,
para curar la lisión
de nuestra primera madre.

IÑIGO LÓPEZ DE MENDOZA, MARQUÉS DE SANTILLANA

1398-1458

SOLDIER and courtier, son and grandson of poets, and kinsman of authors, warriors and statesmen, the first Marqués de Santillana won fame both as a poet and as a writer of prose. His chief prose work is the *Prohemio e Carta que el Marqués de Santillana envió al Condestable de Portugal con las obras suyas* (*c.*1449), a classic of early literary history and poetic theory. In verse, much of his considerable output is erudite in manner and political or didactic in theme. Best known are the *Proverbios*, a collection of 101 stanzas embodying moral precepts, with a prose introduction and glosses; and forty-two " Sonetos, fechos al itálico modo ", which have won their author the distinction of having acclimatized the sonnet-form in Spain. In sharp contrast to these are a number of poems wholly popular in their inspiration, which include the light and graceful *canciones* and *dezires*, and ten examples of the *serranilla*, or hill-song, a type of verse common in early Galician-Portuguese poetry. It is curious that this scholarly aristocrat, who in his *Prohemio e Carta* professed disdain for certain types of popular poetry[1], should himself owe so much of his fame to his delicate ditties on the loves of hill-maidens.

Without being in the first rank of poets, Santillana wrote very much better lyric verse than any author in Castilian who had preceded him. His technique is noteworthy, and, when inspired, which is by no means always, he reaches a very high level. The best of the *canciones* and *dezires* have an extraordinary charm, though many others are artificial or prosaic: on the whole, they have perhaps been over-praised. Critics of the sonnets, on the other hand, have tended to over-stress their technical defects

[1] " Ínfimos son aquellos que sin ningún orden, regla nin cuento fazen estos romances e cantares de que las gentes de baxa e servil condición se alegran." (*Prohemio e Carta*, IX.)

(e.g., awkward handling of the caesura, monotony of accentuation and excess of *agudo*-endings) and to miss the beauty of thought and depth of emotion which many of them can show. The *serranillas*, however, win all hearts: their skilful blending of sensuousness and idealism, their remarkable variety of tone, their rustic atmosphere, the melody of their verse—all these class them, with the finest of the *canciones*, *dezires* and sonnets, as outstanding achievements of mediaeval Spanish poetry.

27. *Soneto V*

"En este quinto soneto el actor (autor) *fabla en nombre del Infante don Enrique, e muestra cómo se quexa por la muerte de la señora Infante* (sic), *doña Cathalina, su muger." None the less, the poem throbs with deep and sincere grief. Note the ingenuous "yo creo" of l. 2 and the melodious phrase "muger mucho amada" (l. 4), the simple dignity of which recalls the famous Biblical tribute, "For she loved much." The octave, unified by a single thought, daringly expressed, of tremendous force and vitality, is followed by a sestet instinct with yearning and caressing sorrow, shot across by a ray of tragic pathos (l. 10) recalling the dead Infanta's youth and culminating in a fine last line, fitting climax to the grief-charged poem. As an exquisite example of a sonnet of universal appeal, it is surprising that it has not received more attention.*

Non solamente al templo divino,
donde yo creo seas receptada,
segunt tu sancto ánimo e benino,
preclara Infante, muger mucho amada;

mas al abismo e centro malino
te seguiría, si fuesse otorgada
a cavallero, por golpe ferrino,
cortar la tela por Cloto filada.

Non lloren la tu muerte, magüer sea
en edat tierna, e tiempo trïunphante;
mas la mi triste vida, que dessea

ir dónde fueres, como fiel amante,
e conseguirte, dulce mia Idea,
e mi dolor acerbo e incessante.

28. *Soneto IX*

" En este nono soneto el actor muestra cómo un día de una grand fiesta vió a la señora suya en cabello." Less technically perfect than Soneto V (cf. the halting seventh line and the agudo-*rhymes of the sestet), this poem succeeds in conveying an impression of intense emotion by the use of florid and hyperbolic imagery, which, in the hands of many other and later poets, would have no meaning whatsoever.*

Non es el rayo de Febo luciente,
nin los filos d'Arabia más fermosos
que los vuestros cabellos luminosos,
nin gema d'estupaça tan fulgente.

Eran ligados d'un verdor placiente
e flores de jazmín, que los ornava ;
e su perfetta belleça mostrava,
qual viva flama o estrella d'Oriente.

Loó mi lengua, magüer sea indina,
aquel buen punto que primero ví
la vuestra imagen e forma divina,

tal como perla e claro rubí,
e vuestra vista társica e benina,
a cuyo esguarde e merced me di.

29. *Soneto XVIII*

The two pairs of simple and ingenuous antitheses with which this sonnet opens have made it famous. Technically, it is a curious mixture of good lines and bad, and once more the agudo-*rhyme invades the sestet, though less harshly. But the sincerity of the author's thought shines right through the poem and the quaintness and aptness of the river-similes (Guadalquivir is, of course, the " Great River " of the Moors) impress it upon the memory.*

Lexos de vos e cerca de cuidado,
pobre de goço e rico de tristeça,
fallido de reposo e abastado
de mortal pena, congoxa e braveça ;

desnudo d'esperança e abrigado
d'inmensa cuita e visto d'aspereça,
la mi vida me fuye, mal mi grado,
la muerte me persigue sin pereça.

Nin son bastantes a satisfacer
la set ardiente de mi grand desseo
Tajo al pressente, nin me socorrer

la enferma Guadiana, nin lo creo:
solo Guadalquevir tiene poder
de me guarir e solo aquel desseo.

30. *Canción*

The best of the canciones *are the simplest. Now and then Santillana showed that he had that uncanny gift, which few Spanish poets have shared with him, of using language almost childish in its simplicity to express lively feeling. So starkly bared in this poem is the lover's primary emotion, especially in the opening* tema, *that no lover will fail to thrill to it. The same high level is kept up throughout till the final stanza slowly raises it to a height of ecstasy surpassed by few love-poems in Spanish before or since.*

Si tú desseas a mí
yo non lo sé;
pero yo desseo a ti
en buena fe.

I

E non a ninguna más;
asy lo ten:
nin es, nin será jamás
otra mi bien.
En tan buen ora te ví
e te fablé
que del todo te me dí
en buena fe.

II

Yo soy tuyo, non lo dubdes,
sin fallir ;
e non piensses al, nin cuides,
sin mentir.
Despues que te conosçí
me captivé,
e sesso e saber perdí
en buena fe.

III

A ti amo e amaré
toda saçón,
e siempre te serviré
con grand raçón :
pues la mejor escojí
de quantas sé,
e non finjo nin fengí
en buena fe.

31. *Serranilla IX*

This subtlest of the Marquis' serranillas *can best be appreciated after a comparison of it with poems of a more conventional kind. The singer is not the stereotyped gallant of fiction, but one who has known passion and abandoned amorous adventure, believing that love has passed him by. The* vaquera, *portrayed in greater detail than usual, is addressed by him throughout as " Señora ", which might be expected to prepare the reader, though it seldom does, for the exquisite finale. For, after the inevitable dialogue—he praising her beauty ; she, having other suitors, bidding him begone ; he protesting that rustic life attracts him—the gallant is not repulsed, as is almost always the case, but accepted. Is the* vaquera *overcome by his courtly mode of address, by his disillusion or by the picturesque frankness (ll. 36-8) with which he professes his rustic proclivities ? Or is she tired of playing off one shepherd-suitor (l. 31) against the other ? We are not told, but, as in the final stanza the tone rises, we forget to ask again. Few poems hint more delicately at love's consummation than the concluding lines of this. V.P.* (I, 258) *is so bold as to compare the beautiful restrained description of the flowers spread like a veil over the crown of love with the finale of San Juan de la Cruz's "Noche obscura"* (*p.* 265, *below*). *The latter poem, even if considered as a panegyric of purely human love, which it was never meant to be, is so infinitely more profound than this that any such comparison must seem superficial. Yet the fact that a competent and sensitive critic could make it throws a startling light on the Marquis' outstanding genius.*

Moçuela de Bores
allá do la Lama
púsom'en amores.

I

Cuidé que olvidado
amor me tenía,
como quien s'avía
grand tiempo dexado
de tales dolores,
que más que la llama
queman amadores.

II

Mas vi la fermosa
de buen continente,
la cara placiente,
fresca como rosa,
de tales colores
qual nunca vi dama
nin otra, señores.

III

Por lo qual: "Señora
(le dixe), en verdat
la vuestra beldat
saldrá desd'agora
dentre estos alcores,
pues meresce fama
de grandes loores."

IV

Dixo: " Cavallero,
tiratvos a fuera:
dexat la vaquera
passar al otero;
ca dos labradores
me piden de Frama,
entrambos pastores."

V

" Señora, pastor
seré si queredes:
mandarme podedes,
como a servidor:
mayores dulçores
será a mi la brama
que oír ruiseñores."

VI

Así concluímos
el nuestro processo
sin facer excesso,
e nos avenimos.
E fueron las flores
de cabe Espinama
los encobridores.

GÓMEZ MANRIQUE

*c.*1412–*c.*1490

A KINSMAN of the first Marqués de Santillana, for whom he often expressed his admiration, and whom he took as a model for his own writing, Gómez Manrique has been somewhat overshadowed by his nephew Jorge, who made his name with a single remarkable poem (p. 98). Nevertheless there is a case for maintaining, with Menéndez y Pelayo, that Gómez Manrique was, apart from Santillana and Mena, " the first poet of his century."[1] The bulk of his 108 poems are undistinguished and conventional, but here and there, like Santillana, he becomes attractively simple, and this simplicity is illustrated in both the extracts here chosen. More artificiality, as well as more art, will be found in most of the *canciones*, though some of these are, of the kind, excellent. More noteworthy are three poems (some might make the number greater) in which we hear a bourdon note of deep solemnity and detect an underlying preoccupation with eternal values—traits more notably illustrated in the masterpiece of the nephew. These poems are the " Coplas para el señor Diego Arias de Ávila," a court official whom the author exhorts to make a worthy and just use of his power ; the " Consolatoria para . . . . . su muy amada mujer ", on the death of their two children within four months of each other ; the " Defunzión del noble cavallero Garcia Laso de la Vega ", a soldier-friend who had been killed by a poisoned arrow in a battle with the Moors.

Gómez Manrique is also the earliest Spanish dramatist known to us by name. His output is slight : a nativity play, " Representación del nacimiento de Nuestro Señor ", a more rudimentary play for Holy Week and two *momos* which are purely secular.

[1] M.P. *Ant.*, VI, lix.

32. *A una Dama que iva cubierta*

Here sincerity is allowed free play and chooses the simplest language for its expression. The only piece of artifice in the poem—the repetitive device which binds it together—enhances the effect of intense devotion conveyed by words almost matter-of-fact in their restraint.

El coraçón se me fué
donde vuestro vulto vi,
e luego vos conosçi
al punto que vos miré;
que no pudo fazer tanto
por mucho que vos cubriese
aquel vuestro negro manto
que no vos reconosciese.

Que debaxo se mostrava
vuestra gracia y gentil aire,
y el cubrir con buen donaire
todo lo magnifestava;
así que con mis enojos
e muy grande turbación
allá se fueron mis ojos
do tenía el coraçón.

33. *Canción para callar al Niño*

The "Representación del nacimiento de Nuestro Señor", written for performance by the nuns of a convent where the author's sister was vicaress, ends with this cradle song, which, like some of the songs later composed by Santa Teresa for her Carmelite foundations, was to be sung to a popular air by the nuns in chorus. Point is given to the first stanza by the preceding scene, in which the Holy Child is presented with the instruments of His Passion. Immature as the song is, its beauty is not wholly that of naïveté. *Fitzmaurice-Kelly surmises that reminiscences of it may have "found their way into Lope de Vega's* Pastores de Belén."[1]

[1] *N.H.*, p. 120.

Callad vos, Señor,
nuestro Redentor,
que vuestro dolor
durará poquito.

Ángeles del cielo,
venid dar consuelo
a este moçuelo
Jhesús tan bonito.

Este fué reparo,
aun que él costó caro,
de aquel pueblo amaro
cativo en Egito.

Este santo dino,
niño tan benino,
por redemir vino
el linaje aflito.

Cantemos gozosas,
ermanas graciosas,
pues somos esposas
del Jesú bendito.

JUAN RODRÍGUEZ DEL PADRÓN

Mid-15th Century

JUAN RODRÍGUEZ DE LA CÁMARA, a native of the Galician town of El Padrón, is supposed to have been a page in the Court of John II and was certainly in the service of Cardinal Juan de Cervantes, for some years Bishop of Tuy. His chief work was an early sentimental novel, *El Siervo libre de amor* (*c.*1440), and in *El Triunfo de las donas* he defended the fair sex against the author of the *Corbacho* and others. But he had also a certain lyric gift and he was reputed, probably without foundation, to be the author of a number of ballads, including the famous "Conde Arnaldos" (p. 148). Tradition has credited him with a love-story which it is customary to compare with the legendary story of Macías, and which is reflected in the ardour of the poem that follows.

34. *Canción*

Cuidado nuevo venido
me da de nueva manera
pena la más verdadera
que jamás he padescido.

Yo ardo sin ser quemado
en bivas llamas d' amor ;
peno sin aver dolor,
muero sin ser visitado
de quien con beldad vencido
me tiene so su bandera.
¡ O mi pena postrimera,
secreto huego encendido !

CARLOS DE GUEVARA

Probably late 15th Century

Nothing at all is known of this Guevara (not, of course, to be confused with Antonio de Guevara, Bishop of Mondoñedo), whose style and merits are very similar to Cartagena's. The first of these *esparsas* contains an effective appeal to Nature; in the second, rays of sincerity succeed in breaking through the paradoxes of a familiar and conventional theme.

35. *Esparsas*

(i)

Las aves andan bolando,
cantando canciones ledas,
las verdes hojas temblando,
las aguas dulces sonando,
los pavos hazen las ruedas:
yo, sin ventura amador,
contemplando mi tristura,
dessago por mi dolor
la gentil rueda d'amor
que hize por mi ventura.

(ii)

Consuélame desconsuelo,
pena triste no descansa,
la tormenta menos mansa
me da vida en este suelo:
lloros son mis buenos sones,
es mi muerte no morir,
dánme gozo mis passiones
porque son las opiniones
que dan fin a mi bevir.

Mi morir que va llegando
esclaresce mis clamores,
que la muerte no penando,
fueran muertos mis dolores :
y partido para 'l cielo,
si quien soy queréis oír,
yo diré : ¡ qué desconsuelo,
yo vestido con un duelo,
que morí por no morir !

JUAN ESCRIVÁ

Late 15th Century

All we know about the life of the Comendador Escrivá is that he was a Valencian and in the year 1497 was Ambassador to the Catholic Monarchs at Rome. But his verses refresh the arid pages of Hernando del Castillo's *Cancionero General* like showers in the desert. He writes, not only as a rule melodiously, and, as nearly always, even on the most conventional themes, with a whimsical fancy, but on occasion with real power: in the finest—which are the shortest—of his poems there is a completely indefinable lyric emotion.

With "Dorar el oro . . . . ." (*C.H.C.*, II, 424) and "Los cabellos de mi amiga . . . . ." (*C.H.C.*, II, 427) the four poems which follow may be considered as among the most typical of his variety and genius. The first, a wistful *villancico*, subtly musical though a little uncertain in its step, is characteristic of his happiest manner. The second is so much more serious in subject and mood that even its verbal melody lies deeper. The third, both in its phraseology and in its convincing sincerity, looks forward to Garcilaso de la Vega.[1] The fourth, by which Escrivá is chiefly known, is an apostrophe to death superficially light, almost nonchalant, in tone, but with a remarkable penetrative quality which is perhaps beyond the range of analysis.

36. *Villancico*

¿ Qué sentís, coraçón mío ?
¿ No dezís ?
¿ Qué mal es el que sentís ?
¿ Qué sentistes aquel día
quando mi señora vistes,
que perdistes alegría
y descanso despedistes ?

[1] E.g., Soneto V, p. 173, below.

¿ Cómo a mí nunca boluistes ?
¿ No dezís ?
¿ Dónde estáis que no venís ?

¿ Qu'es de vos qu'en mí n'os hallo ?
¿ Coraçón, quién os agena ?
¿ Qu'es de vos que, aunque callo,
vuestro mal tan bien me pena ?
¿ Quién os ató tal cadena ?
¿ No dezís ?
¿ Qué mal es el que sentís ?

37. *Canción*

Soledad triste que siento
y cuidados me combaten ;
la gloria del pensamiento
no consiente que me maten
porque biva mi tormento.

Y assí no puedo morir,
ni bivo, pues que no's veo,
aunque biva mi sofrir
y la fe con el desseo :
este gran dolor que siento
y tristezas me combaten ;
la gloria del pensamiento
no consiente que me maten
porque biva mi tormento.

38. *Copla sola*

En aquel punto que os vi
imagen en mí esculpida,
con mis ojos imprimida
dentro en mi alma os metí.
Y sed muy segura d'esto,
qu' estáis tan metida en ella,
que al tiempo qu'e de perdella
dexará forma en mi gesto
del vuestro que irá con ella.

39. *Canción*

Ven muerte tan escondida
que no te sienta comigo,
porqu'el gozo de contigo
no me torne a dar la vida.

Ven como rayo que hiere,
que hasta que ha herido
no se siente su ruido,
por mejor hirir do quiere :
assí sea tu venida,
si no, desde aquí me obligo
qu'el gozo que avré contigo
me dará de nuevo vida.

PEDRO DE CARTAGENA

Late 15th Century

HARDLY anything is known of this gallant and graceful versifier, whose somewhat conventional output is saved from monotony by a combination of fancy and metrical skill. The two short poems to love are typical of his better work; the first of them is particularly interesting for its resemblance to Santa Teresa's "Oh Hermosura . . . ." (p. 189), which suggests that, in penning this love-poem *a lo divino*, the Saint of Ávila was drawing on her memories of secular literature.

40. *Al Amor*

(i)

¡ O amor lleno de extremos !
es tu gloria muy penada,
y muy dulce tu tormento ;
tú nos ciegas, por ti vemos,
tú nos pagas sin dar nada,
descontentas al contento.
¡ O amor tan sin compás !
a quien te plaze desplazes ;
dí, ¿ por qué no mirarás
quán contra tu nombre vas
con las obras que nos hazes ?

(ii)

Si no es amor quien me trata,
qu' es un dolor tan esquivo
de quien yo vencer me dexo ;
si es amor, ¿ por qué me mata ?
si me mata, ¿ cómo que bivo ?
si bivo, ¿ por qué me quexo ?
Quiero sofrir su passión,
tener mi fe en su esperança,
porqu' entre amor y razón
tales diferencias son
qu' el seso no las alcança.

RODRIGO COTA

Late 15th Century

A TOLEDAN of Jewish blood, Cota is a somewhat shadowy figure to whom, with varying but slight degrees of probability, have been ascribed a good many poems generally held to be anonymous. The best known of his authentic works is an allegorical "Diálogo entre el Amor y un Viejo" which, though mediaeval in type, has a vigour and directness which set it at once above the general level of the poems in the *Cancioneros.* The disillusioned old man, " muy retraído ", has shut himself up in a miserable hovel which stands in a " huerta seca y destruida, do la casa del plazer derribada se muestra." Here he is visited by Love, with his attendant ministers, and, after parrying his attacks " en áspera manera ", is finally vanquished. There is more than allegory in that part of the dialogue which describes the climax of Love's blandishments and the submission of " Don Viejo ".

41. *Diálogo entre el Amor y un Viejo*

(Extract)

Por ende, si con dulçura
me quieres obedescer,
yo haré reconoscer
en ti muy nueva frescura :
ponert' e en el coraçón
éste mi bivo alboroço ;
serás en esta sazón
de la misma condición
qu' eras quando lindo moço.

De verdura muy gentil
tu huerta renovaré;
la casa fabricaré
de obra rica, sotil:
sanaré las plantas secas,
quemadas por los friores:
en muy gran simpleza pecas,
viejo triste, si no truecas
tus espinas por mis flores.

El Viejo

Allégate un poco más:
tienes tan lindas razones,
que sofrirt' e que m'encones
por la gloria que me das:
los tus dichos alcahuetes,
con verdad o con engaño,
en el alma me los metes,
por lo dulce que prometes
d'esperar es todo 'l año.

El Amor

Abracémonos entramos,
desnudos sin otro medio;
sentirás en ti remedio,
en tu huerta nuevos ramos.

El Viejo

Vente a mí, muy dulce amor,
vente a mí, braços abiertos;
ves aquí tu servidor,
hecho siervo, de señor,
sin tener tus dones ciertos.

Amor

Hete aquí bien abraçado;
dime, ¿qué sientes agora?

Viejo

Siento ravia matadora,
plazer lleno de cuidado ;
siento fuego muy crescido,
siento mal y no lo veo ;
sin rotura estó herido,
no te quiero ver partido,
ni apartado de deseo.

42. *Esparsa*

This paradoxical little poem, " en que descubre las propiedades del amor ", is a favourite with anthologists, no doubt for its combination of brevity with power. Typically antithetical though it is, it throbs with feeling, and, looked at from the standpoint of form, its terse " revelations "—more properly, perhaps, indictments—lead up to a not ineffective, though far from perfect, climax.

Vista ciega, luz escura,
gloria triste, vida muerta,
ventura de desventura,
lloro alegre, risa incierta ;
hiel sabrosa, dulce agrura,
paz e ira y saña presta
es amor, con vestidura
de gloria que pena cuesta.

VARIOUS POEMS FROM THE CANCIONEROS

THE following short poems, all similar in type, found in Hernández del Castillo's *Cancionero*, are either anonymous or the work of authors who are merely names.

43. *Coplas del Conde de Castro a su Amiga*

Vos sois el bien que me daña,
causando el mal qu' en mí veo;
vos sois mi solo desseo,
sois el plazer que m' engaña:
yo soy el que n' os olvido;
vos sois la que me desama;
yo soy aquel mal querido
que a grandes bozes os llama.

Soy triste quando vos miro,
pensoso quando no os veo;
mirand' os, siempre sospiro;
n' os viendo, siempre os desseo:
y tal es vuestra membrança,
que jamás nunca s' olvida,
y tal es vuestra esperança,
que desespera mi vida.

Vos sois aquella belleza
que da dolor sin medida;
vos sois aquella que olvida
mis males y mi firmeza:
vos sois la nunca vencida;
yo soy quien de vos me venço;
vos sois un triste comienço
que dará fin a mi vida.

Cabo

Quexarme no sé quexar,
olvidaros menos sé ;
ni c' os dexe mi pensar,
no lo consiente mi fe :
mas manda vuestra beldad
que por miralla padezca,
y manda mi voluntad
que por serviros fenezca.

44. *Villancico*

(*Anon.*)

No quiero la muerte, no,
ni el bivir,
porque todo m' es morir.

De la vida desespero
por más muerto no me ver ;
la muerte, por no perder
de serviros, no la quiero ;
mas d'estos males que muero,
el bivir
me mata más qu' el morir.

45. *Canción*

(*Anon.*)

Que no quiero amores
en Ingalaterra,
pues otros mejores
tengo yo en mi tierra.

No quiero ni estimo
ser favorecido ;
de amores me essimo,
qu' es tiempo perdido
seguir a Cupido
en Ingalaterra,
pues otros mejores
tengo yo en mi tierra.

¿ Qué favores puede
darme la fortuna,
por mucho que ruede
el sol ni la luna,
ni muger alguna
en Ingalaterra,
pues otros mejores
tengo yo en mi tierra ?

Que quando allá vaya,
a fe, yo lo fío,
buen galardón aya
del servicio mío ;
que son desvarío
los de Ingalaterra,
pues otros mejores
tengo yo en mi tierra.

46. " *Hermosura tan hermosa . . . .* "

The " Tapia " to whom this and other rather artificial pieces are attributed, and who is not the better-known Juan de Tapia, is perhaps more inspired in his Italian poems, two of which (" Dolce mal, dolce guerra e dolce ingano . . . . .", " Dolce et amar desire che al cuor dicese . . . ."[1]*) recall Sonnets LXI and LXXXII of Boscán. The piece here reproduced may be compared with Nos. 40 and 96.*

Hermosura tan hermosa
que destruye las hermosas
y embaraça las discretas ;
si fuéssedes amorosa,
terníades todas las cosas
más altas y más perfetas ;
mas con vuestro desamor,
quanto gana la belleza,
la crueza desconcierta ;
yo lo sé por mi dolor,
que de lloros y tristeza
ya tengo la vida muerta.

[1] *C.H.C.*, II, 521-4 (Apéndice, Nos. 220, 221).

47. *Canción*
(*attributed to Nicolás Núñez*)

Norte de los mareantes
que en este mar navegamos;
puerto seguro do entramos
huyendo de los levantes
con que a vezes trabucamos.

Pues con tal norte surgidos
en vuestro puerto o baya
la tormenta e travessía
y el temor de ser perdidos
se nos torna en alegría;
assí que, siendo constantes,
que de vista no os perdamos,
aunque tormentas corramos,
huyendo de los levantes,
seguro puerto tomamos.

JUAN DE MENA

1411-1456

Of the pre-Renaissance italianizers in Spanish poetry, Mena, an Andalusian, part of whose youth was spent in Italy, is the most substantial, though not in every respect the best. In his " Laberinto de Fortuna " (also known, from the approximate number of its stanzas, as " Las Trezientas ") he describes an allegorical vision inspired by Dante. Allegorical, too, is the " Coronación dirigida al Marqués de Santillana " (on the same principle dubbed " Las Cincuenta "). His technique, for his time, is advanced—even brilliant—especially in his use of *arte mayor* (p.59); but beneath it there is little for which he will be read to-day. If he continues to live it will be for his historical significance and for a few fine passages, of which the noblest are encomiastic or elegiac, though rather long for reproduction. Two of these are the elegy on the death of the Conde de Niebla and the panegyric of Don Álvaro de Luna, both from the " Laberinto de Fortuna ". A shorter passage from that poem, not inferior to either in quality, laments the death of a young noble, Lorenzo Dávalos, who died in 1441 of wounds received in a rebellion against King John II.

48. *Muerte de Lorenzo Dávalos*
(From " El Laberinto de Fortuna ")

" Aquel que allí vees al cerco travado,[1]
que quiere subir e se falla en el aire,
mostrando su rostro robado donaire
por dos desonestas feridas llagado,
aquel es el Dávalos mal fortunado,

[1] The reference is to the three " wheels " which the poet finds in the Palace of Fortune, representing respectively the past, the present and the future, and each containing seven planetary " circles " of human destiny. The youth has, by dint of labour, begun to progress (*subir*) within his circle, when suddenly fate leaves him " in the air."

aquel es el linpio mancebo Lorenço,
que fizo en un día su fin e comienço:
aquel es el que era de todos amado;

"el mucho querido del señor infante,
que sienpre le fuera señor como padre;
el mucho llorado de la triste madre
que muerto ver pudo tal fijo delante.
¡O dura Fortuna, cruel, tribulante!
por ti se le pierden al mundo dos cosas:
la vida e las lágrimas tan piadosas
que ponen dolores de espada tajante.

"Bien se mostrava ser madre en el duelo
que fizo la triste, después ya que vido
el cuerpo en las andas sangriento tendido
de aquel que criara con tanto recelo:
ofende con dichos crüeles el cielo
con nuevos dolores su flaca salud,
e tantas angustias roban su virtud,
que cae por fuerça la triste en el suelo.

"E rasga con uñas crüeles su cara,
fiere sus pechos con mesura poca,
besando a su fijo la su fría boca,
maldize las manos de quien lo matara,
maldize la guerra do se començara,
busca con ira crueles querellas,
niega a sí mesma reparo de aquéllas,
e tal como muerta biviendo se para.

"Dezía, llorando con lengua raviosa:
'O matador de mi fijo crüel,
mataras a mí, dexaras a él,
que fuera enemiga non tan porfiosa;
fuera la madre muy más dina cosa
para quien mata levar menor cargo,
e non te mostraras a él tan amargo,
nin triste dexaras a mi querellosa.

"'Si antes la muerte me fuera ya dada,
cerrara mis ojos con estas sus manos,
mi fijo, delante de los sus ermanos,

e yo non muriera más de una vegada :
assí morré muchas, desaventurada,
que sola padesco lavar sus feridas
con lágrimas tristes e non gradecidas,
maguer que lloradas por madre cuitada.'

" Assí lamentava la pía matrona
al fijo querido, que muerto tú viste,
faziéndole encima senblante de triste,
segund al que pare faze la leona ;
pues ¿ dónde podría pensar la persona
los daños que causa la triste demanda
de la discordia del reino, que anda
donde non gana ninguno corona ? "

JUAN ÁLVAREZ GATO

c.1430-c.1509

FROM the works of this Madrilenian poet one piece of secular verse is taken, and one of sacred—both, as it happens, written in the same metre. In neither genre did he penetrate far beneath the surface, but in charm and melody he was surpassed by few. The *letra*, it will be observed, bears a close resemblance to the *villancico*, or carol, and is of a type which became very popular in Spain during the sixteenth century.

49. *Cantar endereçado a Nuestro Señor*

Amor, no me dexes,
que me moriré.

Que en ti so yo bivo,
sin ti so cativo ;
si m'eres esquivo
perdido seré.

Si mal no me viene,
por ti se detiene ;
en ti me sostiene
tu gracia y mi fe.

Que el que en ti se ceva,
que truene, que llueva,
no espere ya nueva
que pena le dé.

Que aquel que tú tienes
los males son bienes ;
a él vas y vienes :
muy cierto lo sé.

Amor, no me dexes,
que me moriré.

50. *Letra : Al Nacimiento*

Venida es, venida,
al mundo la vida.

Venida es al suelo
la gracia del cielo
a darnos consuelo
y gloria conplida.

Nacido ha en Belén
Él que es nuestro bien ;
venido es en quien
por Él fué escogida.

En un portalejo,
con pobre aparejo,
servido d'un viejo,
su guarda escogida.

La piedra preciosa,
ni la fresca rosa,
no es tan hermosa
como la parida.

Venida es, venida,
al mundo la vida.

JORGE MANRIQUE

*c.*1440-1479

A SOLDIER-POET, killed in action while fighting for the Catholic Monarchs against Juana *la Beltraneja*, Jorge Manrique was the nephew of Gómez Manrique (p. 76), with whose verse his own shows a striking resemblance, not wholly attributable to imitation. He will be remembered for all time as the author of the famous *coplas* reproduced below; and surprise has often been expressed, not only that he should have written no other outstanding work, but that his remaining poems, about fifty in all, should show so little similarity to his masterpiece. But, although these include some light, artificial and mannered verses, they are by no means all either unfeeling or frivolous in tone. The melancholy and disillusion which permeate the *coplas*, for example, can be found in a number of minor poems—notably in "Con el gran mal que me sobra . . . . ." In "Castillo d'amor" and "Escala d'amor", simplicity and fancy make a combined appeal and emotion breaks through the artificiality of the allegory. The *canciones* are pitched in a lower key, but one of them, "No tardes, Muerte, que muero . . . . . .", recalls the little masterpiece of Escrivá (p. 84), expressing with striking terseness a mood familiar to all. Even the stylistic and technical characteristics of the *coplas* can be found in the minor poems, and their well-known metre (*abc abc def def*, with every third line a short one—the so-called *verso de pie quebrado*) is used in five brief compositions.

51. *Coplas por la Muerte de su Padre*

Written, very probably, soon after the death, on November 11, 1476, of the author's father, Don Rodrigo Manrique, Conde de Paredes, Condestable de Castilla and Maestre de Santiago, this is a lyric which can safely be termed immortal. It expresses, in distinguished and unforgettable language, moods, sentiments and emotions common to all humanity—abounding, as Dr. Johnson said of Gray's Elegy, "*with images which find a mirrour in every mind, and with sentiments to which every bosom returns an echo*". *Though seldom original in its ideas, and indebted, in both form and content, to Gómez Manrique and others, it is unique in the force and intensity with which it conveys these ideas and in the sense of deep solemnity which pervades it. Essentially, one feels, these qualities are inherent in the personality and genius of the author. But they are also enhanced by a subtle technique: the skilful use of contrast in theme, image and phraseology: a deliberate and determined rejection of the purely picturesque; a notable simplicity, amounting almost to austerity, in the presentation of metaphors and illustrations; a happy and melodious use of repetition in word and phrase. Opinions have differed widely as to the suitability of the metre to the theme. Without going so far as Quintana, who thought it inharmonious and disagreeable, we may wonder if a total of 160 "broken" lines in a poem of forty stanzas is not excessive; the continual recurrence of the* quebrado, *which some critics have picturesquely described as an appropriately tolling bell or funeral refrain, seems to make the poem halt, and lag, somewhat in the fashion of the lengthened last line in Spenser's* Faerie Queene. *But with any instrument of his own choosing the poet of genius can work wonders and there will be general agreement that Manrique has done so here.*

Recuerde el alma dormida,
abive el seso y despierte
contemplando
cómo se passa la vida,
cómo se viene la muerte
tan callando:
quán presto se va el plazer,
cómo después de acordado
da dolor,
cómo, a nuestro parecer,
qualquiera tiempo passado
fué mejor.

Y pues vemos lo presente
como en un punto es ido
y acabado,

si juzgamos sabiamente,
daremos lo no venido
por passado.
No se engañe nadie, no,
pensando ha de durar
lo que espera
más que duró lo que vió,
porque todo ha de passar
por tal manera.

Nuestras vidas son los ríos
que van a dar en la mar,
que es el morir;
allí van los señoríos
derechos a se acabar
y consumir;
allí los ríos caudales,
allí los otros medianos
y más chicos,
allegados, son iguales,
los que biven por sus manos
y los ricos.

INVOCACIÓN

Dexo las invocaciones
de los famosos poetas
y oradores;
no curo de sus ficiones,
que traen yerva secreta
sus sabores.
A aquél solo me encomiendo,
aquél solo invoco yo
de verdad,
que en este mundo biviendo,
el mundo no conoció
su deidad.

Este mundo es el camino
para el otro, qu'es morada
sin pesar;

mas cumple tener buen tino
para andar esta jornada
sin errar.
Partimos quando nacemos,
andamos mientra bivimos,
y llegamos
al tiempo que fenecemos;
assí que quando morimos
descansamos.

Este mundo bueno fué
si bien usássemos d' él
como devemos,
porque, según nuestra fe,
es para ganar aquel
que atendemos.
Y aún el Hijo de Dios
para subirnos al cielo
descendió
a nascer acá entre nos,
y bivir en este suelo
do murió.

Ved de quán poco valor
son las cosas tras que andamos
y corremos,
que en este mundo traidor
aun primero que muramos
las perdemos:
d'ellas deshaze la edad,
d'ellas casos desastrados
que acaescen,
d'ellas, por su calidad,
en los más altos estados
desfallecen.

Dezidme, la hermosura,
la gentil frescura y tez
de la cara,
la color y la blancura,
¿quando viene la vejez
quál se para?

Las mañas y ligereza
y la fuerça corporal
de juventud,
todo se torna graveza
quando llega al arraval
de senetud.

Pues la sangre de los godos,
el linage y la nobleza
tan crecida,
¡ por quántas vías e modos
se pierde su gran alteza
en esta vida !
Unos por poco valer,
por quán baxos y abatidos
que los tienen !
Otros que por no tener,
con oficios no devidos
se mantienen.

Los estados y riqueza
que nos dexan a desora
¿ quién lo duda ?
No les pidamos firmeza,
pues que son de una señora
que se muda.
Que bienes son de fortuna
que rebuelve con su rueda
presurosa,
la qual no puede ser una,
ni ser estable ni queda
en una cosa.

Pero digo que acompañen
y lleguen hasta la huessa
con su dueño ;
por esso no nos engañen,
pues se va la vida apriessa
como sueño :
y los deleites de acá
son en que nos deleitamos
temporales,

y los tormentos de allá,
que por ellos esperamos,
eternales.

Los plazeres y dulçores
d' esta vida trabajada
que tenemos,
¿ qué son sino corredores,
y la muerte es la celada
èn que caemos ?
No mirando a nuestro daño
corremos a rienda suelta
sin parar ;
de que vemos el engaño
y queremos dar la buelta,
no ay lugar.

Si fuesse en nuestro poder
tornar la cara fermosa
corporal,
como podemos hazer
el alma tan glorïosa,
angelical,
¡ qué diligencia tan biva
tuviéramos cada hora,
y tan presta,
en componer la cativa,
dexándonos la señora
descompuesta !

Estos reyes poderosos
que vemos por escripturas
ya passadas,
con casos tristes, llorosos,
fueron sus buenas venturas
trastornadas :
assí que no ay cosa fuerte,
que a Papas y Emperadores
y Perlados
assí los trata la muerte
como a los pobres pastores
de ganados.

Dexemos a los Troyanos,
que sus males no los vimos,
ni sus glorias ;
dexemos a los Romanos,
aunque oímos y leímos
sus historias.
No curemos de saber
lo de aquel siglo passado
qué fué d' ello ;
vengamos a lo de ayer,
que también es olvidado
como aquello.

¿ Qué se hizo el Rey Don Juan ?
Los Infantes de Aragón
¿ qué se hizieron ?
¿ Qué fué de tanto galán,
qué fué de tanta invención
como truxeron ?
Las justas e los torneos,
paramentos, bordaduras
e cimeras,
¿ fueron sino devaneos ?
¿ qué fueron sino verduras
de las eras ?

¿ Qué se hizieron las damas,
sus tocados, sus vestidos,
sus olores ?
¿ Qué se hizieron las llamas
de los fuegos encendidos
de amadores ?
¿ Qué se hizo aquel trobar,
las músicas acordadas
que tañían ?
¿ Qué se hizo aquel dançar
y aquellas ropas chapadas
que traían ?

Pues el otro su heredero,
Don Enrique ¡ qué poderes
alcançava !

¡ Quán blando, quán alagüero
el mundo con sus plazeres
se le dava !
Mas verás quán enemigo,
quán contrario, quán crüel
se le mostró ;
aviéndole sido amigo,
quán poco duró con él
lo que le dió.

Las dádivas desmedidas,
los edificios reales
llenos de oro,
las baxillas tan fabridas,
los enriques y rëales
del tesoro ;
los jaezes y cavallos
de su gente y atavíos
tan sobrados,
¿ dónde iremos a buscallos ?
¿ qué fueron sino rocíos
de los prados ?

Pues su hermano el inocente,
que en su vida sucessor
se llamó,
¡ qué corte tan excelente
tuvo y quánto gran señor
que le siguió !
Mas como fuesse mortal,
metiólo la muerte luego
en su fragua.
¡ O jüizio divinal !
quando más ardía el fuego,
echaste agua.

Pues aquel gran Condestable,
Maestre que conocimos
tan privado,
no cumple que d' él se hable,
sino sólo que le vimos
degollado.

Sus infinitos tesoros,
sus villas y sus lugares,
su mandar,
¿ qué le fueron sino lloros ?
¿ qué fueron sino pesares
al dexar ?

Pues los otros dos hermanos,
Maestres tan prosperados
como reyes,
a los grandes y medianos
traxeron tan sojuzgados
a sus leyes ;
aquella prosperidad
que tan alta fué subida
y ensalçada,
¿ qué fué sino claridad
que quando más encendida
fué amatada ?

Tantos duques excelentes,
tantos marqueses y condes
y barones
como vimos tan potentes,
di, muerte, ¿ dó los escondes
y los pones ?
Y sus muy claras hazañas
que hizieron en las guerras
y en las pazes,
quando tú, crüel, te ensañas,
con tu fuerça los atierras
y deshazes.

Las huestes innumerables,
los pendones y estandartes
y vanderas,
los castillos inpunables,
los muros e baluartes
y barreras,
la cava honda chapada,
o qualquier otro reparo
¿ qué aprovecha ?

Quando tú vienes airada,
todo lo passas de claro
con tu flecha.

Aquel de buenos abrigo,
amado por virtuoso
de la gente,
el Maestre Don Rodrigo
Manrique, tan famoso
y tan valiente,
sus grandes hechos y claros
no cumple que los alabe,
pues los vieron,
ni los quiero hazer caros,
pues el mundo todo sabe
quáles fueron.

¡ Qué amigo de amigos !
¡ Qué señor para criados
y parientes !
¡ Qué enemigo de enemigos !
¡ Qué Maestre de esforçados
y valientes !
¡ Qué seso para discretos !
¡ Qué gracia para donosos !
¡ Qué razón !
¡ Quán benigno a los subjetos,
y a los bravos y dañosos
un león !

En ventura Octaviano ;
Julio César en vencer
y batallar ;
en la virtud, Africano ;
Aníbal en el saber
y trabajar.
En la bondad un Trajano ;
Tito en liberalidad
con alegría ;
en su braço, un Archidano ;
Marco Tulio en la verdad
que prometía.

Antonio Pío en clemencia ;
Marco Aurelio en igualdad
del semblante ;
Adriano en eloquencia ;
Theodosio en humanidad
y buen talante.
Aurelio Alexandre fué
en disciplina y rigor
de la guerra ;
un Constantino en la fe ;
Gamelio en el gran amor
de su tierra.

No dexó grandes tesoros,
ni alcançó muchas riquezas
ni baxillas,
mas hizo guerra a los moros,
ganando sus fortalezas
y sus villas ;
y en las lides que venció,
cavalleros y cavallos
se prendieron,
y en este oficio ganó
las rentas e los vasallos
que le dieron.

Pues por su honra y estado
en otros tiempos passados
¿ cómo se huvo ?
Quedando desamparado,
con hermanos y criados
se sostuvo.
Después que hechos famosos
hizo en esta dicha guerra
que hazía,
hizo tratos tan honrosos,
que le dieron muy más tierra
que tenía.

Estas sus viejas historias
que con su braço pintó
en la juventud,

con otras nuevas victorias
agora las renovó
en la senetud.
Por su gran abilidad,
por méritos y ancianía
bien gastada
alcançó la dignidad
de la gran cavallería
del Espada.

E sus villas e sus tierras
ocupadas de tiranos
las halló,
mas por cercos e por guerras
y por fuerças de sus manos
las cobró.
Pues nuestro Rey natural,
si de las obras que obró
fué servido,
dígalo el de Portugal,
y en Castilla quien siguió
su partido.

Después de puesta la vida
tantas vezes por su ley
al tablero;
después de tan bien servida
la corona de su Rey
verdadero;
después de tanta hazaña
a que no puede bastar
cuenta cierta,
en la su villa de Ocaña
vino la muerte a llamar
a su puerta.

(*Habla la Muerte*)

Diziendo: "Buen cavallero,
dexad el mundo engañoso
y su halago;

muestre su esfuerço famoso
vuestro coraçón de azero
en este trago;
y pues de vida y salud
fezistes tan poca cuenta
por la fama,
esfuércese la virtud
para sufrir esta afrenta
que os llama.

"No se os haga tan amarga
la batalla temerosa
que esperáis,
pues otra vida más larga
de fama tan glorïosa
acá dexáis.
Aunque esta vida de honor
tanpoco no es eternal
ni verdadera,
mas con todo es muy mejor
que la otra temporal
perecedera.

"El bivir que es perdurable
no se gana con estados
mundanales,
ni con vida deleitable
en que moran los pecados
infernales;
mas los buenos religiosos
gánanlo con oraciones
y con lloros;
los cavalleros famosos
con trabajos y afliciones
contra moros.

"Y pues vos, claro varón,
tanta sangre derramastes
de paganos,
esperad el galardón
que en este mundo ganastes

por las manos;
y con esta confiança
y con la fe tan entera
que tenéis,
partid con buena esperança
que esta otra vida tercera
ganaréis."

(Responde el Maestre)

"No gastemos tiempo ya
en esta vida mezquina
por tal modo,
que mi voluntad está
conforme con la divina
para todo;
y consiento en mi morir
con voluntad plazentera,
clara, pura,
que querer hombre bivir
quando Dios quiere que muera,
es locura."

Oración

Tú, que por nuestra maldad
tomastes forma servil
y baxo nombre;
Tú que en tu divinidad
juntaste cosa tan vil
como el hombre;
Tú que tan grandes tormentos
sufriste sin resistencia
en tu persona,
no por mis merecimientos,
mas por tu sola clemencia
me perdona.

Cabo

Assí con tal entender,
todos sentidos humanos
conservados,
cercado de su muger,
de hijos y (de) hermanos
y criados,
dió el alma a quien gela dió,
(el qual la ponga en el cielo
y en su gloria),
y aunque la vida murió,
nos dexó harto consuelo
su memoria.

FRAY AMBROSIO MONTESINO

?-*c.*1513

This Franciscan is known chiefly for his translation of Ludolph the Carthusian's *Vita Christi*, one of the sources for the *Ejercicios espirituales* of San Ignacio de Loyola. In 1508, however, he published a considerable *Cancionero*, composed largely of verses of a devout character, including many *romances*. These reveal the most diverse tendencies—social satire, a bent towards popular art, colour, eloquence, fervour, freshness and sincerity.

52. *Coplas a reverencia de San Juan Bautista*

Fray Ambrosio's multi-hued angel represents in an exaggerated form that love of colour which was to be so prominent a characteristic of sixteenth-century poetry. His imagination, in both its visual and its auditory flight, shows a lack of restraint which prevents these coplas *from having more than a historical interest.*

Ofreciendo Zacarías
encienso, según costumbre,
vino a él por altas vías
de las claras jerarquías
un ángel de mansedumbre,

con alas de mil colores,
de tan linda hermosura
y de tales resplandores
que a todos daba temores
su figura.

Sus plumas eran distintas,
azules, moradas, verdes,
tocadas de verdes pintas,
como rosicler de cintas
porque dél mejor te acuerdes.

Otras eran plateadas,
con matiz de resplandor ;
otras como pavonadas
e no bien determinadas
en color.

La beldad de su melena,
si con discreción se aprecia,
era madeja tan buena
como dorada en la vena
del oro fino de Grecia.

Fué su voz tan pavorida
que turbaba los oídos,
tan delgada y recogida
cual no oyeron en su vida
los nascidos.

¡ Oh, qué gala fué de galas
ver al ángel sostenido
en el aire, de sus alas,
no por invenciones malas
ilusoras del sentido !

El cual venía de donde
no viene cosa con mengua,
con tal gesto que responde
al secreto que se esconde
en su lengua.

53. *" No la debemos dormir . . . . . "*

Here we have a very different type of poem, showing a surprising simplicity and sensibility which unite to convey real emotion. The poet's daring in attempting to penetrate the mind of the Virgin as she contemplates the imminence of the mystery of the Incarnation may seem to us excessive, but we can hardly fail to admire it, while the directness with which he attacks his theme is as striking as its originality and boldness.

No la debemos dormir
la noche santa,
no la debemos dormir . . . . .

La Virgen a solas piensa
qué hará
cuando al Rey de luz inmensa
parirá,
si de su divina esencia
temblará,
o qué le podrá decir.

No la debemos dormir
la noche santa,
no la debemos dormir.

GARCÍA DE RESENDE

Early 16th Century

THIS author, secretary to King John II of Portugal, published a Portuguese *Cancioneiro geral* at Lisbon (1516), about one in ten of the authors represented in which wrote in Spanish.

54. "*Mira, gentil dama . . . . .*"

All music as it is, this charming little poem contrives to stress the first lines of its tema, *not merely by repeating them (as shown here by italic type) but by carrying the rhymes of the* tema (abxb) *into each stanza. The second half of the first octave is linked, not to the first half, as is usual, but to the* tema (cddcbaab). *The second half of the second octave* (ebebbaab) *is linked to both.*

Mira, gentil dama,
el tu servidor
cómo está tan triste
con tanto dolor.

Mira, que merezco
no ser desamado,
ni tan olvidado
pues tanto padezco.
Y pues con dolor
mi vida te llama,
mira, gentil dama,
el tu servidor.

Pues tu hermosura
causó mi dolor,
mira mi tristura
y tu disfavor.
No trates peor
el que más te ama,
mira, gentil dama,
el tu servidor.

THE ROMANCERO

In no type of literature is Spain richer than in the *romance*, or ballad ; and; though the composition of *romances* has continued almost without interruption since the Middle Ages, at no later period than between the fifteenth and seventeenth centuries has their production been so abundant and their standard of excellence so high. To the whole corpus of anonymous Spanish ballads composed during that period is given the collective title of *Romancero*.

To some extent ballads vary from country to country, and from age to age, but generally speaking they may be defined as relatively short and popular narrative poems almost bare of description but often with a lyrical tinge, simple in conception and in style, and suitable for recitation or song. The Spanish ballad has come down to us in octosyllabic lines, with a stress on the seventh syllable of each line and the even lines assonancing : it is now generally believed that the lines were sixteen-syllabled and as a rule they are so printed. A few of the longer ballads are written, like the epics, in *tiradas*, or *laisses*, each of which has a different assonance. But as a rule the same assonance holds throughout the poem.

Limitation of space precludes more than the briefest of references here to the various problems connected with the Spanish ballad, the chief of which has to do with its origins. Most modern scholars related ballads to epics, and many even hold that the earliest of them were nothing but fragments of epics edited for separate presentation—a reversal of the position taken up, before the matter was seriously investigated, by the nineteenth-century Romantics, who believed the ballads to have been composed, in the early Middle Ages, by some strange collective " popular " process and the epics to have been derived from them. Tradition, however, did play a part in ballad-development, which took place, though decreasingly as printing became more general, through oral transmission. It was from about 1550 that *Cancioneros* or *Silvas* began to appear with titles qualified by the words *de romances*.

From about the end of the sixteenth century there came out collections more specialized in character and limited in scope, in which the popular element gradually faded out before the erudite and the consciously artistic.

In this vast repertory of verse we have both a picture-gallery representing the entire field of Spanish legend and history, and also an account, in little, of the development of the literary art. But we must not forget the lyrical element in these ballads, which, lying as it does some little way beneath their surface, is apt to be overlooked. A few there are to which their lyrical quality has brought fame. But in the majority lyricism breaks through narrative objectivity—sometimes almost imperceptibly, sometimes with irresistible force—and gives no indication of being an integral and deliberately planned part of the whole.

Various devices are used to create or quicken lyric emotion. One is repetition within the line—twofold:

> Conde Olinos, Conde Olinos, es niño y pasó la mar,

or even threefold:

> Fonte-frida, fonte-frida, fonte-frida y con amor—

which often strikes a sharp emotional chord. Another is parallelism, generally involving repetition but aiming chiefly at laying great emphasis upon some fact, idea or sentiment, which may or may not be lyrical, or at working up the audience to a state of tension. A third is the refrain, which varies in sentiment from the Spanish equivalent of the hearty and almost meaningless English "Tra-la-la" to a phrase as deeply charged both with music and with emotion as "¡Ay de mi Alhama!"

There are also lyric themes in the ballads, both in the superficial sense (e.g. the *malcasada* and "rustic lover" themes, which lend themselves readily to song) and also in the more fundamental sense of stirring the emotions and thus creating an atmosphere in which lyricism can flourish. Such lyric themes are love, patriotism, the supernatural and a vague melancholy corresponding to the Portuguese *saudade* and often intensified by contrast. In the non-historical ballads, the dividing line between narrative and lyric is occasionally a very faint one.

We give here a representative selection of primitive anonymous ballads known as *Romances viejos*: similar compositions of later date, and by known authors, will be found elsewhere in this volume.

The classification is that adopted by most critics, and the only important section unrepresented is the Breton cycle :

I. *Romances históricos.*

(*a*) Romances del Rey Don Rodrigo ;
(*b*) Romances de Bernardo del Carpio ;
(*c*) Romances de Fernán González ;
(*d*) Romances de los Siete Infantes de Lara ;
(*e*) Romances del Cid ;
(*f*) Romances del Rey Don Pedro ;
(*g*) Romances fronterizos.

II. *Romances del Ciclo Carolingio.*

III. *Romances novelescos y líricos.*

I. ROMANCES HISTÓRICOS

(*a*) ROMANCES DEL REY DON RODRIGO

STARTING with the Moorish invasion of Spain in 711, we find a large group of ballads dealing with the seduction by King Roderick, "the last of the Goths", of Count Julian's daughter, La Cava, the consequent betrayal of Roderick by Julian to the Moors, the defeat of the King's forces at Lake Janda, and the destruction of the Gothic kingdom.

55. *El Conde Don Julián*

This ballad is markedly lyrical in tone, its emotion coursing through the twofold channel of patriotism and melancholy. The apostrophe "¡ Madre España . . . . . !", with its swelling national pride, and its wealth of description, so rare in the ballad, is itself a pure lyric. Observe, however, how the whole poem stresses the theme of dolor *(ll. 5a, 5b, 16, 18, 23), which is intensified by the element of mystery in ll. 20, 26 and gives it both poignancy and unity.*

En Ceupta está Julián, en Ceupta la bien nombrada ;
para las partes de aliende quiere enviar su embajada ;
moro viejo la escrebía, y el Conde se la notaba :
después de haberla escripto, al moro luego matara.
Embajada es de dolor, dolor para toda España :
las cartas van al Rey moro, en las cuales le juraba
que si le daba aparejo, le dará por suya España.
Madre España, ¡ ay de ti !, en el mundo tan nombrada,
de las partidas la mejor, la mejor y más ufana,
donde nace el fino oro y la plata no faltaba,
dotada de hermosura, y en proezas extremada ;
por un perverso traidor toda eres abrasada,
todas tus ricas ciudades con su gente tan galana
las domeñan hoy los moros por nuestra culpa malvada,

si no fueran las Asturias, por ser la tierra tan brava.
El triste rey Don Rodrigo, el que entonces te mandaba,
viendo sus reinos perdidos sale a la campal batalla ;
el cual en grave dolor enseña su fuerza brava ;
mas tantos eran los moros, que han vencido la batalla.
No paresce el rey Rodrigo, ni nadie sabe dó estaba.
Maldito de ti, Don Orpas, obispo de mala andanza :
en esta negra conseja uno a otro se ayudaba.
¡ Oh dolor sobre manera ! ¡ Oh cosa nunca cuidada !
Que por sola una doncella, la cual Cava se llamaba,
causen estos dos traidores que España sea domeñada,
y perdido el Rey señor, sin nunca dél saber nada.

56. *Don Rodrigo pierde España*

Here, notably in the justly famous lament "Ayer era rey de España . . . . .", where antithesis also takes a hand, the emotion is intensified throughout by parallelism and repetition. Note the skilful preparation of the atmosphere of disaster in ll. 1-2 ; the descriptive colour, forming a strong contrast to this, in ll. 4-6 ; the initiation of the parallelism, with two phrases of no apparent significance, in ll. 7-8 ; and the gradual working up of the emotional tone, as it proceeds, through ll. 11-12, 39-40, 40-3, 46-8, 50.

Los vientos eran contrarios, la luna estaba crecida,
los peces daban gemidos, por el mal tiempo que hacía,
cuando el rey Don Rodrigo junto a la Cava dormía,
dentro de una rica tienda de oro bien guarnecida.
Trescientas cuerdas de plata que la tienda sostenían ;
dentro había cien doncellas vestidas a maravilla ;
las cincuenta están tañendo con muy extraña armonía ;
las cincuenta están cantando con muy dulce melodía.
Allí hablara una doncella, que Fortuna se decía :
" Si duermes, rey Don Rodrigo, despierta por cortesía,
y verás tus malos hados, tu peor postrimería,
y verás tus gentes muertas y tu batalla rompida,
y tus villas y ciudades destruídas en un día.
Tus castillos, fortalezas, otro señor los regía.
Si me pides quién lo ha hecho, yo muy bien te lo diría :

ese conde Don Julián por amores de su hija ;
porque se la deshonraste y más de ella no tenía.
Juramento viene echando que te ha de costar la vida."
Despertó muy congojado con aquella voz que oía ;
con cara triste y penosa de esta suerte respondía :
" Mercedes a ti, Fortuna, de esta tu mensajería."
Estando en esto allegó uno que nuevas traía,
cómo el conde Don Julián las tierras le destruía.
Apriesa pide el caballo y al encuentro le salía ;
los enemigos son tantos que esfuerzo no le valía ;
que capitanes y gentes huía el que más podía.
Rodrigo deja sus tiendas y del real se salía :
solo va el desventurado, que no lleva compañía.
El caballo de cansado ya mudar no se podía ;
camina por donde quiere, que no le estorba la vía.
El Rey va tan desmayado que sentido no tenía ;
muerto va de sed y hambre, que de velle era mancilla.
Iba tan tinto de sangre que una brasa parecía ;
las armas lleva abolladas, que eran de gran pedrería ;
la espada lleva hecha sierra de los golpes que tenía ;
el almete de abollado en la cabeza se le hundía ;
la cara lleva hinchada del trabajo que sufría.
Subióse encima de un cerro, el más alto que veía ;
dende allí mira su gente cómo iba de vencida.
De allí mira sus banderas y estandartes que tenía,
cómo están todos pisados que la tierra los cubría.
Mira por los capitanes que ninguno parescía ;
mira el campo tinto en sangre, la cual arroyos corría.
El triste de ver aquesto gran mancilla en sí tenía ;
llorando de los sus ojos, de esta manera decía :
" Ayer era rey de España, hoy no lo soy de una villa ;
ayer villas y castillos, hoy ninguno poseía ;
ayer tenía criados y gente que me servía ;
hoy no tengo una almena que pueda decir que es mía.
¡ Desdichada fué la hora, desdichado fué aquel día
en que nací y heredé la tan grande señoría,
pues lo había de perder todo junto y en un día !
¡ Oh muerte ! ¿ por qué no vienes y llevas esta alma mía,
de aqueste cuerpo mezquino, pues se te agradecería ? "

(*b*) ROMANCES DE BERNARDO DEL CARPIO

Bernardo del carpio, a legendary figure typifying nationalistic independence, seems to have been invented by the *juglares* as a patriotic pseudo-historical counterpoise to the French King Charlemagne. His characteristic attitudes in the ballads of this cycle are militant patriotism, defiance of the French and a sturdy independence of his master, King Alfonso the Chaste. The last attitude is emphatically illustrated in the ballad which follows—the only one of its group known to be early in date. The change of assonance after l. 8—unusual in so short a ballad—should be noticed.

57. *Bernardo y el Rey Don Alfonso*

Con cartas y mensajeros el Rey al Carpio envió ;
Bernaldo, como es discreto, de traición se receló :
las cartas echó en el suelo y al mensajero habló :
" Mensajero eres, amigo, no mereces culpa, no ;
mas al Rey que acá te envía dígasle tú esta razón :
que no lo estimo yo a él, ni aun cuantos con él son ;
mas, por ver lo que me quiere, todavía allá iré yo."
Y mandó juntar los suyos ; de esta suerte les habló :
" Cuatrocientos sois, los míos, los que comedes mi pan :
los ciento irán al Carpio, para el Carpio guardar ;
los ciento por los caminos, que a nadie dejen pasar ;
doscientos iréis conmigo para con el Rey hablar ;
si mala me la dijere peor se la he de tornar."
Por sus jornadas contadas a la corte fué a llegar.
" Manténgavos Dios, buen Rey, y a cuantos con vos están."
" Mal vengades vos, Bernaldo, traidor, hijo de mal padre :
dite yo el Carpio en tenencia, tú tómaslo de heredad."
" Mentides, el Rey, mentides, que no dices la verdad ;
que si yo fuese traidor, a vos os cabría en parte.

Acordársevos debía de aquella del Encinal,
cuando gentes extranjeras, allí os trataron tan mal,
que os mataron el caballo, y aun a vos querían matar.
Bernaldo, como traidor, de entre ellos os fué a sacar :
allí me distes el Carpio de juro y de heredad :
prometístesme a mi padre, no me guardastes verdad."
" Prendedlo, mis caballeros, que igualado se me ha."
" ¡ Aquí, aquí, los mis doscientos, los que coméis mi pan !
Que hoy era venido el día que honra habemos de ganar."
El Rey, de que aquesto viera, de esta suerte fué a hablar :
" ¿ Qué ha sido aquesto, Bernaldo, que así enojado te has ?
¿ Lo que hombre dice de burla de veras vas a tomar ?
Yo te dó el Carpio, Bernaldo, de juro y de heredad."
" Aquestas burlas, el Rey, no son burlas de burlar ;
llamástesme de traidor, traidor, hijo de mal padre :
el Carpio yo no lo quiero, bien lo podéis vos guardar,
que cuando yo lo quisiere, muy bien lo sabré ganar."

(*c*) ROMANCES DE FERNAN GONZÁLEZ

A few of the ballads which centre round the hero of Castilian independence (p. 26, above) are as stirring as any in existence. "Castellanos y leoneses . . . . .", perhaps the best of them, begins on a low note, but rises to heights of real eloquence as the figures of the Count and the King emerge from the shadows and are brought into sharp and vivid opposition. The Count's gruff response to the shrill if colourful threats of the King is given greater force by parallelism and antithesis, and these devices, as well as the same note of contrast between the two characters, continue to the end of the narrative. The abruptness with which the poem ends is not felt to be an artistic flaw as it would be in more sophisticated poetry.

58. *Romance del Rey Don Sancho Ordóñez*

Castellanos y leoneses tienen grandes divisiones.
El conde Fernán González y el buen rey Don Sancho Ordóñez,
sobre el partir de las tierras ahí pasan malas razones:
llámanse hideputas, hijos de padres traidores;
echan mano a las espadas, derriban ricos mantones:
no les pueden poner treguas cuantos en la corte son,
pónenselas dos hermanos, aquesos benditos monjes;
el uno es tío del Rey, el otro hermano del Conde.
Pónenlas por quince días, que no pueden por más, non;
que se vayan a los prados que dicen de Carrión.
Si mucho madruga el Rey, el Conde no dormía, no;
el Conde partió de Burgos, y el Rey partió de León.
Venido se han a juntar al vado de Carrión,
y a la pasada del río movieron una cuistión:
los del Rey que pasarían, y los del Conde que non.
El Rey, como era risueño, la su mula revolvió;

el Conde con lozanía su caballo arremetió ;
con el agua y el arena al buen Rey ensalpicó.
Allí hablara el buen Rey, su gesto muy demudado :
" Buen conde Fernán González, mucho sois desmesurado :
si no fuera por las treguas que los monjes nos han dado,
la cabeza de los hombros ya vos la hubiera quitado ;
con la sangre que os sacara yo tiñera aqueste vado."
El Conde le respondiera, como aquel que era osado :
" Eso que decís, buen Rey, véolo mal aliñado ;
vos venís en gruesa mula, yo en ligero caballo ;
vos traéis sayo de seda, yo traigo un arnés tranzado ;
vos traéis alfanje de oro, yo traigo lanza en mi mano ;
vos traéis cetro de rey, yo un venablo acerado ;
vos con guantes olorosos, yo con los de acero claro ;
vos con la gorra de fiesta, yo con un casco afinado ;
vos traéis ciento de mula, yo trescientos de caballo."
Ellos en aquesto estando, los frailes que han allegado :
" ¡ Tate, tate, caballeros ! ¡ Tate, tate, hijosdalgo !
¡ Cuán mal cumplistes las treguas que nos habíades mandado ! "
Allí hablara el buen Rey : " Yo las compliré de grado."
Pero respondiera el Conde : " Yo de pies puesto en el campo."
Cuando vido aquesto el Rey, no quiso pasar el vado ;
vuélvese para sus tierras : malamente va enojado.
Grandes bascas va haciendo, reciamente va jurando
que había de matar al Conde y destruir su condado,
y mandó llamar a cortes ; por los grandes ha enviado :
todos ellos son venidos, sólo el Conde ha faltado.
Mensajero se le hace a que cumpla su mandado :
el mensajero que fué de esta suerte le ha hablado :
" Buen conde Fernán González, el Rey envía por vos,
que váyades a las cortes que se hacían en León ;
que si vos allá vais, Conde, daros han buen galardón,
daros ha a Palenzuela y a Palencia la mayor ;
daros ha las nueve villas, con ellas a Carrión ;
daros ha a Torquemada, la torre de Mormojón.
Buen Conde, si allá no ides, daros hían por traidor."
Allí respondiera el Conde y dijera esta razón :
" Mensajero eres, amigo, no mereces culpa, no ;
que yo no he miedo al Rey, ni a cuantos con él son.
Villas y castillos tengo, todos a mi mandar son,

de ellos me dejó mi padre, de ellos me ganara yo :
los que me dejó mi padre poblélos de ricos hombres ;
los que yo me hube ganado poblélos de labradores ;
quien no tenía más de un buey, dábale otro, que eran dos ;
al que casaba su hija dóle yo muy rico don ;
cada día que amanece, por mí hacen oración ;
no la hacían por el Rey, que no la merece, non ;
él les puso muchos pechos, y quitáraselos yo."

(*d*) ROMANCES DE LOS SIETE INFANTES DE LARA

THE tenth-century story of the murder of the seven sons of Gonzalo Gustios de Lara through the machinations of their kinsman Ruy Velázquez, and of the birth to the stricken father of a half-Moorish son who eventually avenges them will be known to some readers from a nineteenth-century treatment by Ángel de Saavedra, Duque de Rivas (p. 457, below) called *El Moro expósito.* But, as Sr. Menéndez Pidal has shown,[1] the story has its roots deep in Spanish literature.

59. *Las Siete Cabezas*

There are numerous ballads on the Infantes de Lara story, covering its entire range : this which follows represents the moment of its highest emotional tension. Gustios de Lara, father of the Infantes, has been captured and imprisoned at Córdoba by the Moorish chief, Almanzor. Meanwhile the Infantes themselves, with their guardian Nuño Salido, have, through Ruy Velázquez's treachery, been inveigled into an ambush and killed. The eight heads are brought by the Moor in charge of the ambush to Almanzor, who has them mounted on a board and exhibited to their father. Note the absence of rhetorical devices here : the author considers the story poignant enough to convey its emotion unaided, though it may be doubted how far it does so. Occasionally, the matter-of-factness of the narrative descends to bathos. The assonance, it will be noticed, changes from a *to* a-a *at l. 25.*

Pártese el moro Alicante víspera de Sant Cebrián ;
ocho cabezas llevaba, todas de hombres de alta sangre.
Sábelo el rey Almanzor, a recebírselo sale :
aunque perdió muchos moros, piensa en esto bien ganar.

[1] *La Leyenda de los Infantes de Lara*, Madrid, 1934 [*Obras*, Vol. I].

Manda hacer un tablado para mejor las mirar ;
mandó traer un cristiano que estaba en captividad.
Como ante sí lo trujeron, empezóle de hablar ;
díjole : " Gonzalo Gustos, mira quién conocerás ;
que lidiaron mis poderes en el campo de Almenar :
sacaron ocho cabezas, todas son de gran linaje."
Respondió Gonzalo Gustos : " Presto os diré la verdad."
Y, limpiándoles la sangre, asaz se fuera a turbar ;
dijo llorando agramente : " ¡ Conóscolas por mi mal !
La una es de mi carillo ; las otras me duelen más,
de los Infantes de Lara son, mis hijos naturales."
Así razona con ellos como si vivos hablasen :
" ¡ Dios os salve, el mi compadre, el mi amigo leal !
¿ Adónde son los mis hijos que yo os quise encomendar ?
Muerto sois como buen hombre, como hombre de fiar."
Tomara otra cabeza del hijo mayor de edad :
" Sálveos Dios, Diego González, hombre de muy gran bondad,
del conde Fernán González alférez el principal :
a vos amaba yo mucho, que me habíades de heredar."
Alimpiándola con lágrimas volviérala a su lugar,
y toma la del segundo, Martín Gómez que llamaban :
" Dios os perdone, el mi hijo, hijo que mucho preciaba ;
jugador era de tablas el mejor de toda España ;
mesurado caballero, muy buen hablador en plaza."
Y dejándola llorando, la del tercero tomaba :
" Hijo Suero Gustos, todo el mundo os estimaba ;
el rey os tuviera en mucho sólo para la su caza.
Gran caballero esforzado, muy buen bracero a ventaja.
Ruy Gómez, vuestro tío, estas bodas ordenara."
Y, tomando la del cuarto, lasamente la miraba :
" Oh hijo Fernán González (nombre del mejor de España,
del buen conde de Castilla, aquel que vos baptizara),
matador de puerco espín, amigo de gran compaña,
nunca con gente de poco os vieran en alianza."
Tomó la de Ruy Gómez, de corazón la abrazaba :
" ¡ Hijo mío, hijo mío ! ¿ quién como vos se hallara ?
Nunca le oyeron mentira, nunca por oro ni plata ;
animoso, buen guerrero, muy gran feridor de espada,
que a quien dábades de lleno tullido o muerto quedaba."
Tomando la del menor, el dolor se le doblara :

"¡Hijo Gonzalo González, los ojos de Doña Sancha!
¡Qué nuevas irán a ella, que a vos más que a todos ama!
Tan apuesto de persona, decidor bueno entre damas,
repartidor en su haber, aventajado en la lanza.
¡Mejor fuera la mi muerte que ver tan triste jornada!"
Al duelo que el viejo hace toda Córdoba lloraba.
El rey Almanzor, cuidoso, consigo se lo llevaba,
y mandó a una morica lo sirviese muy de gana.
Esta le torna en prisiones y con hambre le curaba.
Hermana era del rey, doncella moza y lozana;
con ésta Gonzalo Gustos vino a perder su saña,
que de ella le nació un hijo que a los hermanos vengara.

(*e*) ROMANCES DEL CID

The Cid ballads, though lightly represented here on account of the space given to the *Cantar* (pp. 1-12, above), form one of the largest and most influential groups of all. They dwell on the earlier part of the Cid's life rather than on the later, say little of the Infantes de Carrión and endow both the Cid and his entourage with qualities very different from those of the sober epic. The two ballads here given date only from the sixteenth century.

60. *Romance de Jimena Gómez*

This episode from the history of the Cid's mocedades, *recalling Guillén de Castro and Corneille, needs little commentary. The Cid has just slain the father of Doña Ximena, who appeals to the King for vengeance. Vivid, picturesque and energetic, the ballad also has unusual dramatic qualities. A few words of introduction and it becomes first-hand drama.*

Día era de los Reyes,   día era señalado,
cuando dueñas y doncellas   al Rey piden aguinaldo,
sino es Jimena Gómez,   hija del conde Lozano,
que, puesta delante el Rey,   de esta manera ha hablado :
" Con mancilla vivo, Rey,   con ella vive mi madre ;
cada día que amanece   veo quien mató a mi padre
caballero en un caballo   y en su mano un gavilán ;
otra vez con un halcón   que trae para cazar,
por me hacer más enojo   cébalo en mi palomar :
con sangre de mis palomas   ensangrentó mi brial.
Enviéselo a decir,   envióme a amenazar
que me cortará mis haldas   por vergonzoso lugar,
me forzará mis doncellas   casadas y por casar ;
matárame un pajecico   so haldas de mi brial.
Rey que no hace justicia   no debía de reinar,
ni cabalgar en caballo,   ni espuela de oro calzar,
ni comer pan a manteles,   ni con la reina holgar,
ni oír misa en sagrado,   porque no merece más."

El Rey de que aquesto oyera comenzara de hablar :
" ¡ Oh válame Dios del cielo ! Quiérame Dios consejar :
si yo prendo o mato al Cid, mis Cortes se volverán ;
y si no hago justicia mi alma lo pagará."
" Tente las tus Cortes, Rey, no te las revuelva nadie,
al Cid que mató a mi padre dámelo tú por igual,
que quien tanto mal me hizo sé que algún bien me hará."
Entonces dijera el Rey, bien oiréis lo que dirá :
" Siempre lo oí decir, y agora veo que es verdad,
que el seso de las mujeres que no era natural :
hasta aquí pidió justicia ; ya quiere con él casar.
Yo lo haré de buen grado, de muy buena voluntad.
Mandarle quiero una carta, mandarle quiero llamar."
Las palabras no son dichas, la carta camino va,
mensajero que la lleva dado la había a su padre.
" Malas mañas habéis, Conde, no vos las quiero quitar,
que cartas que el Rey vos manda no me las queréis mostrar."
" No era nada, mi hijo, sino que vades allá,
quedávos aquí, hijo, yo iré en vuestro lugar."
" Nunca Dios atal quisiese ni Santa María lo mande,
sino que adonde vos fuéredes que vaya yo adelante."

61. *El Cid y el Gafo*

An interesting example of the use which the ballads make of the supernatural. Generally they incline to treat it in a sombre, even in a morbid, way. Here, in addition to creating an atmosphere of weirdness and awe, it is utilized to inculcate a Christian virtue, though one always suspects that the author secretly sympathized with those of the Cid's companions who, rather than sit at table with the leper, changed their hotel. The ballad represents the extreme point reached in the idealization of a popular figure—his metamorphosis from rude warrior to semi-saint.

Ya se parte Don Rodrigo, que de Vivar se apellida,
para visitar Santiago, adonde va en romería.
Despidióse de Fernando, aquese rey de Castilla,
que le dió muchos haberes, sin dones que dado había.
Veinte vasallos consigo levaba en su compañía ;
mucho bien y gran limosna hacía por donde iba :
daba a comer a los pobres y a los que pobreza habían.

Siguiendo por su camino muy grande llanto oía,
que en medio de un tremedal un gafo triste plañía,
dando voces que lo saquen por Dios y Santa María.
Rodrigo, cuando lo oye, para el gafo se venía,
descendiera de la bestia, en tierra se descendía:
en la silla lo subió, delante sí lo ponía;
llegaron a la posada do albergaron aquel día.
Sentados son a cenar, comían a una escudilla.
Gran enojo habían los suyos, de aquesto que el Cid hacía:
no quieren estar presentes, a otra posada se iban.
Hicieron al Cid y al gafo una cama en que dormían
ambos, cuando a media noche, ya que Rodrigo dormía,
un soplo por las espaldas el gafo dado le había;
tan recio fué, que a los pechos a Don Rodrigo salía.
Despertó muy espantado, al gafo buscado había:
no lo hallaba en la su cama, a voces lumbre pedía.
Traídole habían la lumbre, el gafo no parecía;
tornado se había a la cama, gran cuidado en sí tenía
de lo que le aconteciera, mas vió un hombre que a él venía
vestido de paños blancos, y que aquesto le decía:
"¿Duermes o velas, Rodrigo?" "No duermo," le respondía.
"Pero dime quién tú eres que tanto resplandecías."
"San Lázaro soy, Rodrigo, yo, que a te hablar venía;
yo soy el gafo a que tú por Dios tanto bien hacías.
Rodrigo, Dios bien te quiere, otorgado te tenía
que lo que tú comenzares en lides, o en otra guisa,
lo cumplirás a tu honra y crecerás cada día.
De todos serás temido, de cristianos y morisma,
y que los tus enemigos empecerte no podrían;
morirás tú muerte honrada, no tu persona vencida,
tú serás el vencedor, Dios su bendición te envía."
En diciendo estas palabras luego se desparecía.
Levantóse Don Rodrigo y de hinojos se ponía;
dió gracias a Dios del cielo, también a Santa María;
ansí estuvo en oración hasta que fuera de día.
Partiérase a Santiago, su romería cumplía;
De allí se fué a Calahorra adonde el buen Rey yacía.
Muy bien lo había recebido, holgóse con su venida,
lidió con Martín González, y en el campo lo vencía.

(*f*) ROMANCES DEL REY DON PEDRO

THE reign of Peter the Cruel (1350-1369) was stained with many crimes, and any ballad-writers who wished, as most of them did, to hold him up as a fearful example had ample scope. His amours with María de Padilla; the sad fate of his queen, Blanche de Valois (Blanca de Borbón); the murder of his half-brother Fadrique; and, above all, his own death at the hand of his half-brother Henry, who succeeded him—all these incidents, and various others no less grisly, figure in the ballads. Horrors are piled high, especially in the invention of details about the supposed murder of Queen Blanche, which is not known ever to have taken place. Though most of these ballads are on the side of the angels (unlike many of the dramas on the same king, which tend to idealize him), mention should be made of a remarkable late ballad of the artistic type, beginning:

A los pies de Don Enrique   yace muerto el rey Don Pedro,

which sympathizes with the dead king and has a strikingly effective refrain describing the contrasting sympathies of the contending brothers' retinues:

Y los de Enrique
cantan, repican y gritan
" Viva Enrique "; y los de Pedro
clamorean, doblan, lloran
su Rey muerto.

62. *Romance del Hermano del Rey Don Pedro, Don Fadrique, Maestre de Santiago*

The effectiveness of this ballad is heightened by the fact that the murdered man tells the story. Particularly noteworthy are the growing tension of the early lines, the skilful suggestion of the evil atmosphere at court and the presentation of Don Pedro—a figure the more impressive because he has so little to say.

Yo me estaba allá en Coimbra   que yo me la hube ganado,
cuando me vinieron cartas   del rey Don Pedro mi hermano
que fuese a ver los torneos   que en Sevilla se han armado.
Yo Maestre sin ventura,   yo Maestre desdichado,
tomara trece de mula,   veinte y cinco de caballo,
todos con cadenas de oro   y jubones de brocado:
jornada de quince días   en ocho la había andado.
A la pasada de un río,   pasándole por el vado,
cayó mi mula conmigo,   perdí mi puñal dorado,
ahogáraseme un paje   de los míos más privado,
criado era en mi sala   y de mí muy regalado.
Con todas estas desdichas   a Sevilla hube llegado;
a la puerta Macarena   encontré con un ordenado,
ordenado de un Evangelio,   que misa no había cantado:
"Manténgate Dios, Maestre;   Maestre, bien seáis llegado,
hoy te ha nacido hijo,   hoy cumples veinte y un año.
Si te pluguiese, Maestre,   volvamos a baptizallo,
que yo sería el padrino,   tú, Maestre, el ahijado."
Allí hablara el Maestre,   bien oiréis lo que ha hablado:
"No me lo mandéis, señor,   padre, no queráis mandallo,
que voy a ver qué me quiere   el rey Don Pedro mi hermano."
Di de espuelas a mi mula,   en Sevilla me hube entrado;
de que no vi tela puesta   ni vi caballero armado,
fuíme para los palacios   del rey Don Pedro mi hermano.
En entrando por las puertas,   las puertas me habían cerrado;
quitáronme la mi espada,   la que traía a mi lado;
quitáronme mi compañía   la que me había acompañado.
Los míos desque esto vieron   de traición me han avisado,
que me saliese yo fuera   que ellos me pondrían en salvo.
Yo, como estaba sin culpa,   de nada hube curado,
fuíme para el aposento   del rey Don Pedro mi hermano:
"Manténgaos Dios, el Rey,   y a todos de cabo a cabo."
"Mal hora vengáis, Maestre;   Maestre mal seáis llegado:
nunca nos venís a ver   sino una vez en el año,
y esta que venís, Maestre,   es por fuerza o por mandado.
"Vuestra cabeza, Maestre,   mandada está en aguinaldo."
"¿Por qué es aqueso, buen Rey?   Nunca os hice desaguisado,
ni os dejé yo en la lid,   ni con moros peleando."
"Venid acá, mis porteros,   hágase lo que he mandado."
Aun no lo hubo bien dicho,   la cabeza le han cortado;

a doña María de Padilla en un plato la ha enviado :
así hablaba con él como si estuviera sano.
Las palabras que le dice de esta suerte está hablando :
" Aquí pagaréis, traidor, lo de antaño y lo de ogaño,
el mal consejo que diste al rey don Pedro tu hermano."
Asióla por los cabellos, echado se la ha a un alano ;
el alano es del Maestre, púsola sobre un estrado,
a los aullidos que daba atronó todo el palacio.
Allí demandara el Rey : " ¿ Quién hace mal a ese alano ? "
Allí respondieron todos a los cuales ha pesado :
" Con la cabeza lo ha, señor, del Maestre vuestro hermano."
Allí hablara una su tía, que tía era de entrambos :
" ¡ Cuán mal lo mirastes, Rey ! Rey, ¡ qué mal lo habéis mirado !
Por una mala mujer habéis muerto un tal hermano."
Aun no lo había bien dicho, cuando ya le había pesado.
Fuése para doña María, de esta suerte le ha hablado :
" Prendedla, mis caballeros, ponédmela a buen recado,
que yo le daré tal castigo que a todos sea sonado."
En cárceles muy escuras allí la había aprisionado :
él mismo le da a comer, él mismo con la su mano :
no se fía de ninguno, sino de un paje que ha criado.

(g) ROMANCES FRONTERIZOS

THESE " Border Ballads " are both numerous and highly individual, as one would expect, having regard to the idealistic character of the later stages of the Reconquest and to the nearness in date of the events described to the composition of the poems describing them. So varied are they that it is impossible to give any general description of them in a few words, but the briefest selection cannot fail to illustrate the patriotic fervour, the idealism and the emotion reflected in the accounts of that final struggle between the two forces for so long at grips in Spain—Moslems and Christians. Some of the ballads of this group, and more markedly some of the later " Moorish " ballads, sentimentalize the Moors in a way which became common, in prose as well as in verse, during the sixteenth century.

63. *Romance de Abenámar*

This fine ballad has reference to the campaign of John II against Granada in 1431. By Abenámar is meant the Moorish prince who ruled the kingdom for a time as Yusuf IV: he did, in fact, establish contact with King John, so that the poem has that amount of foundation. Its charm, however, lies in its evocative and imaginative quality. It was a wonderful touch to bring the would-be conqueror so near to his prize that in the bright southern light he could pick out the Alhambra, the Mosque and the Alijares Palace and to plant in that context the fierce legend of the architect murdered by the King of Granada lest he should build such another for the Andalusian King. But the true flight into poetry comes at the end of the ballad, where King John addresses Granada in the language of love, promising her a rich dowry if she will wed him, only to hear her reply that she is wedded to another and is not yet his widow

Por Guadalquivir arriba   el buen rey Don Juan camina:
encontrara con un moro   que Abenámar se decía.
El buen Rey desque lo vido   de esta suerte le decía:
" Abenámar, Abenámar,   moro de la morería,
hijo eres de un moro perro   y de una cristiana cativa.
A tu padre llaman Halí   y a tu madre Catalina.
Cuando tú naciste, moro,   la luna estaba crecida,
y la mar estaba en calma,   viento no la rebullía.
Moro que en tal signo nace   no debe decir mentira:
preso tengo un hijo tuyo,   yo le otorgaré la vida,
si me dices la verdad   de lo que te preguntaría.
Moro, si no me la dices,   a ti también mataría."
" Yo te la diré, buen Rey,   si tú me otorgas la vida."
" Dígasmela tú, el moro,   que otorgada te sería.
¿ Qué castillos son aquellos,   que altos son y relucían ? "
" El Alhambra era, señor,   y la otra es la Mezquita;
los otros los Alijares,   labrados a maravilla.
El moro que los labró   cien doblas ganaba al día,
y el día que no los labra   de lo suyo las perdía;
desque los tuvo labrados,   el Rey le quitó la vida
porque no labre otros tales   al Rey del Andalucía.
La otra era Granada,   Granada la noblecida
de los muchos caballeros   y de gran ballestería."
Allí habla el rey Don Juan,   bien oiréis lo que diría:
" Granada, si tú quisieses,   contigo me casaría:
darte he yo en arras y dote   a Córdoba y a Sevilla,
y a Jerez de la Frontera,   que cabe sí la tenía.
Granada, si más quisieses,   mucho más yo te daría."
Allí hablara Granada,   al buen Rey le respondía:
" Casada soy, el rey Don Juan,   casada soy, que no viuda;
el moro que a mí me tiene   bien defenderme querría."

64. *Romance de Alora*

In 1434, Diego de Ribera, Adelantado (Governor) of Andalusia, surrounded the town of Alora (hence " la bien cercada "), which lies to the north-west of Málaga, and was treacherously and mortally wounded as he raised the visor of his helmet while advancing to a parley with the Moorish Governor. This ballad is noteworthy for its picturesque though simple phraseology and for the rapid, nervous progress of its action, but otherwise it hardly deserves as high a place as generations of readers, apparently attracted by its opening half-line, have given it.

Alora, la bien cercada,   tú que estás en par del río,
cercóte el Adelantado   una mañana en domingo,
de peones y hombres de armas   el campo bien guarnecido;
con la gran artillería   hecho te había un portillo.
Viérades moros y moras   todos huir al castillo:
las moras llevaban ropa,   los moros harina y trigo,
y las moras de quince años   llevaban el oro fino,
y los moricos pequeños   llevaban la pasa y higo.
Por cima de la muralla   su pendón llevan tendido.
Entre almena y almena   quedado se había un morico
con una ballesta armada,   y en ella puesto un cuadrillo;
en altas voces decía,   que la gente lo había oído:
"¡Treguas, treguas, Adelantado,   por tuyo se da el castillo!"
Alza la visera arriba,   para ver el que tal le dijo;
asestárale a la frente,   salido le ha al colodrillo.
Sacólo Pablo de rienda,   y de mano Jacobillo,
estos dos que había criado   en su casa desde chicos.
Lleváronle a los maestros,   por ver si será guarido.
A las primeras palabras   el testamento les dijo.

65. *Romance del Rey Moro que perdió Alhama*

This ballad treats (from the Moorish standpoint) the fall (1482) of Alhama, a town situated in the Sierra of the same name, some twenty miles south-east of Loja. It has been familiarized to English readers by Lord Byron in a ballad which begins:

The Moorish King rides up and down
Through Granada's royal town.
From Elvira's gate to those
Of Bibarambla on he goes.
Woe is me, Alhama!

There is some doubt whether the refrain should read as in the text below or as Byron must have read or understood it—" ¡Ay de mí,

Alhama!" The slaughter of the tribe of the Abencerrajes by their rivals the Zegríes and the Gomeles, at the instigation of the King, is one of the best known incidents of the last years of Moorish rule in Granada.

The beauty of the poem is attributable in part to its rhythm and melody, and in part to the contrast between the short clipt sentences of the stanzas, rapped out with the objectivity of a ticker-tape, and the simplicity and pathos of the refrain, which resembles a long-drawn sigh. The vividness of the two pictures—the Moorish King ordering trumpets and pipes to be sounded in the Alhambra and the appearance of the white-bearded old alfaquí—*is of a degree which no translation will render. But a more striking and durable impression is made on the ear even than on the eye: the prophecies are more compelling than the prophet.*

Paseábase el Rey moro   por la ciudad de Granada,
desde la puerta de Elvira   hasta la de Vivarrambla,
"¡Ay de mi Alhama!"
Cartas le fueron venidas   que Alhama era ganada:
las cartas echó en el fuego,   y al mensajero matara.
"¡Ay de mi Alhama!"
Descabalga de una mula,   y en un caballo cabalga;
por el Zacatín arriba   subido se había al Alhambra.
"¡Ay de mi Alhama!"
Como en el Alhambra estuvo,   al mismo punto mandaba
que se toquen sus trompetas,   sus añafiles de plata.
"¡Ay de mi Alhama!"
Y que las cajas de guerra   apriesa toquen al arma,
porque lo oigan sus moros,   los de la Vega y Granada.
"¡Ay de mi Alhama!"
Los moros que el son oyeron   que al sangriento Marte llama,
uno a uno y dos a dos   juntado se ha gran batalla.
"¡Ay de mi Alhama!"
Allí habló un moro viejo,   de esta manera hablara:
"¿Para qué nos llamas, Rey,   para qué es esta llamada?"
"¡Ay de mi Alhama!"
Habéis de saber, amigos,   una nueva desdichada:
que cristianos de braveza   ya nos han ganado Alhama.
"¡Ay de mi Alhama!"

Allí habló un alfaquí   de barba crecida y cana :
" ¡ Bien se te emplea, buen Rey !   ¡ Buen Rey, bien se te empleara ! "
" ¡ Ay de mi Alhama ! "
" Mataste los Bencerrajes,   que eran la flor de Granada ;
cogiste los tornadizos   de Córdoba la nombrada."
" ¡ Ay de mi Alhama ! "
" Por eso mereces, Rey,   una pena muy doblada :
que te pierdas tú y el reino,   y aquí se pierda Granada."
" ¡ Ay de mi Alhama ! "

66. *Romance del Río Verde*

Again we have a ballad made famous by its exordium. Those first three lines, with their reiterated apostrophe and their vivid colour, are not merely easy to remember : they are hard to forget. And the lyrical theme to which they point—the futility and wastefulness of warfare—is far more impressive than the actual narrative which follows. The rest of the poem, in fact, is something of a chronicler's jog-trot, little superior to the average of its kind, though also, like many of the romances fronterizos, *heavy with the atmosphere of disaster. Historically, the ballad is rather muddled, representing the death of Don Alonso de Aguilar on the Río Verde, south-west of Málaga, in 1501, as contemporary with that of Sayavedra in the same locality over half a century earlier. Artistically, the poem would have been greatly improved by the elimination of one of the two heroes.*

¡ Río-Verde, Río-Verde !   ¡ cuánto cuerpo en ti se baña
de cristianos y de moros   muertos por la dura espada !
Y tus ondas cristalinas   de roja sangre se esmaltan ;
entre moros y cristianos   se trabó muy gran batalla.
Murieron duques y condes,   grandes señores de salva,
murió gente de valía   de la nobleza de España.
En ti murió don Alonso,   que de Aguilar se llamaba ;
el valeroso Urdiales   con don Alonso acababa.
Por una ladera arriba   el buen Sayavedra marcha :
natural es de Sevilla,   de la gente más granada ;
tras dél iba un renegado,   de esta manera le habla :

"Date, date Sayavedra, no huigas de la batalla ;
yo te conozco muy bien ; gran tiempo estuve en tu casa,
y en la plaza de Sevilla bien te vide jugar cañas ;
conozco tu padre y madre y a tu mujer doña Clara.
Siete años fuí tu cautivo ; malamente me tratabas,
y ahora lo serás mío, si Mahoma me ayudara,
y tan bien te trataré como tú a mí me tratabas.
Sayavedra, que lo oyera, al moro volvió la cara.
Tiróle el moro una flecha, pero nunca le acertara ;
mas hirióle Sayavedra de una herida muy mala.
Muerto cayó el renegado, sin poder hablar palabra.
Sayavedra fué cercado de mucha mora canalla,
y al cabo quedó allí muerto de una muy mala lanzada.
Don Alonso en este tiempo bravamente peleaba ;
el caballo le habían muerto, y lo tiene por muralla ;
mas cargan tantos de moros, que mal lo hieren y tratan ;
de la sangre que perdía, don Alonso se desmaya :
al fin, al fin, cayó muerto al pie de una peña alta.
También el Conde de Ureña, mal herido, se escapaba,
guiábalo un adalid, que sabe bien las entradas.
Muchos salen tras el Conde, que le siguen las pisadas :
muerto quedó don Alonso ; eterna fama ganara.

II. ROMANCES DEL CICLO CAROLINGIO

Only a fragment remains of the Spanish epic on the theme of the *Chanson de Roland*, but there is ample material for comparison of the French treatment of the Roland-theme with the Spanish. For Charlemagne as a ballad-hero was as popular as his legendary rival Bernardo del Carpio; and the Carolingian ballads, many of which are early in date, show great imaginative flexibility. No group displays more varied emotions and in none is the stage more closely packed with characters: as well as Charlemagne, his twelve Peers and other Peers unknown in French story, we have Roland's bride—"la belle Aude" of the *Chanson de Roland*—King Marsín, Reynaud de Montauban, Gaiferos' bride Julianesa, Charlemagne's son and grandson, to say nothing of an extraordinary character, Durendal, Roland's famous sword, metamorphosed into a knight named Durandarte. This knight is the protagonist in the ballad which follows.

67. *Romance de Durandarte*

In another version of this ballad the death in battle of the imaginary Durandarte is described in greater and more picturesque detail:

Muerto queda Durandarte al pie de una gran montaña,
un canto por cabecera, debajo una verde haya;
todas las aves de la monte alrededor le acompañan.

The Montesinos who mourns him is a son of Charlemagne's daughter, who reappears in the ballad next following. The poem is a curious mixture of tragic and trivial, marred by prolixity and lack of unity, but the final impression which it leaves on the mind is rather of pathos.

"¡Oh Belerma! ¡oh Belerma! por mi mal fuiste engendrada,
que siete años te serví sin de ti alcanzar nada;
agora que me querías muero yo en esta batalla.

No me pesa de mi muerte aunque temprano me llama :
mas pésame que de verte y de servirte dejaba.
¡ Oh mi primo Montesinos ! lo que agora yo os rogaba,
que cuando yo fuere muerto y mi ánima arrancada,
vos llevéis mi corazón adonde Belerma estaba,
y servilda de mi parte, como de vos yo esperaba,
y traelde a la memoria dos veces cada semana ;
y diréisle que se acuerde cuán cara que me costaba ;
y dalde todas mis tierras las que yo señoreaba ;
pues que yo a ella pierdo, todo el bien con ella vaya.
¡ Montesinos, Montesinos ! ¡ mal me aqueja esta lanzada !
El brazo traigo cansado, y la mano del espada :
traigo grandes las heridas, mucha sangre derramada ;
los extremos tengo fríos, y el corazón me desmaya ;
los ojos que nos vieron ir nunca nos verán en Francia.
Abracéisme, Montesinos, que ya se me sale el alma.
De mis ojos ya no veo, la lengua tengo turbada ;
yo vos doy todos mis cargos, en vos yo los traspasaba."
" El Señor en quien creéis, Él oiga vuestra palabra."
Muerto yace Durandarte al pie de una alta montaña,
llorábalo Montesinos, que a su muerte se hallara :
quitándole está el almete, desciñéndole el espada ;
hácele la sepultura con una pequeña daga ;
sacábale el corazón, como él se lo jurara,
para llevar a Belerma, como él se lo mandara.
Las palabras que le dice de allá le salen del alma :
" ¡ Oh mi primo Durandarte ! ¡ primo mío de mi alma !
¡ espada nunca vencida ! ¡ esfuerzo do esfuerzo estaba !
¡ quien a vos mató, mi primo, no sé por qué me dejara ! "

68. *Romance de Rosaflorida*

We shall agree with Menéndez y Pelayo in thinking this a ballad of unusual beauty. The brilliant scene described in the first lines, which in the Golden Age would have been called almost Herreran, forms a fit accompaniment to the lozanía *of the beautiful maiden. More in keeping with the ballad-spirit, however, is the simple and primitive frankness of Rosaflorida's message. Yet both these features combined fail to account for the elusive charm of the poem, which probably derives from the melody and evocative power of the words Rocafrida . . . . . Rosaflorida . . . . . Pascua Florida, dominant in both narrative and description.*

En Castilla está un castillo   que se llama Rocafrida;
al castillo llaman Roca,   y a la fonte llaman Frida.
El pie tenía de oro,   y almenas de plata fina;
entre almena y almena   está una piedra zafira;
tanto relumbra de noche   como el sol a mediodía.
Dentro estaba una doncella   que llaman Rosaflorida;
siete condes la demandan,   tres duques de Lombardía;
a todos les desdeñaba,   tanta es su lozanía.
Enamoróse de Montesinos,   de oídas, que no de vista.
Una noche estando así,   gritos da Rosaflorida;
oyérala un camarero,   que en su cámara dormía.
"¿Qué es aquesto, mi señora?   ¿Qué es esto, Rosaflorida?
O tenedes mal de amores,   o estáis loca sandía."
"Ni yo tengo mal de amores,   ni estoy loca sandía,
mas llevásesme estas cartas   a Francia la bien guarnida;
diéseslas a Montesinos,   la cosa que yo más quería;
dile que me venga a ver   para la Pascua Florida;
darle he yo este mi cuerpo,   el más lindo que hay en Castilla,
si no es el de mi hermana,   que de fuego sea ardida.
Y si de mí más quisiere   yo mucho más le daría:
darle he siete castillos,   los mejores que hay en Castilla."

69. *Romance de Doña Alda*

"La belle Aude", as she is sensitively and skilfully presented in this ballad, surrounded by her three hundred ladies and tortured by her dream, is surely one of the most pathetic figures in all literature. At the beginning of the poem (ll. 3-4, 6-7) parallelism is employed to work up the hearer's emotions to the climax which comes in the dream-narrative, related with considerable economy of language and with great power. The inconsequent tailing-off of the story just as it looks like gathering force for an even greater climax is of course a commonplace of ballad-technique: the one vivid splash of tragic colour (l. 28) is more in character with the Carolingian ballad-group in general than with this particular poem.

En París está doña Alda, la esposa de don Roldán,
trescientas damas con ella para la acompañar:
todas visten un vestido, todas calzan un calzar,
todas comen a una mesa, todas comían de un pan,
si no era doña Alda, que era la mayoral.
Las ciento hilaban oro, las ciento tejen cendal,
las ciento tañen instrumentos para doña Alda holgar.
Al son de los instrumentos doña Alda adormido se ha:
ensoñado había un sueño, un sueño de gran pesar.
Recordó despavorida y con un pavor muy grande,
los gritos daba tan grandes que se oían en la ciudad.
Allí hablaron sus doncellas, bien oiréis lo que dirán:
"¿Qué es aquesto, mi señora, quién es el que os hizo mal?"
"Un sueño soñé, doncellas, que me ha dado gran pesar:
que me veía en un monte en un desierto lugar;
de so los montes muy altos un azor vide volar,
tras dél viene un aguililla que lo ahinca muy mal.
El azor con grande cuita metióse so mi brial;
el aguililla con grande ira de allí lo iba a sacar:
con las uñas lo despluma, con el pico lo deshace."
Allí habló su camarera, bien oiréis lo que dirá:
"Aquese sueño, señora, bien os lo entiendo soltar:
el azor es vuestro esposo que viene de allén la mar;
el águila sedes vos, con la cual ha de casar,
y aquel monte es la iglesia donde os han de velar."
"Si así es, mi camarera, bien te lo entiendo pagar."
Otro día de mañana cartas de fuera le traen;
tintas venían de dentro, de fuera escritas con sangre,
que su Roldán era muerto en la caza de Roncesvalles.

III. ROMANCES NOVELESCOS Y LÍRICOS

THESE two classes of ballad, both of them independent of any cycle, may conveniently be treated together, since romantic and lyrical elements are apt to invade, if not to permeate, any poem belonging to either of them. They incorporate *motifs* common to the ballads of many nations, though frequently, both as to landscape and as to psychology, they are intensely Spanish. Only a very few of the most celebrated of these ballads can be given.

70. *Romance de Blanca Niña*

This and " La bella mal maridada . . . . ." are among the best known Spanish examples of the malcasada *motif : " Blanca Niña" is perhaps the finer of the two, with the greater vividness and sharper dramatic quality of its* oratio recta, *so admirably suited to the atmosphere of stark cruelty. Notable also are the swift, telescoped action, the latent force of the repetitive questions and the implied contrast between the brilliance of l. 1 and the rest of the poem, as typified in l. 4. The thrill of the ballad is produced (as, on a lower level, in " Red Riding-Hood ") by the element of suspense : the reader, guessing how the story will end, remains throughout in a state of tension.*

" Blanca sois, señora mía, más que el rayo del sol :
¿ si la dormiré esta noche desarmado y sin pavor ?
Que siete años había, siete, que no me desarmo, no.
Más negras tengo mis carnes que un tiznado carbón."
" Dormilda, señor, dormilda, desarmado sin temor,
que el Conde es ido a la caza a los montes de León."
" Rabia le mate los perros, y águilas el su halcón,
y del monte hasta casa a él arrastre el morón."
Ellos en aquesto estando su marido que llegó :
" ¿ Qué hacéis, la blanca niña, hija de padre traidor ? "
" Señor, peino mis cabellos, péinolos con gran dolor
que me dejéis a mí sola y a los montes os vais vos."

"Esa palabra, la niña, no era sino traición :
¿ cúyo es aquel caballo que allá bajo relinchó ? "
"Señor, era de mi padre, y envióoslo para vos."
"¿ Cúyas son aquellas armas que están en el corredor ? "
"Señor, eran de mi hermano, y hoy os las envió."
"¿ Cúya es aquella lanza, desde aquí la veo yo ? "
"Tomalda, Conde, tomalda, matadme con ella vos,
que aquesta muerte, buen Conde, bien os la merezco yo."

71. *Romance del Conde Arnaldos*

About this exquisite ballad more perhaps has been written than about any other in Spanish. The intense emotion which it arouses is attributable, not so much to its aptly chosen language and its nervous, forceful style as to its skilful combination of plastic detail (e.g., ll. 3-5) and atmospheric vagueness, its restrained technique, which enhances the sense of the supernatural, and, above all, the expectancy aroused by ll. 1-2 and the atmosphere of mystery which this engenders. The Romantics, both in Spain and abroad, hazarded guesses as to the ballad's meaning : "I suppose some religious allegory is intended,"[1] *wrote Lockhart, and even the sober Milá felt sure the underlying idea was "mystical."*[2] *Had the author purposely cut the ballad short, it might well have been through inability to fulfil the promise of his admirable beginning. But this was clearly not so, for a poem begun with such care would never have been truncated so brusquely, and in any case the only point of such a cut would be to set the audience guessing if the Count embarked or no—a question answered in l. 2 by the verb* hubo.

Sr. Menéndez Pidal, who knows twelve Spanish or Moroccan versions of this ballad,[3] *has advanced a solution by supplying what he asserts to be the "primitive and authentic* dénouement*".*[4] *The Count embarks, and the music of the waves lulls him to sleep, whereupon, from what sinister motive we are not told, the sailors clap him into irons. Awakening, he protests, telling them that he is the Dauphin of France lost at sea seven years before. "In that case,"*

[1] J. G. Lockhart : *Ancient Spanish Ballads*, London, 1870, p. 109.

[2] Cf. R. Menéndez Pidal : *El Romancero*, Madrid, n.d., p. 31.

[3] *Op. cit.*, pp. 18-37.

[4] *Op. cit.*, pp. 24-5.

cries the helmsman, "you are our lost prince Arnaldos whom we have been seeking." So they make for France forthwith and the last line hints at extensive rejoicings.

Though the dénouement *solves a mystery to which one might prefer weaving solutions of one's own, the critic who calls it "commonplace" is surely unduly severe. It has the same artistic qualities as the first part, and, as a moment's thought will show, raises questions only one degree less intriguing. Each part is full of realistic, even trivial detail, but over each the magic quality of mystery is triumphant. "It is thoroughly Castilian", remarks Aubrey Bell with justice, "in its mingling of mysticism and reality."*[1]

¡ Quién hubiese tal ventura   sobre las aguas de mar,
como hubo el Conde Arnaldos   la mañana de San Juan !
Con un falcón en la mano   la caza iba cazar,
vió venir una galera   que a tierra quiere llegar.
Las velas traía de seda,   la ejercia de un cendal,
marinero que la manda   diciendo viene un cantar
que la mar facía en calma,   los vientos hace amainar,
los peces que andan 'nel hondo   arriba los hace andar,
las aves que andan volando   'nel mástel las face posar.
Allí fabló el Conde Arnaldos,   bien oiréis lo que dirá :
" Por Dios te ruego, marinero,   dígasme ora ese cantar."
Respondióle el marinero,   tal respuesta le fué a dar :
" Yo no digo esta canción   sino a quien conmigo va."

72. *Romance de Fonte-frida*

With its repetitions, its parallelisms and its heavily stylized negatives, this allegorical story of the "cool spring", the turtle-dove and the nightingale might easily have become stiff with artificiality, had it not been the work of a poet through and through. It can be appreciated on more planes than one. Not far below the surface of the daintily related narrative lies hard, sordid reality, and below that again a deeper meaning still; yet so completely has the author laid us under the spell of Nature that it never declares itself. Seldom have green trees, meadow flowers and clear water exercised a more potent charm than here.

[1] *Castilian Literature*, Oxford, 1938, p. 109. Cf. J. Fitzmaurice-Kelly: *Chapters on Spanish Literature*, London, 1908, pp. 115-17; William J. Entwistle: *European Balladry*, Oxford, 1939, pp. 179-80.

Fonte-frida, fonte-frida, fonte-frida y con amor,
do todas las avecicas van tomar consolación,
si no es la tortolica que está viuda y con dolor.
Por allí fuera a pasar el traidor de ruiseñor;
las palabras que le dice llenas son de traición:
" Si tú quisieses, señora, yo sería tu servidor."
" Vete de ahí, enemigo, malo, falso, engañador,
que ni poso en ramo verde, ni en prado que tenga flor;
que si el agua hallo clara, turbia la bebía yo;
que no quiero haber marido, porque hijos no haya, no;
no quiero placer con ellos, ni menos consolación.
" ¡ Déjame, triste enemigo, malo, falso, mal traidor,
que no quiero ser tu amiga ni casar contigo, no ! "

73. *Romance de la Lavandera*

This rustic ballad, like " Conde Arnaldos " (which it rivals in suggestiveness) touched (l. 1) with Midsummer magic, must, if regarded as logical narrative, be considered fragmentary and incomplete. But all its beauty and all its meaning derive from its associational pattern—mariner, maiden, sea-shore, rose-tree, golden comb—and its underlying theme of unsatisfied longing. It is, as it were, a narrative of impression, emotion and imagination all compact.

Yo me levantara, madre, mañanica de Sant Juan:
vide estar una doncella ribericas de la mar:
sola lava y sola tuerce, sola tiende en un rosal;
mientras los paños se enjugan, dice la niña un cantar:
" ¿ Dó los mis amores, dó los ? ¿ Dónde los iré a buscar ? "
Mar abajo, mar arriba, diciendo iba un cantar,
peine de oro en las sus manos por sus cabellos peinar.
" Dígasme tú, el marinero, que Dios te guarde de mal,
si los viste, a mis amores, si los viste allá pasar."

74. *Romance de Rosa fresca*

A curiously unsatisfying ballad, resembling " Conde Arnaldos " in giving the impression of being truncated, but with much less happy result. The first three lines tremble with the most poignant of emotions, telling of lost opportunity and a love that was no love at all. The narrative then descends to an inharmoniously lower level, and, lit up only by one lovely image (l. 8), reveals a sordid tale of infidelity. The lover's defence, as we have it, is inconclusive, but there may have been more, and, if only in fairness to the nameless culprit, one would like to hear the end.

¡Rosa fresca, rosa fresca,   tan garrida y con amor,
cuando vos tuve en mis brazos,   no vos supe servir, no,
y agora que os serviría   no vos puedo haber, no!
"Vuestra fué la culpa, amigo,   vuestra fué, que mía no;
enviástesme una carta   con un vuestro servidor,
y en lugar de recaudar,   él dijera otra razón:
que érades casado, amigo,   allá en tierras de León;
que tenéis mujer hermosa   y hijos como una flor."
"Quien os lo dijo, señora,   no vos dijo verdad, no;
que yo nunca entré en Castilla,   ni allá en tierras de León,
sino cuando era pequeño   que no sabía de amor."

75. *Romance de la Constancia*

A pure lyric, known also as the Knight Errant's song, and familiar to all readers of Don Quijote *(I, ii). Translators and commentators have disagreed in several places as to exactly what the picture is intended to represent. My own view is that in l. 5 the traveller is crossing successive ridges parallel with the sea, though whether l. 6 indicates that there are streams to be forded at each descent or is to be taken metaphorically, I cannot say.* Ventura, *despite Professor Entwistle* (op. cit., *p. 185*), *I think emphatically means* "good *fortune." These, however, are minor points beside the poem's high idealism; both as to sentiment and as to artistry l. 7 reaches a pitch of tremendous intensity for which all the antithesis and enumeration of ll. 1-6 prepare us. It will be observed that the ballad has full end-rhymes throughout.*

Mis arreos son las armas,   mi descanso es pelear,
mi cama las duras peñas,   mi dormir siempre velar.
Las manidas son escuras,   los caminos por usar,

el cielo con sus mudanzas ha por bien de me dañar,
andando de sierra en sierra por orillas de la mar,
por probar si mi ventura hay lugar donde avadar.
Pero por vos, mi señora, todo se ha de comportar.

76. *Canción de una Gentil Dama y un Rústico Pastor*

This type of dialogue-ballad, bringing together a man and a woman of unequal social station to discuss love, is common to many literatures. Its popular appeal is due largely to its clear-cut contrasts, strengthened by repeated phrases which link the stanzas together and by a jovial refrain which sets the story going with a swing. Note, too, the pattern-like alternation of "yo" and "tú," the alliteration in "villano vil" and the regular intertwining of consonance (ll. 1-2, 5-6, 9-10, etc.) with assonance (ll. 3-4, 7-8, 11-12, etc.).

"Pastor, que estás en el campo, de amores tan retirado,
yo te vengo a proponer si quisieres ser casado."
"Yo no quiero ser casado," responde el villano vil:
"tengo el ganado en la sierra: a Dios, que me quiero ir."
"Tú, que estás acostumbrado a ponerte esos sajones;
si te casaras conmigo te pusieras pantalones."
"No quiero tus pantalones," responde el villano vil:
"tengo el ganado en la sierra: a Dios, que me quiero ir."
"Tú, que estás acostumbrado a ponerte chamarreta;
si te casaras conmigo, te pondrías tu chaqueta."
"Yo no quiero tu chaqueta," responde el villano vil:
"tengo el ganado en la sierra: a Dios, que me quiero ir."
"Tú, que estás acostumbrado a comer pan de centeno;
si te casaras conmigo, lo comieras blanco y bueno."
"Yo no quiero tu pan blanco," responde el villano vil:
"tengo el ganado en la sierra: a Dios, que me quiero ir."
"Tú, que estás acostumbrado a dormir entre granzones;
si te casaras conmigo, durmieras en mis colchones."
"Yo no quiero tus colchones," responde el villano vil:
"tengo el ganado en la sierra: a Dios, que me quiero ir."
"Si te casaras conmigo, mi padre te diera un coche,
para que vengas a verme, los sábados por la noche."
"Yo no quiero ir en coche," responde el villano vil:
"tengo el ganado en la sierra: a Dios, que me quiero ir."

"Te he de poner una fuente   con cuatro caños dorados,
para que vayas a ella   a dar agua a tu ganado."
"Yo no quiero tu gran fuente,"   responde el villano vil:
"ni mujer tan amorosa   no quiero yo para mí."

77. *Romance del Conde Olinos*

As we have seen, the Spanish ballad is not greatly addicted to the miraculous and supernatural, but in this highly idealistic poem, of Asturian origin, both these elements occur in abundance—some might say in excess. Further, the northern mists seem to have interposed themselves between the sense of the story and the reader's mind: the narrative is a dream-like fairy tale, lacking coherence, internal logic and all sense of time and place, while motifs common to idealistic balladry—such as the horse and the sword endowed with the power of speech, the princess transformed into a dove, and the lovers who turn into intertwining trees—float vaguely around. The pattern-like arrangement of the story, as in "La Dama y el Pastor," is like a sign-post to its unreality, though it also marks the ballad as one pre eminently suited for singing. The refrain-like first and last lines add to the intriguing—and occasionally provoking—sense of mystery which never leaves us.

¡Conde Olinos, Conde Olinos,   es niño y pasó la mar!
Levantóse Conde Olinos   mañanita de San Juan:
llevó su caballo al agua   a las orillas del mar.
Mientras el caballo bebe   él se pusiera a cantar:
"Bebe, bebe, mi caballo;   Dios te me libre de mal,
de los vientos rigurosos   y las arenas del mar."
Bien lo oyó la Reina mora,   de altas torres donde está:
"Escuchad, mis hijas todas;   las que dormís, recordad
y oiredes a la sirena   como canta por la mar."
Respondió la más chiquita,   (¡más le valiera callar!)
"Aquello no es la sirena,   ni tampoco su cantar;
aquél era el Conde Olindos,   que a mis montes va a cazar."
"Mis morillos, mis morillos,   los que me coméis el pan,
id buscar al Conde Olindos,   que a mis montes va a cazar.
Al que me lo traiga vivo,   un reinado le he de dar;

el que me lo traiga muerto   con la Infanta ha de casar :
al que traiga su cabeza,   a oro se la he de pesar."
Po 'l monte de los Acebos,   cien mil morillos se van
en busca del Conde Olindos ;   non le pueden encontrar.
Encontráronlo durmiendo   debajo de un olivar.
" ¿ Qué haces ahí, Conde Olindos ?   ¿ Qué vienes aquí a buscar ?
Si a buscar vienes la muerte,   te la venimos a dar,
si a buscar vienes la vida   de aquí non la has de llevar."
" ¡ Oh, mi espada, oh, mi espada   de buen oro y buen metal;
que de muchas me libraste,   desta non me has de faltar :
y si desta me librases,   te vuelvo a sobredorar ! "
Por la gracia del Dios Padre,   comenzó la espada a hablar :
" Si tú meneas los brazos   cual los sueles menear,
yo cortaré por los moros   como cuchillo por pan."
" ¡ Oh caballo, mi caballo ;   oh, mi caballo ruán,
que de muchas me libraste,   desta non me has de faltar ! "
Por la gracia de Dios Padre,   comenzó el caballo a hablar :
" Si me das la sopa en vino   y el agua por la canal,
las cuatro bandas de moros   las pasaré par a par."
Cuando era medio día,   no halló con quien pelear,
sinon era un perro moro   que non lo pudo matar.
Allí vino una paloma,   blanquita y de buen volar.
"¿ Qué haces ahí, palomita ?   ¿ Qué vienes aquí a buscar? "
" Soy la Infanta, Conde Olinos ;   de aquí te vengo a sacar.
Ya que non queda más qu'ese,   vivo nó habrá de marchar."
Por el campo los dos juntos   se pasean par a par.
La Reina mora los vió,   y ambos los mandó matar :
del uno nació una oliva,   y del otro un olivar :
cuando hacía viento fuerte,   los dos se iban a juntar.
La Reina también los vió,   también los mandó cortar :
del uno nació una fuente,   del otro un río caudal.
Los que tienen mal de amores   allí se van a lavar.
La Reina también los tiene   y también se iba a lavar.
" Corre fuente, corre fuente,   que en ti me voy a bañar."
" Cuando yo era Conde Olinos,   tú me mandaste matar ;
cuando yo era olivar,   tú me mandaste cortar ;
ahora que yo soy fuente,   de ti me quiero vengar :
para todos correré   para ti me he de secar."
¡ Conde Olinos, Conde Olinos,   es niño y pasó la mar !

ANONYMOUS

78. *"Tres morillas me enamoran . . ."*

With about as much sense as a nursery rhyme—the type of verse to which it most nearly conforms—this pleasant little song has won itself a place in Spanish memories through its distinctive refrain, the exotic flavour of which has caught the fancy. The repetitions of ll. 9, 15 and the imperfections of the rhymes are also suggestive of popular poetry.

Tres morillas me enamoran
en Jaén :
Axa y Fátima y Marién.

Tres morillas tan garridas
iban a coger olivas,
y hallábanlas cogidas
en Jaén :
Axa y Fátima y Marién.

Y hallábanlas cogidas,
y tornaban desmaídas
y las colores perdidas,
en Jaén :
Axa y Fátima y Marién.

Tres moricas tan lozanas,
tres moricas tan lozanas
iban a coger manzanas
a Jaén :
Axa y Fátima y Marién.

GARCI SÁNCHEZ DE BADAJOZ

*c.*1460-*c.*1526

A LOVE-POET who suffered unhappiness in love and in his later years is believed to have lost his reason. Though indebted to a number of his contemporaries and predecessors, both in Spain and in Italy, he reaches a high level of technical skill.

79. *Villancico*

Slight as it is, this little poem puts into words the feelings of every pair of lovers at some moment when life tears them asunder. With the exception of the conventional reference to love's "prison" (l. 5), and the mild play on partir *(ll. 6-7), there is nothing about the poem in the least artificial. It is wrung from the very heart of a sensitive lover and its beauty depends on a combination of imagination and sincerity.*

Lo que queda es lo seguro,
que lo que comigo va
desseando os morirá.

Mi anima queda aquí,
señora, en vuestra prisión,
partida del coraçón
del dolor con que partí ;
mas los ojos con que os vi,
y el cuerpo que no os verá,
desseando os morirá.

GIL VICENTE

*c.*1465-*c.*1536

THIS Portuguese dramatist, who wrote one quarter of his plays in Spanish and about half as many again in a mixture of Spanish and Portuguese, is temperamentally as much a lyric poet as a playwright. Fitzmaurice-Kelly considers him "unmatched" as such "till we come to Lope de Vega and Calderón."[1] Both the songs reproduced below are taken from one of his most lyrical plays, the *Auto da Sibilla Cassandra.*

80. "*Muy graciosa es la doncella. . . .*"

"Es tal vez," remarks Dámaso Alonso of this song, "la poesía más sencillamente bella de toda la literatura española."[2] *Even as modified by the "tal vez," this is high praise, but one might fairly demur to the "sencillamente". For the astonishing thing about the poem is the high degree of art which it attains at so early a date. In ll. 1-2 (which, though always printed as part of the first stanza, really form a* tema *to the poem), the interlaced medial and end rhymes initiate the melody, the key to which is the vowel* e, *occurring in stressed words ten times in the fourteen lines, and in end-rhymes eight times. At the conclusion of the first stanza the threefold reiteration of this end-rhyme at such short intervals accelerates the movement of the poem and lends force to the final phrase. In the second and third stanzas, the radical vowels* a-e-e-e *give place to a scheme* a-a-e-e, *which produces the same effect, with the added attraction of variety. Alliteration, suggested rather than imposed upon the reader, enhances the melody. The presentation of the theme is charmingly stylized in a pronounced but delicate pattern. Finally,*

[1] *N.H.*, pp. 162-3.

[2] D.A., p. 542.

with remarkable skill, the author contrives that his unnamed heroine shall never take form, yet shall be real to us out of her sheer, ethereal loveliness. She is one of the best known figures in Spanish poetry—though all that we actually know of her is the fact of her beauty.

Muy graciosa es la doncella,
¡ cómo es bella y hermosa !

Digas tú, el marinero,
que en las naves vivías,
si la nave o la vela o la estrella
es tan bella.

Digas tú, el caballero,
que las armas vestías,
si el caballo o las armas o la guerra
es tan bella.

Digas tú, el pastorcico
que el ganadico guardas,
si el ganado o los valles, o la sierra
es tan bella.

81. "*Dicen que me case yo. . . .*"

The charm of this spirited little song depends upon the smoothness of its rhythm, the rapidity of its action and the bluntness of its refrain. The threefold reiteration of the rhymes quickens the pace, but any other devices, such as the rather prominent alliteration, are quite supererogatory.

Dicen que me case yo :
no quiero marido, no.

Más quiero vivir segura
n'esta sierra a mi soltura,
que no estar en ventura
si casaré bien o no.
Dicen que me case yo :
no quiero marido, no.

Madre, no seré casada,
por no ver vida cansada,
o quizá mal empleada
la gracia que Dios me dió.
Dicen que me case yo :
no quiero marido, no.

No será ni es nacido
tal para ser mi marido ;
y pues que tengo sabido
que la flor yo me la só,
dicen que me case yo :
no quiero marido, no.

JUAN DEL ENCINA

*c.*1468-*c.*1529

THE first in time of Spain's great dramatists, Encina is particularly given to intercalating songs in his plays, and these are much finer than his longer poems or than most of the non-dramatic verses which he included in his *Cancionero* (1496). Musician as well as poet, he composed settings to some of his songs and no less than sixty-eight of these will be found in Barbieri's *Cancionero musical de los siglos XV y XVI* (1890).

82. "*No te tardes, que me muero. . .*"

The music of the refrain, which has recently been re-scored by a contemporary poet (p. 694), is produced by the soft consonants, the echo-rhyme in l. 2 and the double alliteration in t *and* m. *The three like endings in the refrain are answered, as it were, by a similar device in the stanzas, producing in each a climax which in its turn lends stress to the refrain. Only a slight uncertainty in the rhythm mars the music. The theme of the poem is an old one, as are also the metaphors, but the bringing of the "carcelero" into the foreground gives the treatment picturesqueness and originality.*

No te tardes, que me muero,
carcelero;
no te tardes, que me muero.

Apresura tu venida
porque no pierda la vida,
que la fe no está perdida.
Carcelero,
no te tardes, que me muero.

Bien sabes que la tardanza
trae gran desconfianza ;
ven y cumple mi esperanza.
Carcelero,
no te tardes, que me muero.

Sácame desta cadena,
que recibo muy gran pena.
Tu tardanza me condena.
Carcelero,
no te tardes, que me muero.

En el punto que me viste,
sin te vencer me venciste ;
suéltame, pues me prendiste.
Carcelero,
no te tardes, que me muero.

83. " *Tan buen ganadico. . . . . .* "

More consonant-music : this time the rhymes include two sounds of almost vocalic softness—ll *and* r. *Of the forty-five lines of the* villancico, *seventeen end in* ll *and eleven in* r *or* rr, *to say nothing of the occurrence of these consonants medially. No song in the language trips more easily off the tongue : the words are only of importance in that they are sung by a shepherd guarding his sheep. A real shepherd, it may be added, and real sheep—facing real wolves. There is the minimum of artificiality here.*

Tan buen ganadico,
y más en tal valle,
placer es guardalle.

Ganado d' altura,
y más de tal casta,
muy presto se gasta
su mala pastura ;
y en buena verdura,
y más en tal valle,
placer es guardalle.

Ansí que yo quiero
guardar mi ganado,
por todo este prado
de muy buen apero;
con este tempero,
y más en tal valle,
placer es guardalle.

Está muy vicioso
y siempre callando;
no anda balando
ni es enojoso;
antes da reposo
en cualquiera valle:
placer es guardalle.

Conviene guardalla
la cosa preciosa,
que en ser codiciosa
procuran hurtalla.
Ganada sin falla,
y más en tal valle,
placer es guardalle.

[Pastor que se encierra
en valle seguro,
los lobos te juro
que no le dan guerra.
Ganado de sierra
traspuesto en tal valle
placer es guardalle.][1]

Pastor de buen grado
yo siempre sería,
pues tanta alegría
me da este ganado;
y tengo jurado
de nunca dejalle,
mas siempre guardalle.

[1]Cf. p. 713, below.

CRISTÓBAL DE CASTILLEJO

*c.*1490-1550

Ironically, this writer who led the reaction against the italianizing tendencies of Boscán and Garcilaso de la Vega (p. xxxiii), spent most of his own life in the service of Charles V's brother, Ferdinand of Bohemia, out of Spain. His two long poems, a burlesque " Sermón de amores " and a satirical " Diálogo de mujeres ", in which the respective speakers attack and defend women, were not published until shortly before his death, and his collected works appeared only in 1573. The short poems include graceful but artificial love-songs, his most typical work, addressed to a larger number of ladies than one would expect a priest to have fallen in love with ; dreary " Obras morales ", now for the most part forgotten ; " Obras de conversación y pasatiempo ", farcical, ironical or satirical, including satires on literary themes ; and some temperate and tuneful " Obras de devoción ".

One of the literary satires, " Reprensión contra los poetas españoles que escriben en verso italiano ", attacks Boscán and Garcilaso for introducing " foreign " innovations (" nuevo lenguaje mezclado de extranjera poesía ") and contrasts them, greatly to their disadvantage, with Juan de Mena and Jorge Manrique. Castillejo's own verse, however, is the best justification of the italianizers. The metrical grace and melody of the fifteenth-century poets remains, but whatever substance there had been in their poetry has vanished, leaving nothing but compliments, conventions and jingles. It was unfortunate that men who, having found refreshment and recreative power abroad, used it to endow the poetry of their country with new life should have been so sharply censured by a critic who has been well described as " one of the wasted forces in Spanish literature."[1]

The most attractive of Castillejo's verses are those in lighter vein, such as the story, in fabular style, of the " transfiguración de

[1] J. Fitzmaurice-Kelly in *Oxford Book of Spanish Verse*, Oxford, 1913, p. xxiii.

un vizcaíno, gran bebedor de vino",[1] and the sprightly parody of a popular *romance glosado*, which begins: "Tiempo es ya, Castillejo, Tiempo es de andar de aquí."[2] We have preferred, however, to choose two shorter pieces from the "Obras de amores" which are more characteristic both of the man himself and of what he stands for in the history of literature. Both illustrate the musical quality of his verse; but the melodious superficiality of the second should be contrasted with the depth of feeling which in Boscán's sonnets is struggling for expression, though perhaps crudely.

84. *Villancico*

Alguna vez,
oh pensamiento,
serás contento.

Si amor cruel
me hace la guerra.
seis pies de tierra
podrán más que él;
allí, sin él
y sin tormento,
serás contento.

Lo no alcanzado
en esta vida,
ella perdida,
será hallado;
que sin cuidado
del mal que siento,
serás contento.

85. *Villancico*

No pueden dormir mis ojos;
no pueden dormir.

Pero ¿cómo dormirán
cercados en derredor
de soldados de dolor,

[1] *Obras*, *ed.* J. Domínguez Bordona, Madrid, 1926-8, II, 309-14.
[2] *Obras*, III, 18-23.

que siempre en armas están ?
Los combates que les dan,
no los pudiendo sufrir,
no pueden dormir.

Alguna vez, de cansados
de la angustia y del tormento,
se duermen que no lo siento ;
que los hallo transportados ;
pero los sueños pesados
no les quieren consentir
que puedan dormir.

Mas ya que duerman un poco,
están tan desvanecidos,
que ellos quedan aturdidos,
yo poco menos de loco ;
y si los muevo y provoco
con cerrar y con abrir,
no pueden dormir.

JUAN BOSCÁN

*c.*1493-1542

JOAN BOSCÀ ALMUGÀVER—to give his true name to this Catalan poet who lived largely in Castile and wrote in Castilian—was the leader of the movement which infused into Spanish poetry new inspiration and vigour drawn from Italy, and prepared the way for the great poetic achievements of Spain in the Golden Age. He visited Italy when quite young, became a pupil of the Italian humanist Lucio Marineo Sículo, and, on returning to Spain, held a post in Charles V's Court and was appointed tutor to the young Duke of Alba. In 1526, when the Court was at Granada, the Venetian Ambassador and man of letters, Andrea Navagiero, urged him to abandon the native metres in which he had hitherto written his poetry, and to fashion his art on the best Italian models. He did so, at first with some trepidation and difficulty[1], and transformed himself from a merely pleasant versifier into a truly great, though in some respects an unformed, poet. He tells us that he was fortified by the judgment of his friend Garcilaso de la Vega (" el cual, no solamente en mi opinión, mas en la de todo el mundo, ha sido tenido por regla cierta "[2]); this notable friendship was proclaimed to the world by the publication of the works of the two poets in one volume, by Boscán's widow, in the year after his death.

The first three of the four books in this volume comprise the poetical works of Boscán. The verses in native measures (*coplas*, *villancicos* and *canciones*, with two longer poems in *décimas*) have at their worst a certain harshness which their author never wholly overcame, but at their best are extremely melodious. They are mainly conventional and superficial love-poems, however, never touching the poet's inner life. Of the remainder, strongly inspired by Petrarch and sometimes by the Valencian poet Ausiàs March, the best are the ninety-two sonnets, four of the finest of

[1] See preface to Book II of *Obras*, Barcelona, 1543—reprinted, Madrid, 1875.

[2] *Obras*, Madrid, 1875, p. 170.

which are here reproduced as testifying to the variety of the author's themes and methods ; next in merit come eleven *canciones* imitated from Italian *canzoni* ; and, below these, some " Capítulos " and " Epístolas ", a verse allegory in *ottava rima* and a long poem in blank hendecasyllabics, entitled " Historia de Leandro y Hero."

Boscán's great achievements are to have acclimatized the hendecasyllable and transplanted the sonnet-form more successfully than Santillana and others and to have introduced and popularized the *canzone*, the tercet, the *ottava rima* and blank verse. But among his sonnets are some which, though never without their blemishes, are among the finest in sixteenth-century Spain. For the impetus of the new measures taught him that he had something to say, and he said it, though haltingly and crudely, with deep sincerity and true lyric emotion. He is the first Spanish poet who, in the words of his contemporary, Sir Philip Sidney, " looks in his heart and writes."

86. *Soneto VII*

The opening lines follow those of Petrarch's twenty-second sonnet " in vita di M. Laura " (" Solo e pensoso i più deserti campi. . . . . .") but the resemblance stops here, for the Italian poem is lit by the rays of love, whereas the Spanish one is plunged into the gloom of solitude. The poet seems to be endeavouring to reproduce the symptoms of a state of mind actually experienced by him : greater vividness and conciseness of expresion would have improved it, but, though not the highest art, it is manifestly sincere art and an earnest of better to come.

Solo y pensoso en páramos desiertos
mis pasos doy cuidosos y cansados ;
y entrambos ojos traigo levantados,
a ver no vea alguien mis desconciertos.

Mis tormentos allí vienen tan ciertos,
y van mis sentimientos tan cargados,
que aun los campos me suelen ser pesados,
porque todos no están secos y muertos.

Si oyo balar acaso algún ganado,
y la voz del pastor da en mis oídos,
allí se me revuelve mi cuidado ;

y quedan espantados mis sentidos :
¡ cómo ha sido no haber desesperado,
después de tantos llantos doloridos !

87. *Soneto LXIV*

Perhaps this quadripartite sonnet, embodying a fourfold apostrophe, is Boscán's best. Its weakest feature is its somewhat tame conclusion, which contrasts unfortunately with the tremendous power of ll. 1-2, 5-6. This apart, it is a remarkable poem. Commonplace sentiments and well-worn mediaeval metaphors are reinforced with bold paradoxes and antitheses which smash their way like battering-rams through the reader's complacency or indifference.

¡ O gran fuerza de amor, que así enflaqueces
los que nacidos son para ser fuertes,
y les truecas así todas sus suertes
que presto los más ricos empobreces !

¡ O piélago de mar, que te enriqueces
con los despojos de infinitas muertes !
Trágaslos, y después luego los viertes,
porque nunca en un punto permaneces.

¡ O rayo, cuyo efecto no entendemos,
que de dentro nos dejas abrasados,
y de fuera sin mal sanos nos vemos !

¡ O dolencia mortal, cuyos extremos
son menos conocidos y alcanzados
por los tristes que más los padecemos !

88. *Soneto LXXIV*

Here is one complete sustained metaphor—a sonnet wholly allegorical, and, unlike most of Boscán's, wholly suggestive. In what sense does the poet resemble a hermit in the desert? Whom or what are we to understand by the friend believed to be dead? What are the thoughts of the past awakened by his arrival? Answers to these questions will easily be found—but they will not always be the same. It is hard to over-praise this sonnet's evocative quality, particularly the magnificent last line describing the hermit's continual expectancy and opening out a complete panorama to the imagination.

Soy como aquel que vive en el desierto,
del mundo y de sus cosas olvidado,
y a descuido veis donde le ha llegado
un gran amigo, al cual tuvo por muerto.

Teme luego de un caso tan incierto;
pero después que bien se ha segurado,
comienza a holgar pensando en lo pasado,
con nuevos sentimientos muy despierto.

Mas cuando ya este amigo se le parte,
al cual partirse presto le conviene,
la soledad empieza a serle nueva;

con las yerbas del monte no se aviene,
para el yermo le falta toda el arte,
y tiembla cada vez que entra en su cueva.

89. *Soneto LXXXII*

Petrarch's sonnet (CLIII in vita) *" Dolci ire, dolci sdegni, e dolci paci. . . ." produces a strong emotional effect by the repeated use of the melodious word " dolce ". But this lovely meditative sonnet, I think, improves upon its model, which overdoes the effect by using the word ten times in the first quatrain. Boscán's " dulce " is the softest of intermittently sounding bells, almost a poetic angelus—three times in the first quatrain, three times in the second and twice in the sestet—conveying an impression, not only of* dulzura *but of ordered peace, very difficult to define. Marred only by its weak last line, the sonnet creates an atmosphere of intentionally vague but tranquil happiness. The superficially quadripartite construction may be compared with that of LXIV and the use of the word* dulce *with LXI.*

Dulce reposo de mi entendimiento ;
dulce placer fundado sobre bueno ;
dulce saber, que de saber soy lleno,
pues tengo de mi bien conocimiento.

Dulce gozar de un dulce sentimiento,
viendo mi cielo estar claro y sereno,
y dulce revolver sobre mi seno,
con firme concluir, que estoy contento.

Dulce gustar de un no sé qué sin nombre,
que amor dentro en mi alma poner quiso,
cuando mi mal sanó con gran renombre.

Dulce pensar que estoy en paraíso,
sino que en fin me acuerdo que soy hombre,
y en las cosas del mundo tomo aviso.

GARCILASO DE LA VEGA

*c.*1501-1536

THE Toledan Garcí(a) Lasso de la Vega y Guzmán was the typical " Elizabethan " poet—courtier, soldier and man of accomplishments, " tomando, ora la espada, ora la pluma ",[1] like Sir Philip Sidney, with whose life and poetry his own have been compared. He entered the service of Charles V when young, and, for either military or political reasons, spent long periods, including the last four years of his life, in Naples. He died at Nice, on October 13, 1536, from wounds received in a Provençal campaign of the Emperor's, three weeks earlier.

Garcilaso's poems, which were published only in 1543 (p. 166) but quickly became popular, are all, apart from three Latin odes and a handful of *coplas*, in the Italian manner—38 sonnets, five *canciones*, three eclogues, two elegies and an *epístola*. In them he attained much greater technical heights than Boscán and also plumbed greater depths of emotion. Both his musical ear and his poetic sensibility are keener than those of any of his predecessors. His range of themes is limited but within his limits he is superb. In him, for the first time in Spain, the flame of lyric passion burns brightly. He is perhaps the first Spanish poet to sing worthily of love.

His love-poems are based mainly upon a deep, though apparently platonic and unreciprocated attachment for a Portuguese lady, Isabel Freire, who came to Spain, in 1526, with Charles V's portuguese consort; three years later, married a Spanish noble; and in 1533 died at the birth of her third child. (Cf. Sonetos I, II, V, IX, X, XXV and others; Égloga I). But it would also appear (Canción IV; Sonetos VII, XII, XXVIII and others) that in Naples, shortly before his death, he was seized with a new and perhaps less ethereal passion, which is thought (Soneto XXXIV) to have been short-lived.

[1] Égloga III.

Primacy among Garcilaso's works is generally given to the First Eclogue and to about a dozen of his sonnets, all of which throb with restrained emotion. In his lighter vein, the fifth *canción* is inimitable.

90. *Soneto I*

The first lines,[1] *though not the poem as a whole, are inspired by Petrarch (Sonetto XXX* in morte). *A situation, obscure till l. 10, is described with a perfect symmetry corresponding to the perfect restraint of the language. Summarized in prose, the argument seems almost inhumanly dispassionate, and perhaps, had the mathematically precise octave been followed by a sestet in which the poet's passion broke its bounds, the sonnet would have come nearer perfection. Technically, the last line lacks the finality which the sonnet-structure demands, but the architecture is unexceptionable and the strong double link* (acabo . . . . acabar ; acabaré . . . . acabarme) *between octave and sestet allows the strengthening of the contrast by the use of past and future tenses in the two parts respectively. Almost every line, when pondered over, yields up beauty of balance and rhythm. The first, however, with its thrice-repeated* a-o *pattern and the enunciation and echo of its dominant consonant-group,* c-m-p, *is the most remarkable of them all.*

Cuando me paro a contemplar mi estado,
y a ver los pasos por do me ha traído,
hallo, según por do anduve perdido,
que a mayor mal pudiera haber llegado.

Mas cuando del camino estó olvidado,
a tanto mal no sé por dó he venido ;
sé que me acabo, y más he yo sentido
ver acabar conmigo mi cuidado.

Yo acabaré, que me entregué sin arte
a quien sabrá perderme y acabarme,
si quisiere, y aun sabrá querello ;

que, pues mi voluntad puede matarme,
la suya, que no es tanto de mi parte,
pudiendo, ¿ qué hará sino hacello ?

[1] It is curious, not merely how many sonnets, but how many of the greatest sonnets, begin with "When". There are outstanding examples in Petrarch, Ronsard, Du Bellay, Shakespeare, Milton and Keats.

91. *Soneto V*

The appeal of this sonnet depends on quite different qualities. More mellifluous than Soneto I and its equal in technical merit, it is much freer from the taint of artificiality. Graceful throughout, its octave is almost deferential, but the sestet suggests that a kneeling lover has suddenly risen to his feet and flung off the cloak which has hitherto enveloped him. He begins boldly (l. 9); then for a moment (ll. 10-11) retreats behind a protective préciosité*; and finally, returning to his direct and forceful manner, leads us, with rising emotion, to the perfect climax. Ll. 1-8, 10-11 could only be the words of a courtier; ll. 9, 12-14 are the language of all lovers everywhere.*

Escrito está en mi alma vuestro gesto,
y cuanto yo escribir de vos deseo,
vos sola lo escribistes, yo lo leo
tan solo, que aun de vos me guardo en esto.

En esto estoy y estaré siempre puesto;
que, aunque no cabe en mí cuanto en vos veo.
de tanto bien lo que no entiendo creo,
tomando ya la fe por presupuesto.

Yo no nací sino para quereros;
mi alma os ha cortado a su medida;
por hábito del alma misma os quiero.

Cuanto tengo confieso yo deberos;
por vos nací, por vos tengo la vida,
por vos he de morir y por vos muero.

92. *Soneto IX*

Here the merits and methods of Sonetos I and V are combined. The octave is symmetrically constructed and its argument logically developed, while the antitheses reflect the swaying conflict in the poet's mind. But in the sestet (linked by the words diferente . . . . diferencia) *the hitherto suppressed passion threatens to break through the trim phraseology: l. 11 is a real* cri du cœur; *and in l. 14 a new and paradoxical idea is enunciated with a clinching force. Without ever sacrificing restraint, this sonnet shows emotion triumphant over reason.*

Señora mía, si de vos yo ausente
en esta vida turo y no me muero,
paréceme que ofendo a lo que os quiero,
y al bien de que gozaba en ser presente.

Tras este, luego siento otro acidente,
que es ver que, si de vida desespero,
yo pierdo cuanto bien de vos espero,
y así ando en lo que siento diferente.

En esta diferencia mis sentidos
están en vuestra ausencia y en porfía.
No sé ya qué hacerme en mal tamaño.

Nunca entre sí los veo sino reñidos;
de tal arte pelean noche y día,
que sólo se conciertan en mi daño.

93. *Soneto X*

Is this the greatest of Garcilaso's sonnets? At least we can say that it gives to the most poignant grief the most exquisite expression. The unexpected discovery of the "dulces prendas" (no doubt some such reminiscence as a lock of the beloved's hair: cf. Égloga I, ll. 352 ff.) reawakens past emotions and re-kindles the flame of desire. In his distress, the poet revolves each sentiment in his mind. How different is this from those sonnets so closely packed with reasoning! Here, too, each phrase is packed—but with emotion. Light, almost playful beneath the formal disguise of the apostrophe, the poem is heavily charged with suppressed grief, sharply ("dulces . . . . mal", "tanto bien . . . . tan grave dolor," "el bien . . . . el mal") contrasted with past happiness. Its poignancy is enhanced by deep, rich melody, some of the secrets of which can be discovered: the predominance of broad vowels; the "dying fall" of "por mi mal halladas"; the repetition of "dulces"; the frequent use of the soft consonant m *(ll. 1, 3, 4, 11, 14). In the last line sound echoes sense as nowhere else in Garcilaso.*

¡Oh dulces prendas, por mi mal halladas,
dulces y alegres cuando Dios quería!
Juntas estáis en la memoria mía,
y con ella en mi muerte conjuradas.

¿ Quién me dijera, cuando las pasadas
horas, que en tanto bien por vos me vía,
que me habíades de ser en algún día
con tan grave dolor representadas ?

Pues en una hora junto me llevastes
todo el bien que por términos me distes,
llevadme junto el mal que me dejastes.

Si no, sospecharé que me pusistes
en tantos bienes, porque deseastes
verme morir entre memorias tristes.

94. *Égloga I*

In this pastoral lament on the poet's loss of Isabel Freire, the shepherd Salicio bewails the inconstancy of his lady Galatea, after which his comrade Nemoroso, enamoured of one Elisa, mourns her death. Both Salicio (=Garcilaso) and Nemoroso (Lat. nemus = *Sp.* vega) *seem to represent the author, in two contrasting moods of a dissociated personality. In that case Galatea and Elisa would both be Isabel. The stanzas are of fourteen lines, rhyming* ABC ABC cdd EEFeF *(capitals representing lines of 11 syllables and lower-case letters lines of 7). Each of the two laments, which, apart from a courtly dedication to the poet's patron and some stylized* décor, *occupy the entire poem, consists of twelve stanzas. Salicio's complaint, with its lovely refrain : " Salid sin duelo, lágrimas, corriendo," has some exquisitely musical passages (e.g., ll. 99-112), but is less moving than Nemoroso's elegy, in which the very construction of the stanza is twice modified (ll. 263, 276), possibly in order to indicate uncontrollable emotion. The intensification of the poet's grief is observable even in the first stanza (ll. 239-52) ; its images and reminiscences (e.g., ll. 267-81) are intimate and vivid ; and its poignant reflections are of universal application. The finest thing in the whole poem, and perhaps in all Garcilaso, is the closing invocation (ll. 394-407) to the " divine Elisa " dwelling among the immortals in a mythological heaven. It is fitting that, in a poem which ends upon a note of such sublime ecstasy, there should be passages (e.g., ll. 259-62, 372-5, 397-9, 401-4) which may well have inspired Fray Luis de León and San Juan de la Cruz, the sublimest poets of the Golden Age.*

Al Virrey de Nápoles

El dulce lamentar de dos pastores,
Salicio juntamente y Nemoroso,
he de cantar, sus quejas imitando,
cuyas ovejas al cantar sabroso
estaban muy atentas, los amores
de pacer olvidadas escuchando.
Tú, que ganaste obrando
un nombre en todo el mundo,
y un grado sin segundo,
agora estés atento solo y dado
al ínclito gobierno del Estado
albano; agora vuelto a la otra parte,
resplandeciente, armado,
representando en tierra el fiero Marte;

agora de cuidados enojosos
y de negocios libre, por ventura
andas a caza, el monte fatigando
en ardiente jinete, que apresura
el curso tras los ciervos temerosos,
que en vano su morir van dilatando.
Espera, que en tornando
a ser restituído
al ocio ya perdido,
luego verás ejercitar mi pluma
por la infinita, innumerable suma
de tus virtudes y famosas obras;
antes que me consuma,
faltando a ti que a todo el mundo sobras.

En tanto que este tiempo que adivino
viene a sacarme de la deuda un día,
que se debe a tu fama y a tu gloria,
que es deuda general, no sólo mía,
mas de cualquier ingenio peregrino
que celebra lo digno de memoria;
el árbol de victoria
que ciñe estrechamente
tu gloriosa frente
dé lugar a la yedra que se planta

debajo de tu sombra y se levanta
poco a poco, arrimada a tus loores ;
y en cuanto esto se canta,
escucha tú el cantar de mis pastores.

Saliendo de las ondas encendido,
rayaba de los montes el altura
el sol, cuando Salicio, recostado
al pie de un alta haya, en la verdura,
por donde un agua clara con sonido
atravesaba el fresco y verde prado.
Él, con canto acordado
al rumor que sonaba
del agua que pasaba,
se quejaba tan dulce y blandamente
como si no estuviera de allí ausente
la que de su dolor culpa tenía ;
y así, como presente,
razonando con ella, le decía :

SALICIO

¡ Oh, más dura que mármol a mis quejas,
y al encendido fuego en que me quemo,
más helada que nieve, Galatea !
Estoy muriendo, y aun la vida temo ;
témola con razón, pues tú me dejas ;
que no hay, sin ti, el vivir para qué sea.
Vergüenza he que me vea
ninguno en tal estado,
de ti desamparado,
y de mí mismo yo me corro agora.
¿ De un alma te desdeñas ser señora,
donde siempre moraste, no pudiendo
della salir una hora ?
Salid sin duelo, lágrimas, corriendo.

El sol tiende los rayos de su lumbre
por montes y por valles, despertando
las aves y animales y la gente :
cuál por el aire claro va volando,
cuál por el verde valle o alta cumbre

paciendo va segura y libremente,
cuál con el sol presente
va de nuevo al oficio,
y al usado ejercicio
do su natura o menester le inclina :
siempre está en llanto esta ánima mezquina,
cuando la sombra el mundo va cubriendo
o la luz se avecina.
Salid sin duelo, lágrimas, corriendo.

¿ Y tú, desta mi vida ya olvidada,
sin mostrar un pequeño sentimiento
de que por ti Salicio triste muera,
dejas llevar, desconocida, al viento
el amor y la fe que ser guardada
eternamente sólo a mí debiera ?
¡ Oh, Dios ! ¿ Por qué siquiera,
pues ves desde tu altura
esta falsa perjura
causar la muerte de un estrecho amigo,
no recibe del cielo algún castigo ?
Si en pago del amor yo estoy muriendo,
¿ qué hará el enemigo ?
Salid sin duelo, lágrimas, corriendo.

Por ti el silencio de la selva umbrosa,
por ti la esquividad y apartamiento
del solitario monte me agradaba ;
por ti la verde yerba, el fresco viento,
el blanco lirio y colorada rosa
y dulce primavera deseaba.
¡ Ay, cuánto me engañaba !
¡ Ay, cuán diferente era
y cuán de otra manera
lo que en tu falso pecho se escondía !
Bien claro con su voz me lo decía
la siniestra corneja, repitiendo
la desventura mía.
Salid sin duelo, lágrimas, corriendo.

¡ Cuántas veces, durmiendo en la floresta,
reputándolo yo por desvarío,

vi mi mal entre sueños, desdichado!
Soñaba que en el tiempo del estío
llevaba, por pasar allí la siesta,
abrevar en el Tajo mi ganado;
y después de llegado,
sin saber de cuál arte,
por desusada parte
y por nuevo camino el agua se iba.
Ardiendo yo con la calor estiva,
el curso, enajenado, iba siguiendo
del agua fugitiva.
Salid sin duelo, lágrimas, corriendo.

Tu dulce habla ¿en cúya oreja suena?
Tus claros ojos ¿a quién los volviste?
¿Por quién tan sin respeto me trocaste?
Tu quebrantada fe ¿dó la pusiste?
¿Cuál es el cuello que, como en cadena,
de tus hermosos brazos añudaste?
No hay corazón que baste,
aunque fuese de piedra,
viendo mi amada yedra,
de mí arrancada, en otro muro asida,
y mi parra en otro olmo entretejida,
que no se esté con llanto deshaciendo
hasta acabar la vida.
Salid sin duelo, lágrimas, corriendo.

¿Qué no se esperará de aquí adelante,
por difícil que sea y por incierto?
O ¿qué discordia no será juntada?
y juntamente ¿qué tendrá por cierto,
o qué de hoy más no temerá el amante,
siendo a todo materia por ti dada?
Cuando tú enajenada
de mí, cuitado, fuiste,
notable causa diste
y ejemplo a todos cuantos cubre el cielo,
que el más seguro tema con recelo
perder lo que estuviere poseyendo.
Salid fuera sin duelo,
salid sin duelo, lágrimas, corriendo.

Materia diste al mundo de esperanza
de alcanzar lo imposible y no pensado,
y de hacer juntar lo diferente,
dando a quien diste el corazón malvado,
quitándolo de mí con tal mudanza,
que siempre sonará de gente en gente.
La cordera paciente
con el lobo hambriento
hará su ayuntamiento,
y con las simples aves sin ruido
harán las bravas sierpes ya su nido,
que mayor diferencia comprehendo
de ti al que has escogido.
Salid sin duelo, lágrimas, corriendo.

Siempre de nueva leche en el verano
y en el invierno abundo ; en mi majada
la manteca y el queso está sobrado ;
de mi cantar, pues, yo te vi agradada,
tanto que no pudiera el mantüano
Títero ser de ti más alabado.
No soy, pues, bien mirado,
tan disforme ni feo,
que aun agora me veo
en esta agua que corre clara y pura,
y cierto no trocara mi figura
con ese que de mí se está riendo ;
¡ trocara mi ventura !
Salid sin duelo, lágrimas, corriendo.

¿ Cómo te vine en tanto menosprecio ?
¿ Cómo te fuí tan presto aborrecible ?
¿ Cómo te faltó en mí el conocimiento ?
Si no tuvieras condición terrible,
siempre fuera tenido de ti en precio,
y no viera de ti este apartamiento.
¿ No sabes que sin cuento
buscan en el estío
mis ovejas el frío
de la sierra de Cuenca y el gobierno
del abrigado Estremo en el invierno ?

Mas ¡ qué vale el tener, si derritiendo
me estoy en llanto eterno !
Salid sin duelo, lágrimas, corriendo.

Con mi llorar las piedras enternecen
su natural dureza y la quebrantan ;
los árboles parece que se inclinan ;
las aves que me escuchan, cuando cantan,
con diferente voz se condolecen,
y mi morir cantando me adivinan.
Las fieras que reclinan
su cuerpo fatigado
dejan el sosegado
sueño por escuchar mi llanto triste.
Tú sola contra mí te endureciste,
los ojos aun siquiera no volviendo
a los que tú hiciste
salir sin duelo, lágrimas, corriendo.

Mas ya que a socorrer aquí no vienes,
no dejes el lugar que tanto amaste,
que bien podrás venir de mí segura.
Yo dejaré el lugar do me dejaste ;
ven, si por sólo esto te detienes.
Ves aquí un prado lleno de verdura,
ves aquí una espesura,
ves aquí un agua clara,
en otro tiempo cara,
a quien de ti con lágrimas me quejo.
Quizá aquí hallarás, pues yo me alejo,
al que todo mi bien quitarme puede ;
que pues el bien le dejo,
no es mucho que el lugar también le quede.

Aquí dió fin a su cantar Salicio,
y sospirando en el postrero acento,
soltó de llanto una profunda vena.
Queriendo el monte al grave sentimiento
de aquel dolor en algo ser propicio,
con la pasada voz retumba y suena.
La blanca Filomena,

casi como dolida
y a compasión movida,
dulcemente responde al son lloroso.
Lo que cantó tras esto Nemoroso,
decidlo vos, Piérides ; que tanto
no puedo yo ni oso,
que siento enflaquecer mi débil canto.

NEMOROSO

Corrientes aguas puras, cristalinas ;
árboles que os estáis mirando en ellas,
verde prado de fresca sombra lleno,
aves que aquí sembráis vuestras querellas,
yedra que por los árboles caminas,
torciendo el paso por su verde seno ;
yo me vi tan ajeno
del grave mal que siento
que de puro contento
con vuestra soledad me recreaba,
donde con dulce sueño reposaba,
o con el pensamiento discurría
por donde no hallaba
sino memorias llenas de alegría ;

y en este triste valle, donde agora
mi entristezco y me canso en el reposo,
estuve ya contento y descansado.
¡ Oh bien caduco, vano y presuroso !
Acuérdome durmiendo aquí algún hora,
que despertando, a Elisa vi a mi lado.
¡ Oh, miserable hado !
¡ Oh, tela delicada,
antes de tiempo dada
a los agudos filos de la muerte !
Mas convenible suerte
a los cansados años de mi vida,
que es más que el hierro fuerte,
pues que no la ha quebrantado tu partida.

¿ Dó están agora aquellos claros ojos
que llevaban tras sí, como colgada,

mi alma, doquier que ellos se volvían?
¿Dó está la blanca mano delicada,
llena de vencimientos y despojos
que de mí mis sentidos le ofrecían?
Los cabellos que vían
con gran desprecio el oro,
como a menor tesoro,
¿adónde están? ¿Adónde el blando pecho?
¿Dó la coluna que el dorado techo
con presunción graciosa sostenía?
Aquesto todo agora ya se encierra,
por desventura mía,
en la fría, desierta y dura tierra.

¿Quién me dijera, Elisa, vida mía,
cuando en aqueste valle al fresco viento
andábamos cogiendo tiernas flores,
que había de ver con largo apartamiento
venir el triste y solitario día
que diese amargo fin a mis amores?
El cielo en mis dolores
cargó la mano tanto
que a sempiterno llanto
y a triste soledad me ha condenado;
y lo que siento más es verme atado
a la pesada vida y enojosa,
solo, desamparado,
ciego, sin lumbre en cárcel tenebrosa.

Después que nos dejaste, nunca pace
en hartura el ganado ya, ni acude
el campo al labrador con mano llena.
No hay bien que en mal no se convierta y mude:
la mala yerba al trigo ahoga y nace
en su lugar la infelice avena.
La tierra, que de buena
gana nos producía
flores con que solía
quitar en sólo vellas mil enojos,
produce agora en cambio estos abrojos,
ya de rigor de espinas intratable.

Yo hago con mis ojos
crecer, lloviendo, el fruto miserable.

Como al partir del sol la sombra crece,
y en cayendo su rayo se levanta
la negra escuridad que el mundo cubre,
de do viene el temor que nos espanta,
y la medrosa forma en que se ofrece
aquella que la noche nos encubre,
hasta que el sol descubre
su luz pura y hermosa;
tal es la tenebrosa
noche de tu partir, en que he quedado
de sombra y de temor atormentado,
hasta que muerte el tiempo determine
que a ver el deseado
sol de tu clara vista me encamine.

Cual suele el ruiseñor con triste canto
quejarse, entre las hojas escondido,
del duro labrador, que cautamente
le despojó su caro y dulce nido
de los tiernos hijuelos, entretanto
que del amado ramo estaba ausente,
y aquel dolor que siente
con diferencia tanta
por la dulce garganta
despide y a su canto el aire suena,
y la callada noche no refrena
su lamentable oficio y sus querellas,
trayendo de su pena
al cielo por testigo y las estrellas;

desta manera suelto ya la rienda
a mi dolor, y así me quejo en vano
de la dureza de la muerte airada.
Ella en mi corazón metió la mano,
y de allí me llevó mi dulce prenda,
que aquél era su nido y su morada.
¡Ay, muerte arrebatada!
Por ti me estoy quejando

al cielo y enojando
con importuno llanto al mundo todo.
El desigual dolor no sufre modo.
No me podrán quitar el dolorido
sentir, si ya del todo
primero no me quitan el sentido.

Tengo una parte aquí de tus cabellos,
Elisa, envueltos en un blanco paño,
que nunca de mi seno se me apartan.
Descójolos, y de un dolor tamaño
enternecerme siento, que sobre ellos
nunca mis ojos de llorar se hartan.
Sin que de allí se partan,
con suspiros calientes,
más que la llama ardientes,
los enjugo del llanto, y de consuno
casi los paso y cuento uno a uno;
juntándolos, con un cordón los ato.
Tras esto el importuno
dolor me deja descansar un rato.

Mas luego a la memoria se me ofrece
aquella noche tenebrosa, escura,
que siempre aflige esta ánima mesquina
con la memoria de mi desventura.
Verte presente agora me parece
en aquel duro trance de Lucina,
y aquella voz divina,
con cuyo son y acentos
a los airados vientos
pudieron amansar, que agora es muda;
me parece que oigo que a la cruda,
inexorable diosa demandabas
en aquel paso ayuda;
y tú, rústica diosa, ¿dónde estabas?

¿Íbate tanto en perseguir las fieras?
¿Íbate tanto en un pastor dormido?
¿Cosa pudo bastar a tal crueza,
que, comovida a compasión, oído

a los votos y lágrimas no dieras
por no ver hecha tierra tal belleza,
o no ver la tristeza
en que tu Nemoroso
queda, que su reposo
era seguir tu oficio, persiguiendo
las fieras por los montes, y ofreciendo
a tus sagradas aras los despojos ?
¿ Y tú, ingrata, riendo
dejas morir mi bien ante mis ojos ?

Divina Elisa, pues agora el cielo
con inmortales pies pisas y mides,
y su mudanza ves, estando queda,
¿ por qué de mí te olvidas, y no pides
que se apresure el tiempo en que este velo
rompa del cuerpo, y verme libre pueda,
y en la tercera rueda
contigo mano a mano
busquemos otro llano,
busquemos otros montes y otros ríos,
otros valles floridos y sombríos,
donde descanse y siempre pueda verte
ante los ojos míos,
sin miedo y sobresalto de perderte ?

Nunca pusieran fin al triste lloro
los pastores, ni fueran acabadas
las canciones que sólo el monte oía,
si, mirando las nubes coloradas,
al tramontar del sol bordadas de oro,
no vieran que era ya pasado el día.
La sombra se veía
venir corriendo apriesa
ya por la falda espesa
del altísimo monte, y recordando
ambos como de sueño, y, acabando
el fugitivo sol, de luz escaso,
su ganado llevando,
se fueron recogiendo paso a paso.

DIEGO HURTADO DE MENDOZA (THE YOUNGER)

1503-1575

THIS Humanist and historian, not to be confused with the father of the Marqués de Santillana, who bore the same name (p. 51), was one of the leading italianate poets of his day. He wrote verse only as a side-line, however; and has left little that rises above mediocrity.

95. *A un Retrato*

A well constructed sonnet, with excessive alliteration (e.g., ll. 7, 10-11, 12) but cunningly placed enjambements and cæsuræ (cf. ll. 2, 6, 10, 13). Though the poet's treatment of his theme is of no great distinction, it has a flavour of Petrarch and Garcilaso and as an expression of his idealism it is most attractive.

Tu gracia, tu valor, tu hermosura,
muestra de todo el cielo retratada,
como cosa que está sobre natura,
ni pudiera ser vista ni pintada.

Pero ya que en el alma tu figura
tengo, en humana forma abreviada,
tal hice retraerte de pintura,
cual amor te dejó en ella estampada.

No por ambición vana o por memoria
de ti, ni para publicar mis males,
ni por verte más veces que te veo;

mas por sólo gozar de tanta gloria,
señora, con los ojos corporales,
como con los del alma y del deseo.

SANTA TERESA DE JESÚS

1515-1582

THE Carmelite nun who for twenty-five years lived in complete seclusion in her Avilan convent before inaugurating the foundation of the Discalced Reform and incidentally becoming a world-renowned writer, can hardly in any sense be termed a poet save by virtue of the Divine love which continually welled up in her soul. Sometimes, in all probability quite unconsciously, she gave this love truly poetic expression and no anthology can be considered a representative one which fails to reproduce a few examples of her often rude and unpolished verse. This has a surprising range of subject and style. We pass from such a striking and distinguished hymn as "Oh Hermosura, que ecedéis . . . . " to stanzas of frank doggerel in which the author invokes death; then on to an imaginative but rather discursive dialogue between her soul and Christ, contrasting with the famous "Bookmark" (p. 189), which displays a conciseness seldom equalled in Spanish. None of her verses were written for publication, and many of them, platitudinous in the extreme, were intended for the nuns of her foundations to sing at festival processions or at the clothing of some novice. Fortunately the patron saint of humour has preserved one of these—the hymn written to be chanted alternately by the author and her nuns as a prophylactic against the invasion of their rough frieze habits by vermin:

Pues nos dais vestido nuevo,
   Rey celestial,
librad de la mala gente
   este sayal . . . . .

The examples of her verse here given are less dramatic than this, but it may truly and fairly be said that Spanish literature would be the poorer without them.

96. *Villancico:* "*¡Oh Hermosura que ecedéis . . . . !*"

The term villancico *is given to this poem, not very appropriately, by Santa Teresa herself (in a letter to her brother Lorenzo, dated January 2, 1577). It is clearly inspired by, if not directly imitated from, verse of a type found in the* Cancioneros (*Cf. Nos.* 40, 46). *The rhymes betray Santa Teresa's characteristic imperfections but both the thought and the language raise the poem to a considerably higher plane than that of her verses as a whole—indeed, were there not such unimpeachable testimony as to the authorship, one might have doubted its genuineness. In restraint and word-economy it is superior to her "Vivo sin vivir en mí . . . . ." and even this adheres closely to a well-marked tradition.*

¡Oh Hermosura que ecedéis
a todas las hermosuras!
Sin herir dolor hacéis,
y sin dolor deshacéis
el amor de las criaturas.

Oh ñudo que ansí juntáis
dos cosas tan desiguales,
no sé por qué os desatáis,
pues atado fuerza dais
a tener por bien los males.

Juntáis quien no tiene ser
con el Ser que no se acaba:
sin acabar acabáis,
sin tener que amar amáis,
engrandecéis vuestra nada.

97. "*Nada te turbe . . .*"

These nine five-syllabled lines, four of which, it will be observed, assonance in a-a, *were found in Santa Teresa's breviary after her death, and are often known, in their English version at least, as "St. Teresa's Bookmark." They show a remarkable economy of language: seldom, in any modern tongue, can more have been said in fewer words. But what makes them chiefly memorable is the simplicity of their expression and the underlying spirit of implicit trust in God.*

Nada te turbe,
nada te espante,
todo se pasa,
Dios no se muda,
la paciencia
todo lo alcanza ;
quien a Dios tiene
nada le falta :
sólo Dios basta.

98. *Villancico : " Pues el amor . . ."*

Here we have Santa Teresa at her most characteristic, in a genuine villancico *of the type familiar in English as the Christmas carol. Two shepherds, Pascual and Llorente, are celebrating the birth of the Christ-child. As is usual in this kind of poem, they know more about the theology of the Incarnation than far more learned people did for a long time afterwards, but such anachronisms only enhance the naïve charm of the lines and rob them of none of the emotion which lies so near the surface throughout and emerges in the refrain. The poem is evidently a dialogue between the two shepherds, but there is some little doubt, especially in the last stanza, exactly how the parts are divided. This each reader must decide for himself.*

Pues el amor
nos ha dado Dios,
ya no hay que temer,
muramos los dos.

Danos el Padre
a su único Hijo :
hoy viene al mundo
en un pobre cortijo.
¡ Oh, gran regocijo,
que ya el hombre es Dios !
No hay que temer,
muramos los dos.

Mira, Llorente,
qué fuerte amorío,
viene el inocente
a padecer frío;
deja un señorío,
en fin, como Dios.
Ya no hay que temer,
muramos los dos.

Pues ¿cómo, Pascual,
hizo esa franqueza,
que toma un sayal
dejando riqueza?
Mas quiere pobreza,
sigámosle nos;
pues ya viene hombre,
y *muramos los dos.*

Pues ¿qué le darán
por esta grandeza?
Grandes azotes
con mucha crueza.
Oh, qué gran tristeza
será para nos:
si esto es verdad,
muramos los dos.

Pues ¿cómo se atreven,
siendo Omnipotente?
Ha de ser muerto
de una mala gente.
Pues si eso es, Llorente,
hurtémosle nos.
—No ves que él lo quiere,
muramos los dos.

99. "*Mi gallejo, mira quién llama . . .*"

Another Christmas carol, the rustic naïveté of which is as attractive as are its flashes of genuine popular poetry. The speakers are apparently a shepherd and his boy, " keeping watch over their flocks by night"; in the second stanza the scene has shifted to the Bethlehem manger. The shepherd's description of the parentage of the Virgin Mary rather takes one's breath away, but is presumably intended, like the simile which follows, to be, not theological, but poetical.

Mi gallejo, mira quién llama.
—Ángeles son, que ya viene el alba.

Hame dado un gran zumbido
que parecía cantillana.
Mira, Bras, que ya es de día,
vamos a ver la zagala.

Mi gallejo, mira quién llama.
—Ángeles son, que ya viene el alba.

—¿ Es parienta del alcalde,
o quién es esta doncella ?
—Ella es hija de Dios Padre,
relumbra como una estrella.

Mi gallejo, mira quién llama.
—Ángeles son, que ya viene el alba.

ANONYMOUS

100. *Soneto : " No me mueve, mi Dios . . ."*

THE most famous sonnet of religious inspiration in Spanish literature, " No me mueve, mi Dios . . .", used to be attributed, on evidence no longer considered valid, to San Francisco Xavier : other writers credited with it are San Ignacio de Loyola, Fray Pedro de los Reyes and (perhaps the least unlikely of the four) Fray Miguel de Guevara. The attribution of the sonnet to Santa Teresa is fantastic, for, not only does she habitually use native measures, but her art never approaches this author's. Several commentators, on the other hand, have remarked on the similarity of this sonnet, in style, to those of Lope de Vega's *Rimas sacras*, and, if there were any direct evidence that he wrote it, that conclusion would be hard to resist.[1]

The primary appeal of the sonnet, of course, lies in its deep sincerity, but this is reflected, with unusual skill, in the language and versification. The key-note of the poem is the word *mueve*, the repetitions of which are like the strokes of a bell, slow and regular at first (ll. 1, 3, 5a), then quickening (ll. 5b, 7, 8, 9) as the poet warms to his theme. The same word binds the sestet to the octave.

The sincerity of the poem, again, is emphasized by the striking contrast between the motives enumerated in ll. 1-4 and the simple word *Tú* in l. 5 and also by the almost complete absence of epithets. A later age must have thought the bare nouns (" el cielo," " esa cruz," " tu cuerpo," " tus afrentas," " tu muerte," " tu amor ") highly inartistic.

The sestet, exquisitely musical though it is, will perhaps be thought inferior to the octave. The turn of sense, at the words " al fin", is well contrived, but the language recalls that of poems

[1] Cf. p. 710, below and E. Allison Peers : *Studies of the Spanish Mystics*, London, 1927-30, I, 202-3. A translation of the poem into English will be found on p. vi of the same volume.

of a very different kind, full of verbal refinements; "aunque" is an ugly and unpoetical word when it occurs three times in five lines; and the last line, instead of ending triumphantly as its theme demands, gives an impression of something like spent force.

No me mueve, mi Dios, para quererte
el cielo que me tienes prometido,
ni me mueve el infierno tan temido
para dejar por eso de ofenderte.

Tú me mueves, Señor; muéveme el verte
clavado en esa cruz y escarnecido;
muéveme el ver tu cuerpo tan herido;
muévenme tus afrentas y tu muerte.

Muévesme al tu amor en tal manera
que, aunque no hubiera cielo, yo te amara,
y, aunque no hubiera infierno, te temiera.

No me tienes que dar porque te quiera;
que, aunque cuanto espero no esperara,
lo mismo que te quiero te quisiera.[1]

[1] Of the variants quoted by Foulché-Delbosc (cf. p. 710, below), the following alone seem to have any significance: l. 3, el infierno merecido; l. 6, en una cruz; l. 7, ver tu pecho; l. 8, muévenme las angustias de tu muerte; l. 9, muéveme, en fin, tu amor, de tal manera; muévenme, o sumo bien, de tal manera.

GUTIERRE DE CETINA

*c.*1518-*c.*1554

CETINA, a soldier who fought in Italy and travelled in Mexico, was also a poet, largely Italian in his affinities, who produced sonnets by the hundred and poems of other kinds by the score, together with one single madrigal, of only ten lines, which has won its author more renown than all his other compositions put together. His verse is built round his loves for two ladies—an Italian countess whom he addresses as Amarillida, and a certain Dórida, whose identity he keeps a secret. He has little depth of thought ; but for delicacy of expression and sheer music few Spaniards, if any, have surpassed him.

101. *Madrigal*

In this, the ten-line lyric referred to above, the sound almost creates the sense : so satisfying is the poem as music that its meaning hardly matters. It might be called a theme (ll. 1-3) with variations (ll. 4-7) and coda (ll. 8-10). The coda (ll. 1, 9, it will be observed, are identical) both echoes and answers the question of the theme. Much of the charm of the poem is to be found in its light, delicate, almost playful air and in the extraordinary beauty of its melody. This, though in appearance natural, is achieved by a number of devices : the alternation of the five lines of seven syllables each with the five of eleven : aBBcDdCcaA ; *the echo-effects produced by the long and short lines rhyming in pairs ; the alliteration (ll. 3, 6, 7, 10) in that softest of consonants,* m ; *and the skilful repetition of vowels ("... miráis, miráis airados "; " miréis ... ira " " bellos ... quien os ..." ; " menos hermosos .... tormentos rabiosos.")*

Ojos claros, serenos,
si de un dulce mirar sois alabados,
¿ por qué, si me miráis, miráis airados ?

Si cuanto más piadosos,
más bellos parecéis a aquel que os mira,
no me miréis con ira
porque no parezcáis menos hermosos.
¡ Ay, tormentos rabiosos !
Ojos claros, serenos,
ya que así me miráis, miradme al menos.

102. *Madrigal*

Though both in form and in subject a companion-piece to "Ojos claros, serenos . . .", this madrigal is distinctly its inferior. The poet's intention is blurred; the imaginative sequence goes astray. The scheme, aBBcDdCcEE, *is that of "Ojos claros . . .", except for the latter's final* aA, *which, quite apart from the repetition of l. 1 as l. 9, is a more musical conception, though the* a (-ora), *and* e (-ores) *in this poem are almost identical. The medial rhymes and the alliterations in* m, *especially in the final couplet, will be noted: less happy, and introduced for no obvious purpose, are the alliterations in* p *and* b-v *of ll. 3-5. The concluding lines are a sad contrast with those of "Ojos claros . . ."; melodious though they are, they lack the others' delicate equilibrium. The latter poem is a series of scattered impressions; the former is a unity.*

No miréis más, señora,
con tan grande atención esa figura,
no os mate vuestra propia hermosura.
Huid, dama, la prueba
de lo que puede en vos la beldad vuestra.
Y no haga la nuestra
venganza de mi mal piadosa y nueva.
El triste caso os mueva
del mozo convertido entre las flores
en flor, muerto de amor de sus amores.

103. *Anacreóntica*

A pleasant and mellifluous little trifle, mediaeval in its use of assonance, in its metaphors and in its personification of love. The peculiar simplicity and directness of its language give it added distinction.

De tus rubios cabellos,
Dórida, ingrata mía,
hizo el Amor la cuerda
para el arco homicida.
" Ahora verás si burlas
de mi poder," decía ;
y, tomando una flecha,
quiso a mí dirigirla.
Yo le dije : " Muchacho,
arco y arpón retira ;
con esas nuevas armas
¿ quién hay que te resista ? "

104. *Soneto*

Cetina was not the most accomplished of sonneteers ; and both his occasional aciertos *and the familiar and frequently exaggerated devices which he employs must more often than not be credited to Petrarch. In this particular example some of the lines are over-packed, others stumble and others again reveal the difficulty which the poet found in the handling of his instrument. Once more the use of alliteration seems rather pointless. On the other hand, those who know Cetina only from his madrigals might be surprised at finding such emphatic and apparently sincere personal feeling, and one forgives him his flood of rhetorical questions for the sake of the glimpse which he gives into his personality.*

¡ Ay, sabrosa ilusión, sueño süave !
¿ Quién te ha enviado a mí ? ¿ Cómo viniste ?
¿ Por dónde entraste al alma, o qué le diste
a mi secreto por guardar la llave ?
¿ Quién pudo a mi dolor fiero, tan grave,
el remedio poner que tú pusiste ?
Si el ramo tinto en Lete en mí esparciste,
ten la mano al velar que no se acabe.
Bien conozco que duermo y que me engaño,
mientra envuelto en un bien falso, dudoso,
manifiesto mi mal se muestra cierto ;
pero, pues excusar no puedo un daño,
hazme sentir ¡ oh sueño piadoso !
antes durmiendo el bien que el mal despierto.

HERNANDO DE ACUÑA

*c.*1520–*c.*1585

ACUÑA, who belonged to the italianate group of Spanish poets, was, like Garcilaso de la Vega, a soldier and a courtier. A number of long works which he published during his lifetime have little originality and are remembered only by students; his name is perpetuated by a few lyrics which, like Boscán's, were published by his widow soon after his death.

105. *Soneto: Al Rey Nuestro Señor*

Here, as seldom in the sixteenth-century sonnet, we have the authentic trumpet-note. The triumphant finality of the line which closes the octave has made it famous: a cynic once said that there was more than a suggestion about it of the Trinity in Unity. The line which closes the sestet brings the sonnet to a magnificent close. On the other hand, we are all the time in an atmosphere of adulation, which occasionally, as in l. 4, becomes distinctly oppressive. The rhythm of the sonnet is not impeccable.

Ya se acerca, Señor, o es ya llegada
la edad gloriosa en que promete el cielo
una grey, y un pastor solo en el suelo,
por suerte a vuestros tiempos reservada;
ya tan alto principio en tal jornada
os muestra el fin de vuestro santo celo,
y anuncia al mundo para más consuelo
un Monarca, un Imperio y una Espada;
Ya el orbe de la tierra siente en parte
y espera en todo vuestra monarquía
conquistada por vos en justa guerra,
que a quien ha dado Cristo su estandarte,
dará el segundo más dichoso día
en que vencido el mar, venza la tierra.

JORGE DE MONTEMAYOR

c.1520-1561

MONTEMAYOR (more properly, Montemôr) was a Portuguese, and the famous author of the pastoral novel *Diana*, in which are interspersed many of his lyrics. In 1554 he published a *Cancionero* of his verses, and, four years later, an enlarged edition of it. He is at his best in short lyrics, written in short lines—always slight but also always charming.

106. *Villancico*

The opening lines of this song are famous in an adaptation a lo divino *beginning:*

Véante mis ojos,
dulce Jesús bueno.
Véante mis ojos,
muérame yo luego.

In 1571, these lines, sung by a young nun, Isabel de Jesús, in the parlour of her convent, sent Santa Teresa into an ecstasy.[1] *The play made by the song upon the theme of death-in-life as applied to human love is at best artificial and it was only when the mystics applied it to Divine love that it acquired reality. Here it expresses a frankly conventionalized emotion, acceptable enough in its pastoral setting, not least when given so tuneful and so markedly rhythmical an accompaniment.*

Véante mis ojos
y muérame yo luego,
dulce amor mío
y lo que yo más quiero.

[1] Cf. *Obras de Santa Teresa, ed.* P. Silverio de Santa Teresa, Burgos, 1915-24, II, 47, n. 3.

A trueque de verte
la muerte me es vida,
si fueres servida
mejora mi suerte :
que no será muerte
si en viéndote muero,
dulce amor mío,
y lo que yo más quiero.

¿ Dó está tu presencia ?
¿ Por qué no te veo ?
¡ Oh, cuánto un deseo
fatiga en ausencia !
Socorre, paciencia,
que yo desespero
por el amor mío,
y lo que yo más quiero.

LUIS DE CAMOENS
1524-1580

One of the greatest epic poets in world-history and also one of the greatest lyric poets in post-Renaissance Europe, the Portuguese Luis de Camoens (in Portuguese, Luiz de Camões) wrote a number of fine and varied poems in Spanish, two of which are given here as typical both of his mastery of Spanish technique and of his versatility.

107. *Soneto*

Here Camoens is an artist in Herreran Baroque, and his sonnet, in white and gold, studded with epithets evocative of light, is of a truly Herreran magnificence. The new element which he adds is a somewhat artificial symbolism, conscientiously interpreted for us in the sestet, and certainly no great addition to the poem's attractiveness.

El vaso reluciente y cristalino,
de ángeles agua clara y olorosa,
de blanca seda ornado y fresca rosa,
ligado con cabellos de oro fino,
bien claro parecía el don divino
labrado por la mano artificiosa
de aquella blanca ninfa, graciosa
más que el rubio lucero matutino.
Nel vaso vuestro cuerpo se afigura,
rajado de los blandos miembros bellos,
y en el agua vuestra ánima pura;
la seda es la blancura, y los cabellos
son las prisiones, y la ligadura
con que mi libertad fué asida de ellos.

108. *Mote*

But Camoens, as in this mote, *could be a popular poet as well as a cunning artificer. The girl and her receptive mother, the atmosphere of the sea and the appeal to the waves are all characteristic of its type, as, of course, is the metrical form also, while the* estribillo *is traditional. The melody—in the key, as it were, of* m (e.g., *ll. 1, 3-5, 9-12, 17-20, etc.)—suggests the murmur and ripple of the waves. Like Góngora (pp. 316-7), Camoens excelled in the sixteenth-century equivalent of the* mester de joglaría *and of the* mester de clerecía *as well.*

Irme quiero, madre,
a aquella galera,
con el marinero,
a ser marinera.

Madre, si me fuere,
dó quiera que vó,
no lo quiero yo,
que el Amor lo quiere.
Aquel niño fiero
hace que me muera
por un marinero
a ser marinera.

El que todo puede,
madre, no podrá,
pues el alma va,
que el cuerpo se quede.
Con él por quien muero
voy, porque no muera ;
que, si es marinero,
seré marinera.

Es tirana ley
del niño Señor,
que por un amor
se deseche un Rey.
Pues desta manera
quiero irme, quiero,
por un marinero
a ser marinera.

Decid, ondas, ¿ cuándo
vistes vos doncella,
siendo tierna y bella,
andar navegando ?
Mas ¿ qué no se espera
de aquel niño fiero ?
Vea yo quien quiero :
sea marinera.

JUAN DE TIMONEDA

*d.*1583

THIS Valencian is remembered by the historian chiefly as an early and not very original playwright who wrote comedies and farces both in prose and in verse. Neither in the majority of these nor in his anecdotal tales would one suspect him of being a poet and such graceful lyrics as those printed below come as a welcome surprise.

109. "*Veo las ovejas. . . .*"

A charming trifle: though the author does nothing but repeat the same idea, and a stereotyped idea at that, he is a fellow of most excellent fancy and gives the impression of having command of an infinity of variations. The vitality of movement of the poem and the freshness of its open-air imagery hardly need emphasis.

Veo las ovejas
orillas del mar,
no veo el paster
que me hace penar.

Las ovejas veo
orillas del río,
no ve mi deseo
el dulce amor mío.
Miro en derredor
del fresco pinar,
no veo el pastor
que me hace penar.

Los perros y el manso
veo, y su bardina,
mi gloria y descanso,
no veo mezquina.
Por bien qu'el amor
me esfuerza a mirar
no veo el pastor
que me hace penar.

Veo muy esenta
su choza sombría,
sin ver quien sustenta
aquesta alma mía.
Veo mi dolor
crecer y menguar,
no veo el pastor
que me hace penar.

110. "*Hermosura no la he. . . .*"

For a poet to react against physical beauty is rare and the playful bluntness with which Timoneda does this here is altogether delightful. Note, as in Encina (p. 160), the reiterated rhyme, which throws the emphasis forward on to the refrain.

Hermosura no la he.
La gracia Dios me la dé.

Si quiso naturaleza
no dotarme en gentileza,
hame dotado en firmeza
con la cual proclamaré :
la gracia Dios me la dé.

Ser la persona graciosa
es una muy gentil cosa
muy más que no ser hermosa,
y así contino diré :
la gracia Dios me la dé.

Bien sé que mucha hermosura
a veces trae procura
de soberbia y de locura,
por do siempre cantaré :
la gracia Dios me la dé.

FRAY LUIS DE LEÓN

1527-1591

THE life of the Augustinian Fray Luis de León is intimately connected with the University of Salamanca, where he was a professor for close upon thirty years. During his stormy career there, punctuated by numerous enmities and broken by a four-year spell in a prison of the Inquisition, he won a reputation as theologian, philosopher and Biblical critic; but this has long since faded before his more lasting fame as ascetic, mystic and poet. Current views notwithstanding, he is less of a mystic in his verse than in his prose, and even here other tendencies and trends of thought conflict with mystical ideals, which one often feels might gain complete ascendancy over him if he would let them.

Fray Luis' output in verse is not large: rather more than a score of original poems—none of them long—and less than twice that number of translations. Both in inspiration and in technique it tends to be unequal. Some of his lines are almost flung together; his thought can be confused; and even his images, usually so penetrating and so vivid, sometimes lack power. But his general level is high and his finest moments are hardly surpassable: an occasional dimness and insipidity only emphasize by contrast the poetic radiance and the thrusts of irresistible lyrical energy which are his greatest gifts to Spanish literature. His deep sincerity, his ardent desires, his warm affections shine through all his verse and their effect is increased by the simplicity of his language and style. This simplicity greatly enhances his appeal, though at the first contact one may be more attracted by his rich and satisfying Nature imagery and by the "soaring magnificence"[1] of his *saltos líricos*, in which, with some sudden apostrophe or vibrant imperative, he seems to cleave the air.

A less obvious, but no less real, attraction in Luis de León is the light and shade in his poetry. Now he is restless and dynamic,

[1] A. F. G. Bell: *Luis de Leon*, Oxford, 1925, p. 227.

now contented and serene; now his inspiration is pagan, now Christian; now his mood is that of the Old Testament, now that of the New; now his spirit is at peace on earth, now it mounts swiftly to Heaven. These contrasts are the more effective for being suggested rather than openly expressed. Often the poet will pass almost imperceptibly from one manner to another: his scansion may occasionally be at fault, but his intuition, never.

III. *Vida retirada*

This felicitously phrased and frequently quoted poem, probably written early in its author's life, is characteristic only of one phase of his thought and that a relatively superficial one. Like a famous passage in Garcilaso de la Vega's Second Eclogue, it is clearly inspired by Horace's ode "Beatus ille. . . .": none the less it is as subjective in spirit as in form and may suitably be read with the introductory paragraphs to each of the three books of the author's Nombres de Cristo, *which describe the "seguro puerto" that he found at La Flecha, on the banks of the river Tormes. Not everyone will admire the poem's somewhat Epicurean conclusion and there are several phrases in it which would strike most readers as discordant. But its beauty of language, and above all its tone of grave tranquillity, give it a very high place in Spanish poetry. Its greatest moment is perhaps the beginning of the fifth stanza, where the threefold apostrophe soars unexpectedly skywards from the dead level of the Horatian plain.*

¡Qué descansada vida
la del que huye el mundanal ruído,
y sigue la escondida
senda por donde han ido
los pocos sabios que en el mundo han sido!

Que no le enturbia el pecho
de los soberbios grandes el estado,
ni del dorado techo
se admira, fabricado
del sabio Moro, en jaspes sustentado.

No cura si la fama
canta con voz su nombre pregonera,
ni cura si encarama
la lengua lisonjera
lo que condena la verdad sincera.

¿ Qué presta a mi contento
si soy del vano dedo señalado ?
¿ si en busca deste viento
ando desalentado,
con ansias vivas, con mortal cuidado ?

¡ Oh monte ! ¡ oh fuente ! ¡ oh río !
¡ oh secreto seguro deleitoso !
Roto casi el navío,
a vuestro almo reposo
huyo de aqueste mar tempestuoso.

Un no rompido sueño,
un día puro, alegre, libre quiero ;
no quiero ver el ceño
vanamente severo
de a quien la sangre ensalza o el dinero.

Despiértenme las aves
con su cantar sabroso no aprendido ;
no los cuidados graves
de que es siempre seguido
el que al ajeno arbitrio está atenido.

Vivir quiero conmigo,
gozar quiero del bien que debo al cielo
a solas sin testigo,
libre de amor, de celo,
de odio, de esperanzas, de recelo.

Del monte en la ladera
por mi mano plantado tengo un huerto,
que con la primavera
de bella flor cubierto
ya muestra en esperanza el fruto cierto.

Y como codiciosa
por ver y acrecentar su hermosura,
desde la cumbre airosa
una fontana pura
hasta llegar corriendo se apresura.

Y luego sosegada
el paso entre los árboles torciendo,
el suelo de pasada
de verdura vistiendo
y con diversas flores va esparciendo.

El aire el huerto orea,
y ofrece mil olores al sentido:
los árboles menea
con un manso ruído
que del oro y del cetro pone olvido.

Ténganse su tesoro
los que de un falso leño se confían;
no es mío ver el lloro
de los que desconfían
cuando el Cierzo y el Ábrego porfían.

La combatida antena
cruje, y en ciega noche el claro día
se torna, al cielo suena
confusa vocería,
y la mar enriquecen a porfía.

A mí una pobrecilla
mesa de amable paz bien abastada
me basta, y la vajilla
de fino oro labrada
sea de quien la mar no teme airada.

Y mientras miserable-
mente se están los otros abrasando
con sed insaciable
del peligroso mando,
tendido yo a la sombra esté cantando.

A la sombra tendido,
de hiedra y lauro eterno coronado,
puesto el atento oído
al son dulce acordado,
del plectro sabiamente meneado.

112. *A Francisco Salinas*[1]

Salinas, the Professor of Music at Salamanca University, was about a dozen years older than Fray Luis and one of his most intimate friends. This is the greatest poem ever written in Spanish on music and it is a pity, in my view, that some critics have interpreted it as symbolical—a proceeding partly due to a stanza found in some manuscripts only and probably an interpolation made with a definite purpose, which runs as follows:

Ve cómo el gran maestro
a aquesta inmensa cítara aplicado,
con movimiento diestro
produce el son sagrado,
con que este eterno templo es sustentado.

To me, though it uses some of the familiar phrases of mysticism—absorption, rapture, life-giving death—the poem means precisely what it says, and no more. Every music-lover will recognize in it a moving attempt to describe genuine sensations, with a restrained emotion, which, particularly in the last four stanzas, reaches a very high level. A detailed analysis will also reveal one of Luis de León's most remarkable gifts—his skill in canalizing the reader's sensations and carrying them along with him to a climax. Beside such an achievement, the poet's obvious and not over-successful experiments in alliteration (e.g., Stanzas 1, 7, 9) strike one as activities on which his genius is wasted.

El aire se serena
y viste de hermosura y luz no usada,
Salinas, cuando suena
la música extremada
por vuestra sabia mano gobernada.

[1] A critical appreciation of this poem by T. W. Keeble will be found in *B.S.S.*, 1945, XXII, 91-3.

A cuyo son divino
el alma que en olvido está sumida
torna a cobrar el tino
y memoria perdida
de su origen primera esclarecida.

Y como se conoce,
en suerte y pensamientos se mejora:
el oro desconoce
que el vulgo vil adora,
la belleza caduca engañadora.

Traspasa el aire todo
hasta llegar a la más alta esfera,
y oye allí otro modo
de no perecedera
música, que es la fuente y la primera.

Y como está compuesta
de números concordes, luego envía
consonante respuesta,
y entre ambas a porfía
se mezcla una dulcísima harmonía.

Aquí la alma navega
por un mar de dulzura, y finalmente
en él así se anega,
que ningún accidente
extraño o peregrino oye o siente.

¡ Oh desmayo dichoso!
¡ oh muerte que das vida! ¡ oh dulce olvido!
¡ durase en tu reposo
sin ser restituído
jamás aqueste bajo y vil sentido.

A este bien os llamo,
gloria del Apolíneo sacro coro,
amigos a quien amo
sobre todo tesoro,
que todo lo visible es triste lloro.

¡ Oh ! suene de contino,
Salinas, vuestro son en mis oídos,
por quien al bien divino
despiertan los sentidos,
quedando a lo demás adormecidos.

113. *A Diego Olarte : Noche serena*

Olarte (some manuscripts write Loarte or Oloarte) was another of Fray Luis' older friends, whose name, unlike that of the better known Salinas, would probably, but for this magnificent poem, have been forgotten. In its sensitiveness to Nature it has been termed Wordsworthian, but it is much more than that : lovely indeed as is its opening picture of the starry sky, it is when the poet rises from the earthly sphere to the heavenly ("¡ Oh ! despertad, mortales. . . .") that the depths in him call to the depths in us. The three final stanzas, which mark the crisis of his emotion, throb and ring with an eloquence that even he never surpassed.

This is one of the poems frequently, and quite inaccurately, called mystical. Certainly, its attitude of contempt for worldliness and its exhortation to spiritual ambition are found in the mystics, while the " ansia ardiente " of l. 7 recalls San Juan de la Cruz's " con ansias en amores inflamada " (p. 266). But there the resemblance ends. The God of the poem is not immanent, but transcendent ; the Heaven, for all its loveliness, is remote : we are farther from the mystical ideal of Union at the end than at the beginning. Spiritual the poem is in a high degree, but no more.

Cuando contemplo el cielo
de innumerables luces adornado,
y miro hacia el suelo
de noche rodeado,
en sueño y en olvido sepultado ;

el amor y la pena
despiertan en mi pecho un ansia ardiente ;
despiden larga vena
los ojos hechos fuente,
Olarte, y digo al fin con voz doliente :

Morada de grandeza,
templo de claridad y hermosura,
el alma que a tu alteza
nació, ¿ qué desventura
la tiene en esta cárcel baja, escura?

¿ Qué mortal desatino
de la verdad aleja así el sentido,
que, de tu bien divino
olvidado, perdido,
sigue la vana sombra, el bien fingido ?

El hombre está entregado
al sueño, de su suerte no cuidando,
y con paso callado
el cielo vueltas dando
las horas del vivir le va hurtando.

¡ Oh ! despertad, mortales,
mirad con atención en vuestro daño.
¿ Las almas inmortales
hechas a bien tamaño
podrán vivir de sombras y de engaño ?

¡ Ay ! levantad los ojos
a aquesta celestial eterna esfera ;
burlaréis los antojos
de aquesa lisonjera
vida, con cuanto teme y cuanto espera.

¿ Es más que un breve punto
el bajo y torpe suelo, comparado
con ese gran trasunto
do vive mejorado
lo que es, lo que será, lo que ha pasado ?

Quien mira el gran concierto
de aquestos resplandores eternales,
su movimiento cierto,
sus pasos desiguales
y en proporción concorde tan iguales :

la luna cómo mueve
la plateada rueda, y va en pos della
la luz do el saber llueve,
y la graciosa estrella
de Amor le sigue reluciente y bella:

y cómo otro camino
prosigue el sanguinoso Marte airado,
y el Júpiter benino
de bienes mil cercado
serena el cielo con su rayo amado:

rodéase en la cumbre
Saturno, padre de los siglos de oro;
tras él la muchedumbre
del reluciente coro
su luz va repartiendo y su tesoro:

¿Quién es el que esto mira,
y precia la bajeza de la tierra,
y no gime y suspira,
y rompe lo que encierra
el alma, y destos bienes la destierra?

Aquí vive el contento,
aquí reina la paz, aquí asentado
en rico y alto asiento
está el Amor sagrado,
de glorias y deleites rodeado.

Inmensa hermosura
aquí se muestra toda, y resplandece
clarísima luz pura,
que jamás anochece;
eterna primavera aquí florece.

¡Oh campos verdaderos!
¡oh prados con verdad frescos y amenos!
¡riquísimos mineros!
¡oh deleitosos senos,
repuestos valles de mil bienes llenos!

114. *A Felipe Ruiz*

Here again we find spirituality, this time together with a strong infusion of intellectualism and without a trace of mysticism. The Heaven pictured by Fray Luis to his friend, Felipe Ruiz de la Torre y Mota (a poet and scholar of whom very little is known), is a " Heaven of the intellect " : when the poet arrives there it will be as an inquisitive child of the Renaissance, and his main concern will be to see *and* know *the reason for everything. The key-words to the poem are* veré *and* ¿ por qué ? *There is less imaginative and more descriptive force here than in Fray Luis' other great poems and it is significant that three stanzas in the middle of it (8-10) are imitated from Vergil's First Georgic (ll. 316-34). The* moradas *of the final stanza may be situated in the " highest sphere " known to Luis de León, but Santa Teresa knew of* moradas *far higher.*

¿ Cuándo será que pueda
libre desta prisión volar al cielo,
Felipe, y en la rueda
que huye más del suelo
contemplar la verdad pura sin duelo ?
Allí a mi vida junto
en luz resplandeciente convertido
veré distinto y junto
lo que es y lo que ha sido
y su principio propio y escondido.
Entonces veré cómo
la soberana mano echó el cimiento
tan a nivel y plomo,
do estable y firme asiento
posee el pesadísimo elemento.
Veré las inmortales
columnas do la tierra está fundada,
las lindes y señales
con que a la mar hinchada
la Providencia tiene aprisionada.
Por qué tiembla la tierra,
por qué las hondas mares se embravecen :
dó sale a mover guerra
el Cierzo, y por qué crecen
las aguas del Océano y descrecen :

de dó manan las fuentes;
quién ceba y quién bastece de los ríos
las perpetuas corrientes;
de los helados fríos
veré las causas, y de los estíos;

las soberanas aguas
del aire en la región quién las sostiene;
de los rayos las fraguas;
dó los tesoros tiene
de nieve Dios, y el trueno dónde viene.

¿No ves cuando acontece
turbarse el aire todo en el verano?
El día se ennegrece,
sopla el Gallego insano,
y sube hasta el cielo el polvo vano.

Y entre las nubes mueve
su carro Dios, ligero y reluciente;
horrible son conmueve,
relumbra fuego ardiente,
treme la tierra, humíllase la gente.

La lluvia baña el techo,
envían largos ríos los collados:
su trabajo deshecho,
los campos anegados
miran los labradores espantados.

Y de allí levantado
veré los movimientos celestiales,
así el arrebatado
como los naturales,
la causa de los hados, las señales.

Quién rige las estrellas
veré, y quién las enciende con hermosas
y eficaces centellas;
por qué están las dos Osas,
de bañarse en la mar siempre medrosas.

Veré este fuego eterno,
fuente de vida y luz dó se mantiene;
y por qué en el invierno
tan presuroso viene,
quién en las noches largas le detiene.

Veré sin movimiento
en la más alta esfera las moradas
del gozo y del contento,
de oro y luz labradas,
de espíritus dichosos habitadas.

115. *De la Vida del Cielo*

While neither the longest nor the most impressive of the poems, this is, to my mind, the most nearly perfect. The initial evocation of the realms of light; the skilful appeals to sense; the picture of the Good Shepherd, with its single touch of vivid colour; the simple, yet slightly and attractively stylized, description of the progress to the mountain; the aptness and vividness of the phraseology of the whole poem—all these are memorable traits. But the chief beauty is the wonderful apostrophe: "¡Oh son! ¡oh voz! . . .", which crowns the poem and incidentally contains the only passage descriptive of strictly mystical union in the whole of Fray Luis' verse. This stanza is somewhat marred by the weakness of the latter part of the stanza following, though this is exclusively a weakness of form. Aubrey Bell has suggested that in "En la Ascensión", supposed to have been written in the Inquisition prison, the poet is working from his recollection of some painting[1] *: the suggestion seems even apter here.*

Alma región luciente,
prado de bienandanza, que ni al hielo
ni con el rayo ardiente
fallece, fértil suelo,
producidor eterno de consuelo:

de púrpura y de nieve
florida la cabeza coronado,
a dulces pastos mueve
sin honda ni cayado,
el buen Pastor en ti su hato amado.

[1] *Modern Language Review*, 1926, XXI, 172.

Él va, y en pos dichosas
le siguen sus ovejas do las pace
con inmortales rosas,
con flor que siempre nace,
y cuanto más se goza más renace.

Ya dentro a la montaña
del alto bien las guía ; ya en la vena
del gozo fiel las baña,
y les da mesa llena,
Pastor y pasto él solo y suerte buena.

Y de su esfera cuando
la cumbre toca altísimo subido
el sol, él sesteando
de su hato ceñido
con dulce son deleita el santo oído.

Toca el rabel sonoro,
y el inmortal dulzor al alma pasa,
con que envilece el oro,
y ardiendo se traspasa
y lanza en aquel bien libre de tasa.

¡ Oh son ! ¡ oh voz ! ¡ Siquiera
pequeña parte alguna descendiese
en mi sentido, y fuera
de sí el alma pusiese
y toda en ti, oh Amor, la convirtiese !

Conocería dónde
sesteas, dulce Esposo, y desatada
desta prisión adonde
padece, a tu manada
viviera junta, sin vagar errada.

116. *En la Ascensión*

Though there is substance in the criticism that the elegiac tone of this poem is false to the spirit of the Gospel story (" They . . . returned to Jerusalem with great joy " : St. Luke xxiv, 52), it is in all other respects admirable. The author's normal objectivity (to which his frequent use of the yo *must not blind us) becomes positively plastic :*

" one seems to see and hear the upward sweep of wings as in El Greco's Assumption and Giotto's Ascension."[1] *The most surprising feature of the poem, its unconventional, almost conversational opening " ¿ Y dejas. . . . ? ", suggests a comment or a reflection on turning away from such a picture as has been postulated above. The elegiac level of the poem, considered without relation to the Biblical narrative, is very high. Though it palpitates with emotion, it is marred by little conventionality or hyperbole and both imagination and feeling are held in check with masterly restraint. The endings of his poems are not Luis de León's strongest point, but this one, with its heart-wrung antithesis and the " dying fall " of its last line,*

¡ cuán rica tú te alejas !
¡ cuán pobres y cuán ciegos, ay, nos dejas !

is particularly lovely.

¿ Y dejas, Pastor santo,
tu grey en este valle hondo, escuro,
con soledad y llanto ;
y tú, rompiendo el puro
aire, te vas al inmortal seguro ?
¿ Los antes bienhadados,
y los agora tristes y afligidos,
a tus pechos criados,
de ti desposeídos,
a dó convertirán ya sus sentidos ?
¿ Qué mirarán los ojos
que vieron de tu rostro la hermosura,
que no les sea enojos ?
quien oyó tu dulzura
¿ qué no tendrá por sordo y desventura ?
¿ Aqueste mar turbado,
quién le pondrá ya freno ? ¿ quién concierto
al viento fiero, airado ?
¿ estando tú encubierto,
qué norte guiará la nave al puerto ?
¡ Ay ! nube envidïosa
aun deste breve gozo ¿ qué te aquejas ?
¿ dó vuelas presurosa ?
¡ cuán rica tú te alejas !
¡ cuán pobres y cuán ciegos, ay, nos dejas !

[1] *Ibid.*

BALTASAR DEL ALCÁZAR
1530-1606

A TALENTED Sevilian, who threw off light verses as a recreation with an ease rarely equalled even by Spaniards, Alcázar stands quite apart from schools and tendencies, unless his *españolismo* can be said to range him unconsciously on the side of the anti-italianizers. It never occurred to him to publish his verse, and had not his friend Pacheco, on every visit to him, " written something of what he had stored in the treasury of his felicitous memory,"[1] it would probably all have been lost. Little need be said about these poems —they speak for themselves. Wit, humour and irony play about them like the rays of their author's merry and sunny disposition; and such is their facility that one can imagine them tripping off his tongue and the painter-poet writing for dear life lest he should lose anything. Well does Alcázar merit the latter part of Jáuregui's tribute: " no sólo . . . superior a todos, sino entre todos singular."[2]

117. *Cena jocosa*

This sprightly narrative, with its unexpectedly abrupt ending, is a classic example of Alcázar's humorous style. In Rodríguez Marín's edition of his works may be read a somewhat shorter and in other ways different verson, entitled " La Cena ".[3]

En Jaén, donde resido,
vive don Lope de Sosa,
y diréte, Inés, la cosa
más brava dél que has oído.

[1] *Poesías de Baltasar del Alcázar.* Ed. de la Real Academia Española. Madrid, 1910, pp. lvi-lvii.

[2] *Op. cit.*, p. lxxxiii.

[3] *Op. cit.*, pp. 81-4.

Tenía este caballero
un criado portugués—
Pero cenemos, Inés,
si te parece, primero.

La mesa tenemos puesta ;
lo que se ha cenar, junto ;
las tazas y el vino, a punto :
falta comenzar la fiesta.

Rebana pan. Bueno está.
La ensaladilla es del cielo ;
y el salpicón, con su ajuelo,
¿ no miras qué tufo da ?

Comienza el vinillo nuevo
y échale la bendición :
yo tengo por devoción
de santiguar lo que bebo.

Franco fué, Inés, ese toque ;
pero arrójame la bota ;
vale un florín cada gota
deste vinillo haloque.

¿ De qué taberna se trajo ?
Mas ya : de la del cantillo ;
diez y seis vale el cuartillo ;
no tiene vino más bajo.

Por Nuestro Señor, que es mina
la taberna de Alcocer ;
grande consuelo es tener
la taberna por vecina.

Si es o no invención moderna,
vive Dios, que no lo sé ;
pero delicada fué
la invención de la taberna.

Porque allí llego sediento,
pido vino de lo nuevo,
mídenlo, dánmelo, bebo,
págolo y voime contento.

Esto, Inés, ello se alaba ;
no es menester alaballo ;
sola una falta le hallo :
que con la priesa se acaba.

La ensalada y salpicón
hizo fin ; ¿ qué viene ahora ?
La morcilla. ¡ Oh, gran señora,
digna de veneración !

¡ Qué oronda viene y qué bella !
¡ Qué través y enjundias tiene !
Paréceme, Inés, que viene
para que demos en ella.

Pues ¡ sus !, encójase y entre,
que es algo estrecho el camino.
No eches agua, Inés, al vino,
no se escandalice el vientre.

Echa de lo trasaniejo,
porque con más gusto comas :
Dios te salve, que así tomas,
como sabia, mi consejo.

Mas di : ¿ no adoras y precias
la morcilla ilustre y rica ?
¡ Como la traidora pica !
Tal debe tener especias.

¡ Qué llena está de piñones !
Morcilla de cortesanos,
y asada por esas manos,
hechas a cebar lechones.

¡ Vive Dios, que se podía
poner al lado del Rey !
Puerco, Inés, a toda ley,
que hinche tripa vacía.

El corazón me revienta
de placer. No sé de ti
cómo te va. Yo, por mí,
sospecho que estás contenta.

Alegre estoy, vive Dios.
Mas oye un punto sutil:
¿No pusiste allí un candil?
¿Cómo remanecen dos?

Pero son preguntas viles;
ya sé lo que puede ser:
con este negro beber
se acrecientan los candiles.

Probemos lo del pichel.
¡Alto licor celestial!
No es el haloquillo tal,
ni tiene que ver con él.

¡Qué suavidad! ¡Qué clareza!
¡Qué rancio gusto y olor!
¡Qué paladar! ¡Qué color,
todo con tanta fineza!

Mas el queso sale a plaza.
la moradilla va entrando,
y ambos vienen preguntando
por el pichel y la taza.

Prueba el queso, que es extremo:
el de Pinto no le iguala.
Pues la aceituna no es mala:
bien puede bogar su remo.

Pues haz, Inés, lo que sueles:
daca de la bota llena
seis tragos. Hecha es la cena:
levántense los manteles.

Ya que, Inés, hemos cenado
tan bien y con tanto gusto,
parece que será justo
volver al cuento pasado.

Pues sabrás, Inés hermana,
que el portugués cayó enfermo—
Las once dan: yo me duermo:
quédese para mañana.

118. *Modo de vivir en la vejez*

This delightful piece of fun, given in Rodríguez Marín's edition under the title "A Francisco Sarmiento", illustrates not only the quiet, almost solemn, side of Alcázar's humour, but also the extraordinary facility of his style, which flows as readily as prose and yet as mellifluously as the verse of much greater writers.

Deseáis, señor Sarmiento,
saber en estos mis años,
sujetos a tantos daños,
cómo me porto y sustento.

Yo os lo diré en brevedad,
porque la historia es bien breve,
y el daros gusto se os debe
con toda puntualidad.

Salido el sol por Oriente
de rayos acompañado,
me dan un güevo pasado
por agua, blando y caliente,

Con dos tragos del que suelo
llamar yo néctar divino,
y a quien otros llaman vino
porque nos vino del cielo.

Cuando el luminoso vaso
toca en la meridional,
distando por un igual
del Oriente y del Ocaso,

me dan, asada y cocida,
de una gruesa y gentil ave,
con tres veces del süave
licor que alegra la vida.

Después que, cayendo, viene
a dar en el Mar hesperio,
desamparando el imperio
que en nuestro horizonte tiene,

me suelen dar a comer
tostadas en vino mulso,
que el debilitado pulso
restituyen en su ser.

Luego me cierran la puerta
y me entrego al dulce sueño ;
dormido soy de otro dueño :
no sé de mí cosa cierta.

Hasta que, habiendo sol nuevo,
me cuentan cómo he dormido,
y así, de nuevo les pido
que me den néctar y güevo.

Ser vieja la casa es esto ;
veo que se va cayendo ;
voile puntales poniendo,
porque no caiga tan presto.

Mas todo es vano artificio :
que presto dicen mis males
han de faltar los puntales
y allanarse el edificio.

119. *Canción*

" Could not Alcázar write exquisite songs ? " the reader of the foregoing extract may enquire. Indeed he could : here is a canción, *not perhaps as musical as one of the madrigals of his friend the " gran Cetina " (Poesías, etc., p. 173), but at least a notable combination of vivacity and melody. The echo-effect of the short lines (3, 5, 10, 12) is one which the author exploited more openly in other pieces (e.g., " Discurso de unos cuernos averiguados por la hermosa Eco ") and to which, as other writers were to find, Spanish particularly lends itself.*

Aquí, suspiro, te espero :
corre y dile a mi señora
que ya es hora
que mande a su despensero
que me abra,
pues que me dió la palabra
de que seré yo el primero.

Y que éste es tiempo oportuno
de recogerme a su centro,
sin encuentro
de otro opositor alguno,
y, en efeto,
que se luzga, y le prometo
que ha ya tres meses que ayuno.

120. *Epigramas*

Alcázar was also a successful epigrammatist. In the few examples of his skill in this style which follow, it will be noted that his humour takes on a cynical tinge, which reappears long afterwards in Campoamor, that sometimes it is more forced and heavy than elsewhere and that he does not scruple to make a target of physical disability.

A DOS CORCOVADOS

Contemplaba un corcovado
la corcova del vecino,
teniéndose por divino
y al otro por desdichado.

Porque lo que se usa más
es ver ajenos defectos;
tenerse por más perfectos;
traer su corcova atrás.

EPITAFIO A UNA DAMA MUY DELGADA

Yace en esta losa dura
una mujer tan delgada,
que en la vaina de una espada
se trajo a la sepultura.

Aquí al huésped notifique
dura punta o polvo leve
que al pasar no se la lleve,
o al pisarla no se pique.

"CIELO SON TUS OJOS. . . ."

Cielo son tus ojos, Ana ;
cielo dispuesto a llover,
pues siempre suelen tener
nubes, a tarde y mañana,

Relámpagos, agua y nieve,
con perpetuo desconsuelo.
Si Dios no tiene otro cielo,
nunca Dios allá me lleve.

DEFINICIÓN DE UN POETA

Si es poeta el ser ladrón,
más poeta sois que Caco ;
que Horacio no fué tan flaco,
ni Ovidio fué más nasón.

A UNA DAMA MUY MALDICIENTE Y ENFERMA DEL PECHO

Del pecho se queja loca
Leonor, y, a lo que sospecho,
nunca tendrá bueno el pecho
quien tan mal guarda la boca.

ALONSO DE ERCILLA

1533-1594

ERCILLA is remembered as the author of *La Araucana*, the best of a large number of epics, most of them of but slight value as literature, which during the latter part of the sixteenth century were evoked by the exploits of Spain in the New World. It is a huge work of thirty-seven cantos, in *octavas reales*, which appeared at intervals between 1569 and 1590, and was begun a good deal earlier. The main narrative, describing the rebellion of the Araucanian Indians against their conquerors, is diversified by numerous digressions; but about the poem as a whole there is a sense of reality not wholly attributable to its having been written—partly in America—by one who had himself taken part in such scenes as he pictures. Ercilla had a gift for vivid description: true, in so long a poem, as in almost every post-mediaeval epic, there are dreary wastes which it is easier to skip over than to traverse, but the purple patches more than make up for them. The *Araucana* is a book into which one can dip with delight—and dip again and again.

121. *La Araucana*

(*Extract*)

. . . . No sabré encarecer nuestra altiveza,
los ánimos briosos y lozanos,
la esperanza de bienes y riqueza,
las vanas trazas y discursos vanos:
el cerro, el monte, el risco y la aspereza
eran caminos fáciles y llanos,
y el peligro y trabajo exorbitante,
no osaban ya ponérsenos delante.

Íbamos sin cuidar de bastimentos
por cumbres, valles hondos, cordilleras,
fabricando en los llanos pensamientos,
máquinas levantadas y quimeras.
Así ufanos, alegres y contentos
pasamos tres jornadas, las primeras ;
pero a la cuarta, al tramontar del día,
se nos huyó la mentirosa guía.

El mal indicio, la sospecha cierta,
los ánimos turbó más esforzados,
viendo la falsa trama descubierta,
y los trabajos ásperos doblados ;
mas, aunque sin camino y en desierta
tierra, del gran peligro amenazados,
y la hambre y fatiga todo junto
no pudo detenernos sólo un punto.

Pasamos adelante, descubriendo
siempre más arcabucos y breñales,
la cerrada espesura y paso abriendo
con hachas, con machetes y destrales :
otros con pico y azadón rompiendo
las peñas y arraigados matorrales,
do el caballo hostigado y receloso
afírmase seguro el pie medroso.

Nunca con tanto estorbo a los humanos
quiso impedir el paso la natura,
y que así de los cielos soberanos
los árboles midiesen el altura :
ni entre tantos peñascos y pantanos
mezcló tanta maleza y espesura
como en este camino defendido,
de zarzas, breñas y árboles tejido.

También el cielo en contra conjurado,
la escasa y turbia luz nos encubría,
de espesas nubes lóbregas cerrado,
volviendo en tenebrosa noche el día :

y de granizo y tempestad cargado,
con tal furor el paso defendía
que era mayor del cielo ya la guerra
que el trabajo y peligro de la tierra.

Unos presto socorro demandaban
en las hondas malezas sepultados,
otros ¡ ayuda ! ¡ ayuda ! voceaban,
en húmidos pantanos atascados,
otros iban trepando, otros rodaban,
los pies, manos y rostro desollados,
oyendo aquí y allí voces en vano,
sin poderse ayudar ni dar la mano.

Era lástima oír los alaridos,
ver los impedimentos y embarazos,
los caballos sin ánimo caídos,
destrozados los pies, rotos los brazos.
Nuestros sencillos débiles vestidos
quedaban por las zarzas a pedazos,
descalzos y desnudos, sólo armados,
en sangre, lodo y en sudor bañados.

Y demás del trabajo incomportable,
faltando ya el refresco y bastimento,
la aquejadora hambre miserable
las cuerdas apretaba del tormento ;
y el bien dudoso y daño indubitable
desmayaba la fuerza y el aliento,
cortando un dejativo sudor frío
de los cansados miembros todo el brío.

Pero luego también considerando
la gloria que el trabajo aseguraba,
el corazón, los miembros reforzando,
cualquier dificultad menospreciaba ;
y los fuertes opuestos contrastando,
todo lo por venir facilitaba ;
que el valor más se muestra y se parece
cuando la fuerza de contrarios crece.

Así, pues, nuestro ejército rompiendo,
de sólo la esperanza alimentado,
pasaba a puros brazos descubriendo
el encubierto cielo deseado.
Íbanse ya las breñas destejiendo,
y el bosque de los árboles cerrado
desviando sus ramas intrincadas,
nos daban paso y fáciles entradas.

Ya por aquella parte, ya por ésta,
la entrada de la luz desocupando,
el yerto risco y empinada cuesta
iban sus altas cumbres allanando:
la espesa y congelada niebla opuesta,
el grueso vapor húmido exhalando,
así se adelgazaba y esparcía,
que penetrar la vista ya podía.

Siete días perdidos anduvimos
abriendo a hierro el impedido paso,
que en todo aquel discurso no tuvimos
do poder reclinar el cuerpo laso.
Al fin una mañana descubrimos
de Ancud el espacioso y fértil raso,
y al pie del monte y áspera ladera
un extendido lago y gran ribera.

Era un ancho archipiélago, poblado
de innumerables islas deleitosas,
cruzando por el uno y otro lado
góndolas y piraguas presurosas.
¡Marinero jamás desesperado
en medio de las olas fluctuosas
con tanto gozo vió el vecino puerto,
como nosotros el camino abierto!

Luego, pues, en un tiempo arrodillados,
llenos de nuevo gozo y de ternura,
dimos gracias a Dios, que así escapados
nos vimos del peligro y desventura;

y de tantas fatigas olvidados,
siguiendo el buen suceso y la ventura,
con esperanza y ánimo lozano
salimos presto al agradable llano.

El enfermo, el herido, el estropeado,
el cojo, el manco, el débil, el tullido,
el desnudo, el descalzo, el desgarrado,
el desmayado, el flaco, el deshambrido
quedó sano, gallardo y alentado,
de nuevo esfuerzo y de valor vestido,
pareciéndole poco todo el suelo,
y fácil cosa conquistar el cielo.

FERNANDO DE HERRERA

1534-1597

LESS is known of Herrera as a man than of any other Spanish poet of comparable stature since the Renaissance. He was born in Seville ; lived (though not in Holy Orders) upon the proceeds of a benefice there ; mixed with intellectuals, who included the humanist Juan de Mal Lara, the painter Francisco Pacheco, the poet Baltasar del Alcázar and the dramatist Juan de la Cueva, and published a prose *Relación de la guerra de Chipre* (1572), an annotated edition of Garcilaso de la Vega (1580) which involved him in considerable polemic, and (1582) a collection of his own poems. Nothing more is known of him with any certainty, save for one phase of his life essential to an understanding of his work—the love (generally assumed to have been platonic) which he conceived for Doña Leonor de Milán, wife of the Conde de Gelves, and which apparently lasted from about 1559 till her death in 1581. This love inspired most of his verse. The third and tenth Elegies immortalize the sole occasion when she gave his ardour any encouragement :

D'amor tierno llena,
me dixo assí la bella desdeñosa :

. . . . .

" Si en sufrir más me vences, yo t'ecedo
en pura fe i afetos de terneza :
vive d'oi más ya confiado i ledo."
No sé si oí, si fui de su belleza
arrebatado, si perdí el sentido ;
sé que allí se perdió mi fortaleza, etc.[1]

[1] Elegía III. I follow here the C.C. edition (Madrid, 1914), which uses the 1582 text (for the Lepanto ode, the 1572 text), like it modernizing accentuation but retaining Herrera's characteristic orthography and like it giving variants from the posthumous 1619 edition in footnotes. The variants to this present quotation, being trivial, are not given.

The fifth Elegy was apparently written during a profound reaction from the elation which was caused by this experience, and which finds classical expression in a line from Elegía X:

Ya passó mi dolor, ya sé qu'es vida.

Most of the remaining elegies, the magnificent collection of sonnets and a few of the *Canciones* reflect the poet's normal condition of despondency, alternating, however (even within the limits of a single sonnet), with many other moods, and continually illumined by Platonic idealization of the Beloved, joy in Nature, delight in pure self-expression and a technique which in his own day had hardly been surpassed in Spanish poetry. Of this technique the chief features are: a profusion of images (especially of images of fire and light: the two names which he gives to his lady are Luz y Estrella); a great wealth of colour-terms, both direct and allusive; sound-music of extreme beauty—Herrera can hardly ever have inadvertently written a harsh line; hyperbole which, though daring, is seldom felt to be, on the one hand, excessive, or, on the other, an essential part of the poet's art. Alliteration he uses but rarely and then with no very evident purpose. He has greater command of sonnet-technique than Garcilaso, greater warmth of colour, and as a rule greater exuberance of expression, but in general, though he stands between Garcilaso and Góngora, he is nearer to the former than to the latter. Criticism has been apt to magnify the few signs of incipient conceptism which can be found in him and to represent him as a florid and even bombastic writer in whom the Baroque is already well developed.

This error arises chiefly from the over-emphasizing of his few patriotic poems at the expense of the poems of love. For Herrera the heroic poet is completely unlike Herrera the lover. To hymn his country's victories or to lament her defeats he chooses long stanzas of from eight to thirteen hendecasyllabic lines, diversified by occasional heptasyllabics, save where, in addressing Don Juan de Austria after the triumph of the Alpujarras, he uses *liras*. His instrument is not now a key that unlocks hearts but a "trumpet that sings to battle." The "proud full sail of his great verse," the long paragraphs of stanzas, the majestic epithets, the sonorous rhymes, suggest the turgid but often stirring oratory of the Spanish pulpit. Broad, sweeping effects take the place of the vivid, penetrating phrases of the Elegies and Sonnets, and what the language loses in warmth it makes up in energy and vigour. In the patriotic *canciones*, of which the two best are those on Lepanto and Alcazarquivir, Herrera is much less cold and formal than in those to the Condesa de Gelves (V), to St. Ferdinand (VI), and on the exploits of the Bazán family (VIII). In his masterly use of the Old Testament he not only adopted its language but absorbed its spirit and showed for the first time how the poetry of the Psalms and the Major Prophets could be naturalized in his mother tongue. "Divine" was the epithet bestowed upon him in his own day, and he might well have become another Milton—"God-gifted organ-voice" of Spain.

122. *Soneto X*

The image, in this sonnet, emerges as its dominant feature, not merely illustrating, but existing for its own sake. And yet it is hard to know which of the sonnet's beauties to admire most—the vivid and gorgeous picture of the rising sun in the first quatrain, the caressing music of the second or the combination of perfect architecture and restrained emotion in the whole. In the rhetorical questions of ll. 3-4, 8, the emotion is very near the surface but the octave is dominated by its visual, auditory and tactile images with which, to the modern reader at least, rhetorical devices are quite unable to compete.

The sestet can hardly be said to maintain the same level. The almost hurried apostrophe to the moon and stars is much less striking than those which precede it; and, impressive as is the form in which the heavenly bodies are finally marshalled by the poet, that very form leads the reader to expect a conclusion more than usually complete—not a sudden twist of sense which introduces into the sonnet an element entirely new. Further, the two concluding questions are weak in themselves; and, whereas the octave gives the impression of an intense strength of feeling seeking an outlet in hyperbole, the sestet conveys a picture of the weak and almost querulous lover.

Roxo Sol, que con hacha luminosa
cobras el purpuréo i alto cielo
¿ hallaste tal belleza en todo el suelo
qu' iguale a mi serena Luz dichosa ?

Aura suäve, blanda i amorosa
que nos halagas con tu fresco buelo ;
cuando se cubre del dorado velo[1]
mi Luz ¿ tocaste trença[2] más hermosa ?

Luna, onor de la noche, ilustre coro
de las errantes lumbres i fixadas[3]
¿ consideraste tales dos estrellas ?

Sol puro, Aura, Luna, llamas[4] d'oro
¿ oístes vos mis penas nunca usadas ?[5]
¿ vistes Luz más ingrata a mis querellas ?

123. *Soneto XXVII*

This lovely sonnet clearly has reference to the lover's short-lived triumph of 1571 ; the "por quien mísero suspiro" connects it chronologically with the reaction represented by the fifth Elegy, but the tone of the whole poem suggests that it was written during one of the poet's interludes of hopefulness.

The Neo-platonic idealization of the Beloved, conveyed in the octave with the greatest delicacy by means of colour, would itself suffice to give the sonnet the seal of immortality. But with the careless rodigality of immense wealth, the poet, his imagination perhaps kindled by his own phrase "eterna hermosura" (l. 6), mounts higher still in the sestet, and, laying hold of the mystic's supreme image—that of the transformation of union with God—applies it hyperbolically to himself and his lady. The mystical language is sustained until the very end of the poem, where it culminates in a final line of great power.

I can think of no other modern poem the tone of which is so quickly and completely transformed from plaint (l. 4) and plea (l. 8) to the sublimest contemplation. It is a perfect and unfading flower plucked from a rare and precious experience—an undying spark preserved from a fire to which it alone has given immortality.

[1] cuando el oro descubre i rico velo.
[2] trença tocaste.
[3] de los errantes astros i fixados.
[4] Luzes.
[5] ¿ oístes mis dolores nunca usados ?

El color bello en el umor de Tiro
ardió, i la nieve vuestra en llama pura,
cuando, Estrella, bolvistes[1] con dulçura
los ojos[2], por quien mísero suspiro.

Vivo color[3] de lúcido safiro,
dorado[4] cielo, eterna hermosura,
pues mereci alcanzar esta ventura
acoged blandamente mi suspiro.

Con él mi alma, en el celeste fuego
vuestro abrasada, viene, i se trasforma
en la belleza vuestra soberana.

I en tanto gozo, en su mayor sossiego
su bien, en cuantas almas halla, informa;
qu'en el comunicar más gloria gana[5].

124. *Soneto LXI*

The octave, which illustrates Herrera's predilection for rich and brilliant words calling up images of light and fire, is one of the most powerfully visual passages in Spanish. The impression it conveys is not that of a particular woman's beauty, but of a typically Baroque concentration on one aspect of it, exaggerated out of all proportion. Everything else fades beside these brilliant images, evoking light, flame, fire, gold, the burning comet and the blazing sun: the entire octave is a glowing fragment of the hyperbole of love.

The sestet, by contrast, opens soberly: the poet's ardour is tempered, and love's vision is veiled, like the Beloved's beauty. Then it takes us back to hyperbole, which now, however, it wears with a difference. For the language—especially in the telling final line—is perfectly simple, yet so highly is it charged with lyric emotion that it seems, as it were, to be impotently protesting against the restraint imposed upon it.

Cual d'oro era el cabello ensortijado,
i en mil varias lazadas dividido;
i cuanto en más figuras esparcido,
tanto de más centellas ilustrado;

[1] vibrástes. [2] los rayos. [3] esplendor. [4] sereno.

[5] su bien, en cuantos halla, alegre informa;
qu'en el solo menor la gloria gana.

tal, de luzientes hebras coronado,
Febo aparece en llamas encendido ;
tal discurre en el cielo[1] esclarecido
un ardiente cometa arrebatado.

Debaxo el puro, proprio i sutil velo
Amor, gracia, i valor[2], i la belleza
templada en nieve i púrpura se vía.

Pensara que s'abrió esta vez el cielo,
i mostró su poder i su riqueza,
si no fuera la luz de l'alma mía.

125. *Soneto LXII*

In both theme and execution the simple opening lines are suggestive of Shakespeare (e.g., Sonnets XCVII, XCVIII, CIX, CXIII). Then suddenly the poet plunges into a riot of Nature-imagery recalling, for a moment, Shakespeare's "Full many a glorious morning . . ." (XXXIII) but incontestably surpassing it in "heavenly alchemy." The theme is not merely the Beloved's absence, or the Lover's constant remembrance of her, but her immanence in Nature—in the roseate lap of dawn and in the warm rays of the golden sun. The magnificence of this passage is exaggerated, in the sestet, into extravagance ; then, with a suddenness which comes almost as a shock, it gives way (l. 12) to complete sobriety. This double modulation of tone both enhances the brilliance of the rapid movement of ll. 3-11 and also intensifies the slowly penetrating bitterness and desolation of ll. 13-14.

Hazer no puede ausencia que presente
no os vea yo, mi Estrella, en cualquier' ora ;
que cuando sale la purpúrea Aurora[3],
en su rosada falda estáis luziente.

I cuando el Sol alumbra el Orïente[4],
en su dorada[5] imagen os[6] colora ;
i en sus rayos parecen[7] a desora
rutilar los cabellos i la frente[8].

[1] discurre 'n el Polo.
[2] gracia, valor.
[3] no vos tenga mi Estrella ; qu'en la ora que se viste de púrpura l'Aurora.
[4] Cuando Febo esclarece 'l Oriente.
[5] espléndida.
[6] vos.
[7] florecen.
[8] con puro ardor las hebras i la frente.

Cuando ilustra el bellísimo Luzero
el orbe, entre los braços puros veo[1]
de Venus encender[s'] essa belleza.

Allí os hablo, allí suspiro i muero;
mas vos, siempre[2] enemiga a mi desseo,
os mostráis sin dolor a mi tristeza.[3]

126. *Soneto LXXV*

An example of Herrera in his sombrest mood. Figures like the opening one, of the trackless desert, he normally uses, in preference to images of darkness, as foils to his dominant motifs of fire and light. The desolation, it will be observed, is complete: unlike San Juan de la Cruz's Lover (Noche obscura, *St. 3: p. 266), Herrera's is "sin luz, sin guía". The aim of the whole octave seems to be to isolate and intensify that impression.*

In the sestet the tone changes. Depression is succeeded by a suggestion of flaming wrath. Resoluteness emerges: "I shall conquer —or die." Yet the subdued, monotonous note persists: the last words are of death. The final clear-cut alternatives are suggestive of Garcilaso de la Vega, and the last line, alliterating in m, *recalls that of Garcilaso's Soneto X (p. 174). The technique of this sonnet, it may be added, consists largely in alliteration* (tr: *ll. 1, 3, 4;* c: *l. 10;* t: *l. 11;* m: *ll. 5, 7, 13-14), which, however, except in l. 14, seems rather pointless.*

Sigo por un desierto no tratado,
sin luz, sin guía, en confusión perdido,
el vano error, que solo m' a traído
a la miseria del más triste estado.

Cuanto m' alargo más, voi más errado,
i a mayores peligros ofrecido:
dexar atrás el mal m' es defendido;
qu' el passo del remedio está cerrado.

[1] Cuando, onor de los astros, el Luzero
ilustra el orbe, entre los braços veo.

[2] dulce.

[3] despreciáis el dolor en mi tristeza.

En ira enciende el daño manifiesto
al coraçón caído, i cobra aliento,
contra la instante tempestad osando.

O venceré tanto rigor molesto,
o en los concursos de su movimiento
moriré, con mis males acabando.

127. *Canción en alabança de la Divina Magestad por la vitoria del Señor Don Juan*

This noble poem, which hymns the defeat of the Turks at Lepanto in 1571, was written very shortly after the event and published in the following year. Its outstanding achievement is to have translated into Spanish not only the words of Old Testament battle-poetry but also something of its spirit. Source-hunters have traced quotations, or close adaptations, from no less than eight Old Testament books. Two long passages (Exodus xv, 1-19 and Psalm lxxxiii, 3-8, 14-17) seem to have suggested the plan of the poem, with its alternation of paean, narrative and reflection, and to each of them the poet returns in a most striking way at the central point of his song. By means, too, of grandly conceived ideas, aided by deep, sonorous notes compassable by few but he, this "mighty-mouthed inventor of harmonies" has contrived to convey something of the gigantic scale and the elemental tone characterizing those early narratives of battles in which the authors believed the Deity to be taking a direct and personal part. It seems strange that a poet who could achieve this should have written so little more of the same kind.

Cantemos al Señor, que en la llanura
venció del mar al enemigo fiero[1].
Tú, Dios de las batallas, tú eres diestra,
salud, y gloria nuestra.

Tú rompiste las fuerças y la dura
frente de Faraón, feroz guerrero.
Sus escogidos príncipes cubrieron
los abissos del mar, y decendieron
qual piedra en el profundo; y tu ira luego
los tragó, como arista seca el fuego.

[1] venció d'el ancho mar al Trace fiero.

El sobervio tirano, confiado
en el grande aparato de sus naves,
que de los nuestros la cerviz cativa,
y las manos aviva
al ministerio de su duro estado[1],
derribó con los braços suyos graves
los cedros más ecelsos de la cima
y el árbol que más yerto se sublima,
bebiendo agenas aguas, y pisando
el más cerrado y apartado vando[2].

Temblaron los pequeños confundidos
del ímpio furor suyo ; alçó la frente
contra ti, Señor Dios, y enfurecido
ya contra ti se vido
con los armados brazos estendidos
el arrogante cuello del potente[3].
Cercó su coraçón de ardiente saña
contra las dos Esperias, que el mar baña,
porque en ti confiadas le resisten,
y de armas de tu fe y amor se visten.

Dixo aquel, insolente y desdeñoso :
" ¿ No conocen mis iras estas tierras,
y de mis padres los ilustres hechos ?
¿ o valieron sus pechos
contra ellos, con el Úngaro dudoso,[4]
y de Dalmacia y Rodas en las guerras ?
¿ pudo su Dios librallos de sus manos ?
¡ Que Dios salvó a los de Austria y los Germanos !
¿ por ventura podrá su Dios aora
guardallos de mi diestra vencedora ?[5]

[1] al ministerio injusto de su estado.

[2] beviendo agenas aguas, i, atrevido,
pisando el vando nuestro y defendido.

[3] . . . Señor Dios, i, con semblante
i con pecho arrogante
i los armados braços estendidos,
movió el airado cuello aquel potente.

[4] medroso.

[5] ¿ Quién las pudo librar ? ¿ quién de sus manos
pudo salvar los d'Austria i los Germanos ?
¿ Podrá su Dios, podrá por suerte aora
guardallas de mi diestra vencedora ?

Su Roma, temerosa y umillada,
sus canciones[1] en lágrimas convierte;
ella y sus hijos mi furor esperan[2]
quando vencidos mueran.
Francia está con discordia quebrantada,
y en España amenaza orrible muerte
quien onra de la luna las vanderas;
y aquellas gentes en la guerra fieras[3]
ocupadas están en su defensa:
y aunque no, ¿ quién podrá hazerme ofensa ?[4]

Los poderosos pueblos me obedecen,
y con su daño el yugo an consentido[5],
y me dan por salvarse ya la mano;
y su valor es vano,
que sus luzes muriendo se escurecen[6].
Sus fuertes en batalla an perecido[7]
sus vírgenes están en cativerio,
su gloria a buelto al cetro de mi imperio.
Del Nilo a Eufrates y al Danubio frío[8],
quanto el sol alto mira, todo es mío."

Tu, Señor, que no sufres que tu gloria
usurpe quien confía en su grandeza[9],
prevaleciendo en vanidad y en ira,
a este sobervio mira,
que tus templos[10] afea en su vitoria
. . . . [eza][11]
y en sus cuerpos las fieras bravas ceva,[12]
y en su esparcida sangre el odio prueva;[13]
y hecho ya su oprobio[14], dize: "¿ Dónde
el Dios destos está ? ¿ de quién se esconde ?"[15]

[1] los cánticos.

[2] ella i sus hijos tristes m'ira esperan.

[3] i aquellas en la guerra gentes fieras.

[4] i, aunque no, quién hazer me puede ofensa ?

[5] i el cuello con su daño al yugo inclinan.

[6] que sus luzes cayendo s'oscurecen.

[7] Sus fuertes a la muerte ya caminan.

[8] d'el Nilo a Eufrates fertil i Istro frío.

[9] usurpe quien su fuerça, osado estima.

[10] tus aras.

[11] This line is wanting. García de Diego conjectures, e.g., "i tus hijos oprime con dureza." The 1619 edition has: "no dexes que los tuyos assí oprima."

[12] i en sus cuerpos, cruel, las fieras ceve.

[13] prueve.

[14] que, hechos ya su oprobrio.

[15] s'asconde.

¡ Por la gloria devida[1] de tu nombre,
por la vengança de tu muerta gente[2],
y de los presos por aquel gemido[3],
buelve el braço tendido
contra aquel, que[4] aborrece ya ser ombre,
y las onras que a ti se dan consiente,
y tres y quatro vezes su castigo
dobla con fortaleza al enemigo[5];
y la injuria a tu nombre cometida
sea el duro cuchillo[6] de su vida !

Levantó la cabeça el poderoso
que tanto odio te tiene, en nuestro estrago
juntó el consilio[7], y contra nos pensaron
los que en él se hallaron.
" ¡ Venid ! dixeron : y en el mar undoso[8]
hagamos de su sangre un grande lago ;
deshagamos a estos de la gente,
y el nombre de su Cristo juntamente,
y, dividiendo dellos los despojos,
hárten[se] en muerte suya nuestros ojos."

Vinieron de Asia y de la antigua Egito[9],
los Árabes y fieros[10] Africanos,
y los que Grecia junta mal con ellos,
con levantados[11] cuellos,
con gran potencia[12] y número infinito.
Y prometieron con sus duras manos[13]
encender nuestros fines, y dar muerte
con hierro a nuestra juventud más fuerte[14],
nuestros niños prender y las donzellas,
y la gloria ofender[15] y la luz dellas.

[1] ¡ Por la devida gloria . . . . !

[2] por la justa vengança de tu gente.

[3] por aquel de los míseros gemido.

[4] contra este, qu'.

[5] i las onras que zelas tú consiente,
i tres i cuatro vezes el castigo
esfuerça con rigor a tu enemigo.

[6] el hierro contrario.

[7] consejo.

[8] ondoso.

[9] Vinieron d'Asia i portentosa Egito.

[10] i leves.

[11] con los erguidos.

[12] poder.

[13] Y prometer osaron con sus manos.

[14] a nuestra juventud con hierro fuerte.

[15] manchar.

Ocuparon del mar los largos senos,
en silencio y temor puesta la tierra,
y nuestros fuertes súbito cessaron,
y medrosos callaron;
hasta que a los feroces Agarenos[1],
el Señor eligiendo nueva guerra,
se opuso el joven de Austria valeroso[2]
con el claro Español y belicoso;
que Dios no sufre en Babilonia viva
su querida Sión siempre cativa[3].

Qual león a la presa apercibido,
esperavan los ímpios confiados[4]
a los que tú, Señor, eras escudo;
que el coraçón desnudo
de temor, y de fe todo vestido[5],
de tu espíritu estavan confortados[6].
Sus manos a la guerra compusiste,
y a sus braços[7] fortíssimos pusiste
como el arco azerado, y con la espada
mostraste en su favor[8] la diestra armada.

Turbáron[se] los grandes, los robustos
rindiéron[se] temblando, y desmayaron,
y tú pusiste[9], Dios, como la rueda,
como la arista queda
al ímpetu del viento, a estos injustos,
que mil huyendo de uno se pasmaron.
Qual fuego abr[a]sa selvas, y qual llama,
que en las espesas cumbres se derrama[10],
tal en tu ira y tempestad seguiste
y su faz de inominia confundiste[11].

[1] Ocuparon d'el piélago los senos,
puesta en silencio i en temor la tierra,
i cessaron los nuestros valerosos,
i callaron dudosos,
hasta qu'al fiero ardor de Sarracenos.

[2] generoso.

[3] que Dios no sufre ya en Babel cativa
que su Sión querida siempre viva.

[4] sin recelo los ímpios esperavan.

[5] de pavor i de fe i amor vestido.

[6] con celestial aliento confiavan.

[7] i sus braços.

[8] vibraste 'n su favor.

[9] y tú entregaste.

[10] Cual fuego abrasa selvas, cuya llama
en las espessas cumbres se derrama.

[11] convertiste.

Quebrantaste al dragón fiero[1], cortando
las alas de su cuerpo temerosas,
y sus braços terribles no vencidos,
que con hondos gemidos
se retira a su cueva silvos dando,
y tiembla con sus sierpes venenosas[2],
lleno de miedo torpe sus entrañas,
de tu león temiendo las hazañas;
que, saliendo de España, dió un rugido,
que con espanto lo dexó atordido[3].

Oy los ojos se vieron[4] umillados
del sublime varón y su grandeza,
y tú solo, Señor, fuiste exaltado;
que tu día es llegado,
Señor de los ejércitos armados,
sobre la alta cerviz y su dureza,
sobre derechos cedros y estendidos,
sobre empinados montes y crecidos,
sobre torres, y muros, y las naves
de Tiro, que a los tuyos fueron graves.

Babilonia y Egito amedrentada
del fuego y asta temblará sangrienta[5],
y el humo subirá a la luz del cielo,
y, faltos de consuelo,
con rostro oscuro y soledad turbada
tus enemigos llorarán su afrenta.
Y tú[6], Grecia, concorde a la esperança
de Egito[7], y gloria de su confiança,
triste que a ella pareces, no temiendo
a Dios, y en[8] tu remedio no atendiendo,

porque ingrata tus hijas adornaste
en adulterio con tan ímpia gente[9],
que desseava profanar tus frutos,
y con ojos enxutos

[1] al cruel dragón.

[2] se retira a su cueva, do, silvando,
tiembla con sus culebras venenosas.

[3] que lo dexó assombrado i atordido.

[4] Oi se vieron los ojos.

[5] temerá el fuego i l'asta violenta.

[6] Mas tú.

[7] egicia.

[8] y a

[9] en adulterio infame a una ímpia gente.

sus odiösos passos imitaste,
su aborrecible vida y mal presente[1],
por esso Dios se vengará en tu muerte;
que llega a tu cerviz su diestra fuerte
la aguda espada. ¿ Quién será que pueda
tener su mano poderosa queda ?[2]

Mas tú, fuerça del mar, tú, ecelsa Tiro,
que en tus naves estavas gloriösa,
y el término espantavas de la tierra,
y si hazías guerra,
de temor la cubrías con suspiro,
¿ cómo acabaste fiera y orgullosa ?
¿ quién pensó a tu cabeça daño tanto ?
Dios, para convertir tu gloria en llanto,
y derribar tus ínclitos y fuertes,
te hizo perecer con tantas muertes.

Llorad, naves del mar, que es destruída
toda vuestra sobervia y fortaleza :[3]
¿ quién ya tendrá de ti lástima alguna,
tú, que sigues la luna,
Asia adúltera, en vicios sumergida ?
¿ quién mostrará por ti alguna tristeza ?[4]
¿ quién rogará por ti ? Que Dios entiende
tu ira, y la sobervia que te ofende ;[5]
y tus antiguas culpas y mudança[6]
an buelto contra ti a pedir vengança.

Los que vieren tus braços quebrantados
y de tus pinos ir el mar desnudo,
que sus ondas turbaron y llanura,
viendo tu muerte oscura,
dirán de tus estragos espantados :
" ¿ Quién contra la espantosa tanto pudo ? "

[1] su aborrecida vida y mal presente

[2] Dios vengará sus iras en tu muerte,
que llega a tu cerviz con diestra fuerte
l'aguda espada suya. ¿ Quién, cuitada,
reprimirá su mano desatada ?

[3] vuestra vana soberbia i pensamiento.

[4] ¿ quién mostrará un liviano sentimiento ?

[5] Qu'a Dios enciende
tu ira i l'arrogancia que t'ofende.

[6] i tus viejos delitos i mudança.

El Señor, que mostró su fuerte mano,
por la fe de su príncipe cristiano
y por el nombre santo de su gloria,
a España le concede[1] esta vitoria.

Bendita, Señor, sea tu grandeza,
que después de los daños padecidos,
después de nuestras culpas y castigo,
rompiste al enemigo
de la antigua sobervia la dureza.
Adórente, Señor, tus escogidos;
confiesse quanto cerca el ancho cielo
tu nombre, o nuestro Dios, nuestro consuelo
y la cerviz rebelde, condenada,
padesca en bravas llamas abrasada.

A ti solo la gloria
por siglos de los siglos, a ti damos
la onra, y umillados te adoramos[2].

128. *Canción por la pérdida del Rei Don Sebastián*

This lament for the defeat of the Portuguese by the Moors and the loss of their King, the headstrong and adventurous Sebastian, at Alcazarquivir (August 4, 1578) was first published in 1582. In plan, language and spirit, it is closely allied, like the Lepanto ode, to Old Testament narrative and it makes direct use of the prophecy of Isaiah xiii, 9-11, 17-18 and of the story of the proud tree in Daniel iv, 7-11. Yet, although the poet succeeds in applying the righteous wrath of the Prophets to the tragedy caused by Sebastian's imprudence in disregarding the advice of his wise counsellors, his use of his sources is both less direct and less apt. On the other hand, he was more fitted by temperament, as also by his experience, to lament defeats than to hymn victories, and the intensity of the emotion instinct in this ode is perhaps even greater than that in its predecessor.

Voz de dolor, i canto de gemido,
i espíritu de miedo, embuelto en ira,
hagan principio acerbo a la memoria

[1] a su España concede.

[2] In the 1619 edition the last three lines are omitted.

d'aquel día fatal aborrecido
que Lusitania mísera suspira,
desnuda de valor, falta de gloria;
i la llorosa istoria
assombre con orror funesto i triste
dend' el Africo Atlante i seno ardiente
hasta do el mar d'otro color se viste,
i do el límite roxo d' Oriënte,
i todas sus vencidas gentes fieras
vên tremolar de Cristo las vanderas.

¡ Ai de los que passaron, confiados
en sus cavallos i en la muchedumbre
de sus carros, en ti, Libia desierta;
i en su vigor i fuerças engañados,
no alçaron su esperança a aquella cumbre
d' eterna luz; mas con sobervia cierta
se ofrecieron la incierta
vitoria; i sin bolver a [D]ios sus ojos,
con ierto cuello i coraçón ufano
sólo atendieron siempre a los despojos!
I el [S]anto d' Israel abrió su mano,
i los dexó, i cayó en despeñadero
el carro, i el cavallo i cavallero.

Vino el día cruel, el día lleno
d' indinación, d' ira i furor, que puso
en soledad i en un profundo llanto
de gente, i de plazer el reino ageno.
El cielo no alumbró, quedó confuso
el nuevo sol, presago de mal tanto;
i con terrible espanto
el Se[ñ]or visitó sobre sus males,
para umillar los fuertes arrogantes,
i levantó los bárbaros no iguales,
que con osados pechos i constantes
no busquen oro, mas con crudo hierro
venguen la ofensa i cometido ierro.[1]

[1] no busquen oro: mas con hierro airado
la ofensa venguen i el error culpado.

Los ímpios i robustos, indinados,
las ardientes espadas desnudaron
sobre la claridad i hermosura
de tu gloria i valor, i no cansados
en tu muerte, tu onor todo afearon,
mesquina Lusitania sin ventura;
i con frente segura
rompieron sin temor con fiero estrago
tus armadas escuadras i braveza.
L' arena se tornó sangriento lago,
la llanura con muertos, aspereza;
cayó en unos vigor, cayó denuedo,
mas en otros desmayo i torpe miedo.

¿ Son éstos, por ventura, los famosos,
los fuertes i belígeros varones[1]
que conturbaron con furor la tierra,
que sacudieron reinos poderosos,
que domaron las órridas naciones,
que pusieron desierto en cruda guerra
cuanto enfrena i encierra
el mar Indo, i feroces destruyeron
grandes ciudades? ¿ dó la valentía?[2]
¿ cómo assí s' acabaron, i perdieron
tanto eroico valor en sólo un día;
i lexos de su patria derribados,
no fueron justamente sepultados?

Tales fueron aquestos, cual hermoso
cedro del alto Líbano, vestido
de ramos, hojas con ecelsa alteza;
las aguas lo criaron poderoso,
sobre empinados árboles subido,
i se multiplicaron en grandeza
sus ramos con belleza;
i, estendiendo su sombra, s' anidaron
las aves que sustenta el grande cielo,

[1] los fuertes, los belígeros varones.

[2] ¿ . . . . cuanto el mar Indo encierra;
i sobervias ciudades destruyeron?
¿ dó el coraçón seguro i la osadía?

i en sus hojas las fieras engendraron,
i hizo a mucha gente umbroso velo :
no igualó en celsitud i hermosura
jamás árbol alguno a su figura.

Pero elevóse con su verde cima,
i sublimó la presunción su pecho,
desvanecido todo i confiado,
haziendo de su alteza sólo estima.
Por esso Dios lo derribó deshecho,
a los ímpios i agenos entregado,
por la raíz cortado ;
qu' opresso de los montes arrojados,
sin ramos i sin hojas, i desnudo,
huyeron dél los ombres espantados,
que su sombra tuvieron por escudo ;
en su ruina i ramos cuantas fueron
las aves i las fieras se pusieron.

Tú, infanda Libia, en cuya seca arena
murió el vencido reino Lusitano,
i s' acabó su generosa gloria,
no estés alegre i d' ufanía llena,
porque tu temerosa i flaca mano
uvo sin esperança tal vitoria,
indina de memoria ;
que si el justo dolor mueve a vengança
alguna vez el Español corage,
despedaçada con aguda lança,
compensarás muriendo el hecho ultrage ;
i Luco amedrentado al mar inmenso
pagará d' Africana sangre el censo.

FRANCISCO DE LA TORRE

*c.*1534-*c.*1594

So little is known of this poet, whose affinities are with Luis de León (p. 205) and the Salamancan group, that at one time his name was thought to be only a pseudonym. A collection of his verse was first published in 1631 by Quevedo (p. 359); it consists of one long poem and rather less than a hundred short ones of which over two-thirds are sonnets. Technically, these productions have merit: some of them are indebted to Italy, while others are of native growth. Their correctness, however, inclines to frigidity and there is little individuality behind them.

129. *La Cierva*

An early example of a poem fettered by passion for epithet—a foretaste of eighteenth-century pseudo-classicism. The fourteen-lined stanzas have grace, dignity and poise, but their slow, winding motion, though appropriate enough to the form, soon becomes tedious: as we follow the fortunes of Torre's cierva *we think wistfully of the simple, poignant allusive reference to the* ciervo *in San Juan de la Cruz (p. 259). Nearly the whole of the scanty colour in the poem is concentrated in the fourth stanza, but even here the unreality of the epithets pursues us. More attractive are the musical quality of individual lines, the veiled melancholy and the evocations of Nature delicately suggested in refined, aristocratic language. Torre is a less robust Garcilaso, with a circumscribed and tenuous appeal.*

Doliente cierva, que el herido lado
de ponzoñosa y cruda yerba lleno,
buscas la agua de la fuente pura,
con el cansado aliento y con el seno
bello de la corriente sangre hinchado,
débil y descaída tu hermosura.

¡ Ay ! que la mano dura,
que tu nevado pecho
ha puesto en tal estrecho,
gozosa va con tu desdicha, cuando
cierva mortal, viviendo estás penando
tu desangrado y dulce compañero
el regalado y blando
pecho pasado del veloz montero.

Vuelve cuitada, vuelve al valle, donde
queda muerto tu amor ; en vano dando
términos desdichados a tu suerte ;
morirás en su seno, reclinando
la beldad, que la cruda mano esconde
delante de la nube de la muerte.
Que el paso duro y fuerte,
ya forzoso y terrible,
no puede ser posible
que le excusen los cielos, permitiendo
crudos astros que mueras padeciendo
las asechanzas de un montero crudo
que te vino siguiendo
por los desiertos de este campo mudo.

Mas ¡ ay ! que no dilatas la inclemente
muerte, que en tu sangriento pecho llevas,
del crudo amor vencido y maltratado ;
tú con el fatigado aliento pruebas
a rendir el espíritu doliente
en la corriente de este valle amado.
Que el ciervo desangrado,
que contigo la vida
tuvo por bien perdida,
no fué tan poco de tu amor querido,
que habiendo tan cruelmente padecido,
quieras vivir sin él, cuando pudieras
librar el pecho herido
de crudas llagas y memorias fieras.

Cuando por la espesura deste prado,
como tórtolas solas y queridas,
solos y acompañados anduvistes :

cuando de verde mirto y de floridas
violetas, tierno acanto y lauro amado
vuestras frentes bellísimas ceñistes
cuando las horas tristes,
que ausentes y queridos,
con mil mustios bramidos
ensordecistes la ribera umbrosa
del claro Tajo, rica y venturosa
con vuestro bien, con vuestro mal sentida :
cuya muerte penosa
no deja rastro de contenta vida.

Agora el uno, cuerpo muerto lleno
de desdén y de espanto, quien solía
ser ornamento de la selva umbrosa :
tú, quebrantada y mustia, al agonía
de la muerte rendida, el bello seno
agonizando, el alma congojosa,
cuya muerte gloriosa,
en los ojos de aquellos
cuyos despojos bellos
son victorias del crudo amor furioso,
martirio fué de amor, triunfo glorioso,
con que corona y premia dos amantes
que del siempre rabioso
trance mortal salieron muy triunfantes.

Canción, fábula un tiempo, y caso agora
de una cierva doliente, que la dura
flecha del cazador dejó sin vida,
errad por la espesura
del monte, que de gloria tan perdida
no hay sino lamentar su desventura.

FRANCISCO DE FIGUEROA

*c.*1536-*c.*1617

ANOTHER poet of the Salamancan group, closely allied in style to Francisco de la Torre and like him often indebted to Italy. Though quoted by Cervantes, and apparently widely known in his lifetime, Figueroa's verses were not published until 1625. On the technical side his principal achievement was the acclimatization in Spain of the never very popular blank verse.

130. *Soneto*

Though marred by meaningless alliterations (ll. 2, 5, 7-8, 12-14, etc.) and by affected, often somewhat nebulous images (ll. 1-2, 3-4, 11), this sonnet attains distinction in its choice of epithets and achieves at least one noteworthy line. The general effect is of veiled beauty: the only colour is a dim white; the only clear details are the fair white hands with delicate fingers spread.

Blancas y hermosas manos, que colgado
tenéis de cada dedo mi sentido,
hermoso y bello cuerpo, que escondido
tenéis a todo el bien de mi cuidado,

divino y dulce rostro, que penado
tenéis mi corazón después que os vido,
¿ por qué ya no borráis de vuestro olvido
al que de sí por vos vive olvidado ?

Volved con buen semblante ya, señora,
aquesos ojos llenos de hermosura ;
¡ sacad esta vuestra alma a dulce puerto !

Mirad que me es mil años cada hora
y es mengua que quien vió vuestra figura
muera ya tantas veces siendo muerto.

131. *Madrigal*

A tissue of conceits on the noun parte *and the two senses of the verb* partir, *derivatives of which appear ten times in the ten lines of the poem. The device cannot be called very effective: contrast Figueroa's method with that of Sánchez de Badajoz (p. 156), who is seeking to convey very much the same sentiment. But the poem is an interesting and quite clever example of early Spanish conceptism.*

Triste de mí que parto, mas no parto ;
que el alma, que es de mí la mejor parte,
ni partirá, ni parte,
de quien jamás el pensamiento aparto :
si parte el cuerpo triste, el alma queda
gozosa, ufana y leda :
sí ; mas del alma el cuerpo parte, y temo,
¡ o doloroso extremo !
que en esta de los dos triste partida,
por fuerza he de partirme de la vida.

FRANCISCO DE MEDRANO

1570-*c.*1606

THE researches of Rodríguez Marín and Dámaso Alonso have thrown much light on the life of this hitherto little-known Sevilian poet, whose works appeared only in 1617 at the end of a forgotten epic by a fellow-Sevilian. A friend of Arguijo, Rioja and other members of the Sevilian group, he shares with them a tendency to use brilliant colour. But his Horatian bent, his normal sobriety of diction and his warmth of feeling ally him rather to Fray Luis de León than to the exuberant poets of the south.

132. *Soneto*

This richly figured and gorgeously coloured sonnet shows some conformity with the Herreran type. Medrano is particularly addicted to greens and blues, used generally, as here, in conjunction with white or gold. The symmetry of the poem enhances the semi-conventional effect produced by the colours, as does the repetition, in the last line, of the phrase in the first which sets its key.

Borde Tormes de perlas sus orillas
sobre las yerbas de esmeralda, y Flora
hurte para adornarlas a la aurora
las rosas que arrebolan sus mejillas.

Viertan las turquesadas maravillas
y junquillos dorados que atesora
la rica gruta, donde el viejo mora,
sus dríadas en cándidas cestillas,

para que pise Margarita ufana,
tierra y agua llenando de favores;
mas si uno y otro mira con desvío,

ni las ninfas de Tormes viertan flores,
ni rosas hurte Flora a la mañana,
ni su orilla de perlas borde el río.

133. *Soneto : A Don Juan de Arguijo, contra el artificio*

Written " volviendo el autor de Roma y de Madrid a Sevilla ", this sonnet to Arguijo is a variant on the theme, so popular in Spanish literature, that " God made the country and man made the town." Note particularly the feeling for wild Nature (ll. 5-6). A striking contrast to the preceding sonnet, this poem abandons colour, convention and artifice for a moral theme developed in somewhat oratorical language. One thing alone the two poems have in common—their pictures of the river and its surrounding countryside. Not content, like most Andalusians, with conventionalizing and personifying the Guadalquivir, Medrano seems to have been fascinated by its dynamic aspect—" cómo corre eternamente ". Both when he paints and when he moralizes it is the course of a river to the sea that most often attracts him, just as, long previously, it had attracted Jorge Manrique (p. 100).

Cansa la vista el artificio humano
cuanto mayor más presto ; la más clara
fuente y jardín compuestos dan en cara
que nuestro ingenio es breve y nuestra mano.

Aquel, aquel descuido soberano
de la naturaleza, en nada avara,
con luenga admiración suspende y para
a quien lo advierte con sentido sano.

Ver cómo corre eternamente un río,
cómo el campo se tiende en las llanuras,
y en los montes se anuda y se reduce,

grandeza es siempre nueva y grata, Argío,
tal, pero es el autor que las produce
¡ oh Dios inmenso ! en todas tus criaturas.

SAN JUAN DE LA CRUZ

1542-1591

THIS outstanding figure of the Counter-Reformation, Santa Teresa's co-pioneer in the Discalced Carmelite Reform, has also the distinction of being one of Spain's greatest poets. And yet the entire body of verse which he produced totals less than one thousand lines, more than half of which aim solely at edification and can hardly be described as poetry at all. The quality of his three greatest poems, however, has certainly never been surpassed in Spanish literature and their finest passages may stand beside the work of any poet in history.

San Juan de la Cruz began to write verse while incarcerated at Toledo by some fellow-friars who did not relish his zeal as a reformer. First, it would seem, he tried his hand at some simple doctrinal stanzas beginning *In principio erat Verbum.* Then he composed a poem, also doctrinal in content, but in a more attractive metre and of considerable lyric power, generally entitled, after its refrain, " Aunque es de noche ". In his next flight—a far higher one—he wrote the first thirty stanzas of the superb " Cántico espiritual ", which he completed after regaining his liberty. His other two masterpieces are " Noche obscura " and " Llama de amor viva " : these, with the " Cántico espiritual ", form the bases of the four prose treatises which have won their author his fame as a mystical writer and a Doctor of the Church Universal. A striking specimen of his simpler style is the allegory *a lo divino* of the shepherd-boy who died of love.

What heights San Juan de la Cruz would have reached had he devoted himself to pure poetry it is difficult to imagine. Writing as he did with his mystical interpretation always in the forefront of his mind, his soaring imagination must have been continually impeded : only a mind disciplined in the highest degree could have accepted the restraints which his exegetical aims imposed upon him. How far the beauty of form which makes his poetry the sweetest music in the Spanish language is the result of assiduous care, and how far it is natural to him, no one can say. He handles Garcilaso de la Vega's *lira* more ably than Garcilaso himself and the poems which he describes in general terms as "coplas del alma" make it clear that he was familiar with the *Cancioneros.* But to call him a conscious and skilful artist is not to deny that he was also one of the world's great natural singers—at any rate when he was singing, as every mystic does, of love.

To enumerate his gifts is unnecessary when we have his work before us. His intense vitality, his rich and vivid imagery, and the boldness and freedom with which he moves in the highest regions known to man are qualities possessed in comparable measure by very few. Not far below these come his picturesqueness, the power with which he can communicate emotion, his inspired use of Nature and the liquid melody of his numbers. Seldom in the history of literature has so much been enshrined in so little.

134. *Canciones a lo divino de Cristo y el Alma*

In these unassuming quatrains we have a transparent pastoral allegory: the shepherd-boy represents Christ; his love, the human soul; and the villain who tries to part them, Satan. Though they show rather less than usual of their author's formal skill, their simplicity is never prosaic. The boldness with which a conventional theme is adapted to its high purpose and the intensification of the pathos of the subject by the use of a recurrent rhyme and a refrain reach a fitting crisis in the final picture of the Crucifixion of Our Lord, quite Franciscan in its delicacy and tenderness.

Un pastorcico solo está penado,
ajeno de placer y de contento,
y en su pastora puesto el pensamiento,
y el pecho del amor muy lastimado.

No llora por haberle amor llagado,
que no le pena verse así afligido,
aunque en el corazón está herido;
mas llora por pensar que está olvidado.

Que sólo de pensar que está olvidado
de su bella pastora, con gran pena
se deja maltratar en tierra ajena,
el pecho del amor muy lastimado.

Y dice el Pastorcico : ¡ Ay, desdichado
de aquel que de mi amor ha hecho ausencia,
y no quiere gozar la mi presencia,
y el pecho por su amor muy lastimado !

Y a cabo de un gran rato se ha encumbrado
sobre un árbol do abrió sus brazos bellos,
y muerto se ha quedado, asido de ellos,
el pecho del amor muy lastimado.

135. *Cántico espiritual*[1]

This longest of San Juan de la Cruz's poems might well have originated in a cry of loneliness wrung from him in his prison by a sense of complete abandonment and deep desolation. Such a cry we find in its two opening lines, which introduce the poet's description of the Bride's quest for her Spouse and their subsequent union. There are certain inequalities in the poem : an occasional phrase, or even stanza, is barely comprehensible apart from its mystical interpretation ; the sequence of events is imperfect and suggestive of a work composed by instalments ; the conclusion is no real conclusion at all and is an anti-climax into the bargain. On the other hand, some of the finest stanzas are of hardly surpassable beauty ; notable use is made of Nature, both as viewed directly and as seen through the eyes of Hebrew poets ; and the whole poem throbs with every kind of emotion, from a tremulous feminine tearfulness to the proud ring of virile possession. We have here a remarkable combination of white-hot inspiration with a swiftly developing but not yet perfected technique. " One day," reports a nun to whom San Juan de la Cruz acted as spiritual director, " I asked him if God gave him those words which were so comprehensive and so lovely. And he answered : ' Daughter, sometimes God gave them to me and at other times I sought them.' "

ESPOSA

¿ A dónde te escondiste,
amado, y me dejaste con gemido ?
Como el ciervo huiste,
habiéndome herido ;
salí tras ti clamando, y eras ido.

[1] The full title of the poem is " Canciones entre el alma y el Esposo," but the short titles of this and the two following poems, borrowed from the treatises which form commentaries upon them, are more commonly used.

Pastores, los que fuerdes
allá por las majadas al otero,
si por ventura vierdes
aquel que yo más quiero,
decilde que adolezco, peno y muero.

Buscando mis amores,
iré por esos montes y riberas,
ni cogeré las flores,
ni temeré las fieras,
y pasaré los fuertes y fronteras.

PREGUNTA A LAS CRIATURAS

Oh bosques y espesuras,
plantadas por la mano del Amado,
oh prado de verduras,
de flores esmaltado,
decid si por vosotros ha pasado.

RESPUESTA DE LAS CRIATURAS

Mil gracias derramando,
pasó por estos sotos con presura,
y yéndolos mirando,
con sola su figura
vestidos los dejó de hermosura.

ESPOSA

¡ Ay, quién podrá sanarme !
Acaba de entregarte ya de vero,
no quieras enviarme
de hoy más ya mensajero,
que no saben decirme lo que quiero.

Y todos cuantos vagan
de ti me van mil gracias refiriendo,
y todos más me llagan
y déjame muriendo
un no sé qué que quedan balbuciendo.

Mas, ¿ cómo perseveras,
oh vida, no viviendo donde vives,
y haciendo porque mueras,
las flechas que recibes,
de lo que del Amado en ti concibes ?

¿ Por qué, pues has llagado
a aqueste corazón, no le sanaste ?
Y pues me le has robado,
¿ por qué así le dejaste,
y no tomas el robo que robaste ?

Apaga mis enojos,
pues que ninguno basta a deshacellos
y véante mis ojos,
pues eres lumbre dellos,
y sólo para ti quiero tenellos.

Descubre tu presencia,
y máteme tu vista y hermosura ;
mira que la dolencia
de amor, que no se cura
sino con la presencia y la figura.

¡ Oh cristalina fuente,
si en esos tus semblantes plateados
formases de repente
los ojos deseados,
que tengo en mis entrañas dibujados !

Apártalos, Amado,
que voy de vuelo.

ESPOSO

Vuélvete, paloma,
que el ciervo vulnerado
por el otero asoma,
al aire de tu vuelo, y fresco toma.

ESPOSA

Mi Amado, las montañas,
los valles solitarios nemorosos,
las ínsulas extrañas,
los ríos sonorosos,
el silbo de los aires amorosos.

La noche sosegada
en par de los levantes de la aurora,
la música callada,
la soledad sonora,
la cena, que recrea y enamora.

Nuestro lecho florido,
de cuevas de leones enlazado,
en púrpura tendido,
de paz edificado,
de mil escudos de oro coronado.

A zaga de tu huella
las jóvenes discurren al camino
al toque de centella,
al adobado vino,
emisiones de bálsamo Divino.

En la interior bodega
de mi amado bebí, y cuando salía
por toda aquesta vega,
ya cosa no sabía,
y el ganado perdí, que antes seguía.

Allí me dió su pecho,
allí me enseñó ciencia muy sabrosa,
y yo le di de hecho
a mí, sin dejar cosa ;
allí le prometí de ser su esposa.

Mi alma se ha empleado,
y todo mi caudal en su servicio :
ya no guardo ganado,
ni ya tengo otro oficio ;
que ya sólo en amar es mi ejercicio.

Pues ya si en el ejido,
de hoy más no fuere vista ni hallada,
diréis que me he perdido,
que andando enamorada,
me hice perdidiza, y fuí ganada.

De flores y esmeraldas
en las frescas mañanas escogidas,
haremos las guirnaldas,
en tu amor florecidas,
y en un cabello mío entretejidas.

En solo aquel cabello,
que en mi cuello volar consideraste,
mirástele en mi cuello,
y en él preso quedaste,
y en uno de mis ojos te llagaste.

Cuando tú me mirabas,
tu gracia en mí tus ojos imprimían :
por eso me adamabas
y en eso merecían
los míos adorar lo que en ti vían.

No quieras despreciarme,
que si color moreno en mí hallaste,
ya bien puedes mirarme,
después que me miraste,
que gracia y hermosura en mí dejaste.

Cogednos las raposas,
que está ya florecida nuestra viña,
en tanto que de rosas
hacemos una piña,
y no parezca nadie en la montiña.

Detente, Cierzo muerto ;
ven, Austro, que recuerdas los amores,
aspira por mi huerto,
y corran sus olores,
y pacerá el Amado entre las flores.

ESPOSO

Entrádose ha la Esposa
en el ameno huerto deseado,
y a su sabor reposa,
el cuello reclinado
sobre los dulces brazos del Amado.

Debajo del manzano,
allí conmigo fuiste desposada,
allí te di la mano,
y fuiste reparada,
donde tu madre fuera violada.

A las aves ligeras,
leones, ciervos, gamos saltadores,
montes, valles, riberas,
aguas, aires, ardores,
y miedos de las noches veladores :

Por las amenas liras
y canto de serenas os conjuro
que cesen vuestras iras,
y no toquéis al muro,
porque la Esposa duerma más seguro.

ESPOSA

Oh ninfas de Judea,
en tanto que en las flores y rosales
el ámbar perfumea,
morá en los arrabales,
y no queráis tocar nuestros umbrales.

Escóndete, Carillo,
y mira con tu haz a las montañas,
y no quieras decillo ;
mas mira las compañas
de la que va por ínsulas extrañas.

ESPOSO

La blanca palomica
al Arca con el ramo se ha tornado,
y ya la tortolica
al socio deseado
en las riberas verdes ha hallado.

En soledad vivía,
y en soledad ha puesto ya su nido,
y en soledad la guía
a solas su querido,
también en soledad de amor herido.

ESPOSA

Gocémonos, Amado,
y vámonos a ver en tu hermosura
al monte u al collado,
do mana el agua pura ;
entremos más adentro en la espesura.

Y luego a las subidas
cavernas de la piedra nos iremos,
que están bien escondidas,
y allí nos entraremos,
y el mosto de granadas gustaremos.

Allí me mostrarías
aquello que mi alma pretendía
y luego me darías
allí tú, vida mía,
aquello que me diste el otro día.

El aspirar del aire,
el canto de la dulce Filomena,
el soto y su donaire,
en la noche serena
con llama que consume y no da pena.

Que nadie lo miraba,
Aminadab tampoco parecía,
y el cerco sosegaba,
y la caballería
a vista de las aguas descendía.

136. *Noche obscura*[1]

As the "Cántico" may have sprung from a cry of desolation uttered in the prison cell, so this, the most nearly perfect of the poems, may possibly have been inspired by the author's escape. Its more conscious art and the suggestions in it of spiritual serenity indicate a

[1] Or, more correctly, "Canciones del alma que se goza de haber llegado al alto estado de la perfección, que es la unión con Dios, por el camino de la negación espiritual."

later date, and the blunt, matter-of-fact lines, round which is woven so much beauty, are in fact an exact description of the flight from the Toledo prison :

En una noche obscura . . . .
salí sin ser notada,
estando ya mi casa sosegada.

For pure melody, and for restrained emotion, it would be hard to find forty lines of verse to surpass these : the vowel-play, the languishing cadences, and above all the perfect last line are sheer delight. Further formal beauty is attributable to the use of repetition, already experimented with in the " Cántico " ; to the short vigorous phrases, none of them ever brusque or harsh ; and to the vividness of the few and simple images. But there is beauty here, too, of a still higher kind. Note the construction of the poem, as precise as that of a drama—the emotional tone rising until the climax of the fifth stanza is reached, then continuing on a lower but well-sustained level to the end of the seventh, when it sinks to rest with a placid but unmistakable finality. Note, too, the interplay of the themes of darkness and light—light which is darkness, darkness which is light—culminating in the threefold apostrophe which endows night with the qualities of dawn. And even now we have taken no account of the sublimity of San Juan's great argument—the journey of the soul to union with God—to the height of which he rises with complete and apparently effortless perfection.

En una noche obscura,
con ansias en amores inflamada,
¡ oh dichosa ventura !
salí sin ser notada,
estando ya mi casa sosegada.

A escuras, y segura,
por la secreta escala disfrazada,
¡ oh dichosa ventura !
a escuras, y en celada,
estando ya mi casa sosegada.

En la noche dichosa,
en secreto, que nadie me veía,
ni yo miraba cosa,
sin otra luz y guía,
sino la que en el corazón ardía.

Aquesta me guiaba
más cierto que la luz del mediodía,
a donde me esperaba
quien yo bien me sabía,
en parte donde nadie parecía.

¡ Oh noche, que guiaste,
oh noche amable más que el alborada :
oh noche, que juntaste
Amado con amada,
amada en el Amado transformada !

En mi pecho florido,
que entero para él solo se guardaba,
allí quedó dormido,
y yo le regalaba,
y el ventalle de cedros aire daba.

El aire de la almena,
cuando yo sus cabellos esparcía,
con su mano serena
en mi cuello hería,
y todos mis sentidos suspendía.

Quedéme, y olvidéme,
el rostro recliné sobre el Amado.
Cesó todo, y dejéme,
dejando mi cuidado
entre las azucenas olvidado.

137. *Llama de amor viva*[1]

Here the soul is experiencing the most profound and intimate communion with God, and, by piling image upon image, the poet seems to be striving to express the ineffable. With each stanza the tone changes : from deep and fervent yearning (St. 1) to ejaculatory apostrophe charged with emotion (St. 2) ; thence to a rich and picturesque sustained metaphor (St. 3) and (St. 4) a majestic finale in which the dignified tread of the verse conveys a remarkable impression of complete confidence and satisfying security. Once again sound is a perfect

[1] The full title is : " Canciones del alma en la íntima comunicación de unión de amor de Dios."

minister to sense: the interlacing vowels of the feminine endings; the faint suggestions of alliteration; the predominance of liquid consonants; the deep, dark vowels which give dignity to such key-words as "resplandores", "profundas cavernas", "amoroso", "enamoras"; the play on the vowels a *and* e *in another of the few absolutely flawless "last lines" in Spanish poetry—these are some of the means by which this consummate artist attained effects of the greatest brilliance. And yet, when one turns back to the poem after reading the glowing commentary upon it much of which is itself a poem, one forgets all this, faced now with the sublimity of the experience which it succeeds to such an amazing extent in impressing upon the sensitive reader.*

¡ Oh llama de amor viva,
que tiernamente hieres
de mi alma en el más profundo centro !
Pues ya no eres esquiva,
acaba ya si quieres,
rompe la tela deste dulce encuentro.

¡ Oh cauterio suave !
¡ Oh regalada llaga !
¡ Oh mano blanda ! ¡ Oh toque delicado,
que a vida eterna sabe,
y toda deuda paga !
Matando, muerte en vida la has trocado.

¡ Oh lámparas de fuego,
en cuyos resplandores
las profundas cavernas del sentido,
que estaba obscuro y ciego,
con extraños primores
calor y luz dan junto a su querido !

¡ Cuán manso y amoroso
recuerdas en mi seno,
donde secretamente solo moras :
y en tu aspirar sabroso
de bien y gloria lleno
¡ cuán delicadamente me enamoras !

LUIS BARAHONA DE SOTO
1548-1595

BARAHONA DE SOTO's major work is *Las Lágrimas de Angélica* (1586), an imitation of Ariosto overpraised by Cervantes and esteemed by critics both temperamentally and chronologically as far apart as Lope de Vega and Luzán. "Ariosto en tono menor," it is called by Valbuena Prat,[1] who reminds us that it is the apparent source of Espinosa's *Fábula del Genil* and represents its author as marking one stage in the evolution from Herrera to Góngora. This, however, seems to me an exaggeration: not only did Barahona de Soto, in one of his sonnets, satirize Herrera's art but his art as a whole is less Baroque than either Herrera's or Espinosa's.

138. *Madrigal*

A fable-like story pleasantly told in melodious verse. The poet's Cupid is somewhat unconvincing and here and there (e.g., ll. 10-11) one finds a certain frigidity of metaphor. But the total effect, though never of dazzling attractiveness, is quite agreeable.

Un panal, lleno de sutil rocío,
de blanca miel hurtaba codicioso
Amor para su boca,
más dulce que el panal al gusto mío,
y no de mi reposo,
cuando una abeja toca,
con celo venenoso,
su tierna mano, atrevidilla y loca.
El niño con un ¡ ay ! tan doloroso
que arder hiciera el frío

[1] V.P., II, 141.

y enternecer lo duro de una roca,
la mano tiende y muéstrala herida
a su piadosa madre, que, temiendo
del caro hijo la ultrajada vida,
venido había corriendo ;
y al hijo, que pedía
por qué ponzoña en animal cabía
de quien tan dulce miel fué producida,
respóndele riendo :
" Más dulce es, aunque falsa, tu alegría,
y mas ponzoña en ti se esconde y cría."

ANONYMOUS

139. *Epístola moral a Fabio*

ONE of two poems to be wrested from Rioja (cf. p. 345: its "Fabio" is probably an imaginary or conventional personage, unconnected with Rodrigo Caro's) has been attributed both to Caro and to Medrano (p. 255), but is now generally credited to a Sevilian captain, Andrés Fernández de Andrada, who lived early in the seventeenth century but of whom we know practically nothing more. Though a moral poem in tercets is not a particularly attractive form, it fully merits the high praise which has been given it: Valbuena Prat calls it " the most finished example of its genre ",[1] while Montoliu (a Catalonian, it should be observed) hails it as an " expresión tan cabal del alma nacional castellana " and as a " joya única y perfecta " of Castilian literature.[2] Not all would go so far as this, though its defence of moderation and contentment against ambition is a perennial theme in that literature and both its grave, austere, dignified spirit and the sobriety and restraint of its language are wholly in keeping with the national character. It will be remembered, too, for its terse maxims, its homely but telling metaphors and an occasional touch of the sublime. But perhaps its greatest quality is an indescribable serenity, which it owes not only to its author's personal character but also to his extraordinary ear for rhythm. On it flows, like an imperturbable strong-running stream, a melodic picture of stoic tranquillity in the midst of confusion and unrest.

The poem lacks colour, warmth and (as most readers will think) emotion, though one constantly senses hidden depths of feeling which familiarity, to some extent, enables one to penetrate. Comparison is unavoidable with the author's fellow-Horatian, Luis de León, who soars oftener and higher, but in purity of expression seldom equals the *anónime sevillano* and never surpasses him. On the secular plane he might be termed the counterpart of the greater Spanish mystics.

[1] V.P., II, 178. [2] Mont., pp. 284-5.

Fabio, las esperanzas cortesanas
prisiones son do el ambicioso muere
y donde al más activo[1] nacen canas.

El que no las limare o las rompiere,
ni el nombre de varón ha merecido,
ni subir al honor que pretendiere.

El ánimo plebeyo y abatido
elija[2], en sus intentos temeroso,
primero[3] estar suspenso que caído;

que el corazón entero y generoso
al caso adverso inclinará la frente,
antes que la rodilla al poderoso.

Más triunfos, más coronas[4] dió al prudente
que supo retirarse, la fortuna,
que al que esperó obstinada y locamente.

Esta invasión terrible e importuna
de contrarios sucesos nos espera
desde el primer sollozo de la cuna:

dejémosla pasar como a la fiera
corriente del gran Betis, cuando airado
dilata hasta los montes su ribera.

Aquel entre los héroes es contado
que el premio mereció, no quien le alcanza
por vanas consecuencias del estado.

Peculio es propio ya de la privanza
cuanto de Astrea fué, cuanto regía
con su temida espada y su balanza.

El oro, la maldad, la tiranía
del inicuo procede y pasa al bueno:
¿qué espera la virtud, o qué confía?

Ven[5] y reposa en el materno seno
de la antigua Romúlea, cuyo clima
te será más humano y más sereno;

[1] Some versions have "astuto." A few other variants are given in succeeding footnotes.

[2] procure.

[3] antes.

[4] Más coronas, más triunfos.

[5] Vente.

adonde, por lo menos, cuando oprima
nuestro cuerpo la tierra, dirá alguno:
" ¡ Blanda le sea ! " al derramarla encima;

donde no dejarás la mesa ayuno
cuando te falte en ella el pece raro,
o cuando su pavón nos niegue Juno.

Busca, pues, el sosiego dulce y caro,
como, en la oscura noche del Egeo,
busca el piloto el eminente faro;

que si acortas y ciñes tu deseo,
dirás: " Lo que desprecio he conseguido ",
que la opinión vulgar es devaneo.

Más precia[1] el ruiseñor su pobre nido
de pluma y leves pajas, más sus quejas,
en el bosque[2] repuesto y escondido,

que agradar lisonjero las orejas
de algún príncipe insigne, aprisionado
en el metal de las doradas rejas.

¡ Triste de aquel que vive destinado
a esa antigua colonia de los vicios,
augur de los semblantes del privado !

Cese el ansia y la sed de los oficios,
que acepta el don y burla del intento
el ídolo a quien haces sacrificios.

Iguala con la vida el pensamiento,
y no le pasarás de hoy a mañana,
ni quizá de un momento a otro momento.

Casi no[3] tienes ni una sombra vana
de nuestra antigua Itálica, y ¿ qué esperas ?
¡ O error perpetuo de la suerte humana !

Las enseñas grecianas, las banderas
del senado y romana monarquía
murieron, y pasaron sus carreras.

¿ Qué es nuestra vida más que un breve día,
do, apenas sale el sol, cuando se pierde
en las tinieblas de la noche fría ?

[1] quiere. [2] monte. [3] Apenas.

¿ Qué más que el heno, a la mañana verde,
seco a la tarde ? ¡ O ciego desvarío !
¿ Será que de este sueño me[1] recuerde ?

¿ Será que pueda ver que me desvío
de la vida viviendo, y que está unida
la cauta muerte al simple vivir mío ?

Como los ríos, que en veloz corrida
se llevan a la mar, tal soy llevado
al último suspiro de mi vida.

De la pasada edad ¿ qué me ha quedado ?
o ¿ qué tengo yo a dicha en la que espero
sino ninguna[2] noticia de mi hado ?

¡ Oh, si acabase, viendo cómo muero,
de aprender a morir, antes que llegue
aquel forzoso término postrero,

antes que aquesta mies inútil siegue
de la severa muerte dura mano
y a la común materia se la entregue !

Pasáronse las flores del verano,
el otoño pasó con sus racimos,
pasó el invierno con sus nieves cano ;

las hojas que en las altas selvas vimos
cayeron, y nosotros, a porfía,
en nuestro engaño inmóviles vivimos.

Temamos al Señor, que nos envía
las espigas del año, y la hartura,
y la temprana lluvia y la tardía.

No imitemos la tierra siempre dura
a las aguas del cielo y al arado,
ni la vid cuyo fruto no madura.,

¿ Piensas acaso tú que fué criado
el varón para rayo de la guerra,
para sulcar el piélago salado,

para medir el orbe de la tierra
y el cerco donde[3] el sol siempre camina ?
¡ O, quien así lo entiende,[4] cuánto yerra !

[1] se. [2] alguna. [3] por do. [4] piensa.

Esta nuestra porción alta y divina,
a mayores acciones es llamada
y en más nobles objetos se termina.

Así aquella, que al hombre solo es dada,
sacra razón y pura me despierta,
de esplendor y de rayos coronada;

y en la fría región dura y desierta
de aqueste pecho, enciende nueva llama,
y la luz vuelve a arder que estaba muerta.

Quiero, Fabio, seguir a quien me llama,
y callado pasar entre la gente,
que no afecto a los nombres ni la fama.

El soberbio tirano del Oriente
que maciza las torres de cien codos
del cándido metal, puro y luciente,

apenas puede ya comprar los modos
del pecar; la virtud es más barata,
ella consigo misma ruega a todos.

¡Pobre de[1] aquel que corre y se dilata
por cuantos son los climas y los mares,
perseguidor del oro y de la plata!

Un ángulo me basta entre mis lares,
un libro y un amigo, un sueño breve
que no perturben deudas ni pesares:

esto tan solamente es cuanto debe
naturaleza al simple[2] y al discreto,
y algún manjar común, honesto y leve.

No, porque así te escribo, hagas conceto
que pongo la virtud en ejercicio;
que aun esto fué difícil a Epiteto.

Basta al que empieza aborrecer el vicio
y el ánimo enseñar a ser modesto:
después le será el cielo más propicio.

Despreciar el deleite no es supuesto
de sólida virtud, que aun el vicioso
en sí proprio le nota de molesto;

[1] Mísero [2] parco.

mas no podrás negarme cuán forzoso
este camino sea al alto asiento,
morada de la paz y del reposo.

No sazona la fruta en un momento
aquella Inteligencia, que mensura
la duración de todo a su talento.

Flor la vimos primero,[1] hermosa y pura,
luego materia acerba y desabrida,
y perfecta[2] después, dulce y madura.

Tal la humana prudencia[3] es bien que mida
y dispense y comparta[4] las acciones
que han de ser compañeras de la vida.

No quiera Dios que imite estos[5] varones
que gritan en las[6] plazas, macilentos,
de la virtud infames histriones;

esos inmundos trágicos, atentos
al aplauso común, cuyas entrañas
son infectos y oscuros[7] monumentos.

¡ Cuán callada que pasa las montañas
el aura, respirando mansamente !
¡ Qué gárrula y sonante[8] por las cañas !

¡ Qué muda la virtud por el prudente !
¡ Qué redundante y llena de ruído
por el vano, ambicioso y aparente !

Quiero imitar al pueblo en el vestido,
en las costumbres sólo a los mejores,
sin presumir de roto y mal ceñido.

No resplandezca el oro y las colores
en nuestro traje, ni tampoco sea
igual al de los dóricos cantores.

Una mediana vida yo posea,
un estilo común y moderado,
que no lo note nadie que lo vea.

[1] ayer. [2] sabrosa. [3] natura.
[4] y compase y dispense. [5] siga los. [6] moran nuestras.
[7] oscuros e infaustos. [8] sonora.

En el plebeyo barro mal tostado
hubo ya quien bebió, tan ambicioso
como en el vaso múr(r)ino preciado;

y alguno tan ilustre y generoso
que usó, como si fuera plata neta,[1]
de cristal transparente y luminoso.

Sin la templanza ¿ viste tú perfeta
alguna cosa ? ¡ O muerte ! ven callada,
como sueles venir en la saeta,

no en la tonante máquina, preñada
de fuego y de rumor, que no es mi puerta
de doblados metales fabricada.

Así, Fabio, me enseña descubierta
su esencia la verdad,[2] y mi albedrío
con ella se compone y se concierta.

No te burles de ver cuánto confío
ni al arte de decir, vana y pomposa,
el ardor atribuyas de este brío.

¿ Es por ventura menos poderosa
que el vicio la virtud, o menos fuerte ?[3]
No la arguyas de flaca y temerosa.

La codicia, en las manos de la suerte,
se arroja al mar, la ira a las espadas,
y la ambición se ríe de la muerte.

Y ¿ no serán siquiera tan osadas
las opuestas acciones, si las miro
de más ilustres genios[4] ayudadas ?

Ya, dulce amigo, huyo y me retiro
de cuanto simple amé ; rompí los lazos.
Ven y verás[5] al alto[6] fin que aspiro,
antes que el tiempo muera en nuestros brazos.

[1] fuese vil gabeta. [2] virtud. [3] la virtud ? ¿ Es menos fuerte ?
[4] de más nobles objetos. [5] sabrás. [6] grande.

LUPERCIO LEONARDO DE ARGENSOLA

1559-1613

This Aragonese writer and his younger brother Bartolomé (who was in Holy Orders) had somewhat similar careers. Each in turn was appointed Chronicler of Aragon and each in turn served as Secretary of State to the Conde de Lemos, Viceroy of Naples. In literature, both stand for the native tradition and for the Classical ideal. Italian influence they betray only in the rarest reminiscences of Petrarch and they foreshadow the Baroque age only in an occasional and temporary exuberance. They often imitate Horace and Juvenal; their diction is sober; their outlook on life, sane; they are seldom purely lyrical; the chief gifts they bring to literature are balance, proportion and restraint. It seemed, said Lope de Vega, as if they had come from Aragon to reform the language of the poets of Castile—and the dictum is applicable to more than language.

Lupercio left only half as much verse as Bartolomé, partly because of his shorter life and partly because he destroyed a great part of his own manuscript. He was rather the more elegant and polished of the two; his technical standards were high; he wrote (as his brother remarked) for "exquisite wits". The sonnet was just the type of instrument to suit him, and his best sonnets, though hardly inspired, are notable *objets d'art*. Most of his longer poems —*canciones*, *epístolas*, *tercetos*, etc.—are both diffuse and dull. The best known of them are some remote and conventional tercets on Aranjuez; a satire of nearly 600 lines, "A Flora", also known as "La Marquesilla"; and Canción II, "A la Esperanza", the opening of which is pleasantly Horatian, but the ending prosaic to the last degree. His love-poems have every known artifice but not a sign of feeling or a breath of passion.

140. *Soneto*

Except for the use of the word temo, *there is nothing personal about this sonnet : part of its attractiveness, indeed, lies in its detachment. But it has one memorable characteristic. The octave, with its Horatian imagery and its concise language, so closely packed that it inclines to obscurity, is complete in itself, and the sestet, as it opens, shows every sign of petering out in platitudinous observations upon death. Then, at l. 12, comes an unexpected twist of thought and all the talk about perils and slavery and death is seen to have been only a preface to the true theme of the poem. " What I really fear," says the poet, " is the mere thought that I may be forgotten. And that thought casts a shadow over me. For to be forgotten is to exist no longer and not to exist is the worst of all possible fates."*[1] *The sudden introduction of an insufficiently prepared theme may perhaps, in view of its effectiveness, be forgiven. But it is questionable whether the treatment of the theme is not somewhat forced and its sentiment unnatural. The poet, however, laughs last. Answers spring quickly to the reader's mind—but the sonnet is over !*

Technically it is an excellent piece of work, rounded off by a striking final line, which, incidentally, contains no less than four synalephas.

No temo los peligros del mar fiero
ni de un scita la odiosa servidumbre,
pues alivia los hierros la costumbre,
y al remo grave puede hacer ligero.

Ni oponer este pecho por terrero
de flechas a la inmensa muchedumbre ;
ni envuelta en humo la dudosa lumbre,
ver y esperar el plomo venidero.

Mal que tiene la muerte por extremo,
no le debe temer un desdichado ;
mas antes escogerle por partido.

La sombra sola del olvido temo,
porque es como no ser un olvidado,
y no hay mal que se iguale al no haber sido.

[1] Cf. Herrera's more vivid and impressive reference to the same theme :

En el silencio de la noche fría
me hiere el miedo del eterno olvido.

(*Poesías*, ed. García de Diego, Madrid, 1914 (C.C.), p. 52).

141. *Soneto*

This, perhaps, is the most impressive of Lupercio's sonnets, though the qualities it displays are quite unrelated to his typical balance and sobriety. Exuberance and bravado of language, force and vividness of imagery are its characteristics: from the bold and striking figure of the very first line, Lupercio points, not back to Castillejo, but forward to Góngora. Then come two magnificent word-pictures, each of only two lines, but glowing with autumnal splendour. First, the Aragonese river Ebro (Iberus), unwontedly swollen (insolente *is to be taken in the Latin sense*) *after the heavy rains, overflowing its banks, flooding its bridges and submerging the surrounding meadows. And then the Aragonese Sierra del Moncayo, that*

Excelso monte, cuya frente altiva
cubre de nubes tan escuro velo. . .[1]

of another of Lupercio's sonnets, newly unveiling its lofty snow-crowned brow. The succeeding images—a sunset which we hardly see, the howling wind sweeping ocean and forest, and the people taking refuge from it—are less vivid than these but make a striking contribution to the general effect. The final tercet, with its suggestion of that desengaño *so often found in the Baroque, is something of an anti-climax; but, though the pictures fade and there is no powerful thought to bind them together, the music keeps up its majesty to the very end.*

Lleva[2] tras sí los pámpanos octubre,
y con las grandes lluvias insolente,
no sufre Ibero márgenes ni puente,
mas antes los vecinos campos cubre.

Moncayo, como suele, ya descubre
coronada de nieve la alta frente;
y el sol apenas vemos en oriente,
cuando la opaca tierra nos lo encubre.

Sienten el mar y selvas ya la saña
del Aquilón, y encierra su bramido
gente en el puerto y gente en la cabaña.

Y Fabio, en el umbral de Tais tendido,
con vergonzosas lágrimas lo baña,
debiéndolas al tiempo que ha perdido.

[1] *Ed. cit.*, p. 286.

[2] Or, as in the *Flores de poetas ilustres*, "llevó."

LUPERCIO O BARTOLOMÉ LEONARDO DE ARGENSOLA

142. *Soneto*

This aristocratic companion-piece to the merry satires of Góngora and Quevedo must be the most modern sonnet that the Golden Age ever produced. There is not a word in it that dates and it would be a gilding of the lily to insist upon its liveliness and charm. Note the unaffected, conversational opening; the natural and technically admirable progression from octave to sestet; the heightening, by paradox and antithesis, of the gentle irony; and the exclamation of mock dismay which brings a perfect sonnet to a perfect close.

First published in the second edition of Luzán's Poética *(1789), the sonnet was then attributed to Lupercio, but the best evidence now available gives it to his brother Bartolomé.*

Yo os quiero conceder[1], Don Juan, primero,
que aquel blanco y carmín[2] de Doña Elvira
no tiene de ella más, si bien se mira,
que el haberle costado su dinero.

Pero también que me confieses quiero[3]
que es tanta la beldad de su mentira
que en vano a competir con ella aspira
belleza igual de rostro verdadero.

Mas ¿ qué mucho que yo perdido ande
por un engaño tal, pues que sabemos
que nos engaña así naturaleza ?

Porque ese cielo azul que todos vemos
¡ ni es cielo, ni es azul ! ¡ Lástima grande
que no sea verdad tanta belleza !

[1] confesar.

[2] color.

[3] Pero tras eso confesaros quiero.

BARTOLOMÉ LEONARDO DE ARGENSOLA

1562-1631

In his longer poems, Bartolomé Leonardo is little, if at all, superior to Lupercio, though he differs from him in giving greater prominence to religion. His love-poems are as devoid of feeling as of reality. In poems of moral or religious inspiration, however, he often writes with genuine sincerity and even emotion. His sonnets have perhaps less technical skill than Lupercio's but they have certainly greater poetic force and soar in more rapid flights to higher levels of thought and feeling. Occasionally one finds in him a somewhat elusive semi-mystical strain which rewards study.

143. *Soneto*

The remarkable feature of this poem is its complete domination by the metaphor of the phœnix. Except for the rather weak l. 8, the octave is a masterpiece of pure impressiveness. But even through the sestet, a somewhat forced application of the metaphor to the author's experience, the initial impression persists, and saves the poem from anything like triviality.

De antigua palma en la suprema altura
con los sacros olores del oriente,
para su parto y muerte juntamente,
hace la fénix nido y sepultura.

Mueve las alas para arder segura,
que el fuego a su esperanza está obediente ;
y así, sus llamas fieles más luciente
la restituyen a la edad futura.

Desta manera en la sagrada palma
de vuestro alto valor arder presume
mi pensamiento alegre entre sus ramas ;

que vuestro ardor da vida al que consume ;
y así, no es temerario el que a sus llamas
entrega el gran depósito del alma.

144. *Soneto*

Save in one single respect, this sonnet has, I think, been overrated by anthologists, who invariably reproduce it, and by critics, who all but unanimously term it "magnificent" or "splendid" and consider it Bartolomé's masterpiece. The opening invocation is telling enough and even suggestive of restrained emotion. But the ten lines of complaint which follow grow weaker as they proceed, and the unnatural inversions lead to some obscurity. The complaint concludes with a pointlessly alliterating tercet, which draws vague pictures of unspecified "iniquitous hands" waving "victorious palms" and of a very abstract "virtue" sighing at the rejoicing of some anonymous "unjust" person over a "triumph" of which nothing further is known. The confusion is not cleared up by the projection into it of a "celestial nymph"—who for some mysterious reason is "laughing". But the single line she utters transforms the poem entirely and deserves all the adjectives which have been showered upon the sonnet as a whole. The trenchant "¡Ciego!" cuts right into the verbiage—one might almost say "explodes" among it—and the question which follows not only dispels the querulousness of the plaints, but, with that indefinable suggestiveness which so often accompanies great poetry, opens up a new world of thought. Further, it introduces a figure from the language of mysticism which raises the last line of the poem far above the level of the rest.

"Dime, Padre común, pues eres justo,
¿por qué ha de permitir tu providencia
que, arrastrando prisiones la inocencia,
suba la fraude a tribunal augusto?

"¿Quién da fuerzas al brazo que robusto
hace a tus leyes firme resistencia,
y que el celo, que más la reverencia,
gima a los pies del vencedor injusto?

"Vemos que vibran vitoriosas palmas
manos inicuas, la virtud gimiendo
del triunfo en el injusto regocijo."

Esto decía yo, cuando riendo
celestial ninfa apareció, y me dijo:
"¡Ciego! ¿Es la tierra el centro de las almas?"

145. *Soneto*

Here the poet carries us to the realms of mysticism, to the very threshold of the Illuminative Life. "The loving-kindness of the Lord is overthrowing the soul's idols and once more light is pouring into the interior castle. May the affections be ready for the knife and the purifying fire." That is the octave's noble theme, nobly and poetically expressed. The sestet changes the figure and calls upon the contemplative's two ministers, silence and solitude, to shut out from him the distracting activities of sense. No profane eye must witness the clothing of the spirit in that eternal light beside which all temporal light is as darkness.

It might be argued that the change of metaphor is too sudden and too complete for the preservation of the sonnet's artistic unity, and the language of the whole poem may sound a little strange to those accustomed to the terminology of Santa Teresa and San Juan de la Cruz. But it cannot be denied that this is a remarkable sonnet and it is strange that it should previously have almost entirely escaped notice.

Ya tu piedad magnánima derriba
mis ídolos, Señor ; ya por ti espero
que restituya el resplandor primero
a mi templo interior su luz nativa.

Animoso el afecto se aperciba
para víctima al fuego verdadero ;
sienta el furor del religioso acero,
pues que no ha de arder víctima viva.

Silencio y soledad, ministros puros
de alta contemplación, tended el velo
a profanos sentidos inferiores.

No acechen cómo ciñe el tercer cielo
la mente de tan limpios resplandores,
que a todos los visibles deja escuros.

JOSEF DE VALDIVIELSO
1560-1638

One of the best of the many minor poets who wrote upon religious themes, Valdivielso, a Toledan priest, is known chiefly for a *Romancero espiritual* (1612), which contains verses written to be sung at the Exposition of the Blessed Sacrament, for a long and somewhat mediocre narrative poem to St. Joseph and for some *autos sacramentales* not unworthy to be compared with those of better-known authors.

146. *Villancico al encerrar el Santísimo Sacramento*

Though perhaps normally at his best in verse of popular, even rustic, inspiration, Valdivielso left a few superlatively good poems of a highly personal kind, of which this is one. Note its unity, the simplicity of its central thought and its almost complete absence of imagery.

Ya no verán mis ojos
cosa que les dé placer,
hasta volveros a ver.

Quien llenar pudo el deseo
del bien que en veros se encierra,
¿ qué podrá ver en la tierra,
que no le parezca feo ?
En Vos cuanto quiero veo
y sin Vos no hay qué querer
hasta volveros a ver.

Cuando mirándoos estoy,
estoy otro del que fuí,
que sin veros no me vi,
y mirándoos, veo quién soy :
tras Vos con los ojos voy,
pues no los he menester
hasta volveros a ver.

Si os vais, divino manjar,
llevad mis ojos tras Vos :
que ojos que vieron a Dios,
¿ qué pueden sin Dios mirar ?
Veros, Señor, es gozar,
y no veros padecer
hasta volveros a ver.

147. *Letra a un Crucifijo*

The touch of poetry in the refrain of this letra *brings out its hidden emotion and redeems it from a possible charge of affectation. Its deeply personal note, its display of almost womanly feeling and its reference to the trees keeping guard over the sleeping Christ suggest a comparison with Lope de Vega's " Pues andáis en las palmas " (pp. 299-301), of which it is also the equal in verbal melody.*

Vientecico murmurador,
que lo miras y andas todo,
haz el son con las hojas del olmo,
mientras duerme mi lindo amor.

En la cama estrecha y dura
se durmió después de cena,
por hacer suya mi pena,
y su sueño mi soltura :
duerme como otro Sansón,
atado el bien de mis ojos.
Haz el son con las hojas del olmo,
mientras duerme mi lindo amor.

No perturbes su quietud,
que duerme mal quien bien ama,
y duerme en la Cruz por cama
el sueño de la salud :
duerme, y no su corazón,
que me vela cuidadoso.
Haz el son con las hojas del olmo,
mientras duerme mi lindo amor.

Durmióse con pesadilla,
y sacó, de amor deshecho,
a su esposa de su pecho,
como Adán de su costilla ;
la cabeza me inclinó,
por verme en su pecho roto.
Haz el son con las hojas del olmo,
mientras duerme mi lindo amor.

LOPE FÉLIX DE VEGA CARPIO

1562-1635

THE crowded and adventurous life of Lope de Vega, Spain's most prolific, and in some ways most remarkable, dramatist, is as well known to us as Herrera's is shrouded in mystery. As a boy he wrote verses, ran away from school, became page to a Bishop, and perhaps attended the University of Alcalá de Henares. As a young man he was banished from Castile on a charge of libel, ran away with a lady and made her his wife, fought in the " Invincible " Armada, and, on his return to Spain, became secretary to the young Duke of Alba. He had begun writing plays when very young; yet his first success was not a play, but a long narrative poem on San Isidro, Patron of Madrid (1599). He soon became Spain's uncrowned laureate, and thenceforward, until his death, wrote and published voluminously; as early as 1619, he claimed to have finished 900 plays and twelve books of prose and verse, as well as a vast mass of unpublished opuscules. He married again, lost his second wife, and then, although his private life had been anything but exemplary, took Holy Orders. He was the leading literary man of his day, in request everywhere: though he had many domestic sorrows, his public life was one unclouded triumph. He continued writing plays almost to the day of his death. And primarily he will always be known by these—" animated and picturesque, gay and reckless . . . a picture of a restricted and more or less imaginary society, so lifelike and so minute as to be unrivalled."[1]

No short selection from the poems of this extraordinary genius can do him justice, for his output, in non-dramatic as in dramatic verse, is as varied as it is immense. Besides writing verse epics, satires, burlesques and romances totalling many thousands of lines, together with many hundreds of shorter poems, such as sonnets, eclogues, elegies, odes, epistles and ballads, he intercalated some of his most charming lyrics in his prose works (notably in *La Arcadia*,

[1] H. Butler Clarke: *History of Spanish Literature*, London, 1893, p. 168.

El Peregrino en su patria, *Los Pastores de Belén* and *La Dorotea*) and in his dramas. The pieces which follow are all examples of his shorter poems, and complete in themselves. Through them we shall look at him from two standpoints—as a writer of cultured verse, standing in the line of Boscán, Garcilaso and Herrera, and as a popular poet, a descendant of the ballad-writers, the Marqués de Santillana and Castillejo.

In the former sphere his greatest achievements are his sonnets, secular and devout, from the collections entitled *Rimas humanas* and *Rimas sacras* respectively. With a much stronger sense of form than might be expected of so prolific a writer, he fashioned his instrument skilfully, though it is apt to be a somewhat lifeless one save when he sings of love. Of human love, with all its moods and facets, in verses full of warmth and colour, tending to the hyperbolic and occasionally fringing on conceptism. But more intensely and movingly of Divine love. He was a great sinner, and knew it, but he sang of his own unworthiness, of the goodness of God and of his constant longings to serve Him. Not all who read him will understand, for

> La lengua del amor a quien no sabe
> lo que es amor, ¡ qué bárbara parece ![1]

But all will surely sense the emotion which pulsates and throbs in some of his white-hot lines :

> ¡ O quién muriera por tu amor ardiendo
> en vivas llamas, dulce Jesús mío ![2]

> Ponme a la sombra de tu cruz divina,
> y vengan contra mí fuego, aire, tierra,
> mar, hierro, engaño, envidia, infierno y muerte.[3]

> Luz que ilumina el sol, las once esferas,
> luz ¿ quién es luz, sino tu luz hermosa ?[4]

As a popular poet Lope seems to infuse into his simple verses all the vivacity, spontaneity and freshness which permeate his dramas. To these must be added a delicacy and grace hardly surpassed in Spain ; an emotion skilfully controlled but ever and anon threatening to break its bonds ; and a fancy which can play not only impishly but ethereally, and " ride on the curl'd clouds " at the bidding of this Spanish Prospero. These little poems—

1 *Rimas sacras*, XX (*Ed. cit.*, XIII, 185).
2 *Op. cit.*, XL (XIII, 195).
3 *Op. cit.*, LXXXV (XIII, 217).
4 *Op. cit.*, XXXIV (XIII, 192).

many of them in the etymological sense of the word "lyrics"—often use the simplest and least conventional language, yet are instinct with the very essence of poetry. Some of them are found in the plays—"Deja las avellanicas" in *El Villano en su rincón;* "Velador que el castillo velas" in *Las Almenas de Toro;* "Blanca me era yo" in *El Gran Duque de Muscovia;* etc. But here again Lope's fancy was never brighter, just as his emotion was never deeper, than when he was treating sacred themes. And among the loveliest and most inspiring of his little songs are those which enliven the rather arid pages of *Los Pastores de Belén*, a prose narrative describing the early history of the Holy Family.

The same traits, together with a rapidity of movement found also in the action of his dramas, are characteristic of Lope's *romances*, most of which, in subject, are either pastoral or Moorish. At their worst, they charm and captivate by their formal perfection; but more frequently they are distinguished by a soaring fancy or a restrained emotion which gives them real power. Sometimes, again, Lope's conceptist tendencies find an outlet in this kind of verse, and he enjoys lurking among the thickets of this native Spanish growth to play games of hide-and-seek with his reader. In any or all of these moods (which often change as rapidly as thought) he is unfailingly delightful. The achievement of having written so much, and yet written so well, is more remarkable in his poems even than in his dramas.

SONNETS

Of the seven sonnets which follow, the first three are from the *Rimas humanas*; the remainder from the *Rimas sacras*.

148. *Rimas Humanas: Soneto IV*

Lope de Vega is not often merely (or even recognizably) Petrarchan: like Herrera, and perhaps more markedly than he, the Phœnix of Wits has absorbed much from Petrarch, but has assimilated it completely into his poetic system. Now and again, however, he draws directly and noticeably upon the Italian poet or his Spanish devotees—most strikingly in the first sonnet of the Rimas sacras:

Cuando me paro a contemplar mi estado,
y a ver los pasos por donde he venido[1]. . . .

[1] *Ed. cit.*, XIII, 175.

which closely follows Garcilaso's first sonnet (p. 172, above) and Petrarch's Sonetto XXX in morte. *A second example, recalling Boscán's eighty-second sonnet (p. 170, above) and Petrarch's Sonetto CLIII* in vita *("Dolci ire. . . ."), is this, the fourth of the* Rimas humanas, *which may be considered as representative of that collection.*

Rodríguez Marín relates ll. 1-4 to the death of Lope's wife Isabel ("Belisa") and supposes that he met the lady who inspired it on the day before that happening. Montesinos (C.C., *LXVIII*, 47) *demurs to the implication of heartlessness which such a hypothesis implies and to the inconsistency of his calling his late wife, of whom he was certainly very fond, "sin igual", and yet of terming the day on which he met his new love (who would not have been flattered at the open partition of allegiance) "alegre". This critic's suggestion is that the day referred to is the eve of the Assumption of Our Lady—a hypothesis which admirably suits the spirit and language of the quatrain, and, in my view, hardly admits of question (cf. Petrarch : Sonetto III* in vita *: "Era 'l giorno ch'al Sol si scoloraro. . . .")*

Neither the music of the poem—especially of its three concluding lines—nor its idealistic, Petrarchan tone will need any emphasis. Admirably constructed, on a threefold plan of exposition, climax and crisis of emotion, it treats a single idea with consummate skill. Without containing any one line or phrase of unforgettable brilliance, it may fairly be described as approaching perfection.

Era la alegre víspera del día,
que la que sin igual nació en la tierra
de la cárcel mortal y humana guerra
para la patria celestial salía.

Y era la edad en que más viva ardía
la nueva sangre que mi pecho encierra,
cuando el consejo y la razón destierra
la vanidad, que el apetito guía ;

cuando amor me enseñó la vez primera
de Lucinda en su sol los ojos bellos
y me abrasó, como si rayo fuera.

Dulce prisión y dulce arder por ellos ;
sin duda que su fuego fué mi esfera
que con verme morir descanso en ellos.[1]

[1] Note the rhyme-scheme of the sestet (*cdcdcd*) and the "identical" rhymes of ll. 12, 14. Both are common in Lope.

149. *Rimas Humanas : Soneto XXXII*

Again the poet idealizes love, and again in a poem impeccable as to form, with an emotional tension which rises all the way through till it reaches that final line which so fittingly concludes it. The figures of speech, it is true, have little originality or vividness, but their cumulative effect, enhanced by Lope's favourite device of brief enumerations, is considerable. For emotion can be evoked as readily by oratorical play with familiar ideas as by the unexpected enunciation of novel ones. None the less, there is a somewhat chilly objectivity in the sonnet which shuts it out from real greatness, and perhaps this trait is the more noticeable just because in Lope's lyric poetry the personal note is heard with such frequency.

Si gasta el mar la endurecida roca
con el curso del agua tierna y blanda,
si el Español que entre los Indios anda
con largo trato a su amistad provoca ;

si al ruego el aspid la fiereza apoca,
si el fuego al hierro la dureza ablanda,
no yerra amor, cuando esperar le manda
un imposible a mi esperanza loca.

Que el tiempo, que las rocas enternece,
Indios, aspides, hierros, bien podría
sirviendo, amando, cuanto amor concede ;

por más que mi desdicha os endurece,
Señora, enterneceros algún día,
que un inmortal amor todo lo puede.

150. *Rimas Humanas : Soneto XLIII*

On a first reading, one would call this merely a collection of pretty conceits, of the "twopence coloured" variety, in a setting—an engaste, *shall we say?—of perfect form. About the correctness of this definition, as far as it goes, there would be no dispute. Fancy is allowed to run riot, and only acceptance of the hyperboles makes the poem even tolerable. Every reader will remark upon the excellence of the construction. Note how the theme-word on which the poem opens is caught up at l. 5, as are also the key-words to ll. 4, 8 in l. 14—*

an exquisite " last line ", satisfying alike to eye, ear and brain. Note also the increasing tension of the emotional tone with the double repetition of " Ahora sí. . . ." in the sestet. A perception, in fact, of the emotion with which the poem is charged is the key to a true appreciation of it. The constantly recurring words " ojos ", " azul ", "luz ", " cielo " carry more than their ordinary meaning; the hyperboles are not mere artificialities; it is not by chance that the personal note is struck in the first line. Just as the scent of a flower is brought out by the warmth of a room, so the fragrance of this sonnet will yield itself increasingly to the reader in whom it finds a receptive atmosphere. Mere artificiality soon cloys, but here familiarity will reveal ever greater beauty.

Ojos, por quien llamé dichoso al día,
en que nací, para morir por veros,
que por salir de noche a ser luceros,
cercáis de azul la luz que al sol la envía ;

hermosos ojos, que del alma mía
un inmortal engaste pienso haceros
de envidia del zafir, que por quereros
entre cristal y rosa el cielo cría.

Ahora sí, que vuestras luces bellas
son de mi noche celestial consuelo,
pues en azul engaste vengo a vellas.

Ahora sí, que sois la luz del suelo,
ahora sí, que sois ojos estrellas,
que estáis en campo azul, color de cielo.

151. *Rimas Sacras : Dios, Centro del alma*

Notwithstanding commentators' frequent application of the word "mystical" to the Rimas sacras, *there is scarcely anything in them which merits such description—only a love for, and a trust in, God which is, as it were, mysticism's raw material. This poem, however —one of the " named " sonnets of that collection—develops an idea often found in mystical literature, especially in literature inspired by St. Augustine, applying it, with the help of one vivid metaphor, to the master-theme of the author's sacred verse—his own sinfulness and*

God's mercy. Even had the sonnet less technical excellence (marred only, to the modern ear, by the identical rhyme in ll. 12, 14) its manifest and eager sincerity would give it distinction. But the impression which it makes upon the mind is due also to a formal characteristic—the repetition of the dominant idea, like the low, deep note of a bell, suggestive of the insistent appeal described in the line

aunque me buscas tú del alma adentro.

Si fuera de mi amor verdad el fuego,
él caminara a tu divina esfera,
pero es cometa que corrió ligera
con resplandor que se deshizo luego.

¡ Qué deseoso de tus brazos llego
cuando el temor mis culpas considera !
Mas si mi amor en ti no persevera,
¿ en qué centro mortal tendrá sosiego ?

Voy a buscarte, y cuanto más te encuentro,
menos reparo en ti, Cordero manso,
aunque me buscas tú del alma adentro.

Pero dime, Señor : si hallar descanso
no puede el alma fuera de su centro,
y estoy fuera de ti ¿ cómo descanso ?

152. *Rimas Sacras : Soneto XIV*

This poignant and moving sonnet, built on the Scriptural theme of the Good Shepherd, reveals Lope's full technical perfection. It might be objected that the idea of the fashioning of a crook from the wood of the True Cross (ll. 3-4) is both inartistic and artificial, but the allegorical significance of the phrase is so evident that one hardly thinks of it as a metaphor. The repetition of the theme-word at the opening of the sestet gives added force to the chief beauty of the poem—the sudden, almost startling, modulation of thought in ll. 13-14 and the resolution of the melody in a fresh key ; or, to use a more obvious metaphor, the vanishing of the picture : "My sheep hear My voice, and I know them, and they follow Me" and the emergence of another : "Behold, I stand at the door and knock." Since the formal charm of the poem is as much auditory as visual, the musical figure will be felt to be as appropriate as the pictorial. Its melody consists largely in skilful vowel-play and in a rippling alliteration of consonants (especially in ll. 9-11) the effect of which is largely subconscious. A reading of the sonnet aloud will show how much of its power depends on the slowing-up of the rate at the end of the sestet, and this is aided, first, by the sudden stop at the end of l. 12, and then by the threefold repetition of accented a *in l. 14.*

Pastor, que con tus silbos amorosos
me despertaste del profundo sueño;
tú, que hiciste cayado de ese leño
en que tiendes los brazos poderosos:

vuelve los ojos a mi fe piadosos,
pues te confieso por mi amor y dueño
y la palabra de seguirte empeño
tus dulces silbos y tus pies hermosos.

Oye, Pastor, que por amores mueres,
no te espante el rigor de mis pecados,
pues tan amigo de rendidos eres.

Espera, pues, y escucha mis cuidados—
pero ¿ cómo te digo que me esperes
si estás para esperar los pies clavados ?

153. *Rimas Sacras : Soneto XVIII*

Here, in his opening picture, Lope seems to have returned to the closing image of Soneto XIV, as though its possibilities had struck him afresh, and the whole of the octave consists in a most skilful intensification of it by the addition of telling and affecting detail. Some, nevertheless, may think the figure in ll. 7-8 excessively artificial. Characteristic of the entire poem is its twofold and alternating appeal to eye and ear. But to me its most effective moment is its simplest—the poignancy of the conclusion, expressed though its sentiments are in almost colloquial language, which gains in force from its contrast with the phrase "Hermosura soberana", so rich with memories of St. Augustine, and charged with a cumulative emotion of centuries.

¿ Qué tengo yo, que mi amistad procuras ?
¿ Qué interés se te sigue, Jesús mío,
que a mi puerta, cubierto de rocío,
pasas las noches del invierno escuras ?

¡ Oh, cuánto fueron mis entrañas duras,
pues no te abrí ! ¡ Qué extraño desvarío
si de mi ingratitud el hielo frío
secó las llagas de tus plantas puras !

¡ Cuántas veces el ángel me decía :
Alma, asómate ahora a la ventana,
verás con cuánto amor llamar porfía !

¡ Y cuántas, Hermosura soberana :
Mañana le abriremos, respondía,
para lo mismo responder mañana !

154. *Rimas Sacras : Soneto XLVI*

The opening of the octave, simple in form, is followed by a torrent of Baroque metaphor, recalling (both in type and in detail) the language of the seventh chapter of the Song of Solomon. The sestet, by comparison, is something of an anti-climax, though it is saved by a final hyperbole which is in full harmony with the spirit of the octave. The application of the imagery of physical beauty is the more effective as coming from a poet for whom this beauty had so strong an appeal.

No sabe qué es amor quien no te ama,
celestial hermosura, esposo bello :
tu cabeza es de oro, y tu cabello
como el cogollo que la palma enrama ;

tu boca como lirio, que derrama
licor al alba ; de marfil tu cuello ;
tu mano el torno, y en su palma el sello,
que el alma por disfraz jacintos llama.

¡ Ay Dios ! ¿ en qué pensé cuando, dejando
tanta belleza, y las mortales viendo,
perdí lo que pudiera estar gozando ?

Mas si del tiempo que perdí me ofendo,
tal prisa me daré, que un hora amando
venza los años que pasé fingiendo.

LOS PASTORES DE BELÉN

155. *¿Dónde vais, zagala. . . .?*

This lyric, which, like the two following it, is taken from Los Pastores de Belén, *is a gloss on St. Luke i, 39-40 (" And Mary arose in those days, and went into the hill country with haste, into a city of Juda; and entered into the house of Zacharias, and saluted Elisabeth.") The preceding lines of the prose narrative describe the Virgin's journey in picturesque but hyperbolic terms:*

> *¿Dijérasle si quería compañía? No; que llevaba la de Dios y sus ángeles. ¿Dijérasle si quería algún regalo? No; que bien regalada iría de todo el cielo, y por donde quiera que pasaba, los árboles se inclinar an a servirla, los unos con sus frutas, y los otros con sus sombras.*[1]

This language is fully in harmony with that of the last stanza of the poem, but this is its less admirable part, contrasting unnaturally with the simplicity of the first stanza and conflicting with the mystical appeal of the refrain. It is this refrain that makes the poem so memorable, lighting it up with one brilliant flash of imagination and transforming the figure of the zagala *so that we see in her the Mother of God.*

Later in the same work comes a lyric on the Epiphany with similar inspiration, beginning:

Reyes, que venís por ellas,
no busquéis estrellas ya,
porque donde el sol está
no tienen luz las estrellas.[2]

¿Dónde vais, zagala,
sola en el monte?
Mas quièn lleva el sol
no teme la noche.

[1] *Ed. cit.*, XVI, 43.

[2] *Ed. cit.*, XVI, 374.

¿ Dónde vais, María,
divina esposa,
madre gloriosa
de quien os cría ?
¿ Que haréis, si el día
se va al Ocaso,
y en el monte acaso
la noche os coge ?
Mas quien lleva el sol
no teme la noche.

El ver las estrellas
me causa enojos,
pero vuestros ojos
más lucen que ellas.
Ya sale con ellas
la noche escura,
a vuestra hermosura
la luz se esconde.
Mas quien lleva el sol
no teme la noche.

156. "*Campanitas de Belén. . . .*"

In their careless style, their simple language and their sudden excursion (ll. 9-11) into onomatopoeia, these stanzas (of unequal length, it will be observed) recall the traditional English carol. The effect of the onomatopoeia is rather skilfully, and not too obviously, enhanced by the leonine rhymes and also by the alliteration " tocan, tocan y tañen ", which is echoed all through the poem. The simplicity of the language, it should be added, is somewhat marred by the image in l. 3 and also by the paradoxical opening of the last stanza.

Campanitas de Belén,
tocad al Alba, que sale
vertiendo divino aljófar,
sobre el sol que della nace,
que los ángeles tocan,
tocan y tañen.

Que es Dios hombre el sol,
y el Alba su madre :
din, din, din, que vino en fin,
don, don, don, San Salvador,
dan, dan, dan, que hoy nos le dan,
tocan y tañen a gloria en el cielo,
y en la tierra tocan a paz.

En Belén tocan al Alba
casi al primer arrebol,
porque della sale el sol,
que de la noche nos salva.
Si las aves hacen salva
al Alba del sol que ven,
Campanitas de Belén,
tocad al Alba, que sale
vertiendo divino aljófar,
sobre el sol que della nace,
que los ángeles tocan,
tocan y tañen.

Este sol se hiela y arde
de amor y frío en su Oriente,
para que la humana gente
el cielo sereno aguarde,
y aunque dicen que una tarde
se pondrá en Jerusalén,
Campanitas de Belén,
tocad al Alba, que sale
vertiendo divino aljófar,
sobre el sol que della nace,
que los ángeles tocan,
tocan y tañen.

157. " *Pues andáis en las palmas. . . .*"

This so-called " Cantarcillo de la Virgen ", a Christmas cradle-song, is generally printed without the romances *which introduce it. But in reality the simple and charming, if slightly sentimental, picture of the " niña bella "—emphatically a Murillo Virgin—is as essential a background to the cradle-song as is a recitative in an oratorio to its aria. The perfect simplicity and appropriateness of the Virgin's language, which at once calls for notice, contrasts very strikingly with a most florid and decorative prose passage immediately preceding the* romances, *in which the shepherd Aminadab successfully rivals the Baroque similitudes of the* Song of Solomon.

The aria (if the term may be permitted) gains in beauty from the change of metre. It is of course the picturesque figure of the palm-trees that has made it famous, but to this, which occupies the refrain and the first stanza only, must be added the exquisite melody of the whole. Montesinos hardly exaggerates when he describes the poem as " ese maravilloso ' Pues andáis en las palmas ', sin igual en nuestra poesía ". (C.C., *LXXV*, 47).

La niña a quien dijo el ángel
que estaba de gracia llena,
cuando de ser de Dios madre
le trujo tan altas nuevas,

ya le mira en un pesebre,
llorando lágrimas tiernas,
que obligándose a ser hombre
también se obliga a sus penas.

" ¿ Qué tenéis, dulce Jesús ? "
le dice la niña bella.
" ¿ Tan presto sentís, mis ojos,
el dolor de mi pobreza ?

Yo no tengo otros palacios
en que recibiros pueda,
sino mis brazos y pechos,
que os regalan y sustentan.

No puedo más, amor mío,
porque si yo más pudiera,
vos sabéis que vuestros cielos
envidiaran mi riqueza ".

El niño recién nacido
no mueve la pura lengua,
aunque es la sabiduría
de su Eterno Padre inmensa,

mas revelándole al alma
de la Virgen la respuesta,
cubrió de sueño en sus brazos
blandamente sus estrellas.

Ella entonces, desatando
la voz regalada y tierna,
así tuvo a su armonía
la de los cielos suspensa :

Pues andáis en las palmas,
ángeles santos,
que se duerme mi niño,
tened los ramos.

Palmas de Belén,
que mueven airados
los furiosos vientos
que suenan tanto,
no le hagáis ruido,
corred más paso,
que se duerme mi niño,
tened los ramos.

El niño divino,
que está cansado
de llorar en la tierra,
por su descanso
sosegar quiere un poco
del tierno llanto,
que se duerme mi niño,
tened los ramos.

Rigurosos hielos
le están cercando ;
ya veis que no tengo
con qué guardarlo.
Ángeles divinos,
que vais volando,
que se duerme mi niño,
tened los ramos.

LA DOROTEA

158. "*A mis soledades voy. . . .*"

At first sight a rather rambling composition of twenty-eight four-lined stanzas with a lazy and pleasant assonance in e-o, *written in the natural style of a letter, this most celebrated of the verse-interludes in the* Dorotea *grows greatly on the reader with familiarity. Whimsical, paradoxical, subtle—with more than a touch about it, indeed, of conceptism—it should be read by the side of the preceding popular lyrics if it is to convey an idea of Lope's versatility. The playfulness of the opening lines soon gives place to serious reflection and biting satire: yet the tone of the whole poem remains deceptively light—it might be a more trifle. The personal angle merits notice. The* autorretrato *just escapes being a confession: the reader is eager to know more, but the poet keeps him at arm's length with mocking irony. The epigrammatical cast of the stanzas, too, is striking: each stanza is drawn with two or three bold and rapid strokes; each is complete in itself.*

A mis soledades voy,
de mis soledades vengo,
porque para andar conmigo
me bastan mis pensamientos.

No sé qué tiene la aldea
donde vivo y donde muero,
que con venir de mí mismo
no puedo venir más lejos.

Ni estoy bien ni mal conmigo,
mas dice mi entendimiento
que un hombre, que todo es alma,
está cautivo en su cuerpo.

Entiendo lo que me basta,
y solamente no entiendo
cómo se sufre a sí mismo
un ignorante soberbio.

De cuantas cosas me cansan
fácilmente me defiendo,
pero no puedo guardarme
de los peligros de un necio.

Él dirá que yo lo soy,
pero con falso argumento,
que humildad y necedad
no caben en un sujeto.

La diferencia conozco,
porque en él y en mí contemplo
su locura en su arrogancia,
mi humildad en mi desprecio.

O sabe naturaleza
más que supo en este tiempo,
o tantos que nacen sabios
es porque lo dicen ellos.

" Sólo sé que no sé nada ",
dijo un filósofo, haciendo
la cuenta con su humildad,
adonde lo más es menos.

No me precio de entendido,
de desdichado me precio,
que los que no son dichosos
¿ cómo pueden ser discretos ?

No puede durar el mundo,
porque dicen, y lo creo,
que suena a vidrio quebrado
y que ha de romperse presto.

Señales son del juicio
ver que todos le perdemos,
unos por carta de más,
otros por carta de menos.

Dijeron que antiguamente
se fué la verdad al cielo :
tal la pusieron los hombres
que desde entonces no ha vuelto.

En dos edades vivimos
los proprios y los ajenos ;
la de plata los extraños
y la de cobre los nuestros.

¿ A quién no dará cuidado,
si es español verdadero,
ver los hombres a lo antiguo
y el valor a lo moderno ?

Todos andan bien vestidos,
y quéjanse de los precios,
de medio arriba, romanos,
de medio abajo, romeros.

Dijo Dios que comería
su pan el hombre primero
en el sudor de su cara,
por quebrar su mandamiento,

y algunos inobedientes
a la vergüenza y al miedo,
con las prendas de su honor
han trocado los efectos.

Virtud y filosofía
peregrinan como ciegos :
el uno se lleva al otro,
llorando van y pidiendo.

Dos polos tiene la tierra,
universal movimiento :
la mejor vida, el favor ;
la mejor sangre, el dinero.

Oigo tañer las campanas,
y no me espanto, aunque puedo,
que en lugar de tantas cruces
haya tantos hombres muertos.

Mirando estoy los sepulcros,
cuyos mármoles eternos
están diciendo sin lengua
que no lo fueron sus dueños.

¡ Oh, bien haya quien los hizo,
porque solamente en ellos
de los poderosos grandes
se vengaron los pequeños !

Fea pintan a la envidia,
yo confieso que la tengo
de unos hombres que no saben
quién vive pared en medio.

Sin libros y sin papeles,
sin tratos, cuentas ni cuentos,
cuando quieren escribir
piden prestado el tintero.

Sin ser pobres ni ser ricos
tienen chimenea y huerto ;
no los despiertan cuidados,
ni pretensiones, ni pleitos.

Ni murmuraron del grande
ni ofendieron al pequeño ;
nunca, como yo, firmaron
parabién ni Pascuas dieron.

Con esta envidia que digo
y lo que paso en silencio,
a mis soledades voy,
de mis soledades vengo.

159. " *Pobre barquilla mía. . . .*"

In this poem, as in the last, the intimate tone is tempered by the sustained metaphor. There is, however, a deeper undercurrent of pathos here, which grows in profundity right down to the last stanza. The most attractive formal characteristic of the poem is its rapidity of movement : a single assonance maintained for 128 lines need not involve monotony or languidness—when the author is Lope de Vega. Among the reasons for this may be noted the alternating of description, reflection, exclamation and interrogation, the use of short, concise phrases, often of parallel construction, such as the couplet on which the poem ends ; and of course the picturesqueness and colour which mark it throughout.

¡ Pobre barquilla mía
entre peñascos rota,
sin velas desvelada,
y entre las olas sola !

¿ Adónde vas perdida,
adónde, di, te engolfas ?
Que no hay deseos cuerdos
con esperanzas locas.

Como las altas naves
te apartas animosa
de la vecina tierra
y al fiero mar te arrojas.

Igual en las fortunas,
mayor en las congojas,
pequeña en las defensas,
incitas a las ondas.

Advierte que te llevan
a dar entre las rocas
de la soberbia envidia,
naufragio de las honras.

Cuando por las riberas
andabas costa a costa,
nunca del mar temiste
las iras procelosas.

Segura navegabas,
que por la tierra propia
nunca el peligro es mucho
adonde el agua es poca.

Verdad es que en la patria
no es la virtud dichosa,
ni se estimó la perla
hasta dejar la concha.

Dirás que muchas barcas,
con el favor en popa,
saliendo desdichadas,
volvieron venturosas.

No mires los ejemplos
de las que van y tornan,
que a muchas ha perdido
la dicha de las otras.

Para los altos mares
no llevas cautelosa
ni velas de mentiras,
ni remos de lisonjas.

¿ Quién te engañó, barquilla ?
Vuelve, vuelve la proa,
que presumir de nave
fortunas ocasiona.

¿ Qué jarcias te entretejen ?
¿ Qué ricas banderolas
azote son del viento
y de las aguas sombra ?

¿ En qué gavia descubres,
del árbol alta copa,
la tierra en perspectiva,
del mar incultas orlas ?

¿ En qué celajes fundas
que es bien echar la sonda,
cuando, perdido el rumbo,
erraste la derrota ?

Si te sepulta arena,
¿ qué sirve fama heroica ?
que nunca desdichados
sus pensamientos logran.

¿ Qué importa que te ciñan
ramas verdes o rojas,
que en selvas de corales
salado césped brota ?

Laureles de la orilla
solamente coronan
navíos de alto bordo
que jarcias de oro adornan.

No quieras que yo sea,
por tu soberbia pompa,
Faetonte de barqueros
que los laureles lloran.

Pasaron ya los tiempos
cuando, lamiendo rosas,
el céfiro bullía
y suspiraba aromas.

Ya fieros huracanes
tan arrogantes soplan,
que, salpicando estrellas,
del sol la frente mojan.

Ya los valientes rayos
de la vulcania forja
en vez de torres altas
abrasan pobres chozas.

Contenta con tus redes
a la playa arenosa
mojado me sacabas ;
pero vivo, ¿ qué importa ?

Cuando de rojo nácar
se afeitaba la aurora,
más peces te llenaban
que ella lloraba aljófar.

Al bello sol que adoro,
enjuta ya la ropa,
nos daba una cabaña
la cama de sus hojas.

Esposo me llamaba,
yo la llamaba esposa,
parándose de envidia
la celestial antorcha.

Sin pleito, sin disgusto,
la muerte nos divorcia :
¡ ay de la pobre barca
que en lágrimas se ahoga !

Quedad sobre la arena,
inútiles escotas,
que no ha menester velas
quien a su bien no torna.

Si con eternas plantas
las fijas luces doras,
¡ oh, dueño de mi barca !
y en dulce paz reposas,

merezca que le pidas
al bien que eterno gozas
que a donde estás me lleve,
más pura y más hermosa.

Mi honesto amor te obligue,
que no es digna victoria
para quejas humanas
ser las deidades sordas.

Mas ¡ ay que no me escuchas !
Pero la vida es corta :
viviendo, todo falta,
muriendo, todo sobra.

160. " *Beatus ille. . . .*"

Lope de Vega attempted several treatments of Horace's " Beatus ille . . . . " ; this, which is set, somewhat anachronistically, in Los Pastores de Belén *(1612), may profitably be compared with Luis de León's " Vida retirada " (p. 206, above). Neither in felicity of language nor in rhythm and melody is the poem comparable with its author's best, but in dignity and serenity it stands high among Spanish adaptations of its subject.*

Among its anachronisms is an interesting reference to the conceptist author of the day

—no habla desvelado
en sutiles sentencias y concetos,
ni inventa voces nuevas—

who, in 1612, was becoming more and more common : here the Lope of the popular lyrics is apparently pointing at the Lope of the more Baroque sonnets.

¡ Cuán bienaventurado
aquel puede llamarse justamente,
que sin tener cuidado
de la malicia y lengua de la gente,
a la virtud contraria,
la suya pasa en vida solitaria !

¡ Dichoso el que no mira
del altivo señor las altas casas,
ni de mirar se admira
fuertes colunas oprimiendo basas,
en las soberbias puertas,
a la lisonja eternamente abiertas !

Los altos frontispicios,
con el noble blasón de sus pasados,
los bélicos oficios,
de timbres y banderas coronados,
desprecia y tiene en menos
que en el campo los olmos, de hojas llenos.

Ni sufre al confiado
en quien puede morir, y que al fin muere,
ni humilde al levantado
con vanas sumisiones le prefiere,
sin ver que no hay coluna
segura en las mudanzas de fortuna.

Ni va sin luz delante
del señor poderoso, que atropella
sus fuerzas arrogante,
pues es mejor de noche ser estrella,
que por la compañía
del sol dorado no lucir de día.

¡ Dichoso el que, apartado
de aquellos que se tienen por discretos,
no habla desvelado
en sutiles sentencias y concetos,
ni inventa voces nuevas,
más de ambición que del ingenio pruebas !

Ni escucha al malicioso
que todo cuanto ve le desagrada,
ni al crítico enfadoso
teme la esquiva condición, fundada
en la calumnia sola,
fuego activo del oro que acrisola.

Ni aquellos arrogantes
por el verde laurel de alguna ciencia,
que llaman ignorantes
los que tiene por sabios la experiencia,
porque la ciencia en suma
no sale del laurel, mas de la pluma.

No da el saber el grado,
sino el ingenio natural, del arte
y estudio acompañado,
que el hábito y los cursos no son parte,
ni aquella ilustre rama,
faltando lo esencial para dar fama.

¡ Oh, cuántos hay que viven
a sus cortas esferas condenados !
Hoy lo que ayer escriben,
ingenios como espejos que, quebrados,
muestran siempre de un modo
lo mismo en cualquier parte que en el todo.

¡ Dichoso, pues, mil veces
el solo que en su campo, descuidado
de vanas altiveces,
cuanto rompiendo va con el arado
baña con la corriente
del agua que destila de su frente !

El ave sacra a Marte
le despierta del sueño perezoso,
y el vestido sin arte
traslada presto al cuerpo, temeroso
de que la luz del día
por las quiebras del techo entrar porfía.

Revuelve la ceniza,
sopla el humoso pino mal quemado ;
el animal se eriza
que estaba entre las pajas acostado.
Ya la tiniebla huye
y lo que hurtó a la luz le restituye.

El pobre almuerzo aliña,
come y da de comer a los dos bueyes,
y en el barbecho o viña,
sin envidiar los patios de los reyes,
ufano se pasea
a vista de las casas de su aldea.

Y son tan derribadas,
que aun no llega el soldado a su aposento,
ni sus armas colgadas
de sus paredes vió, ni el corpulento
caballo estar atado
al humilde pesebre del ganado.

Caliéntase el enero,
al rededor de sus hijuelos todos,
a un roble, ardiendo entero,
y allí cantando de diversos modos
de la extranjera guerra,
duerme seguro y goza de su tierra.

Ni deuda en plazo breve,
ni nave por la mar su paz impide,
ni a la fama se atreve;
con el reloj del sol sus horas mide,
y la incierta postrera
ni la teme cobarde ni la espera.

POPULAR LYRICS

161. *Trébole*

No song in the language exhales more of the aroma of the countryside or in so few words gives a clearer and fuller picture of village life and customs than does this lyric from the drama Peribáñez. *There is far more in it than the author consciously put there and its picturesqueness is matched by its melody: slight and unpretentious though it is, it must be considered an outstanding example of its author's lyric skill.*

Trébole, ¡ ay Jesús, cómo huele !
Trébole, ¡ ay Jesús, qué olor !

Trébole de la casada
que a su esposo quiere bien ;
de la doncella también
entre paredes guardada,
que fácilmente engañada
sigue su primer amor.
Trébole, ¡ ay Jesús, cómo huele !
Trébole, ¡ ay Jesús, qué olor !

Trébole de la soltera
que tantos amores muda ;
trébole de la viuda
que otra vez casarse espera,
tocas blancas por defuera
y faldellín de color.
Trébole, ¡ ay Jesús, cómo huele !
Trébole, ¡ ay Jesús, qué olor !

162. " *Blancas coge Lucinda . . .*"

This Lucinda of El Caballero de Illescas *was clearly no less a beauty than Lope's Lucinda of the* Rimas humanas : *possibly the one had some of the reflected charms of the other. A more sophisticated artifice informs this song and the rustic atmosphere of the last gives place to an aristocratic setting. The outrageous hyperboles, each more daring than its predecessor, take the reader by storm. Why does he accept them without a murmur? Is it for their picturesqueness? For their melody? For their ingenuousness and candour? In any case, by the time he comes to the end of the lyric he is completely convinced of the truth of the poet's initial assertion and contentedly adds a* quod erat demonstrandum *of his own.*

Blancas coge Lucinda
las azucenas
y en llegando a sus manos
parecen negras.

Cuando sale el alba
Lucinda bella
sale más hermosa,
la tierra alegra.

Con su sol enjuga
sus blancas perlas ;
si una flor le quita
dos mil engendra.

Porque son sus plantas
de primavera
y como cristales
sus manos bellas.

Y ansí, con ser blancas
las azucenas,
en llegando a sus manos
parecen negras.

163. "*A los verdes prados . . .*"

In this lyric from Con su pan se lo coma *we should imagine ourselves back in the Middle Ages were it not evident on reflection how much the language has gained since the time of the Marqués de Santillana. These sixteen alliterating lines give us back the rustic atmosphere, the simplicity of thought and the naïve conventionalisms of a past day : note in particular the short clipt clauses matching the ideas and impressions, the repetitions, the parallelisms, the inversions of phrase, and the formal balance as between the first two stanzas and again as between the last two. And yet, when we have analyzed the poem to the very last word, its chief beauties—those of evocative phraseology and nimble fancy—have escaped us.*

A los verdes prados
baja la niña,
ríense las fuentes,
las aves silban.

A los prados verdes
la niña baja,
las fuentes se ríen,
las aves cantan.

Con el alto pino
calle la oliva
y a la gala de Fabio
todas se rindan.

Con las azucenas
callen las rosas
y a la gala de Fabio
se rindan todas.

LUIS DE ARGOTE Y GÓNGORA

1561-1627

EVER since he began to write, the Cordoban prebendary Luis de Góngora (he adopted his mother's surname) has been alternately neglected, attacked and overpraised for his strikingly individual type of poetry: at the moment his star is high, the reaction which in due course will inevitably follow the apotheosis induced by the third centenary of his death not having yet begun.

It used to be maintained that Góngora had two successive "periods"—that in his youth his work was simple and natural but that in middle age he suddenly became obscure; or, to express it in the less measured language of his contemporary critic, Francisco de Cascales, that he turned from an "angel of light" into an "angel of darkness." This, however, will not do. Except for a few apprentice-pieces, hardly one of his poems is untouched by conceptism or cultism, both of which tendencies had been growing up concurrently with the development of Spanish poetry in the direction of the Baroque. And at the same time, he frequently returned to a comparatively simple style, even in the years following the completion of his two longer cultist works: *Polifemo* and the *Soledades*. Rather than two "periods", we should distinguish three "manners" in Góngora: the simple and popular; the simple and semi-academic; the wholly academic and obscure. The last manner is found in its most concentrated form between about 1609 and 1615; and that is the only chronological generalization which is beyond dispute.

So highly individual is the blend of conceptism and cultism (p. xxxiv) which characterizes Góngora's interpretation of the Baroque that it has become known in criticism as Gongorism. Generally speaking, Gongorism embraces conceptism, but it is inseparable from, and dominated by, cultism, which, in lesser men, is often intensified by an exaggerated estimate of the value of their own pearls, or of the swinishness of those before whom they propose to cast them. Opponents of cultism attribute this glorification of form, which enlists all the numerous resources of Baroque art, to penury of thought. But that is not necessarily so—and with Góngora, as his sonnets alone show, it was certainly not so. He was gifted with an extraordinary visual imagination, which developed as he used it. He could leap so rapidly from image to image that few could follow him and he took an exuberant delight in building up edifices of decoration around ideas and impressions in themselves simple. That was his idea of beauty: his reader may not share it, any more than he will necessarily share the view that scaling Alpine peaks is a form of enjoyment, but if he has any poetic sensibility he will not fail to recognize Góngora as a genius.

Some of the most notable traits of Gongoristic poetry are more trivial and more conventional than others, and some more than others are particularly his own. Briefly, we shall find in his cultist poems a great fondness for latinized constructions, for neologisms based on Greek or Latin and for allusions to Classical mythology; a tremendous richness of colour, luminosity and image—Herreran "magnificence" raised to a very high power; a heaping of metaphors one upon another—sometimes a metaphorization of metaphors—till they smother the original idea; an extreme indulgence in inversion, antithesis, paradox, litotes, chiasmus and, above all, hyperbole.

There is exaggeration in all this: one may well feel that by protesting too much Góngora made it hard to believe in his essential sincerity and that by decorating too much he destroyed one kind of beauty at birth in order to create another. But to call Gongorism, as Menéndez y Pelayo does, "poetic nihilism,"[1] betrays the critic's own failure to appreciate Góngora's conception of poetry. A more tolerant criticism will recognize that, while Góngora excelled in simple and semi-popular verse, both his affections and his talents led him in the direction of the Baroque, and that, in hammering out a poetic ideal of his own, he was making a contribution of great value to Spanish literature. Such criticism may hesitate between placing the best of the sonnets or *Polifemo* at the summit of his achievement and it may legitimately hold that in the *Soledades* he overreached himself: there is force in Jáuregui's reference to "unas poesías desalmadas", some of which "sólo contienen un adorno o vestidura de palabras. . . . sin alma ni cuerpo". Yet, even when there is little soul in

[1] *Historica de las ideas estéticas en España*, Madrid, 1890-1907, III, 483.

Góngora's verse, the wealth and energy of his dynamic imagination enriched the language to an extent until recently unrealized. Though his preoccupation with form may run away with him, he is always to be reckoned with; where, as in many of his shorter poems, he maintains a perfect balance between form and content, he is, in that particular field, supreme.

164. *Letrilla*

This best-known of Góngora's simpler poems is only slightly later than " La más bella niña. . . ." (p. 325). There is no suggestion in it of immaturity, however: here and there, indeed (e.g., ll. 17-18), there are indications of the author's later manner. First cousin, in subject and tone, to " Don Dinero " (p. 363)—and a near relative of Lazarillo de Tormes *and Espronceda's " El Mendigo " (p. 487)—it often reminds one of Quevedo at his best. The author is the complete realist (and therefore always popular with Spaniards) and the complete hedonist. The satirical pictures are audacious, unconventional and incredibly vivid: alternately idealistic and material, they crowd through the memory like dissolving views, the longest to linger being the deliciously contrasted images of the final stanza. The devices which the author uses to produce his effects are perhaps a thought too obvious: the short line rounding off each stanza; alliteration (e.g., in* m *and* p*: ll. 4-15); phrases, whether picturesque (ll. 19-20) or alliterative (ll. 22, 26 and the* p, t, t, p *of ll. 39-42), which stick in the mind; repetitions or plays upon words* (gobierno, *ll. 3, 5;* dorado, *ll. 10, 12;* pasar, *ll. 31, 34). But the virtuosity of so young an apprentice in the use of them is certainly noteworthy.*

Ándeme yo caliente,
y ríase la gente.

Traten otros del gobierno
del mundo y sus monarquías,
mientras gobiernan mis días
mantequillas y pan tierno,
y las mañanas de invierno
naranjada y aguardiente,
y ríase la gente.

Coma en dorada vajilla
el príncipe mil cuidados
como píldoras dorados ;
que yo en mi pobre mesilla
quiero más una morcilla
que en el asador reviente,
y ríase la gente.

Cuando cubra las montañas
de plata y nieve el enero
tenga yo lleno el brasero
de bellotas y castañas,
y quien las dulces patrañas
del rey que rabió me cuente,
y ríase la gente.

Busque muy en hora buena
el mercader nuevos soles ;
yo conchas y caracoles
entre la menuda arena,
escuchando a Filomena
sobre el chopo de la fuente,
y ríase la gente.

Pase a media noche el mar,
y arda en amorosa llama
Leandro por ver su dama ;
que yo más quiero pasar
del golfo de mi lagar
la blanca o roja corriente,
y ríase la gente.

Pues Amor es tan cruel
que de Píramo y su amada
hace tálamo una espada,
do se junten ella y él,
sea mi Tisbe un pastel,
y la espada sea mi diente,
y ríase la gente.

165. *Soneto*

Here we enter the orbit of the Baroque with an imposing introduction (l. 1), a quite Herreran hyperbole (ll. 2-4) and an erection of highly ornate metaphor (ll. 7-8) around the simple word " golden ". The octave pictures youth ; the sestet, under the identical conventions, age : each preserves the closest relation with the central theme. Finally, on the heels of the most audacious (ll. 12-13) of the sonnet's hyperboles, comes the last line—its greatest triumph—with its suggestion of passion in the repetition of the verb and its mots propres *contrasting so effectively with the preceding periphrases :*

goza, goza el color, la luz, el oro.

The force of this final line, which contains the poem's entire point and drives home its moral, is increased by the constructional and grammatical dependence upon it of the whole. This sonnet, more than most, needs reading aloud for a full appreciation of its beauty.

Ilustre y hermosísima María,
mientras se dejan ver a cualquier hora
en tus mejillas la rosada aurora,
Febo en tus ojos y en tu frente el día ;

y mientras con gentil descortesía
mueve el viento la hebra voladora
que la Arabia en sus venas atesora
y el rico Tajo en sus arenas cría ;

antes que de la edad Febo eclipsado
el claro día vuelva en noche obscura,
huya la aurora del mortal nublado ;

antes que lo que hoy es rubio tesoro
venza a la blanca nieve su blancura,
goza, goza el color, la luz, el oro.

166. *Soneto*

A companion-piece, perhaps, to the preceding sonnet : the themes are identical and the constructions with mientras *similar, though in this sonnet the moral fills the entire sestet. The octave opens with the most daring, yet most luxuriant, of hyperboles, its effect enhanced by the interlacing alliterations in* l *and* m. *To expatiate upon the rich visual appeal of the whole poem would be mere self-indulgence: the brilliance of its colours and images entirely conceals the almost mechanical precision with which the author catalogues his lady's charms* (cabello . . . . frente . . . . labio . . . .cuello), *to recapitulate them in a different order at the opening of the sestet (l. 9) and again (l. 11) in symbolic shape. Less apparent, perhaps, than this pictorial quality is the swelling of the sestet to its crisis (l. 11) before it slowly descends to its inexorable close. The last line, for sheer power, is one of the most remarkable finales in Spanish literature. Its concluding word not only represents an absolute in sense, but contains the most lightly pronounced of Spanish consonants, so that the line shades off into almost pure vowel. The four caesurae, too, slow down the reader's pace, producing a natural* rallentando *effect which emphasizes the solemnity of the theme.*

Mientras, por competir con tu cabello,
oro bruñido, el sol relumbra en vano;
mientras con menosprecio enmedio el llano
mira tu blanca frente el lirio bello;

mientras a cada labio, por cogello,
siguen más ojos que al clavel temprano,
y mientras triunfa con desdén lozano
del luciente cristal tu gentil cuello;

goza cuello, cabello, labio y frente,
antes que lo que füé en tu edad dorada
oro, lirio, clavel, cristal luciente,

no sólo en plata o vïola trocada
se vuelva, mas tú y ello juntamente
en tierra, en polvo, en humo, en sombra, en nada.

167. *Soneto*

Completely objective save for the slightest of personal touches at the beginning (l. 1) and end (l. 12), this sonnet is a Baroque exercise in playful delicacy of expression and vividness of colour. The effect of the hyperbole in ll. 3-4, disarming in its grace, is offset by the simplicity with which the colours are introduced into the octave—verde . . . .

blanco . . . . verde . . . . rojo . . . . *The dainty word-pictures culminate fitly in the comparison of the flowers with the stars (cf. Calderón : p. 384, below), which sets a seal upon the poem's idealism.*

Al tramontar del sol la ninfa mía,
de flores despojando el verde llano,
cuantas truncaba la hermosa mano,
tantas el blanco pie crecer hacía.

Ondeábale el viento que corría
el oro fino con error galano,
cual verde hoja de álamo lozano
se mueve al rojo despuntar del día ;

mas luego que ciñó sus sienes bellas
de los varios despojos de su falda,
término puesto al oro y a la nieve,

juraré que lució más su guirnalda,
con ser de flores, la otra ser de estrellas,
que la que ilustra el cielo en luces nueve.

168. *Soneto : Al Escorial*

A majestic poem, admirably exemplifying the author's habit of transposing into light and colour and conveying a remarkably vivid sense of grandeur and dignity. The introductory adjectives in l. 1 would seem to have been picked out with deliberate care : each adds something to the impression so precisely elaborated. A similar attempt at precision may be deduced from the striking lines (7-8) which round off the octave. Between these two sober, yet highly expressive, phrases comes a flood of hyperbole (ll. 2-6), symbolic rather than plastic, and not felt, in its context, to be excessive. In the panegyric of Philip II which forms the sestet we have a more measured eloquence and the peroration is impersonal and grave.

Sacros, altos, dorados capiteles
que a las nubes robáis los arreboles,
Febo os teme por más lucientes soles,
y el cielo por gigantes más crüeles.

Depón tus rayos, Júpiter ; no celes
los tuyos, sol ; de un templo son faroles
que al mayor mártir de los españoles
erigió el mayor rey de los fieles.

Religiosa grandeza del monarca
cuya diestra real al Nuevo Mundo
abrevia y el Oriente se le humilla,

perdone el tiempo, lisonjee la parca
la verdad desta octava maravilla,
los años deste Salomón segundo.

169. *Soneto : A la ciudad de Córdoba y su fertilidad*

None of Góngora's topographical sonnets surpasses this, on its author's birthplace. Flawless and highly artistic in form, its use of the caesura—contrast the bipartite lines (1, 4, 5), the tripartite (2, 13, 14) and the quadripartite (6, 8, 10)—gives it a poise which admirably controls its emotion. Note how the emotional crescendo *in l. 7 is checked in l. 8 and passion is dominated by feeling for form. No less attractive is the turn of thought in the sestet which introduces the contrast with Granada—a merely emotional contrast, it will be observed, leading to a powerful peroration.*

¡ Oh excelso muro, oh torres levantadas
de honor, de majestad, de gallardía !
¡ Oh gran río, gran rey de Andalucía,
de arenas nobles, ya que no doradas !

¡ Oh fértil llano, oh sierras encumbradas,
que privilegia el cielo y dora el día !
¡ Oh siempre gloriosa patria mía,
tanto por plumas cuanto por espadas !

Si entre aquellas ruinas y despojos
que enriquece Genil y Darro baña
tu memoria no fué alimento mío,

nunca merezcan mis ausentes ojos
ver tus muros, tus torres y tu río,
tu llano y sierra, ¡ oh patria, oh flor de España !

170. *Soneto: Al Guadalquivir*

At first this seems to be a pure Nature-sonnet. With firm, sweeping strokes the author personifies the "Great River" of Andalusia, describes its rise and traces its course. His aim is apparently to convey, not picturesqueness, but magnificence and power: the epithets, especially those which conclude the octave, have evidently been selected with care. Then, with "A mí. . . ." (l. 9), the poem becomes simple, personal and slightly plaintive, and, perhaps, slightly deteriorates. Save for the fine "ilustremente enamorado", the epithets are now less evocative and the concluding question is a weak one. For all her grace, Clori cannot in fact compare with Betis and the last three words of the sonnet sound almost like an afterthought.

Rey de los otros ríos caudaloso,
que en fama claro, en ondas cristalino,
tosca guirnalda de robusto pino
ciñe tu frente y tu cabello undoso;

pues dejando tu nido cavernoso,
de Segura en el monte más vecino,
por el suelo andaluz tu real camino
tuerces, soberbio, raudo y espumoso:

a mí, que de tus fértiles orillas
piso, aunque ilustremente enamorado,
la noble arena con humilde planta,

dime si entre las rubias pastorcillas
has visto, que en tus aguas se han mirado,
beldad cual la de Clori, o gracia tanta.

171. *Romance*

Written before its author was twenty, this ballad seems to have been inspired by the popular lyric of the Middle Ages. The language could hardly be simpler. The characters conform to mediaeval type —the melancholy girl-wife, widowed by her husband's departure for the wars, and the mother, ever receptive to her complaints. The refrain embodies that primitive form of the appeal to Nature frequently found in rudimentary literature. The antitheses are of a naïve an' simple type, appropriate to the characters into whose mouths they are put, and of a kind that any popular poet might invent. There is no high art here, but there is music, lyric emotion and a sensibility to the spirit of past ages.

La más bella niña
de nuestro lugar,
hoy viuda y sola
y ayer por casar,
viendo que sus ojos
a la guerra van,
a su madre dice
que escucha su mal:
Dejadme llorar,
orillas del mar.

Pues me distes, madre,
en tan tierna edad
tan corto el placer,
tan largo el pesar,
y me cautivastes
de quien hoy se va
y lleva las llaves
de mi libertad,
dejadme llorar,
orillas del mar.

En llorar conviertan
mis ojos, de hoy más,
el sabroso oficio
del dulce mirar,
pues que no se pueden
mejor ocupar,
yéndose a la guerra
quien era mi paz.
Dejadme llorar,
orillas del mar.

No me pongáis freno
ni queráis culpar ;
que lo uno es justo,
lo otro por demás.
Si me queréis bien,
no me hagáis mal ;
harto peor fuera
morir y callar.
Dejadme llorar,
orillas del mar.

Dulce madre mía,
¿ quién no llorará,
aunque tenga el pecho
como un pedernal,
y no dará voces
viendo marchitar
los más verdes años
de mi mocedad ?
Dejadme llorar,
orillas del mar.

Váyanse las noches,
pues ido se han
los ojos que hacían
los míos velar ;
váyanse, y no vean
tanta soledad,
después que en mi lecho
sobra la mitad.
Dejadme llorar,
orillas del mar.

172. *Romance*

Góngora was still only a young man when he wrote this ballad, but artistically it is an advance on the last. Though his language remains relatively simple (where was the struggle between love and duty ever more briefly yet more pungently described than in ll. 23-4?), his descriptions have more force and picturesqueness, and the action (ll. 12-17) is of a studied rapidity. The antitheses, too, if excessive in number, are the result of thought and planning, for they introduce the story (ll. 1-4), form an essential part of the plot (ll. 21-4, 33-40), enter into the characterization (ll. 37-9, 44) and (ll. 45-8) resolve the conflict of the dramatic action. The poem conveys the impression of an artificiality deliberately decided upon: continued indefinitely, it would pall, but in a narrative of this length it is quite attractive.

Servía en Orán al Rey
un español con dos lanzas,
y con el alma y la vida
a una gallarda africana,

tan noble como hermosa,
tan amante como amada,
con quien estaba una noche
cuando tocaron al arma.

Trescientos Cenetes eran
de este rebato la causa,
que los rayos de la luna
descubrieron las adargas;

las adargas avisaron
a las mudas atalayas,
las atalayas los fuegos,
los fuegos a las campanas;

y ellas al enamorado,
que, en los brazos de su dama,
oyó el militar estruendo
de las trompas y las cajas.

Espuelas de honor le pican
y freno de amor le para;
no salir es cobardía,
ingratitud es dejalla.

Del cuello pendiente ella,
viéndole tomar la espada,
con lágrimas y suspiros
le dice aquestas palabras:

" Salid al campo, Señor,
bañen mis ojos la cama ;
que ella me será también,
sin vos, campo de batalla.

" Vestíos y salid apriesa,
que el General os aguarda ;
yo os hago a vos mucha sobra
y vos a él mucha falta.

" Bien podéis salir desnudo,
pues mi llanto no os ablanda ;
que tenéis de acero el pecho
y no habéis menester armas."

Viendo el español brioso
cuánto le detiene y habla,
le dice así : " Mi señora,
tan dulce como enojada,

" porque con honra y amor
yo me quede, cumpla y vaya ;
vaya a los moros el cuerpo,
y quede con vos el alma.

" Concededme, dueño mío,
licencia para que salga
al rebato en vuestro nombre,
y en vuestro nombre combata."

173. *Romance*

The first four lines of this song, which form one of the most popular of Spanish refrains (they are used by Calderón in El Alcalde de Zalamea) *are in themselves remarkable for a picturesqueness, simplicity and aphoristic economy of words which conceal genuine emotion. Some of this becomes explicit in Góngora's treatment. The evocation of the rosemary flowers, with its single touch of colour, remains the most memorable trait in the poem ; but the application of the figure to the suspicions and quarrels of lovers is no mere trite idea picturesquely conveyed—it opens the way to more serious and satisfying reflections at which the actual lines themselves can hardly be said to hint. With one exception (l. 24), all the other figures in the poem are natural and simple; and the conciseness of the language (e.g. ll. 7-12, 27-8), together with a metrical grace which need not be laboured, gives the argument point and verve.*

Las flores del romero,
niña Isabel,
hoy son flores azules,
mañana serán miel.

Celosa estás, la niña,
celosa estás de aquel
dichoso, pues le buscas,
ciego, pues no te ve,
ingrato, pues te enoja,
y confiado, pues
no se disculpa hoy
de lo que hizo ayer.
Enjuguen esperanzas
lo que lloras por él;
que celos entre aquellos
que se han querido bien
hoy son flores azules,
mañana serán miel.

Aurora de ti misma,
que cuando a amanecer
a tu placer empiezas,
te eclipsa tu placer.
Serénense tus ojos,
y más perlas no des,
porque al Sol le está mal
lo que a la Aurora bien.
Desata como nieblas
todo lo que no ves;
que sospechas de amantes
y querellas después
hoy son flores azules,
mañana serán miel.

174. "*¡ Oh bella Galatea. . . . !*" (Polifemo)

Polifemo, *or the* Fábula de Polifemo y Galatea (*1613*), *is a narrative poem of some five hundred lines, in* octavas reales *based on the Ovidian story of the love of Acis and the nymph Galatea, of the wooing of Galatea by the Cyclopean Polyphemus and of the transformation of Acis, on Galatea's prayer, into a river when the giant attempts to slay him. Though its ornate art is now definitely cultist, and its metaphors are often so stereotyped as to be meaningless or so highly developed that they resemble overblown roses, it has a Lopean vigour and a titanic range and power which somehow recall the personality of another great poet, Christopher Marlowe. Like Marlowe, too, Góngora can on occasion be a very sweet singer, and, even in the midst of his Baroque narrative, the lyric note is sometimes heard. Parts of the passage here excerpted (ll. 361-464), though delivered by the giant in his " horrenda voz " as he makes heavy love to Galatea, are an outstanding example of this. Other no less beautiful, and more sensuous, passages describe the singing of the nightingale as Galatea reclines in the shade (ll. 177-84), the arrival of Acis (ll. 189 ff.) and the meeting and embraces of the two lovers (ll. 249 ff.). For the reader who can accept the Baroque there are beauties on every page, if not in every stanza, of this poem, in which narrative exercises a salutary restraint upon Góngora's tendency to over-luxuriate, and all his decorativeness never destroys the purity of his line.*

" ¡ Oh bella Galatea, más süave
que los claveles que tronchó la Aurora ;
blanca más que las plumas de aquel ave
que dulce muere y en las aguas mora ;
igual en pompa al pájaro que, grave,
su manto azul de tantos ojos dora
cuantas el celestial zafiro estrellas !
¡ Oh tú, que en dos incluyes las más bellas !

" Deja las ondas, deja el rubio coro
de las hijas de Tetis, y el mar vea,
cuando niega la luz un carro de oro,
que en dos la restituye Galatea.

Pisa la arena, que en la arena adoro
cuantas el blanco pie conchas platea,
cuyo bello contacto puede hacerlas,
sin concebir rocío, parir perlas.

" Sorda hija del mar, cuyas orejas
a mis gemidos son rocas al viento ;
o dormida te hurten a mis quejas
purpúreos troncos de corales ciento,
o al disonante número de almejas
—marino, si agradable no, instrumento—
coros tejiendo estés, escucha un día
mi voz, por dulce, cuando no por mía.

" Pastor soy ; mas tan rico de ganados,
que los valles impido más vacíos,
los cerros desparezco levantados,
y los caudales seco de los ríos :
no los que, de sus ubres desatados,
o derivados de los ojos míos,
leche corren y lágrimas ; que iguales
en número a mis bienes son mis males.

" Sudando néctar, lambicando olores,
senos que ignora aun la golosa cabra
corchos me guardan, más que abeja flores
liba inquïeta, ingenïosa labra ;
troncos me ofrecen árboles mayores,
cuyos enjambres, o el Abril los abra,
o los desate el Mayo, ámbar destilan,
y en ruecas de oro rayos del Sol hilan.

" Del Júpiter soy hijo de las ondas,
aunque pastor, si tu desdén no espera
a que el Monarca de esas grutas hondas
en trono de cristal te abrace nuera ;
Polifemo te llama, no te escondas,
que tanto esposo admira la ribera,
cual otro no vió Febo más robusto,
del perezoso Volga al Indo adusto.

" Sentado, a la alta palma no perdona
su dulce fruto mi robusta mano ;
en pie, sombra capaz es mi persona
de innumerables cabras el verano.
¿ Qué mucho si de nubes se corona
por igualarme la montaña en vano,
y en los cielos, desde esta roca, puedo
escribir mis desdichas con el dedo ?

" Marítimo Alción, roca eminente
sobre sus huevos coronaba, el día
que espejo de zafiro fué luciente
la playa azul, de la persona mía ;
miréme, y lucir vi un sol en mi frente
cuando en el cielo un ojo se veía :
neutra el agua dudaba a cuál fe preste,
o al cielo humano, o al Cíclope celeste.

" Registra en otras puertas el venado
sus años, su cabeza colmilluda
la fiera cuyo cerro levantado
de helvecias picas es muralla aguda ;
la humana suya el caminante errado
dió ya a mi cueva, de piedad desnuda,
albergue hoy por tu causa al peregrino,
do halló reparo, si perdió camino.

" En tablas dividida, rica nave
besó la playa miserablemente,
de cuantas vomitó riquezas, grave,
por las bocas del Nilo el Orïente.
Yugo aquel día, y yugo bien süave,
del fiero mar a la sañuda frente
imponiéndole estaba, si no al viento,
dulcísimas coyundas mi instrumento.

" Cuando, entre globos de agua, entregar veo
a las arenas ligurina haya,
en cajas los aromas del Sabeo,
en cofres las riquezas de Cambaya ;

delicias de aquel mundo, ya trofeo
de Scila que, ostentado en nuestra playa,
lastimoso despojo fué dos días
a las que esta montaña engendra Harpías.

"Segunda tabla a un ginovés mi gruta
de su persona fué, de su hacienda:
la una reparada, la otra enjuta.
Relación del naufragio hizo horrenda.
Luciente paga de la mejor fruta
que en yerbas se recline, en hilos penda,
colmillo fué del animal que el Ganges
sufrir muros le vió, romper falanges.

"Arco, digo, gentil, bruñida aljaba,
obras ambas de artífice prolijo,
y de malaco rey a deida java
alto don, según ya mi huésped dijo.
De aquél la mano, de ésta el hombro agrava:
convencida la madre, imita al hijo:
serás a un tiempo, en estos horizontes,
Venus del mar, Cupido de los montes."

175. "*Era del año la estación florida. . .*" (Las Soledades)

Many, even most, poetry-lovers can enjoy Polifemo *as a whole, but the* Soledades, *in which line is apt to disappear altogether beneath adornment, and narrative is, of set purpose, reduced almost to a minimum, will appeal, except in snatches, only to the few. Regarded from the standpoint of Góngora's conception of poetry, however, it stands at the summit of his achievements. The slightness of the story and the irregularity of the metre he chose gave him an increased scope, of which he took full advantage, and the fluid medium which his art now attained harmonizes perfectly with his dynamic idealism and the imaginative progression which this demanded. Begun in 1613, and never completed, the work, though over four times the length of* Polifemo, *was to have been twice as long as it is. The first canto* ("*Soledad de los campos*") *and nearly all the second* ("*Soledad de las riberas") were completed; the third ("Soledad de las selvas") and fourth ("Soledad del yermo") were never written.*

The two passages here selected exemplify Góngora's descriptive and lyric manner respectively. It is in the first, which consists of the opening lines of the "Soledad primera", that the reader can best study the poet's method. It is spring (ll. 1-14); and a shipwrecked youth, clinging to a plank (ll. 15-21: note the use of metaphor within metaphor here), is thrown up on a headland (ll. 22-8). He kisses the sand, throws his plank away (ll. 29-33), dries his clothes in the sun (ll. 34-41) and begins to explore his surroundings (ll. 42-51). Spying the flickering light of a distant cottage (ll. 52-61), with a cry of relief and hope (ll. 62-4), he sets off for it (ll. 65-83), aided by a dog which barks at him with the object of frightening him away (ll. 84-9). In due course he reaches it and finds that it is inhabited by some goatherds, who give him a simple greeting (ll. 90-3).

Era del año la estación florida
en que el mentido robador de Europa
—media luna las armas de su frente,
y el Sol todos los rayos de su pelo—
luciente honor del cielo,
en campos de zafiro pace estrellas;
cuando el que ministrar podía la copa
a Júpiter mejor que el garzón de Ida,
—náufrago, y desdeñado, sobre ausente—
lagrimosas de amor dulces querellas
da al mar; que condolido,
fué a las ondas, fué al viento
el mísero gemido,
segundo de Arión dulce instrumento.

Del siempre en la montaña opuesto pino
al enemigo Noto,
piadoso miembro roto
—breve tabla—delfín no fué pequeño
al inconsiderado peregrino
que a una Libia de ondas su camino
fió, y su vida a un leño.

Del Océano pues antes sorbido,
y luego vomitado
no lejos de un escollo coronado
de secos juncos, de calientes plumas
—alga todo y espumas—,
halló hospitalidad donde halló nido
de Júpiter el ave.

Besa la arena, y de la rota nave
aquella parte poca
que le expuso en la playa dió a la roca :
que aun se dejan las peñas
lisonjear de agradecidas señas.

Desnudo el joven, cuanto ya el vestido
Océano ha bebido,
restituir le hace a las arenas ;
y al sol lo extiende luego,
que, lamiéndolo apenas
su dulce lengua de templado fuego,
lento lo embiste, y con süave estilo
la menor onda chupa al menor hilo.

No bien pues de su luz los horizontes
—que hacían desigual, confusamente
montes de agua y piélagos de montes—
desdorados los siente,
cuando—entregado el mísero extranjero
en lo que ya del mar redimió fiero—
entre espinas crepúsculos pisando,
riscos que aun igualara mal, volando,
veloz, intrépida ala
—menos cansado que confuso—, escala.

Vencida al fin la cumbre
—del mar siempre sonante,
de la muda campaña
árbitro igual e inexpugnable muro—,
con pie ya más seguro
declina al vacilante

breve esplendor de mal distinta lumbre :
farol de una cabaña
que sobre el ferro está, en aquel incierto
golfo de sombras anunciando el puerto.

" Rayos ", les dice, " ya que no de Leda
trémulos hijos, sed de mi fortuna
término luminoso." Y—recelando
de invidïosa bárbara arboleda
interposición, cuando
de vientos no conjuración alguna—
cual, haciendo el villano
la fragosa montaña fácil llano,
atento sigue aquella
—aun a pesar de las tinieblas bella,
aun a pesar de las estrellas clara—
piedra, indigna tiara,
—si tradición apócrifa no miente—
de animal tenebroso, cuya frente
carro es brillante de nocturno día :
tal, diligente, el paso
el joven apresura,
midiendo la espesura
con igual pie que el raso,
fijo—a despecho de la niebla fría—
en el carbunclo, norte de su aguja,
o el Austro brame o la arboleda cruja.

El can ya, vigilante,
convoca, despidiendo al caminante ;
y la que desviada
luz poca pareció, tanta es vecina,
que yace en ella la robusta encina,
mariposa en cenizas desatada.

Llegó pues el mancebo, y saludado,
sin ambición, sin pompa de palabras,
de los conducidores fué de cabras,
que a Vulcano tenían coronado.

176. "*Ven, Himeneo, ven. . . .*" (LAS SOLEDADES)

Among other rustic experiences, the young castaway is taken to see a village festival which centres around a wedding. He is presented to the bridegroom and then to the father of the lovely bride, who,

con silencio afable,
beldad parlera, gracia muda ostenta. (*ll.* 732-3)

The sight of her arouses conflicting emotions within him, and "his memory doffs black plumes" (l. 746), for he himself, in the past, has been unhappy in love. He would probably have wept (ll. 755-6) had not at this moment the sound of rustic instruments been heard, and two choirs appeared, composed respectively of youths and of maidens (ll. 757-61). Bride and bridegroom come out (ll. 762-7) and the choirs begin their song (ll. 768-73).

The Belgian critic L.-P. Thomas describes these stanzas as "ces strophes ailées", "un des plus remarquables épithalames que connaisse l'histoire des littératures".[1] *This is high but not excessive praise. The genuine lyric note in Góngora is invariably one of great beauty, and here his stylized manner is shot through with flashes of appealing simplicity. As always, his mastery of technique (notably, in these stanzas, of caesura, repetition and rhyme) is unrivalled, and the melody of the lovely refrain is matched by the vowel-play in each stanza. To many, this bridal song, though not the most typical part of the* Soledades, *will seem its chief attraction.*

CORO I

Ven, Himeneo, ven donde te espera
con ojos y sin alas un Cupido,
cuyo cabello intonso dulcemente
niega el vello que el vulto ha colorido:
el vello, flores de su primavera,
y rayos el cabello de su frente.
Niño amó la que adora adolescente,
villana Psiques, ninfa labradora
de la tostada Ceres. Esta, ahora,
en los inciertos de su edad segunda
crepúsculos, vincule tu coyunda
a su ardiente deseo.
Ven, Himeneo, ven; ven, Himeneo.

[1] *Góngora* (Cent chefs d'œuvre étrangers). Paris, n.d., p. 33.

CORO II

Ven, Himeneo, donde, entre arreboles
de honesto rosicler, previene el día,
aurora de sus ojos soberanos,
virgen tan bella, que hacer podría
tórrida la Noruega con dos soles,
y blanca la Etiopia con dos manos.
Claveles del abril, rubíes tempranos,
cuantos engasta el oro del cabello,
cuantas, del uno ya y del otro cuello
cadenas, la concordia engarza rosas,
de sus mejillas, siempre vergonzosas,
purpúreo son trofeo.
Ven, Himeneo, ven; ven, Himeneo.

CORO I

Ven, Himeneo, y plumas no vulgares
al aire los hijuelos den alados
de las que el bosque bellas ninfas cela;
de sus carcajes, éstos, argentados,
flechen mosquetas, nieven azahares;
vigilantes aquéllos, la aldehuela
rediman del que más o tardo vuela,
o infausto gime pájaro nocturno;
mudos coronen otros por su turno
el dulce lecho conyugal, en cuanto
lasciva abeja al virginal acanto
néctar le chupa hibleo.
Ven, Himeneo, ven; ven, Himeneo.

CORO II

Ven, Himeneo, y las volantes pías
que azules ojos con pestañas de oro
sus plumas son, conduzgan alta diosa,
gloria mayor del soberano coro.
Fíe tus nudos ella, que los días
disuelvan tarde en senectud dichosa;

y la que Juno es hoy a nuestra esposa,
casta Lucina—en lunas desiguales—
tantas veces repita sus umbrales,
que Níobe inmortal la admire el mundo,
no en blanco mármol, por su mal fecundo,
escollo hoy del Leteo.
Ven, Himeneo, ven; ven, Himeneo.

CORO I

Ven, Himeneo, y nuestra agricultura
de copia tal a estrellas deba amigas
progenie tan robusta, que su mano
toros dome, y de un rubio mar de espigas
inunde liberal la tierra dura;
y al verde, joven floreciente llano
blancas ovejas suyas hagan, cano,
en breves horas caducar la hierba;
oro le expriman líquido a Minerva,
y—los olmos casando con las vides—
mientras coronan pámpanos a Alcides
clava empuñe Liëo.
Ven, Himeneo, ven; ven, Himeneo.

CORO II

Ven, Himeneo, y tantas le dé a Pales
cuantas a Palas dulces prendas esta
apenas hija hoy, madre mañana.
De errantes lilios unas la floresta
cubran: corderos mil, que los cristales
vistan del río en breve undosa lana;
de Aracnes otras la arrogancia vana
modestas acusando en blancas telas,
no los hurtos de amor, no las cautelas
de Júpiter compulsen: que, aun en lino,
ni a la pluvia luciente de oro fino,
ni al blanco cisne creo.
Ven, Himeneo, ven; ven, Himeneo.

177. *Letrilla*

This skipping little tune, which the repetition of the vowels i, o *seems to relate to the pipe or the flute, is a sprightly commentary on the capriciousness of Dame Fortune. Its whole tone says, as plainly as anything can : " And who cares ? " The same devices as before are here : contrast (implicit in the theme), alliteration (ll. 5, 6, 8, 17, etc.), comic or audacious illustrations. Needless to say, the lightness of the tone is matched by the briskness of the metre : in such a fundamental matter of artistry, Góngora would never fail.*

Da bienes fortuna
que no están escritos :
cuando pitos flautas,
cuando flautas pitos.

¡ Cuán diversas sendas
suele seguir
en el repartir
honras y haciendas !
A unos da encomiendas,
a otros sambenitos.
Cuando pitos flautas,
cuando flautas pitos.

A veces despoja
de choza y apero
al mayor cabrero,
y a quien se le antoja
la cabra más coja
pare dos cabritos.
Cuando pitos flautas,
cuando flautas pitos.

Porque en una aldea
un pobre mancebo
hurtó solo un huevo,
al sol bambolea,
y otro se pasea
con cien mil delitos.
Cuando pitos flautas,
cuando flautas pitos.

178. *Letrilla*

Later in date than any of Góngora's late cultist poems, this letrilla *could hardly fail to show signs of cultism. But, though it represents a fairly advanced stage of progress from the Herreran to the Gongorine, it cannot be described as Gongoristic. Its moral is that of Calderón's famous flower-sonnet (p. 383), but additional point is given to the moral in the refrain by the unusual, even paradoxical, suggestion that the flowers are to learn it from the poet, not the poet from the flowers. It is perhaps chiefly an excuse for playing with flowers—carnation, jasmine, wallflower and sunflower. The last stanza is the weakest: even the " Methuselah of flowers " could not furnish a peroration to compete with the dramatic stroke which concludes the stanza on the wallflower (ll. 39-40) and gives the poem its true climax.*

Aprended, flores, en mí
lo que va de ayer a hoy,
que ayer maravilla fuí,
y hoy sombra mía aun no soy.

La aurora ayer me dió cuna,
la noche ataúd me dió,
sin luz muriera, si no
me la prestara la luna,
pues de vosotras ninguna
deja de morir así.

Aprended, flores, en mí
lo que va de ayer a hoy,
que ayer maravilla fuí,
y hoy sombra mía aun no soy.

Consuelo dulce el clavel
es a la brevedad mía,
pues quien me concedió un día,
dos apenas le dió a él;
efímeras del vergel,
yo cárdena, él carmesí.

Aprended, flores, en mí
lo que va de ayer a hoy,
que ayer maravilla fuí,
y hoy sombra mía aun no soy.

Flor es el jazmín si bella,
no de las más vividoras,
pues dura pocas más horas
que rayos tiene de estrella ;
si el ámbar florece, es ella
la flor que contiene en sí.

Aprended, flores, en mí
lo que va de ayer a hoy,
que ayer maravilla fuí,
y hoy sombra mía aun no soy.

Aunque el alhelí grosero
en fragancia y en color,
más días ve que otra flor,
pues ve los de un mayo entero ;
morir maravilla quiero,
y no vivir alhelí.

Aprended, flores, en mí
lo que va de ayer a hoy,
que ayer maravilla fuí,
y hoy sombra mía aun no soy.

A ninguna flor mayores
términos concede el sol
si no es al girasol,
matusalén de las flores ;
ojos son aduladores
cuantas en él hojas vi.

Aprended, flores, en mí
lo que va de ayer a hoy,
que ayer maravilla fuí,
y hoy sombra mía aun no soy.

JUAN DE ARGUIJO
*c.*1567-1623

An accomplished musician, cunning with the lute and skilful in song, this Sevilian poet and patron of letters carried the technical art of sonnet-making to a very high pitch. Admirable as they are in form, however, his sonnets are apt to be frigidly objective and only now and then can one sense the faintest glow of feeling. Though in many respects akin to Herrera, he has less warmth and colour, and is also less ornate. He invariably has the air of the virtuoso.

179. *Soneto*

Perfect symmetry of form, sobriety of style and a regard for the mot propre *which imprints itself on the mind: all these traits bring this sonnet into complete harmony with its subject. The epithets are perhaps a little too obvious and too evenly distributed, but the author is so evidently anxious to leave no loose ends that the critic, if not enthusiastic, is content, in the spirit of Eumelo himself, to commend his neatness.*

En segura pobreza vive Eumelo
con dulce libertad, y le mantienen
las simples aves, que engañadas vienen
a los lazos y liga sin recelo.

Por mejor suerte no importuna al çielo,
ni se muestra envidioso a la que tienen
los que con ansia de subir sostienen
en flacas alas el incierto vuelo.

Muerte tras luengos años no le espanta,
ni la recibe con indigna queja,
mas con sosiego grato y faz amiga.

Al fin, muriendo con pobreza tanta,
ricos juzga sus hijos, pues les deja
la libertad, las aves y la liga.

180. *Soneto*

Here, as so often in the Golden Age sonnet, we have a rather trite theme illustrated by a series of pictures. The first of these (ll. 1-4) has great vividness and power ; the second (ll. 5-8) is weaker visually, but the sound swells with the rising storm and the last line almost shudders with the thunder. The sestet admirably reflects the returning calm ; then leads to a conclusion, clear-cut without being over-stressed, and of striking verbal pungency. The most interesting of the sonnet's technical merits is the varying of the position of the caesura in the octave, a device which in ll. 1-4 lends an impression of rapidity to the description of the storm.

Yo vi del rojo sol la luz serena
turbarse, y que en un punto desparece
su alegre faz, y en torno se oscurece
el cielo con tiniebla de horror llena.

El austro proceloso airado suena,
crece su furia, y la tormenta crece,
y en los hombros de Atlante se estremece
el alto Olimpo y con espanto truena ;

mas luego vi romperse el negro velo
deshecho en agua, y a su luz primera
restituirse alegre el claro día,

y de nuevo esplendor ornado el cielo
miré, y dije : ¿ Quién sabe si le espera
igual mudanza a la fortuna mía ?

RODRIGO CARO
1573-1647

181. *A las Ruinas de Itálica*

CHARACTERISTIC of eighteenth-century pre-romanticism in England and France was a keen sensitiveness to the emotions associated with ruins. In Spain this trait is found in the Baroque period of the Golden Age. One of the most famous poems on this subject is the ode to the ruins of Itálica, long thought to be Rioja's, but now generally attributed to Rodrigo Caro, an archaeologist and historian of Utrera. It must be admitted that the poem, perhaps rated unduly high in the past, has all the coldness and plasticity which would be expected in one of his profession. It consists of six seventeen-lined stanzas, with the short lines occurring in the middle of each stanza, and a *silva*-like propensity for rhymes in couplets, which the author was not always skilful enough to prevent from jingling. (The actual scheme is ABCABCcddEFFEGGHH). It achieves a level of poetic eloquence as high as Herrera's. The author knew all the tricks of his trade: he was a master of *enjambement* and wrote in verse-paragraphs which sweep on irresistibly, each of them to be cut off no less inexorably by a line of magnificent finality. He knew his audiences and could hold them spellbound merely by varying the position of a single emphatic word (ll. 79-83). He had a considerable feeling for language and a great gift for communicating emotional tone. That and more can be said in his favour: on the debit side is his complete inability to move the reader, or even to touch him. Already one begins to feel the petrifying effect of the inevitable epithet and the stiffening of sensibility into rhetoric.

Estos, Fabio, ¡ ay dolor ! que ves ahora
campos de soledad, mustio collado,
fueron un tiempo Itálica famosa.
Aquí de Cipïón la vencedora
colonia fué ; por tierra derribado
yace el temido honor de la espantosa
muralla, y lastimosa
reliquia es solamente.
De su invencible gente
sólo quedan memorias funerales,
donde erraron ya sombras de alto ejemplo.
Este llano fué plaza, allí fué templo ;
de todo apenas quedan las señales.
Del gimnasio y las termas regaladas
leves vuelan cenizas desdichadas ;
las torres, que desprecio al aire fueron,
a su gran pesadumbre se rindieron.

Este despedazado anfiteatro,
impio honor de los dioses, cuya afrenta
publica el amarillo jaramago,
ya reducido a trágico teatro,
¡ oh fábula del tiempo ! representa
cuánta fué su grandeza y es su estrago.
¿ Cómo en el cerco vago
de su desierta arena
el gran pueblo no suena ?
¿ Dónde, pues fieras hay, está el desnudo
luchador ? ¿ Dónde está el atleta fuerte ?
Todo despareció : cambió la suerte
voces alegres en silencio mudo.
Mas aun el tiempo da en estos despojos
espectáculos fieros a los ojos ;
y miran tan confusos lo presente
que voces de dolor el alma siente.

Aquí nació aquel rayo de la guerra,
gran padre de la patria, honor de España,
pío, felice, triunfador Trajano ;
ante quien muda se postró la tierra

que ve del sol la cuna, y la que baña
el mar, también vencido, gaditano.
Aquí de Elio Adriano,
de Teodosio divino,
de Silio peregrino
rodaron de marfil y oro las cunas.
Aquí ya de laurel, ya de jazmines,
coronados los vieron los jardines,
que ahora son zarzales y lagunas.
La casa para el César fabricada,
¡ ay ! yace de lagartos vil morada.
Casas, jardines, Césares murieron,
y aun las piedras que de ellos se escribieron.

Fabio, si tú no lloras, pon atenta
la vista en luengas calles destruídas,
mira mármoles y arcos destrozados,
mira estatuas soberbias que violenta
Némesis derribó, yacer tendidas ;
y ya en alto silencio sepultados
sus dueños celebrados.
Así a Troya figuro,
así a su antiguo muro ;
y a ti, Roma, a quien queda el nombre apenas,
—¡ oh patria de los dioses y los reyes !—
y a ti, a quien no valieron justas leyes,
fábrica de Minerva, sabia Atenas :
emulación ayer de las edades,
hoy cenizas, hoy vastas soledades ;
que no os respetó el hado, no la muerte,
¡ ay ! ni por sabia a ti, ni a ti por fuerte.

Mas ¿ para qué la mente se derrama
en buscar al dolor nuevo argumento ?
Basta ejemplo menor, basta el presente :
que aun se ve el humo aquí, aun se ve la llama,
aun se oyen llantos hoy, hoy ronco acento.
Tal genio o religión fuerza la mente
de la vecina gente,
que refiere admirada

que en la noche callada
una voz triste se oye, que llorando
" ¡ Cayó Itálica !," dice ; y lastimosa
Eco reclama " ¡ Itálica ! " en la hojosa
selva, que se le opone resonando
" ¡ Itálica ! " : y el caro nombre oído
de Itálica renuevan el gemido
mil sombras nobles en su gran ruïna.
¡ Tanto aun la plebe a sentimiento inclina !

Esta corta piedad, que agradecido
huésped a tus sagrados Manes debo,
les dó y consagro, Itálica famosa.
Tú (si lloroso don han admitido
las ingratas cenizas, de que llevo
dulce noticia asaz, si lastimosa)
permíteme, piadosa
usura a tierno llanto,
que vea el cuerpo santo
de Geroncio, tu mártir y prelado.
Muestra de su sepulcro algunas señas,
y cavaré con lágrimas las peñas
que ocultan su sarcófago sagrado.
Pero mal pido el único consuelo
de todo el bien que airado quitó el cielo.
Goza en las tuyas sus reliquias bellas
para envidia del mundo y las estrellas.

LUIS MARTÍN DE LA PLAZA

1577-*c*.1625

THOUGH substantially represented in Espinosa's *Flores* (p. 350), Luis Martín de la Plaza is chiefly a translator and adapter of Italian poetry and shows little originality. He is known almost exclusively by the madrigal reproduced below.

182. *Madrigal*

" Artificiality made tolerable by a charming fancy " might be a verdict on this madrigal, which is adapted from Tasso. Whether as a tactful comment on an unfortunate incident or as the most delicate of compliments to " mi ninfa " it would be unlikely to have missed its mark. Perfect rhythm and a haunting melody combine to make it the more acceptable. The last line cunningly suggests the light, swift movements of the bee.

Iba cogiendo flores,
y guardando en la falda,
mi ninfa, para hacer una guirnalda ;
mas primero las toca
a los rosados labios de su boca,
y les da de su aliento los olores ;
y estaba, por su bien, entre una rosa
un abeja escondida,
su dulce humor hurtando,
y como en la hermosa
flor de los labios se halló, atrevida
la picó, sacó miel, fuése volando.

PEDRO ESPINOSA
1578-1650

IN the history of literature Espinosa—the best of a group of poets from Antequera—is most generally known as an anthologist: his *Flores de poetas ilustres de España* (1605), unique in its day, was called, by as modern a critic as Gallardo, " a golden book—the finest treasury of Spanish poetry that we possess." But he is also of importance as a creative writer; and his poems, most of which (including all the best) were written before he had reached his late thirties, represent a notable milestone on the path which led to Gongorism. Their decorative elements (" el ornato de mis versos ", in his own phrase[1]) include ambitious light-effects, ostentation in colour, abundant flower-imagery, and a preoccupation with the magnificent in Nature and the flamboyant in the work of man. His language was free neither of conceptism nor of cultism, though he attacked the latter in a much-quoted satirical sonnet (" Rompe la niebla de una gruta escura. . . ."). His longer poems, the chief of which is the overrated " Fábula del Genil ", an ornate treatment of a trivial mythological theme, are, generally speaking, inferior to his sonnets and to such charming trifles as the madrigal " En una red prendiste tu cabello. . . .". His religious poetry, too, is not to be despised. In the latter part of his life he took Orders, and the long odes which he terms " psalms ", with other of his sacred poems, have a vein of deep and evident sincerity. But these must not be confused with such early religious verse, mainly descriptive and panegyric in intention and Baroque in form, as the *canción* " Al Bautismo de Jesús " and the sonnet " A la Asunción de la Virgen María ".[2] The standard of his technique, it should be added, is a high one.

[1] " No te admire el ornato de mis versos " (" A Crisalda " : Canción).

[2] For a critical appreciation of this sonnet by Audrey Lumsden, see *B.S.S.*, 1942, XIX, 101-3.

183. *Soneto*

An early love-poem, illustrating the poise and balance of Espinosa's verse, his handling of the caesura and his treatment of the poetic element of light. There are indications of immaturity in the sonnet's technique—notably in its use of hyperbole—but much more striking is the impression which it produces of latent power.

El sol a noble furia se provoca
cuando sin luz lo dejas descontento,
y, por gozarte, enfrena el movimiento
el aura, que de gloria se retoca ;

tus bellos ojos y tu dulce boca,
de luz divina y de oloroso aliento,
envidia el claro sol y adora el viento,
por lo que el uno ve y el otro toca.

Ojos y boca, que tenéis costumbre
de darme vida, honraos con más despojos ;
mi ardiente amor vuestra piedad invoca.

Fáltame aliento, y fáltame la lumbre :
¡ Prestadme vuestra luz, divinos ojos !
¡ Beba yo vuestro aliento, dulce boca !

184. *A la Navegación de San Raimundo desde Mallorca a Barcelona*

This florid ode, as characteristic of Espinosa's ornate manner as the Fábula del Genil *and the sonnet on Our Lady's Assumption, belongs, like those poems, to his twenties. His exuberance of language—partly native, partly temperamental—is united to an evident sense of growing power, and produces a Baroque picture which the subject of it—the twelfth-century Dominican Saint Ramon de Penyafort, who is supposed to have walked across the Mediterranean from Majorca to the main-*

land—would certainly never have recognized. Nowhere is Espinosa more lavish with his palette—white, blue and gold, lemon and carmine, purple, green and silver—and nowhere has he in so short a space more words evocative of colour and light : nieve, argentería, rubio, acije, esmeralda, nácar, diamante, claridades, *and literally dozens of others. From the moment of executing the first bold strokes of the dazzling picture with which the poem opens, he displays all the panoply of his art. The grandeur of the ocean is enhanced by the verbal and pictorial magnificence of a high-soaring, all-embracing imagination. The poetical potentialities of the heavens—dawn and day ; sun, moon, and all the stars of light—are called in to increase the effect. Shimmering light, rainbow hues, glittering jewels, subtle shades of colour—all these favourite devices of Espinosa's art illumine a canvas crowded with figures, some impressive, some fantastic, but none negligible. The* silva-*like stanzas (six of nineteen lines each, arranged aBbACdD-ecfEFxgGHhII, with a* coda-*stanza of eight lines) add to the effect of dignity which is never lost.*

Tiran yeguas de nieve
el carro de cambiante argentería
sobre que viene el día
con rubias trenzas, de quien perlas llueve ;
la alcatifa sembrada de diamantes
se borda y se matiza
de génuli, carmín y azul ceniza,
cuando de sus alcobas,
cerúleas, espumantes,
sale Neptuno horrendo,
quitando de la frente el musgo y ovas,
alborotado con el sordo estruendo
que hacen los tritones,
que en torno van de un manto
que el agua corta, que sustenta un santo ;
y recostado en azul tridente,
con arrugada frente,
mira el barco veloz que va volando,
sus erizadas ondas despreciando.

De claridades bellas
vido pintada y rica la canoa ;
que la luna era proa,
la popa el sol, y lo demás estrellas ;
y, viendo aquesta maravilla santa,
bebe el delgado viento
y a un caracol torcido le da aliento ;
y en el profundo estrecho,
oyendo furia tanta,
Doris, con miedo helado,
los azules hijuelos llegó al pecho ;
aparecieron sobre el mar salado
los escamosos dioses,
a quien Neptuno pide
apriesa el carro que las ondas mide ;
encima sube, a los caballos grita
y a volar los incita,
hasta que al venerable Santo llega,
y con espuma los tritones ciega.

Parece el mar que bulle
brocado azul, de plata la entretela,
por donde el carro vuela,
que, por más gala, a veces se zabulle ;
de nácares cubiertas las espaldas,
relumbra el dios que rige
fieros caballos de color de acije,
que con las ondas chocan,
del cual, entre esmeraldas
y sanguinos corales,
los cabellos al pecho helado tocan,
de quien manan clarísimos cristales,
y sobre el carro verde,
un caudaloso río
de las barbas preñadas de rocío ;
y los que deste triunfo allí se admiran
también del viejo miran
que las canas, por más ornato, aforra
de una arrugada concha, en vez de gorra.

Arrojan los delfines
por las narices blanca espuma en arco
sobre el profundo charco,
y, destilando de las verdes crines
aljófar, las nereidas asomaron
y las dulces sirenas
sobre pintadas conchas de ballenas;
Tritón, Forco y Proteo
delante se mostraron,
cuando salió rigiendo
un caballo marino el dios Nereo,
que con hendido pie va el mar hendiendo.
La escuadra de las ninfas
ligera en torno zarpa,
midiendo acentos en discante y harpa;
y tú, Raimundo, sobre el pobre manto,
miras la fiesta, en tanto,
que hace a tu santísima persona
el turquesado mar de Barcelona.

Con ligera pujanza
el Rey te sigue y con hinchadas velas,
en tanto que tú vuelas,
venciendo tu barquillo su esperanza;
tórnase cana espuma el mar cerúleo;
los remeros que bogan
del movimiento del batir se ahogan;
abriendo cuevas hondas,
con movimiento hercúleo,
herrados espolones
rompen las crespas y sonantes ondas;
tiemblan con los furiosos empellones
las galeras de abeto;
los forzados, remando,
arroyos de sudor iban sudando,
y el Rey entiende que un lugar no pasa;
en cólera se abrasa,
y, arrebatado de un dolor interno,
vierte el coraje por el rostro tierno.

Mas tú, tomando tierra,
y religiosa admiración la orilla,
sacudes la barquilla
que te libró de la tormenta y guerra,
y así la cuelgas en sagrado templo
como cuando, devoto,
la tabla al templo consagró el piloto.
Los hombres que miraron
el caso sin ejemplo,
siguiéndote infinitos,
en confusos tropeles te cercaron,
hiriendo las estrellas con los gritos ;
mas tú, ¡ oh padre Raimundo !
del tropel te adelantas
con rostro humilde y sosegadas plantas,
y, en tu celda encerrado,
del Rey lloras y gimes el pecado ;
el cual, tomando puerto apriesa apriesa,
se arrepiente, te busca, y se confiesa.

Canción, que, navegando,
vas tras de san Raimundo,
con el favor de don Andrés de Córdoba,
no al ábrego bramando
ni al piélago profundo
temas : porque la virgen Panopea
te ha prometido cierto
buen tiempo, mar tranquilo, dulce puerto.

185. *Soneto*

Here we have a somewhat more mature example of Espinosa's style. The direction in which his genius has turned is still evident but his colours are soberer and his flights more restrained. The most striking trait of the poem is of course its use of the fourteen-syllable ("alejandrino") line, lending itself admirably to the impression of solemn dignity which, whether unconsciously or of set purpose, Espinosa conveys in a large proportion of his verse. So successful is he here that it is surprising he should not have made greater use of this line elsewhere—and, indeed, that it should have been left to the Modernists to exploit its potentialities to the full. The language of the sonnet has less distinction, and its figures have perhaps less life, than those of other of Espinosa's poems; possibly its vitality is to some extent stifled by an abundance of epithet, which in its turn may have been induced by the length of the line. But, while admittedly not superlative, the standard of the poem is a high one.

Como el triste piloto que por el mar incierto
se ve, con turbios ojos, sujeto de la pena
sobre las corvas olas, que, vomitando arena,
lo tienen de la espuma salpicado y cubierto,

cuando, sin esperanza, de espanto medio muerto,
ve el fuego de Santelmo lucir sobre la antena,
y, adorando su lumbre, de gozo el alma llena,
halla su nao cascada surgida en dulce puerto,

así yo el mar sulcaba de penas y de enojos,
y, con tormenta fiera, ya de las aguas hondas
medio cubierto estaba, la fuerza y luz perdida,

cuando miré la lumbre ¡ oh Virgen ! de tus ojos,
con cuyos resplandores, quietándose las ondas
llegué al dichoso puerto donde escapé la vida.

186. *Plegaria*

Except in its use of antithesis and in its final images, this fragment is in no way typical of Espinosa's art. It will serve, on the other hand, to represent in small compass the unadorned sincerity and fervour of his psalmos *and* canciones *which have had to be omitted in favour of his more characteristic verse. The world of sense and sensuousness has fallen away from him; and, to quote San Juan de la Cruz, there are now only two realities for him—God and his soul.*

Ausente llamo al que presente adoro :
concede Tú a las lágrimas que lloro,
yo, solitario tuyo, en tierra fría,
dulce Jesús, merezca en mi porfía,
ciego, a mi Sol ; y pobre, a mi Tesoro.

JUAN DE TARSIS, CONDE DE VILLAMEDIANA
1580-1622

A courtier, assassinated in his prime by political enemies, Villamediana is best known for his skilful but bitter and often cruelly satiric epigrams, as well as for his numerous sonnets, in which he affects a mild form of Gongorism. All these were published in book form seven years after his death.

187. *Soneto: Al Retiro de las Ambiciones de la Corte*

Written somewhat in the spirit of Fray Luis de León (of whom—p. 207, ll. 31-2—there is a definite and probably intentional reminiscence in the last tercet), this sonnet shows a certain decline from his standard and style. The language of the octave grows more inflated as it proceeds and the first of the two tercets is lacking in clarity. As a whole, nevertheless, though not inspired, the poem has dignity and repose.

Si para mal contentos hay sagrado,
dulce quietud del ánimo lo sea
en esta soledad donde granjea
aviso y no fatigas el cuidado.

El metal en la lluvia desatado
sobre ambiciosa mano lograr vea
quien aun con los engaños lisonjea
de sus áulicas pompas adulado.

Sirenas sean lisonja de su oído
que adulterando a la razón las llaves,
cierren la puerta del mejor sentido.

Yo entre estas mansas ondas, a las aves
en canto ni adulado ni aprendido
deberé el desmentir fatigas graves.

188. *Epigramas*

A DON PEDRO VERGEL, ALGUACIL DE CORTE, ENTRANDO EN LA PLAZA DE TOROS

¡ Qué galán que entró Vergel
con cintillo de diamantes !
Diamantes que fueron antes
de amantes de su mujer.

AL MARQUÉS DE MALPICA[1]

Cuando el marqués de Malpica,
caballero de la llave,
con su silencio replica,
dice todo cuanto sabe.

[1] The Marquis in question was eulogized by Lope de Vega, who at one time served him as secretary. His position of *Caballero de la llave* would be termed in English "Gentleman of the King's Bedchamber."

FRANCISCO DE QUEVEDO

1580-1645

A COURTIER, who, like many such in his age, fell from favour and suffered exiles and imprisonments, Quevedo, as a man of letters, was endowed with a fecundity and versatility exceeded by few save Lope de Vega. Primarily he is known as the author of two prose masterpieces, the satirical *Sueños* and the picaresque *Vida del Buscón.* But he also wrote other satires, biographies, literary pamphlets and prose works on morals, philosophy and religion; yet none the less his poetical works are of almost as great bulk as his works in prose. The fertility and variety of his verse, and the high degree of merit which he attained in each of the types to which he set his hand, are astonishing. He was as adept in exotic or Classical forms as in the popular Spanish tradition, and he excelled in verse of every mood and tone. Some critics think him at his best in subtle irony, in biting satire, in broad humour or in glancing wit. Others, with equal justification, describe him as unsurpassed in his grave, reflective mood, sometimes marked by an almost pagan morbidity, sometimes by a deep and firm Christian faith. But he also wrote the most brilliant occasional verse, complimentary trifles, love poems (both in the old forms and in the new), burlesques, *jácaras*, epigrams, translations and imitations from Hebrew, Greek and Latin, elegies, panegyrics, comedies, *entremeses*, *loas*—and (incredible as it may seem), a great deal more. A few representative examples of his serious, his satirical and his jovial mood are all that can here be given, for Quevedo is the anthologist's despair.

189. *Soneto : Desde la Torre*

The " gran don Josef " of l. 11 was the author's friend González de Salas, who described the sonnet as having been sent him by Quevedo shortly before the latter's imprisonment. Astrana Marín, however[1],

[1] *Obras completas (en verso) de D.F. de Q.*, Madrid, 1932, p. 424, n.

believes it to be considerably earlier, and reproduces the autograph, which differs verbally in six lines, and in l. 11 reads

restituye, D. Juan, *docta la imprenta.*

Solitude, the theme of the poem, is a favourite one with Spanish poets and the solace of reading is delightfully described in ll. 3-4. The reference to " silent music " in l. 7 may well be an intentional allusion to San Juan de la Cruz's Cántico espiritual *(p. 262, l. 3, above). The octave of the sonnet is marked alike by distinction and charm, but it must be confessed that the sestet declines, both constructionally and euphonically, from its standard.*

Retirado en la paz de estos desiertos,
con pocos, pero doctos libros juntos,
vivo en conversación con los difuntos
y escucho con mis ojos a los muertos.

Si no siempre entendidos, siempre abiertos,
o enmiendan, o secundan mis asuntos ;
y en músicos callados contrapuntos
al sueño de la vida hablan despiertos.

Las grandes almas que la muerte ausenta,
de injurias de los años, vengadora,
libra ¡ oh gran don Josef ! docta la emprenta.

En fuga irrevocable huye la hora ;
pero aquella el mejor cálculo cuenta
que en la lección y estudios nos mejora.

190. *Soneto*

The heading of this sonnet—" Afectos varios de su corazón, fluctuando en las ondas de los cabellos de Lisi "—gives a clear indication of its nature. It is an attractive piece of conceptist poetry. In the very first line, imagination, spurred by love, flies away on the wings of hyperbole and never descends anywhere near to earth. The poet may be " thirsting for beauty " as his heart suffers each of the sea-changes he describes, but the reader bathes in it, and absorbs it in every pore, until (and this is so often the case with the reader of Baroque poetry) he is sated with it. There is gold in the first line of the sonnet, gold in the last, and, lest for a single moment the impression should fade, gold in the middle. Then upon a tempest of gold is superimposed Leander's sea of fire, Icarus' burning wings and the burning phœnix, all lit by that purest burning light— " *luz ardiente y pura* " *—which illumines the whole atmosphere to which the poet has brought us. One hardly stops to think what the poem means—one hardly even cares, so gorgeous is it.*

En crespa tempestad del oro undoso
nada golfos de luz ardiente y pura
mi corazón, sediento de hermosura,
si el cabello deslazas generoso.

Leandro en mar de fuego proceloso
su amor ostenta, su vivir apura ;
Ícaro en senda de oro mal segura
arde sus alas por morir glorioso.

Con pretensión de fénix, encendidas
sus esperanzas, que difuntas lloro,
intenta que su muerte engendre vidas.

Avaro y rico, y pobre en el tesoro,
el castigo y la hambre imita a Midas,
Tántalo en fugitiva fuente de oro.

191. *Soneto*[1]

Technically a fine sonnet, with a strong opening, a remarkable crescendo of intensity and a conclusion of impressive finality. The initial alliteration in m *(l. 1) is less appropriate to the theme than that which follows in* c *(ll. 3-4). But the appeal of the poem is pictorial rather than musical. Note how each of the three scenes* (patria, campo, casa) *is more detailed, as well as being more intimate, than the last. The first (ll. 1-4) shows us only* " *walls* "—" *muros. . . . desmoronados* ". *The second (ll. 5-8) gives two quite well defined pictures. In the third (ll. 9-12) the eye rests (ll. 13-14) on one object after another. And corresponding to the increasingly intense impressions of desolation there is a progression of emotion, so that the reader is completely prepared for the grisly conclusion when it comes. Quevedo's sonnet must be acclaimed as a highly individual treatment of a subject common to universal experience.*

[1] For a critical appreciation of this sonnet by S. Griswold Morley, see *B.S.S.*, 1941, XVIII, 226-8.

Miré los muros de la patria mía,
si un tiempo fuertes, ya desmoronados,
de la carrera de la edad cansados
por quien caduca ya su valentía.

Salíme al campo ; vi que el sol bebía
los arroyos del hielo desatados,
y del monte quejosos los ganados
que con sombras hurtó su luz al día.

Entré en mi casa ; vi que, amancillada,
de anciana habitación era despojos ;
mi báculo, más corvo y menos fuerte.

Vencida de la edad sentí mi espada,
y no hallé cosa en que poner los ojos
que no fuese recuerdo de la muerte.

192. *Soneto*

This second of a number of poems which Quevedo wrote on old age and death offers a striking contrast with " Miré los muros. . . ." The one is detached and contemplative ; the other, subjective, dynamic. Instead of displaying carefully selected and prepared pictures, it records the thoughts that flit through the mind of the man growing old—trite or original, abstract or figured, they all go down. Not one of the images (except perhaps that of ll. 7-8) is in the least developed, yet the sonnet is a most moving evocation of the fear of death. Note how the slow, sombre pace of ll. 1-2 quickens in ll. 9-11, to express disquiet and urgency, and how l. 14, which logically opens up a completely new train of thought, might emotionally be an expression of panic, the final question being interpretable as sheer bravado.

Todo tras sí lo lleva el año breve
de la vida mortal, burlando el brío
al acero valiente, al mármol frío
que contra el tiempo su dureza atreve.

Antes que sepa andar el pie, se mueve
camino de la muerte, donde envío
mi vida oscura : pobre y turbio río,
que negro mar con altas ondas bebe.

Todo corto momento es paso largo
que doy, a mi pesar, en tal jornada,
pues, parado y durmiendo, siempre aguijo.

Breve suspiro, y último, y amargo,
es la muerte, forzosa y heredada;
mas si es ley y no pena, ¿ qué me aflijo ?

193. *Letrilla satírica*

So charming an example of Quevedo's ironic vein, with its inimitable and unforgettable personification, familiar to Spaniards from popular proverbs, of "Mr. Money", can hardly be said to need a commentary. It will suffice to draw attention to the lightness, combined with sureness, of touch (as in the second stanza), to the plays upon words (e.g., on the coins blanca, cuarto, escudo), *to the lilt of the whole poem (especially of the refrain) and to the echo-effect produced by the shortness of the last line.*

Poderoso caballero
es don Dinero.

Madre, yo al oro me humillo;
él es mi amante y mi amado,
pues de puro enamorado
anda contino amarillo;
que pues, doblón o sencillo,
hace todo cuanto quiero,
poderoso caballero
es don Dinero.

Nace en las Indias honrado,
donde el mundo le acompaña;
viene a morir en España,
y es en Génova enterrado.
Y pues quien le trae al lado
es hermoso, aunque sea fiero,
poderoso caballero
es don Dinero.

Es galán y es como un oro;
tiene quebrado el color,
persona de gran valor,
tan cristiano como moro.
Pues que da y quita el decoro
y quebranta cualquier fuero,
poderoso caballero
es don Dinero.

Son sus padres principales,
y es de nobles descendiente,
porque en las venas de Oriente
todas las sangres son reales;
y pues es quien hace iguales
al rico y al pordiosero,
poderoso caballero
es don Dinero.

¿A quién no le maravilla
ver en su gloria sin tasa
que es lo más ruin de su casa
doña Blanca de Castilla?
Mas pues que su fuerza humilla
al cobarde y al guerrero,
poderoso caballero
es don Dinero.

Sus escudos de armas nobles
son siempre tan principales,
que sin sus escudos reales
no hay escudos de armas dobles;
y pues a los mismos nobles
da codicia su minero,
poderoso caballero
es don Dinero.

Por importar en los tratos
y dar tan buenos consejos,
en las casas de los viejos
gatos le guardan de gatos.
Y pues él rompe recatos
y ablanda al juez más severo,
poderoso caballero
es don Dinero.

Es tanta su majestad
(aunque son sus duelos hartos)
que, aun con estar hecho cuartos,
no pierde su calidad ;
pero, pues da autoridad
al gañán y al jornalero,
poderoso caballero
es don Dinero.
Nunca vi damas ingratas
a su gusto y afición ;
que a las caras de un doblón
hacen sus caras baratas ;
y pues las hace bravatas
desde una bolsa de cuero,
poderoso caballero
es don Dinero.
Más valen en cualquier tierra
(¡ mirad si es harto sagaz !)
sus escudos en la paz
que rodelas en la guerra.
Pues al natural destierra
y hace propio al forastero,
poderoso caballero
es don Dinero.

194. *Soneto : A una Nariz*

The nasal protuberance has always lent itself, more than most parts of the human body, to caricature : in modern literature the outstanding piece of humour of this type is to be found in Rostand's Cyrano de Bergerac :

. . . C'est un roc ! . . . c'est un pic ! . . . c'est un cap !
Que dis-je, c'est un cap ? . . . C'est une péninsule !

Quevedo can hardly be as expansive and as versatile in fourteen lines as Rostand in fifty, but, by his absurd hyperboles, by repetition for effect, by the use of superlatives and most of all by his flair for the apt phrase, he manages to pack as much fun into a sonnet as anyone had ever done before or has done since. Note how the opening absurdity captures the reader from the first moment. The delicate reference to Ovid's name "Naso" is more obvious than the pun in the last line, where Annas, the Jewish High Priest, is introduced, not merely because Jews are normally represented with prominent noses, but to permit the ironic interpretation of his name as "a-nasal". This is perhaps a little far-fetched, but it will not obscure the delicious mock intensity with which the sonnet rises to its close.

Érase un hombre a una nariz pegado,
érase una nariz superlativa,
érase una nariz sayón y escriba,
érase un peje espada muy barbado.

Era un reloj de sol mal encarado,
érase una alquitara pensativa,
érase un elefante boca arriba,
era Ovidio Nasón más narizado.

Érase un espolón de una galera,
érase una pirámide de Egito:
las doce tribus de narices era.

Érase un naricísimo infinito,
muchísimo nariz, nariz tan fiera
que en la cara de Anás fuera delito.

195. *Soneto: Contra los Hipócritas*

The full title is "Contra los hipócritas y fingida virtud de monjas y beatas, en alegoría del cohete." The "alegoría", or extended figure of speech filling the entire sonnet, is an apt one, skilfully turned in memorable language, though it might perhaps have been more appropriately applied than to hypocrites and beatas. *The proverbial tang of l. 4 is perhaps the sonnet's most attractive feature, with the possible exception of the neat antithesis and the verbal finality of l. 14. It will be observed that the sestet is constructed upon two rhymes instead of the more usual three.*

No digas, cuando vieres alto el vuelo
del cohete, en la pólvora animado,
que va derecho al cielo encaminado,
pues no siempre quien sube llega al cielo.

Festivo rayo que nació del suelo,
en popular aplauso confiado,
disimula el azufre aprisionado:
traza es la cuerda, y es rebozo el velo.

Si le vieres en alto radïante,
que con el firmamento y sus centellas
equivoca su sitio y su semblante,

¡oh, no le cuentes tú por una dellas!
Mira que hay fuego artificial farsante,
que es humo y representa las estrellas.

196. *Diálogo entre Galán y Dama*

The tone of this charming and sprightly trifle is similar to that of most of Quevedo's theatrical diálogos *and* bailes, *some of which, however, contain topical allusions now difficult of interpretation. The movement of the poem suggests, as no doubt it was meant to do, an old-world dance, and the frequent echo of the thematic phrase "-oro" adds to its naturally musical quality. It is interesting to observe how the conceptist note enters even so simple a piece, though its sense, of course, is of little importance by comparison with its melody. One would hardly recognize its author as the fierce satirist of the* Sueños *or as the sombre poet who wrote the sonnets on death.*

GALÁN: Como un oro, no hay dudar,
eres, niña, y yo te adoro.

DAMA: *Niño, pues soy como un oro,*
con premio me he de trocar.

GALÁN: De oro tus cabellos son,
rica ocupación del viento.

DAMA: Pues a sesenta por ciento
daré cada repelón.

GALÁN: ¿Qué precio habrá que consuele
oro que rizado mata?

DAMA: Como me dé el trueco en plata,
dejaré que me repele.

GALÁN: No hay plata para pagar
prisión que vale un tesoro.
DAMA: *Niño, pues soy como un oro,*
con premio me he de trocar.
GALÁN: ¿ Tan grande es la estimación
del oro, a tanto se extiende ?
DAMA: Hasta el orozuz pretende
ventajas contra el vellón.
GALÁN: ¿ Oro que codicia el alba
vendes por cosa del suelo ?
DAMA: Págame tú en plata el pelo,
que yo me quedaré calva.
GALÁN: Quien lo quisiere comprar,
pierde al amor el decoro.
DAMA: *Niño, pues soy como un oro,*
con premio me he de trocar.

197. *Letrilla*

Here, as the refrain alone will suggest, we pass from pointed irony to strident satire. Superficially, Quevedo may appear not to have changed his technique, and, like others which he wrote in the same strain, the piece has certainly its lighter moments. But his word-play, whether complicated, as in the second stanza, or simple, as in the third, is more often bitter than amusing, and his smoothly flowing stanzas seem at times to have a rhetorical ring.

Toda esta vida es hurtar:
no es el ser ladrón afrenta,
que como este mundo es venta
en él es propio robar.
Nadie verás castigar
porque hurta plata o cobre;
que al que azotan es por pobre
de suerte, favor y trazas.
Este mundo es juego de bazas,
que sólo el que roba triunfa y manda.

El escribano recibe
cuanto le dan sin estruendo,
y con hurtar escribiendo,
lo que hurta no se escribe.
El que bien hurta bien vive ;
y es linaje más honrado
el hurtar que el ser hurtado ;
suple faltas, gana chazas.
Que este mundo es juego de bazas,
que sólo el que roba triunfa y manda.
Mejor es, si se repara,
para ser gran caballero,
el ser ladrón de dinero
que ser Ladrón de Guevara.
El alguacil con su vara,
con sus leyes el letrado,
con su mujer el casado,
hurtan en públicas plazas.
Que este mundo es juego de bazas,
que sólo el que roba triunfa y manda.
El juez en injustos tratos
cobra de mala opinión,
porque hasta en la pasión
es parecido a Pilatos.
Protector es de los gatos,
porque rellenarlos gusta :
sólo la botarga es justa,
que en lo demás hay hilazas.
Este mundo es juego de bazas,
que sólo el que roba triunfa y manda.
Hay muchos rostros exentos,
hermosos, cuanto tiranos,
que viven como escribanos
de fes y conocimientos :
por el que beben los vientos,
es al que la capa comen ;
no hay suerte que no le tomen
con embustes y trapazas.
Este mundo es juego de bazas,
que sólo el que roba triunfa y manda.

ANTONIO MIRA DE AMESCUA

*c.*1574-1644

MIRA DE AMESCUA is primarily a dramatist of the school of Lope de Vega, somewhat overshadowed, like all his contemporaries, by the transcendent genius of the Master. The lyric poem, given below, which is chiefly associated with his name is in reality of doubtful authorship and ascribed to him only on the authority of Baltasar Gracián, who quoted from it before it was first published in a seventeenth-century anthology, anonymously.

198. *Canción real a una mudanza*

I

Ufano, alegre, altivo, enamorado,
cortando el aire el suelto jilguerillo,
sentóse en el pimpollo de una haya ;
y con el pico de marfil nevado,
entre el pechuelo verde y amarillo,
las plumas concertó pajiza y baya ;
y celoso se ensaya
a discantar en alto contrapunto
sus celos y amor junto ;
y al ramillo y al prado y a las flores,
libre y gozoso, cuenta sus amores.
Mas ¡ ay ! que en este estado
el cazador cruel, de astucia armado,
escondido le acecha,
y al tierno corazón aguda flecha
tira con mano esquiva,
y envuelto en sangre viva le derriba.
¡ O vida malograda,
imagen de mi suerte desdichada !

II

De la custodia del amor materno
el corderillo juguetón se aleja,
enamorado de la yerba y flores,
y por la libertad y pasto tierno
el cándido licor olvida y deja,
por quien hizo a su madre mil amores :
sin conocer temores,
de la florida primavera bella
el vario manto huella
con brincos licenciosos,
y pace tallos tiernos y sabrosos.
Mas ¡ ay ! que en un otero
dió en la boca del lobo carnicero,
que en partes diferentes
le dividió con sus voraces dientes ;
y a convertirse vino
en purpúreo el dorado vellocino.
¡ O inocencia ofendida,
breve bien, caro pasto, corta vida !

III

Rica con sus penachos y copetes,
ufana y loca, con altivo vuelo
se remonta la garza a las estrellas ;
y aliñando sus blancos martinetes,
procura parecer allá en el cielo
la reina sola de las aves bellas ;
y por ser ella de ellas
la que más altanera se remonta,
ya se encubre y trasmonta
a los ojos del lince más atentos,
y se contempla reina de los vientos.
Mas ¡ ay ! que en la alta nube
el águila la ve y al cielo sube,
donde con pico y garra

el pecho candidísimo desgarra
del bello airón, que quiso
volar tan alto con tan poco aviso.
¡ Ay, pájaro altanero,
de mi suerte retrato verdadero !

IV

Al son de las belígeras trompetas
y al rimbombar del sonoroso parche,
forma escuadrón el general gallardo ;
con relinchos, bufidos y corvetas,
pide el caballo que la gente marche,
trocando en paso presuroso el tardo.
Tocó el clarín bastardo
la esperada señal de arremetida,
y en batalla rompida,
teniendo cierta del vencer la gloria,
oyó su gente que gritó victoria.
Mas ¡ ay ! que el desconcierto
del capitán bisoño y poco experto,
por no guardar el orden
causó en su gente general desorden ;
y, la ocasión perdida,
el vencedor perdió victoria y vida.
¡ Ay Fortuna contraria,
en mis prósperos fines siempre varia !

V

Al cristalino y mudo lisonjero
la altiva dama en su beldad se goza,
contemplándose Venus en la tierra ;
el más soberbio corazón de acero
con su vista enternece y alboroza,
y es de las libertades dulce guerra :
el desamor destierra
de donde pone sus divinos ojos,
que de ellos son despojos

los castos de Diana,
y en su belleza se contempla ufana.
Mas ¡ ay ! que un accidente
apenas puso el pulso intercadente,
cuando cubrió de manchas,
cárdenas ronchas y viruelas anchas,
el bello rostro hermoso,
trocándole en horrible y espantoso.
¡ Ay beldad malograda,
muerta luz, turbio sol y flor pisada !

VI

Sobre frágiles leños, y con alas
de lienzo débil, que del mar son carros,
el mercader surcó las claras olas ;
llegó a la India, y rico de bengalas,
aromas, perlas, nácares bizarros,
dió vuelta a las riberas españolas :
tremoló banderolas,
flámulos, estandartes, gallardetes ;
dió premio a los grumetes
por haber descubierto
de la querida patria el dulce puerto.
Mas ¡ ay ! que estaba ignoto
a la experiencia y ciencia del piloto
en la barra un peñasco,
donde chocando de la nave el casco,
dió a fondo, hechos mil piezas,
mercader, esperanzas y riquezas.
¡ Pobre bajel, figura
del que anegó mi próspera ventura !

Mi pensamiento, con ligero vuelo,
ufano, alegre, altivo, enamorado,
sin conocer temores la memoria,
se remontó, señora, hasta tu cielo ;
y contrastando su desdén helado,
venció mi fe, gritó el amor victoria ;
y en la sublime gloria
de tu beldad se retrataba el alma ;

el mar de amor en calma
mi navecilla con su viento en popa
llevaba navegando a toda ropa.
Mas ¡ ay ! que mi contento
fué el pajarillo y corderillo exento,
fué la garza altanera,
fué el capitán que la victoria espera,
fué la Venus del mundo,
fué la nave del piélago profundo ;
que por diversos modos
todas las muertes padecí de todos.

Canción, ve a la coluna
que sustentó mi próspera fortuna,
y verás que si entonces
te pareció de mármoles y bronces,
hoy es mujer, y en suma
breve bien, fácil viento, leve espuma.

TIRSO DE MOLINA

*c.*1583-1648

ANY extensive account of this famous playwright, whose real name was Gabriel Téllez, belongs to a volume on Spanish drama. He was undoubtedly one of Spain's three greatest dramatists, though his excellence came to be recognized somewhat later than that of Lope de Vega and Calderón. Here it must suffice to note that he carried on the tradition, initiated by Encina and Timoneda, of weaving the most graceful of lyrics into his dramas.

199. "*Segadores, afuera, afuera. . . .*"

A charming example of the "reaping song," taken from the play La Mejor Espigadera. *The whole, it will be noted, has only two rhymes. It is hard to say which is the more attractive—the melodious refrain, with its "popular", rather than correct, end-rhyme, or the gay fancy, so appropriate to the type of song, which plays on the theme.*

Segadores, afuera, afuera :
dejen llegar a la espigaderuela.

Si en las manos que bendigo
fuera yo espiga de trigo,
que me hiciera harina digo
y luego torta o bodigo,
porque luego me comiera.

Segadores, afuera, afuera :
dejen llegar a la espigaderuela.

JUAN DE JÁUREGUI

1583-1641

JÁUREGUI, a Sevilian, was not only a painter and a poet but a critic of cultism (p. xxxvi), against which he wrote a *Discurso poético* (1624), to say nothing of an " Antidote " to Góngora's *Soledades.* None the less, there is a cultist side to his own verses, which consist chiefly of some translations and a collection of *Rimas* (1618). He may perhaps be best described as an Herreran marching with his poetic age.

200. *Soneto*

Not merely because of the verbal resemblance in its final line, but because of the depth of sincerity which it leaves as its chief impression, this love-sonnet is distinctly reminiscent of the love-sonnet a lo divino *"No me mueve, mi Dios. . . ." (p. 194). Together with the subjective note, however, is heard the ring of conventional eloquence, just as the conventional figures of speech are relieved by only one real and brilliant, if slightly inconsequent, metaphor (ll. 5-6). Yet there is a haunting appeal about the sonnet which fixes it in the memory.*

Jamás por larga ausencia, amada Flora,
sentir podrá mi fe mudanza alguna,
bien que me engolfe y lleve la fortuna
por la remota mar hircana o mora.

Si en cada espuma que levanta agora,
brillando el agua al rayo de la luna,
naciesen Venus ciento, y cada una
fuese de un nuevo amor engendradora ;

y éstos y aquéllas con igual denuedo
cuidasen aumentar el fuego mío,
ni se aumentara, ni mi fe creciera ;

y aunque de acrecentalla desconfío,
vivo en eterno afán, porque no puedo
quereros tanto como yo quisiera.

201. *Soneto*

Here we have a more typical example of Jáuregui's style, which at first sight appears to be a retrogression to the artificialities of the early italianate period. But there persists the subjective note, conveying so clear an impression of sincerity, and there is a compelling attractiveness in the smoothly flowing verse.

Si en el amado pecho más constante
teme el olvido el amador ausente,
porque en la ausencia el tiempo no consiente
memoria o voluntad perseverante ;

yo, que en presencia (miserable amante)
no fuí correspondido, y al presente
mi ausencia Filis no recela o siente,
¿ qué olvido espero a su rigor bastante ?

Esta imaginación, al alma asida,
mil muertes puede darme, y yo con ella
ser puedo a mis tormentos homicida ;

mas como agradan a su causa bella
tanto mis males, me reserva en vida ;
que es mayor mal que lo será el perdella.

FRANCISCO DE RIOJA
1583-1659

A SEVILIAN, Rioja writes with an Andalusian exuberance, not untempered, however, by Classical restraint. His celebrity has suffered since he was despoiled of two fine poems now supposed to have been the respective work of Andrada and Caro (pp. 271, 345), but among poems certainly his are a number which, for grace and dignity, purity of line and richness of colour, are worthy of a place beside any others which the age produced.

202. *Silva*

Though not adventurous in versification, Rioja apparently revelled in the complications of that combination of seven- and eleven-syllabled lines known as the silva *and it is worth one's while to study the ingenious scheme of this poem, which for convenience we divide here into three stanzas, none of which has the same rhymes as any other.*

1. *abcCDDBaxA.*
2. *abaBCDBEED.*
3. *AAbCcDDeeFF.*

It will be observed that out of the thirty-one lines sixteen rhyme in couplets, ten of them in the last stanza.

Another characteristic of the piece is its use of words expressive (or, as more usually in Rioja, suggestive) of colour. The impressions here are all of various shades of deep red, a warm, glowing colour which greatly appealed to him, especially in flowers (cf. Silvas VI, VII, VIII). Never has red burned more brilliantly than in the central image of ll. 19-20. There are numerous rhetorical devices : hyperbole, conceptism, repetition used for oratorical effect (ll. 21, 23-4). But there is also an evident desire, not merely to moralize about the flower, but to paint it (cf. p. 669, below) : this comes out in the author's care for detail (e.g., ll. 15-17) as well as for colour. For all its conceptism, the silva *compares favourably with Calderón's better-known sonnet* *(p. 383)* *on the same theme.*

The thought of the poem resolves itself into a series of closely related meditations (ll. 1-10, 11-15, 16-20, 21-7, 28-31) of an elegiac rather than a moral type. But it is not for its thought that the silva *can still be enjoyed.*

Pura, encendida rosa,
émula de la llama
que sale con el día,
¿ cómo naces tan llena de alegría
si sabes que la edad que te da el cielo
es apenas un breve y veloz vuelo ?
Y ni valdrán las puntas de tu rama
ni tu púrpura hermosa
a detener un punto
la ejecución del hado presurosa.
El mismo cerco alado
que estoy viendo riente,
ya temo amortiguado,
presto despojo de la llama ardiente.
Para las hojas de tu crespo seno
te dió Amor de sus alas blandas plumas,
y oro de su cabello dió a tu frente.
¡ O fiel imagen suya peregrina !
Bañóte en su color sangre divina
de la deidad que dieron las espumas.
Y esto, purpúrea flor, esto ¿ no pudo
hacer menos violento el rayo agudo ?
Róbate en una hora,
róbate licencioso su ardimiento
el color y el aliento :
tiendes aun no las alas abrasadas
y ya vuelan al suelo desmayadas :
tan cerca, tan unida
está al morir tu vida,
que dudo si en sus lágrimas la aurora
mustia tu nacimiento o muerte llora.

ESTEBAN MANUEL DE VILLEGAS

1589-1669

Most of Villegas' verse seems to have been written in his youth: some of it, according to himself, when he was no more than fourteen. His *Poesías eróticas o amatorias* (1617-18) are largely of Classical inspiration and occasionally experimental. In later life Villegas entered the legal profession, left amatory verse for satire, fell foul of the Inquisition and employed the evening of a disillusioned life in translating the *De Consolatione* of Boethius.

203. *Cantilena VII: De un Pajarillo*

A rather pointless little poem—superior, however, to its author's more pretentious effusions—which at first glance looks charmingly simple but is soon seen to have a number of expressions (e.g., ll. 4, 6, 8) quite out of character with the theme.

Yo vi sobre un tomillo
quejarse un pajarillo,
viendo su nido amado,
de quien era caudillo,
de un labrador robado.
Vile tan congojado
por tal atrevimiento
dar mil quejas al viento,
para que al cielo santo
lleve su tierno llanto,
lleve su triste acento.
Ya con triste armonía,
esforzando el intento,
mil quejas repetía;
ya cansado callaba,
y al nuevo sentimiento
ya sonoro volvía;

ya circular volaba,
ya rastrero corría;
ya, pues, de rama en rama
al rústico seguía,
y saltando en la grama,
parece que decía:
" Dame, rústico fiero,
mi dulce compañía";
y a mí que respondía
el rústico: " No quiero."

204. *Cantilena VIII: A Lidia*

Like a similar poem by Cetina (p. 197), this Cantilena has a directness which goes far towards neutralizing the artificiality of its metaphors. The sonorous rhymes and the frequent repetition of the musical word amor *bring out the melody of the smoothly running stanzas.*

Lleguen esos rubíes
con que graciosa ríes,
bella Lidia, a mi boca,
pues amor los provoca,
y espárzanse sus mieles
como esparcirlas sueles.
Lleguen, que Amor lo quiere,
Amor, que sana e hiere;
Amor, hijo de Marte,
que reina en toda parte;
Amor, que si atosiga,
luego cura y mitiga;
Amor, niño gracioso
que con fuego amoroso
nos hizo en todo iguales.
Lleguen, pues, tus corales,
Lidia, ¿ quién te acobarda?
¿ No ves que, si se tarda
un punto, un solo instante,
tu regalado beso,
perderás un amante
y yo perderé el seso?

PEDRO CALDERÓN DE LA BARCA

1600-1681

Calderón, who, in drama, dominates the later period of the Golden Age as Lope de Vega dominates the earlier, devoted himself to little beside drama, and his lyric poetry is deeply embedded in his plays—indeed, it is engrained in their very texture and inseparable from any one of them. "His drama," says Ernest Mérimée, "is one of the most *lyrical* that exists. . . . In far higher degree than the aspiring lyrists of his time he possessed in brain and ear and veins what he himself, in truly Spanish phrase, styled *la música de la sangre*." He cannot, therefore, be adequately represented in this anthology by means of extracts, and the two sonnets which follow, both taken from *El Príncipe constante*, must be considered only as an indication of the spirit which permeated his dramas. It should be added that, though he belongs to the Baroque period, he is considerably more elaborate in his formal poems, such as the sonnet, than elsewhere.

205. *Soneto*

Calderón's treatment of the theme of Rioja's well-known silva *(p. 378) is found in an idyllic scene between the Christian prince, Don Fernando, who gives* El Príncipe constante *its title, and Fénix, a Moorish princess, daughter of his captor. He brings her flowers, symbolic (as he says) of his own fate,*

> *pues nacieron con la aurora*
> *y murieron con el día.*

A vivacious dialogue between them follows, in the course of which Don Fernando (very unnaturally, it must be allowed) breaks into this sonnet.

It has distinction and grace, though little resemblance to reality. The critical reader may well exclaim that pompa *(l. 1) is no word to apply to a rose, that the rainbow-metaphor (ll. 5-6) is meaningless and that the figure of l. 4, besides being as frigid as the night it describes, fails to drive home the full force of the contrast. These defects may be admitted—yet the sonnet remains great. Its construction is impeccable. In the octave, the reality lies beneath the words, and its technically magnificent finale (l. 8) is the conclusion of the whole matter. Yet the sestet is not superfluous; with paradox and antithesis it generalizes from the poet's images, its terseness contrasting superbly with the floridity of the octave. Unfortunately for the sonnet considered as such, though less so when rendered dramatically, the last line is by no means the strongest.*

Éstas, que fueron pompa y alegría,
despertando al albor de la mañana,
a la tarde serán lástima vana,
durmiendo en brazos de la noche fría.

Este matiz, que al cielo desafía,
iris listado de oro, nieve y grana,
será escarmiento de la vida humana:
¡ tanto se emprende en término de un día !

A florecer las rosas madrugaron,
y para envejecerse florecieron:
cuna y sepulcro en un botón hallaron.

Tales los hombres sus fortunas vieron:
en un día nacieron y expiraron;
que pasados los siglos, horas fueron.

206. *Soneto*

It is the same scene and Fénix may be said to out-sonnet Fernando, especially if her lines are considered from the Baroque standpoint. Flowers, she has just said, are like stars, and, if he can read his fate in the life of a rose, she sees her life reflected in a star.

The initial picture seems to us stilted and unreal, but l. 5 introduces a beautiful passage which makes the speaker's chief point and thenceforward the sonnet flows steadily and musically on. The underlying sentiment, it may be added, is in character throughout.

Esos rasgos de luz, esas centellas
que cobran con amagos superiores
alimentos del sol en resplandores,
aquello viven que se duele de ellas.

Flores nocturnas son ; aunque tan bellas,
efímeras padecen sus ardores ;
pues si un día es el siglo de las flores,
una noche es la edad de las estrellas.

De esa, pues, primavera fugitiva
ya nuestro mal, ya nuestro bien se infiere :
registro es nuestro, o muera el sol o viva.

¿ Qué duración habrá que el hombre espere,
o qué mudanza habrá, que no reciba
de astro que cada noche nace y muere ?

SOR JUANA INÉS DE LA CRUZ
1651-1695

THIS Mexican nun, whose passions belied her habit, is the most distinguished Gongorist of the New World. Often her love poetry is characterized by remarkable vitality and an almost mystical fervour; and both here and elsewhere the sensibility of her nature combines with gracefulness of style to produce the finest poetry. The familiar *redondillas* which follow, though simpler and more objective than much of her work, are typical of her feminism.

207. *Redondillas*

Hombres necios que acusáis
a la mujer sin razón,
sin ver que sois la ocasión
de lo mismo que culpáis;

si con ansia sin igual
solicitáis su desdén,
¿ por qué queréis que obren bien
si las incitáis al mal ?

Combatís su resistencia,
y luego con gravedad
decís que fué liviandad
lo que hizo la diligencia.

Parecer quiere el denuedo
de vuestro parecer loco
al niño que pone el coco
y luego le tiene miedo.

Queréis con presunción necia
hallar a la que buscáis,
para pretendida, Tais,
y en la posesión, Lucrecia.

¿ Qué humor puede ser más raro
que el que, falto de consejo,
él mismo empaña el espejo
y siente que no esté claro ?

Con el favor y el desdén
tenéis condición igual,
quejándoos, si os tratan mal,
burlándoos, si os quieren bien.

Opinión ninguna gana,
pues la que más se recata,
si no os admite, es ingrata,
y si os admite, es liviana.

Siempre tan necios andáis
que con desigual nivel
a una culpáis por cruel
y a otra por fácil culpáis.

Pues ¿ cómo ha de estar templada
la que vuestro amor pretende,
si la que es ingrata ofende
y la que es fácil enfada ?

Mas entre el enfado y pena
que vuestro gusto refiere,
bien haya la que no os quiere
y quejáos enhorabuena.

Dan vuestras amantes penas
a sus libertades alas,
y después de hacerlas malas
las queréis hallar muy buenas.

¿ Cuál mayor culpa ha tenido
en una pasión errada :
la que cae de rogada
o el que ruega de caído ?

O ¿ cuál es más de culpar
aunque cualquiera mal haga :
la que peca por la paga
o el que paga por pecar ?

Pues ¿ para qué os espantáis
de la culpa que tenéis ?
Queredlas cual las hacéis
o hacedlas cual las buscáis.

Dejad de solicitar,
y después, con más razón,
acusaréis la afición
de la que os fuere a rogar.

Bien con muchas armas fundo
que lidia vuestra arrogancia,
pues en promesa e instancia
juntáis diablo, carne y mundo.

NICOLÁS FERNÁNDEZ DE MORATÍN
1737-1780

LIKE his more famous son Leandro, though lacking the genius for comedy which has made that son immortal, Moratín *padre* devoted himself almost exclusively to drama. His frigid tragedies, however, written in the pseudo-Classical style which dominated most of the eighteenth century, are remembered only by historians: to the ordinary reader, he is the author of the admirable *quintillas*, "Fiesta de toros en Madrid", and of some rather superficially attractive *romances*.

208. *Fiesta de toros en Madrid*

In this fresh and lively piece of verse narrative, Moratín seems to have exchanged the spirit of the eighteenth century for that of the late sixteenth. The action moves briskly, blending effectively with description; incidents are presented in dramatic form, with spirit and skill; epithets are apt and not excessive in number; and there is brilliance, without any garishness, of colour. Not the least pleasing feature of the poem is the evident zest with which it is written, especially in the central part, which describes the appearance of the unknown knight, soon identified as Rodrigo de Vivar ("algunos le llaman Cid"), gives a vivid and lifelike picture of the bull as it awaits him, and then, with gathering power, narrates the details of the fight which ends with the Cid's victory. Particularly noticeable is the poet's complete mastery of his chosen instrument: although, according to Lope de Vega, "las relaciones piden los romances", Moratín is nowhere as successful with his romances *as with these* quintillas, *and it is doubtful if there is any place in Spanish literature where that stanza is used to greater effect.*

Madrid, castillo famoso
que al rey moro alivia el miedo,
arde en fiestas en su coso
por ser el natal dichoso
de Alimenón de Toledo.

Su bravo alcaide Aliatar,
de la hermosa Zaida amante,
las ordena celebrar,
por si la puede ablandar
el corazón de diamante.

Pasó, vencida a sus ruegos,
desde Aravaca a Madrid;
hubo pandorgas y fuegos,
con otros nocturnos juegos
que dispuso el adalid.

Y en adargas y colores,
en las cifras y libreas,
mostraron los amadores,
y en pendones y preseas,
la dicha de sus amores.

Vinieron las moras bellas
de toda la cercanía,
y de lejos muchas de ellas:
las más apuestas doncellas
que España entonces tenía.

Ajá de Jetafe vino,
y Zahara la de Alcorcón,
en cuyo obsequio muy fino
corrió de un vuelo el camino
el moraicel de Alcabón.

Jarifa de Almonacid,
que de la Alcarria en que habita
llevó a asombrar a Madrid
su amante Audalla, adalid
del castillo de Zorita.

De Adamuz y la famosa
Meco llegaron allí
dos, cada cual más hermosa,
y Fátima la preciosa,
hija de Alí el alcadí.

El ancho circo se llena
de multitud clamorosa,
que atiende a ver en su arena
la sangrienta lid dudosa,
y todo en torno resuena.

La bella Zaida ocupó
sus dorados miradores
que el arte afiligranó,
y con espejos y flores
y damascos adornó.

Añafiles y atabales,
con militar armonía,
hicieron salva, y señales
de mostrar su valentía
los moros más principales.

No en las vegas de Jarama
pacieron la verde grama
nunca animales tan fieros,
junto al puente que se llama,
por sus peces, de Viveros,

como los que el vulgo vió
ser lidiados aquel día ;
y en la fiesta que gozó,
la popular alegría
muchas heridas costó.

Salió un toro del toril
y a Tarfe tiró por tierra,
y luego a Benalguacil ;
después con Hamete cierra
el temerón de Conil.

Traía un ancho listón
con uno y otro matiz
hecho un lazo por airón
sobre la inhiesta cerviz
clavado con un arpón.

Todo galán pretendía
ofrecerle vencedor
a la dama que servía :
por eso perdió Almanzor
el potro que más quería.

El alcaide muy zambrero
de Guadalajara huyó
mal herido al golpe fiero,
y desde un caballo overo
el moro de Horche cayó.

Todos miran a Aliatar,
que, aunque tres toros ha muerto,
no se quiere aventurar,
porque en lance tan incierto
el caudillo no ha de entrar.

Mas viendo se culparía,
va a ponérsele delante :
la fiera le acometía,
y sin que el rejón la plante
la mató una yegua pía.

Otra monta acelerado :
le embiste el toro de un vuelo,
cogiéndole entablerado ;
rodó el bonete encarnado
con las plumas por el suelo.

Dió vuelta hiriendo y matando
a los de a pie que encontrara,
el circo desocupando,
y emplazándose, se para,
con la vista amenazando.

Nadie se atreve a salir :
la plebe grita indignada,
las damas se quieren ir,
porque la fiesta empezada
no puede ya proseguir.

Ninguno al riesgo se entrega
y está en medio el toro fijo,
cuando un portero que llega
de la puerta de la Vega,
hincó la rodilla, y dijo :

" Sobre un caballo alazano,
cubierto de galas y oro,
demanda licencia urbano
para alancear a un toro
un caballero cristiano."

Mucho le pesa a Aliatar ;
pero Zaida dió respuesta
diciendo que puede entrar,
porque en tan solemne fiesta
nada se debe negar.

Suspenso el concurso entero
entre dudas se embaraza,
cuando en un potro ligero
vieron entrar por la plaza
un bizarro caballero,

sonrosado, albo color,
belfo labio, juveniles
alientos, inquieto ardor,
en el florido verdor
de sus lozanos abriles.

Cuelga la rubia guedeja
por donde el almete sube,
cual mirarse tal vez deja
del sol la ardiente madeja
entre cenicienta nube.

Gorguera de anchos follajes,
de una cristiana primores,
en el yelmo los plumajes
por los visos y celajes
verjel de diversas flores.

En la cuja gruesa lanza,
con recamado pendón,
y una cifra a ver se alcanza
que es de desesperación,
o a lo menos de venganza.

En el arzón de la silla
ancho escudo reverbera
con blasones de Castilla,
y el mote dice a la orilla :
Nunca mi espada venciera.

Era el caballo galán,
el bruto más generoso,
de más gallardo ademán :
cabos negros, y brioso,
muy tostado, y alazán.

Larga cola recogida
en las piernas descarnadas,
cabeza pequeña, erguida,
las narices dilatadas,
vista feroz y encendida.

Nunca en el ancho rodeo
que da Betis con tal fruto
pudo fingir el deseo
más bella estampa de bruto,
ni más hermoso paseo.

Dió la vuelta al rededor ;
los ojos que le veían
lleva prendados de amor :
" ¡ Aláh te salve ! " decían,
" ¡ Déte el Profeta favor ! "

Causaba lástima y grima
su tierna edad floreciente :
todos quieren que se exima
del riesgo, y él solamente
ni recela ni se estima.

Las doncellas, al pasar,
hacen de ámbar y alcanfor
pebeteros exhalar,
vertiendo pomos de olor,
de jazmines y azahar.

Mas cuando en medio se para,
y de más cerca le mira
la cristiana esclava Aldara,
con su señora se encara,
y así la dice, y suspira :

" Señora, sueños no son ;
así los cielos, vencidos
de mi ruego y aflicción,
acerquen a mis oídos
las campanas de León,

" como ese doncel, que ufano
tanto asombro viene a dar
a todo el pueblo africano,
es Rodrigo de Vivar,
el soberbio castellano."

Sin descubrirle quién es,
la Zaida desde una almena
le habló una noche cortés,
por donde se abrió después
el cubo de la Almudena.

Y supo que, fugitivo
de la corte de Fernando,
el cristiano, apenas vivo,
está a Jimena adorando
y en su memoria cautivo.

Tal vez a Madrid se acerca
con frecuentes correrías
y todo en torno la cerca:
observa sus saetías,
arroyadas y ancha alberca.

Por eso le ha conocido:
que en medio de aclamaciones,
el caballo ha detenido
delante de sus balcones,
y la saluda rendido.

La mora se puso en pie
y sus doncellas detrás:
el alcaide que lo ve,
enfurecido además,
muestra cuán celoso esté.

Suena un rumor placentero
entre el vulgo de Madrid:
no habrá mejor caballero,
dicen, en el mundo entero,
y algunos le llaman Cid.

Crece la algazara, y él,
torciendo las riendas de oro,
marcha al combate crüel:
alza el galope, y al toro
busca en sonoro tropel.

El bruto se le ha encarado
desde que le vió llegar,
de tanta gala asombrado,
y al rededor le ha observado
sin moverse de un lugar.

Cual flecha se disparó
despedida de la cuerda,
de tal suerte le embistió:
detrás de la oreja izquierda
la aguda lanza le hirió.

Brama la fiera burlada;
segunda vez acomete,
de espuma y sudor bañada,
y segunda vez la mete
sutil la punta acerada.

Pero ya Rodrigo espera,
con heroico atrevimiento,
el pueblo mudo y atento:
se engalla el toro y altera,
y finge acometimiento.

La arena escarba ofendido,
sobre la espalda la arroja
con el hueso retorcido;
el suelo huele y le moja
en ardiente resoplido.

La cola inquieto menea,
la diestra oreja mosquea,
vase retirando atrás,
para que la fuerza sea
mayor, y el ímpetu más.

El que en esta ocasión viera
de Zaida el rostro alterado,
claramente conociera
cuánto le cuesta cuidado
el que tanto riesgo espera.

Mas ¡ay, que le embiste horrendo
el animal espantoso!
jamás peñasco tremendo
del Cáucaso cavernoso
se desgaja, estrago haciendo,

ni llama así fulminante
cruza en negra oscuridad.
con relámpagos delante,
al estrépito tronante
de sonora tempestad,

como el bruto se abalanza
en terrible ligereza;
mas rota con gran pujanza
la alta nuca, la fiereza
y el último aliento lanza.

La confusa vocería
que en tal instante se oyó
fué tanta, que parecía
que honda mina reventó,
o el monte y valle se hundía.

A caballo como estaba
Rodrigo, el lazo alcanzó
con que el toro se adornaba:
en su lanza le clavó
y a los balcones llegaba.

Y alzándose en los estribos,
le alarga a Zaida, diciendo:
"Sultana, aunque bien entiendo
ser favores excesivos,
mi corto don admitiendo,

"si no os dignáredes ser
con él benigna, advertid
que a mí me basta saber
que no le debo ofrecer
a otra persona en Madrid."

Ella, el rostro placentero,
dijo, y turbada: "Señor,
yo le admito y le venero,
por conservar el favor
de tan gentil caballero."

Y besando el rico don,
para agradar al doncel,
le prende con afición
al lado del corazón
por brinquiño y por joyel.

Pero Aliatar el caudillo
de envidia ardiendo se ve,
y, trémulo y amarillo,
sobre un tremecén rosillo
lozaneándose fué.

Y en ronca voz, " Castellano,"
le dice, " con más decoros
suelo yo dar de mi mano,
si no penachos de toros,
las cabezas del cristiano.

" Y si vinieras de guerra
cual vienes de fiesta y gala,
vieras que en toda la tierra,
al valor que dentro encierra
Madrid, ninguno se iguala."

" Así," dijo el de Vivar,
" respondo ", y la lanza al ristre
pone, y espera a Aliatar ;
mas sin que nadie administre
orden, tocaron a armar.

Ya fiero bando con gritos
su muerte o prisión pedía,
cuando se oyó en los distritos
del monte de Leganitos
del Cid la trompetería.

Entre la Monclova y Soto
tercio escogido emboscó,
que, viendo como tardó,
se acerca, oyó el alboroto,
y al muro se abalanzó.

Y si no vieran salir
por la puerta a su señor,
y Zaida a le despedir,
iban la fuerza a embestir :
tal era ya su furor.

El alcaide, recelando
que en Madrid tenga partido,
se templó disimulando,
y por el parque florido
salió con él razonando.

Y es fama que, a la bajada,
juró por la cruz el Cid
de su vencedora espada
de no quitar la celada
hasta que gane a Madrid.

GASPAR MELCHOR DE JOVELLANOS
1744-1811

THE works of this versatile author reveal him as a writer of tragedy (*Pelayo*, 1769) and of sentimental or *larmoyante* comedy (*El Delincuente honrado*, 1774), as an economist (*Informe sobre la ley agraria*, 1795) and as a politician (*Memoria en defensa de la Junta Central*, 1810). As a poet, he was greatly respected by the so-called "Salamancan School"—a group loosely connected with Salamanca and united chiefly by admiration for the similar group which flourished in the sixteenth century (p. 250), the greatest figure in which was Luis de León. But Jovellanos was not himself very successful as a writer of verse, though he helped to bring back to Spanish poetry some of the subjectivity and sentiment which it had lost.

209. *Epístola de Fabio a Anfriso*

Through the conventionality of this epistle there breaks a genuine emotion, and the description of El Paular (a fourteenth-century Carthusian monastery in the Guadarrama mountains: cf. p. 643) palpitates with sensibility. The pictures of the countryside, if here and there somewhat stereotyped, clearly indicate first-hand observation; and the epithets are apt and expressive. Other pre-Romantic traits are the imposition of the author's personality, the restless striving after the elusive and perhaps unattainable, and the note of gentle and resigned melancholy, on which, it will be observed, the poem ends. In the latter part of it there are numerous reminiscences—including verbal reminiscences—of Fray Luis de León.

Credibile est illi numen inesse loco.
OVIDIO

Desde el oculto y venerable asilo,
do la virtud austera y penitente
vive ignorada, y del liviano mundo
huída, en santa soledad se esconde,
el triste Fabio al venturoso Anfriso,
salud en versos flébiles envía ;

salud le envía a Anfriso, al que inspirado
de las mantuanas musas, tal vez suele
al grave son de su celeste canto
precipitar del viejo Manzanares
el curso perezoso, tal süave
suele ablandar con amorosa lira
la altiva condición de sus zagalas.
¡ Pluguiera a Dios, oh Anfriso, que el cuitado,
a quien no dió la suerte tal ventura,
pudiese huir del mundo y sus peligros !
¡ Pluguiera a Dios, pues ya con su barquilla
logró arribar a puerto tan seguro,
que esconderla supiera en este abrigo,
a tanta luz y ejemplos enseñado !
Huyera así la furia tempestuosa
de los contrarios vientos, los escollos
y las fieras borrascas, tantas veces
entre sustos y lágrimas corridas.
Así también del mundanal tumulto
lejos, y en estos montes guarecido,
alguna vez gozara del reposo,
que hoy desterrado de su pecho vive.

Mas ¡ ay de aquel que hasta en el santo asilo
de la virtud arrastra la cadena,
la pesada cadena, con que el mundo
oprime a sus esclavos ! ¡ Ay del triste
en cuyo oído suena con espanto,
por esta oculta soledad rompiendo,
de su señor el imperioso grito !

Busco en estas moradas silenciosas
el reposo y la paz, que aquí se esconden,
y sólo encuentro la inquietud funesta,
que mis sentidos y razón conturba.

Busco paz y reposo, pero en vano
los busco, oh caro Anfriso ; que estos dones,
herencia santa, que al partir del mundo
dejó Bruno en sus hijos vinculada,
nunca en profano corazón entraron
ni a los parciales del placer se dieron.

Conozco bien que, fuera de este asilo,
sólo me guarda el mundo sinrazones,
vanos deseos, duros desengaños,
susto y dolor ; empero todavía
a entrar en él no puedo resolverme.
No puedo resolverme, y despechado
sigo el impulso del fatal destino
que a muy más dura esclavitud me guía.
Sigo su fiero impulso, y llevo siempre
por todas partes los pesados grillos
que de la ansiada libertad me privan.

De afán y angustia el pecho traspasado,
pido a la muda soledad consuelo
y con dolientes quejas la importuno.
Salgo al ameno valle, subo al monte,
sigo del claro río las corrientes,
busco la fresca y deleitosa sombra,
corro por todas partes, y no encuentro
en parte alguna la quietud perdida.

¡ Ay, Anfriso ! ¡ qué escenas a mis ojos,
cansados de llorar, presenta el cielo !
Rodeado de frondosos y altos montes
se extiende un valle, que de mil delicias
con sabia mano ornó naturaleza.
Pártele en dos mitades, despeñado
de las vecinas rocas, el Lozoya,
por su pesca famoso y dulces aguas.
Del claro río sobre el verde margen
crecen frondosos álamos, que al cielo
ya erguidos alzan las plateadas copas,
o ya, sobre las aguas encorvados,
en mil figuras, miran con asombro
su forma en los cristales retratada.
De la siniestra orilla un bosque umbrío
hasta la falda del vecino monte
se extiende : tan ameno y delicioso
que le hubiera juzgado el gentilismo
morada de algún dios, o a los misterios
de las silvanas Dríadas guardado.

Aquí encamino mis inciertos pasos,
y en su recinto umbrío y silencioso,
mansión la más conforme para un triste,
entro a pensar en mi cruel destino.
La grata soledad, la dulce sombra,
el aire blando y el silencio mudo
mi desventura y mi dolor adulan.
No alcanza aquí del padre de las luces
el rayo acechador, ni su reflejo
viene a cubrir de confusión el rostro
de un infeliz en su dolor sumido.
El canto de las aves no interrumpe
aquí tampoco la quietud de un triste,
pues sólo de la viuda tortolilla
se oye tal vez el lastimero arrullo,
tal vez el melancólico trinado
de la angustiada y dulce Filomena.
Con blando impulso el céfiro süave,
las copas de los árboles moviendo,
recrea el alma con el manso ruido;
mientras al dulce soplo desprendidas
las agostadas hojas, revolando,
bajan en lentos círculos al suelo;
cúbrenle en torno, y la frondosa pompa
que al árbol adornara en primavera,
yace marchita, y muestra los rigores
del abrasado estío y seco otoño.

Así también de juventud lozana
pasan, oh Anfriso, las livianas dichas.
Un soplo de inconstancia, de fastidio
o de capricho femenil las tala
y lleva por el aire, cual las hojas
de los frondosos árboles caídas.
Ciegos empero, y tras su vana sombra
de contino exhalados, en pos de ellas
corremos hasta hallar el precipicio
do nuestro error y su ilusión nos guían.
Volamos en pos de ellas, como suele
volar a la dulzura del reclamo

incauto el pajarillo. Entre las hojas
el preparado visco le detiene;
lucha cautivo por huir, y en vano;
porque un traidor, que en asechanza atisba,
con mano infiel la libertad le roba,
y a muerte le condena, o cárcel dura.

¡Ah, dichoso el mortal de cuyos ojos
un pronto desengaño corrió el velo
de la ciega ilusión! ¡Una y mil veces
dichoso el solitario penitente,
que, triunfando del mundo y de sí mismo,
vive en la soledad libre y contento!
Unido a Dios por medio de la santa
contemplación, le goza ya en la tierra;
y, retirado en su tranquilo albergue,
observa reflexivo los milagros
de la naturaleza, sin que nunca
turben el susto ni el dolor su pecho.

Regálanle las aves con su canto,
mientras la aurora sale refulgente
a cubrir de alegría y luz el mundo.
Nácele siempre el sol claro y brillante,
y nunca a él levanta conturbados
sus ojos, ora en el oriente raye,
ora, del cielo a la mitad subiendo,
en pompa guíe el reluciente carro,
ora con tibia luz, más perezoso,
su faz esconda en los vecinos montes.
Cuando en las claras noches cuidadoso
vuelve desde los santos ejercicios,
la plateada luna en lo más alto
del cielo mueve la luciente rueda
con augusto silencio; y recreando
con blando resplandor su humilde vista,
eleva su razón, y la dispone
a contemplar la alteza y la inefable
gloria del Padre y Criador del mundo.
Libre de los cuidados enojosos
que en los palacios y dorados techos

nos turban de contino, y entregado
a la inefable y justa Providencia,
si al breve sueño alguna pausa pide
de sus santas tareas, obediente
viene a cerrar sus párpados el sueño
con mano amiga, y de su lado ahuyenta
el susto y las fantasmas de la noche.

¡ Oh suerte venturosa, a los amigos
de la virtud guardada ! ¡ Oh dicha, nunca
de los tristes mundanos conocida !
¡ Oh monte impenetrable ! ¡ Oh bosque umbrío !
¡ Oh valle deleitoso ! ¡ Oh solitaria,
taciturna mansión ! ¡ Oh quién, del alto
y proceloso mar del mundo huyendo
a vuestra eterna calma, aquí seguro
vivir pudiera siempre, y escondido !

Tales cosas revuelvo en mi memoria,
en esta triste soledad sumido.
Llega en tanto la noche, y con su manto
cobija el ancho mundo. Vuelvo entonces
a los medrosos claustros. De una escasa
luz el distante y pálido reflejo
guía por ellos mis inciertos pasos,
y en medio del horror y del silencio,
¡ oh fuerza del ejemplo portentosa !
mi corazón palpita, en mi cabeza
se erizan los cabellos, se estremecen
mis carnes, y discurre por mis nervios
un súbito rigor que los embarga.
Parece que oigo que del centro oscuro
sale una voz tremenda, que, rompiendo
el eterno silencio, así me dice :
" Huye de aquí, profano ; tú, que llevas
de mundanas pasiones lleno el pecho,
huye de esta morada, do se albergan
con la virtud humilde y silenciosa
sus escogidos ; huye, y no profanes
con tu planta sacrílega este asilo."

De aviso tal al golpe confundido,
con paso vacilante voy cruzando
los pavorosos tránsitos, y llego
por fin a mi morada, donde ni hallo
el ansiado reposo, ni recobran
la suspirada calma mis sentidos.
Lleno de congojosos pensamientos
paso la triste y perezosa noche
en molesta vigilia, sin que llegue
a mis ojos el sueño, ni interrumpan
sus regalados bálsamos mi pena.
Vuelve por fin con la risueña aurora
la luz aborrecida, y en pos de ella
el claro día a publicar mi llanto
y dar nueva materia al dolor mío.

FÉLIX MARÍA DE SAMANIEGO

1745-1801

The essentially prosaic eighteenth century found itself at home with the verse fable, though its only outstanding fabulists were Samaniego and Iriarte. Samaniego is at his best with old and often hackneyed themes, which, by an agile use of language and metre, he successfully naturalizes and stamps with his own personality. As the two fables which follow will show, his style has also considerable variety. " La Lechera " tends to the descriptive and lyrical, and the length at which the author details the milkmaid's day-dreams allows him ample scope for his sly and subtle humour. Only in the last two stanzas, curiously reminiscent, both in rhythm and in sentiment, of Luis de León, does he begin to moralize. In " La Gallina de los huevos de oro ", on the other hand, the author's manner is terse, matter-of-fact and epigrammatic, while the " moral " occupies nearly half the poem. Where Samaniego seldom, if ever, varies is in the closely woven texture of his verses and the excellence of his rhymes.

210. *La Lechera*

Llevaba en la cabeza
una Lechera el cántaro al mercado
con aquella presteza,
aquel aire sencillo, aquel agrado,
que va diciendo a todo el que lo advierte :
" ¡ Yo sí que estoy contenta con mi suerte ! "

Porque no apetecía
más compañía que su pensamiento,
que alegre la ofrecía
inocentes ideas de contento,
marchaba sola la feliz Lechera,
y decía entre sí de esta manera :

"Esta leche, vendida,
en limpio me dará tanto dinero,
y con esta partida
un canasto de huevos comprar quiero,
para sacar cien pollos, que al estío
me rodeen cantando el *pío*, *pío*.

"Del importe logrado
de tanto pollo mercaré un cochino;
con bellota, salvado,
berza, castaña, engordará sin tino;
tanto, que puede ser que yo consiga
ver cómo se le arrastra la barriga.

"Llevarélo al mercado;
sacaré de él sin duda buen dinero:
compraré de contado
una robusta vaca y un ternero
que salte y corra toda la campaña
hasta el monte cercano a la cabaña."

Con este pensamiento
enajenada, brinca de manera
que a su salto violento
el cántaro cayó. ¡Pobre Lechera!
¡Qué compasión! Adiós leche, dinero,
huevos, pollos, lechón, vaca y ternero.

¡Oh loca fantasía,
qué palacios fabricas en el viento!
Modera tu alegría;
no sea que, saltando de contento
al contemplar dichosa tu mudanza,
quiebre su cantarillo la esperanza.

No seas ambiciosa
de mejor o más próspera fortuna;
que vivirás ansiosa
sin que pueda saciarte cosa alguna.
No anheles impaciente el bien futuro,
mira que ni el presente está seguro.

211. *La Gallina de los Huevos de Oro*

Érase una Gallina que ponía
un huevo de oro al dueño cada día.
Aun con tanta ganancia mal contento,
quiso el rico avariento
descubrir de una vez la mina de oro,
y hallar en menos tiempo más tesoro.
Matóla ; abrióla el vientre de contado ;
pero después de haberla registrado,
¿ qué sucedió ? : que, muerta la Gallina,
perdió su huevo de oro y no halló mina.

¡ Cuantos hay que teniendo lo bastante,
enriquecerse quieren al instante,
abrazando proyectos
a veces de tan rápidos efectos,
que sólo en pocos meses,
cuando se contemplaban ya marqueses
contando sus millones,
se vieron en la calle sin calzones !

JOSÉ IGLESIAS DE LA CASA
1748-1791

Iglesias, quite undeservedly one of the least known of the Salamancans, brings to poetry, as José Cadalso brought to prose, a restlessness sometimes mounting to intense passion—" la inquietud que en mi interior yo siento," as he terms it, more graphically than poetically, in his sixth Idyll. More commonly, however, his mood is one of disillusion and profound melancholy. His attitude to Nature is notable (for his day) in its appreciation of the " natural desorden " of the country, and he is one of a small number of eighteenth-century poets who have panegyrized solitude. In his thoughts and feelings he often foreshadows the Romantics, though he writes in the main like a man of his own time.

212. *La Soledad*

¡ De qué apagado lustre, cuán pequeñas
son las humanas fábricas, medidas
con aquellas grandezas que perdidas
tiene el desierto entre sus mudas peñas !
¡ De alteza y esplendor cuán pocas señas
tienen las más preciadas,
con el arte adornadas !
¡ Qué primor mendigado, qué pobreza,
las de más precio y de mayor grandeza !

Los artesones de oro sustentados
en dóricas columnas, y a par de ellos,
de azules vetas y de lazos bellos,
ricos jaspes y pórfidos preciados,
si al principio admiraban, ya observados,
enfadan a dos días ;
cansan las simetrías
de cuadros y tapices, y el aseo
del más pintado alcázar queda feo.

Son tibios los colores y pinceles
que el mundo más celebra y solemniza,
puestos junto los riscos que entapiza
mayo galán de alfombras y doseles;
de sus lirios lo azul, de sus claveles
el rosicler variado,
y aquel color dorado
de un ya maduro trigo, y aquel fresco
con que su aliento bulle en lo brutesco.

Aquel confuso amontonar de cosas
arrojadas acaso y diferentes;
acá hiedra, allá espinas, allá fuentes,
riscos, peñascos, ríos, flores, rosas;
unos lejos, que mucho más vistosas
las cosas nos volvieron,
que de cerca se vieron;
un pedazo de playa, una montaña,
que al cielo sube y a la vista engaña.

Vese la entrada de un pendiente risco,
de un bello mirador el corvo techo,
alfombra dando rústico antepecho,
de alegres rejas un vistoso aprisco,
de hiedras entoldado y de lentisco,
donde el jazmín, ventana
teje a la vid lozana,
y de sus grumos hace que se cuaje
la red de su tejido ventanaje.

Pues subiendo a su cumbre y antepecho,
y el campo que descubre registrando,
en lo que advierte absorto contemplando,
muda estatua el más sabio queda hecho;
del mar profundo un ancho y largo trecho
los ojos ser no dudan
espejos que se mudan,
viendo en sus crespas olas, de aire llenas,
los delfines cruzar, saltar ballenas.

Vese del tiempo y humedad cubierta
la hueca peña de menudas flores,
parte en sombras y parte en resplandores,

jaspeada aquí, allá verde y allá yerta,
formando un todo de hermosura engerta
sus metales lucidos
y extraños coloridos,
y esmaltando la tez que los remata
de granos de oro y escarchada plata.

El risco altivo de un diluvio entero
de luciente cristal las selvas moja,
que en espantoso son al mar se arroja
desde aquel desigual despeñadero ;
y de una peña en otra a lo postrero
del monte en larga suma,
hirviendo da su espuma ;
haciendo antes pedazos por los riscos
cristales, flores, perlas y lentiscos.

Por otra parte el monte alza sus pinos,
que al parecer se esconden en el cielo ;
cubren de rocas y boscaje el suelo
entre tajadas peñas los espinos ;
trepa la hiedra, suben remolinos
de flores y de yerba
por señuelo a la cierva
y presto gamo, que por ellas salta,
y de verlas temblar se sobresalta.

Silban por entre almeces y algarrobos
las mirlas, las calandrias y jilgueros ;
las liebres y gazapos placenteros
retozan por la grama y dan corcovos ;
huyen los ciervos, rumian los escobos
las cabras ; sin recelos
saltan los conejuelos
y en las peñas se esconden, y en sus quiebras,
pintadas roscas hacen las culebras.

Todo esto al son del bosque y el ruido
del agua, que en cascadas se despeña
del monte, que batió su crespa greña,
y el canto de las aves, no aprendido ;

de aquí se goza el ánimo embebido
y lleno de dulzura
con tan varia pintura,
sin otras muchas nuevas maravillas,
resacas de la mar y sus orillas.

Que el natural desorden con que puso
el tiempo experto estos rasguños bellos
es el mayor primor y gala en ellos,
bien que arrojados en montón confuso;
y tanto los brutescos descompuso,
y en tan distinta forma
sus aspectos trasforma,
que parece los hizo en competencia
del artificio de la humana ciencia,
y sobre todo, donde de su dueño
el gran tesoro y gran caudal se infiere,
es que se da de balde a quien lo quiere,
grande sea, mediano o ya pequeño;
no hay puerta ni cancel, desvío o ceño,
que en todas ocasiones,
momentos y sazones,
siempre está para el gusto y el provecho
puesto el rico tapiz y el toldo hecho.

Ora cruzando vaya los desiertos
de algún inculto bosque, o engolfado,
al frío escita o al burnés tostado,
en mitad de los mares encubiertos,
o en el del Sur, sobre peñascos yertos,
rompa de sus canales
los helados cristales,
cuyos tumbos la playa y el arena
de blanco nácar y mariscos llena.

O bien se baje donde el suelo ardiente
la línea equinoccial, midiendo el día,
su curso arranca, lleno de alegría,
con alas de oro encima de su frente;
que allí en aquellos páramos sin gente,

si el mundo tiene hoy día
allí tierra baldía,
sus solitarios y ásperos espacios
de los reyes humillan los palacios.

Que aun contemplando aquí el humor fecundo
que sus anchos desiertos fertiliza,
con medroso ignorar de que cenizas
allí el rojo calor no vuelva al mundo,
o que en su ignoto piélago profundo
las olas encrespadas,
en hueco tumbo alzadas,
entre las rocas quiebre y se consuma,
trocada su altivez en blanca espuma ;

o imaginando estrellas nunca vistas
de Europa, o sus alturas no tocadas
de humano pie jamás, siempre engastadas
en pastas de diamantes y amatistas,
si aun fuesen más que el Agon tiene aristas
mis curiosos cuidados,
los hallará colmados
del deleite que causan peregrino
estos bosquejos del pincel divino.

TOMÁS DE IRIARTE

1750-1791

IRIARTE, temperamentally a satirist and polemist, and a writer of great verve and spontaneity, specialized in *Fábulas literarias*, which gave him scope for originality and also for indirect but effective assaults upon his enemies. But more important to literature is the constructive aspect of his fables, which form a novel type of treatise on the art of writing. Like Samaniego, Iriarte has a great command of language and metre: his verses, however, are apt to be more loosely knit and show fewer signs of effort. To the delightfully malicious " El Burro flautista " quite an old-world atmosphere is given by the use of assonance and refrain. In " La Ardilla y el Caballo " there is a metrical flexibility unequalled (except perhaps occasionally by Arjona) until the poems of Espronceda appeared nearly sixty years later.

213. *El Burro Flautista*

Esta fabulilla,
salga bien o mal,
me ha ocurrido ahora
por casualidad.

Cerca de unos prados
que hay en mi lugar
pasaba un borrico
por casualidad.

Una flauta en ellos
halló que un zagal
se dejó olvidada
por casualidad.

Acercóse a olerla
el dicho animal,
y dió un resoplido
por casualidad.

En la flauta el aire
se hubo de colar,
y sonó la flauta
por casualidad.

"¡Oh!" dijo el borrico,
"¡Qué bien sé tocar!
¿Y dirán que es mala
la música asnal?"

Sin reglas del arte
borriquitos hay
que una vez aciertan
por casualidad.

214. *La Ardilla y el Caballo*

Mirando estaba una ardilla
a un generoso alazán,
que dócil a espuela y rienda,
se adestraba en galopar.

Viéndole hacer movimientos
tan veloces y a compás,
de aquesta suerte le dijo
con muy poca cortedad:

"Señor mío,
de ese brío,
ligereza
y destreza
no me espanto,
que otro tanto
suelo hacer, y acaso más.
Yo soy viva,
soy activa,
me meneo,
me paseo,
yo trabajo,
subo y bajo,
no me estoy quieta jamás."

El paso detiene entonces
el buen potro, y muy formal
en los términos siguientes
respuesta a la ardilla da:
" Tantas idas
y venidas,
tantas vueltas
y revueltas
(quiero, amiga,
que me diga),
¿ son de alguna utilidad ?
Yo me afano,
mas no en vano.
Sé mi oficio,
y en servicio
de mi dueño
tengo empeño
de lucir mi habilidad."

Con que algunos escritores
ardillas también serán
si en obras frívolas gastan
todo el calor natural.

JUAN MELÉNDEZ VALDÉS

1754-1817

To Meléndez Valdés must be given the highest place among the Salamancan poets, if not, indeed, among the whole of the pre-Romantics. His love of Nature is not only sincere and intense but of such intimacy as to be at times almost Wordsworthian. His landscapes are much more vivid and particularized than those of most pseudo-Classics. He outdoes Iglesias, and anticipates the Romantics, in preferring the " grato desorden " of the country to " odiosas ciudades ", with their

tristes jardines
hijos míseros del arte ;[1]

He is also a pre-Romantic in his sentimentalizations over human types, as well as over Nature, and in his subjectivity, his melancholy and his disillusion. Yet he is still bound closely to his age and much of his work suffers distressingly from conventionality. The technique of his art is superior to its thought and language ; in its restraint and poise, it is generally in the best sense Classical.

215. *La Tarde*

Ya el Héspero delicioso,
entre nubes agradables,
cual precursor de la noche,
por el Occidente sale ;

desde allí, con su almo brillo
deshaciendo mil celajes,
a los ojos se presenta
cual un hermoso diamante.

[1] Romance XXXIV : " La Tarde ;" Oda XXXII : " Del vivir de las flores."

Las sombras que le acompañan
se apoderan de los valles,
y sobre la mustia hierba
su fresco rocío esparcen.

Su corona alzan las flores,
y de un aroma süave,
despidiéndose del día,
embalsaman todo el aire.

El sol afanado vuela,
y sus rayos celestiales
contemplar tibios permiten,
al morir, su augusta imagen ;

símil a un globo de fuego
que en vivas centellas arde,
y en la bóveda parece
del firmamento enclavarse,

él de su altísima cumbre
veloz se despeña, y cae
del Océano en las aguas,
que a recibirlo se abren.

¡ Oh ! ¡ qué visos ! ¡ qué colores !
¡ qué ráfagas tan brillantes
mis ojos embebecidos
registran de todas partes !

Mil sutiles nubecillas
cercan su trono, y mudables,
el cárdeno cielo pintan
con sus graciosos cambiantes.

Los reverberan las aguas,
y parece que retrae
indeciso el sol sus pasos,
y en mirarlos se complace.

Luego vuelve, huye y se esconde,
y deja en poder la tarde
del Héspero, que en los cielos
alza su pardo estandarte,

como un cendal delicado,
que en su ámbito inmensurable,
en un momento extendido,
veloz al suelo se abate,

a que en tan rápida fuga
su vislumbre centellante,
envuelto en débiles nieblas,
ya sin pábulo desmaye.

Del nido al caliente abrigo
vuelan al punto las aves,
cual al seno de una peña,
cual a lo hojoso de un sauce;

y a sus guaridas los toscos
selváticos animales,
temblando al sentir la noche,
se precipitan cobardes.

Suelta el arador sus bueyes;
y entre sencillos afanes,
para el redil los ganados
volviendo van los zagales;

suena un confuso balido,
gimiendo que los separen
del dulce pasto, y las crías
corren, llamando a sus madres.

Lejos las chozas humean,
y los montes más distantes
con las sombras se confunden,
que sus altas cimas hacen.

De ellas a la excelsa esfera
asomando desiguales
estas sombras en un velo
a la vista impenetrable,

el universo parece
que, de su acción incesante
cansado, el reposo anhela,
y al sueño va a abandonarse.

Todo es paz, silencio todo,
todo en estas soledades
me conmueve, y hace dulce
la memoria de mis males.

El verde oscuro del prado,
la niebla que en ondas se abre
allá sobre el hondo río,
los árboles de su margen,

su deleitosa frescura,
los vientecillos que baten
entre las flores las alas,
y sus esencias me traen,

me enajenan y me olvidan
de las odiosas ciudades
y de sus tristes jardines,
hijos míseros del arte.

Liberal naturaleza,
porque mi pecho se sacie,
me brinda con mil placeres
en su copa inagotable.

Yo me abandono a su impulso;
dudosos los pies no saben
dó se vuelven, dó caminan,
dó se apresuran, dó paren.

Cruzo la tendida vega
con inquietud anhelante
por si en la fatiga logro
que mi espíritu se calme;

mis pasos se precipitan;
mas nada en mi alivio vale,
que agigantadas las sombras
me siguen para aterrarle.

Trepo, huyéndolas, la cima,
y al ver sus riscos salvajes,
"¡Ay! exclamo, ¡quién, cual ellos,
insensible se tornase!"

Bajo del collado al río,
y entre las lóbregas calles.
de altos árboles, el pecho
más pavoroso me late.

Miro las tajadas rocas,
que amenazan desplomarse
sobre mí, tornar oscuros
sus cristalinos raudales.

Llénanme de horror sus sombras,
y el ronco fragoso embate
de las aguas, más profundo
hace este horror, y más grave.

Así, azorado y medroso,
al cielo empiezo a quejarme
de mis amargas desdichas,
y a lanzar dolientes ayes ;

mientras de la luz dudosa
espira el último instante,
y el manto la noche tiende,
que el crepúsculo deshace.

216. *Elegía : El Melancólico. A Jovino*

Cuando la sombra fúnebre y el luto
de la lóbrega noche el mundo envuelven
en silencio y horror ; cuando en tranquilo
reposo los mortales las delicias
gustan de un blando saludable sueño ;
tu amigo solo, en lágrimas bañado,
vela, Jovino, y al dudoso brillo
de una cansada luz, en tristes ayes,
contigo alivia su dolor profundo.

¡ Ah ! ¡ cuán distinto en los fugaces días
de sus venturas y soñada gloria
con grata voz tu oído regalaba,
cuando ufano y alegre, seducido

de crédula esperanza al fausto soplo,
sus ansias, sus delicias, sus deseos
depositaba en tu amistad paciente,
burlando sus avisos saludables!
Huyeron prestos como frágil sombra,
huyeron estos días, y al abismo
de la desdicha el mísero ha bajado.

Tú me juzgas feliz. . . . ¡ Oh si pudieras
ver de mi pecho la profunda llaga,
que va sangre vertiendo noche y día!
¡ Oh si del vivo, del letal veneno,
que en silencio le abrasa, los horrores,
la fuerza conocieses! ¡ Ay Jovino!
¡ Ay amigo! ¡ Ay de mí! Tú solo a un triste,
leal confidente en su miseria extrema,
eres salud y suspirado puerto.
En tu fiel seno, de bondad dechado,
mis infelices lágrimas se vierten,
y mis querellas sin temor piadoso
las oye, y mezcla con mi llanto el tuyo.
Ten lástima de mi: tú solo existes,
tú solo para mí en el universo.
Doquiera vuelvo los nublados ojos,
nada miro, nada hallo que me cause
sino agudo dolor o tedio amargo.
Naturaleza, en su hermosura varia,
parece que a mi vista en luto triste
se envuelve umbría, y que sus leyes rotas,
todo se precipita al caos antiguo.

Sí, amigo, sí: mi espíritu, insensible
del vivaz gozo a la impresión süave,
todo lo anubla en su tristeza oscura,
materia en todo a más dolor hallando,
y a este fastidio universal que encuentra
en todo el corazón perenne causa.
La rubia aurora entre rosadas nubes
plácida asoma su risueña frente,
llamando al día; y desvelado me oye
su luz modesta, maldecir los trinos

con que las dulces aves la alborean,
turbando mis lamentos importunos.
El sol, velando en centellantes fuegos
su inaccesible majestad, preside
cual rey al universo, esclarecido
de un mar de luz que de su trono corre.
Yo, empero, huyendo dél, sin cesar llamo
la negra noche, y a sus brillos cierro
mis lagrimosos fatigados ojos.
La noche melancólica al fin llega,
tanto anhelada ; a lloro más ardiente,
a más gemidos su quietud me irrita.
Busco angustiado el sueño ; de mí huye
despavorido, y en vigilia odiosa
me ve desfallecer un nuevo día,
por él clamando detestar la noche.

Así tu amigo vive : en dolor tanto,
Jovino, el infelice, de ti lejos,
lejos de todo bien, sumido yace.
¡ Ay ! ¿ dónde alivio encontraré a mis penas ?
¿ Quién pondrá fin a mis extremas ansias,
o me dará que en el sepulcro goce
de un reposo y olvido sempiternos ? . . .
Todo, todo me deja y abandona.
La muerte imploro, y a mi voz la muerte
cierra dura el oído ; la paz llamo,
la suspirada paz, que ponga al menos
alguna leve tregua a las fatigas
en que el llagado corazón guerrea :
con fervorosa voz en ruego humilde
alzo al cielo las manos ; sordo se hace
el cielo a mi clamor ; la paz que busco,
es guerra y turbación al pecho mío.

Así huyendo de todos, sin destino,
perdido, extraviado, con pie incierto,
sin seso corro estos medrosos valles ;
ciego, insensible a las bellezas que ora
al ánimo doquiera reflexivo
Natura ofrece en su estación más rica.

Un tiempo fué que, de entusiasmo lleno,
yo las pude admirar, y en dulces cantos
de gratitud holgaba celebrarlas
entre éxtasis de gozo, el labio mío.
¡ Oh cómo entonces las opimas mieses,
que de dorada arista defendidas,
en su llena sazón ceden al golpe
del abrasado segador ! ¡ Oh cómo
la ronca voz, los cánticos sencillos
con que su afán el labrador engaña,
entre sudor y polvo revolviendo
el rico grano en las tendidas eras,
mi espíritu inundaran de alegría !
Los recamados centellantes rayos
de la fresca mañana, los tesoros
de llama inmensos que en su trono ostenta
majestuoso el sol, de la tranquila
nevada luna el silencioso paso,
tanta luz como esmalta el velo hermoso
con que en sombras la noche envuelve el mundo,
melancólicas sombras, jamás fueran
vistas de mí, sin bendecir humilde
la mano liberal que omnipotente
de sí tan rica muestra hacernos sabe ;
jamás lo fueran sin sentir batiendo
mi corazón en celestial zozobra.

Tú lo has visto, Jovino ; en mi entusiasmo
perdido, dulcemente fugitivas
volárseme las horas. . . . Todo, todo
se trocó a un infeliz : mi triste musa
no sabe ya sino lanzar suspiros,
ni saben ya sino llorar mis ojos,
ni más que padecer mi tierno pecho.
En él su hórrido trono alzó la oscura
melancolía, y su mansión hicieran
las penas veladoras, los gemidos,
la agonía, el pesar, la queja amarga,
y cuanto monstruo en su delirio infausto
la azorada razón abortar puede.

¡ Ay ! ¡ si me vieses elevado y triste,
inundando mis lágrimas el suelo,
en él los ojos, como fría estatua
inmóvil y en mis penas embargado,
de abandono y dolor imagen muda !
¡ Ay ! ¡ si me vieses ¡ ay ! en las tinieblas
con fugaz planta discurrir perdido,
bañado en sudor frío, de mí propio
huyendo, y de fantasmas mil cercado !

¡ Ay ! ¡ si pudieses ver . . . el devaneo
de mi ciega razón, tantos combates,
tanto caer, y levantarme tanto :
temer, dudar, y de mi vil flaqueza
indignarme afrentado, en vivas llamas
ardiendo el corazón al tiempo mismo !
¡ Hacer al cielo mil fervientes votos,
y al punto traspasarlos . . . el deseo . . .
la pasión, la razón ya vencedoras . . .
ya vencidas huir ! . . . Ven, dulce amigo,
consolador y amparo ; ven y alienta
a este infeliz, que tu favor implora.
Extiende a mí la compasiva mano,
y tu alto imperio a domeñar me enseñe
la rebelde razón ; en mis austeros
deberes me asegura en la escabrosa
difícil senda que temblando sigo.
La virtud celestial y la inocencia
llorando huyeran de mi pecho triste,
y en pos de ellas la paz ; tú conciliarme
con ellas puedes, y salvarme puedes.
No tardes, ven, y poderoso templa
tan insano furor ; ampara, ampara
a un desdichado que al abismo, que huye,
se ve arrastrar por invencible impulso,
y abrasado en angustias criminales,
su corazón por la virtud suspira.

NICASIO ÁLVAREZ DE CIENFUEGOS

1764-1809

CIENFUEGOS, another Salamancan, is at his best a poet of great imaginative power ; and even below the level of his best he can attract by his outbursts of emotion, by the freshness and spontaneity of his poetic diction and by the boldness of his imagery. He has his quiet moments, too, in which he rejoices in solitude : cf. the opening of " El Otoño ", a poem which also illustrates a treatment of Nature in the main objective, or even picturesque and ornamental. Cienfuegos' average standard of merit, however, is not high, and few of his poems are unspoiled by conventionality, monotony or anti-climax.

217. *El Otoño*

¡ Oh, salve, salve, soledad querida,
do en los halagos del Abril hermoso
vine a cantar en medio a los amores
mi eterno desamor ! ¡ Salve, oh florida,
oh calma vega ! A tu feliz reposo
torno otra vez, y entre tus nuevas flores
enjugando el sudor que a Sirio ardiente
pagó en tributo lánguida mi frente,
veré al otoño levantarse ufano
sobre la árida tumba del verano.

Sí, le veré ; que la balanza justa
las sombras y la luz igual partiendo,
en sus frescos palacios aprisiona
voluble al sol, que de su sien augusta
la diadema inflamada desciñendo,
de rayos más benignos se corona.
" Otoño ", clama de su carro de oro ;
y otoño al punto, entre el favonio coro,
que Agosto adormeció, la faz alzando,
el florido frescor vuela soplando.

A su dulce volar ¡ cuál reverdece
la tierra, enriqueciendo su ancho manto
de opulento verdor ! La tuberosa
del albo cáliz en su honor florece,
y la piramidal, y tú, oh amaranto,
de más largo vivir. Tu flor pomposa,
que adornaba de Mayo los amores,
hoy halla frutos donde vió las flores ;
oyó quejarse al ruiseñor, primero,
y ya recibe su cantar postrero.
Tú le viste brillante y florecido
a este rico peral, que ora, agobiado
del largo enjambre de su prole hermosa,
la frente inclina. Céfiro atrevido,
de una poma tal vez enamorado,
bate rápido el ala sonorosa,
y la besa, y la deja, y torna amante,
y mece las hojitas, e inconstante
huye y torna a mecer, y cae su amada,
y toca el polvo con la faz rosada.
¡ Otoño, otoño ! ¿ le miráis que llega
de colina en colina vacilante
resaltando ? ¡ Evohé ! salid, oh hermosas,
a recibirle al monte y a la vega,
suspendiendo a los hombros el vacante
hondo mimbre. Corred, y en pampanosas
guirnaldas coronad mi temulenta
sien. Dadme yedras, que ardo en violenta
sed báquica. ¡ Evohé ! cortad ; que opimos
entre el pámpano caigan los racimos.
¡ Mil veces Evohé ! que ya resuena,
rechinando, el lagar. ¡ Cuál, ay, corriendo
el padre Baco, en ríos espumantes
se precipita, y de la cuba llena
la ancha capacidad, que tiembla hirviendo !
Copa, copa ; mis labios anhelantes
se bañen en el néctar de Lieo.
Hijos de Ceres, vuestro duro empleo
cesa ; imitad mis báquicos furores,
que ya el año premió vuestros sudores.

Conmigo enloqueced. Ya está vacía,
mi copa rellenad, y en torno ruede,
y los ecos repitan retumbando
cien veces. ¡ Evohé ! La selva umbría
se adelanta hacia mí ; ya retrocede,
ya gira en derredor. ¡ Cuál, ay, saltando
los peñascos y montes de su asiento,
vuelan ligeros por el vago viento !
Tierra y cielo se mueven. Luego, luego
cien copas. ¡ Evohé ! dad a mi fuego.
Otras ciento me dad ; y que el arado,
rompiendo el seno a la fecunda Ceres,
la esperanza asegure en rubios granos
al futuro vivir, y desvelado
siembre nuevo placer. ¡ Ah ! los placeres
cual humo pasan, y recuerdos vanos
dejan en su lugar. ¿ Veis cuál fallece
la alegría otoñal ? Ya palidece
el hojoso verdor, y el claro cielo
llora cubierto en nebuloso velo.
El gozo es llanto. En los vapores lanza
el escorpión su bárbaro veneno,
y abre las puertas de la tumba fría.
Muere el infante, mísera esperanza
de la madre infeliz, que entre su seno
le está viendo morir. En tanto impía
vuela la muerte al trono de himeneo,
huella al amor, y un bárbaro trofeo
allí levanta, a la afligida esposa
cubriendo el lecho de viudez sombrosa.
¡ Tristeza universal ! ¿ quién ¡ ay ! me diera
volar a otra región do más tardío
lanzase otoño el postrimer aliento ?
¡ Que del Betis corriendo la ribera,
no oyese todavía al canto mío
mezclar el ruiseñor su tierno acento !
Entre los bosques de Minerva errante,
la diestra armada del bastón pujante,
el árbol de la paz despojaría
y en ríos de oro el suelo regaría,

u oprimiendo el ijar del espumante
caballo, las selvosas espesuras
penetrara, las fieras persiguiendo.
¿ Oís, oís que el eco retumbante
hinche el aire de acentos ladradores
y de agudos relinchos ? Al estruendo
huye el ciervo, se esconde, para, mira,
y tornando el ladrar, trémulo gira
por entre el laberinto montuoso,
en otro tiempo su feliz reposo.

En vano, en vano en su favor implora
a su bosque. Las ramas alevosas,
que galán de las selvas le aclamaron,
¡ oh fortuna cruel ! prenden ahora
de su frente las galas ambiciosas
que en silencio mil veces retrataron
las ondas claras del arroyo amigo.
Ya todo se mudó ; que su enemigo
llega, y el triste por huir se agita,
y más se enreda cuanto más se irrita.

No hay ya salud, que el ladrador ardiente
le ve y se arroja, y a su cuerpo airoso
se abalanza amagando, y, no exorable,
la majestad humilla de su frente.
¡ Ciervo infeliz ! tendido, sanguinoso,
rodeado de muerte inevitable,
los ojos tristes por la vez postrera
alza al bosque do vió la luz primera ;
y entre el acero que sus gracias hiere,
y recuerdos amargos, llora y muere.

Así tal vez del hombre la alegría
espira en el dolor ; y así sucede
a la risa otoñal el desconsuelo
que a la estación brumal árido guía ;
ya nos rodea ; sustentar no puede
la selva su ambición ; pálido el suelo
se encubre con las hojas que, bajando
por el aire, en mil orbes circulando
lentas van ; caen, y yace lastimero
el selvoso frescor de un año entero.

¡ Cuál silban en las ramas combatiendo,
hijos de oscuridad, los roncos vientos,
vedando a Ceres su vigor fecundo !
Brama el mar, y los ríos con estruendo
arrastran los torrentes vïolentos
en turbias hondas con horror profundo.
Avecitas de Abril, huid ligeras
del Nilo a las benéficas riberas.
Aquí ya no hay placer ; ha muerto Flora,
otoño espira, y nos dejó la aurora.

Huyó cual sueño el anüal contento,
que alargaba mentida mi esperanza,
y se llevó un otoño de mi vida.
Otro en pos volará, y en un momento,
marchita flor mi juvenil pujanza,
la edad madura en lo que fué perdida,
con albo pelo y encorvada frente
me arrastrará la ancianidad doliente,
y do pose la planta vacilante,
la tumba abierta miraré delante.

Presto será que solo y apartado
de todo cuanto amé, llore extranjero
en este mundo muerto a mis placeres.
Vanamente el Octubre empampanado
renovará las risas placentero.
¡ Mísero yo ! perdidos mis quereres,
sin amigos, sin padres, sin amores,
¿ a quién me volveré ? ¿ cuál ser piadoso
enjugará mi llanto congojoso ?

Doquier publicará naturaleza
mi destierro. Vendrá el Abril florido
ya sin mi juventud, sin las delicias
de un ya distante amor, de una belleza,
polvo, sueño fugaz. Saldrá encendido
Agosto, recordando las primicias
de mi Apolo ; ¡ oh dolor ! murió su canto
para siempre. De invierno entre el espanto
oiré que de su helado monumento
mudo me llama el paternal acento.

¡ Oh soledad, oh bárbara amargura
de un ser aislado ! Mi tristeza os llama ;
volad, amigos, que con tiernos lazos
estrechándome, huirá mi desventura.
¡ Pueda en medio de vos, pobre, sin fama,
merecer vuestro amor, y en vuestros brazos
venturoso vivir eternamente !
¡ Pueda aprender de vos, la calma frente
posando en vuestros dulces corazones,
de la santa virtud las instrucciones !

Y cuando ya la muerte se levante
a romper nuestra unión, pruebe conmigo
su hierro. ¡ Oh muerte, en mi cerviz descarga
tu primero furor ! ¡ Jamás quebrante
mi corazón del doloroso amigo
que ya bebe su fin, la escena amarga !
¡ Ah, precédalos yo ! ¡ pueda mi lecho
mirarlos rodear, y entre su pecho,
con su amor olvidando mi tormento,
darles al fin mi postrimer aliento !

¡ Oh recreo feliz del alma mía !
¡ Oh mis amigos ! Cuando yazca helado,
de mi arroyo querido en la ribera
un sepulcro me alzad, de sombra fría
de cipreses y adelfas rodeado ;
amadme siempre ; y cuando otoño muera,
mis cenizas con lágrimas regando,
decid : " Nicasio ", y repetid clamando :
" Hombre tierno y amigo afectuoso,
fué su otoño en nosotros delicioso ".

JOSÉ MARCHENA
1768-1821

MARCHENA, like Blanco y Crespo—the better known of the two in England, because it was there that he settled, adopting the name of Blanco White—was a cleric who abandoned his Orders and exiled himself from Spain. At a time when the French Revolution was at its height he went to France and was adopted by the revolutionaries and their successors: in 1808, when he returned to Spain, it was as Murat's secretary. Both in France and in Spain he wrote voluminously, and his verse, which turns largely on freedom, has a fire and a vigour which give it attractiveness in excess of its technical merits.

218. *Apóstrofe a la Libertad*

¡ Oh lauro inmarcesible, oh glorioso
hado de nación libre, quien te alcanza
llamarse con verdad puede dichoso !
¡ Libertad, libertad ! tú la esperanza
eres de cuanto espíritu brioso
el despotismo en sus mazmorras lanza.
Los pueblos que benéfica visitas,
a vida nueva al punto resucitas.

El pueblo de Minerva, el de Quirino,
si la historia pregona sus loores,
y si con esplendor lucen divino,
del tiempo y del olvido vencedores,
a la libertad deben su destino.
La libertad regó las bellas flores
que la sien de Fabricio y Decio ornaron,
y a Foción y a Aristides coronaron.

A Jéfferson y a Wáshington inflamas
en tu sagrado amor, y otro hemisferio
consume luego entre voraces llamas
los monumentos de su cautiverio.
Tu santo ardor por la nación derramas,
y de las leyes fundas el imperio,
siempre absoluto, porque siempre justo,
que la igualdad social mantiene augusto.

MANUEL MARÍA DE ARJONA

1771-1820

LIKE the Golden Age, the eighteenth century had a Sevilian School as well as an earlier Salamancan one: this took its rise in an Academia de Letras Humanas, founded at Seville in 1793. Though the nearer of the two to the Romantic movement in time, the Sevilian School was the farther from it in spirit. Arjona, however, if over-florid in form, is more subjective and more sensitive to Nature than the rest of the group. He was also its chief metrist, experimenting (somewhat uneasily, it is true, and not always successfully) in forms and devices that had been forgotten for two centuries. The metrical variety in "La Fortuna justa", the alternation of stresses in the sapphics entitled "La Diosa del bosque" and the short lines of the "Cantilenas" all clearly denote originality, and suggest taste. Intrinsically, the "Cantilenas", which seem to bring us near the mediaeval revival so characteristic of the Romantic movement in Spain, are more attractive than the Classically-inspired poems, though Arjona is not to be despised as a Horatian.

219. *Cantilenas*

Pastorcito del alma,
no me abandones;
que cercan mi camino
mil salteadores.

Esta selva vecina
llena está de leones,
y sus fieros rugidos
estremecen los bosques.

¡Ay! qué difícil,
¡Ay! qué intrincada
es esta senda toda,
pastor del alma.

Fatigada y rendida,
quiero sentarme,
pero temo traiciones
por todas partes.

Ay de mí, desdichada,
mísera pastorcilla,
que mi amante me deja
entregada a mí misma.

Sufro cuitada
mi cruda suerte,
y sólo gozo ¡ ay triste !
sombras de muerte.

Ni aun la cumbre del monte
donde tú habitas,
las lágrimas me dejan
que yo perciba.

¿ Me volveré a mi patria
y al olvidado suelo ?
Mas ni tú, amante, quieres,
ni yo puedo, ni quiero.

Sigue constante,
triste pastora ;
que en tan dichosa empresa
morir es gloria.

Y si el tigre te asalta,
si el oso fiero,
si el dragón sanguinario,
no tengas miedo.

De tu amor en las alas
lograrás sublimarte,
y sus necios furores
despreciarás triunfante.

¡ Ay amor mío !
Sin luz ni guía,
me bastarán las armas
de mi osadía.

MANUEL JOSÉ QUINTANA

1772-1857

So much has the fame of Quintana shrunk with the passage of time that it is difficult to picture him, during the latter part of his long life, as a figure towering above his fellows. Not only was he a dramatist and a dramatic critic, the biographer of nine great Spaniards, the author of some good mouth-filling odes, the editor of a justly famous anthology of Spanish poetry and a much-valued contributor to the literary Press, but he was a statesman, a patriot, a fierce lover of independence, and a man who during the political vicissitudes of his middle life had suffered both severely and bravely for his opinions. From 1830 onwards he brooded like a celestial genius over the kaleidoscopic literary scene and no writer, however revolutionary, dared refer to him otherwise than with deep respect.

In passing from the man to his poems one cannot avoid a certain bathos: so hollow is their eloquence to us now, so turgid their language, that it is difficult to recapture the profound emotion by which they would seem to have been inspired. They are rigid in form, with neither the colour nor the music of the odes of Herrera, which in some other respects they resemble; and, while their dignity and nobility make them fully worthy of preservation, they have come down to us only as flowers of art stiffly frozen and unlikely now ever to thaw.

220. *A España, después de la Revolución de Marzo*

This, perhaps the most personal and moving of Quintana's odes, is dated April 1808, and celebrates the rising at Aranjuez against Charles IV and Godoy which had taken place in the preceding month, a few days before the entry of French troops into Madrid. So soon after the events to which it refers was it written that its author had perhaps no time to polish it as he might later have desired, with the result that some of its heat and emotion remain.

¿ Qué era, decidme, la nación que un día
reina del mundo proclamó el destino,
la que a todas las zonas extendía
su cetro de oro y su blasón divino ?
Volábase a occidente,
y el vasto mar Atlántico sembrado
se hallaba de su gloria y su fortuna.
Do quiera España : en el preciado seno
de América, en el Asia, en los confines
del África, allí España. El soberano
vuelo de la atrevida fantasía
para abarcarla se cansaba en vano ;
la tierra sus mineros le rendía,
sus perlas y coral el Oceano,
y donde quier que revolver sus olas
él intentase, a quebrantar su furia
siempre encontraba costas españolas.

Ora en el cieno del oprobio hundida,
abandonada a la insolencia ajena,
como esclava en mercado, ya aguardaba
la ruda argolla y la servil cadena.
¡ Qué de plagas, oh Dios ! Su aliento impuro,
la pestilente fiebre respirando,
infestó el aire, emponzoñó la vida ;
la hambre enflaquecida
tendió sus brazos lívidos, ahogando
cuanto el contagio perdonó ; tres veces
de Jano el templo abrimos,
y a la trompa de Marte aliento dimos ;
tres veces ¡ ay ! Los dioses tutelares
su escudo nos negaron, y nos vimos
rotos en tierra y rotos en los mares.
¿ Qué en tanto tiempo viste
por tus inmensos términos, oh Iberia ?
¿ Qué viste ya sino funesto luto,
honda tristeza, sin igual miseria,
de tu vil servidumbre acerbo fruto ?

Así, rota la vela, abierto el lado,
pobre bajel a naufragar camina,
de tormenta en tormenta despeñado,
por los yermos del mar ; ya ni en su popa
las guirnaldas se ven que antes le ornaban,
ni en señal de esperanza y de contento
la flámula rïendo al aire ondea.
Cesó en su dulce canto el pasajero,
ahogó su vocería
el ronco marinero,
terror de muerte en torno le rodea,
terror de muerte silencioso y frío ;
y él va a estrellarse al áspero bajío.

Llega el momento, en fin ; tiende su mano
el tirano del mundo al occidente
y fiero exclama : " ¡ El occidente es mío ! "
Bárbaro gozo en su ceñuda frente
resplandeció, como en el seno obscuro
de nube tormentosa en el estío
relámpago fugaz brilla un momento
que añade horror con su fulgor sombrío.
Sus guerreros feroces
con gritos de soberbia el viento llenan ;
gimen los yunques, los martillos suenan,
arden las forjas. ¡ Oh vergüenza ! ¿ Acaso
pensáis que espadas son para el combate
las que mueven sus manos codiciosas ?
No en tanto os estiméis : grillos, esposas,
cadenas son que en vergonzosos lazos
por siempre amarren tan inertes brazos.

Estremecióse España
del indigno rumor que cerca oía,
y al grande impulso de su justa saña
rompió el volcán que en su interior hervía.
Sus déspotas antiguos
consternados y pálidos se esconden ;
resuena el eco de venganza en torno,

y del Tajo las márgenes responden :
" ¡ Venganza ! " ¿ Dónde están, sagrado río,
los colosos de oprobio y de vergüenza
que nuestro bien en su insolencia ahogaban ?
Su gloria fué, nuestro esplendor comienza ;
y tú, orgulloso y fiero,
viendo que aun hay Castilla y castellanos,
precipitas al mar tus rubias ondas,
diciendo : " ¡ Ya acabaron los tiranos ! "

¡ Oh triunfo ! ¡ Oh gloria ! ¡ Oh celestial momento !
¿ Con qué puede ya dar el labio mío
el nombre augusto de la patria al viento ?
Yo le daré ; mas no en el arpa de oro
que mi cantar sonoro
acompañó hasta aquí ; no aprisionado
en estrecho recinto, en que se apoca
el numen en el pecho
y el aliento fatídico en la boca.
Desenterrad la lira de Tirteo,
y el aire abierto a la radiante lumbre
del sol, en la alta cumbre
del riscoso y pinífero Fuenfría,
allí volaré yo, y allí cantando
con voz que atruene en rededor la sierra,
lanzaré por los campos castellanos
los ecos de la gloria y de la guerra.

¡ Guerra, nombre tremendo, ahora sublime,
único asilo y sacrosanto escudo
al ímpetu sañudo
del fiero Atila que a occidente oprime !
¡ Guerra, guerra, españoles ! En el Betis
ved del Tercer Fernando alzarse airada
la augusta sombra ; su divina frente
mostrar Gonzalo en la imperial Granada ;
blandir el Cid su centellante espada,
y allá sobre los altos Pirineos,
del hijo de Jimena
animarse los miembros giganteos.

En torvo ceño y desdeñosa pena
ved cómo cruzan por los aires vanos;
y el valor exhalando que se encierra
dentro del hueco de sus tumbas frías,
en fiera y ronca voz pronuncian: " ¡ Guerra ! "

" ¡ Pues qué ! ¿ Con faz serena
vierais los campos devastar opimos,
eterno objeto de ambición ajena,
herencia inmensa que afanando os dimos ?
Despertad, raza de héroes: el momento
llegó ya de arrojarse a la victoria;
que vuestro nombre eclipse nuestro nombre,
que vuestra gloria humille nuestra gloria.
No ha sido en el gran día
el altar de la patria alzado en vano
por vuestra mano fuerte.
Juradlo, ella os lo manda: *¡ Antes la muerte
que consentir jamás ningún tirano !* "

Sí, yo lo juro, venerables sombras;
yo lo juro también, y en este instante
ya me siento mayor. Dadme una lanza,
ceñidme el casco fiero y refulgente;
volemos al combate, a la venganza;
y el que niegue su pecho a la esperanza,
hunda en el polvo la cobarde frente.
Tal vez el gran torrente
de la devastación en su carrera
me llevará. ¿ Qué importa ? ¿ Por ventura
no se muere una vez ? ¿ No iré, expirando,
a encontrar nuestros ínclitos mayores ?
" ¡ Salud, oh padres de la patria mía,
yo les diré, salud ! La heroica España
de entre el estrago universal y horrores
levanta la cabeza ensangrentada,
y vencedora de su mal destino,
vuelve a dar a la tierra amedrentada
su cetro de oro y su blasón divino."

221. *Al Armamento de las Provincias Españolas contra los Franceses*

This ode, though evoked by an even more inspiring manifestation of Spanish love of freedom than the March rising (it is dated July 1808), provides a better example of what a critic has aptly described as Quintana's " well-ordered warmth ".[1] *Not only are the exclamations and questions more rhetorical, while the personal note is less frequently heard, but there is a frigidity about the entire poem which prevents it from ever catching fire. Often (" Hoy lo vuelve a anunciar. . . .") it is pedestrian, even prosaic.*

" Eterna ley del mundo aquesta sea :
en pueblos o cobardes o estragados
que ruede a su placer la tiranía ;
mas si su atroz porfía
osa insultar a pechos generosos
donde esfuerzo y virtud tienen asiento,
estréllese al instante,
y de su ruina brote el escarmiento."
Dijo así Dios : con letras de diamante
su dedo augusto lo escribió en el cielo,
y en torrentes de sangre a la venganza
mandó después que lo anunciase al suelo.

Hoy lo vuelve a anunciar. En justa pena
de tu vicioso y mísero abandono
en ti su horrible trono
sentó el numen del mal, Francia culpable ;
y sacudiendo el cetro abominable,
cuanto sus ojos ven, tanto aniquila.
El genio atroz del insensato Atila,
la furia que el mortífero estandarte
llevaban de Timur, mandan al lado
de tu feroz sultán ; ellos le inspiran,
y ya en su orgullo a esclavizar se atreve
cuanto hay del mar de Italia a los desiertos,
faltos siempre de vida y siempre yertos,
do reina el polo engendrador de nieve.

[1] I. L. McClelland : *The Origins of the Romantic Movement in Spain*, Liverpool, 1937, p. 337.

Llega, España, tu vez ; al cautiverio
con nefario artificio
tus príncipes arrastra, y en su mano
las riendas de tu imperio
logró tener, y se ostentó tirano.
Ya manda, ya devasta ; sus soldados
obedeciendo en torpe vasallaje
al planeta de muerte que los guía,
trocaron en horror el hospedaje,
y la amistad en servidumbre impía.
¿ Adónde pues huyeron,
pregunta el orbe estremecido, adónde
la santa paz, la noble confianza,
la no violada fe ? Vanas deidades,
que sólo ya los débiles imploran.
Europa sabe, de escarmiento llena,
que la fuerza es la ley, el Dios que adoran
esos atroces vándalos del Sena.

Pues bien, la fuerza mande, ella decida ;
nadie incline a esta gente fementida
por temor pusilánime la frente ;
que nunca el alevoso fué valiente.
Alto y feroz rugido
la sed de guerra y la sangrienta saña
anuncia del león ; con bronco acento
ensordeciendo el eco en la montaña,
a devorar su presa
las águilas se arrojan por el viento.
Sola la sierpe vil, la sierpe ingrata
al descuidado seno que la abriga
callada llega y ponzoñosa mata.
Las víboras de Alcides
son las que asaltan la adorada cuna
de tu felicidad. Despierta, España,
despierta, ¡ ay Dios ! Y tus robustos brazos,
haciéndolas pedazos
y esparciendo sus miembros por la tierra,
ostenten el esfuerzo incontrastable
que en tu naciente libertad se encierra.

Ya se acerca zumbando
el eco grande de clamor guerrero,
hijo de indignación y de osadía.
Asturias fué quien le arrojó primero.
¡ Honor al pueblo astur ! Allí debía
primero resonar. Con igual furia
se alza, y se extiende adonde en fértil riego
del Ebro caudaloso y dulce Turia
las claras ondas abundancia brotan ;
y como en selvas estallante fuego
cuando las alas de Aquilón le azotan,
que de pronto a calmar ni vuelto en lluvia
Júpiter basta, ni los anchos ríos
que oponen su creciente a sus furores ;
los ecos libradores
vuelan, cruzan, encienden
los campos olivíferos del Betis,
y de la playa Cántabra hasta Cádiz
el seno azul de la agitada Tetis.

Álzase España, en fin ; con faz airada
hace a Marte señal, y el Dios horrendo
despeña en ella su crujiente carro ;
al espantoso estruendo,
al revolver de su terrible espada,
lejos de estremecerse, arde y se agita,
y vuela en pos el español bizarro.
" ¡ Fuera tiranos ! " grita
la muchedumbre inmensa. ¡ Oh voz sublime,
eco de vida, manantial de gloria !
Esos ministros de ambición ajena
no te escucharon, no, cuando triunfaban
tan fácilmente en Austerlitz y en Jena ;
aquí te oirán y alcanzarás victoria ;
aquí te oirán saliendo
de pechos esforzados, varoniles ;
y la distancia medirán, gimiendo,
que de hombres hay a mercenarios viles.

Fuego noble y sublime, ¿ a quién no alcanzas ?
Lágrimas de dolor vierte el anciano
porque su débil mano
el acero a blandir ya no es bastante ;
lágrimas vierte el ternezuelo infante ;
y vosotras también, madres, esposas,
tiernas amantes, ¿ qué furor os lleva
en medio de esas huestes sanguinosas ?
Otra lucha, otro afán, otros enojos
guardó el destino a vuestros miembros bellos,
deben arder en vuestros negros ojos.
" ¿ Queréis ", responden, " darnos por despojos
a esos verdugos ? No : con pecho fuerte
lidiando a vuestro lado,
también sabremos arrostrar la muerte.
Nosotras vuestra sangre atajaremos ;
nosotras dulce galardón seremos
cuando, de lauro y de floridos lazos
la vencedora frente coronada,
reposo halléis en nuestros tiernos brazos ".

¿ Y tú callas, Madrid ? Tú, la señora
de cien provincias, que cual ley suprema
adoraban tu voz, ¿ callas ahora ?
¿ Adónde están el cetro, la diadema,
la augusta majestad que te adornaba ?
" No hay majestad para quien vive esclava ;
ya la espada homicida
en mí sus filos ensayó primero.
Allí cayó mi juventud sin vida :
yo, atada al yugo bárbaro de acero,
exánime suspiro,
y aire de muerte y de opresión respiro."

¡ Ah ! respira más bien aura de gloria.
¡ Oh corona de Iberia ! Alza la frente,
tiende la vista ; en iris de bonanza
se torna al fin la tempestad sombría.
¿ No oyes por el oriente y mediodía

de guerra y de matanza
resonar el clamor ? Arde la lucha,
retumba el bronce, los valientes caen,
y el campo, de humor rojo hecho ya un lago,
descubre al mundo el espantoso estrago.
Así sus llanos fértiles Valencia
ostenta, así Bailén, así Moncayo ;
y es fama que las víctimas de Mayo
lívidas por el aire aparecían ;
que a su alarido horrendo
las francesas falanjes se aterraban ;
y ellas, su sangre con placer bebiendo,
el ansia de venganza al fin saciaban.

Genios que acompañáis a la victoria,
volad, y apercibid en vuestras manos
lauros de Salamina y de Platea,
que crecen cuando lloran los tiranos.
De ellos ceñido el vencedor se vea
al acercarse al capitolio ibero :
ya llega, ¿ no le veis ? Astro parece
en su carro triunfal, mucho más claro
que tras tormenta el sol. Barred las calles
de ese terror que las yermaba un día ;
que el júbilo las pueble y la alegría ;
los altos coronad, henchid los valles,
y en vuestra boca el apacible acento,
y en vuestras manos tremolando el lino,
" Salve ", exclamad, " libertador divino,
salve," y que en ecos mil lo diga el viento,
y suba resonando al firmamento.

Suba, y España mande a sus leones
volar rugiendo al alto Pirineo,
y allí alzar el espléndido trofeo,
que diga : " Libertad a las naciones."
Tal es, ¡ oh pueblo grande ! ¡ oh pueblo fuerte !
el premio que la suerte
a tu valor magnánimo destina.

Así resiste la robusta encina
al temporal ; arrójanse silbando
los fieros huracanes,
en su espantoso vértigo llevando
desolación y ruina ; ella resiste.
Crece el furor, redoblan su pujanza,
braman, y tiembla en rededor la esfera.
¿ Qué importa que a la verde cabellera
este ramo y aquél falte, arrancado
del ímpetu del viento, y luego muera ?
Ella resiste ; la soberbia cima
más hermosa al Olimpo al fin levanta,
y entre tanto meciéndose en sus hojas,
céfiro alegre la victoria canta.

ALBERTO LISTA Y ARAGÓN

1775-1848

IN Alberto Lista the Sevilian School had a critic of distinction, whose creative work forms a curious link between past and future. On the one hand, he declared that his model in " form, expression and language " was the seventeenth-century Rioja ; on the other, he himself served as model, or at least as mentor, to that Romantic of the Romantics, Espronceda. In another epoch, both as critic and as poet, he might have been greater ; yet his academic muse, which found in Golden Age poetry what he characteristically terms a " delirio raciocinado ", is sometimes better than its own inspiration might suggest. Some of his *romances*, too, are quite charming.

222. *El Amor inmortal*

Beginning like any example of Golden Age amatory verse, this poem soon betrays its new modality through the emphasis which it lays on the moral qualities of the beloved. Venus, endowed with eighteenth-century humanitarianism, becomes a sort of Lady Bountiful, and the sensuous exuberance of Golden Age art is refined into the most bloodless of abstractions.

En tus hermosos ojos templar pudo
el dios de los amores
aquel arpón tan dulce como agudo,
que para herirme coronó de flores.

De ese cabello de oro, que enajena
mi pecho enamorado,
pudo tejer la plácida cadena
que a tus plantas me tiene aprisionado.

O en los lirios del seno, o en la rosa
del cándido semblante
pudo labrar la cárcel deliciosa
que preparaba a tu feliz amante.

La juventud, la gracia halagadora,
el talle torneado,
esa risa más dulce que la aurora
cuando ilumina el soñoliento prado;

tu hechicera mirada, tu festivo
candor, tu hablar suave
el corazón más fiero y más esquivo
domar pudiera; y el amor lo sabe.

Mas no con rayo que mudables vientos
apaguen, quiso herirme,
ni en caducos y frágiles cimientos
labrar una pasión constante y firme.

Yo vi en ti el puro asilo do se anida
la cándida inocencia,
y al blando sentimiento la fe unida,
y en verde juventud dócil prudencia.

Yo vi cuán compasiva e indulgente
con apacible agrado
tu hermosa mano alivia al indigente,
tu dulce hablar consuela al desgraciado.

Yo lo vi y te adoré, y en llama eterna
el pecho me encendiste;
que la santa virtud, la piedad tierna,
del crudo tiempo al huracán resiste.

Deshójase la flor de la hermosura,
se agostan los placeres,
y allá en la margen de la tumba oscura,
deleite encantador, ni aun sombra eres.

En ti, mi dulce bien, cuando tu aurora
florece placentera,
amo el carmín, que no se descolora,
amo la luz, que siempre reverbera.

¡ Ay! este amor de mi felice vida
será el postrer aliento,
y su llama inmortal correspondida
arderá más allá de aquel momento.

223. *Zoraida*

In its form almost as unlike a mediaeval poem as Nicolás Moratín's "Fiesta de toros en Madrid" (*p. 388*), *this Moorish ballad preserves much of the mediaeval spirit. Note the simplicity of the language, the directness of the address, and faint suggestions of colour, to which characteristics may be added an almost voluptuous smoothness and an effective interlacing, in the endings of the lines, of* agudo *and* llano. *First published by J. M. de Cossío in 1927, this is hardly the type of poem hitherto associated with the cold and academic Lista.*

El grato esplendor de la aurora
sobre el Genil va a despuntar,
y su luz que el mundo colora
la vuelvo a ver para llorar.

Dueño querido de mi suerte,
Abenamar, mi dulce amor,
¿ por qué a los campos de la muerte
te arrebató ciego el valor ?

Tu indigno rival me condena,
tirano y vil, a esta prisión ;
mas libre está de tu cadena
la pura fe del corazón.

Yo le aborrezco y tierna lloro
muerto quizá mi amado bien,
y lejos del dueño que adoro
gimo en poder del fiero Hacén.

El tirano, ay Dios, me asegura
que Abenamar no existe ya,
su lengua alevosa y perjura
por mi dolor, ¿ cierta será ?

Mas no ; tú me engañas, malvado ;
eres cruel como traidor,
y oprime un pecho enamorado
no tanto el mal como el temor.

Pero si es verdad que en la guerra
hierro fatal le traspasó,
no hay en el cielo ni en la tierra
quien pueda hacer que viva yo.

Zoraida en el sepulcro helado
a Abenamar se enlazará ;
la muerte que te la ha robado,
perdido bien, te la dará.

JUAN NICASIO GALLEGO
1777-1853

GALLEGO wrote but few poems, and he is known to the general reader by only one of them—" El Dos de Mayo ", an ode on the historic uprising of May 2, 1808, which followed the entry of the French into the Spanish capital. This ode begins and ends upon a note of gloom, and the " fatídicos colores " which came most naturally to the author's palette may seem at first sight rather repellent. But within the limits of pseudo-Classical convention the body of the poem is as fine a diatribe against an unprincipled aggressor as can well be imagined. The fierceness of the invective hurled at the enemy contrasts magnificently with the panegyric to the capital's gallant defenders. For relief there are glimpses of picturesque background, though they are prolonged no more than the emotional tension demands. The splendid climax of the penultimate stanza (" ¡ Venganza y guerra ! . . . ¡ Guerra y venganza ! ") forms the true conclusion of the poem, the relapse into its initial mood serving as a dignified and effective coda.

224. *El Dos de Mayo*

Animus meminisse horret, luctuque refugit.
Virg., En. II.

Noche, lóbrega noche, eterno asilo
del miserable que, esquivando el sueño,
en tu silencio pavoroso gime,
no desdeñes mi voz ; letal beleño
presta a mis sienes, y en tu horror sublime
empapada la ardiente fantasía,
da a mi pincel fatídicos colores
con que el tremendo día
trace al fulgor de vengadora tea,
y el odio irrite de la patria mía,
y escándalo y terror al orbe sea.

¡ Día de execración ! La destructora
mano del tiempo le arrojó al averno ;
mas ¿ quién el sempiterno
clamor con que los ecos importuna
la madre España en enlutado arreo
podrá atajar ? Junto al sepulcro frío,
al pálido lucir de opaca luna,
entre cipreses fúnebres la veo :
trémula, yerta, desceñido el manto,
los ojos moribundos
al cielo vuelve, que le oculta el llanto ;
roto y sin brillo el cetro de dos mundos
yace entre el polvo, y el león guerrero
lanza a sus pies rugido lastimero.

¡ Ay, que cual débil planta
que agosta en su furor hórrido viento,
de víctimas sin cuento
lloró la destrucción Mantua afligida !
Yo vi, yo vi su juventud florida
correr inerme al huésped ominoso.
Mas ¿ qué su generoso
esfuerzo pudo ? El pérfido caudillo
en quien su honor y su defensa fía,
la condenó al cuchillo.
¿ Quién ¡ ay ! la alevosía,
la horrible asolación habrá que cuente,
que, hollando de amistad los santos fueros,
hizo furioso en la indefensa gente
ese tropel de tigres carniceros ?

Por las henchidas calles
gritando se despeña
la infame turba que abrigó en su seno,
rueda allá rechinando la cureña,
acá retumba el espantoso trueno,
allí el joven lozano,
el mendigo infeliz, el venerable
sacerdote pacífico, el anciano
que con su arada faz respeto imprime,
juntos amarra su dogal tirano.

En balde, en balde gime,
de los duros satélites en torno,
la triste madre, la afligida esposa
con doliente clamor ; la pavorosa
fatal descarga suena,
que a luto y llanto eterno la condena.

¡ Cuánta escena de muerte ! ¡ Cuánto estrago !
¡ Cuántos ayes doquier ! Despavorido
mirad ese infelice
quejarse al adalid empedernido
de otra cuadrilla atroz: " ¡ Ah ! ¿ qué te hice ? "
exclama el triste, en lágrimas deshecho.
" Mi pan y mi mansión partí contigo,
te abrí mis brazos, te cedí mi lecho,
templé tu sed, y me llamé tu amigo ;
y ¿ hora pagar podrás nuestro hospedaje
sincero, franco, sin doblez ni engaño,
con dura muerte y con indigno ultraje ? "
¡ Perdido suplicar ! ¡ Inútil ruego !
El monstruo infame a sus ministros mira,
y con tremenda voz gritando : " ¡ Fuego ! "
tinto en su sangre el desgraciado espira.

Y en tanto ¿ dó se esconden ?
¿ Dó están ¡ oh cara patria ! tus soldados,
que a tu clamor de muerte no responden ?
Presos, encarcelados
por jefes sin honor, que, haciendo alarde
de su perfidia y dolo,
a merced de los vándalos te dejan,
como entre hierros el león, forcejan
con inútil afán. Vosotros sólo,
fuerte Daoiz, intrépido Velarde,
que osando resistir al gran torrente
dar supisteis en flor la dulce vida
con firme pecho y con serena frente ;
si de mi libre musa
jamás el eco adormeció a tiranos,
ni vil lisonja emponzoñó su aliento,

allá del alto asiento
a que la acción magnánima os eleva,
el himno oíd que a vuestro nombre entona,
mientras la fama alígera le lleva
del mar de hielo a la abrasada zona.

Mas ¡ ay ! que en tanto sus funestas alas,
por la opresa metrópoli tendiendo,
la yerma asolación sus plazas cubre,
y al áspero silbar de ardientes balas,
y al ronco son de los preñados bronces,
nuevo fragor y estrépito sucede.
¿ Oís cómo rompiendo
de moradores tímidos las puertas,
caen estallando de los fuertes gonces ?
¡ Con qué espantoso estruendo
los dueños buscan, que medrosos huyen !
Cuanto encuentran destruyen,
bramando, los atroces foragidos,
que el robo infame y la matanza ciegan.
¿ No veis cuál se despliegan,
penetrando en los hondos aposentos,
de sangre y oro y lágrimas sedientos ?

Rompen, talan, destrozan
cuanto se ofrece a su sangrienta espada.
Aquí, matando al dueño, se alborozan,
hieren allí su esposa acongojada ;
la familia asolada
yace espirando, y con feroz sonrisa
sorben voraces el fatal tesoro.
Suelta, a otro lado, la madeja de oro,
mustio el dulce carmín de su mejilla,
y en su frente marchita la azucena,
con voz turbada y anhelante lloro,
de su verdugo ante los pies se humilla
tímida virgen, de amargura llena ;
mas con furor de hiena,
alzando el corvo alfanje damasquino,
hiende su cuello el bárbaro asesino.

¡ Horrible atrocidad ! . . . ¡ Treguas, oh musa,
que ya la voz rehusa
embargada en suspiros mi garganta !
Y en ignominia tanta,
¿ será que rinda el español bizarro
la indómita cerviz a la cadena ?
No, que ya en torno suena
de Palas fiera el sanguinoso carro,
y el látigo estallante
los caballos flamígeros hostiga.
Ya el duro peto y el arnés brillante
visten los fuertes hijos de Pelayo.
Fuego arrojó su ruginoso acero :
" ¡ Venganza y guerra ! " resonó en su tumba ;
" ¡ Venganza y guerra ! " repitió Moncayo ;
y al grito heroico que en los aires zumba,
" ¡ Venganza y guerra ! " claman Turia y Duero.
Guadalquivir guerrero
alza al bélico son la regia frente,
y del Patrón valiente
blandiendo altivo la nudosa lanza,
corre gritando al mar : " ¡ Guerra y venganza ! "

¡ Oh sombras infelices
de los que aleve y bárbara cuchilla
robó a los dulces lares !
¡ Sombras inultas que en fugaz gemido
cruzáis los anchos campos de Castilla !
La heroica España, en tanto que al bandido
que a fuego y sangre, de insolencia ciego,
brindó felicidad, a sangre y fuego
le retribuye el don, sabrá piadosa
daros solemne y noble monumento.
Allí en padrón cruento
de oprobio y mengua, que perpetuo dure,
la vil traición del déspota se lea,
y altar eterno sea
donde todo español al monstruo jure
rencor de muerte que en sus venas cunda,
y a cien generaciones se difunda.

ÁNGEL DE SAAVEDRA, DUQUE DE RIVAS
1791-1865

Both in non-dramatic verse and in drama, Rivas was in the forefront of the Romantic movement, which, at the end of long years of preparation, began to assert itself soon after the death of Ferdinand VII in 1833. He was never the leader of that movement (which, in fact, had no leader at all) ; and when, after a decade of somewhat chequered success, it receded before a more comprehensive conception and eclectic ideal of art, he made no attempt to save it. After all, he had lived both his youth and his early manhood in the atmosphere of pseudo-classicism, and youthful habit dies hard.

Rivas' lyric poems are few and of no great merit. But in narrative verse, which he wrote with an ease unusual even in the fluent Spaniard, he was stronger than in lyric or drama, though it is with drama that he is most commonly associated. His *Moro expósito* (1834), a typically nineteenth-century re-presentation of the mediaeval legend of the Infantes de Lara (p. 128), was the first long poem of the new literary epoch, and upon its appearance was hailed as unique of its kind. In his *Romances históricos* (1841) he presented brilliant pictures from Spanish history ranging from the times of Peter the Cruel to the almost contemporary War of Independence against Napoleon. Finally, three longer poems (*Leyendas* : 1854) treated legend much as the preceding volume had treated history, but with greater latitude as to metre and greater freedom in theme and in technique.

Though in many respects careless and superficial, Rivas' works mark the beginning of a new epoch in narrative poetry, which was to be succeeded at the end of the century by a renaissance in the lyric. He popularized both the long and the short narrative poem, stimulated the mediaeval revival, and encouraged many able writers to return to the native octosyllabics and to make use of modern artistry in re-telling the stories of the past.

EL MORO EXPÓSITO

(*Extracts*)

Here, in twelve cantos comprising something like fifteen thousand lines, Rivas tells a story of Moslem and Christian Spain. Mudarra, a foundling Moor educated in the Cordoban court, is in love with Kerima, daughter of Giafar, a Moorish statesman. Giafar, opposed to the match, plots against Mudarra, who slays him in ignorance of his identity. Zaide, the youth's tutor, then tells him that he (Mudarra) is the son of Zahira, the Caliph's late sister, and a Christian noble named Lara. Many years before, through the treachery of a kinsman, Rui-Velázquez, Lara's seven sons had been ambushed in battle and murdered by Giafar, who had displayed their heads to the unhappy father, then the Caliph's prisoner. Of the love of Lara and Zahira, who visited him in prison, concludes Zaide, Mudarra was born. The youth then sets out for Christian Burgos to find his father, now old and blind, and to avenge himself on Rui-Velázquez, whom he challenges and kills in a duel. Kerima then comes to Burgos, to be baptized and married to Mudarra, but at the altar she renounces him, to become the Bride of Christ, since she cannot marry the man who has slain her father.

225. *Mudarra y Zaide*

At the beginning of Canto III Mudarra has just killed Giafar. Night is falling, and Zaide, vaguely uneasy, awaits the youth, who should have come to him some time before. At last he appears :

Pronto le reconoce. . . . ¡ Sí . . . Mudarra !
Ya le recibe mudo en su regazo.

Note, in the passage which follows, the exaggerated language which the Romantics so much favoured ; the effectiveness of the short, rapid phrases which lead up to the revelation of l. 18 ; the elements of fatalism and mystery, both characteristic of the poem ; and the use made of Nature in the provision of a setting for Zaide's story. The seven cypresses (l. 70), it may be added, wave in the breeze " con lúgubre rumor " (but with a great lack of humour) when Zaide comes to the story of the seven heads, reproduced in the extract which follows this.

Mas ¡ en qué situación llega el mancebo !
¡ Oh santo Dios, en qué terrible estado !
Pálido, alienta apena, en torno gira
los ojos, que terror pintan y espanto ;

desceñido el turbante al viento ondea,
desnudo el hierro muéstrase en su mano ;
y hierro, y mano, y manga, todo es sangre,
y sus miembros temblor, nieve su tacto.

Zaide su estado advierte ; cuanto mira
le está de horror el corazón ahogando ;
cuájasele la sangre, y confundido,
prorrumpe así con balbuciente labio :

" ¡ Oh Mudarra ! . . . ¿ Qué es esto ? . . . ¡ Ay, hijo mío !
¿ Qué golpe amaga a este infelice anciano ?
¡ Mudarra ! . . . ¿ No respondes ? " El mancebo,
al conocido acento en sí tornando,

alza la faz, lanza un gemido, y dice :
" Al padre de Kerima muerte he dado."
Y con nuevo terror quiere esconderse
del tierno Zaide en los amigos brazos.

" ¡ Cómo ! " pregunta el viejo, " ¿ has dado muerte
a Giafar ? " " A Giafar ", responde ahogado
el mísero garzón ; y Zaide exclama :
" ¿ Quién penetra tus miras, cielo santo ?

" ¡ Oh poderoso Alá ! . . . Ciertas, terribles
son tus venganzas : sí, la eterna mano
que las estrellas rige, inexorable
pesa sobre la frente del malvado.

" ¡ Oh joven ! De las iras del Eterno
es ya ministro tu inocente brazo.
Alzate, torna en ti ; noble principio
a tus venganzas sin saberlo has dado.

" Álzate, torna en ti : llegó el momento
de la revelación ; llena los altos
destinos a que el cielo te encamina ;
cúmplanse sus decretos soberanos."

Tales palabras, del turbado joven
el corazón confuso reanimaron ;
lumbre de gloria relució en sus ojos,
cesó de pronto su abatido espanto ;

sintió su sangre hervir, miró el anillo,
el misterioso anillo que la mano
adornó de Zahira ; estremecióse,
y la diestra estrechó del viejo sabio.

Éste, resuelto, " sígueme ", le dice ;
" ven conmigo al jardín, y de los astros
allí en presencia, con el fiero adorno
de esas ropas, que sangre están manando,

" y con esa invencible cimitarra
firme en tu diestra, escucha de mi labio
la maldad de los hombres, los desastres
que presidieron a tu origen claro,

" y la alta obligación que el cielo impuso
a tu nacer. El tiempo no perdamos,
pues debes para siempre estas riberas
dejar antes que el sol tienda sus rayos."

¡ Ay ! . . . Las palabras últimas de Zaide
el pecho de Mudarra traspasaron.
Tembló, fijó la planta, quedó inmoble,
y un suspiro lanzó. Viéndole el ayo,

con gran resolución y fuerte diestra
le ase y sacude la siniestra mano,
y " ¡ Oh Mudarra ! . . . ¡ oh Mudarra ! . . . en este instante
no vil temblor, esfuerzo es necesario ",

grítale, y ante sí firme le impele :
y entrambos pasan del castillo el atrio,
y en gran silencio, del jardín caminan
por las calles de adelfas y naranjos.

Llegan a un sitio de él, donde sus puntas
siete cipreses jóvenes alzando,
una cuadrada losa circundaban
bruñida y sin emblema ni epitafio :

sitio donde Mudarra muchas veces,
con la atención de los primeros años
del docto Zaide oyó doctos consejos,
y de honra y de virtud sublimes rasgos;

y do siempre curioso preguntara
lo que guardaba aquel pulido mármol,
recibiendo tan sólo por respuesta
tiernas caricias, lágrimas y abrazos.

Páranse, pues, allí; sobre la losa
se asientan mudos y abatidos ambos,
y alza la faz al vaporoso cielo,
sin prorrumpir palabra, el noble anciano.

Su marchito semblante iluminaba,
por la cándida barba resbalando,
el claror de la luna, que triunfante
de las nubes reinaba en el espacio.

Su venerable rostro las señales,
y los ojos de lágrimas preñados,
daban de quien recuerda atroces hechos
y le falta la voz para contarlos.

Mudarra en sus facciones juveniles,
vuelta la espalda al disco plateado,
de obscuridad cubiertas, escondía
inquietud, atención, dolor y espanto.

Estaba el viento en calma; blandamente
el aura hería los desnudos ramos;
reinaba hondo silencio; pero Zaide
rompiólo al fin . . . . . .

226. *Lara y las Siete Cabezas*

Zaide relates how Lara, in prison, is visited by Giafar, who announces that he has a present for him. This proves to be the heads of his seven sons. Mudarra starts up in horror at this unexpected climax to the story.

The passage, which illustrates Rivas' rather crude and prolix handling of the horrible and grotesque, may be compared with the ballad-version of the same incident on pp. 128-30, above.

Quedando en pie Mudarra, hondo suspiro
arrojó Zaide, y con cansada lengua
anudó el hilo de la horrible historia,
y prosiguió en decir de esta manera :

" Sí, el noble Lara, el desdichado padre
vió de sus siete hijos las cabezas
encima del bufete, en una fila,
y por orden de edad, ¡ ay triste ! puestas.

" Aunque desfiguradas y espantables,
cual de lejos traídas, y entre yerbas,
espíritus y sales conservadas,
distinguió en cada cual las propias señas.

" En estatua de hielo convertido,
fijos los ojos, sin moverse, en ellas,
y los latidos del hinchado pecho
dando tan sólo en él de vida muestras,

" quedó Lara infeliz . . . ¡ Ah ! ¿ cómo puede
mi débil voz la situación horrenda
con palabras pintar ? . . . Padre es preciso,
padre es preciso ser para entenderla.

" Un esclavo que oculto allí con otros,
por orden de Giafar, estaba alerta,
mil veces me ha contado de aquel día
hasta las circunstancias más pequeñas.

" Sin habla Gustios, o mejor, sin vida,
estuvo sin moverse una gran pieza :
luego un temblor ligero, imperceptible
apareció en sus miembros, y en violenta

" convulsión terminó ; pero tornando
a la inmovilidad, gira y pasea
los ojos, cual los ojos de un espectro,
por una y otra de las siete prendas.

" Sonrisa amarga agita un breve instante
sus labios sin color, y en tanto queman
sus mejillas dos lágrimas, y luego
los tiernos hijos a nombrar comienza,

"los ojos enclavando en el que nombra,
y esperando tal vez, ¡ ay ! su respuesta :
¡ Diego ! . . ¡ Martín ! . . ¡ Fernando ! . . ¡ Suero ! . . ¡ Enrico !
¡ Veremundo ! . . *¡ Gonzalo !* . . y cuando llega

"a este nombre, dos veces lo repite ;
y recobrando esfuerzo y vida nueva,
entrambas manos trémulas extiende,
agarra de Gonzalo la cabeza,

"y la alza ; pero al verla sin el cuerpo,
un grito arroja y súbito la suelta,
cual si hecha de encendido hierro fuese.
Empero torna a asirla, se la lleva

"a los labios, y un beso en la insensible
mejilla imprime. . . . La frialdad horrenda,
la ascosa fetidez sufrir no pudo,
y como cuerpo muerto cayó en tierra.

"Aquel resto infeliz del hijo suyo
cayó sobre su pecho, y desde él rueda
por la alfombra, dejando sucio rastro
de sangre helada, corrompida y negra.

"Ni aun Giafar, ya saciado de venganza,
pudo aguantar más tiempo tal escena ;
y huyó a esconderse cual se esconde el tigre,
cansado de exterminio, en su caverna."

227. *Córdoba y Burgos en el siglo décimo*

The title here given to this extract, which introduces Canto VI, is the sub-title of the entire poem. The Moro expósito *was intended to be, not only the amplification of a mediaeval legend, but also a tale of two cities. The civilization of Moorish Córdoba (Rivas' birthplace) is contrasted, greatly to its advantage, with that of Christian Burgos : the author is thus enabled to vary his local colour as well as to make full use of the Romantic device of antithesis.*

The interpolation of the personal note (ll. 17 ff.) is highly characteristic both of Rivas and of romanticism in Spain : an even more striking example occurs in Espronceda's Diablo Mundo *(p. 500). The richness of detail hardly needs emphasis. More colour might perhaps have been expected, but one of the curious features of Rivas' colour-scheme, here illustrated, is his predilection for white.*[1] *The most striking characteristic of the passage, however, is the impression it conveys of a contrast which the author both imagines and feels.*

Otra escena se ofrece ante mis ojos :
ya no son las florestas y campiñas
por donde el curso majestuoso extiende
Guadalquivir, gran rey de Andalucía ;

ni la sierra feraz que al puro cielo,
ignorando que hay nieve, alza la cima
de peñascos y musgo coronada,
de flores odorantes y de olivas ;

mientras verjeles, huertas y jardines
sus deliciosas faldas entapizan,
embalsamando el vaporoso ambiente,
que azahares y jazmín blando respira ;

ni la insigne ciudad, cuyo alto nombre,
gigantesco poder y gloria antigua
la fama ensalza, las historias cuentan,
y su templo y sus muros testifican.

¡ Córdoba insigne ! . . . ¡ Oh patria, dulce patria !
en cuyo seno de la luz del día
gocé la primer vez, en cuyo seno
disfruté el tierno amor y las caricias,

tesoro de la infancia. Si en tus bosques,
encantadas llanuras y colinas,
de mi niñez y juventud llenaron
las horas, que han pasado fugitivas,

de tu grandeza insigne los recuerdos,
volando en torno de la mente mía
las sombras de tus héroes generosos,
cual de una planta nueva en torno giran

las mariposas del risueño Mayo
jamás mi amor a ti, jamás se entibia,
ni de mi pensamiento un punto sales,
desde que arrastro en extranjeros climas

[1] Cf. E. Allison Peers : *Rivas, a Critical Study*, New York, Paris, 1923, pp. 309-13.

la vida, ha tantos años sustentada
con el amargo pan de la desdicha,
y aun más con la esperanza de que al cabo
logren en ti reposo mis cenizas.

Tú reinas en mi pecho, aunque mi mente,
de tus héroes en pos, hoy por distintas
tierras se espacie y por remotos siglos,
sus hazañas buscando esclarecidas.

Sí, de Mudarra y del prudente Zaide
se arroja en pos mi suelta fantasía,
del imperio andaluz salva los lindes,
y vuela por los campos de Castilla.

Obscuro el cielo entre reacias nubes,
y entre nieblas oculto blanquecinas ;
desnudo el suelo, donde invierno crudo
su rigor y sus sañas ejercita ;

y un horizonte de hórridas montañas,
que con peñascos áridos se erizan,
do nacen sólo verdinegros pinos,
y que abruman las nieves me lo indican.

Allí el Arlanza, allí : si en el estío
ufano se corona con espigas,
ahora entre hielos ásperos sus aguas,
turbias y perezosas se deslizan.

Ya la ciudad descubro belicosa,
que es de los Condes castellanos silla.
¡ De la corte de Hixcen el poderoso,
en todo cuán diversa y cuán distinta !

No, cual Córdoba, al cielo de zafiro
alza opulenta las gallardas cimbrias
Burgos naciente, ni de mármol y oro
alminares altísimos empina.

Gruesos muros levanta y torreones
de tosca piedra, donde el sol no brilla ;
pero que a las tormentas y huracanes,
y al furor de la guerra desafían.

No de riquezas bárbaras henchidos
sus palacios están, ni de exquisitas
telas del rico Oriente entapizados,
ni el regalo y las ciencias los habitan.

No suena, al despuntar la clara aurora,
la voz del almuhedén, que el nuevo día
anunciando a los hombres, a que acudan
con sus ruegos al templo les convida.

En su lugar la atmósfera ensordecen
gruesas campanas de metal, que vibran
melancólicos sones, convocando
a celebrar las prácticas divinas.

No en las calles la voz de las escuelas
se escucha, ni el bullicio y alegría
en abundantes plazas, ni el estruendo
de talleres, telares y oficinas ;

sólo resuena en Burgos el martillo
que sobre el duro ayunque se ejercita,
en arneses tornando el fuerte acero,
ya templado en las fraguas encendidas ;

el monótono canto de los coros
de conventos, parroquias y capillas,
y el confuso rumor de un pueblo pobre
y taciturno, que en las calles gira.

Y los campos. . . . ¡ Oh Dios, cuán diferentes !
allá los labradores en cuadrilla,
casi desnudos, y cantando ledos
tras de los tardos bueyes fecundizan

los pingües sulcos, y feraz cosecha,
premio de su sudor, segura miran ;
mientras pobre gañán aquí, luchando
con tierra ingrata y con adusto clima,

en pos de ágiles mulas rompe el suelo,
temiendo de su afán y su fatiga
el fruto ver en su verdor talado
por invasoras huestes enemigas ;

o robado si no, cuando maduro,
por el monje sagaz, por la codicia
del tirano señor, o con violencia
por foragidos que en el monte habitan.

Finalmente, aquel siglo el sol eterno
en las tierras de Betis descubría
un imperio ilustrado y poderoso,
una grande nación, acorde y rica,

ya en la alta cumbre, y anunciando acaso
su próximo descenso y su rüina
el supremo poder de sus monarcas
y del pueblo el amor a las delicias;

y en la que Arlanza con sus aguas mide,
un estado naciente, una conquista,
gobierno sin vigor, inciertas leyes,
crasa ignorancia a la pobreza unida,

bandos feroces; mas tan noble brío,
constancia tal y tanta valentía,
que presagiaban la grandeza inmensa
que los cielos guardaban a Castilla.

ROMANCES HISTÓRICOS

228. *El Alcázar de Sevilla*

In Rivas' Romances históricos, *much more than in the mediaeval* romances, *description blends with action. The first canto of* "*El Alcázar de Sevilla*", *here reproduced, is pure description, and the story—the murder of Don Fadrique by Peter the Cruel—does not begin till the third and last. Once again we find the personal note intruding into a description which is purely picturesque, leading in the most leisurely way to a point (l. 101) at which the atmosphere—a typically Romantic atmosphere—can be created.*

Magnífico es el Alcázar
con que se ilustra Sevilla,
deliciosos sus jardines,
su excelsa portada rica.

De maderos entallados
en mil labores prolijas,
se levanta el frontispicio
de resaltadas cornisas ;

y hay en ellas un letrero
donde, con letras antiguas,
Don Pedro hizo estos palacios
esculpido se divisa.

Mal dicen en sus salones
las modernas fruslerías ;
mal en sus soberbios patios
gente sin barba y ropilla.

¡ Cuántas apacibles tardes,
en la grata compañía
de chistosos sevillanos
y de sevillanas lindas,

recorrí aquellos verjeles,
en cuya entrada se miran
gigantes de arrayán hechos
con actitudes distintas !

Las adelfas y naranjos
forman calles extendidas,
y un obscuro laberinto
que a los hurtos de amor brinda.

Hay en tierra surtidores
escondidos ; se improvisan,
saltando entre los mosaicos
de pintadas piedrecillas,

y a los forasteros mojan,
con algazara y con risa
de los que ya escarmentados
el chasco pesado evitan.

En las tardes del estío,
cuando al ocaso declina
el sol entre leves nubes,
que de oro y grana matiza ;

aquel trasparente cielo
con ráfagas purpurinas,
cortado por un celaje
que el céfiro manso riza ;

aquella atmósfera ardiente
en que fuego se respira,
¡ qué languidez dan al cuerpo !
¡ qué temple al alma divina !

De los baños, tan famosos
por quien los gozó, la vista,
la del soberbio edificio,
obra gótica y morisca,

tétrico en partes, en partes
alegre, y en el que indican
los dominios diferentes,
ya reparos, ya ruinas ;

con recuerdos y memorias
de las edades antiguas
y de los modernos años,
embargan la fantasía.

El azahar y los jazmines,
que si los ojos hechizan,
embalsaman el ambiente
con los aromas que espiran ;

de las fuentes el murmurio,
la lejana gritería
que de la ciudad, del río,
de la alameda contigua

de Triana y de la puente
confusa llega y perdida,
con el son de las campanas
que en la alta Giralda vibran ;

forman un todo encantado,
que nunca jamás se olvida,
y que, al recordarlo, siempre
mi alma y corazón palpitan.

Muchas deliciosas noches,
cuando aún ardiente latía
mi ya helado pecho, alegres,
de concurrencia escogida

vi aquellos salones llenos ;
y a la juventud, cuadrillas
o contradanzas bailando
al son de orquestas festivas.

En las doradas techumbres
los pasos, la charla y risas
de las parejas gallardas,
por amor tal vez unidas,

con el son de los violines
confundidos se extendían,
acordes ecos hallando
por las esmaltadas cimbrias.

Mas ¡ ay ! aquellos pensiles
no he pisado un solo día,
sin ver (¡ sueños de mi mente !)
la sombra de la Padilla,

lanzando un hondo gemido,
cruzar leve ante mi vista,
como un vapor, como un humo,
que entre los árboles gira ;

ni entré en aquellos salones,
sin figurárseme erguida,
del fundador la fantasma
en helada sangre tinta :

ni en el vestíbulo obscuro,
el que tiene en la cornisa
de los reyes los retratos,
el que en columnas estriba,

al que adornan azulejos
abajo, y esmalte arriba,
el que muestra en cada muro
un rico balcón, y encima

el hondo artesón dorado,
que lo corona y atrista,
sin ver en tierra un cadáver.
Aún en las losas se mira

una tenaz mancha obscura. . . .
¡ Ni las edades la limpian ! . . .
¡ Sangre ! ! ¡ Sangre ! ! . . . ¡ Oh cielos, cuántos
sin saber lo que es la pisan !

229. *Los Dos Hermanos*

The final stanzas of the poem " El Fratricidio " tell how, after his defeat at Montiel by his half-brother, Henry of Trastamara, Peter the Cruel was trapped by Henry and slain in a duel. They give a good idea of Rivas' lively narrative style, marred, to modern ears, by the fantastic expressions common in such contexts, but vivid and realistic to a degree. " Claquín " is the French knight Bertrand du Guesclin, who enters into the story disguised as a priest.

Ni Enrique a Pedro conoce,
ni Pedro a Enrique : apartólos
el cielo hace muchos años,
años de agravios y enconos,

un mar de rugiente sangre,
de huesos un promontorio,
de crímenes un abismo
poniendo entre el uno y otro.

Don Enrique fué el primero
que con satánico tono,
" ¿ Quién de estos dos es," prorrumpe,
" el objeto de mis odios ? "

" Vil bastardo," le responde
Don Pedro iracundo y torvo,
" yo soy tu Rey ; tiembla, aleve ;
hunde tu frente en el polvo."

Se embisten los dos hermanos ;
y don Enrique, furioso
como tigre embravecido,
hiere a don Pedro en el rostro.

Don Pedro, cual león rugiente,
¡ Traidor ! grita ; por los ojos
lanza infernal fuego, abraza
a su armado hermano, como

a la colmena ligera
feroz y forzudo el oso,
y traban lucha espantosa
que el mundo contempla absorto.

Caen al suelo, se revuelcan,
se hieren de un lado y otro,
la tierra inundan en sangre,
lidian cual canes rabiosos.

Se destrozan, se maldicen,
dagas, dientes, uñas, todo
es de aquellos dos hermanos
a saciar la furia poco.

Pedro a Enrique al cabo pone
debajo, y se apresta ansioso,
de su crueldad o justicia
a dar nuevo testimonio ;

cuando Claquín (¡ oh desgracia !
en nuestros debates propios
siempre ha de haber extranjeros
que decidan a su antojo),

cuando Claquín, trastornando
la suerte, llega de pronto,
sujeta a don Pedro, y pone
sobre él a Enrique alevoso,

diciendo el aventurero
de tal maldad en abono :
" Sirvo en esto a mi señor ;
ni rey quito, ni rey pongo."

No duró más el combate ;
de su rey en lo más hondo
del corazón, la corona
busca Enrique, hunde hasta el pomo

el acero fratricida,
y con él el puño todo
para asegurarse de ella,
para agarrarla furioso.

Y la sacó . . . goteando
¡ ¡ ¡ sangre ! ! ! . . . De funesto gozo
retumbó en el campo un *viva*,
y el infierno repitiólo.

JOSÉ MARÍA DE HEREDIA

1803-1839

A CUBAN, who lived in Spain during the years immediately preceding the brief vogue of the Romantic movement, Heredia (not to be confused with the Frenchman of the same name, who wrote *Les Trophées*) is remembered chiefly for his poem "Niágara" (1824). Conceived and executed though it is (and by no means unsuccessfully) in the grand manner of the literary age that was drawing to a close, it exhibits all the marks of pre-Romantic poetry: in places, for a poem of its type and epoch, it has remarkable power. This seems to depend much less on a technique which the author had apparently studied with some care (e.g., the alliteration in *t*(*r*) of ll. 9-11 contrasting with that in *m* of ll. 12-13 and echoing a contrast of sense) than upon an unusual success in the choice of appropriate language. The principal effect of both technique and vocabulary, however, is cumulative, deriving from the momentum of the rhythm and the weight of the grandiose imagery. The purely descriptive passages have more force than their moral application, which, though meant no doubt to serve as a climax, errs through being over-emphatic and rhetorical. The final stanzas are disproportionately subjective, and the concluding lines, in sentiment though not in form, are weak.

230. *Niágara*[1]

Dadme[2] mi lira, dádmela, que siento
en mi alma estremecida y agitada
arder la inspiración. ¡Oh! ¡cuánto tiempo
en tinieblas pasó, sin que mi frente
brillase con su luz! . . . Niágara undoso,
sola tu faz sublime ya podría[3]
tornarme el don divino, que ensañada
me robó del dolor la mano impía.

[1] The orthographic variants found in the edition of 1832 (see p. 715, below) are given in the following footnotes.

[2] Templad.

[3] Tu sublime terror sólo podría.

Torrente prodigioso, calma, acalla[1]
tu trueno aterrador: disipa un tanto
las tinieblas que en torno te circundan,
y[2] déjame mirar[3] tu faz serena,
y de entusiasmo ardiente mi alma llena.
Yo digno soy de contemplarte: siempre,
lo común y mezquino desdeñando,
ansié por lo terrífico y sublime.
Al despeñarse el huracán furioso,
al retumbar sobre mi frente el rayo,
palpitando gocé: vi al Oceano
azotado del[4] austro proceloso
combatir mi bajel, y ante mis plantas
sus abismos abrir,[5] y amé el peligro,[6]
y sus iras amé: mas su fiereza
en mi alma no dejara
la profunda impresión que tu grandeza.

Corres sereno y majestuoso,[7] y luego
en ásperos peñascos quebrantado,
te abalanzas violento, arrebatado,
como el destino irresistible y ciego.
¿ Qué voz humana describir podría
de la sirte rugiente
la aterradora faz? El alma mía
en vagos pensamientos[8] se confunde,
al contemplar la[9] férvida corriente,
que en vano quiere la turbada vista
en su vuelo seguir al borde ancho[10]
del precipicio altísimo: mil olas,
cual pensamiento rápidas pasando,
chocan y se enfurecen,
y otras mil y otras mil ya las alcanzan,
y entre espuma y fragor desaparecen.
Mas llegan . . . saltan . . . el[11] abismo horrendo

[1] calla. [2] *Omits* y. [3] contemplar. [4] por.

[5] vórtice hirviente abrir. [6] *Continues*: . . . . el peligro.
Mas del mar la fiereza
en mi alma no produjo . . . .

[7] Sereno corres, majestuoso.

[8] en vago pensamiento. [9] al mirar esa. [10] obscuro.

[11] *Begins a new stanza and reads*: ¡ Ved ! ¡ llegan, saltan ! El . . . .

devora los torrentes despeñados;
crúzanse en él mil iris, y asordados
vuelven los bosques el fragor tremendo.
Al golpe violentísimo en las peñas[1]
rómpese el agua,[2] y salta, y una nube
de revueltos vapores
cubre el abismo en remolinos, sube,
gira en torno, y al cielo
cual pirámide inmensa se levanta,
y por sobre los bosques[3] que le cercan
al solitario cazador espanta.

Mas ¿ qué en ti busca mi anhelante vista
con inquieto afanar ?[4] ¿ Por qué no miro
alrededor de tu caverna inmensa
las palmas ¡ ay ! las palmas deliciosas,
que en las llanuras de mi ardiente patria
nacen del sol a la sonrisa, y crecen,
y al soplo de la brisa[5] del Océano
bajo un cielo purísimo se mecen ?

Este recuerdo a mi pesar me viene. . . .
Nada ¡ oh Niágara ! falta a tu destino,
ni otra corona que el agreste pino
a tu terrible majestad conviene.
La palma, y mirto, y delicada rosa,
muelle placer inspiren y ocio blando
en frívolo jardín : a ti la suerte
guardó más digno objeto y más[6] sublime.
El alma libre, generosa y fuerte[7]
viene, te ve, se asombra.
Menosprecia los frívolos deleites,[8]
y aun se siente elevar cuando te nombra.

[1] En las rígidas peñas.

[2] *Continues* : . . . . el agua : vaporosa nube
con elástica fuerza
llena el abismo en torbellino, sube,
gira en torno, y al éter
luminosa pirámide levanta . . . .

[3] montes.

[4] con inútil afán ?

[5] las brisas.

[6] objeto, más.

[7] generosa, fuerte.

[8] El mezquino deleite menosprecia.

¡ Dios, Dios de la verdad ![1] En otros climas
[vi monstruos execrables,
blasfemando tu nombre sacrosanto,
sembrar error y fanatismo impío,
los campos inundar en sangre y llanto,
de hermanos atizar la infanda guerra,
y desolar frenéticos la tierra.
Vilos, y el pecho se inflamó a su vista
en grave indignación. Por otra parte][2]
vi mentidos filósofos, que osaban
escrutar tus misterios, ultrajarte,
y de impiedad al lamentable abismo
a los míseros hombres arrastraban :
por eso siempre te buscó mi mente[3]
en la sublime soledad : ahora
entera se abre a ti ; tu mano siente
en esta inmensidad que me circunda,
y tu profunda voz baja a mi seno[4]
de este raudal en el eterno trueno.

¡ Asombroso torrente !
¡ Cómo tu vista mi[5] ánimo enajena
y de terror y admiración me llena !
¿ Dó tu origen está ? ¿ Quién fertiliza
por tantos siglos tu inexhausta fuente ?
¿ Qué poderosa mano
hace que al recibirte
no rebose en la tierra el Oceano ?

Abrió el Señor su mano omnipotente,
cubrió tu faz de nubes agitadas,
dió su voz a tus aguas despeñadas
y ornó con su arco tu terrible frente.[6]

Miro tus aguas que incansables corren,
como el largo torrente de los siglos

[1] ¡ Omnipotente Dios !

[2] *The bracketed lines are not in the 1st edition.*

[3] por eso te buscó mi débil mente.

[4] hiere mi seno.

[5] el.

[6] *Continues, without indentation* :
¡ Ciego, profundo, infatigable corres,
como el torrente obscuro de los siglos
en insondable eternidad ! . . . . ¡ Al hombre
huyen así las ilusiones gratas,
los florecientes días
y despierta al dolor !

rueda en la eternidad : así del hombre
pasan volando los floridos días,
y despierta al dolor. . . . ¡ Ay ! ya[1] agostada
siento mi juventud, mi faz marchita,[2]
y la profunda pena que me agita
ruga mi frente de dolor nublada.

Nunca tanto sentí como este día
mi mísero aislamiento, mi abandono,[3]
mi[4] lamentable desamor. . . . ¿ Podría[5]
una alma apasionada y borrascosa
sin amor ser feliz ? . . . ¡ Oh ! ¡ Si una hermosa
digna de mí me amase
y de este abismo al borde turbulento
mi vago pensamiento
y mi andar solitario[6] acompañase !
¡ Cuál gozara al mirar su faz cubrirse[7]
de leve palidez, y ser más bella
en su dulce terror, y sonreírse
al sostenerla en[8] mis amantes brazos ! . . .
¡ Delirios de virtud ! . . . ¡ Ay ! desterrado,
sin patria, sin amores,
sólo miro ante mí llanto y dolores.

¡ Niágara poderoso !
Oye mi última voz : en pocos años[9]
ya devorado habrá la tumba fría
a tu débil cantor. ¡ Duren mis versos
cual tu gloria inmortal ! Pueda piadoso,
al contemplar tu faz algún viajero,[10]
dar un suspiro a la memoria mía.
Y yo, al hundirse el sol en Occidente,
vuele gozoso do el Criador me llama,[11]
y al escuchar los ecos de mi fama
alce en las nubes la radiosa frente.

[1] *Omits* ya. [2] yace mi juventud ; mi faz, marchita ; [3] mi soledad y mísero abandono.

[4] y. [5] *Continues* : en edad borrascosa
sin amor ser feliz ? ¡ Oh ! si una hermosa
mi cariño fijase,

[6] y ardiente admiración. [7] ¡ Cómo gozara, viéndola cubrirse. [8] *Omits* en.

[9] ¡ Adiós ! ¡ Adiós ! Dentro de pocos años. [10] viéndote algún viajero. [11] Y al abismarse Febo en occidente,
feliz yo vuele do el Señor me llama.

JUAN AROLAS
1805-1849

Of the minor Romantics, Arolas, a Valencian priest who wrote more than one would have expected about love, and died insane, is remembered chiefly for his *Orientales* and neo-mediaeval ballads. These, by their energy and zest, recall Rivas, and by their colour, Zorrilla. Critics have also compared Arolas with Chateaubriand, and in a number of passages he plagiarizes Hugo, Lamartine and Byron. He is not, then, a very original genius; yet in his day he was popular for the richness of his language, for the lilt of his varied metres and for the florid and somewhat superficial brilliance of his imagination.

231. *A una Bella*

It is in Arolas' love-lyrics that we see most of the man. Though in the main they conform to his usual florid style, they are more subjective than the mediaeval and oriental poems and simpler and more apparently sincere than those inspired by religion. In this, one of the most familiar of them, a typically Romantic melancholy blends with imagery of exotic languor to produce a curious effect of remoteness, while a somewhat Lamartinian use of the refrain enhances the emotion of the poem and gives it unity.

Sobre pupila azul con sueño leve
tu párpado cayendo amortecido
se parece a la pura y blanca nieve
que sobre las violetas reposó.
Yo el sueño del placer nunca he dormido:
Sé más feliz que yo.

Se asemeja tu voz en la plegaria
al canto del zorzal de indiano suelo,
que sobre la pagoda solitaria
los himnos de la tarde suspiró.
Yo sólo esta oración dirijo al cielo :
"Sé más feliz que yo."

Es tu aliento la esencia más fragante
de los lirios del Arno caudaloso,
que brotan sobre un junco vacilante
cuando el céfiro blando los meció.
Yo no gozo su aroma delicioso :
Sé más feliz que yo.

El amor, que es espíritu de fuego
que de callada noche se aconseja
y se nutre con lágrimas y ruego
en tus purpúreos labios se escondió.
Él te guarde el placer y a mí la queja :
Sé más feliz que yo.

Bella es tu juventud en sus albores
como un campo de rosas del Oriente ;
al ángel del recuerdo pedí flores
para adornar tu sien, y me las dió.
Yo decía al ponerlas en tu frente :
"Sé más feliz que yo."

Tu mirada vivaz es de paloma :
como la adormidera del desierto
causa dulce embriaguez, hurí de aroma
que el cielo de topacio abandonó.
Mi suerte es dura, mi destino incierto :
Sé más feliz que yo.

232. *La hermosa Halewa*

Though not perhaps one of the best, this is certainly a highly typical "Oriental", the characteristics of which are so obvious that they need no enumeration. In a poem of this kind we are taken back for the first time (if Zorrilla is considered as later than Arolas) to the florid, colour-laden magnificence of Herrera and Espinosa, though Arolas lacks both the restraint of these and their power. Atmosphere is given by the lavish use of local colour, the crudity of which (as of other sensuous impressions) reflects the crudity, not to say violence, of the theme.

El prudente Almanzor, Emir glorioso,
el Cordobés imperio dirigía ;
Hixén su rey en el harén dichoso
los blandos sueños del placer dormía.

Cisnes de oro purísimo, labrados
sobre conchas de pórfido en las fuentes,
en medio de jardines regalados
derramaban las linfas transparentes.

Los limpios baños de marmóreas pilas
do el agua pura mil esencias toma
cercaban lirios y agrupadas lilas
de tintas bellas y profuso aroma.

Damascos y alcatifas tunecinas
del palacio adornaban los salones,
perlas en colgaduras purpurinas,
perlas en recamados almohadones.

Olores del Arabia respiraban
lechos de blanda pluma en los retretes
y las fuentes de plata reflejaban
del alcázar los altos minaretes.

Del regio templo celebrada diosa,
Halewa fué en su plácida fortuna
ídolo del monarca por hermosa,
tierna como una lágrima en la cuna.

Feliz si de un esclavo que sabía
enamorar con trova cariñosa
más amor no aprendiera que armonía
al son del arpa dulce y sonorosa.

Iba el docto mancebo modulando
los ayes del amor en vario tono,
la bella favorita suspirando
hizo el primer desprecio al regio trono.

Un día. . . . Nunca el sol su rayo activo
lanzó con más ardor, ni más hermoso
fué el pensil y la sombra del olivo,
para gozar del celestial reposo.

Sediento del halago y del cariño,
buscaba Hixén los suspirados lazos
y cual sus juegos inocente niño,
apetecía el rey tiernos abrazos.

¡ Infeliz ! ¡ ah ! repara aquella rosa
que el roedor insecto ha deshojado,
no muevas, no, la planta vagarosa ;
la tumba del dolor está a tu lado.

Vió en la gruta que al fin de los andenes
se cubre con la hiedra trepadora,
dormir con frescas rosas en las sienes
la inconstante beldad que el pecho adora.

Vió dormido al esclavo : frescas flores
coronaban su sien ; su labio impuro
en sueños murmuraba sus amores
y el desliz de otro labio más perjuro.

El arpa sobre el césped olvidada
con el viento sus fibras conmovía .
y de su docto dueño enamorada
parece que lloraba su agonía.

Ruge el león y silva la serpiente
por ofendido amor, la mujer llora
y el hombre con la sangre delincuente
lava el torpe baldón que le desdora.

Suspira Hixén ; su corazón desgarra
una furia infernal ; su mano lleva
al puño de la corva cimitarra
y abre los ojos la infeliz Halewa.

Los abre para ver el golpe airado
contra el siervo que amaba su belleza,
el lívido cadáver a su lado
y fuera de los hombros la cabeza.

Sangre vió en su vestido y en su velo,
que en sangre se tiñó la gruta y senda
al rodar la cabeza por el suelo
en temblor frío y convulsión horrenda.

A lóbrega mazmorra es arrastrada
por seis esclavos negros. ¡ Ah ! su lloro
de aljófar puro y tímida mirada
no pueden doblegar a esquivo moro.

La nueva luz del nebuloso día
vió en la punta de un palo en los jardines
la cabeza del siervo horrenda y fría
y con gotas de sangre los jazmines.

JOSÉ DE ESPRONCEDA

1808-1842

TEMPERAMENTALLY, Espronceda was far more of a Romantic than Rivas, and, being considerably younger, he was never (despite the influence of his schoolmaster, Alberto Lista) so thoroughly grounded in pseudo-classicism. His passion for freedom, his surrender of judgment to impulse, and his love of rebellion make his entire life a Romantic poem—

un poema
con lances raros y revuelto asunto.[1]

In his verse (and he wrote little but lyrical and narrative poetry), imagination, spontaneity, inconsequence of theme and tone, indifference to convention and predilection for experiment make him the almost perfect Romantic—in practice, that is to say, for of literary theories he had none. The keys to his attitude towards life are restlessness, cynicism and disillusion, which, with certain minor traits, make up what it is customary to call Byronism. Though in many ways careless of form, he was a natural artist, and he has some noteworthy effects in metre and diction. It was a sad loss to literature when he died, worn out by the intensity of his living, at thirty-four.

233. *Canción del Pirata*

It would have taken more than the timid metrical innovations of Arjona to prepare the public for this breezy kind of verse which, early in the short career of the Romantic review El Artista *(1835), began to blow through its pages. So much variety, in metre and in spirit, could seldom have been packed into so short a poem. With the placid introductory* octavillas *contrasts the brusque manner of the pirate captain, conveyed in short, sharp lines and in two alternating*

[1] *El Diablo Mundo*, Canto I. *Ed. cit.*, p. 389.

measures. Yet note how this type of stanza, with its eight lines and its two agudo *endings, can convey, not only bluntness and truculence (ll. 23-30) or a devil-may-care courage (ll. 71-8), but also (ll. 90-3) a totally unexpected languor. This poem alone must have made it clear to the Spanish public that there had appeared a young artist of extraordinary promise.*

Con diez cañones por banda,
viento en popa, a toda vela,
no corta el mar, sino vuela
un velero bergantín :
bajel pirata que llaman
por su bravura el *Temido*,
en todo mar conocido
del uno al otro confín.

La luna en el mar riela,
en la lona gime el viento,
y alza en blando movimiento
olas de plata y azul ;
y ve el capitán pirata,
cantando alegre en la popa,
Asia a un lado, al otro Europa,
y allá a su frente Stambul.

" Navega, velero mío,
sin temor,
que ni enemigo navío,
ni tormenta, ni bonanza
tu rumbo a torcer alcanza,
ni a sujetar tu valor.

" Veinte presas
hemos hecho
a despecho
del inglés,
y han rendido
sus pendones
cien naciones
a mis pies.

" *Que es mi barco mi tesoro,*
que es mi Dios la libertad,
mi ley la fuerza y el viento,
mi única patria la mar.

" Allá muevan feroz guerra
ciegos reyes
por un palmo más de tierra ;
que yo tengo aquí por mío
cuanto abarca el mar bravío,
a quien nadie impuso leyes.

" Y no hay playa,
sea cualquiera,
ni bandera
de esplendor,
que no sienta
mi derecho
y dé pecho
a mi valor.

" *Que es mi barco mi tesoro. . . .*

" A la voz de '¡ barco viene ! '
es de ver
cómo vira y se previene
a todo trapo a escapar ;
que yo soy el rey del mar,
y mi furia es de temer.

" En las presas
yo divido
lo cogido
por igual :
sólo quiero
por riqueza
la belleza
sin rival.

" *Que es mi barco mi tesoro. . . .*

" ¡ Sentenciado estoy a muerte !
Yo me río :
no me abandone la suerte,

y al mismo que me condena
colgaré de alguna entena,
quizá en su propio navío.

" Y si caigo
¿ qué es la vida ?
Por perdida
ya la di,
cuando el yugo
del esclavo,
como un bravo,
sacudí.

" *Que es mi barco mi tesoro. . . .*

" Son mi música mejor
aquilones ;
el estrépito y temblor
de los cables sacudidos ;
del negro mar los bramidos
y el rugir de mis cañones.

" Y del trueno
al son violento,
y del viento
al rebramar,
yo me duermo
sosegado,
arrullado
por el mar.

" *Que es mi barco mi tesoro,*
que es mi Dios la libertad,
mi ley la fuerza y el viento,
mi única patria la mar."

234. *El Mendigo*

Like the pirate, the beggar was a common type in Romantic literature, but a pathetic, sentimental type, far removed from this bold, indolent, open-air beggar, first cousin to the pirate, a rebel in whom the most pronounced individualism blends with an ironic humour.

Though the metrical innovations of this poem, also first published in 1835, were even more striking than those of the "Canción del Pirata", it is in the conception of the beggar himself that its chief originality resides.

Mío es el mundo: como el aire libre,
otros trabajan porque coma yo:
todos se ablandan si doliente pido
una limosna por amor de Dios.

El palacio, la cabaña
son mi asilo,
si del ábrego el furor
troncha el roble en la montaña,
o que inunda la campaña
el torrente asolador.

Y a la hoguera
me hacen lado
los pastores
con amor,
y sin pena
y descüidado
de su cena
ceno yo;
o en la rica
chimenea,
que recrea
con su olor,
me regalo
codicioso
del banquete
suntüoso
con las sobras
de un señor.

Y me digo: el viento brama,
caiga furioso turbión;
que al son que cruje de la seca leña,
libre me duermo sin rencor ni amor.

Mío es el mundo: como el aire libre. . . .

Todos son mis bienhechores,
y por todos
a Dios ruego con fervor ;
de villanos y señores
yo recibo los favores
sin estima y sin amor.

Ni pregunto
quiénes sean,
ni me obligo
a agradecer ;
que mis rezos
si desean,
dar limosna
es un deber.
Y es pecado
la riqueza ;
la pobreza
santidad :
Dios a veces
es mendigo,
y al avaro
da castigo,
que le niegue
caridad.

Yo soy pobre y se lastiman
todos al verme plañir,
sin ver son mías sus riquezas todas,
que mina inagotable es el pedir.

Mío es el mundo : como el aire libre. . . .

Mal revuelto y andrajoso,
entre harapos
del lujo sátira soy,
y con mi aspecto asqueroso
me vengo del poderoso,
y adonde va, tras él voy.

Y a la hermosa
que respira
cien perfumes,

gala, amor,
la persigo
hasta que mira,
y me gozo
cuando aspira
mi punzante
mal olor.
Y las fiestas
y el contento
con mi acento
turbo yo,
y en la bulla
y la alegría
interrumpen
la armonía
mis harapos
y mi voz.

Mostrando cuán cerca habitan
el gozo y el padecer,
que no hay placer sin lágrimas, ni pena
que no transpire en medio del placer.

Mío es el mundo : como el aire libre. . . .

Y para mí no hay *mañana,*
ni hay *ayer ;*
olvido el bien como el mal,
nada me aflige ni afana ;
me es igual para mañana
un palacio, un hospital.

Vivo ajeno
de memorias,
de cuidados
libre estoy ;
busquen otros
oro y glorias,
yo no pienso
sino en hoy.

Y doquiera
vayan leyes,
quiten reyes,
reyes den ;
yo soy pobre,
y al mendigo,
por el miedo
del castigo,
todos hacen
siempre bien.
Y un asilo donde quiera
y un lecho en el hospital
siempre hallaré, y un hoyo donde caiga
mi cuerpo miserable al expirar.
Mío es el mundo : como el aire libre,
otros trabajan porque coma yo :
todos se ablandan, si doliente pido
una limosna por amor de Dios.

235. *A Jarifa, en una orgía*

Here, especially in ll. 57-64, 75-6, which are among the lines most frequently quoted from his poetry, Espronceda draws back the veil from his own personality and reveals the Weltanschauung *of a typical Romantic. All his turbulence of spirit, confused idealism and self-conscious disillusionment are here : the swagger of the more objective "Pirata" and "Mendigo" is transformed into a subjective, Byronic bitterness, in which, it will be observed, the suicide motif appears. Throbbing with passion and bitter pain, eloquent with such sincerity as had not been heard in Spanish poetry for two hundred years, "A Jarifa" also reaches a high level of artistry. It is crowded with alliteration, vowel-play, antithesis and such-like devices. Yet so compelling is the poet's earnestness that we yield to their influence without knowing they are there. The two striking double changes of metre, of the type found in the* Nuits *of Espronceda's contemporary, Alfred de Musset, aptly indicate variations in the emotional tone.*

Trae, Jarifa, trae tu mano,
ven y pósala en mi frente,
que en un mar de lava hirviente
mi cabeza siento arder.

Ven y junta con mis labios
esos labios que me irritan,
donde aún los besos palpitan
de tus amantes de ayer.

¿ Qué la virtud, la pureza ?
¿ Qué la verdad y el cariño ?
Mentida ilusión de niño
que halagó mi juventud.

Dadme vino : en él se ahoguen
mis recuerdos ; aturdida
sin sentir huya la vida ;
paz me traiga el ataúd.

El sudor mi rostro quema,
y en ardiente sangre rojos
brillan inciertos mis ojos,
se me salta el corazón.

Huye, mujer ; te detesto,
siento tu mano en la mía,
y tu mano siento fría,
y tus besos hielo son.

¡ Siempre igual ! Necias mujeres,
inventad otras caricias,
otro mundo, otras delicias,
¡ Oh maldito sea el placer !

Vuestros besos son mentira,
mentira vuestra ternura,
es fealdad vuestra hermosura,
vuestro gozo es padecer.

Yo quiero amor, quiero gloria,
quiero un deleite divino,
como en mi mente imagino,
como en el mundo no hay ;

y es la luz de aquel lucero
que engañó mi fantasía,
fuego fatuo, falso guía
que errante y ciego me trae.

¿ Por qué murió para el placer mi alma
y vive aún para el dolor impío ?
¿ Por qué si yazgo en indolente calma,
siento, en lugar de paz, árido hastío ?

¿ Por qué este inquieto, abrasador deseo ?
¿ Por qué este sentimiento extraño y vago,
que yo mismo conozco un devaneo,
y busco aún su seductor halago ?

¿ Por qué aun fingirme amores y placeres
que cierto estoy de que serán mentira ?
¿ Por qué en pos de fantásticas mujeres
necio tal vez mi corazón delira,

si luego, en vez de prados y de flores,
halla desiertos áridos y abrojos,
y en sus sandios o lúbricos amores
fastidio sólo encontrará y enojos ?

Yo me arrojé, cual rápido cometa,
en alas de mi ardiente fantasía :
doquier mi arrebatada mente inquieta
dichas y triunfos encontrar creía.

Yo me lancé con atrevido vuelo
fuera del mundo en la región etérea,
y hallé la duda, y el radiante cielo
vi convertirse en ilusión aérea.

Luego en la tierra la virtud, la gloria
busqué con ansia y delirante amor,
y hediondo polvo y deleznable escoria
mi fatigado espíritu encontró.

Mujeres vi de virginal limpieza
entre albas nubes de celeste lumbre ;
yo las toqué, y en humo su pureza
trocarse vi, y en lodo y podredumbre.

Y encontré mi ilusión desvanecida
y eterno e insaciable mi deseo ;
palpé la realidad y odié la vida :
sólo en la paz de los sepulcros creo.

Y busco aún y busco codicioso,
y aun deleites el alma finge y quiere :
pregunto y un acento pavoroso
" ¡ Ay ! " me responde, " desespera y muere.

" Muere, infeliz : la vida es un tormento,
un engaño el placer ; no hay en la tierra
paz para ti, ni dicha, ni contento,
sino eterna ambición y eterna guerra.

" Que así castiga Dios el alma osada,
que aspira loca, en su delirio insano,
de la verdad para el mortal velada
a descubrir el insondable arcano."

¡ Oh ! cesa : no, yo no quiero
ver más, ni saber ya nada ;
harta mi alma y postrada,
sólo anhela descansar.

En mí muera el sentimiento,
pues ya murió mi ventura,
ni el placer ni la tristura
vuelvan mi pecho a turbar.

Pasad, pasad en óptica ilusoria,
y otras jóvenes almas engañad :
nacaradas imágenes de gloria,
coronas de oro y de laurel, pasad.

Pasad, pasad, mujeres voluptuosas,
con danza y algazara en confusión ;
pasad como visiones vaporosas
sin conmover ni herir mi corazón.

Y aturdan mi revuelta fantasía
los brindis y el estruendo del festín,
y huya la noche y me sorprenda el día
en un letargo estúpido y sin fin.

Ven, Jarifa ; tú has sufrido
como yo ; tú nunca lloras ;
mas ¡ ay triste ! que no ignoras
cuán amarga es mi aflicción.

Una misma es nuestra pena,
en vano el llanto contienes. . . .
Tú también, como yo, tienes
desgarrado el corazón.

236. *El Estudiante de Salamanca* (*Extract*)

In this, his only complete narrative poem (1839), Espronceda rings changes on the legend of Don Juan, and, with the aid of much Romantic paraphernalia and of his own exquisite art, describes the dreadful fate of his villain-hero, Don Félix de Montemar, who has seduced the lovely but somewhat doll-like Elvira. On this broad canvas, Espronceda puts into practice the lessons of experience and experiment in a way which, though a few of its artificialities tend to date, most readers feel to be extraordinarily modern. Contrasts—of clarity and vagueness, of light and darkness, of virtue and vice ; the alternation of lyrical and dramatic passages with narrative and descriptive ; a maximum of metrical variety ; an evocative and sensitive use of light and colour ; the successful creation of a supernatural atmosphere, in which alone such a story as this could live—these are the principal traits of the poem which in attractiveness as in literary merit its author never surpassed.

The first canto, given in full below, illustrates Espronceda's method of etching his dramatis personæ *sharply against a dim and sinister background, his use of contrast in character-drawing, and of course (as almost any passage in the poem must) the same parallel changes of metre and tone which we have already studied.*

Era más de media noche,
antiguas historias cuentan,
cuando, en sueño y en silencio,
lóbrega envuelta la tierra,
los vivos muertos parecen,
los muertos la tumba dejan.
Era la hora en que acaso
temerosas voces suenan
informes, en que se escuchan

tácitas pisadas huecas,
y pavorosas fantasmas
entre las densas tinieblas
vagan, y aúllan los perros
amedrentados al verlas;
en que tal vez la campana
de alguna arruinada iglesia
da misteriosos sonidos
de maldición y anatema,
que los sábados convoca
a las brujas a su fiesta.
El cielo estaba sombrío,
no vislumbraba una estrella,
silbaba lúgubre el viento,
y allá en el aire, cual negras
fantasmas, se dibujaban
las torres de las iglesias,
y del gótico castillo
las altísimas almenas,
donde canta o reza acaso
temeroso el centinela.
Todo, en fin, a media noche
reposaba, y tumba era
de sus dormidos vivientes
la antigua ciudad que riega
el Tormes, fecundo río,
nombrado de los poetas,
la famosa Salamanca,
insigne en armas y letras,
patria de ilustres varones,
noble archivo de las ciencias.

Súbito rumor de espadas
cruje y un ¡ ay ! se escuchó;
un ¡ ay ! moribundo, un ¡ ay !
que penetra el corazón,
que hasta los tuétanos hiela
y da al que lo oyó temblor;
un ¡ ay ! de alguno que al mundo
pronuncia el último adiós.

El ruido
cesó,
un hombre
pasó
embozado,
y el sombrero
recatado
a los ojos
se caló.
Se desliza
y atraviesa
junto al muro
de una iglesia,
y en la sombra
se perdió.

Una calle estrecha y alta,
la calle del Ataúd,
cual si de negro crespón
lóbrego eterno capuz
la vistiera, siempre oscura,
y de noche sin más luz
que la lámpara que alumbra
una imagen de Jesús,
atraviesa el embozado,
la espada en la mano aún,
que lanzó vivo reflejo
al pasar frente a la cruz.

Cual suele la luna tras lóbrega nube
con franjas de plata bordarla en redor,
y luego si el viento la agita, la sube
disuelta a los aires en blanco vapor:

así vaga sombra de luz y de nieblas,
mística y aérea dudosa visión,
ya brilla, o la esconden las densas tinieblas.
cual dulce esperanza, cual vana ilusión.

La calle sombría, la noche ya entrada,
la lámpara triste ya pronta a expirar,
que a veces alumbra la imagen sagrada
y a veces se esconde la sombra a aumentar,

el vago fantasma que acaso aparece,
y acaso se acerca con rápido pie,
y acaso en las sombras tal vez desparece,
cual ánima en pena del hombre que fué,

al más temerario corazón de acero
recelo inspirara, pusiera pavor;
al más maldiciente feroz bandolero
el rezo a los labios trajera el temor.

Mas no al embozado, que aún sangre su espada
destila, el fantasma terror infundió,
y, el arma en la mano con fuerza empuñada,
osado a su encuentro despacio avanzó.

Segundo Don Juan Tenorio,
alma fiera e insolente,
irreligioso y valiente,
altanero y reñidor:

siempre el insulto en los ojos,
en los labios la ironía,
nada teme y todo fía
de su espada y su valor.

Corazón gastado, mofa
de la mujer que corteja,
y hoy, despreciándola, deja
la que ayer se le rindió.

Ni el porvenir temió nunca,
ni recuerda en lo pasado
la mujer que ha abandonado,
ni el dinero que perdió.

Ni vió el fantasma entre sueños
del que mató en desafío,
ni turbó jamás su brío
recelosa previsión.

Siempre en lances y en amores,
siempre en báquicas orgías,
mezcla en palabras impías
un chiste a una maldición.

En Salamanca famoso
por su vida y buen talante,
al atrevido estudiante
le señalan entre mil;

fueros le da su osadía,
le disculpa su riqueza,
su generosa nobleza,
su hermosura varonil.

Que su arrogancia y sus vicios,
caballeresca apostura,
agilidad y bravura
ninguno alcanza a igualar:

que hasta en sus crímenes mismos,
en su impiedad y altiveza,
pone un sello de grandeza
don Félix de Montemar.

Bella y más pura que el azul del cielo,
con dulces ojos lánguidos y hermosos,
donde acaso el amor brilló entre el velo
del pudor que los cubre candorosos;
tímida estrella que refleja al suelo
rayos de luz brillantes y dudosos,
ángel puro de amor que amor inspira,
fué la inocente y desdichada Elvira.

Elvira, amor del estudiante un día,
tierna y feliz y de su amante ufana,
cuando al placer su corazón se abría,
como al rayo del sol rosa temprana:
del fingido amador que la mentía,
la miel falaz que de sus labios mana
bebe en su ardiente sed, el pecho ajeno
de que oculto en la miel hierve el veneno.

Que no descansa de su madre en brazos
más descuidado el candoroso infante
que ella en los falsos lisonjeros lazos
que teje astuto el seductor amante:

dulces caricias, lánguidos abrazos,
placeres ¡ ay ! que duran un instante,
que habrán de ser eternos imagina
la triste Elvira en su ilusión divina.

Que el alma virgen que halagó un encanto
con nacarado sueño en su pureza
todo lo juzga verdadero y santo,
presta a todo virtud, presta belleza.
Del cielo azul al tachonado manto,
del sol radiante a la inmortal riqueza,
al aire, al campo, a las fragantes flores,
ella añade esplendor, vida y colores.

Cifró en don Félix la infeliz doncella
toda su dicha, de su amor perdida ;
fueron sus ojos a los ojos de ella
astros de gloria, manantial de vida.
Cuando sus labios con sus labios sella,
cuando su voz escucha embebecida,
embriagada del dios que la enamora,
dulce le mira, extática le adora.

237. *El Diablo Mundo*

(Extracts)

El Diablo Mundo *(1841), which its author left unfinished at his death, is the most Byronic of his works : picturesqueness and literary artistry are forgotten by a poet reaching out to intellectual and emotional heights which he never quite scales. The* Faust-*like story harmonizes with the poem's somewhat inchoate form : the stanzas, as they ramble on, suggest a complete indifference to plan. On the other hand,* El Diablo Mundo *reveals much of Espronceda's inner life, and its second canto, "A Teresa"—a digression apostrophizing his dead mistress—perhaps tells us more about his character than he ever intended. So, careless, verbose, ill-knit and crude though it often is, this poem will always have to be reckoned with in any attempt to understand its author.*

Two typically revealing extracts are here given—from Cantos I and II respectively. The first not only illustrates Espronceda's pseudo-philosophy of desengaño, *but also describes his methods and ideals as a writer. The second introduces the digression "A Teresa", the whole of which, with its varied emotional nuances, its passionate climax and its savagely bitter conclusion, must be read before it can be fairly judged.*

(i)

Dicha es soñar cuando despierto sueña
el corazón del hombre su esperanza,
su mente halaga la ilusión risueña,
y el bien presente al venidero alcanza :
y tras la aérea y luminosa enseña
del entusiasmo, el ánimo se lanza
bajo un cielo de luz y de colores,
campos pintando de fragantes flores.

Dicha es soñar, porque la vida es sueño,
lo que fingió tal vez la fantasía,
cuando embriagada en lánguido beleño,
a las regiones del placer nos guía :
dicha es soñar, y el rigoroso ceño
no ver jamás de la verdad impía :
dicha es soñar y en el mundano ruido
vivir soñando y existir dormido.

Y un sueño a la verdad pasa la vida,
sueño al principio de dorada lumbre,
senda de flores mil, fácil subida
que a un monte lleva de lozana cumbre ;
después vereda áspera y torcida,
monte de insuperable pesadumbre,
donde cansada de una en otra breña,
llora la vida y lo pasado sueña.

Sueños son los deleites, los amores,
la juventud, la gloria, la hermosura ;
sueños las dichas son, sueños las flores,
la esperanza, el dolor, la desventura :
triunfos, caídas, bienes y rigores
el sueño son que hasta la muerte dura,
y en incierto y continuo movimiento
agita al ambicioso pensamiento.

Siento no sea nuevo lo que digo,
que el tema es viejo y la palabra rancia,
y es trillado sendero el que ahora sigo,
y caminar por él ya es arrogancia.
En la mente, lector, se abre un postigo,
sale una idea y el licor escancia
que brota el labio y que la pluma vierte,
y en palabras y frases se convierte.

Nihil novum sub sole, dijo el sabio,
nada hay nuevo en el mundo : harto lo siento.
Que, como dicen vulgarmente, rabio
yo por probar un nuevo sentimiento :
palabras nuevas pronunciar mi labio,
renovado sentir mi pensamiento,
ansío, y girando en dulce desvarío,
ver nuevo siempre el mundo en torno mío.

Uniforme, monótono y cansado
es sin duda este mundo en que vivimos ;
en Oriente de rayos coronado,
el sol que vemos hoy, ayer le vimos :
de flores vuelve a engalanarse el prado,
vuelve el Otoño pródigo en racimos,
y tras los hielos del invierno frío,
coronado de espigas el estío.

¿ Y no habré yo de repetirme a veces,
decir también lo que otros ya dijeron,
a mí a quien quedan ya sólo las heces
del rico manantial en que bebieron ?
¿ Qué habré yo de decir que ya con creces
no hayan dicho tal vez los que murieron,
Byron y Calderón, Shakspear, Cervantes,
y tantos otros que vivieron antes ?

¿ Y aun asimismo acertaré a decirlo ?
¿ Saldré de tanto enredo en que me he puesto ?
Ya que en mi cuento entré ¿ podré seguirlo,
y el término tocar que me he propuesto ?

Y aunque en mi empeño logre concluirlo,
¿ a ti no te será nunca molesto,
¡ oh caro comprador ! que con zozobra
imploro en mi favor comprar mi obra ?

Nada menos te ofrezco que un poema
con lances raros y revuelto asunto,
de nuestro mundo y sociedad emblema,
que hemos de recorrer punto por punto :
si logro yo desenvolver mi tema,
fiel traslado ha de ser, cierto trasunto
de la vida del hombre y la quimera
tras de que va la Humanidad entera.

Batallas, tempestades, amoríos,
por mar y tierra, lances, descripciones
de campos y ciudades, desafíos,
y el desastre y furor de las pasiones,
goces, dichas, aciertos, desvaríos,
con algunas morales reflexiones
acerca de la vida y de la muerte,
de mi propia cosecha, que es mi fuerte.

En varias formas, con diverso estilo,
en diferentes géneros, calzando
ora el coturno trágico de Esquilo,
ora la trompa épica sonando,
ora cantando plácido y tranquilo,
ora en trivial lenguaje, ora burlando,
conforme esté mi humor, porque a él me ajusto,
y allá van versos donde va mi gusto.

(ii)

¿ Por qué volvéis a la memoria mía,
tristes recuerdos del placer perdido,
a aumentar la ansiedad y la agonía
de este desierto corazón herido ?
¡ Ay ! que de aquellas horas de alegría,
le quedó al corazón solo un gemido,
y el llanto que al dolor los ojos niegan
lágrimas son de hiel que el alma anegan.

¿ Dónde volaron ¡ ay ! aquellas horas
de juventud, de amor y de ventura,
regaladas de músicas sonoras,
adornadas de luz y de hermosura ?
Imágenes de oro bullidoras,
sus alas de carmín y nieve pura,
al sol de mi esperanza desplegando,
pasaban ¡ ay ! a mi alredor cantando.

Gorjeaban los dulces ruiseñores,
el sol iluminaba mi alegría,
el aura susurraba entre las flores,
el bosque mansamente respondía,
las fuentes murmuraban sus amores. . . .
¡ Ilusiones que llora el alma mía !
¡ Oh ! cuán süave resonó en mi oído
el bullicio del mundo y su rüido !

Mi vida entonces cual guerrera nave
que el puerto deja por la vez primera,
y al soplo de los céfiros süave,
orgullosa despliega su bandera,
y al mar dejando que a sus pies alabe,
su triunfo en roncos cantos, va velera,
una ola tras otra bramadora
hollando y dividiendo vencedora.

¡ Ay ! en el mar del mundo, en ansia ardiente
de amor volaba, el sol de la mañana
llevaba yo sobre mi tersa frente,
y el alma pura de su dicha ufana :
dentro de ella el amor cual rica fuente
que entre frescura y arboledas mana,
brotaba entonces abundante río
de ilusiones y dulce desvarío.

Yo amaba todo : un noble sentimiento
exaltaba mi ánimo, y sentía
en mi pecho un secreto movimiento,
de grandes hechos generoso guía :

la libertad con su inmortal aliento,
santa diosa mi espíritu encendía,
contino imaginando en mi fe pura
sueños de gloria al mundo y de ventura.

. . . .

Yo desterrado en extranjera playa,
con los ojos extático seguía
la nave audaz que en argentada raya
volaba al puerto de la patria mía :
yo cuando en Occidente el sol desmaya,
solo y perdido en la arboleda umbría,
oír pensaba el armonioso acento
de una mujer, al suspirar del viento.

¡ Una mujer ! En el templado rayo
de la mágica luna se colora,
del sol poniente al lánguido desmayo,
lejos entre las nubes se evapora ;
sobre las cumbres que florece el Mayo
brilla fugaz al despuntar la aurora,
cruza tal vez por entre el bosque umbrío,
juega en las aguas del sereno río.

¡ Una mujer ! Deslízase en el cielo
allá en la noche desprendida estrella ;
si aroma el aire recogió en el suelo,
es el aroma que le presta ella.
Blanca es la nube que en callado vuelo
cruza la esfera, y que su planta huella,
y en la tarde la mar olas la ofrece
de plata y de zafir, donde se mece.

Mujer que amor su ilusión figura,
mujer que nada dice a los sentidos,
ensueño de suavísima ternura,
eco que regaló nuestros oídos ;
de amor la llama generosa y pura,
los goces dulces del placer cumplidos,
que engalana la rica fantasía,
goces que avaro el corazón ansía.

¡ Ay ! aquella mujer, tan sólo aquélla
tanto delirio a realizar alcanza,
y esa mujer tan cándida y tan bella
es mentida ilusión de la esperanza :
es el alma que vívida destella
su luz al mundo cuando en él se lanza,
y el mundo con su magia y galanura
es espejo no más de su hermosura :

es el amor que al mismo amor adora,
el que creó las sílfides y ondinas,
la sacra ninfa que bordando mora
debajo de las aguas cristalinas :
es el amor que recordando llora
las arboledas del Edén divinas,
amor de allí arrancado, allí nacido,
que busca en vano aquí su bien perdido.

¡ Oh llama santa ! ¡ celestial anhelo !
¡ sentimiento purísimo ! ¡ memoria
acaso triste de un perdido cielo,
quizá esperanza de futura gloria !
¡ Huyes y dejas llanto y desconsuelo !
¡ Oh mujer, que en imagen ilusoria
tan pura, tan feliz, tan placentera,
brindó el amor a mi ilusión primera ! . . .

MANUEL DE CABANYES

1808-1833

A PRE-ROMANTIC of rare quality, cut off in youth just as he was completing his one collection of verse, *Preludios de mi lira*, Cabanyes might easily have become an outstanding figure in the decade dominated by Rivas and Espronceda, if not the fashioner and leader of a Romantic school. Even when so young, he struck out for " independence " in poetry—

Sobre sus cantos la expresión del alma
vuela sin arte : números sonoros
desdeña y rima acorde ; son sus versos
cual su espíritu libres.[1]

As one would expect of a Catalonian who grew up during the reign of Ferdinand VII, there is an element of rebellion, as well as of patriotism, in his verse, but the judgment, based on a single poem " A Cintio ", which makes him a Byronist, is wholly without justification. Two simple *canciones*—one a love lyric, which shows its author growing rapidly out of the eighteenth century ; the other a simple song of freedom—are no less characteristic of his sentiment and technique. Both are polished and concise and make effective use of repetition.

238. *Canción*

Yo te adoré, cuando la vez primera
recato y gracias admirara en ti :
yo te adoré cuando benignas viera
tus lumbres bellas dirigirse a mí.

Cuando tu voz oí melodïosa
yo te creyera un ángel del Señor,
y te adoré cuando por fin piadosa
me prometiste sempiterno amor.

[1] " La Independencia de la poesía." *Ed. cit.*, p. 49.

Yo te adoré cuando un destino impío
lejos de ti, mi Nice, me arrancó,
y la corriente del extraño río
mi llanto fiel mil veces aumentó.

Yo te amaré, yo te seré constante
mientra a la noche siga el rosicler,
siga la sombra a la deidad radiante,
goce al afán, quebrantos al placer.

Cuando la luz yo dejaré del mundo
y de mi tumba el mármol abriré;
entonces aún mi labio moribundo
repetirá: "Te adoro, te adoré."

239. *Canción del esclavo*

Por los jardines de mi patrio suelo
tiende natura el manto floreal;
mas ¡ ay ! la niebla que encapota el cielo
no desvanece el Sol de Libertad.

Nuncias de goce, encantadoras Bellas
en mi aflicción prométenme solaz;
mas pasan ¡ ay ! cual pálidas estrellas,
que no esclarece el Sol de Libertad.

Sólo me queda el consolar del llanto
y un harpa ¡ ay Dios ! que no será inmortal:
con el cantor perecerá su canto
que no inflamara el Sol de Libertad.

No, jamás diga el eco de la Historia
mi nombre esclavo, al siglo que vendrá.
¡ Ay ! turbios son los rayos de la gloria
si no los hiere el Sol de Libertad.

Muramos pues, la inmerecida afrenta
sólo el sepulcro puede ya ocultar:
feliz si un día plácido calienta
mi frío tronco el Sol de Libertad.

NICOMEDES PASTOR DÍAZ

1811-1863

In lyric poetry the Romantic movement developed rather later than in the other *genres* and it was not until the year 1840 that collections of verse descended upon the public like a flood. One of the poets of this *annus mirabilis* was the Galician, Nicomedes Pastor Díaz, whose Romantic disillusion later found vent in a novel, *De Villahermosa a la China* (1858). He described his verses, not unfairly, as " suspiros, desahogos, gemidos solitarios de un corazón que . . . gime y llora solamente por haber nacido." But, though often crude, nebulous or fantastic, they are usually graceful and always convey the impression of sincerity. Their melodious quality, too, foreshadows a development which, with many others, was to take place at the end of the century.

240. *La Mariposa negra*

Here we have one of Díaz's experiments in symbolism, a tendency which had much less vogue in Spain than in France. The Romantics, no less than the pseudo-Classicists, cherished their conventionalities and for these a certain allowance must be made in any estimate of the qualities of a poem of this type. Those susceptible to the Romantic manner would no doubt find it attractive, and even moving ; present-day readers, unable to do this, will grant that its conception is a striking one, out of which the poet strives to extract the greatest possible effect. The stanza, if somewhat artificial, has an effective rhyme-scheme (abbcaddc) *and the* lleno *and* agudo *endings are a happy blend.*

Borraba ya del pensamiento mío
de la tristeza el importuno ceño :
dulce era mi vivir, dulce mi sueño,
dulce mi despertar.

Ya en mi pecho era lóbrego vacío
el que un tiempo rugió volcán ardiente;
ya no pasaban negras por mi frente
nubes que hacen llorar.

Era una noche azul, serena, clara,
que embebecido en plácido desvelo,
alcé los ojos en tributo al cielo,
de tierna gratitud.
Mas ¡ ay ! que apenas lánguido se alzara
este mirar de eterna desventura,
turbarse vi la lívida blancura
de la nocturna luz.

Incierta sombra que mi sien circunda,
cruzar siento en zumbido revolante,
y con nubloso vértigo incesante
a mi vista girar.
Cubrió la luz incierta, moribunda,
con alas de vapor, informe objeto;
cubrió mi corazón terror secreto
que no puedo calmar.

No, como un tiempo, colosal quimera
ni atónita atención amedrentaba;
mis oídos profundo no aterraba
acento de pavor:
que fué la aparición vaga y ligera:
leve la sombra aérea y nebulosa;
que fué sólo una negra mariposa
volando en derredor.

No, cual suele, fijó su giro errante
la antorcha que alumbraba mi desvelo;
de su siniestro misterioso vuelo
la luz no era el imán.
¡ Ay ! que sólo el fulgor agonizante
en mis lánguidos ojos abatidos,
ser creí de sus giros repetidos
secreto talismán.

Lo creo, sí . . . que a mi agitada suerte
su extraña aparición no será en vano.
Desde la noche de ese infausto arcano
¡ Ay Dios ! . . . aun no dormí.
¿ Anunciaráme próxima la muerte ?
¿ O es más negro su vuelo repentino ? . . .
Ella trae un mensaje del Destino. . . .
Yo . . . ¡ no le comprendí !

Ya no aparece sólo entre las sombras ;
doquier me envuelve su funesto giro ;
a cada instante sobre mí la miro
mil círculos trazar.
Del campo entre las plácidas alfombras,
del bosque entre el ramaje la contemplo :
y hasta bajo las bóvedas del templo. . . .
y ante el sagrado altar.

" Para calmar mi frenesí secreto
cesa un instante, negra mariposa :
tus leves alas en mi frente posa ;
tal vez me aquietarás. . . . "
Mas redoblando su girar inquieto
huye, y parece que a mi voz se aleja,
y revuelve, y me sigue, y no me deja. . . .
¡ ni se para jamás !

A veces creo que un sepulcro amado
lanzó, bajo esta larva aterradora,
el espíritu errante, que aun adora
mi yerto corazón.
Y una vez ¡ ay ! extático y helado,
la vi, la vi. . . . creciendo de repente
mágica desplegar sobre mi frente
nueva transformación.

Vi tenderse sus alas como un velo,
sobre un cuerpo fantástico colgadas,
en rozagante túnica trocadas,
so un manto funeral.

Y el lúgubre zumbido de su vuelo
trocóse en voz profunda melodiosa,
y trocóse la negra mariposa
en Genio celestial.

Cual sobre estatua de ébano luciente
un rostro se alza en ademán sublime,
do en pálido marfil su sello imprime
sobrehumano dolor ;
y de sus ojos el brillar ardiente,
fósforo de visión, fuego del cielo,
hiere en el alma . . . ¡ como hiere el vuelo
del rayo vengador !

" Un momento ¡ gran Dios ! " mis brazos yertos
desesperado la tendí gritando :
" ¡ Ven de una vez, la dije sollozando,
ven y me matarás ! "
Mas ¡ ay ! que, cual las sombras de los muertos,
sus formas vanas a mi voz retira,
y de nuevo circula, y zumba y gira. . . .
y no para jamás. . . .

¿ Qué potencia infernal mi mente altera ?
¿ De dónde viene esta visión pasmosa ?
Ese Genio . . . esa negra mariposa,
¿ Qué es ? . . . ¿ Qué quiere de mí ? . . .
En vano llamo a mi ilusión, quimera ;
no hay más verdad que la ilusión del alma :
verdad fué mi quietud, mi paz, mi calma. . . .
verdad. . . . ¡ que ya perdí !

Por ocultos resortes agitado
vuelvo al llanto otra vez hondo y doliente,
y mi canto otra vez vuela y mi mente
a esa extraña región,
do sobre el cráter de un abismo helado
las nieves del volcán se derritieron. . . .
al fuego que ligeras encendieron
dos alas de crespón.

GERTRUDIS GÓMEZ DE AVELLANEDA

1814-1873

Though a Cuban by birth, La Avellaneda, as she is invariably called, lived all her life in Spain and belongs to the history of Spanish literature. She is often described as Spain's greatest woman writer after Santa Teresa—but it must be confessed that she comes a long way after, for, though a fertile producer of novel, drama and lyric verse, she seldom achieves excellence anywhere. In verse she was an Eclectic, dexterous but not very original in technique, much given to translation and the pseudo-Classical grand manner. She has many moods, varying from Quintanesque oratory to a feebly Lamartinian pathos. Her best moments are Romantic: these, however, are not when she dilates on conventional Romantic themes, but when her preoccupation with art is overwhelmed by deep feeling. Then, all too rarely, one feels that she was indeed a poet.

241. *Soledad del Alma*

These lines, written to be recited to music, are more notable for their music than for their sentiment, which is commonplace to a degree. Though having neither the skill nor the ambition of her great fellow-American, Rubén Darío (p. 580), who, through sheer force of genius, was to revolutionize Spanish poetry, she shows at times considerable aptitude for the melodious long line, which she uses here. Against the smoothness of some of her alliterations and elisions, however, have to be set the harshness and jerkiness of others, and to-day we think of such a poem as this chiefly as an earnest of what was to come.

Huyeron veloces—cual nubes que el viento arrebata—
los breves momentos de dicha que el cielo me dió . . . .
¿ Por qué mi existencia, ya inútil, su curso dilata,
si el término ansiado a su espalda perdido dejó ?

¿ Qué resta ¡ ay ! qué resta de tanta ferviente esperanza ?
¿ Qué resta de tanto inefable continuo anhelar ? . . .
¡ Recuerdo infecundo, cadáver que apenas alcanza
galvánica fuerza por solo un minuto a agitar !

La flor delicada—que apenas existe una aurora—
tal vez largo tiempo al ambiente le deja su olor. . . .
Mas ¡ ay ! que del alma las flores, que un día atesora,
muriendo marchitas no dejan perfume en redor.

La luz esplendente del astro fecundo del día,
se apaga, y sus huellas aun forman hermoso arrebol. . . .
Mas ¡ ay ! cuando al alma le llega su noche sombría,
¿ qué guarda del fuego sagrado que ha sido su sol ?

Se rompe, gastada, la cuerda del arpa armoniosa,
y aun su eco difunde en los aires fugaz vibración. . . .
Mas ¡ todo el silencio profundo, de muerte espantosa,
si da un pecho amante el postrero tristísimo son !

Sale la aurora risueña, de flores vestida,
dándole al cielo y al campo variado color ;
todo se anima sintiendo brotar nueva vida,
cantan las aves, y el aura suspira de amor.

Llega la tarde, de místico encanto colmada ;
triste acaricia los campos la luz al morir ;
busca el rebaño en silencio su dulce majada ;
tornan las aves, pïando, su nido a cubrir.

Luego la noche solemne su manto despliega ;
bordan estrellas lucientes la etérea región ;
todo hace pausa . . . la vida su impulso sosiega. . . .
Reina en el mundo tranquilo feliz inacción.

Mas nada, ni noche, ni aurora, ni tarde indecisa,
cambian del alma desierta la lúgubre faz . . . .
A ella no llegan crepúsculo, aroma ni brisa. . . .
A ella no brindan las sombras ensueños de paz.

Vista los campos de flores gentil primavera,
doren las mieses los besos del cielo estival,
pámpanos ornen de otoño la faz placentera,
lance el invierno brumoso su aliento glacial.

Siempre perdidas—vagando en su estéril desierto—
siempre abrumadas del peso de vil nulidad,
gimen las almas do el fuego de amor está muerto. . . .
¡ Nada hay que pueble o anime su gran soledad !

242. *A Él*

Here we are in a very different atmosphere. The intensity of the poet's emotion has dispersed her conventional metaphors and broken up her neatly turned phrases. Her lover has betrayed, or deserted, her. She sees everything with a clarity reflected in words so terse and brusque that, but for the fire which breaks out from beneath them, they would have little to do with poetry. Her vibrant energy contrasts strangely with her profession of meek resignation to the Divine will ; and yet, unusual as is her method of expression, one never doubts her sincerity.

No existe lazo ya : todo está roto :
plúgole al cielo así : ¡ bendito sea !
Amargo cáliz con placer agoto :
mi alma reposa al fin : nada desea.

Te amé, no te amo ya : piénsolo al menos.
¡ Nunca, si fuere error, la verdad mire !
Que tantos años de amarguras llenos
trague el olvido ; el corazón respire.

Lo has destrozado sin piedad : mi orgullo
una vez y otra vez pisaste insano. . . .
Mas nunca el labio exhalará un murmullo
para acusar tu proceder tirano.

De graves faltas vengador terrible,
dócil llenaste tu misión : ¿ lo ignoras ?
No era tuyo el poder que irresistible
postró ante ti mis fuerzas vencedoras.

Quísolo Dios y fué : ¡ gloria a su nombre !
Todo se terminó : recobro aliento.
¡ Ángel de las venganzas ! ya eres hombre. . .
Ni amor ni miedo al contemplarte siento.

Cayó tu cetro, se embotó tu espada. . . .
Mas ¡ ay ! ¡ cuán triste libertad respiro !
Hice un mundo de ti, que hoy se anonada,
y en honda y vasta soledad me miro.

¡ Vive dichoso tú ! Si en algún día
ves este adiós que te dirijo eterno,
sabe que aun tienes en el alma mía
generoso perdón, cariño tierno.

ENRIQUE GIL Y CARRASCO
1815-1846

ANOTHER Romantic who, like Larra and Espronceda, died all too young, Gil is remembered chiefly for a charming regionalist novel: *El Señor de Bembibre* (1844). Had he lived, he might have made a greater name with his poems, the melancholy charm of which still has power.

243. *La Violeta*

Highly subjective and mildly elegiac in type, this melodious poem is typical of the Romantic lyric in its least aggressive form. Even if its lingering sweetness may seem to him too long drawn out, the sensitive reader will not fail to respond to an appeal evoked in a manner as modest and unassuming as the tiny flower which forms its subject. To the poet's contemporaries the final stanzas of the poem were given an added pathos by his early death in a foreign land.

Flor deliciosa en la memoria mía,
ven mi triste laúd a coronar,
y volverán las trovas de alegría
en sus ecos tal vez a resonar.

Mezcla tu aroma a sus cansadas cuerdas;
yo sobre ti no inclinaré mi sien,
de miedo, pura flor, que entonces pierdas
tu tesoro de olores y tu bien.

Yo, sin embargo, coroné mi frente
con tu gala en las tardes del Abril,
yo te buscaba orillas de la fuente,
yo te adoraba tímida y gentil.

Porque eras melancólica y perdida,
y era perdido y lúgubre mi amor ;
y en ti miré el emblema de mi vida
y mi destino, solitaria flor.

Tú allí crecías olorosa y pura
con tus moradas hojas de pesar ;
pasaba entre la yerba tu frescura,
de la fuente al confuso murmurar.

Y pasaba mi amor desconocido,
de un arpa oscura al apagado son,
con frívolos cantares confundido
el himno de mi amante corazón.

Yo busqué la hermandad de la desdicha
en tu cáliz de aroma y soledad,
y a tu ventura asemejé mi dicha,
y a tu prisión mi antigua libertad.

¡ Cuántas meditaciones han pasado
por mi frente mirando tu arrebol !
¡ Cuántas veces mis ojos te han dejado
para volverse al moribundo sol !

¡ Qué de consuelos a mi pena diste
con tu calma y tu dulce lobreguez,
cuando la mente imaginaba triste
el negro porvenir de la vejez !

Yo me decía : " Buscaré en las flores
seres que escuchen mi infeliz cantar,
que mitiguen con bálsamo de olores
las ocultas heridas del pesar."

Y me apartaba, al alumbrar la luna,
de ti, bañada en moribunda luz,
adormecida en tu vistosa cuna,
velada en tu aromático capuz.

Y una esperanza el corazón llevaba
pensando en tu sereno amanecer,
y otra vez en tu cáliz divisaba
perdidas ilusiones de placer.

Heme hoy aquí : ¡ cuán otros mis cantares !
¡ cuán otro mi pensar, mi porvenir !
Ya no hay flores que escuchen mis pesares,
ni soledad donde poder gemir.

Lo secó todo el soplo de mi aliento,
y naufragué con mi doliente amor :
lejos ya de la paz y del contento,
mírame aquí en el valle del dolor.

Era dulce mi pena y mi tristeza ;
tal vez moraba una ilusión detrás :
mas la ilusión voló con su pureza,
mis ojos, ¡ ay ! no la verán jamás.

Hoy vuelvo a ti, cual pobre viajero
vuelve al hogar que niño le acogió ;
pero mis glorias recobrar no espero,
sólo a buscar la huesa vengo yo.

Vengo a buscar mi huesa solitaria
para dormir tranquilo junto a ti,
ya que escuchaste un día mi plegaria,
y un ser hermano en tu corola vi.

Ven mi tumba a adornar, triste viola,
y embalsama mi oscura soledad ;
sé de su pobre césped la aureola
con tu vaga y poética beldad.

Quizá al pasar la virgen de los valles,
enamorada y rica en juventud,
por las umbrosas y desiertas calles
do yacerá escondido mi ataúd,

irá a cortar la humilde violeta
y la pondrá en su seno con dolor,
y llorando dirá : " ¡ Pobre poeta !
¡ Ya está callada el arpa del amor ! "

JOSÉ ZORRILLA

1817-1893

ESPRONCEDA was born a Romantic ; Rivas achieved romanticism ; Zorrilla had romanticism thrust upon him. Just as he was setting out on his career, still a mere boy, the short-lived vogue of the Romantic movement began : a dramatist, he found the stage swept temporarily all but clean of classicism ; a poet, he leapt into fame, when barely out of his teens, at the grave of the young Romantic Larra, by declaiming some highly emotional verses which were greeted with quite disproportionate praise. After Rivas' semi-retirement and Espronceda's death, he was accounted for a full generation the foremost poet in Spain : and, though in drama he dallied with eclecticism, in lyric and narrative poetry he remained a Romantic through and through.

His lyric poems, incurably picturesque, harp on three strings—mystery, melancholy and religiosity : at times we hear in them a more robust note, that of profound faith in Church and country. " He tenido presentes dos cosas," he wrote in 1838 : " la patria en que nací y la religión en que vivo."[1] When he emerged in his true colours, as a narrative poet, this double inspiration became more pronounced, as did also his determination to follow his bent, unfettered by convention and precept, wherever it led him. So he wrote more and more in the invitingly elastic *leyenda*-form, and indulged, often somewhat obviously, in such devices as colloquial asides to his readers and oratorical repetitions. In his fantastic plots, in his attachment to the supernatural, and in his use of Nature as a background to his narrative, he is often superficial and sometimes crudely puerile. His poems have no longer much intrinsic appeal, but they live by virtue of being documents of their age and by the zest with which they exteriorize that double inspiration just referred to, which nowhere has more vitality and power than in Spain.

[1] For the context of this phrase, see *H.R.M.S.*, II, 204-5.

244. *A la memoria desgraciada del joven literato Don Mariano José de Larra*

These are the lines that made Zorrilla famous. "De en medio de nosotros", wrote Nicomedes Pastor Díaz of that memorable funeral, "y como si saliera debajo de aquel sepulcro, vimos brotar y aparecer un joven, casi un niño, para todos desconocido. Alzó su pálido semblante, clavó en aquella tumba y en el cielo una mirada sublime, y dejando oír una voz que por primera vez sonaba en nuestros oídos, leyó en cortados y trémulos acentos los versos . . . que . . . no pudo concluir. . . . Nuestro asombro fué igual a nuestro entusiasmo."[1] *To-day the faults of the piece are obvious enough ; but it has the particular interest of voicing two related ideas characteristic of Spanish nineteenth-century poetry, as also of French* (e.g., *Vigny and Baudelaire*) *—the essential loneliness of the poet and the sacredness of his mission. Both these ideas recur again and again in Zorrilla's verse.*

Ese vago clamor que rasga el viento
es la voz funeral de una campana :
vano remedo del postrer lamento
de un cadáver sombrío y macilento
que en sucio polvo dormirá mañana.

Acabó su misión sobre la tierra,
y dejó su existencia carcomida,
como una virgen al placer perdida
cuelga el profano velo en el altar.
Miró en el tiempo el porvenir vacío,
vacío ya de ensueños y de gloria,
y se entregó a ese sueño sin memoria,
que nos lleva a otro mundo a despertar.

Era una flor que marchitó el estío,
era una fuente que agotó el verano ;
ya no se siente su murmullo vano,
ya está quemado el tallo de la flor.
Todavía su aroma se percibe,
y ese verde color de la llanura,
ese manto de yerba y de frescura
hijos son del arroyo creador.

[1] *Obras de Nicomedes Pastor Díaz*, Madrid, 1866-7, III, 44-5.

Que el poeta en su misión,
sobre la tierra que habita
es una planta maldita
con frutos de bendición.

Duerme en paz en la tumba solitaria
donde no llegue a tu cegado oído
más que la triste y funeral plegaria
que otro poeta cantará por ti.
Esta será una ofrenda de cariño
más grata, sí, que la oración de un hombre,
pura como la lágrima de un niño,
¡ memoria del poeta que perdí !

Si existe un remoto cielo
de los poetas mansión,
y solo le queda al suelo
ese retrato de yelo,
fetidez y corrupción ;

¡ Digno presente por cierto
se deja a la amarga vida !
¡ Abandonar un desierto
y darle a la despedida
la fea prenda de un muerto !

Poeta, si en el *no ser*
hay un recuerdo de ayer,
una vida como aquí
detrás de ese firmamento. . . .
conságrame un pensamiento
como el que tengo de ti.

245. *Oriental*

Nowhere is Zorrilla more picturesque than in poems inspired by Moorish themes, of which this " Oriental " is an example drawn from his juvenilia. *Note the somewhat crude use of colour and the almost childish alliterations (e.g., ll. 2, 3, 32, 35, 37-9) but also the flair for striking phrases and vivid pictures : the first line alone has kept the poem alive in Spanish memories.*

Dueña de la negra toca,
la del morado monjil,
por un beso de tu boca
diera a Granada Boabdil.

Diera la lanza mejor
del cenete más bizarro,
y con su fresco verdor
toda una orilla del Darro.

Diera las fiestas de toros,
y, si fueran en sus manos,
con las zambras de los moros
el valor de los cristianos.

Diera alfombras orientales,
y armaduras y pebetes,
y diera. . . . ¡ que tanto vales !
hasta cuarenta jinetes.

Porque tus ojos son bellos ;
porque la luz de la aurora
sube al oriente desde ellos,
y el mundo su lumbre dora.

Tus labios son un rubí
partido por gala en dos. . . .
Le arrancaron para ti
de la corona de un Dios.

De tus labios la sonrisa,
la paz de tu lengua mana. . . .
leve, aérea, como brisa
de purpurina mañana.

¡ Oh, qué hermosa nazarena
para un harén oriental,
suelta la negra melena
sobre el cuello de cristal,

en lecho de terciopelo,
entre una nube de aroma,
y envuelta en el blanco velo
de las hijas de Mahoma !

Ven a Córdoba, cristiana,
sultana serás allí,
y el sultán será ¡ oh sultana !
un esclavo para ti.

Te dará tanta riqueza,
tanta gala tunecina,
que has de juzgar tu belleza
para pagarle, mezquina.

Dueña de la negra toca,
por un beso de tu boca
diera un reino Boabdil ;
y yo por ello, cristiana,
te diera de buena gana
mil cielos, si fueran mil.

246. *Granada*
(*Extract*)

Perhaps the best known of Zorrilla's lyric poems, this fine apostrophe to Granada is taken from the first book of his long but unfinished work of that title, published in 1852. No evocation in verse of a Spanish city—and such evocations are legion—is more completely impregnated with its spirit than this : it is still learned, and loved, by lovers of Andalusia. Imagination and expression run riot through musical lines which thrill with sensuous emotion ; and (as more markedly elsewhere in Granada) *local colour has a prominent place. Zorrilla is always most effective as a lyric poet when, as here, his main preoccupation is narrative.*

¡ Granada ! Ciudad bendita
reclinada sobre flores,
quien no ha visto tus primores
ni vió luz, ni gozó bien.
Quien ha orado en tu mezquita
y habitado tus palacios,
visitado ha los espacios
encantados del Edén.

Paraíso de la tierra
cuyos mágicos jardines
con sus manos de jazmines
cultivó celeste hurí,
la salud en ti se encierra,
en ti mora la alegría,
en tus sierras nace el día,
y arde el sol de amor por ti.

Tus fructíferas colinas,
que son nidos de palomas,
embalsaman los aromas
de un florido eterno Abril:
de tus fuentes cristalinas
surcan cisnes los raudales:
bajan águilas rëales
a bañarse en tu Genil.

Gayas aves entretienen
con sus trinos y sus quejas
el afán de las abejas
que en tus troncos labran miel:
y en tus sauces se detienen
las cansadas golondrinas
a las playas argelinas
cuando emigran en tropel.

En ti como en un espejo
se mira el profeta santo:
la luna envidia el encanto
que hay en tu dormida faz:
y al mirarte a su reflejo
el arcángel que la guía
un casto beso te envía,
diciéndote: "Duerme en paz."

El albor de la mañana
se esclarece en tu sonrisa,
y en tus valles va la brisa
de la aurora a reposar.

¡ Oh Granada, la sultana
del deleite y la ventura !
quien no ha visto tu hermosura
al nacer debió cegar.

¡ Aláh salve al Nazarita,
que derrama sus tesoros
para hacerte de los Moros
el alcázar imperial !
¡ Aláh salve al rey que habita
los palacios que en ti eleva !
¡ Aláh salve al rey que lleva
tu destino a gloria tal !

Las entrañas de tu sierra
se socavan noche y día ;
dan su mármol a porfía
Geb-Elvira y Macaël ;
ensordécese la tierra
con el son de los martillos,
y aparecen tus castillos
maravillas del cincel.

Ni un momento de reposo
se concede : palmo a palmo,
como a impulso de un ensalmo,
se levanta por doquier
el alcázar portentoso
que, mofándose del viento,
será eterno monumento
de tu ciencia y tu poder.

Reverbera su techumbre
por las noches, a lo lejos,
de las teas a la lumbre
que iluminan sin cesar
los trabajos misteriosos,
y a sus cárdenos reflejos
van los Genios sus preciosos
aposentos a labrar.

¿ De quién es ese palacio
sostenido en mil pilares,
cuyas torres y alminares
de inmortales obras son ?
¿ Quién habita el regio espacio
de sus cámaras abiertas ?
¿ Quién grabó sobre sus puertas
atrevido su blasón ?

¿ De quién es aquella corte
de galanes africanos
que la cruzan tan ufanos
de su noble Amir en pos ?
En su alcázar y en su porte
bien se lee su nombre escrito :
Al-hamar. Aláh bendito,
Es la ALHAMBRA. ¡ Gloria a Dios !

247. *Justicias del Rey Don Pedro.*

To bring one of the best of Zorrilla's narrative poems into the compass of an anthology is impossible, for his best are his longest, and the full charm of his easy, prolix and picturesque style cannot be experienced save by familiarity. The following brief sketch, however, gives some idea of the method of the leyendas, *of which he says (in the preface to the* Vigilias del Estío) :

Lector, no hay en sus renglones
más que viejas tradiciones
y acaso fábulas bellas.
No tienen más intención
que hacer humilde memoria
de nuestra pasada historia,
de nuestra fe y religión.

It is also of interest as illustrating an aspect of the character of Peter the Cruel—that of the rey justiciero*—complementary to the more obvious one which we have already observed (pp. 134-6, 467-73).*

I

Cuando su luz y su sombra
mezclan la noche y la tarde,
y los objetos se sumen
en la sombra impenetrable,
en un postigo excusado,
que a una callejuela sale,
de una casa cuya puerta
principal da a la otra calle,
dos hombres que se despiden
se ven, aunque no se sabe
ni cuál de los dos se queda,
ni cuál de los dos se parte.
Ambos mirándose atentos,
ambos un pie hacia adelante,
parados en el dintel
están, y entrambos iguales.
Por fin el más viejo de ellos,
hundiendo el mustio semblante
entre el sombrero y la capa
en ademán de marcharse,
torció la cabeza a un lado,
pronunciando un *no* tan grave,
que bien se vió que era el fin
de las pláticas de enantes.
Sin duda el otro, entendido,
no encontró qué replicarle,
pues, bajando la cabeza,
callóse por un instante.
" Buenas noches," dijo el viejo.
Tartamudeó un " Dios te guarde "
el otro ; mas, decidiéndose,
hizo hacia el viejo un avance.
" Mírelo bien, y cuidado
no se arrepienta, compadre."
" Nunca eché más que una cuenta."
" Piénselo bien, y no pase
sin contar lo que va de él
a don Juan de Colmenares."

" Señor," replicó el anciano,
" en tiempos tan deplorables
ya sé que lo pueden todo
los ricos y los audaces."
" Pues mire lo que le importa ;
que rico y audaz, señales
son con que marca la fama
a los que en mi casa nacen."

Callaron por un momento,
y, continuando mirándose,
dijo el viejo tristemente,
aunque en tono irrevocable :
" Nunca lo esperé de vos ;
mas tampoco vos ni nadie
puede esperar más de mí."
" Pues entonces adelante :
idos, buen viejo, con Dios,
que estoy de prisa y es tarde."

Cerró la puerta de golpe
a escuchar sin esperarse
una respuesta que el viejo
tuvo tentación de darle :
y acaso por su fortuna
quedó a tal punto en la calle
para dársela a la puerta,
donde la deshizo el aire.
Volvió el anciano la espalda,
y, en dos golpes desiguales,
sus pasos descompasados
pueden de lejos contarse ;
porque sus pies, impedidos,
deben a su edad y achaques
una muleta que marcha
un pie que los suyos antes.
La esquina a espacio traspuso,
y a poco otro hombre más ágil,
saliendo por el postigo,
siguió en silencio su alcance.

Túvose al volver la esquina ;
tendió los ojos sagaces
y enderezó los oídos
atento por todas partes ;
mas, no oyendo ni escuchando
de qué poder recelarse,
tomando el rastro del viejo,
echó por la misma calle.

II

En un aposento ambiguo,
medio portal, medio tienda,
que hace asimismo las veces
de cocina y de despensa,
pues da su entrada a la calle,
y en confuso ajuar ostenta
camas, hormas y un caldero
colgado en la chimenea,
hay seis personas distintas
que hacen al pie de la letra
(salvo el padre, que está ausente),
una raza verdadera.
Un mozo de viente abriles ;
una muchacha risueña
de diez y seis ; tres muchachos
y una anciana de sesenta.
Y aunque a las veces nos turban
engañosas apariencias,
zapateros son de oficio,
si a espacio se considera,
que está la estancia aromada
con vapores de pez negra ;
que ribetea la moza,
y que el mozo maja suela.
" Mucho tarda," dijo el último,
" padre, esta noche, Teresa."
" Ya ha tiempo que ha anochecido."
" Muchacho, atiza esa vela,
y deja quieto ese bote."

Y esto diciendo en voz recia
el mozo, siguió en silencio
cada cual en su tarea ;
el chico sitiando al bote,
ribeteando la doncella,
majando el mozo a compás,
y dormitando la vieja.

Con monótonos murmullos
arrullaban esta escena
el son de la escasa lluvia
de un aguacero que empieza,
el no interrumpido son
con que hierve la caldera,
y el tumultuoso chasquido
con que la luz chisporrea.
" ¿ Las nueve son ? " dijo el mozo.
" Eso las ánimas suenan
con sus campanas," repuso
santiguándose Teresa.
" ¡ Las ánimas, y aun no viene ! "
Y, echando atrás la silleta,
se puso el mancebo en pie,
y encaminóse a la puerta.
Al ruido que hizo en el cuarto,
despertándose la vieja,
dijo : " ¿ Rezáis a las ánimas ? "
" Sí, señora, estése queda."
Asió el mancebo la aldaba ;
mas la había alzado apenas
cuando un espantoso golpe
venció la puerta por fuera.
¡ Muerto soy ! dijo una voz.
Cayó un embozado en tierra,
y vióse un hombre que huía
al fin de la callejuela.
En derredor del caído
se agolparon, que aun conserva
algún resto de la vida
que le arrancan a la fuerza :

mas no bien le desenvuelven,
por ver piadosos si alienta,
un grito descompasado
lanzó . . . la familia entera.
Blasfemó el mozo con ira,
desmayóse la doncella,
y la anciana y los muchachos
el llanto a la par revientan.
" Padre, ¿ quién fué ? " preguntaba,
sosteniendo la cabeza
del anciano moribundo,
el hijo, que llora y tiembla.
Echóle triste mirada
su padre, como quien lega
su razón y su justicia
en quien se fija con ella.
" *Juan. . . .* "
" ¿ Qué Juan ?"
" *De Colmenares,*"
balbuceó con torpe lengua,
y sobre el brazo del hijo
dobló la faz macilenta.

Reinó un silencio solemne
por un instante en la escena,
y a reunirse empezaron
vecinos de ambas aceras.
Llegó la justicia al punto,
y mientras *justicia* ella,
partió por la turba el mozo
en faz de intención siniestra.
" ¿ Dónde va ? " dijo un corchete.
" Siendo yo su sangre mesma
¿ adónde sino al culpable ? "
" Soy con vos."
" Enhorabuena."
" Por si acaso, va seguro,"
dijo para sí el de presa,
mientras el mozo, resuelto,
ganó a una esquina la vuelta.

III

Son treinta días después,
y el mismo lugar y hora,
la misma vieja y los chicos
con mesa, mancebo y moza.
Cada cual en su tarea
sigue en paz, aunque se nota
que todos tienen los ojos
del mancebo en la faz torva.
Él, sin embargo, en silencio
prosigue en tanto su obra,
sin levantar la cabeza,
que sobre el pecho se apoya.
Tan doblada la mantiene,
que apenas la llama roja
que da la luz, alumbrarle
las cejas fruncidas logra;
y alguna vez que el reflejo
las negras pupilas toca,
tan viva luz reverberan
que chispas parece brotan.
La verdad es, que una lágrima
que a sus párpados asoma
viene anunciando un torrente
en que el corazón se ahoga.
Y el mozo, por no aumentar
de los suyos la congoja,
a duras penas le tiene
dentro el pecho y le sofoca.
Largo rato así estuvieron
en atención afanosa,
todos mirando al mancebo,
y éste mirando a sus hormas;
hasta que al cabo Teresa,
más sentida o más curiosa,
le dijo: "¿Estás malo, Blas?"
Y a su voz limpia y sonora
siguió otro largo intervalo
de larga atención dudosa.

Nada el hermano responde,
mas ella su afán redobla,
que no hay temor que la tenga
la valla de una vez rota.
" ¡ Cómo estás tan cabizbajo. . . . ! "
Y aquí Blas interrumpióla.
" ¿ Y qué tengo que decir
a quien sin padre y sin honra
debe vivir para siempre ? "
Y aquí la familia toda
rompió en ahogados sollozos
a tan infausta memoria.
Sosegóse, y siguió Blas
en voz lamentable y honda :
" Él rico, y nosotros pobres ;
débil la justicia, y poca,
y el Rey en caza y en guerra,
¿ qué puede alcanzar quien llora ? "
" ¿ Qué, por libre se atrevieron. . . . ? "
" Poco menos, pues sus doblas
pudieran más con los jueces
que las leyes."
" ¡ Las ignoran ! "
dijo indignada Teresa.
" ¡ No, hermana ! Las acogotan,"
contestó Blas, sacudiendo
su mazo con ciega cólera.
Siguió en silencio otro espacio,
y otra vez Teresa torna :
" Mas la sentencia ¿ cuál fué ? "
dijo, y calló vergonzosa.
" ¿ La sentencia ? " gritó Blas,
revolviendo por las órbitas
los negros y ardientes ojos.
" ¿ La sentencia pides ? Óyela."
Todos se echaron de golpe
sobre la mesilla coja,
que vaciló al recibirles,
a oír lo que tanto importa.
" Sabéis que el de Colmenares

hoy pingüe prebenda goza
en la iglesia, y que, a Dios gracias,
y a mi diligencia propia,
se le probó que dió muerte
a padre (que en paz reposa).
Pues bien : no sé por qué diablos
de maldita jerigonza
de conspiración que dicen
que con su muerte malogra,
dieron por bien muerto a padre,
y al clérigo . . ."
"¿ Le perdonan ? "
" No, vive Dios, le condenan.
¡ Mas ved qué dogal le ahoga !
Condénanle a que en un año
no asista a coro, mas cobra
su renta ; es decir, le mandan
que no trabaje y que coma."

Tornó a su silencio Blas,
y a sus sollozos la moza,
ella cosiendo sus cintas,
y él machacando sus hormas.

IV

Está la mañana limpia,
azul, transparente, clara,
y el sol, de entre nubes rojas,
espléndida luz derrama.
Toda es tumulto Sevilla,
músicas, vivas y danzas ;
todo movimiento el suelo,
toda murmullos el aura.
Cruzan literas y pajes,
monjes, caballeros, guardias,
vendedores, alguaciles,
penachos, pendones, mangas ;
flota el damasco y las plumas
en balcones y ventanas,
y atraviesan besamanos

donde no caben palabras ;
descórrense celosías,
tapices visten las tapias,
los abanicos ondulan
y los velos se levantan.
Cuantas hermosas encierra
Sevilla, a su gloria saca ;
cuantos buenos caballeros
en sus fortalezas guarda ;
ellos porque son galanes,
y ellas porque son bizarras,
las unas porque la adornen,
los otros para admirarlas.
Óyense al lejos clarines,
y chirimías y cajas,
y a lengua suelta repican
esquilones y campanas.
Mas no vienen los hidalgos
armados hasta las barbas,
ni el pálido rostro asoman
las bellas amedrentadas ;
que no doblan los tambores
en son agudo de alarma,
ni las campanas repican
a rebato arrebatadas :
que es *la procesión del Corpus*,
que ya traspone las gradas
del atrio, y el rey don Pedro
acompañándola baja.
Padillas y Coroneles
y Alburquerques se adelantan,
con Osorios y Guzmanes,
pompa ostentando sobrada.
Y bajo un palio don Pedro,
de ocho punzones de plata,
descubierta la cabeza
y armado hasta el cuello, marcha.
　En torno suyo el Cabildo
diez individuos encarga
que de escuderos le sirvan

en comisión poco santa ;
mas tiempos son tan ambiguos
los que estos monjes alcanzan,
que tanto arrastran ropones,
como broqueles embrazan.
Entre ellos se ve a don Juan
de Colmenares y Vargas,
que deja por vez primera
la reclusión de su casa,
no porque el año ha cumplido,
sino porque el año paga,
y doblas redimen culpas
si se confiesan doradas.
   Rosas deshojan sobre ellos
las hermosísimas damas,
y toda es flores la calle
por donde la corte pasa.
Envidia de las más bellas
salió a un balcón del alcázar
la hermosísima Padilla,
origen de culpas tantas.
Hízola venia don Pedro,
y, al responderle la dama,
soltó sin querer un guante,
y ¡ ojalá no le soltara !
Lanzóse a tomar la prenda
muchedumbre cortesana :
muchos llegaron a un tiempo,
mas nadie tomarla osaba,
que fuera acción peligrosa,
aparte de lo profana.
Partiendo la diferencia,
salió de la fila santa
el bizarro Colmenares
con intención de tomarla.
Mas no bien dejó su mano
del palio el punzón de plata,
y puso desde él al Rey
cuatro pasos de distancia,
cuando un mancebo iracundo,

con irresistible audacia,
se echó sobre él, y en el pecho
le asestó dos puñaladas.

Cayó don Juan ; quedó el mozo
sereno en pie entre los guardias,
que le asieron, y don Pedro
se halló con él cara a cara.
La procesión se deshizo ;
volvió gigante la fama
el caso de boca en boca,
y ya prodigios contaban.
Juntáronse los soldados
recelando una asonada ;
cercaron al Rey algunos,
y llenó al punto la plaza
la multitud, codiciosa
de ver la lucha empezada
entre el sacrílego mozo
y el sanguinario Monarca.
Duró un instante el silencio,
mientras el Rey devoraba
con sus ojos de serpiente
los ojos del que le ultraja.

" ¿ Quién eres ? " dijo por fin
dando en tierra una patada.
" Blas Pérez," contestó el mozo
con voz decidida y clara.
Pálido el rey de coraje,
asióle por la garganta,
y así en voz ronca le dijo,
que la cólera le ahogaba :
" ¿ Y yendo tu Rey aquí,
¡ voto a Dios ! por qué no hablaste,
si con ocasión te hallaste
para obrar con él así ? "

Soltóse Blas de la mano
con que el Rey le sujetaba,
y, señalando al difunto,

repuso tras breve pausa :
" Mató a mi padre, señor,
y el tribunal, por su oro,
privóle un año del coro,
que, en vez de pena, es favor."
" Y si vende el tribunal
la justicia encomendada,
¿ no es mi justicia abonada
para quien justicia mal ? "
" Cuando el miedo o la malicia,"
dijo Blas, " tuercen la ley,
nadie se fía en el Rey,
medido por su justicia."

Calló Blas, y calló el Rey
a respuesta tan osada,
y los ojos de don Pedro
bajo las cejas chispeaban.
Tendiólos por todas partes,
y al fuego de sus miradas,
de aquellos en quien las puso
palidecieron las caras.
Temblaron los más audaces,
y el pueblo ansioso esperaba
una explosión en don Pedro
más recia que sus palabras.
Rompió el silencio por fin,
y en voz amistosa y blanda,
el interrumpido diálogo
así con el mozo entabla :
" ¿ Qué es tu oficio ? "
" Zapatero."
" No han de decir ¡ vive Dios !
que a ninguno de los dos
en mi sentencia prefiero."

Y encarándose don Pedro
con los jueces que allí estaban,
dando un bolsillo a Blas Pérez,
dijo en voz resuelta y alta :

" Pesando ambos desacatos,
si con no rezar cumple él
en un año, cumples fiel
no haciendo en otro zapatos."

Tornóse don Pedro al punto,
y brotó la turba osada
murmullos de la nobleza
y aplausos de la canalla.
Mas viendo el Rey que la fiesta
mucho en ordenarse tarda,
echando mano al estoque,
dijo así, ronco de rabia :
" ¡ La procesión adelante,
o meto cuarenta lanzas
y acaban ¡ voto a los cielos !
los salmos a cuchilladas ! "

Y como consta a la Iglesia
que es hombre el Rey de palabra,
siguieron calle adelante
palio, pendones y mangas.

RAMÓN DE CAMPOAMOR

1817-1901

BEGINNING his career as an almost pure Romantic (*Ternezas y flores*, 1840), Campoamor quickly reacted in the direction of realism (*Doloras*, 1846), returning after a few years to a formless and vaguely symbolic romanticism (*Colón*, 1853; *El Drama Universal*, 1869), but eventually resuming the realistic manner (*Pequeños Poemas*, 1872; *Humoradas*, 1886-8) by which he is principally known. In the *Doloras* one finds little poetry, but much observation and understanding of human nature, though these, on occasion, are cheerfully sacrificed for some mordant or witty epigram. Some of Campoamor's most typical pieces are packed with thought and wisdom; others, built upon hollow antitheses, are no more than superficially clever. It should be observed that, hard-headed as Campoamor seems, sentimentality often lies just below the surface of his verses.

Three examples of epigrammatic verse from the *Doloras* are here given—the second and the third corresponding respectively to the two types just described—followed by "¡ Quién supiera escribir!", a poem in which Campoamor achieved something really unique. This spirited imaginary dialogue between the lover and the *cura* who acts as village letter-writer, recorded in one of Campoamor's favourite metres, is really an essay in *costumbrismo* clothed in a novel form; but it is also the highly sympathetic study of a human being, which plays surely, skilfully and with progressive intensity upon the emotions.

248. *Todo y Nada*

"¡ Cuánta dicha y cuánta gloria!"
dije, entre humillado y fiero,
leyendo una vez la historia
del emperador Severo.

Y cuando a verle llegué
subir a Rey desde el lodo,
" Yo, en cambio," humilde exclamé,
no fuí nada, y nada es todo."

Mas con humildad mayor,
vi que al fin de la jornada
exclamó el emperador :
" Yo fuí todo, y todo es nada."

249. *Hastío*

Sin el amor que encanta,
la soledad de un ermitaño espanta.
¡ Pero es más espantosa todavía
la soledad de dos en compañía !

250. *La Vuelta al Hogar*

I

Después de un viaje por mar,
volviendo hacia su alquería,
oye Juan con alegría
las campanas del lugar.

II

Llega, y maldice lo incierto
de las venturas humanas,
al saber que las campanas
tocan por su padre a muerto.

251. *¡ Quién supiera escribir !*

I

" Escribidme una carta, señor Cura."
" Ya sé para quién es."
" ¿ Sabéis quién es, porque una noche oscura
Nos visteis juntos ? " " Pues."

"Perdonad; mas...." "No extraño ese tropiezo.
La noche.... la ocasión....
Dadme pluma y papel. Gracias. Empiezo:
Mi querido Ramón:"
"¿Querido?... Pero, en fin, ya lo habéis puesto...."
"Si no queréis...." "¡Sí, sí!"
"*¡Qué triste estoy!* ¿No es eso?" "Por supuesto."
"*¡Qué triste estoy sin ti!*
Una congoja, al empezar, me viene...."
"¿Cómo sabéis mi mal?"
"Para un viejo, una niña siempre tiene
el pecho de cristal.
¿Qué es sin ti el mundo? Un valle de amargura.
¿Y contigo? Un edén."
"Haced la letra clara, señor Cura,
que lo entienda eso bien."
"*El beso aquel que de marchar a punto*
te di...." "¿Cómo sabéis?..."
"Cuando se va y se viene y se está junto
siempre... no os afrentéis....
Y si volver tu afecto no procura,
tanto me harás sufrir...."
"¿Sufrir y nada más? No, señor Cura,
¡que me voy a morir!"
"¿Morir? ¿Sabéis que es ofender al cielo?..."
"Pues, sí, señor, ¡morir!"
"Yo no pongo *morir.*" "¡Qué hombre de hielo!
¡Quién supiera escribir!"

II

"¡Señor Rector, señor Rector! En vano
me queréis complacer,
si no encarnan los signos de la mano
todo el ser de mi ser.
Escribidle, por Dios, que el alma mía
ya en mí no quiere estar;
que la pena no me ahoga cada día....
porque puedo llorar.

Que mis labios, las rosas dé su aliento,
no se saben abrir;
que olvidan de la risa el movimiento
a fuerza de sentir.

Que mis ojos, que él tiene por tan bellos,
cargados con mi afán,
como no tienen quien se mire en ellos,
cerrados siempre están.

Que es, de cuantos tormentos he sufrido,
la ausencia el más atroz;
que es un perpetuo sueño de mi oído
el èco de su voz. . . .

Que siendo por su causa, ¡ el alma mía
goza tanto en sufrir ! . . .
Dios mío ¡ cuántas cosas le diría
si supiera escribir ! . . ."

III

Epílogo

" Pues, señor, ¡ bravo amor ! Copio y concluyo :
A don Ramón. . . . En fin,
que es inútil saber para esto arguyo
ni el griego ni el latín."

PABLO PIFERRER
1817-1848

PIFERRER was a Catalonian whose modest but attractive *Composiciones poéticas*, with those of two less able contemporaries, Juan Francisco Carbó and José Semís, were published after his death, in 1851. Influenced strongly by Scott, he was best in the neo-mediaeval ballad; his most prominent qualities are a command of rhythm and melody. In his *canción* to spring he makes effective use of the whole-line and half-line refrain; the slow-moving even lines are suggestive of one of the slow dances common in Catalonia, to which the *gaita*, or bagpipe, provides the music; but the distinction of the poem lies in its semi-symbolism, which intensifies and exalts the vivid reminiscences of the countryside.

252. *Canción de la Primavera*

Ya vuelve la primavera,
suene la gaita, ruede la danza:
tiende sobre la pradera
el verde manto de la esperanza.

Sopla caliente la brisa;
suene la gaita, ruede la danza:
las nubes pasan aprisa,
y el azur muestran de la esperanza.

La flor ríe en su capullo;
suene la gaita, ruede la danza:
canta el agua en su murmullo
el poder santo de la esperanza.

¿ La oís que en los aires trina ?
Suene la gaita, ruede la danza.
" Abrid a la golondrina,
que vuelve en alas de la esperanza."

Niña, la niña modesta,
suene la gaita, ruede la danza :
el mayo trae tu fiesta
que el logro trae de tu esperanza.

Cubre la tierra el amor ;
suene la gaita, ruede la danza :
el perfume engendrador
al seno sube de la esperanza.

Todo zumba y reverdece :
suene la gaita, ruede la danza.
Cuanto el son y el verdor crece,
tanto más crece toda esperanza.

Sonido, aroma y color
(suene la gaita, ruede la danza)
únense en himnos de amor,
que engendra el himno de la esperanza.

Morirá la primavera :
suene la gaita, ruede la danza :
mas cada año en la pradera
tornará el manto de la esperanza.

La inocencia de la vida
(calle la gaita, pare la danza)
no torna una vez perdida.
¡ Perdí la mía ! ¡ ay mi esperanza !

GABRIEL GARCÍA TASSARA
1817-1875

GARCÍA TASSARA, a Sevilian like his greater contemporary Bécquer, might have been a much better poet had he lived in more propitious times. He had fire and vigour, imagination and a sense of art, but he seems to have found it hard to shake off conventionality—both in style and occasionally also in subject. Though chiefly remembered for his political satires, written in mid-century, he shows more promise as a much younger man, but at no time in his life can he long sustain a high level: he is a poet of shreds and flashes.

253. *Himno al Mesías*

Baja otra vez al mundo,
baja otra vez, ¡ Mesías !
De nuevo son los días
de tu alta vocación ;
y en su dolor profundo
la humanidad entera
el nuevo oriente espera
de un sol de redención.

Corrieron veinte edades
desde el supremo día
que en esa cruz te veía
morir Jerusalén ;
y nuevas tempestades
surgieron y bramaron,
de aquellas que asolaron
el primitivo Edén.

De aquellas que le ocultan
al hombre su camino
con ciego torbellino
de culpa y expiación;
de aquellas que sepultan
en hondos cautiverios
cadáveres de imperios
que fueron y no son.

Sereno está en la esfera
el sol del firmamento:
la tierra en su cimiento
inconmovible está:
la blanca primavera,
con su gentil abrazo,
fecunda el gran regazo
que flor y fruto da.

Mas ¡ay! que de las almas
el sol yace eclipsado;
mas ¡ay! que ha vacilado
el polo de la fe;
mas ¡ay! que ya tus palmas
se vuelven al desierto:
no crecen, no, en el huerto
del que tu pueblo fué.

Tiniebla es ya la Europa:
ella agotó la ciencia,
maldijo su creencia,
se apacentó con hiel;
y rota ya la copa
en que su fe bebía,
se alzaba y te decía:
¡Señor! yo soy Luzbel.

Mas ¡ay! que contra el cielo
no tiene el hombre rayo,
y en súbito desmayo
cayó de ayer a hoy;
y en son de desconsuelo,
y en llanto de impotencia,
hoy clama en tu presencia:
Señor, tu pueblo soy.

No es, no, la Roma atea
que entre aras derrocadas
despide a carcajadas
los dioses que se van :
es la que humilde rea,
baja a las catacumbas,
y palpa entre las tumbas
los tiempos que vendrán.

Todo ¡ Señor ! diciendo
está los grandes días
de lutos y agonías,
de muerte y orfandad ;
que del pecado horrendo
envuelta en el sudario,
pasa por un Calvario
la ciega humanidad.

Baja ¡ oh Señor ! no en vano
siglos y siglos vuelan ;
los siglos nos revelan
con misteriosa luz
el infinito arcano
y la virtud que encierra,
trono de cielo y tierra,
tu sacrosanta cruz.

Toda la historia humana
¡ Señor ! está en tu nombre.
Tú fuiste Dios del hombre,
Dios de la humanidad.
Tu sangre soberana
es su Calvario eterno :
tu triunfo del infierno
es su inmortalidad.

¿ Quién dijo, Dios clemente,
que Tú no volverías,
y a horribles gemonías
y a eterna perdición,
condena a esta doliente
raza del ser humano
que espera de tu mano
su nueva salvación ?

Sí, Tú vendrás. Vencidos
serán con nuevo ejemplo
los que del santo templo
apartan a tu grey.
Vendrás y confundidos
caerán con los ateos
los nuevos fariseos
de la caduca ley.

¿ Quién sabe si ahora mismo
entre alaridos tantos
de tus profetas santos
la voz no suena ya ?
Ven, saca del abismo
a un pueblo moribundo ;
Luzbel ha vuelto al mundo
y Dios ¿ no volverá ?

¡ Señor ! En tus juicios
la comprensión se abisma ;
mas es siempre la misma
del Gólgota la voz.
Fatídicos auspicios
resonarán en vano ;
no es el destino humano
la humanidad sin Dios.

Ya pasarán los siglos
de la tremenda prueba ;
ya nacerás, ¡ luz nueva
de la futura edad !
Ya huiréis, ¡ negros vestiglos
de los antiguos días !
Ya volverás ¡ Mesías !
en gloria y majestad.

ADELARDO LÓPEZ DE AYALA

1828-1879

LÓPEZ DE AYALA made his name chiefly as an Eclectic dramatist of the generation preceding that dominated by the neo-Romantic Echegaray. As a poet, however, and particularly as a sonneteer, he is by no means negligible. Delicacy and grace are his ruling traits, rather than passion or power, and he is sometimes most charming when most unequal, especially in his lyrics on love. In the religious sonnet here reproduced, which is somewhat marred by the unrelieved monotony of the *agudo* endings, he first gives us a nineteenth-century treatment of a paradoxical theme common in devotional poetry of the sixteenth—a notable example can be found in Santa Teresa[1]—and then expresses an aspiration with a sincere directness also suggestive of the sixteenth-century ascetics and mystics.

254. *Plegaria*

¡ Dame, Señor, la firme voluntad,
compañera y sostén de la virtud ;
la que sabe en el golfo hallar quietud
y en medio de las sombras claridad :

la que trueca en tesón la veleidad
y el ocio en perenal solicitud,
y las ásperas fiebres en salud,
y los torpes engaños en verdad !

Y así conseguirá mi corazón
que los favores que a tu amor debí,
te ofrezcan algún fruto en galardón. . . .

Y aun tú, Señor, conseguirás así
que no llegue a romper mi confusión
la imagen tuya que pusiste en mí.

[1] *Obras, ed. cit.*, VI, 111-2.

FEDERICO BALART
1831-1905

BALART, who wrote principally in late middle age, may stand for a number of post-Romantic poets—Ruiz Aguilera, Bartrina and Querol are three of them—writing in a minor key and on a note of disillusion. In a study of literary *desengaño* they would all have to be reckoned with, but viewed in relation to the nineteenth century as a whole they can take only a secondary place. Balart's sonnet " Visión ", from the collection *Horizontes* (1894), will show how a Romantic inspiration still had power even so long after the Romantic movement was dead.

255. *Visión*

Por los ámbitos lóbregos de un sueño
vi cruzar un fantasma peregrino
que, envuelto en nube de fulgor divino,
me llamaba mirándome risueño.

Seguirle quise con ardiente empeño,
fascinado y extático y sin tino ;
pero, al tocar su manto purpurino,
veloz huyó, mirándome con ceño.

Sentido de su rápida mudanza,
" ¿ Por qué," dije, " te places en mi daño ? "
Y él, al desvanecerse en lontananza,

" Yo soy," me dijo con semblante huraño,
" para quien no me logra, la Esperanza ;
para quien me consigue, el Desengaño."

GASPAR NÚÑEZ DE ARCE

1832-1903

Núñez de Arce's verse is generally thought of as the expression of his political Liberalism and of the element of *desengaño* in his philosophy of life. Many of his poems found in the collection significantly named *Gritos del combate* may, in fact, be described as a commentary on the stormy decade which ended with the restoration of the Bourbon monarchy: they were written, he himself said, "bajo la impresión de dolorosos y transcendentales sucesos, y en medio del fragor de la lucha." Such are the sonnet "A España" (1866), the epistle "La Duda" (1868), the "Estrofas" of 1870 and the ode to Castelar (1873). But to what extent their author was a true *desengañado* is another matter. If we disregard the poems which echo Romantic sentimentality and melancholy and isolate those which seem to express genuine feeling, we shall find that an early tendency to disillusion, accompanied by loss of faith ("Treinta Años"), becomes intensified by the impact of external events ("La Duda"), but that, on the other hand, most of his poems contain happier and brighter reflections: the latest in date of them is entitled "¡ Sursum, corda!"

256. *¡ Excelsior!*

This brief meditation on idealism and effort, full of hope and faith, was written in 1872, during the short reign of Amadeo, when Núñez de Arce's apprehensiveness as to the future of his country was temporarily stilled. Its terseness and force are as far from the discursiveness of the longer poems as is its noble idealism from the rather plaintive disillusion of "Treinta Años" and "Tristezas". It is certainly one of its author's poems best worth preserving.

¿ Por qué los corazones miserables,
por qué las almas viles,
en los fieros combates de la vida
ni luchan ni resisten ?

El espíritu humano es más constante
cuanto más levanta ;
Dios puso el fango en la llanura, y puso
la roca en la montaña.

La blanca nieve que en los hondos valles
derrítese ligera,
en las altivas cumbres permanece
inmutable y eterna.

257. *Tristezas*

Completed on June 30, 1874, at a time when Spain's future was again in the melting-pot, "Tristezas" returns to the theme of doubt and desengaño. *An extended pictorial contrast, replete with outworn Romantic imagery and terminology, between the religiosity of the author's boyhood and the disillusion of his middle age, leads him to a description of his present state ("Entre tinieblas desespero y dudo. . . .") which he develops at some length and rather repetitively. Then comes the other side of the picture. The age, of which he is a child, has also changed : the ship is drifting helplessly on the sea and the shore is far distant. In despair, the poet clutches once more at his early beliefs (ll. 1-12) : only the power of Christ can save the world.*

Cuando recuerdo la piedad sincera
con que en mi edad primera
entraba en nuestras viejas catedrales,
donde postrado ante la cruz de hinojos
alzaba a Dios mis ojos,
soñando en las venturas celestiales ;

hoy que mi frente atónito golpeo,
y con febril deseo
busco los restos de mi fe perdida,
por hallarla otra vez, radiante y bella
como en la edad aquella,
¡ desgraciado de mí ! diera la vida.

¡ Con qué cándido amor, niño inocente,
prosternaba mi frente
en las losas del templo sacrosanto !
Llenábase mi joven fantasía
de luz, de poesía,
de mudo asombro, de terrible espanto.

Aquellas altas bóvedas que al cielo
levantaban mi anhelo ;
aquella majestad solemne y grave ;
aquel pausado canto, parecido
a un doliente gemido,
que retumbaba en la espaciosa nave ;

las marmóreas y austeras esculturas
de antiguas sepulturas,
aspiración del arte a lo infinito ;
la luz que por los vidrios de colores
sus tibios resplandores
quebraba en los pilares de granito,

haces de donde en curva fugitiva,
para formar la ojiva
cada ramal subiendo se separa,
cual del rumor de multitud que ruega,
cuando a los cielos llega,
surge cada oración distinta y clara ;

en el gótico altar inmoble y fijo
el santo Crucifijo,
que extiende sin vigor sus brazos yertos,
siempre en la sorda lucha de la vida,
tan áspera y reñida
para el dolor y la humildad abiertos ;

el místico clamor de la campana
que sobre el alma humana
de las caladas torres se despeña,
y anuncia y lleva en sus aladas notas
mil promesas ignotas
al triste corazón que sufre y sueña ;

todo elevaba mi ánimo tranquilo
a más sereno asilo,
religión, arte, soledad, misterio. . . .
todo en el templo secular hacía
vibrar el alma mía,
como vibran las cuerdas de un salterio.

Y a esta voz interior que solo entiende
quien crédulo se enciende
en fervoroso y celestial cariño,
envuelta en sus flotantes vestiduras
volaba a las alturas,
virgen sin mancha, mi oración de niño.

Su rauda, viva y luminosa huella
como fugaz centella
traspasaba el espacio, y ante el puro
resplandor de sus alas de querube,
rasgábase la nube
que me ocultaba el inmortal seguro.

¡ Oh anhelo de esta vida transitoria !
¡ Oh perdurable gloria !
¡ Oh sed inextinguible del deseo !
¡ Oh cielo, que antes para mí tenías
fulgores y armonías,
y hoy tan obscuro y desolado veo !

Ya no templas mis íntimos pesares,
ya al pie de tus altares
como en mis años de candor no acudo.
Para llegar a ti perdí el camino,
y errante y peregrino
entre tinieblas desespero y dudo.

Voy espantado sin saber por dónde ;
grito, y nadie responde
a mi angustiada voz ; alzo los ojos
y a penetrar la lobreguez no alcanzo ;
medrosamente avanzo,
y me hieren el alma los abrojos.

Hijo del siglo, en vano me resisto
a su impiedad, ¡ oh Cristo !
Su grandeza satánica me oprime.
Siglo de maravillas y de asombros,
levanta sobre escombros
un Dios sin esperanza, un Dios que gime,

¡ y ese Dios no eres tú ! No tu serena
faz, de consuelos llena,
alumbra y guía nuestro incierto paso.
Es otro Dios incógnito y sombrío :
su cielo es el vacío,
sacerdote el Error, ley el Acaso.

¡ Ay ! No recuerda el ánimo suspenso,
un siglo más inmenso,
más rebelde a tu voz, más atrevido :
entre nubes de fuego alza su frente,
como Luzbel, potente ;
pero también, como Luzbel, caído.

A medida que marcha y que investiga,
es mayor su fatiga,
es su noche más honda y más obscura,
y pasma, al ver lo que padece y sabe,
cómo en su seno cabe
tanta grandeza y tanta desventura.

Como la nave sin timón y rota,
que el ronco mar azota,
incendia el rayo y la borrasca mece
en piélago ignorado y proceloso,
nuestro siglo-coloso
con la luz que le abrasa resplandece.

¡ Y está la playa mística tan lejos ! . . .
a los tristes reflejos
del sol poniente se colora y brilla.
El huracán arrecia, el bajel arde,
y es tarde, es ¡ ay ! muy tarde
para alcanzar la sosegada orilla.

¿ Qué es la ciencia sin fe ? Corcel sin freno,
a todo yugo ajeno,
que al impulso del vértigo se entrega,
y al través de intrincadas espesuras,
desbocado y a obscuras
avanza sin cesar y nunca llega.

¡ Llegar ! ¿ A dónde ? . . . El pensamiento humano
en vano lucha, en vano
su ley oculta y misteriosa infringe.
En la lumbre del sol sus alas quema,
y no aclara el problema,
ni penetra el enigma de la Esfinge.

¡ Sálvanos, Cristo, sálvanos, si es cierto
que tu poder no ha muerto !
Salva a esta sociedad desventurada,
que bajo el peso de su orgullo mismo
rueda al profundo abismo,
acaso más enferma que culpada.

La ciencia audaz, cuando de ti se aleja,
en nuestras almas deja
el germen de recónditos dolores,
como al tender el vuelo hacia la altura,
deja su larva impura
el insecto en el cáliz de las flores.

Si en esta confusión honda y sombría
es, Señor, todavía
raudal de vida tu palabra santa,
di a nuestra fe desalentada y yerta :
" ¡ Anímate y despierta ! "
como dijiste a Lázaro : " ¡ Levanta ! "

258. *La Luz y las Tinieblas*

Though it falls outside the Gritos de combate *proper, the preface to which was dated three months after the Restoration (March 9, 1875), this poem (October 5, 1876) is of the same inspiration. Combat between light and darkness, truth and error: which will triumph? This time the poet's reply to that oft-answered question is indeterminate. Neither will triumph: the conflict will continue world without end.*

La fiera, la titánica batalla
dura y persiste aún:
es el combate entre la ciega sombra
y la fecunda luz.

¡ Ni un instante de tregua y de reposo !
En la tierra, en el mar,
en el espacio, en la conciencia humana
siempre lidiando están.

Al través de los siglos que se empujan
con sorda confusión,
ruedan mezclados la verdad, el día,
la noche y el error.

¿ Quién vencerá por fin ? ¿ La negra sombra ?
¿ La excelsa claridad ? . . .
¡ Ay, no lo preguntéis ! La horrenda lucha
nunca terminará.

Cuando la creación rota y deshecha
vuelva al caos otra vez ;
cuando desierta, impenetrable y muda,
la inmensidad esté ;

en el seno del tiempo, en el espacio
sin mundos y sin sol
seguirá eterno el duelo formidable
entre Satán y Dios.

GUSTAVO ADOLFO BÉCQUER

1836-1870

This Andalusian, a Romantic born out of due time, and the subtlest poet of his age, wrote a number of charming and sometimes powerful tales—prose equivalents of Zorrilla's *leyendas*, though composed with greater art—but it is as a writer of verse that he will be immortal. Some critics would describe him as the first truly lyric poet Spain had known for two and a half centuries: not, certainly, for as long as that had any poet shown such imagination, sensibility and gift for song. Some of his works were published in periodicals during his lifetime, but they were not collected until the year after his tragically early death and it was only in the following decade that men began to appreciate his greatness. Though he wrote in what may be called the "pseudo-Romantic" period, his poetry is of the purest quality, free from all the exaggerations of the Romantic mode.

RIMAS

Bécquer's total output in verse consists of seventy-nine short poems, bearing no names save for their collective title of "Rimas". Their theme is love; but the Romantic mist in which they are veiled has baffled the critics' efforts at reconstruction. In their subtlety, and in the intangibility of their expression, lies their chief beauty: denuded of anecdote, they resemble much present-day poetry in the high degree of their malleability to the imagination. Analyzed, they will be found to contain, in the purest form, all the elements which the preceding generation had dubbed "Romantic"—subjectivity, melancholy, disillusion and an intense sensibility to Nature. To these add a delicate sense of colour, a great wealth of imagery and an exquisite command of melody: the rest is indefinable. Another feature of the "Rimas" is their homogeneity of merit: so uniformly high is their standard of beauty that one can select from them almost at random, though always with the feeling that justice demands the inclusion of the whole.

259. *Rima V*

Espíritu sin nombre,
indefinible esencia,
yo vivo con la vida
sin formas de la idea.

Yo nado en el vacío
del sol tiemblo en la hoguera,
palpito entre las sombras
y floto con las nieblas.

Yo soy el fleco de oro
de la lejana estrella ;
yo soy de la alta luna
la luz tibia y serena.

Yo soy la ardiente nube
que en el ocaso ondea ;
yo soy del astro errante
la luminosa estela.

Yo soy nieve en las cumbres,
soy fuego en las arenas,
azul onda en los mares,
y espuma en las riberas.

En el laúd soy nota,
perfume en la violeta,
fugaz llama en las tumbas,
y en las ruinas hiedra.

Yo atrueno en el torrente,
y silbo en la centella,
y ciego en el relámpago,
y rujo en la tormenta.

Yo río en los alcores,
susurro en la alta yerba,
suspiro en la onda pura,
y lloro en la hoja seca.

Yo ondulo con los átomos
del humo que se eleva,
y al cielo lento sube
en espiral inmensa.

Yo, en los dorados hilos
que los insectos cuelgan,
me mezco entre los árboles
en la ardorosa siesta.

Yo corro tras las ninfas
que en la corriente fresca
del cristalino arroyo
desnudas juguetean.

Yo, en bosques de corales,
que alfombran blancas perlas,
persigo en el Océano
las náyades ligeras.

Yo, en las cavernas cóncavas,
do el sol nunca penetra,
mezclándome a los gnomos,
contemplo sus riquezas.

Yo busco de los siglos
las ya borradas huellas,
y sé de esos imperios
de que ni el nombre queda.

Yo sigo en raudo vértigo
los mundos que voltean,
y mi pupila abarca
la creación entera.

Yo sé de esas regiones
a do un rumor no llega,
y donde informes astros
de vida un soplo esperan.

Yo soy sobre el abismo
el puente que atraviesa;
yo soy la ignota escala
que el cielo une a la tierra.

Yo soy el invisible
anillo que sujeta
el mundo de la forma
al mundo de la idea.

Yo, en fin, soy ese espíritu,
desconocida esencia,
perfume misterioso,
de que es vaso el poeta.

260. *Rima XI*

" Yo soy ardiente, yo soy morena,
yo soy el símbolo de la pasión ;
de ansia de goces mi alma está llena.
¿ A mí me buscas ? " " No es a ti ; no."

" Mi frente es pálida ; mis trenzas de oro
puedo brindarte dichas sin fin ;
yo de ternura guardo un tesoro.
¿ A mí me llamas ? " " No ; no es a ti."

" Yo soy un sueño, un imposible,
vano fantasma de niebla y luz ;
soy incorpórea, soy intangible ;
no puedo amarte." " ¡ Oh, ven ; ven tú ! "

261. *Rima XV*

Cendal flotante de leve bruma,
rizada cinta de blanca espuma,
rumor sonoro
de arpa de oro,
beso del aura, onda de luz,
eso eres tú.

Tú, sombra aérea, que cuantas veces
voy a tocarte, te desvaneces
como la llama, como el sonido,
como la niebla, como el gemido
del lago azul.

En mar sin playas onda sonante,
en el vacío cometa errante
largo lamento
del ronco viento,
ansia perpetua de algo mejor,
eso soy yo.

¡ Yo, que a tus ojos en mi agonía
los ojos vuelvo de noche y día ;
yo, que incansable corro y demente
tras una sombra, tras la hija ardiente
de una visión !

262. *Rima XVII*

Hoy la tierra y los cielos me sonríen ;
hoy llega al fondo de mi alma el sol ;
hoy la he visto . . . la he visto y me ha mirado. . . .
¡ Hoy creo en Dios !

263. *Rima LIII*

Volverán las oscuras golondrinas
en tu balcón sus nidos a colgar,
y otra vez con el ala a sus cristales
jugando llamarán.

Pero aquellas que el vuelo refrenaban
tu hermosura y mi dicha al contemplar,
aquellas que aprendieron nuestros nombres.
Ésas . . . ¡ no volverán !

Volverán las tupidas madreselvas
de tu jardín las tapias a escalar,
y otra vez a la tarde, aun más hermosas,
sus flores se abrirán.

Pero aquellas cuajadas de rocío,
cuyas gotas mirábamos temblar
y caer, como lágrimas del día. . . .
Ésas . . . ¡ no volverán !

Volverán del amor en tus oídos
las palabras ardientes a sonar ;
tu corazón de su profundo sueño
tal vez despertará.

Pero mudo y absorto y de rodillas,
como se adora a Dios ante su altar,
como yo te he querido . . . desengáñate,
¡ así no te querrán !

264. *Rima LXVIII*

No sé lo que he soñado
en la noche pasada ;
triste, muy triste debió ser el sueño,
pues despierto la angustia me duraba.

Noté, al incorporarme,
húmeda la almohada,
y por primera vez sentí, al notarlo,
de un amargo placer henchirse el alma.

Triste cosa es el sueño
que llanto nos arranca ;
mas tengo en mi tristeza una alegría. . . .
¡ Sé que aún me quedan lágrimas !

265. *Rima LXXV*

¿ Será verdad que cuando toca el sueño
con sus dedos de rosa nuestros ojos,
de la cárcel que habita huye el espíritu
en vuelo presuroso ?

¿ Será verdad que, huésped de las nieblas,
de la brisa nocturna al tenue soplo,
alado sube a la región vacía
a encontrarse con otros ?

¿ Y allí, desnudo de la humana forma,
allí, los lazos terrenales rotos,
breves horas habita de la idea
el mundo silencioso ?

¿ Y ríe y llora, y aborrece y ama,
y guarda un rastro del dolor y el gozo,
semejante al que deja cuando cruza
el cielo un meteoro ?

¡ Yo no sé si ese mundo de visiones
vive fuera o va dentro de nosotros ;
pero sé que conozco a muchas gentes
a quienes no conozco !

ROSALÍA CASTRO DE MURGUÍA

1837-1885

ROSALÍA CASTRO, a Galician, wrote much verse in her own language, but her Castilian volume, *En las Orillas del Sar* (1884), contains poems noteworthy for a sincerity, a sensitiveness and a lyric quality which few nineteenth-century poets surpassed. She lacks power, and sometimes depth—her verses have all the modesty of Gil's violet; but there will always be some whom they will attract by their fragrance.

The poems which follow illustrate her characteristic moods: subjectivity, melancholy, disillusion blended with religious faith, aspiration to the unattainable. They show, too, that she could on occasion be as vivid and picturesque as was consonant with the permeation of her work by a Galician *saudade*.

266. *Las Campanas*

Yo las amo, yo las oigo,
cual oigo el rumor del viento,
el murmurar de la fuente
o el balido del cordero.

Como los pájaros, ellas,
tan pronto asoma en los cielos
el primer rayo del alba,
le saludan con sus ecos.

Y en sus notas, que van prolongándose
por los llanos y los cerros,
hay algo de candoroso,
de apacible y de halagüeño.

Si por siempre enmudecieran,
¡ qué tristeza en el aire y el cielo !
¡ qué silencio en las iglesias !
¡ qué extrañeza entre los muertos !

267. *Hora tras hora. . . .*

Hora tras hora, día tras día,
entre el cielo y la tierra que quedan
eternos vigías,
como torrente que se despeña
pasa la vida.

Devolvedle a la flor su perfume
después de marchita ;
de las ondas que besan la playa
y que unas tras otras besándola expiran,
recoged los rumores, las quejas,
y en planchas de bronce grabad su armonía.

Tiempos que fueron, llantos y risas,
negros tormentos, dulces mentiras,
¡ ay ! ¿ en dónde su rastro dejaron,
en dónde, alma mía ?

SALVADOR RUEDA

1857-1933

It is in Rueda, if we take these poets in their chronological order, that we first feel the invigorating breath of the Darian revolution: in him not only does true poetry re-appear, expressing itself in confident tones that almost drown the exquisite whispers of Bécquer, but language and metric, both in their triumphs and in their shortcomings and exaggerations, constantly suggest the Modernists, of whom Rubén Darío is generally considered the first in date. In reality, though the interactions between them were close in both directions, Rueda may more properly be thought of as Rubén's disciple. But whether he be considered as initiating the revolution, or as following it, he remains a poet to be read for his own sake—unequal, and at times uninspired, but generally touched with a divine fire, which has never been quenched in Spanish letters since his day.

268. *Candilazo*

Here we can see a conception of the poetic art in process of transformation. The poem was published in 1891, yet its language is still studded with phrases recalling pseudo-Classical clichés of a century earlier, each noun complete with its appropriate epithet. At the same time the author is clearly attempting to create and leave in the mind vivid impressions, especially impressions of his images of light. In metric, the strong natural stresses give the piece a new vitality: we are back in the days of arte mayor, *with occasional rough and halting lines but with a virility and vigour, long absent from Spanish verse, which more than compensates for them. Finally, the melodious assonances in* a-a *remind us what a wealth of resources the Spanish language had in waiting for the pioneers of the renewed art.*

Por la erguida cresta de negra montaña
viene la tormenta ceñuda y airada;
le antecede el viento que dobla las cañas,
cimbrea los juncos y agita las parras.

Chispazos de lluvia vibrando se clavan
en el suelo, ansioso de frescura y agua ;
las tejas repican con voces cascadas,
y dan las veletas sus notas metálicas.

El duro granizo extiende y desata
de cables tendidos la sábana blanca,
y las fuertes cuentas rebotan y saltan
en árboles, piedras, paseros y casas.

Del plátano verde por las hojas anchas,
alzan los granizos sonoras escalas ;
la parra es un tímpano que vibra y que encanta,
el sauce una lira y el álamo un arpa.

Las voces de auxilio que tristes se exhalan,
en ruido de vientos perdidas cabalgan ;
deshecho su idilio, los pastores vagan
tras de sus dispersos rebaños de cabras.

Es todo un lamento, un llover de lágrimas ;
batallan los vientos con la fuerza humana,
y la luz funesta del trágico drama
es la del relámpago que lívido pasa.

De la lluvia luego, pacífica y mansa
el eco uniforme resuena en las ramas ;
el iris brillante que enciende sus bandas
con arco de triunfo los cielos escala.

Brilla el *candilazo* en huertas, montañas,
collados y ríos, laderas y playas ;
la mar resplandece a fuego dorada ;
los lagos son oro, las crestas son llamas.

Muestra el horizonte candelas de grana ;
el cielo se incendia ; los montes se abrasan ;
destellan las fuentes, y en ellas igualan
corales las piedras, rubíes las aguas.

Cuando lejos suena la recia tronada,
entre el candilazo que todo lo inflama,
sobre los granizos los niños se agarran
para hollar la alfombra de perlas nevadas.

269. *Idilio*

More successful in the long line than La Avellaneda, Rueda can at times write quite Darian hexameters. That particular line is well suited to the languor of his somewhat sentimental theme, and he brings also to the double task of creating melody and atmosphere a by no means despicable dexterity in handling such devices as alliteration, onomatopœia and regional vocabulary. His rhymes are full and sonorous and his concern to convey clear impressions by means of the mot propre *does not, as in some of his otherwise excellent pieces, lead him to neologize.*

Entre el sopor de la siesta que duerme Galicia lozana,
junto a la fuente que ronda zumbando clamante abejorro,
medio entreabierta la boca encendida, de olor a manzana,
bebe una moza las gotas del arco movible del chorro.

Y bajo d'él, colocando la herrada que trajo a la fuente,
mira llenarse la tosca vasija de inquietos albores,
como si rosas de recias espumas y luz floreciente
se desflecasen en mil carcajadas y locos temblores.

Entre el ardor de la brisa gallega, la moza suspira;
y bajo el arco de carne florida del pecho oloroso,
la juventud balancea, temblando con ritmo de lira,
la plenitud de los senos redondos de mármol glorioso.

De su mociño, remota en el aire, le viene la queja,
y con los dedos, tapando de pronto del caño el ruido,
con la avaricia que bebe la esponja, se ensancha su oreja,
y a los ramales del viento le arranca del hombre el sonido.

" Por las praderas te busco, le dice la copla de llanto,
por las vertientes y al pie de las aguas que rompen sus flecos,
por los apriscos, y lloro de ovejas contesta a mi canto;
por los torrentes y sólo a mis ayes responden sus ecos.

" ¡ Cuándo será que mis ojos te miren, arisca paloma,
y que la risa reviente tus labios de roja granada,
y bajo el chorro que forme cayendo tu risa de aroma,
ponga mi pecho y en luces rebose cual fondo de herrada ! "

Ella contesta con voz clara y dulce : " Te espero en la fuente,
ven y al ganado cortemos la hierba del campo moreno,
y con mi pelo, que es trigo de Julio y es oro riente,
ata si quieres, con manos de novio, los haces del heno."

Y hacia el cantar dirigiendo el amante la planta briosa,
halla en la fuente la moza que sueña del agua al conjuro,
y al contemplarlo, del pecho rotundo la curva ambiciosa
triunfal balancea los prietos racimos del seno maduro.

Él la sujeta, feliz en sus brazos, que tiemblan latentes,
ella resiste la lucha amorosa con giros fugaces,
hasta que al fin, al prenderla de nuevo los brazos potentes,
dan entre risas, jugando y corriendo, del heno en los haces.

Y entre el sopor de la siesta campestre que evoca a Virgilio,
mientras que duermen al son de las ramas del lago de Seira,
finge la fuente la gaita del Norte que arrulla el idilio,
como si Pan estuviese tocando la alegre muñeira.

270. *Los Pavos reales*

In one of his phases, Rueda paid considerable attention to the sonnet, a medium which he conceived as adapted to essentially objective art. His " century of sonnets " entitled Piedras preciosas *(1900) inclines to the symbolistic, though it is not without reminiscences of earlier modes. The sonnet which follows, from the volume* Fuente de salud *(1906), is better than most of these, and notable for its aptness of epithet and its vivid colour. The use of the first personal pronoun must not blind one to the poet's quite Parnassian plasticity. Opinions may be divided as to the skill with which he uses the dodecasyllabic line but there will be no gainsaying the beauty and effectiveness of the sonnet's close.*

Cuando vuelvo cantando de los trigales
ya al morir entre púrpuras el sol caído,
en medio del paisaje hieren mi oído
con su grito estridente los pavos reales.

Me escondo tras las ramas de los frutales,
y al ave egregia acecho sin hacer ruido,
y miro los colores de su vestido
y su moño de breves flechas triunfales.

Repitiendo su canto que el aire aleja,
hace el amor en torno de su pareja
y alza la cola augusta de hebras lustrosas.

Y a los ojos abriendo sus galas sumas,
deja brillar cien rosas sobre cien plumas,
y cien iris prendidos a las cien rosas.

271. *Viaje real*

With the foregoing sonnet may be contrasted this somewhat later one (1910), memorable for its imaginative symbolism, its evocative language, its masterly handling of the caesura, and the slow, measured tread of its verse.

Un elefante inmenso mandóme un rey de Oriente
con un castillo encima del espaldar gigante,
y en el castillo puso bajo un dosel triunfante
un trono como un ágata de luz resplandeciente.

Como corona brava del risco de mi frente
colgó sobre él un águila de vista rutilante,
y dando vuelta en torno del épico elefante
le ató ricas gualdrapas de brillo sorprendente.

A recorrer mis reinos del ritmo castellano
voy en mi torre altiva ; mi trono soberano,
mujer de luz, te ofrezco bañado en pedrería.

Desde el castillo, te echo larga escalera de oro ;
sube, y en mis Estados te aclamarán en coro
diosa de cien Naciones, reina de la Poesía.

MIGUEL DE UNAMUNO
1864-1936

FROM the purely literary standpoint, it might be thought excessive to devote much space to Unamuno's verse, since he is chiefly known by his prose and it is in that medium that some of his most poetical moments are perpetuated. But the fact is that, wherever Unamuno is spoken of, it must be at length, so complex and so overmastering is his personality. His life, for that of a University professor, was a stormy one. A native of Bilbao, a graduate of Madrid, he was appointed, at twenty-seven, to the Chair of Greek at Salamanca, where he might easily have spent the rest of his life in an atmosphere of tranquillity. But Unamuno was not created for tranquillity. Already he had abandoned the Catholicism of his childhood for a faith which he had hewn out for himself—he was a freethinker and an intensely religious one. When war with the United States robbed Spain of her last American colonies, he became an outstanding writer of the so-called "Generation of '98," which urged on the defeated nation an attitude of introspective humility, a policy of europeanization and a clean cut with past errors. In 1901 he was appointed Rector of Salamanca University, a post which later, for political reasons, he forfeited. His outspoken and sometimes eccentric interventions in politics brought him into disfavour with the Dictatorship of 1923—and the world heard for the first time of Fuerteventura, one of the Canary Islands, because he was exiled there. Later, set free, he settled for a time in the French Basque country. When the Republic came he returned to Spain, but still lived tempestuously, though once again in his beloved Salamanca. He died six months after the outbreak of the Civil War.

Thus introduced, Unamuno may best be left to speak for himself, which he does in his verse as decisively as in the *Vida de Don Quijote y Sancho* and *Del Sentimiento trágico de la vida*, or in his travel-books, novels, essays and plays. Perhaps verse is a more fitting medium for one who, in Antonio Machado's phrase, is essentially "donquijotesco,"[1] and whose attitude to life, whether he called it religion or philosophy, was so largely intuitive. Provided that it be not subjected to academic standards, by which it would often be found wanting, his virile poetry may safely be described as some of the greatest of the century.

The poems included in this selection are representative of different facets of Unamuno's poetic genius. First come three "regional" pieces which express the divided affections of the Basque who was to spend the greater part of his life in Salamanca and to draw so much inspiration from the pure air of Castile. Next, two philosophical poems characteristically picturesque, paradoxical and individualistic, the second instinct with the loveliest melody. Then a selection from a large number of pieces which might be termed "religious"—a characteristically restless sonnet and an extract from his long poem built on the famous painting "El Cristo de Velázquez." Finally, some lines in Unamuno's playful-serious vein, so familiar to those who knew him, suggested by the question of a little boy for whom he had made a toy bird out of paper (one of his favourite pastimes): "Y el pájaro ¿ habla ?"

272. *Vizcaya*

Las montañas de mi tierra
en el mar se miran,
y los robles que las visten
salina respiran.

De mi tierra el mar bravío
briza a las montañas,
y ellas se duermen sintiendo
mar en las entrañas.

¡ Oh mi Vizcaya, marina
tierra montañesa,
besan al cielo tus cumbres
y el mar te besa !

Tu hondo mar y tus montañas
llevo yo en mí mismo,
copa me diste en los cielos,
raíz en el abismo.

[1] Antonio Machado: *Poesías completas*, Madrid, 1936, p. 246.

273. *Castilla*

Tú me levantas, tierra de Castilla,
en la rugosa palma de tu mano,
al cielo que te enciende y te refresca,
al cielo, tu amo.

Tierra nervuda, enjuta, despejada,
madre de corazones y de brazos,
toma el presente en ti viejos colores
del noble antaño.

Con la pradera cóncava del cielo
lindan en torno tus desnudos campos,
tiene en ti cuna el sol y en ti sepulcro
y en ti santuario.

Es todo cima tu extensión redonda
y en ti me siento al cielo levantado,
aire de cumbre es el que se respira
aquí, en tus páramos.

¡ Ara gigante, tierra castellana,
a ese tu aire soltaré mis cantos,
si te son dignos bajarán al mundo
desde lo alto !

274. *Salamanca*

Salamanca, Salamanca,
renaciente maravilla,
académica palanca
de mi visión de Castilla.

Oro en sillares de soto
de las riberas del Tormes ;
de viejo saber remoto
guardas recuerdos conformes.

Hechizo salmanticense
de pedantesca dulzura ;
gramática del Brocense,
florón de literatura.

¡ Ay mi Castilla latina
con raíz gramatical,
ay tierra que se declina
por luz sobrenatural !

275. *Soneto*

Vuelve hacia atrás la vista, caminante,
verás lo que te queda de camino;
desde el oriente de tu cuna, el sino
ilumina tu marcha hacia adelante.

Es del pasado el porvenir semblante;
como se irá la vida así se vino;
cabe volver las riendas del destino
como se vuelve del revés un guante.

Lleva tu espalda reflejado el frente;
sube la niebla por el río arriba
y se resuelve encima de la fuente;

la lanzadera en su vaivén se aviva;
desnacerás un día de repente;
nunca sabrás dónde el misterio estriba.

276. *¿Qué es tu vida, alma mía. . . .?*

¿Qué es tu vida, alma mia? ¿Cuál tu pago?
¡Lluvia en el lago!
¿Qué es tu vida, alma mía, tu costumbre?
¡Viento en la cumbre!
¿Cómo tu vida, mi alma, se renueva?
¡Sombra en la cueva!
¡Lluvia en el lago!
¡Viento en la cumbre!
¡Sombra en la cueva!
Lágrimas es la lluvia desde el cielo,
y es el viento sollozo sin partida,
pesar la sombra sin ningún consuelo,
y lluvia y viento y sombra hacen la vida.

277. *El Cristo de Velázquez*
(*Extract*)

¿En qué piensas Tú, muerto, Cristo mío?
¿Por qué ese velo de cerrada noche
de tu abundosa cabellera negra
de nazareno cae sobre tu frente?

Miras dentro de Ti, donde está el reino
de Dios ; dentro de Ti, donde alborea
el sol eterno de las almas vivas.
Blanco tu cuerpo está como el espejo
del padre de la luz, del sol vivífico ;
blanco tu cuerpo al modo de la luna
que muerta ronda en torno de su madre,
nuestra cansada vagabunda tierra ;
blanco tu cuerpo está como la hostia
del cielo de la noche soberana,
de ese cielo tan negro como el velo
de tu abundosa cabellera negra
de nazareno.
Que eres, Cristo, el único
Hombre que sucumbió de pleno grado,
triunfador de la muerte, que a la vida
por Ti quedó encumbrada. Desde entonces
por Ti nos vivifica esa tu muerte,
por Ti la muerte se ha hecho nuestra madre,
por Ti la muerte es el amparo dulce
que azucara amargores de la vida ;
por Ti, el Hombre muerto que no muere,
blanco cual luna de la noche. Es sueño,
Cristo, la vida, y es la muerte vela.
Mientras la tierra sueña solitaria,
vela la blanca luna ; vela el Hombre
desde su cruz, mientras los hombres sueñan ;
vela el Hombre sin sangre, el Hombre blanco
como la luna de la noche negra ;
vela el Hombre que dió toda su sangre
porque las gentes sepan que son hombres.
Tú salvaste a la muerte. Abres tus brazos
a la noche, que es negra y muy hermosa,
porque el sol de la vida la ha mirado
con sus ojos de fuego ; que a la noche
morena la hizo el sol y tan hermosa.
Y es hermosa la luna solitaria,
la blanca luna en la estrellada noche,
negra cual la abundosa cabellera
negra del nazareno. Blanca luna

como el cuerpo del Hombre en cruz, espejo
del sol de vida, del que nunca muere.
Los rayos, Maestro, de tu suave lumbre
nos guían en la noche de este mundo,
ungiéndonos con la esperanza recia
de un día eterno. Noche cariñosa,
¡ oh noche, madre de los blandos sueños,
madre de la esperanza, dulce Noche,
noche oscura del alma, eres nodriza
de la esperanza en Cristo salvador !

278. *Irrequietum Cor*

Recio Jesús ibero, el de Teresa,
Tú que en la más recóndita morada
del alma mueres, cumple la promesa
que entre abrazos de fe diste a la amada.

Gozó dolor sabroso, Quijotesa
a lo divino, que dejó asentada
nuestra España inmortal cuya es la empresa :
sólo existe lo eterno ; ¡ Dios o nada !

Si Él se hizo hombre para hacernos dioses,
mortal para librarnos de la muerte,
¿ qué mucho, osado corazón, que así oses

romper los grillos de la humana suerte
y que en la negra vida no reposes
bregando sin cesar por poseerte ?

279. *A una Pajarita de papel*

¡ Habla, que lo quiere el niño !
¡ Ya está hablando !
El Hijo del Hombre, el Verbo
encarnado
se hizo Dios en una cuna
con el canto
de la niñez campesina,
canto alado. . . .

¡ Habla, que lo quiere el niño !
¡ Hable tu papel, mi pájaro !
Háblale al niño que sabe
voz del alto,
la voz que se hace silencio
sobre el fango. . . .
Háblale al niño que vive
en su pecho a Dios criando. . . .
Tú eres la paloma mística,
tú el Santo
Espíritu que hizo el hombre
con sus manos. . . .
Habla a los niños, que el reino
tan soñado
de los cielos es del niño
soberano ;
¡ del niño, rey de los sueños !
¡ corazón de lo creado !
¡ Habla, que lo quiere el niño !
¡ Ya está hablando ! . . .

RUBÉN DARÍO
1867-1916

THE name of the Nicaraguan poet Rubén Darío[1] is as indelibly engraved upon the history of Spanish literature as that of any Spaniard, because, with his coming to Spain, Spanish poetry was reborn.

A youth of extraordinary precocity, an omnivorous reader in both Spanish and French, a born traveller and cosmopolitan, Rubén was writing prose and poetry for Nicaraguan papers at fourteen, published his first volume at eighteen and travelled in Central and South America before visiting Spain in 1892. Thanks largely to Juan Valera's review of his best-known early collection, *Azul* (1888), his reputation as a poet of new technique and inspiration had preceded him; and, besides being made much of by the leading men of letters, he was welcomed by many who, though still hardly more than boys, were to become the poets of the new generation. "Y yo le grito: ¡Salve!" wrote one of these, Antonio Machado (p. 621),

a la bandera
flamígera que tiene
esta hermosa galera,-
que de una nueva España a España viene.[2]

After leaving Spain, he travelled still more widely in America, made a short stay in Paris and then for a time lived in Buenos Aires. Here he published a book of verse called *Prosas profanas* (1896) which first gave a comprehensive idea of his command of language and metre and later played an important part in the history of the movement known as Modernism Returning to Spain early in 1899, he found that the youths of five years earlier were rapidly becoming Spain's foremost writers; allying himself

[1] His legal name was Félix Rubén García Sarmiento. "Darío," however, was not a pseudonym, but an ancestral name which had been adopted by his father, Manuel García, so that the son was never known by any other.

[2] *Op. cit.*, p. 241.

with them, he became from that time the acknowledged leader of contemporary Spanish poetry. For the rest of his life he lived chiefly between Spain and France, travelling widely in both countries, spending long periods in their capitals, and writing, among much else, *España contemporánea* (1901) and his best collection of verse, *Cantos de vida y esperanza* (1905). His visits to the Western Hemisphere, however, were frequent; much of his later work (e.g., *Canto a la Argentina:* 1910) was Hispano-American in inspiration; and, when he died, worn out by his restless living, at the early age of forty-nine, it was in his own country.

Much has been written upon the sources of Rubén Darío's inspiration: some have looked upon him as essentially French; others, as essentially Spanish. The truth is, he was essentially Rubén Darío. From his earliest years he had lived in closest intimacy with the two literatures and he was great enough to absorb what seemed to him best in both and make it part of his own genius. But, in so far as his debts can be estimated, he owed more to Spain than to France. He drank avidly of France, but his roots were deep in Spain. "Si Francia fué la tierra de sus ilusiones", a critic has said, "España lo fué de sus realidades y sus triunfos."[1] But he himself got closer to the heart of the matter when he wrote: "Mi esposa es de mi tierra; mi querida, de París."[2]

Rubén Darío's work was not, then, merely to import French modes and measures into Spain, and to naturalize them there, as Garcilaso de la Vega had naturalized the modes and measures of Italy. He was the leader, less of a neo-Romantic Revolt than of a Revival. Nearly all the metrical forms and usages that he was credited with having invented, discovered in France or adapted according to French rule or custom, he had in reality found in mediaeval or Golden Age Spain and revived or re-created by means of his marvellous vitality.

Vitality, in the fullest sense of that word, was Rubén Darío's great gift to literature and to Spain. Surging through both the content and the form of his work, it is perhaps the more obvious in the latter—in, for example, the extraordinary flexibility of his alexandrines and the sensitiveness and skill with which he adapted

[1] Arturo Torres-Rioseco: *Rubén Darío: Casticismo y americanismo*, Harvard University Press, 1931, p. 165.

[2] *Prosas profanas*, Madrid., n.d. (1920), p. 10; *Obras poéticas completas*, Madrid, 1932, p. 714.

them to every kind of mood; in his demonstrations that the Classical hexameter, which had been but timidly essayed by Spaniards, could be used by them as confidently as by the natives of any other country; in the boldness with which he re-introduced *enjambements* of a type hardly known since Calderón. And to such specific indications, which space curtails, must be added more general ones: the discovery of a new world of colour and music, the revivification of well-worn themes, the creation of new atmospheres and the energizing of the verse-form with the poetic spirit.

With the name of Darío is generally connected the literary manifestation known as Modernism—a "direction" or a "mode", rather than a "movement" or a "school", which an acute critic has gone so far as to call a label for the "forma hispánica de la crisis universal de las letras y del espíritu que inicia hacia 1885 la disolución del siglo XIX."[1] This association of Modernism with the greatest of its exponents is justified. For, although the ideals which it sought to implant had arisen, independently of him, both in Spain and in Spanish America, it was he who carried them with the greatest distinction into practice and to whom poets in both continents looked as to their chief exponent. Spanish Modernism, reacting against the now effete and prosaic eclecticism which fifty years before had arisen to stem the Classical-Romantic conflict, was essentially, though not superficially or in appearance, a second Romantic movement.

¡ Románticos somos ! ¿ Quién que es no es romántico ?[2]

It claimed and assumed a freedom to assimilate what and whence it would; it revived, and to some extent conventionalized, Romantic attitudes of thought and feeling, including the mediaeval elements which the Romantic Revival had itself drawn out of the past; it reached out confidently and innovated boldly in the sphere of vocabulary and versification. Thus it comprehends many lesser movements, among them movements as nearly antithetical as Parnassianism and Symbolism. Like the modes which had preceded it, Modernism was not without its exaggerations: sentimentality, verbosity, artificiality, bombast have attempted to use it as their justification, as they had previously used Romanticism. But, considered broadly, it is one of the three or four most

[1] O., p. xv.

[2] Rubén Darío: "Canción de los pinos" (*Canto errante*, Madrid, 1907, p. 99).

significant landmarks in the history of Spanish poetry and none of the poets who follow in this survey failed to undergo its influence.

280. *Sonatina*

The fairy-tale world which flits in and out of Azul *is encountered again in this well-known piece from* Prosas profanas, *so often looked down upon because of the triviality of its theme and the artificiality with which that theme is treated. The key to an understanding of it, however, lies in the title. It is, from beginning to end, a piece of music, in which sense only sets off the appropriateness of sound. One might suppose that the six-lined stanza, rhyming* aabccb, *with the* b-*endings invariably masculine and the remainder feminine, would very soon become monotonous. But not in the hands of Rubén Darío, with his nimble manipulation of cæsuræ, his skilful use of alliteration and repetition and above all his marvellous ear for melody and rhythm. Never before had the potentialities of Spanish as an instrument of purely rhythmical verse so clearly asserted themselves. The light, rapid movement of the piece, too, not only carries the reader along with it, but blends perfectly with the fairy-tale atmosphere of theme and language.*

La princesa está triste. . . . ¿ Qué tendrá la princesa ?
Los suspiros se escapan de su boca de fresa,
que ha perdido la risa, que ha perdido el color.
La princesa está pálida en su silla de oro,
está mudo el teclado de su clave sonoro,
y en un vaso olvidada se desmaya una flor.

El jardín puebla el triunfo de los pavos reales.
Parlanchina, la dueña dice cosas banales,
y vestido de rojo piruetea el bufón.
La princesa no ríe, la princesa no siente ;
la princesa persigue por el cielo de Oriente
la libélula vaga de una vaga ilusión.

¿ Piensa acaso en el príncipe de Golconda o de China,
o en el que ha detenido su carroza argentina
para ver de sus ojos la dulzura de luz,
o en el rey de las islas de las rosas fragantes,
o en el que es soberano de los claros diamantes,
o en el dueño orgulloso de las perlas de Ormuz ?

¡ Ay ! la pobre princesa de la boca de rosa
quiere ser golondrina, quiere ser mariposa,
tener alas ligeras, bajo el cielo volar ;
ir al sol por la escala luminosa de un rayo,
saludar a los lirios con los versos de Mayo,
o perderse en el viento sobre el trueno del mar.

Ya no quiere el palacio, ni la rueca de plata,
ni el halcón encantado, ni el bufón escarlata,
ni los cisnes unánimes en el lago de azur.
Y están tristes las flores por la flor de la corte ;
los jazmines de Oriente, los nelumbos del Norte,
de Occidente las dalias y las rosas del Sur.

¡ Pobrecita princesa de los ojos azules !
Está presa en sus oros, está presa en sus tules,
en la jaula de mármol del palacio real ;
el palacio soberbio que vigilan los guardas,
que custodian cien negros con sus cien alabardas,
un lebrel que no duerme y un dragón colosal.

¡ Oh, quién fuera hipsipila que dejó la crisálida !
(La princesa está triste. La princesa está pálida.)
¡ Oh visión adorada de oro, rosa y marfil !
¡ Quién volara a la tierra donde un príncipe existe
(La princesa está pálida. La princesa está triste)
más brillante que el alba, más hermoso que Abril !

" ¡ Calla, calla, princesa," dice el hada madrina ;
" en caballo con alas hacia acá se encamina,
en el cinto la espada y en la mano el azor,
el feliz caballero que te adora sin verte,
y que llega de lejos, vencedor de la Muerte,
a encenderte los labios con su beso de amor ! "

281. *Verlaine : Responso*

This half-Christian, half-pagan responso, *written after the death of Verlaine, uses a variation of the author's favourite six-lined stanza, but the scheme (14.14.9.14.14.9.) so closely resembles the*

12.12.8.12.12.8. of the corresponding stanza of the French Romantics that one may assume direct indebtedness. The tone, as would be expected, contrasts strikingly with that of " Sonatina ", and each of the author's resources ministers to it. The movement is grave and slow ; the vocabulary dignified to the point of pretentiousness ; the keynote of the poem sonority.

Padre y maestro mágico, liróforo celeste,
que al instrumento olímpico y a la siringa agreste
diste tu acento encantador ;
¡ Panida ! ¡ Pan tú mismo, que coros condujiste
hacia el propíleo sacro que amaba tu alma triste,
al son del sistro y del tambor !

Que tu sepulcro cubra de flores Primavera,
que se humedezca el áspero hocico de la fiera,
de amor, si pasa por allí ;
que el fúnebre recinto visite Pan bicorne ;
que de sangrientas rosas el fresco abril te adorne,
y de claveles de rubí.

Que si posarse quiere sobre la tumba el cuervo,
ahuyenten la negrura del pájaro protervo
el dulce canto del cristal
que Filomela vierta sobre tus tristes huesos,
o la harmonía dulce de risas y de besos
de culto oculto y florestal.

Que púberes canéforas te ofrenden el acanto,
que sobre tu sepulcro no se derrame el llanto,
sino rocío, vino, miel :
que el pámpano allí brote, las flores de Citeres,
y que se escuchen vagos suspiros de mujeres
bajo un simbólico laurel.

Que si un pastor su pífano bajo el frescor del haya,
en amorosos días, como en Virgilio, ensaya,
tu nombre ponga en la canción ;
y que la virgen náyade, cuando ese nombre escuche,
con ansias y temores entre las linfas luche,
llena de miedo y de pasión.

De noche, en la montaña, en la negra montaña
de las Visiones, pase gigante sombra extraña,
sombra de un Sátiro espectral;
que ella al centauro adusto con su grandeza asuste;
de una extra-humana flauta la melodía ajuste
a la harmonía sideral.

Y huya el tropel equino por la montaña vasta;
tu rostro de ultratumba bañe la luna casta
de compasiva y blanca luz;
y el Sátiro contemple sobre un lejano monte
una cruz que se eleve cubriendo el horizonte
y un resplandor sobre la cruz.

282. *Cantos de Vida y Esperanza*

A semi-autobiographical poem, prefacing the collection of the same title, with no very notable features in vocabulary or metre—giving the impression, in fact, of being rather carelessly written. The sidelights thrown by the poet, in familiar phrases, upon his character and literary tastes will give the reader food for thought and discussion. More elusive is the curious naïveté of tone, sometimes breaking into a half-defiant candour, and very strongly recalling (e.g., in the fourth, fifth and twelfth stanzas) similar confessions by Espronceda. This is a poem of capital importance for an understanding of its author.

Yo soy aquel que ayer no más decía
el verso azul y la canción profana,
en cuya noche un ruiseñor había
que era alondra de luz por la mañana.

El dueño fuí de mi jardín de sueño,
lleno de rosas y de cisnes vagos;
el dueño de las tórtolas, el dueño
de góndolas y liras en los lagos;

y muy siglo diez y ocho y muy antiguo
y muy moderno; audaz, cosmopolita;
con Hugo fuerte y con Verlaine ambiguo,
y una sed de ilusiones infinita.

Yo supe de dolor desde mi infancia;
mi juventud . . . ¿ fué juventud la mía ?
Sus rosas aun me dejan su fragancia—
una fragancia de melancolía. . . .

Potro sin freno se lanzó mi instinto;
mi juventud montó potro sin freno;
iba embriagada y con puñal al cinto;
si no cayó, fué porque Dios es bueno.

En mi jardín se vió una estatua bella;
se juzgó mármol y era carne viva;
un alma joven habitaba en ella,
sentimental, sensible, sensitiva.

Y tímida ante el mundo, de manera
que, encerrada en silencio, no salía
sino cuando en la dulce primavera
era la hora de la melodía. . . .

Hora de ocaso y de discreto beso;
hora crepuscular y de retiro;
hora de madrigal y de embeleso
de " te adoro ", de " ¡ ay ! " y de suspiro.

Y entonces era en la dulzaina un juego
de misteriosas gamas cristalinas,
un renovar de notas del Pan griego
y un desgranar de músicas latinas,

con aire tal y con ardor tan vivo,
que a la estatua nacían de repente
en el muslo viril patas de chivo
y dos cuernos de sátiro en la frente.

Como la Galatea gongorina
me encantó la marquesa verleniana,
y así juntaba a la pasión divina
una sensual hiperestesia humana;

todo ansia, todo ardor, sensación pura
y vigor natural; y sin falsía,
y sin comedia y sin literatura . . . :
si hay un alma sincera, ésa es la mía.

La torre de marfil tentó mi anhelo;
quise encerrarme dentro de mí mismo,
y tuve hambre de espacio y sed de cielo
desde las sombras de mi propio abismo.

Como la esponja que la sal satura
en el jugo del mar, fué el dulce y tierno
corazón mío, henchido de amargura
por el mundo, la carne y el infierno.

Mas, por gracia de Dios, en mi conciencia
el Bien supo elegir la mejor parte;
y si hubo áspera hiel en mi existencia,
melificó toda acritud el Arte.

Mi intelecto libré de pensar bajo,
bañó el agua castalia el alma mía,
peregrinó mi corazón y trajo
de la sagrada selva la armonía.

¡Oh, la selva sagrada! ¡Oh, la profunda
emanación del corazón divino
de la sagrada selva! ¡Oh, la fecunda
fuente cuya virtud vence al destino!

Bosque ideal que lo real complica,
allí el cuerpo arde y vive y Psiquis vuela;
mientras abajo el sátiro fornica,
ebria de azul deslíe Filomela.

Perla de ensueño y música amorosa
en la cúpula en flor del laurel verde,
Hipsipila sutil liba en la rosa,
y la boca del fauno el pezón muerde.

Allí va el dios en celo tras la hembra,
y la caña de Pan se alza del lodo;
la eterna vida sus semillas siembra,
y brota la armonía del gran Todo.

El alma que entra allí debe ir desnuda,
temblando de deseo y fiebre santa,
sobre cardo heridor y espina aguda:
así sueña, así vibra y así canta.

Vida, luz y verdad, tal triple llama
produce la interior llama infinita ;
el Arte puro como Cristo exclama :
¡ Ego sum lux et veritas et vita !

Y la vida es misterio, la luz ciega
y la verdad inaccesible asombra ;
la adusta perfección jamás se entrega,
y el secreto ideal duerme en la sombra.

Por eso ser sincero es ser potente ;
de desnuda que está, brilla la estrella ;
el agua dice el alma de la fuente
en la voz de cristal que fluye d'ella.

Tal fué mi intento, hacer del alma pura
mía una estrella, una fuente sonora,
con el horror de la literatura
y loco de crepúsculo y de aurora.

Del crepúsculo azul que da la pauta
que los celestes éxtasis inspira,
bruma y tono menor—¡ toda la flauta !—
y Aurora, hija del Sol—¡ toda la lira !

Pasó una piedra que lanzó una honda ;
pasó una flecha que aguzó un violento.
La piedra de la honda fué a la onda,
y la flecha del odio fuése al viento.

La virtud está en ser tranquilo y fuerte ;
con el fuego interior todo se abrasa ;
se triunfa del rencor y de la muerte,
¡ y hacia Belén . . . la caravana pasa !

283. *Salutación del Optimista*

The first magnificent line of this poem—repeated at its close—is probably the best-known hexameter-line in all Spanish, as the poem itself is deservedly the best known of all Spanish exercises in this measure. Torres-Rioseco believes that Darío knew nothing, when he wrote these lines, of previous attempts of the kind in his own language, though he may very probably have been familiar with Longfellow's Evangeline. *The hexametric poem, however, held one pitfall for the Modernists—it tempted them to indulge their weakness for long, sonorous words, expressive or no; and it must be owned that Darío occasionally falls down here. The theme of the poem is on the same high level as the language—a notable tribute to the spiritual unity of the Hispanic peoples to come from a Spanish-American poet so soon after the '98 disasters.*

Ínclitas razas ubérrimas, sangre de Hispania fecunda,
espíritus fraternos, luminosas almas, ¡ salve !
Porque llega el momento en que habrán de cantar nuevos himnos
lenguas de gloria. Un vasto rumor llena los ámbitos; mágicas
ondas de vida van renaciendo de pronto;
retrocede el olvido, retrocede engañada la muerte;
se anuncia un reino nuevo, feliz sibila sueña,
y en la caja pandórica de que tantas desgracias surgieron
encontramos de súbito, talismánica, pura, riente,
cual pudiera decirla en sus versos Virgilio divino,
la divina reina de luz, ¡ la celeste Esperanza !

Pálidas indolencias, desconfianzas fatales que a tumba
o a perpetuo presidio condenasteis al noble entusiasmo,
ya veréis al salir del sol en un triunfo de liras,
mientras dos continentes, abonados de huesos gloriosos,
del Hércules antiguo la gran sombra soberbia evocando,
digan al orbe: la alta virtud resucita
que a la hispana progenie hizo dueña de siglos.

Abominad la boca que predice desgracias eternas;
abominad los ojos que ven sólo zodiacos funestos;
abominad las manos que apedrean las ruinas ilustres,
o que la tea empuñan o la daga suicida.
Siéntense sordos ímpetus de las entrañas del mundo;
la inminencia de algo fatal hoy conmueve a la tierra;
fuertes colosos caen, se desbandan bicéfalas águilas,
y algo se inicia como vasto social cataclismo
sobre la faz del orbe. ¿ Quién dirá que las savias dormidas
no despierten entonces en el tronco del roble gigante
bajo el cual se exprimió la ubre de la loba romana ?

¿ Quién será el pusilánime que al vigor español niegue músculos
y que al alma española juzgase áptera y ciega y tullida ?
No es Babilonia ni Nínive enterrada en olvido y en polvo,
ni entre momias y piedras reina que habita el sepulcro,
la nación generosa, coronada de orgullo inmarchito,
que hacia el lado del alba fija las miradas ansiosas,
ni la que tras los mares en que yace sepulta la Atlántida,
tiene su coro de vástagos, altos, robustos y fuertes.

Únanse, brillen, secúndense tantos vigores dispersos ;
formen todos un solo haz de energía ecuménica.
Sangre de Hispania fecunda, sólidas, ínclitas razas,
muestren los dones pretéritos que fueron antaño su triunfo.
Vuelva el antiguo entusiasmo, vuelva el espíritu ardiente
que regará lenguas de fuego en esa epifanía.
Juntas las testas ancianas ceñidas de líricos lauros
y las cabezas jóvenes que la alta Minerva decora,
así los manes heroicos de los primitivos abuelos,
de los egregios padres que abrieron el surco pristino,
sientan los soplos agrarios de primaverales retornos
y el rumor de espigas que inició la labor triptolémica.

Un continente y otro renovando las viejas prosapias,
en espíritu unidos, en espíritu y ansias y lengua,
ven llegar el momento en que habrán de cantar nuevos himnos.

Latina estirpe verá la gran alba futura,
en un trueno de música gloriosa, millones de labios
saludarán la espléndida luz que vendrá del Oriente,
Oriente augusto en donde todo lo cambia y renueva
la eternidad de Dios, la actividad infinita.
Y así sea esperanza la visión permanente en nosotros.
¡ Ínclitas razas ubérrimas, sangre de Hispania fecunda !

284. *A Roosevelt*

Taken, like the foregoing piece, from the Cantos de vida y esperanza, *this poem is noteworthy almost wholly for its subject. It was addressed to Theodore Roosevelt, at a time when his " Big Stick " policy was antagonizing the Latin-American peoples, whose cause the poet takes up against the potential invader with a savage but dignified irony and a finely-controlled passion. Here and there the rhetoric verges dangerously on rant and some of the effects employed are facile, even childish. But these flaws are insignificant beside the positive achievements of the poem—notably the handling of the emotional tension as it first rises and then falls, before rising again, in the final section, to its tremendous climax. Unlike most of his other work though this may be, Darío would be remembered by the people of two continents had he written nothing beside.*

¡ Es con voz de la Biblia, o verso de Walt Whitman,
que habría que llegar hasta ti, Cazador !
¡ Primitivo y moderno, sencillo y complicado,
con un algo de Wáshington y cuatro de Nemrod !
Eres los Estados Unidos,
eres el futuro invasor
de la América ingenua que tiene sangre indígena,
que aun reza a Jesucristo y aun habla en español.

Eres soberbio y fuerte ejemplar de tu raza ;
eres culto, eres hábil ; te opones a Tolstoy.
Y domando caballos, o asesinando tigres,
eres un Alejandro-Nabucodonosor.
(Eres un profesor de Energía,
como dicen los locos de hoy.)

Crees que la vida es incendio,
que el progreso es erupción ;
que en donde pones la bala
el porvenir pones.
No.
Los Estados Unidos son potentes y grandes.
Cuando ellos se estremecen hay un hondo temblor
que pasa por las vértebras enormes de los Andes.
Si clamáis, se oye como el rugir del león.
Ya Hugo a Grant lo dijo : " Las estrellas son vuestras."
(Apenas brilla, alzándose, el argentino sol
y la estrella chilena se levanta . . .) Sois ricos.
Juntáis al culto de Hércules el culto de Mammón ;
y alumbrando el camino de la fácil conquista,
la Libertad levanta su antorcha en Nueva York.

Mas la América nuestra, que tenía poetas
desde los viejos tiempos de Netzahualcoyotl,
que ha guardado las huellas de los pies del gran Baco,
que el alfabeto pánico en un tiempo aprendió ;
que consultó los astros, que conoció la Atlántida,
cuyo nombre nos llega resonando en Platón,
que desde los remotos momentos de su vida
vive de luz, de fuego, de perfume, de amor,
la América del grande Moctezuma, del Inca,
la América fragante de Cristóbal Colón,
la América católica, la América española,
la América en que dijo el noble Guatemoc :
" Yo no estoy en un lecho de rosas " ; esa América
que tiembla de huracanes y que vive de amor ;
hombres de ojos sajones y alma bárbara, vive.
Y sueña. Y ama, y vibra ; y es la hija del Sol.
Tened cuidado. ¡ Vive la América española !
Hay mil cachorros sueltos del León español.
Se necesitaría, Roosevelt, ser por Dios mismo,
el Riflero terrible y el fuerte Cazador,
para poder tenernos en vuestras férreas garras.

Y, pues contáis con todo, falta una cosa : ¡ Dios !

285. *Canción de Otoño en Primavera*

Here we return to something very much like the romanticism of the early nineteenth century. This canción *is included as an illustration of Rubén's great versatility, which never allowed him to confine himself to one mode or one style. Save for occasional refinements, it might have been written either by Espronceda or by any one of his contemporaries. Its chief originality is in its adoption, and method of treatment, of the characteristically Darian enneasyllabic line.*

Juventud, divino tesoro,
¡ ya te vas para no volver !
Cuando quiero llorar, no lloro . . .
y a veces lloro sin querer . . .

Plural ha sido la celeste
historia de mi corazón.
Era una dulce niña, en este
mundo de duelo y aflicción.

Miraba como el alba pura;
sonreía como una flor.
Era su cabellera obscura
hecha de noche y de dolor.

Yo era tímido como un niño.
Ella, naturalmente, fué,
para mi amor hecho de armiño,
Herodías y Salomé . . .

Juventud, divino tesoro,
¡ya te vas para no volver! . . .
Cuando quiero llorar, no lloro,
y a veces lloro sin querer . . .

La otra fué más sensitiva,
y más consoladora y más
halagadora y expresiva,
cual no pensé encontrar jamás.

Pues a su continua ternura
una pasión violenta unía.
En un peplo de gasa pura
una bacante se envolvía . . .

En brazos tomó mi ensueño
y lo arrulló como a un bebé . . .
Y le mató, triste y pequeño,
falto de luz, falto de fe . . .

Juventud, divino tesoro,
¡te fuiste para no volver!
Cuando quiero llorar, no lloro,
y a veces lloro sin querer . . .

Otra juzgó que era mi boca
el estuche de su pasión;
y que me roería, loca,
con sus dientes el corazón;

poniendo en un amor de exceso
la mira de su voluntad,
mientras eran abrazo y beso
síntesis de la eternidad ;

y de nuestra carne ligera
imaginar siempre un Edén,
sin pensar que la Primavera
y la carne acaban también . . .

Juventud, divino tesoro,
¡ ya te vas para no volver !
Cuando quiero llorar, no lloro,
y a veces lloro sin querer . . .

¡ Y las demás ! En tantos climas,
en tantas tierras, siempre son,
si no pretextos de mis rimas,
fantasmas de mi corazón.

En vano busqué a la princesa
que estaba triste de esperar.
La vida es dura. Amarga y pesa.
¡ Ya no hay princesa que cantar !

Mas a pesar del tiempo terco,
mi sed de amor no tiene fin ;
con el cabello gris, me acerco
a los rosales del jardín . . .

Juventud, divino tesoro,
¡ ya te vas para no volver !
Cuando quiero llorar, no lloro,
y a veces lloro sin querer . . .

¡ Mas es mía el Alba de oro !

286. *Soneto a Cervantes*

This variant of the conventional sonnet, technically noteworthy for its three short lines and strong cæsuræ, may be remembered as an example of the many poems in which Rubén Darío pays tribute to great

Spanish writers. It anticipates the simplicity and reaction from rhetoric of such later poets as Unamuno and Antonio Machado. Contrast the simple, almost conversational language (" Pero Cervantes es buen amigo . . . Es para mí . . . Así le admiro y quiero ") of the author who wrote

Si hay un alma sincera, ésa es la mía

with that of the ornate and decorative, or sonorous poems reprinted above. Yet there is also distinction in the expression of the sonnet, especially in its fine conclusion.

Horas de pesadumbre y de tristeza
paso en mi soledad. Pero Cervantes
es buen amigo. Endulza mis instantes
ásperos, y reposa mi cabeza.

Él es la vida y la naturaleza,
regala un yelmo de oros y diamantes
a mis sueños errantes.
Es para mí : suspira, ríe y reza.

Cristiano y amoroso y caballero
parla como un arroyo cristalino.
Así le admiro y quiero,

viendo cómo el destino
hace que regocije al mundo entero
la tristeza inmortal de ser divino.

287. *Marcha triunfal*

Here, as in " Sonatina " (p. 583), Darío's wonderful ear and the rhythmic possibilities of the Spanish language combine to convey a particular atmosphere which would be partially apprehended even by a hearer ignorant of the meaning of the words. As we gaze on the brilliant scene and listen to the martial amphibrachs tramping past to the accompaniment of drum and clarion the thing seems so easy. But the author has called up all his visual and auditory art : repetition (note its force in ll. 1-2), the alternation of long lines and short (the gamut ranges from 21 syllables to 3), alliteration, synalepha, enjambement, colour metaphor, hyperbole, personification, and, of course, the skilful handling of stress. True, this is not the highest type of art, but it is exquisite of its type, and it is perhaps not too much to say, with Ángel Valbuena Prat, of the auditory, if not of the pictorial effect of the poem, " en lo exterior no tiene rival en toda la historia del verso de lengua castellana."[1]

¡ Ya viene el cortejo !
¡ Ya viene el cortejo ! Ya se oyen los claros clarines.
La espada se anuncia con vivo reflejo ;
ya viene, oro y hierro, el cortejo de los paladines.

Ya pasa debajo los arcos ornados de blancas Minervas y Martes,
los arcos triunfales en donde las Famas erigen sus largas trompetas,
la gloria solemne de los estandartes,
llevados por manos robustas de heroicos atletas.
Se escucha el ruido que forman las armas de los caballeros,
los frenos que mascan los fuertes caballos de guerra,
los cascos que hieren la tierra,
y los timbaleros,
que el paso acompasan con ritmos marciales.
¡ Tal pasan los fieros guerreros
debajo los arcos triunfales !

Los claros clarines de pronto levantan sus sones,
su canto sonoro,
su cálido coro,
que envuelve en un trueno de oro
la augusta soberbia de los pabellones.
Él dice la lucha, la herida venganza,
las ásperas crines,
los rudos penachos, la pica, la lanza,
la sangre que riega de heroicos carmines
la tierra ;
los negros mastines
que azuza la muerte, que rige la guerra.

[1] V.P., II, 795.

Los áureos sonidos
anuncian el advenimiento
triunfal de la Gloria ;
dejando el picacho que guarda sus nidos,
tendiendo sus alas enormes al viento,
los cóndores llegan. ¡ Llegó la victoria !

Ya pasa el cortejo.
Señala el abuelo los héroes al niño :
" Ved cómo la barba del viejo
los bucles de oro circundan de armiño."
Las bellas mujeres aprestan coronas de flores,
y bajo los pórticos vense sus rostros de rosa ;
y la más hermosa
sonríe al más fiero de los vencedores.
¡ Honor al que trae cautiva la extraña bandera !
¡ Honor al herido y honor a los fieles
soldados que muerte encontraron por mano extranjera !
¡ Clarines ! ¡ Laureles !

Las nobles espadas de tiempos gloriosos
desde sus panoplias saludan las nuevas coronas y lauros
—Las viejas espadas de los granaderos, más fuertes que osos,
hermanos de aquellos lanceros que fueron centauros—.
Las trompas guerreras resuenan ;
de voces los aires se llenan . . .
—A aquellas antiguas espadas,
a aquellos ilustres aceros,
que encarnan las glorias pasadas—.
¡ Y al sol que hoy alumbra las nuevas victorias ganadas,
y al héroe que guía su grupo de jóvenes fieros,
al que ama la insignia del suelo materno,
al que ha desafiado, ceñido el acero y el arma en la mano,
los soles del rojo verano,
las nieves y vientos del gélido invierno,
la noche, la escarcha
y el odio y la muerte, por ser por la patria inmortal,
saludan con voces de bronce las trompas de guerra, que tocan la marcha
triunfal !

RAMÓN MARÍA DEL VALLE-INCLÁN
1869-1935

PRIMARILY a novelist, and as truly a poet in his novels (particularly in the *Sonatas* and *Flor de santidad*) as anywhere, Valle-Inclán has also achieved great distinction in verse, as a Modernist of pronounced individuality. While there are several phases in his poetic evolution, his best work is perhaps that of the collection *Aromas de leyenda* (1907), the source of the first two extracts which follow. Here one forgets the Modernistic devices which, on occasion, he can indulge to the full, as (to use a conventional verb in anything but a conventional sense) the poet " re-creates " the sights and sounds of the countryside of his native Galicia. He touches other sides of life too—the eerie, the tragic, the grotesque, the disillusioned, the legendary, the courtly, the cosmopolitan—but his chief contribution to Spanish poetry is his intense sensibility and the great command of language which enables him to give expression to its most delicate nuances. Nor can one ever forget the music of his verse, instinct as it is with the most elusive melody.

288. *Prosas de Dos Ermitaños*

A queer, naïve little leyenda, *with its haunting enneasyllabic lines and its clipt assonances ringing changes on six masculine endings like the slightly cracked bells of a country church. The conversation of the two Galician saints, with its curious litany-like movement, sounds as unreal as it was no doubt intended to be and harmonizes exquisitely with the mediaeval setting. Note the interplay of images of light and darkness and the few masterly strokes in the first stanza which give the piece its atmosphere of gloom.*

En la austera quietud del monte
y en la sombra de un peñascal,
nido de buitres y de cuervos
que el cielo cubren al volar,
razonaban dos ermitaños :
San Serenín y San Gundián.

" San Serenín, padre maestro,
tu grande saber doctoral
que aconseja a papas y reyes,
¿ puede mi alma aconsejar
y un cirio de cándida cera
encender en su oscuridad ? "

" San Gundián, padre maestro
y definidor teologal,
confesor de papas y reyes
en toda la cristiandad,
el cirio que encienda mi mano
ninguna luz darte podrá."

" San Serenín, padre maestro,
mis ojos quieren penetrar
en el abismo de la muerte,
el abismo del bien o del mal
adonde vuelan nuestras ánimas,
cuando el cuerpo al polvo se da."

" San Gundián, padre maestro,
¿ quién el trigo contó al granar,
y del ave que va volando
dice en dónde se posará,
y de la piedra de la onda
y de la flecha, adónde van ? "

" San Serenín, padre maestro
como los ríos a la mar,
todas las cosas en el mundo
hacen camino a su final,
y el ave y la flecha y la piedra
son en el aire Eternidad."

"San Gundián, padre maestro,
todo el saber en eso da :
cuanto es misterio, en el misterio
ha de ser por siempre jamás,
hasta que el cirio de la muerte
nos alumbre en la Eternidad."

"San Serenín, padre maestro,
esa luz que no apagarán
todas las borrascas del mundo,
mi aliento quisiera apagar.
¡ El dolor de sentir la vida
en la otra vida seguirá ! "

"San Gundián, padre maestro,
mientras seas cuerpo mortal
y al cielo mires, en el día
la luz del sol te cegará,
y en la noche las negras alas
del murciélago Satanás."

Callaron los dos ermitaños
y se pusieron a rezar.
San Serenín, como más viejo,
tenía abierto su misal,
y en el misal la calavera
abría su vacío mirar.

289. *Milagro de la Mañana*

The poems in Aromas de leyenda *are built upon snatches of Galician popular poetry, of which the couplet at the end of this piece is an example. Short though it is, this evocation of a Galician morning is a fragment of perfect artistry. A critic once said that Valle-Inclán's poetry is "full of little definite sounds"*[1] *: hear them in these lines. But every phrase, almost every word, brings its quota of beauty to the whole. One after another, they sink into the reader's mind, until it thrills to re-awakening Nature's glory.*

[1] A. F. G. Bell : *Contemporary Spanish Literature*, London, 1926, p. 206.

Tañía una campana
en el azul cristal
de la santa mañana.

Oración campesina
que temblaba en la azul
santidad matutina.

Y en el viejo camino
cantaba un ruiseñor,
y era de luz su trino.

La campana de aldea
le dice con su voz,
al pájaro, que crea.

La campana aldeana
en la gloria del sol
era alma cristiana.

Al tocar esparcía
aromas del rosal
de la Virgen María.

Esta santa conseja
la recuerda un cantar
en una fabla vieja.

Campana, campaniña do Pico Sacro,
toca por que floreza a rosa do milagro.

290. *Rosa del Caminante*

This sonnet, from a later collection (El Pasajero, *1920*), *is more highly developed and less idealized art. To the same essential gifts as we find in* Aromas de leyenda *it adds greater maturity of expression and greater variety of tone. A suggestion of the affectation so characteristic of Valle-Inclán in certain of his moods is found in the title of the poem : each of these lyrics is a " rose ", plucked in a " moment " which it reawakens.*

Álamos fríos en un claro cielo
—azul con timideces de cristal—
sobre el río la bruma como un velo,
y las dos torres de la catedral.

Los hombres secos y reconcentrados,
las mujeres deshechas de parir:
rostros obscuros llenos de cuidados,
todas las bocas clásico el decir.

La fuente seca. En torno el vocerío,
los odres a la puerta del mesón,
y las recuas que bajan hacia el río,

y las niñas que acuden al sermón.
¡Mejillas sonrosadas por el frío
de Astorga, de Zamora, de León.

291. *Rosa vespertina*

Here we have still more virtuosity—in enjambements, *repetitions and echo-rhymes, for example: perhaps just a little too much. There is also (l. 3) a rather striking neologism—and Valle-Inclán, like all Modernists, neologizes freely when it suits him:* amapol *is created from* amapola (*cf.* arrebol) *to describe the glow of a scarlet sunset. This is the first of many glowing colours which we find in the poem—and, though the early Romantics were attracted by colour, they never learned to use it with the same skill as the best of the Modernists. Not since the last of the Herrerans laid down his paint-brush had the colourist's art reached such a height as now.*

Anochece. En la aldea
un gallo cacarea
mirando el amapol
del Sol.

Vacas y recentales
pacen en los herbales,
y canta una mocina
albina.

El refajo de grana
de la niña aldeana
enciende al cristalino
lino.

En el fondo del prado
el heno agavillado,
entre llovizna y bruma
perfuma.

Por la verde hondonada,
la luz anaranjada
que la tarde deslíe
ríe.

Y abre sobre la loma
su curva policroma,
el arco que ventura
augura.

Y toda azul, la hora
tiene el alma que llora
y reza, de una santa
infanta.

Con el rumor de un vuelo
tiembla el azul del cielo,
y un lucero florece.
Anochece.

JOSÉ MARÍA GABRIEL Y GALÁN
1870-1905

OLD-FASHIONED by the standards of the time at which he wrote, this poet of the Salamancan countryside found inspiration partly in the Salamancan poets of the past, but chiefly in his own love of Nature. Standing aloof from literary feuds, owning allegiance to no school, and uninterested in literary innovations, he is content to use traditional metres and (unless we except his poems in dialect) traditional language, and to write on such well-worn themes as family life, Nature and religion. For some years a schoolmaster, he sprang from the plough, and, before his early death, returned to it. His popularity resembles that of Robert Burns, some of whose limitations he shares also. Moving and beautiful, for example, as is his poem " El Cristo de Velázquez ", it cannot compare with that of Unamuno (p. 576) on the same theme. Apart from his *casticidad*, he has little of the spirit of the '98 Generation, and, in general, it is in description, rather than in reflection, that he excels.

292. *El Ama*

In this poem, which won a prize in the Juegos Florales held at Salamanca in 1901, is found almost the whole of Gabriel y Galán's art, and so near the surface does it lie that little comment upon it is necessary. All the themes above enumerated are here, together with an emotion which, reinforced now and again by a simple technique of eloquence, compensates for much that is prosaic, over-obvious and trivial. The gravity, the tranquillity, the contentment which make the atmosphere of the poem are all typically rural; the love of the tierra, *which has inspired so many Spanish writers during the past century, reaches the point of a finely restrained passion—the emotion of Antonio Machado, one might say, without his ideas.*

I

Yo aprendí en el hogar en qué se funda
la dicha más perfecta,
y para hacerla mía
quise yo ser como mi padre era
y busqué una mujer como mi madre
entre las hijas de mi hidalga tierra.
Y fuí como mi padre, y fué mi esposa
viviente imagen de la madre muerta.
¡ Un milagro de Dios, que ver me hizo
otra mujer como la santa aquella !

Compartían mis únicos amores
la amante compañera,
la patria idolatrada,
la casa solariega,
con la heredada historia,
con la heredada hacienda.
¡ Qué buena era la esposa
y qué feraz mi tierra !
¡ Qué alegre era mi casa
y qué sana mi hacienda,
y con qué solidez estaba unida
la tradición de la honradez a ellas !

Una sencilla labradora, humilde
hija de obscura castellana aldea ;
una mujer trabajadora, honrada,
cristiana, amable, cariñosa y seria,
trocó mi casa en adorable idilio
que no pudo soñar ningún poeta.

¡ Oh, cómo se suaviza
el penoso trajín de las faenas
cuando hay amor en casa
y con él mucho pan se amasa en ella
para los pobres que a su sombra viven,
para los pobres que por ella bregan !
¡ Y cuánto lo agradecen, sin decirlo,

y cuánto por la casa se interesan
y cómo ellos la cuidan,
y cómo Dios la aumenta !

Todo lo pudo la mujer cristiana,
logrólo todo la mujer discreta.

La vida en la alquería
giraba en torno de ella
pacífica y amable,
monótona y serena. . . .

¡ Y cómo la alegría y el trabajo,
donde está la virtud se compenetran !

Lavando en el regato cristalino
cantaban las mozuelas,
y cantaba en los valles el vaquero,
y cantaban los mozos en las tierras,
y el aguador camino de la fuente,
y el cabrerillo en la pelada cuesta. . .
¡ Y yo también cantaba,
que ella y el campo hiciéronme poeta !

Cantaba el equilibrio
de aquel alma serena,
como los anchos cielos,
como los campos de mi amada tierra ;
y cantaba también aquellos campos,
los de las pardas onduladas cuestas,
los de los mares de enceradas mieses,
los de las mudas perspectivas serias,
los de las castas soledades hondas,
los de las grises lontananzas muertas. . . .

El alma se empapaba
en la solemne clásica grandeza
que llenaba los ámbitos abiertos
del cielo y de la tierra.

¡ Qué plácido el ambiente,
qué tranquilo el paisaje, qué serena
la atmósfera azulada se extendía
por sobre el haz de la llanura inmensa !

La brisa de la tarde
meneaba, amorosa, la alameda,
los zarzales floridos del cercado,
los guindos de la vega,
las mieses de la hoja,
la copa verde de la encina vieja. . . .

¡ Monorrítmica música del llano,
qué grato tu sonar, qué dulce era !

La gaita del pastor en la colina
lloraba las tonadas de la tierra,
cargadas de dulzuras,
cargadas de monótonas tristezas,
y dentro del sentido
caían las cadencias,
como doradas gotas
de dulce miel que del panal fluyeran.

La vida era solemne ;
puro y sereno el pensamiento era ;
sosegado el sentir, como las brisas ;
mudo y fuerte el amor, mansas las penas,
austeros los placeres,
raigadas las creencias,
sabroso el pan, reparador el sueño,
fácil el bien y pura la conciencia.

¡ Qué deseos el alma
tenía de ser buena,
y cómo se llenaba de ternura
cuando Dios le decía que lo era !

II

Pero bien se conoce
que ya no vive ella ;
el corazón, la vida de la casa
que alegraba el trajín de las tareas ;
la mano bienhechora
que con las sales de enseñanzas buenas
amasó tanto pan para los pobres
que regaban, sudando, nuestra hacienda.

¡ La vida en la alquería
se tiñó para siempre de tristeza !

Ya no alegran los mozos la besana
con las dulces tonadas de la tierra
que al paso perezoso de las yuntas
ajustaban sus lánguidas cadencias.

Mudos de casa salen,
mudos pasan el día en sus faenas,
tristes y mudos vuelven
y sin decirse una palabra cenan ;
que está el aire de casa
cargado de tristeza,
y palabras y ruidos importunan
la rumia sosegada de las penas.

Y rezamos, reunidos, el Rosario,
sin decirnos por quién . . . pero es por ella.
Que aunque ya no su voz a orar nos llama,
su recuerdo querido nos congrega,
y nos pone el Rosario entre los dedos
y las santas plegarias en la lengua.

¡ Qué días y qué noches !
¡ Con cuánta lentitud las horas ruedan
por encima del alma que está sola
llorando en las tinieblas !

Las sales de mis lágrimas amargan
el pan que me alimenta ;
me cansa el movimiento,
me pesan las faenas,
la casa me entristece
y he perdido el cariño de la hacienda.

¡ Qué me importan los bienes
si he perdido mi dulce compañera !

¡ Qué compasión me tienen mis criados
que ayer me vieron con el alma llena
de alegrías sin fin que rebosaban
y suyas también eran !

Hasta el hosco pastor de mis ganados,
que ha medido la hondura de mi pena,
si llego a su majada
baja los ojos y ni hablar quisiera ;
y dice al despedirme : " Ánimo, amo ;
haiga mucho valor y *haiga pacencia. . . .* "

Y le tiembla la voz cuando lo dice,
y se enjuga una lágrima sincera,
que en la manga de la áspera zamarra
temblando se le queda. . . .

¡ Me ahogan estas cosas,
me matan de dolor estas escenas !

¡ Que me anime, pretende, y él no sabe
que de su choza en la techumbre negra
le he visto yo escondida
la dulce gaita aquella
que cargaba el sentido de dulzuras
y llenaba los aires de cadencias ! . . .

¿ Por qué ya no la toca ?
¿ Por qué los campos su tañer no alegra ?

Y el atrevido vaquerillo sano
que amaba a una mozuela
de aquellas que trajinan en la casa,
¿ por qué no ha vuelto a verla ?
¿ por qué no canta en los tranquilos valles ?
¿ por qué no silba con la misma fuerza ?
¿ por qué no quiere restallar la honda ?
¿ por qué está muda la habladora lengua,
que al amo le contaba sus sentires
cuando el amo le daba su licencia ?

" ¡ El ama era una santa ! . . . "
me dicen todos, cuando me hablan de ella.

" ¡ Santa, santa ! ", me ha dicho
el viejo señor cura de la aldea,
aquel que le pedía
las limosnas secretas
que de tantos hogares ahuyentaban
las hambres y los fríos y las penas.

¡ Por eso los mendigos
que llegan a mi puerta
llorando se descubren
y un Padrenuestro por *el ama* rezan !

El velo del dolor me ha obscurecido
la luz de la belleza.

Ya no saben hundirse mis pupilas
en la visión serena
de los espacios hondos,
puros y azules, de extensión inmensa.

Ya no sé traducir la poesía,
ni del alma en la médula me entra
la intensa melodía del silencio,
que en la llanura quieta
parece que descansa,
parece que se acuesta.

Será puro el ambiente, como antes,
y la atmósfera azul será serena,
y la brisa amorosa
moverá con sus alas la alameda,
los zarzales floridos,
los guindos de la vega,
las mieses de la hoja,
la copa verde de la encina vieja. . . .

Y mugirán los tristes becerrillos,
lamentando el destete, en la pradera ;
y la de alegres recentales dulces,
tropa gentil, escalará la cuesta
balando plañideros
al pie de las dulcísimas ovejas ;
y cantará en el monte la abubilla,
y en los aires la alondra mañanera
seguirá derritiéndose en gorjeos,
musical filigrana de su lengua. . . .

Y la vida solemne de los mundos
seguirá su carrera
monótona, inmutable,
magnífica, serena. . . .

Mas, ¿ qué me importa todo,
si el vivir de los mundos no me alegra,
ni el ambiente me baña en bienestares,
ni las brisas a música me suenan,
ni el cantar de los pájaros del monte
estimula mi lengua,
ni me mueve a ambición la perspectiva
de la abundante próxima cosecha,
ni el vigor de mis bueyes me envanece,
ni el paso del caballo me recrea,
ni me embriaga el olor de las majadas,
ni con vértigos dulces me deleitan
el perfume del heno que madura
y el perfume del trigo que se encera ?
Resbala sobre mí sin agitarme
la dulce poesía en que se impregnan
la llanura sin fin, toda quietudes,
y el magnífico cielo, todo estrellas.
Y ya mover no pueden
mi alma de poeta,
ni las de Mayo auroras nacarinas
con húmedos vapores en las vegas,
con cánticos de alondra y con efluvios
de rocïadas frescas,
ni estos de otoño atardeceres dulces
de manso resbalar, pura tristeza
de la luz que se muere
y el paisaje borroso que se queja. . . .
ni las noches románticas de Julio,
magníficas, espléndidas,
cargadas de silencios rumorosos
y de sanos perfumes de las eras ;
noches para el amor, para la rumia
de las grandes ideas,
que a la cumbre al llegar de las alturas
se hermanan y se besan. . . .
¡ Cómo tendré yo el alma
que resbala sobre ella
la dulce poesía de mis campos
como el agua resbala por la piedra !

Vuestra paz era imagen de mi vida
¡ oh campos de mi tierra !
pero la vida se me puso triste
y su imagen de ahora ya no es ésa :
en mi casa, es el frío de mi alcoba,
es el llanto vertido en sus tinieblas ;
en el campo, es el árido camino
del barbecho sin fin que amarillea.

Pero yo ya sé hablar como mi madre
y digo como ella
cuando la vida se le puso triste :
" ¡ Dios lo ha querido así ! ¡ Bendito sea ! "

MANUEL MACHADO
1874-1947

BORN in Seville, the son of an authority on folk-lore, Manuel Machado went to Madrid when quite young and soon became a Madrileño by adoption. In his verse, however, he is more of an Andalusian, though its outstanding characteristics are not so much regional as artistic. In word-music (especially in vowel-play), in his use of colour, in his metrical technique, in his vivid portraits rich with detail, he is one of the most accomplished of Rubén Darío's Spanish disciples. Nearly all his best poems are highly objective, and, at his most advanced, he attains a degree of Parnassianism rare in Spain. He has been called superficial, and it is true that he seldom writes both thoughtfully and well, but his artistic gifts are of so high a quality that it seems ungrateful to demand of him anything more than he gives.

293. *Cantares*

These melodious lines serve as preface to a collection of the same name, the poems in which are reminiscent of various well-known forms of Andalusian folk-music. Picturesqueness and atmosphere are its key-notes, but the onomatopœia of the second stanza is also noteworthy.

Vino, sentimiento, guitarra y poesía
hacen los cantares de la patria mía. . . .
Cantares. . . .
Quien dice cantares, dice Andalucía.

A la sombra fresca de la vieja parra
un mozo moreno rasguea la guitarra. . . .
Cantares. . . .
Algo que acaricia y algo que desgarra.

La prima que canta y el bordón que llora. . . .
y el tiempo callado se va hora tras hora.
Cantares. . . .
Son dejos fatales de la raza mora.

No importa la vida, que ya está perdida,
y después de todo, ¿ qué es eso, la vida ? . . .
Cantares. . . .
Cantando la pena, la pena se olvida.

Madre pena, suerte, pena, madre, muerte,
ojos negros, negros, y negra la suerte. . . .
Cantares. . . .
En ellos el alma del alma se vierte.

Cantares. Cantares de la patria mía ;
cantares son sólo los de Andalucía.
Cantares. . . .
No tiene más notas la guitarra mía.

294. *Felipe IV*

An exquisite and memorable verbal rendering of Velázquez's famous picture. Note the vividness of the colours picked out against the background of deep black and the striking individuality of each of the adjectives—cansado, cobarde, generoso, silencioso, galán. *Note above all the skill with which the poet leaves on the reader's memory that final impression of the white, blue-veined regal hand.*

Nadie más cortesano ni pulido
que nuestro Rey Felipe, que Dios guarde,
siempre de negro hasta los pies vestido.

Es pálida su tez como la tarde,
cansado el oro de su pelo undoso
y de sus ojos, el azul, cobarde.

Sobre su augusto pecho generoso
ni joyeles perturban ni cadenas
el negro terciopelo silencioso.

Y, en vez de cetro real, sostiene apenas,
con desmayo galán, un guante de ante
la blanca mano de azuladas venas.

295. *Figulinas*

Here we come back from painting to music—or, rather, turn aside to musical portraiture. The vowels are cunningly varied, and the short, clipt phrases, often of no more than four syllables, are cut off sharply, so as to convey precisely the opposite impression to that produced by "Otoño" (p. 618)—an impression of liveliness and gaiety. In the second and fifth stanzas (or, more correctly, "movements") the symmetrical half-lines suggest the advance and retire of a courtly dance. One has only to read the poem aloud two or three times to see *the little princess dancing.*

¡ Qué bonita es la princesa !
¡ qué traviesa !
¡ qué bonita
la princesa pequeñita
de los cuadros de Watteau !

Yo la miro, ¡ yo la admiro,
yo la adoro !
Si suspira, yo suspiro ;
si ella llora, también lloro ;
si ella ríe, río yo !

Cuando alegre la contemplo,
como ahora, me sonríe,
. . . . y otras veces su mirada
en los aires se deslíe
pensativa. . . .

¡ Si parece que está viva
la princesa de Watteau !
Al pasar la vista hiere,
elegante,
y ha de amarla quien la viere.

. . . Yo adivino en su semblante
que ella goza, goza y quiere,
vive y ama, sufre y muere. . . .
¡ como yo !

296. "*Es la mañana . . . . .*"

These lines have been compared with Verlaine's

La lune blanche
Luit dans les bois

though the resemblances are chiefly of a general kind—the Spaniard's use of the impair, *his determined* enjambements *and his characteristically unfinished ending following the abrupt and almost defiant cæsura of the final line. Verlaine certainly never did anything better. From the quiet opening phrase on one vowel, reminiscent of a pianist's introductory chords, the musician passes directly to his subject, built almost wholly on the two broad vowels* a, o, *and giving an effect of spaciousness and tranquillity, enhanced by the repetitions in ll. 3, 5, 6. After the golden sunrise has faded into the blue, the tranquillity is broken by the shrill front-vowel* i (*l.* 9), *representing the laughing river. The third stanza, with its full rhymes and repeated vowels, becomes reflective and so leads to the fourth, which (the conclusion apart) takes up the tone of the first. None of Manuel Machado's poems is more successfully and uniformly melodious than this.*

Es la mañana.
El sol está
—nácar y grana—
peinado ya.
Y el campo, ahora,
dora y colora.

Su oro deslíe
en el azul.
El río ríe.
La brisa el tul
nocturno pliega.
. . . . Y huyendo juega.

Luz inocente
de paz y amor,
cielo riente,
santo calor,
bálsamo amable,
inenarrable.

Clara mañana,
tu luz así
—nácar y grana—
descienda a mí.
Y que yo sea
bueno. . . . Y que crea.

297. *Otoño*

Here is an exquisite blending of sound with sense in purest melody. The piece has three movements. The marked brusqueness of the opening of the second movement, which is made up of two parts, is intensified by the use (ll. 7-8) of a grammatically unconnected adjective and adverb. The second part of the movement leads by a skilful modulation into the third, which repeats the main trend of the first. The atmosphere of monotony and languor with which the poem is charged is perfectly conveyed by the feminine endings, by the repetition of nada *and by the predominance of the vowels* a, o. *A poem which packs so much art into so few lines and wears it with such grace is the best answer to critics who accuse the poet of superficiality.*

En el parque yo solo. . . .
Han cerrado,
y olvidado :
en el parque viejo, solo
me han dejado.

La hoja seca
vagamente
indolente
roza el suelo. . . .
Nada sé,
nada quiero,
nada espero.
Nada. . . .
¡ Solo
en el parque me han dejado
olvidado
. . . y han cerrado !

298. *Castilla*

A masterpiece of plasticity. The story is that of the opening scene of the Cantar de Mío Cid *(pp. 2-3) and in his first five lines Manuel Machado paints a picture, as sharp and objective as can be, of that vast, arid, inexorable, sun-drenched Castilian desert. Every detail of the scene which follows is etched with perfect clarity. But it is a cold, detached picture—a picture* seen, *not* felt*—which it is instructive to compare with the keenly felt Castilian poems of the author's brother Antonio (pp. 621 ff.).*

El ciego sol se estrella
en las duras aristas de las armas,
llaga de luz los petos y espaldares
y flamea en las puntas de las lanzas.

El ciego sol, la sed y la fatiga.
Por la terrible estepa castellana,
al destierro, con doce de los suyos
—polvo, sudor y hierro—el Cid cabalga.

Cerrado está el mesón a piedra y lodo. . . .
Nadie responde. Al pomo de la espada
y al cuento de las picas el postigo
va a ceder. . . . ¡ Quema el sol, el aire abrasa !

A los terribles golpes,
de eco ronco, una voz pura, de plata
y de cristal, responde. . . . Hay una niña
muy débil y muy blanca
en el umbral. Es toda
ojos azules y en los ojos lágrimas.
Oro pálido nimba
su carita curiosa y asustada.

" Buen Cid, pasad. . . . El rey nos dará muerte,
arruinará la casa,
y sembrará de sal el pobre campo
que mi padre trabaja. . . .
Idos. El cielo os colme de venturas. . . .
¡ En nuestro mal, oh Cid, no ganáis nada ! "

Calla la niña y llora sin gemido. . . .
Un sollozo infantil cruza la escuadra
de feroces guerreros
y una voz inflexible grita : " ¡ En marcha ! "

El ciego sol, la sed y la fatiga.
Por la terrible estepa castellana,
al destierro, con doce de los suyos
—polvo, sudor y hierro—el Cid cabalga.

299. *Oliveretto de Fermo*

One of the most finished pieces of work turned out even by Manuel Machado. Not one person in a thousand who reads it knows anything of this prince of the Italian Renaissance ; not one in a hundred thousand has visited his palace near the Adriatic shore. Yet to the reader with imagination these disjointed enigmatic phrases call up a whole biography. Note the exquisite restraint ; the perfect word-economy ; the careful, even mathematically precise, construction ; the tripartite division of the first two lines and the last ; the quadripartite division of the poem itself ; the even distribution of the emphasis ; the paradox in the second line ; the irony in the sixth ; and, above all, the conclusion. For the beautifully rounded form of the last line, which would seem to be trying to convince one that there was not a single thing more that could be said about the prince, is entirely at odds with its content. "¿Un cuadro? . . . ¿un puñal? . . . ¿un soneto?" repeats the reader. A flood of questions comes to his lips. Why? . . . Where? . . . How? . . . And, while he is framing them, the picture vanishes, leaving its unknown hero an ineradicable memory.

Fué valiente, fué hermoso, fué artista.
Inspiró amor, terror y respeto.
En pintarle gladiando desnudo
ilustró su pincel Tintoretto.
Machiavelli nos narra su historia
de asesino elegante y discreto.
César Borgia lo ahorcó en Sinigaglia. . . .
Dejó un cuadro, un puñal y un soneto.

ANTONIO MACHADO

1875-1939

Though, like his brother, a native of Seville, Antonio Machado, who died an exile in Southern France shortly before the end of the Spanish Civil War, was more of a Castilian than of an Andalusian in his poetry. He was also a thinker : in his *Soledades, Galerías y otros poemas* (1907) he describes his interior life of meditation lived in the retreats (*soledades*) of the mind and the secret corridors (*galerías*) of the soul. And he was a man of '98 : perhaps of all his poems the greatest are those in which he muses on Spain's past and future. In form, he was indebted to Rubén Darío : but, notwithstanding the picturesque tribute (p. 580) which he paid him, he never embraced literary Modernism, nor, great artist though he is, was he primarily interested in technique. The Parnassianism of his brother Manuel was alien to him : he is in the truest and deepest sense subjective. And everything he wrote was dominated by his noble personality. Of few modern Spanish writers could it be more confidently said : " He was a great man."

300. *Retrato*

Beginning in a light-hearted autobiographical vein, this preface to the collection Campos de Castilla *(1907-1917) expresses, in a frequently quoted stanza, the attitude of the poet, and of most of his contemporaries, to the rival literary modes over which battles had been fought in the preceding century. It then moves to a loftier plane and the high seriousness of the last three stanzas is as characteristic as anything that their author ever wrote.*

Mi infancia son recuerdos de un patio de Sevilla,
y un huerto claro donde madura el limonero ;
mi juventud, veinte años en tierra de Castilla ;
mi historia, algunos casos que recordar no quiero.

Ni un seductor Mañara, ni un Bradomín he sido
—ya conocéis mi torpe aliño indumentario—,
mas recibí la flecha que me asignó Cupido,
y amé cuanto ellas pueden tener de hospitalario.

Hay en mis venas gotas de sangre jacobina,
pero mi verso brota de manantial sereno;
y, más que un hombre al uso que sabe su doctrina,
soy, en el buen sentido de la palabra, bueno.

Adoro la hermosura, y en la moderna estética
corté las viejas rosas del huerto de Ronsard;
mas no amo los afeites de la actual cosmética,
ni soy un ave de esas del nuevo gay-trinar.

Desdeño las romanzas de los tenores huecos
y el coro de los grillos que cantan a la luna.
A distinguir me paro las voces de los ecos,
y escucho solamente, entre las voces, una.

¿ Soy clásico o romántico ? No sé. Dejar quisiera
mi verso, como deja el capitán su espada:
famosa por la mano viril que la blandiera,
no por el docto oficio del forjador preciada.

Converso con el hombre que siempre va conmigo
—quien habla solo espera hablar a Dios un día—;
mi soliloquio es plática con este buen amigo
que me enseñó el secreto de la filantropía.

Y al cabo, nada os debo; debéisme cuanto he escrito.
A mi trabajo acudo, con mi dinero pago
el traje que me cubre y la mansión que habito,
el pan que me alimenta y el lecho en donde yago.

Y cuando llegue el día del último viaje,
y esté al partir la nave que nunca ha de tornar,
me encontraréis a bordo ligero de equipaje,
casi desnudo, como los hijos de la mar.

301. *A Orillas del Duero*

To the years which Antonio Machado spent in the remote Castilian city of Soria we owe a number of his first patriotic poems, the titles of two of which are almost identical. Both are at once powerfully evocative of the Castilian landscape and deeply moving for the grave and sober eloquence inspired by the author's concern for his country. One of them (" Orillas del Duero ") is remembered chiefly by its fine atmosphere :

¡ Castilla varonil, adusta tierra,
Castilla del desdén contra la suerte,
Castilla del dolor y de la guerra,
tierra inmortal, Castilla de la muerte ![1]

The other, here printed, is at once more significant and more substantial. Note the curious crescendo-diminuendo *movement in its emotional tone—the matter-of-fact opening, the increasingly imaginative description, the sudden enkindling of the theme at the mention of the Duero, the prolonged apostrophe which marks the poem's greatest height, the gradual relaxation of tension as the poet abandons himself to reflection, and finally the slow, almost dreamy* coda. *The assertion made of Spain, " Desprecia cuanto ignora," and the question " ¿ Espera, duerme o sueña ? " are perhaps the most pregnant judgments on that country ever packed into so few words.*

Mediaba el mes de julio. Era un hermoso día.
Yo, solo, por las quiebras del pedregal subía,
buscando los recodos de sombra, lentamente.
A trechos me paraba para enjugar mi frente
y dar algún respiro al pecho jadeante ;
o bien, ahincando el paso, el cuerpo hacia adelante
y hacia la mano diestra vencido y apoyado
en un bastón, a guisa de pastoril cayado,
trepaba por los cerros que habitan las rapaces
aves de altura, hollando las hierbas montaraces
de fuerte olor—romero, tomillo, salvia, espliego.
Sobre los agrios campos caía un sol de fuego.

Un buitre de anchas alas con majestuoso vuelo
cruzaba solitario el puro azul del cielo.
Yo divisaba, lejos, un monte alto y agudo,
y una redonda loma cual recamado escudo,
y cárdenos alcores sobre la parda tierra
—harapos esparcidos de un viejo arnés de guerra—,

[1] *Ed. cit.*, CII, p. 115.

las serrezuelas calvas por donde tuerce el Duero
para formar la corva ballesta de un arquero
en torno a Soria.—Soria es una barbacana,
hacia Aragón, que tiene la torre castellana—.
Veía el horizonte cerrado por colinas
obscuras, coronadas de robles y de encinas ;
desnudos peñascales, algún humilde prado
donde el merino pace y el toro, arrodillado
sobre la hierba, rumia ; las márgenes del río
lucir sus verdes álamos al claro sol de estío,
y, silenciosamente, lejanos pasajeros,
¡ tan diminutos !—carros, jinetes y arrieros—
cruzar el largo puente, y bajo las arcadas
de piedra ensombrecerse las aguas plateadas
del Duero.

El Duero cruza el corazón de roble
de Iberia y de Castilla.
¡ Oh, tierra triste y noble,
la de los altos llanos y yermos y roquedas,
de campos sin arados, regatos ni arboledas ;
decrépitas ciudades, caminos sin mesones,
y atónitos palurdos sin danzas ni canciones
que aun van, abandonando el mortecino hogar,
como tus largos ríos, Castilla, hacia la mar !

Castilla miserable, ayer dominadora,
envuelta en sus andrajos desprecia cuanto ignora.
¿ Espera, duerme o sueña ? ¿ La sangre derramada
recuerda, cuando tuvo la fiebre de la espada ?
Todo se mueve, fluye, discurre, corre o gira ;
cambian la mar y el monte y el ojo que los mira.
¿ Pasó ? Sobre sus campos aun el fantasma yerra
de un pueblo que ponía a Dios sobre la guerra.

La madre en otro tiempo fecunda en capitanes
madrastra es hoy apenas de humildes ganapanes.
Castilla no es aquella tan generosa un día,
cuando Myo Cid Rodrigo el de Vivar volvía,
ufano de su nueva fortuna y su opulencia,

a regalar a Alfonso los huertos de Valencia ;
o que, tras la aventura que acreditó sus bríos,
pedía la conquista de los inmensos ríos
indianos a la corte, la madre de soldados,
guerreros y adalides que han de tornar, cargados
de plata y oro, a España, en regios galeones,
para la presa cuervos, para la lid leones.
Filósofos nutridos de sopa de convento
contemplan impasibles el amplio firmamento ;
y si les llega en sueños, como un rumor distante,
clamor de mercaderes de muelles de Levante,
no acudirán siquiera a preguntar ¿ qué pasa ?
Y ya la guerra ha abierto las puertas de su casa.

Castilla miserable, ayer dominadora,
envuelta en sus harapos desprecia cuanto ignora.

El sol va declinando. De la ciudad lejana
me llega un armonioso tañido de campana
—ya irán a su rosario las enlutadas viejas—.
De entre las peñas salen dos lindas comadrejas ;
me miran y se alejan, huyendo, y aparecen
de nuevo ¡ tan curiosas ! . . . Los campos se obscurecen.
Hacia el camino blanco está el mesón abierto
al campo ensombrecido y al pedregal desierto.

302. *Recuerdos*

In this poem, written " *en el tren—Abril 1912* ", *during a journey southward, we see the Andalusian in Machado contending with the Castilian. Its descriptive brilliance, its verbal melody and the caressing smoothness of its rhythm hardly need emphasis.*

¡ Oh Soria, cuando miro los frescos naranjales
cargados de perfume, y el campo enverdecido,
abiertos los jazmines, maduros los trigales,
azules las montañas y el olivar florido ;

Guadalquivir corriendo al mar entre vergeles ;
y al sol de abril los huertos colmados de azucenas,
y los enjambres de oro, para libar sus mieles
dispersos en los campos, huir de sus colmenas ;
yo sé la encina roja crujiendo en tus hogares,
barriendo el cierzo helado tu campo empedernido ;
y en sierras agrias sueño—¡ Urbión, sobre pinares !
¡ Moncayo blanco, al cielo aragonés, erguido !—
Y pienso : Primavera, como un escalofrío
irá a cruzar el alto solar del romancero,
ya verdearán de chopos las márgenes del río.
¿ Dará sus verdes hojas el olmo aquel del Duero ?
Tendrán los campanarios de Soria sus cigüeñas,
y la roqueda parda más de un zarzar en flor ;
ya los rebaños blancos, por entre grises peñas,
hacia los altos prados conducirá el pastor.

¡ Oh, en el azul, vosotras, viajeras golondrinas
que vais al joven Duero, rebaños de merinos,
con rumbo hacia las altas praderas numantinas,
por las cañadas hondas y al sol de los caminos ;
hayedos y pinares que cruza el ágil ciervo,
montañas, serrijones, lomazos, parameras,
en donde reina el águila, por donde busca el cuervo
su infecto expoliario ; menudas sementeras
cual sayos cenicientos, casetas y majadas
entre desnuda roca, arroyos y hontanares
donde a la tarde beben las yuntas fatigadas,
dispersos huertecillos, humildes abejares ! . . .

¡ Adiós, tierra de Soria ; adiós el alto llano
cercado de colinas y crestas militares,
alcores y roquedas del yermo castellano,
fantasmas de robledos y sombras de encinares !

En la desesperanza y en la melancolía
de tu recuerdo, Soria, mi corazón se abreva.
Tierra de alma, toda, hacia la tierra mía,
por los floridos valles, mi corazón te lleva.

En el tren.—Abril 1912.

303. *Consejos*

The philosophy which Machado learned in the school of meditation often finds expression in short epigrammatical poems, somewhat similar to the Doloras *of Campoamor. But occasionally, as here, he expands one of these and gives it more substantial form.*

Sabe esperar, aguarda que la marea fluya,
—así en la costa un barco—sin que al partir te inquiete.
Todo el que aguarda sabe que la victoria es suya ;
porque la vida es larga y el arte es un juguete.
Y si la vida es corta
y no llega la mar a tu galera,
aguarda sin partir y siempre espera,
que el arte es largo y, además, no importa.

304. *España, en paz*

Over-reminiscent, perhaps, at the beginning, of the oratorical verse of the late eighteenth century, this reflective poem, written three months after the outbreak of the War of 1914-18, shows more fire than its author generally displays. Considered as a whole, it is more notable for nobility of sentiment than for excellence of form.

En mi rincón moruno, mientras repiquetea
el agua de la siembra bendita en los cristales,
yo pienso en la lejana Europa que pelea,
el fiero Norte, envuelto en lluvias otoñales.

Donde combaten galos, ingleses y teutones,
allá, en la vieja Flandes y en una tarde fría,
sobre jinetes, carros, infantes y cañones
pondrá la lluvia el velo de su melancolía.

Envolverá la niebla el rojo expolario
—sordina gris al férreo claror del campamento—,
las brumas de la Mancha caerán como un sudario
de la flamenca duna sobre el fangal sangriento.

Un César ha ordenado las tropas de Germania
contra el francés avaro y el triste moscovita,
y osó hostigar la rubia pantera de Britania.
Medio planeta en armas contra el teutón milita.

¡ Señor ! La guerra es mala y bárbara ; la guerra,
odiada por las madres, las almas entigrece ;
mientras la guerra pasa, ¿ quién sembrará la tierra ?
¿ Quién segará la espiga que junio amarillece ?

Albión acecha y caza las quillas en los mares ;
Germania arruina templos, moradas y talleres ;
la guerra pone un soplo de hielo en los hogares,
y el hambre en los caminos, y el llanto en las mujeres.

Es bárbara la guerra y torpe y regresiva ;
¿ por qué otra vez a Europa esta sangrienta racha
que siega el alma y esta locura acometiva ?
¿ Por qué otra vez el hombre de sangre se emborracha ?

La guerra nos devuelve las podres y las pestes
del Ultramar cristiano ; el vértigo de horrores
que trajo Atila a Europa con sus feroces huestes ;
las hordas mercenarias, los púnicos rencores ;
la guerra nos devuelve los muertos milenarios
de cíclopes, centauros, Heracles y Teseos ;
la guerra resucita los sueños cavernarios
del hombre con peludos mammuthes giganteos.

¿ Y bien ? El mundo en guerra y en paz España sola.
¡ Salud, oh buen Quijano ! Por si este gesto es tuyo,
yo te saludo. ¡ Salve ! Salud, paz española,
si no eres paz cobarde, sino desdén y orgullo.

Si eres desdén y orgullo, valor de ti, si bruñes
en esa paz, valiente, la enmohecida espada,
para tenerla limpia, sin tacha, cuando empuñes
el arma de tu vieja panoplia arrinconada ;
si pules y acicalas tus hierros para, un día,
vestir de luz, y erguida : *heme aquí, pues, España,*
en alma y cuerpo, toda, para una guerra mía,
heme aquí, pues, vestida para la propia hazaña,
decir, para que diga quien oiga : *es voz, no es eco,*
el buen manchego habla palabras de cordura ;
parece que el hidalgo amojamado y seco
entró en razón, y tiene espada a la cintura ;
entonces, paz de España, yo te saludo.
Si eres
vergüenza humana de esos rencores cabezudos

con que se matan miles de avaros mercaderes,
sobre la madre tierra que los parió desnudos ;
si sabes como Europa entera se anegaba
en una paz sin alma, en un afán sin vida,
y que una calentura cruel la aniquilaba,
que es hoy la fiebre de esta pelea fratricida ;
si sabes que esos pueblos arrojan sus riquezas
al mar y al fuego—todos—para sentirse hermanos
un día ante el divino altar de la pobreza,
gabachos y tudescos, latinos y britanos,
entonces, paz de España, también yo te saludo,
y a ti, la España fuerte, si, en esta paz bendita,
en tu desdeño esculpes, como sobre un escudo,
dos ojos que avizoran y un ceño que medita.

305. *A Don Francisco Giner de los Ríos*

This is one of the finest poems ever written in Spanish : for sheer grandeur, I know nothing that can touch it since San Juan de la Cruz. Don Francisco Giner de los Ríos, a nineteenth-century educator, whose character, no less than his life-work and ideals, inspired a rare devotion in his followers, had just died (1915) and was to be buried in the heights north-west of Madrid, his much-loved Guadarrama Mountains. Machado's elegy is as remarkable for its word-economy (e.g., ll. 11-14), for its vivid description of the road to the Sierra and for the gentle cadences of its assonancing feminine endings as for the loftiness of its theme, which clothes in never-to-be-forgotten language the idealism alike of the master and of the disciple. We have here a perfect marriage between thought and art

Como se fué el maestro,
la luz de esta mañana
me dijo : Van tres días
que mi hermano Francisco no trabaja.
¿ Murió ? . . . Sólo sabemos
que se nos fué por una senda clara,
diciéndonos : Hacedme
un duelo de labores y esperanzas.

Sed buenos y no más, sed lo que he sido
entre vosotros : alma.
Vivid, la vida sigue,
los muertos mueren y las sombras pasan ;
lleva quien deja y vive el que ha vivido.
¡ Yunques, sonad ; enmudeced, campanas !

Y hacia otra luz más pura
partió el hermano de la luz del alba,
del sol de los talleres,
el viejo alegre de la vida santa.
. . . Oh, sí, llevad, amigos,
su cuerpo a la montaña,
a los azules montes
del ancho Guadarrama.
Allí hay barrancos hondos
de pinos verdes donde el viento canta.
Su corazón repose
bajo una encina casta,
en tierra de tomillos, donde juegan
mariposas doradas. . . .
Allí el maestro un día
soñaba un nuevo florecer de España.

FRANCISCO VILLAESPESA

1877-1935

This brilliant and facile Andalusian, one of Rubén Darío's first Spanish disciples, gave rein to the exuberance of his temperament and achieved an enormous output, marred by an inevitable superficiality. At its best, his highly picturesque and decorative work is full of charm, most of all when his theme allows him to indulge in Andalusian colour. A super-Zorrilla, with his Romantic qualities reinforced by the influence of Modernism, he has also less-known moods of introspection, melancholy, iconoclasm and rebellion suggestive rather of Espronceda. In none of these moods is he negligible, though neither is he in any of them a poet of depth or significance.

306. *La Rueca*

This lyric, in the tradition of the sixteenth century, is taken from one of Villaespesa's early collections (Rapsodias, 1905), *as an example of his simpler manner. Despite a frequently obtrusive artificiality, its tunefulness and rhythm, enhanced by an alternate slowing and quickening of pace, give it a genuine attraction.*

La Virgen cantaba,
la dueña dormía. . .
La rueca giraba
loca de alegría.

—¡ Cordero divino,
tus blancos vellones
no igualan al lino
de mis ilusiones !

Gira, rueca mía,
gira, gira al viento. . . .
¡ Amanece el día
de mi casamiento !

¡ Hila con cuidado
mi velo de nieve,
que vendrá el Amado
que al altar me lleve !

Se acerca. . . . Lo siento
cruzar la llanura. . . .
Sueña la ternura
de su voz el viento. . . .

¡ Gira, rueca loca,
gira, gira, gira !
¡ Su labio suspira
por besar mi boca !

¡ Gira, que mañana
cuando el alba cante
la clara campana,
llegará mi Amante !

¡ Cordero divino,
tus blancos vellones
no igualan al lino
de mis ilusiones !—

La luz se apagaba ;
la dueña dormía ;
la Virgen hilaba,
y sólo se oía

la voz crepitante
de la leña seca. . . .
¡ y el loco y constante
girar de la rueca !

307. *Animae rerum*

Here, by delving more deeply than he was wont into experience, the author attains an unwontedly high level of poetry. Conceived though they are in the conventionally Romantic manner, his sensations ring true and he contrives to convey something of his own emotions to his reader.

Al mirar del paisaje la borrosa tristeza
y sentir de mi alma la sorda pena obscura,
pienso, a veces, si esta dolorosa amargura
surge de mí o del seno de la Naturaleza.

Contemplando el paisaje lluvioso en esta hora
y sintiendo en los ojos la humedad de mi llanto,
ya no sé, confundido de terror y de espanto,
si lloro su agonía o si él mis penas llora.

A medida que sobre los valles anochece
todo se va borrando, todo desaparece. . . .
El labio, que recuerda, un dulce nombre nombra.

Y en medio de este obscuro silencio, de esta calma,
ya no sé si es la sombra quien invade mi alma
o si es que de mi alma va surgiendo la sombra.

308. *Las Fuentes de Granada*

Despite his having devoted many of his collections of lyrics to Granada and other parts of "Moorish" Spain, Villaespesa's most famous Granadine passage comes from a drama, El Alcázar de las perlas *(1912). It is needless to dwell on its over-ornate language, not felt perhaps to be out of place in its luxuriant setting, especially since, unlike so many of its kind, the poem is not spoiled by an excessive orientalism. On the technical side, one notes the effectiveness of the varying length of the lines, the boldness of the* enjambements *and the use made of alliteration and onomatopœia in the conveying of sensuous impressions.*

Las fuentes de Granada. . . .
¿ Habéis sentido,
en la noche de estrellas perfumada,
algo más doloroso que su triste gemido ?
Todo reposa en vago encantamiento
en la plata flúida de la luna.
Entre el olor a nardos que se aspira en el viento,
la frescura del agua es como una
mano que refrescase la sien calenturienta.

El agua es como el alma de la ciudad. Vigila
su sueño, y al oído
del silencio le cuenta
las leyendas que viven a pesar del olvido,
¡ y bajo las estrellas de la noche tranquila
tiene palpitaciones de corazón herido !
¡ La voz del agua es santa !
Quien la profunda música de su acento adivina
comprenderá algún día la palabra divina. . . .
¡ El agua es guzla donde Dios sus misterios canta !
Las fuentes de Granada. . . .
¿ Habéis sentido,
en la noche de estrellas perfumada,
algo más doloroso que su triste gemido ?
Una, gorgoteante, suspira entre las flores
de un carmen, esperando la mano de un ensueño
que abra a la blanca luna sus clavos surtidores
para dar a la noche sus diamantes de sueño ;
y mientras sobre el mármol, una a una, desgrana
las perlas de los ricos collares de sultana,
algunas se despeñan como ecos de torrente,
y entre las alamedas descienden rumorosas,
arrastrando en el vivo fulgor de su corriente,
en féretros de espuma, cadáveres de rosas.
Otra por las paredes resbala, lentamente,
y entre las verdes hiedras lagrimear se siente,
como si poco a poco, por una estrecha herida,
se fuese desangrando hasta quedar sin vida.
Las hay ciegas, y en ellas
llora toda la móvil plata de las estrellas.
Hay en el aire tanta humedad que da frío.
La noche, un fresco aroma acuático deslíe.
El agua llora, gime, suspira, canta y ríe,
y dominando el gárrulo y eterno murmurío,
se oyen plañir las roncas serenatas del río.

La sangre de Granada corre por esas fuentes,
y en el hondo silencio de las noches serenas,
al escuchar sus músicas sobre los viejos puentes
la sentimos que corre también por nuestras venas.

Aduerme nuestro espíritu su musical encanto ;
bebemos el ensueño de sus respiraciones ;
penetra hasta la carne en lentas filtraciones
y huye por nuestros ojos en un furtivo llanto. . . .
Las fuentes de Granada. . . .
¿ Habéis sentido,
en la noche de estrellas perfumada,
algo más doloroso que su triste gemido ?

ENRIQUE DÍEZ-CANEDO

1879-1944

THOUGH a poet of slender output, limited range and modest ambitions, Díez-Canedo, a native of Badajoz but a Madrileño by adoption, has in general been rated far below his merits. He was an excellent critic, and to his effective self-criticism may well be due the high level of his verse. The gravity of its tone, the restraint of its emotion and the profoundly religious spirit which underlies it relate him to Antonio Machado and Unamuno. A keen student and lover of France, with long and intimate experience of the culture of Spanish America, he is occasionally inclined to be derivative. His poems on Madrilenian subjects, too, fringe the prosaic. But of the remainder there stand out a large proportion, many of them on the simplest themes, whose universality of touch should give them a permanent place in Spanish literature.

309. *Viejo Semanario*

This pleasant, if in no way distinguished, piece, from an early collection, La Visita del sol *(1907), is characteristic of the intimate atmosphere in which Díez-Canedo finds himself most at home. Turning over his books, playing with his children, or walking round Madrid, he can observe what so many others, doing the same things, have overlooked. It is in that sense, perhaps, more than in any other, that he is a poet: the poet of the ordinary man.*

Este tomo de un viejo semanario, que tiene
los años que tendría mi abuelo, si viviera,
de tan amable guisa mis horas entretiene
como cuando sus folios volví por vez primera.

Y encuentro en él tan suave, tan íntima fragancia,
me llena el corazón de tal melancolía,
que pienso si se habrá quedado en él mi ínfancia
como esta flor, hoy seca, que no sé quién pondría.

Es un amigo viejo que sabe muchas cosas ;
cien historias ingenuas refiere con cariño,
y a veces, cuando escucho sus frases candorosas,
pienso : " Este pobre anciano tiene cosas de niño."

Grabados en madera, toscos, que reproducen
efigies de caudillos, exóticos paisajes ;
versos que hablan de tumbas, de aceros que relucen
en torvas callejuelas ; relatos de viajes

a regiones de Oriente, magníficas, lejanas ;
novelas en que al héroe da el triunfo un amuleto ;
y, traducidas, tétricas baladas alemanas
en que se ve a caballo pasar un esqueleto ;

todo, desde la infancia, lo tengo tan presente,
con relieve tan puro, firme y extraordinario,
que hoy florecen mis versos de la vieja simiente
que tú dejaste en mí, vetusto semanario ;

vetusto semanario que hoy, cuando a mis congojas
juveniles huyendo, torno a tu amor, abiertas
dejas al paso mío, con sólo abrir tus hojas,
del encantado alcázar de mi niñez las puertas.

310. *Soldado*

The father is watching his little son playing with his tin soldiers. On that commonplace sight he builds a lay sermon of extraordinary force and verve, its points emphasized and driven home by the shortness of the stanzas and the continually recurring staccato note on which the poem ends.

¡ Soldado !
Tu sable y tu escopeta ;
tu ros y tu caballo.

¡ Soldado !
Huestes imaginarias
siguen tu voz de mando.

¡ Soldado !
Frunces el ceño y huyen
dispersos los contrarios.

¡ Soldado !
Toda la casa llena
de estrépito tu paso.

Bien lo adivinas, hijo ;
¿ quién te hizo adivinarlo ?
Si eres como yo quiero,
tendrás que ser soldado.

Soldado, aunque no quieras,
pero soldado raso,
sin galones ni estrellas,
en combate diario.
Soldado, aunque no quieras,
sólo con que hable alto
tu corazón y escuche
lo que hablan tus hermanos.

¡ Soldado !
Firme sin juramentos
y sin hazañas bravo.

¡ Soldado !
Soldado a todas horas,
alerta y arma al brazo.

¡ Soldado !
Contra el odio y la guerra,
contra todo lo falso,
contra todo lo impuro.
¡ Soldado !

311. *Oración en el Jardín*

From the technical standpoint this poem would have gained by being written in stanzaic form, instead of in the single paragraph of blank verse, which fails to distinguish the successive stages of the thought. But, so far as the thought is concerned, the imagination which illumines it and the feeling with which it is expressed, no poet of the '98 Generation ever wrote anything better.

Yo me quiero morir como se muere
todos los años el jardín, y luego
renacer de igual modo que renace
todos los años el jardín. Se han ido
los pájaros ; volaron en pos de ellos
las hojas, pero no tenían alas.
No me quiero morir como las hojas,
ni quiero ser el árbol de perenne
verdor adusto, ni el arbusto dócil
cortado en seto, sino el árbol libre,
desnudo atleta que en el suelo ahinca
las fuertes plantas y en el aire tuerce
los recios brazos : no el verdor eterno,
sino la fronda renovada, el fruto
cuando el año lo envíe. Aquí me tienes,
Señor, desnudo como el árbol. Dame
tu bautismo de lluvias y tu crisma
de sol, y dame vestiduras nuevas,
inmaculadas. El jardín de invierno
callado está : mi corazón callado.
Habla tú ; luego, vísteme de hojas.
Algo de tus palabras, al moverse,
repetirán, como inspiradas lenguas.

EDUARDO MARQUINA
1879-1946

An able and successful dramatist, Marquina, a typical Romantic and a no less typical Spaniard, laboured to break down the walls that separate the genres, producing such things as "leyendas dramáticas", "comedias poéticas" and a "cuento de pueblo en cuatro actos y en verso". In the pure lyric he is less Romantic, and also less good, than in drama: if he has his fine and inspired moments, moving by virtue of their sensitiveness or virility, he can also be superficial, or trivial, or imitative, or prosaic, or over-decorative—and he too often is. It seems likely that posterity, while preserving some of his best plays, which have great lyric moments, will gradually forget the rest, and with them a large proportion of his non-dramatic poetry.

312. *Se pinta el mar*

In the oddly un-elegiac Elegías (*1905*), *in which, rather than in a collection often preferred to them, the vigorously allegorical* Vendimión (*1909*), *lies some of Marquina's most inspired lyricism, he is never happier than when he writes of the sea, with which, as a native of Barcelona, he was familiar from childhood. The interplay of Nature and human love, a theme which he develops in many different ways, is particularly aptly treated in his sea-poems, of which "Se pinta el mar" is one of the best.*

La tierra es toda vida
y el mar es todo amor.
En el mar hay escondida
una fuerza más grande que la vida:
la tierra es criatura, y el mar es creador.

Todo el mar es misterio resonante
y palabra inicial:
nada hay a espaldas de él, nada hay delante:
el mar es una eternidad constante
y un movimiento en lo inmortal.

Escapa al pertinaz conocimiento
y prolonga en fantasmas la visión:
el mar es elemento,
hermano del pensamiento
y lecho azul de la imaginación.

Las mujeres suspiran
cuando a la tarde miran
la gran fatiga, hecha pasión, del mar:
toda mujer quisiera
en una noche encapotada y fiera
estarse a solas abrazando al mar.

Los marineros de canosa frente,
estatuas que ha esculpido su garra omnipotente,
pasan como hombres tipos a la orilla del mar:
llevan en sus pupilas el misterio
y tienen un hablar de magisterio,
mamado en su nodriza, la recia tempestad.

A las mozas alegres de la costa,
cuando más lindas van, se les agosta
en sólo un día toda su beldad:
prometidas tal vez a un fiero esposo,
pierden en un abrazo misterioso,
como la tierra en Junio, toda su majestad.

Los barrios, junto al mar, de pescadores,
son hornos de fantásticas mentiras,
cunas de unos deseos buscadores,
que se echan a volar emprendedores
renuevos de la tierra en arriesgadas jiras.

Las noches, en las casas marineras,
vienen con aparato de quimeras
poniendo luces rojas en todas las ventanas:
detrás de los cristales arden unas pupilas
espiando las sombras intranquilas
y en atisbo de barcas lejanas.

Entre las rocas de la costa alzada
se oye un extraño hablar, de madrugada,
de gentes que en la noche vigilaron :
las barcas, animadas de un deseo,
tienen un misterioso balanceo
y nunca se están quietas en donde las dejaron.

Las casas de los pueblos marineros
abren todas al mar sus agujeros :
rejas y puertas y ventanas
toda la vida, de la mar, esperan :
al monte sólo irán cuando se mueran,
al quieto cementerio de las tapias enanas.

¡ Oh, mar ! ¡ Oh, extraño mar ! ¡ Oh, gran misterio !
¡ Oh ! ¡ No saben tus gentes el imperio
que ejerces en sus almas !
Tú has sabido, a través de las edades,
garantir con tus altas tempestades
la majestad suprema de tus calmas.

¡ Santo mar, fuerza nueva, agua querida,
adobo espiritual de nuestra vida,
campo siempre fecundo a la mirada !
¡ Sólo tú, cuando un ansia la enajena,
pones la gracia de una paz serena
en la pupila fácil de la Amada !

ENRIQUE DE MESA

1879-1929

MESA, like the less sophisticated Gabriel y Galán (p. 605), and more exclusively than the Sevilian-born Antonio Machado (p. 621), is a poet of Castile, and a better example than either of a writer of real talent whose inspiration derives from a limited phase of his experience. He combines with extraordinary success a Classical restraint and the spontaneity of the born singer. Beginning as a Modernist, he returned increasingly, as he grew older, to the mediaeval Spanish forms of the *Romanceros* and *Cancioneros*. He yielded, too, more and more, to his love for the Sierra de Guadarrama (pp. 629-30), which inspires the collection *Andanzas serranas* (1910) and illumines *El Silencio de la Cartuja* (1916), a verse description of a journey made in spring-time to the Carthusian monastery of El Paular (p. 400). He is no great thinker; his meditations, even in the Carthusian silence, are somewhat shallow; but his sensitiveness and power of expression more than compensate for deficiencies in thought. Unfortunately, his output was all too slight and he died without having wholly fulfilled his promise.

313. *Sin Caballero*

A vivid evocation of the Don Quixote country, taken from the Cancionero Castellano *(1911), in which the physical qualities of the landscape may be intended to symbolize (in the spirit of the '98 Generation) Spain's moral state. This symbolism is heightened by the emphasis laid on the antithetical figures of Don Quixote and Sancho Panza (note particularly ll. 18, 22-5). The last stanza, in which the antithetical ideas are subtly fused, seems to glimpse the possibilities of a better world. Even if we reject, or ignore, this interpretation of the piece, however, it would be difficult to find a contemporary poem which is its superior in choice and economy of words.*

Un molino,
perezoso a par del viento.
Un son triste de campana.
Un camino
que se pierde polvoriento,
surco estéril de la tierra castellana.

Ni un rebaño
por las tierras. Ni una fuente
que dé alivio al caminante.
Como antaño,
torna al pueblo, lentamente,
triste y flaco sucesor de Rocinante.

Una venta.
Un villano, gordo y sucio,
de miserias galeote. . . .
Soñolienta
la andadura de su rucio.
¡ No aparece en la llanada Don Quijote !

Terruñero
de la faz noblota y ancha,
descendiente del labriego castellano.
Escudero,
ya no tienes caballero ;
ya no templas con prudencia de villano
las locuras del hidalgo de la Mancha.

314. *Voz del Agua*

This purest of lyrics—from the same collection as the preceding poem, yet in every way so unlike it—is given by its author the subtitle " madrigal ". Sheer music, for which no recipe can be provided, it is as near as human effort will ever come to the carefree song of the bird or the laughing brook, unless another song in this Cancionero—*that with the refrain*

¿ Porqué corriendo te quejas,
arroyo de Garcisancho ?—[1]

be taken as rivalling it.

[1] " ¿ Por qué corriendo te quejas . . . . ? " *Ed. cit.*, pp. 67-70.

Era pura nieve,
y los soles me hicieron cristal.
Bebe, niña, bebe
la clara pureza de mi manantial.

Canté entre los pinos
al bajar desde el blanco nevero ;
crucé los caminos,
di armonía y frescura al sendero.

No temas que, aleve,
finja engaños mi voz de cristal.
Bebe, niña, bebe
la clara pureza de mi manantial.

Allá, cuando el frío,
mi blancura las cumbres entoca ;
luego, en el estío,
voy cantando a morir en tu boca.

Tan sólo soy nieve,
no me enturbian ponzoña ni mal.
Bebe, niña, bebe
la clara pureza de mi manantial.

315. "*Y la gloria del sol. . . .*"

Has anyone, in prose or poetry, succeeded in conveying as much of the atmosphere of Castile as Mesa does in these hendecasyllables? Every substantive, every epithet goes home to the reader's sensibility. A magnificent piece of word-imagery.

Y la gloria del sol es un triunfo
en un cielo de azur. La rubia parva
—pan de la vida y oro de la tierra—
tendida sobre el heno de los campos,
gime bajo los trillos, como gimen
las espigas de ensueño maceradas
por trillos de dolor. Cerca, las cumbres,
los fuertes robles, las roquedas bravas,

el cielo castellano, zarco y limpio,
el regio manto del pinar que pende
desde los hombros del hercúleo monte.
Y la albura de nieve, en que los ojos
beben blanca pureza. Y los regatos
con su voz de cristal. Y las canciones
del pinar centenario, en que la brisa
finge manso oleaje. ¡ Oh !, que mi alma
por la tierra se esparza y se difunda,
y sienta amor por todo lo creado ;
por la piedra y el árbol, por las aves,
por la fontana pura, donde ríe,
hecha cristal, la nieve de las cimas.
Y que el torrente de la sangre bulla,
y sea el corazón todo una llama.
Y que las mieles del amor se viertan
en labios de mujer. ¡ Oh los aromas
de la pródiga tierra florecida,
aliento de mujer sana y fecunda !
Hay que vivir la vida intensamente,
y gozar, y sufrir. Que el alma roja
vibre y llegue a romperse de ventura.
Y si la muerte con su voz nos llama,
y nos ofrece sus morenos brazos
nuestra madre la tierra, que los huesos,
al pudrirse en su entraña, críen flores.
Y que las corten femeninas manos.
Y que se enreden en los negros rizos
de una mujer que por amor suspire.

316. *La Hora dulce*

The last poem was a picture : this (from El Silencio de la Cartuja*), is no less vividly pictorial, yet at the same time is music. An excellent example of Mesa's handling of his favourite octosyllabic measure, noteworthy for its melodious rhymes, and also for its use of colour, to which its author is much less addicted than are most of his contemporaries.*

¡ Oh crepúsculos divinos
del dulce sol otoñal
en las claras de los pinos,
linderos del roquedal !

Esplende el cielo azulado
con viva lumbre carmín.
Suena lejos, apagado,
ronco, el ladrar de un mastín.

Una franja luminosa,
allá en el crestón frontero,
baña en suave tinta rosa
la blancura del nevero.

Cruza la trocha un regato,
todo espumas y rumor :
gobierna un zagal el hato
—sucia nieve en el verdor— ;

y al eco de su silbido,
sube desde la quebrada
el quejumbroso balido
de una oveja desmandada.

El creciente de la luna
es de nácar en el cielo.
Sobre la muerta laguna
alza un águila su vuelo.

Y dos cuervos, que del llano
retornan hacia sus nidos,
al cruzar el altozano
lanzan discordes graznidos.

JUAN RAMÓN JIMÉNEZ

1881

WHAT kind of judgment posterity will pass upon the poetry of Juan Ramón Jiménez is a matter on which the views of present-day critics widely diverge. But as to his position in the history of literature there is no doubt. He has served as a most powerful and effective link between Rubén Darío and the poets of to-day. He, better than any of his contemporaries, was able to absorb from Modernism the elements which he judged likely to be of most abiding value, and to pass them on, in a refined and re-modernized form, to a generation which never knew the high priest of Modernism save through his writings.

Like Rubén Darío, Juan Ramón Jiménez began writing when very young, and had published more than twenty collections of verse by the time he was thirty-five. From the very beginning he has charm, melody and sensibility, but his mannerisms, exaggerations and neologisms mar his early volumes, which he has himself publicly declared to have the value only of *borradores*. After 1917, however, the date of his *Diario de un poeta recién casado*, he began to write less freely and more carefully, to issue " anthologies " of his own poetry and to work towards an aim which henceforth becomes more dominant in Spanish lyricism : *poesía pura*. " Ni más nuevo, al ir, ni más lejos," he sets as his motto in the *Diario*,—" más hondo : la depuración constante de lo mismo."[1] In much of his later work we find the very quintessence of poetry; mature technique; the predominance of imagination; controlled sensibility; penetrating imagery; the simplicity of genius.

317. *Nocturno*

The recording of sensation rather than thought, a subjectivity which is only apparent, a bolder use of metaphor than any which Spanish poetry

[1] *Diario de un poeta recién casado*, Madrid, 1917 [p. 14].

had previously known—these are the characteristic notes of one of the best of Jiménez's juvenilia. *Its peculiar beauty centres in the images of water and reflected light, floating slowly to the surface from the depths of poetic sensibility.*

La luna me echa en el alma
honda, un agua de deslumbres,
que me la deja lo mismo
que un pozo templado y dulce.

Entonces, mi fondo, bueno
para todos, sube, sube,
y abre, al nivel del prado
del mundo, su agua de luces.

Agua que une estrella y flor,
que llama a la sed con lumbres
celestes, donde están, náufragos
de amor, los reinos azules.

318. *Pastoral*

This charmingly descriptive piece, with its haunting refrain, goes back to an earlier tradition. It would be quite superfluous to comment upon the poet's apt use of detail, his blending of imagination with description and his effective evocation of the daily melancholy of sunset.

Ya vienen ahí las carretas. . . .
—Lo han dicho el pinar y el viento,
lo ha dicho la luna de oro,
lo han dicho el humo y el eco. . . .—
Son las carretas que pasan
estas tardes, al sol puesto,
las carretas que se llevan
del monte los troncos muertos.

¡ Cómo lloran las carretas,
camino de Pueblo Nuevo !

Los bueyes vienen soñando,
a la luz de los luceros,
en el establo caliente
que sabe a madre y a heno.
Y detrás de las carretas,
caminan los carreteros,
con la aijada sobre el hombro
y los ojos en el cielo.

¡ Cómo lloran las carretas,
camino de Pueblo Nuevo !

En la paz del campo, van
dejando los troncos muertos
un olor fresco y honrado
a corazón descubierto.
Y cae el Ángelus desde
la torre del pueblo viejo,
sobre los campos talados
que huelen a cementerio.

¡ Cómo lloran las carretas,
camino de Pueblo Nuevo !

319. *Elejía pura*[1]

The identification of himself with the more quietly penetrative aspects of Nature is one of the most individual notes of Juan Ramón Jiménez's poetry. He combines, too, vivid though simple description with word-music of a high order.

Amo el paisaje verde por el lado del río.
El sol, entre la fronda, ilusiona el poniente ;
y, sobre flores de oro, el pensamiento mío,
crepúsculo del alma, se va con la corriente.

¿ Al mar ? ¿ Al cielo ? ¿ Al mundo ? ¿ Qué sé yo. . . . ?
Las estrellas
suelen bajar al agua, traíd as por la brisa. . . .
Medita el ruiseñor. . . . Las penas son más bellas,
y sobre la tristeza florece la sonrisa.

[1] The use of *j* for *g* before *e* and *i* is an idiosyncrasy of the poet.

320. *Tenebrae*

Read aloud, these lines attract one by the melody of liquid and sibilant consonants and cunningly grouped, repeated vowels. The eye, however, is caught rather by the poet's crude laying-on of colour, typical of his early collections, while the mind finds it hard to adjust itself to the transference of the validity of colour-images. But these visual and auditory impressions should not obscure the poet's real achievement—the subtlety, hitherto unapproached in Spain, with which emotion is conveyed through symbols.

Todo el ocaso es amarillo limón.
En el cenit cerrado, bajo las nubes mudas,
bandadas negras de pájaros melancólicos
rayan, constantes, el falso cielo de lluvia.

Por el jardín, sombrío, de los plúmbeos nimbos,
las rosas tienen una morada veladura,
y el crepúsculo vago, que cambia las verdades,
pone en todo, al rozarlo, no sé qué gasas húmedas.

Lívido, deslumbrado del amarillo, torvo
del plomo, en mis oídos, como un moscardón, zumba
una ronda monótona, que yo no sé de dónde
viene. . . . , que deja lágrimas. . . . , que dice : " Nunca. . . .
Nunca. . . ."

321. *El Poeta a caballo*

Again ear and eye receive widely different impressions : the ear, in the pulsating rhythm, detects the trotting of the horse ; the eye cannot escape from the continually reiterated " tranquilidad violeta "—another typical juanramoniano *colour-transference. But conflicting with the brightness of the colour and the unusually emphatic rhythm, both found in the refrain, is an imprecision of form—unfinished sentences and inconsequent repetitions—which harmonizes well with the reflective mood of the body of the poem.*

¡ Qué tranquilidad violeta,
por el sendero, a la tarde !
A caballo va el poeta. . . .
¡ Que tranquilidad violeta !

La dulce brisa del río,
olorosa a junco y agua,
le refresca el señorío. . . .
La brisa leve del río. . . .

A caballo va el poeta. . . .
¡ Qué tranquilidad violeta !

Y el corazón se le pierde,
doliente y embalsamado,
en la madreselva verde. . . .
Y el corazón se le pierde. . . .

A caballo va el poeta. . . .
¡ Qué tranquilidad violeta !

Se está la orilla dorando. . . .
El último pensamiento
del sol la deja soñando. . . .
Se está la orilla dorando. . . .

¡ Qué tranquilidad violeta,
por el sendero, a la tarde !
A caballo va el poeta. . . .
¡ Qué tranquilidad violeta !

322. *Mar, nada*

Until quite modern times, Castilian poetry (unlike Catalan, Galician and Basque) said little of the sea, which has come into its own only in this twentieth century. It was Juan Ramón who first gave it this new vogue and no one has treated the theme more suggestively or sensitively than he. In this wonderful poem, with its sinuous rhythm and its sense-echoing sounds, the long, placid lines, the occasional short, brusque words dominated by the consonant r, *the repetition of* mar, nada, *give an inescapable impression of the waves, now monotonous in their tranquillity, now dashing fiercely against the rocks. And there is more in the poem than this. It seethes with a sense of savage frustration expressed in distorted views of the outside world. Its sea is a vision of sterile desolation, presented against a background of sordid futility, and to this symbolic meaning the artistry also ministers, as in the descending scale of mournful vowels (ll. 13-17) leading to the black abyss. Both in tone and in technique the poem is reminiscent of Walt Whitman. There is no finer example in Spanish of the expression of powerful emotion through the medium of external description.*

Los nubarrones tristes
le dan sombras al mar.
El agua,
manchada férreamente,
parece un duro campo llano
de minas agotadas
(en no sé qué arruinamiento
de fluentes escorias,
de líquidas ruinas).

¡ Qué subir y caer, qué barajeo,
qué quita y pon
de oscuros planos desolados !

¿ Un mar sin su virtud de mar, un agua inútil
sin mar, un mar perdido,
un mar de olvido y de pasado,
un negro mar de nada,
de acumulada, trastornada nada ?

¡ Nada !
(La palabra, aquí, encuentra
hoy, para mí, su sitio,
en catástrofe yerta,
como un cadáver de palabra
que se tendiera en su sepulcro
natural.)
¡ Nada y mar !

323. " *El barco entra. . . .* "

Here again we have pure and vivid description, though overlaid with reflection, the lack of detail in which leaves freedom for the most varied associations. The impressions of tranquillity, as the boat glides in through the blackness of the night, and of the drowsiness of the watchers, seem ineffaceable : yet with the challenging exclamation " ¡ Oh vela real nuestra. . . . ! " the poem comes to life in the mind before sinking back once more into the darkness.

El barco entra, opaco y negro,
en la negrura trasparente
del puerto inmenso.
Paz y frío.
—Los que esperan
están aún dormidos con su sueño,
tibios en ellos, lejos todavía y yertos dentro de él,
de aquí, quizás . . . .

¡ Oh vela real nuestra, junto al sueño
de duda de los otros ! ¡ Seguridad, al lado
del sueño inquieto por nosotros !—
Paz. Silencio.
Silencio que, al romperse. con el alba,
hablará de otro modo.

TOMÁS MORALES
1885-1921

Among the immediate followers of Rubén Darío was a little group of poets from the Canary Islands, of whom the most gifted was Tomás Morales. He excelled in verse full of rich, ornate and brilliant imagery, for which he found ample inspiration in his *tierra*, and his command of form was complete enough to enable him to cultivate this type of literature with a sureness of touch, at its best, surpassed only by that of Rubén himself. Without any doubt, as his magnificent "Oda al Atlántico" will alone attest, he is the greatest contemporary poet of the sea. The two sonnets here given—the first and last of a group—are of similar type, and, though of necessity cramped by the confines of form, they are perhaps even more remarkable examples of the poet's virtuosity. Nowhere in Spanish has the fourteen-syllable Alexandrine been used to greater effect; nowhere else, as here, can one hear the authentic rolling of the waves.

324. *Poemas del Mar*

I

Puerto de Gran Canaria sobre el sonoro Atlántico,
con sus faroles rojos en la noche calina,
y el disco de la luna bajo el azul romántico
rielando en la movible serenidad marina. . . .

Silencio de los muelles en la paz bochornosa,
lento compás de remos en el confín perdido,
y el leve chapoteo del agua verdinosa
lamiendo los sillares del malecón dormido;

fingen en la penumbra fosfóricos trenzados
las mortecinas luces de los barcos anclados,
brillando entre las ondas muertas de la bahía. . . .

y de pronto, rasgando la calma, sosegado,
un cantar marinero, monótono y cansado,
vierte en la noche el dejo de su melancolía. . . .

FINAL

Yo fuí el bravo piloto de mi bajel de ensueño,
argonauta ilusorio de un país presentido,
de alguna isla dorada de quimera o de sueño
oculta entre las sombras de lo desconocido. . . .

Acaso un cargamento magnífico encerraba
en su cala mi barco, ni pregunté siquiera ;
absorta mi pupila las tinieblas sondaba,
y hasta hube de olvidarme de clavar mi bandera.

Y llegó el viento Norte, desapacible y rudo ;
el poderoso esfuerzo de mi brazo desnudo
logró tener un punto la fuerza del turbión ;

para lograr el triunfo luché desesperado,
y cuando ya mi cuerpo desfalleció cansado
una mano en la noche me arrebató el timón. . . .

SALVADOR DE MADARIAGA

1886

STATESMAN, diplomat and professor, historian, dramatist, essayist and literary critic, Salvador de Madariaga has played so many parts in his life that he would probably consider himself in only a very minor degree a poet. His *Romances de ciego*, however, and a striking little short-lined " soneto a la española," here reproduced, have become widely known, together with his fine elegies on the deaths of Unamuno (p. 573) and García Lorca (p. 677). The latter of these elegies is among the few poems inspired by the Civil War of 1936-9 which is sure to live; in the former the author shows himself in poetry, as he had already done in other spheres, to be in the authentic line of the Generation of '98. The elegies were first collected in a trilingual volume entitled *Rosa de cieno y ceniza*, a remarkable tribute to this poet's virtuosity, which also contains a graphic and nimble descriptive poem " El Corzo ", and a short but impressive " Himno a España ", somewhat in the Darian mode, but throbbing with the sternly restrained emotion of an exile.

325. *Abandono*

Razón de la sinrazón
que en mi ser vas penetrando,
me doblego ante tu mando
con íntima desazón.

Rompiste la trabazón
del porqué, del cómo y cuándo,
y así te fuí abandonando
alma, juicio y corazón.

Te entregué hasta mis laureles. . . .
Y no queda en los vergeles
de lo que fué mi albedrío

otra cosa que cederte
que el ciprés recto y sombrío
de la idea de la muerte.

326. *El Corzo*

Aire al galope, corzo,
del prado breve huésped,
apenas con pie leve besa el césped
cuando otra vez al viento
vierte en flúido escorzo
su raudo movimiento,
ráfaga viva, corzo,
imagen presurosa,
esquivo pensamiento. . . .

Río, sierpe sedosa,
sueño de cielo en agua diluído,
mirada luminosa
que sobrevive el agua en que ha vivido—
aire al galope, el corzo aquí ha venido
para aplacar la sed que le atormenta,
quizá para esconderse
o quizá para verse
en el espejo líquido del río,
vibrándole las formas y colores,
suspenso de sí mismo en el vacío. . . .

Alamos tembladores,
almas abiertas a la luz y al viento ;
cipreses soñadores
que, vestidos de verde macilento,
yerguen su tenso anhelo
hacia la etérea bóveda del cielo—
por entre aquestos troncos, con el viento,
fluye, ráfaga viva,
el corzo que se esquiva
del álamo al ciprés, y se diluye
en el río del aire,
así como el donaire
se diluye en el goce que de él fluye. . . .

Colina, roca viva,
que el tiempo mordisquea y no destruye,
y deja patinada,
perfil que sobre el cielo .

corta el bisel buído
de la mirada—
al ápice ha subido,
huído,
aire al galope, el corzo,
posando su pie leve
sobre la roca breve
para aspirar con místico alborozo
el aire de la altura
que ha frotado la nieve
y que ha afilado el yelo.

El corzo
recógese en escorzo
y arrojando hacia atrás la roca breve,
en un súbito salto
al cielo da el asalto,
ráfaga viva vuelta hacia lo alto.

327. *Himno a España*

¡ Nuestra España ! Tierra hermosa. En aventura y andanza
la he mirado palmo a palmo y admirado lanza a lanza.
Por espada tiene el sol y por escudo la piedra ;
por casco crestas de yelo, por brial encina y yedra.
Su cofia es azul de cielo y sobre su pecho altivo
lleva un manto de madroños, cada madroño un olivo.
La fuerza anima en su pecho y la gracia en sus modales :
bajo corpiño de césped, coraza de pedernales,
sus alfanjes cinco ríos, sus almenas cinco montes :
sus fosos los cuatro mares ; sus sueños cuatro horizontes,
cuatro vastos horizontes que se le van agrandando
hasta abarcar todo el mundo con Isabel y Fernando.

JOSÉ MORENO VILLA
1887

A MALAGUEÑO, like the younger poets Prados (p. 683) and Altolaguirre (p. 699), and also a historian and an art critic, Moreno Villa, as soon as he began to write verse, took the post-Modernist path, showing a predilection for Andalusian *coplas* and at the same time reaching out to current modes in a highly individual way. His temperament and upbringing incline him to introspection and gravity of mood : had he been born a decade or so earlier, he would have been an outstanding figure in the Generation of '98. Of the poems which follow, the first, retaining some Modernistic motifs, is, both in style and in content, typically of his *tierra* ; the two others, individual, serious and reflective, are typically himself.

328. *Galeras de plata*

Galeras de plata por el río azul. . . .
¿ Dónde vais, afanes de mi juventud ?

Abiertas las velas y los estandartes,
reís en las febles entrañas del aire.

Galeras de plata por el río azul,
que sois los ensueños de mi juventud.

¿ No habrá un banco donde las proas encallen ?
¡ Ay, la irresistencia del agua y del aire !

Galeras de plata por el río azul.
¿ Se irá la ufanía de mi juventud ?

Los ojos del puente son chicos. . . . Si caben.
—¿ Pasaron ?
—Palomas pasaron suaves. . . .

Sobre una de ellas, por el río azul,
¡ Emperatriz blanca, te alejabas tú !

329. *Ritmo roto*

He perdido el ritmo
y sólo veo fealdad ;
deshechas las arquitecturas ;
los colores sin separar ;
las palabras, vasos
rotos, que cortan la verdad.

He perdido el ritmo
y sólo veo mi maldad.
No entiendo mis palabras viejas
ni tampoco lo que es suspirar.
El bien se quebró en mi alma
y no lo pegaré jamás.

¿ Son los años ? ¡ Dime !
Yo sólo supe meditar ;
y acaso, acaso se deforme
el mundo con el pensar.
¡ Dime ! ¡ Dime ! ¿ Dónde hallo el ritmo
de dulce y hondo compás ?

¿ En el mundo de las personas ?
¿ En la selva montaraz ?
¿ En el río, en el cielo ? ¿ En dónde ?

Dios me pudiera mandar
un afinador, de su cielo,
para este armonio que anda mal :
que decae, disuena y chilla,
y es la avellana de mi mal.

330. *La Verdad*

Un renglón hay en el cielo para mí.
Lo veo, lo estoy mirando ;
no lo puedo traducir,
es cifrado.
Lo entiendo con todo el cuerpo ;
no sé hablarlo.

PEDRO SALINAS

1892

LIKE Díez-Canedo, this Madrileño is an accomplished literary critic, and his output, though not extensive, is of a high quality. No Spanish poet has ever written more convincingly or penetrated more deeply into the reader's mind and heart. Simple, to the point of bareness, competely free from affectations and meretricious devices, he exemplifies the apparent artlessness of the greatest art and enters farther into the soul of poetry than most of his contemporaries.

331. "*No te veo....*"

One of the most poignantly moving poems in contemporary Spanish literature. Behind a wall of art as delicate and fragile as that which it pictures, beat waves of emotion, perfectly controlled. In the climax, the last four lines, the emotion almost breaks its bounds. What will happen between "to-day" and "to-morrow"? Where will the loved one be "to-morrow"? Is the "wall" distance, death, or the changes wrought by time? To each his own interpretation, provided he remembers that the wall is "fragile". These are a few, but are far from being all, of the reflections and emotions which the poem creates for us.

No te veo. Bien sé
que estás aquí, detrás
de una frágil pared
de ladrillos y cal, bien al alcance
de mi voz, si llamara.
Pero no llamaré.

Te llamaré mañana,
cuando al no verte ya,
me imagine que sigues
aquí cerca, a mi lado,
y que basta hoy la voz
que ayer no quise dar.
Mañana . . . cuando estés
allá detrás de una
frágil pared de vientos,
de cielos y de años.

332. " *¿ Lloverá otra vez mañana. . . .?* "

Like the preceding poem, this is from Salinas' early volume Presagios *(1923), which contains some of his best work. A whole world of experience is built around a simple, conversational question. As behind the words " No te veo ", so behind four monosyllables " Yo no lo sé ", lie volumes of emotion. In this poem, however, the author gives rein to his delicate fancy and his powerful imagination, so that, like the masterpieces of San Juan de la Cruz, the lines may be taken at their face value, as a " nature poem ", a " spring song ", and nothing more.*

" ¿ Lloverá otra vez mañana ? "
¿ Alma, tú me lo preguntas ?
Yo no lo sé.
Brillando están las estrellas
como niñas bien bañadas
en el gran río del día ;
ahora
limpias y gozosas saltan
por el campo azul del cielo.
El árbol tiene un verdor
sin usar y es un chiquillo
que lloraba por tener
vestido nuevo y la madre
primavera se lo dió.
La brisa es más fresca ; el alma
siente que pasa por ella

algo nuevo, que es un cauce
que estuvo seco y que vuelve
a conducir su caudal.
Y un gozo nunca sentido,
un verdor, unas estrellas
y un río que vuelve a andar
son un augurio bien claro.
Alma, tú me lo preguntas :
" ¿ Lloverá otra vez mañana ? "
Yo no sé más.

333. *Orilla*

Another fine sea-piece—an enigma, one might say, with its solution in the last line. Every phrase has its significance and its charm, embroidering the simple idea that, but for the distant flecks of foam—" white roses "—this July sea would appear quite motionless. Contrast the descriptive intensity of ll. 1-2 with the descriptive range of ll. 6-8, and the almost dramatic force of ll. 7-8 with the tranquil and satisfying close in l. 9.

¿ Si no fuera por la rosa
frágil, de espuma, blanquísima,
que él, a lo lejos, se inventa,
quién me iba a decir a mí
que se le movía el pecho
de respirar, que está vivo,
que tiene un ímpetu dentro,
que quiere la tierra entera,
azul, quieto, mar de julio ?

334. *Mirar lo invisible*

A backward glance to that Romantic vagueness which the Romantics called " northern ", to Romantic emotions heightened by the sensibility of the modern poet and defined by his consummate artistry. The problem, presented in a sharpened form and resolved by a solution which is no solution at all, is of universal applicability. Its skilful presentation intrigues the reader, compels his attention, then haunts him. A poem not easily forgotten.

La tarde me está ofreciendo
en la palma de su mano,
hecha de enero y de niebla,
vagos mundos desmedidos
de esos que yo antes soñaba,
que hoy ya no quiero.
Y cerraría los ojos
para no verlo. Si no
los cierro
no es por lo que veo.
Por un mundo sospechado
concreto y virgen detrás,
por lo que no puedo ver
llevo los ojos abiertos.

JORGE GUILLÉN

1893

ANOTHER Castilian, who, like Salinas, spent much of his early manhood in Seville, and, like him too, emigrated to the United States. Less simple than Salinas and of a more limited appeal, he is an intellectual who has carried *depuración* to a very fine art and is intent on *poesía pura*—or, as he prefers to call it, *poesía simple*—of which Onís goes so far as to term him " la manifestación más alta en España."[1] In *Cántico* (1936), which, rather than a collection of poems, is a single creative effort, Guillén has left a poetic testament ranking with the work of García Lorca and Antonio Machado as one of the modern period's most significant achievements.

335. *Primavera delgada*

A poem of impressions and sensations, notable for its skill in progression, for its use of suspense and climax, for the smooth flow of its verse and for the melody of the assonances in which the short lines echo the long.

Cuando el espacio, sin perfil, resume
con una nube

su vasta indecisión a la deriva. . . .
¿ dónde la orilla ?

Mientras el río con el rumbo en curva
se perpetúa

buscando sesgo a sesgo, dibujante,
su desenlace,

mientras el agua, duramente verde,
niega sus peces

[1] O., p. 1086.

bajo el profundo equívoco reflejo
de un aire trémulo. . . .

Cuando conduce la mañana, lentas,
sus alamedas

gracias a las estelas vibradoras
entre las frondas,

a favor del avance sinuoso
que pone en coro

la ondulación suavísima del cielo
sobre su viento

con el curso tan ágil de las pompas,
que agudas bogan. . . .

¡ Primavera delgada entre los remos
de los barqueros !

336. *Beato Sillón*

Whether building them, as in the next poem, according to the traditional plan, or whether, as here, giving variety to that plan by a bold use of the cæsura, Guillén is particularly successful in his décimas. *This little poem, full of dignity, nobility and a serene optimism, is more than worthy of the vessel in which its author places it.*

¡ Beato sillón ! La casa
corrobora su presencia
con la vaga intermitencia
de su invocación en masa
a la memoria. No pasa
nada. Los ojos no ven :
saben. El mundo está bien
hecho ; el instante lo exalta
a marea, de tan alta,
de tan alta, sin vaivén.

337. *La Rosa*

Yo vi la rosa ; clausura
primera de la armonía,
tranquilamente futura.
Su perfección sin porfía
serenaba al ruiseñor,
cruel en el esplendor
espiral del gorgorito.
Y al aire ciñó el espacio
con plenitud de palacio,
y fué ya imposible el grito.

338. *Esos Cerros*

This is perhaps one of the most attractive of Guillén's poems ; and although, as a rule, he is almost exclusively cerebral, it comes near to touching the emotions. It is a symphony in grey : indeed, it is greyness itself, for greyness captures the untrodden solitudes and takes their place, till the entire scene, with all the unseen beyond stretching out towards oblivion, is filled with nothing else. The ethereal diaphaneity of this poem may be contrasted with the opaque quality of Jiménez's " Mar, nada " (p. 652).

¿ Pureza, soledad ? Allí : son grises.
Grises intactos que ni el pie perdido
sorprendió, soberanamente leves.
Grises junto a la Nada, melancólica,
bella, que el aire acoge como un alma,
visible de tan fiel a un fin ; la espera.
—¡ Ser, ser, y aun más remota, para el humo,
para los ojos de los más absortos,
una Nada amparada : gris intacto
sobre tierna aridez, gris de esos cerros !

GERARDO DIEGO

1896

INDEBTED to, and inspired by, Juan Ramón Jiménez as were the younger post-Modernist poets, they were not content merely to follow him. Individuals and groups struck out for themselves in all directions, some with considerable *acierto* and some with none. About 1919, with the emergence of a vocal but not very productive group of so-called " Ultraístas ", began a period of remarkable poetic activity which even the catastrophic and cataclysmic years that followed the Second Republic have not succeeded in arresting. The features which most phases of this activity have in common are the rejection of Modernism—at any rate, in its superficial manifestations—and the quest for *poesía pura*. With one exception no attempt will be made to label or classify the poets who follow: the exception is Gerardo Diego, whose *creacionismo*, like that of Huidobro (*d.*1948) in America, more nearly represents the present-day tendency of poetry that any of the other modes, some of which had more reality and significance than the rest, whose names may or may not pass into history.

Creacionismo, as its name suggests, aims at making poetry creative and vital. " La poesía es la creación," says Diego, in his anthology *Poesía española*. " No reflejo de algo, sino apariencia, ilusión de sí propia. Imagen libre, creada y creadora." *Creacionismo*, like the *literatura de vanguardia* in general, has reacted completely against the conventions that poetry should be content with describing, with painting or with singing:

> ¿ Por qué cantáis la rosa, oh poetas ?
> *¡ Hacedla florecer en el poema !*[1]

" Crear lo que nunca veremos, esto es la Poesía."[2]

[1] Huidobro: "Arte poética." O., p. 1129. [2] Diego, pp. 264-5.

339. *Romance del Duero*

One of the achievements of the vanguardistas, *as of the Romantics of a century earlier, is the revival and the revitalization of the mediaeval ballad. The extraordinary malleability of this type of poem, in the hands of masters of verse through successive ages, is a testimony to its genuinely native quality. This particular ballad, presumably inspired by "Río-Verde. . . ." (p. 141), shows that the simple devices of mediaeval art can be combined with the most modern and sophisticated use of imagery and that the form can be as successfully reflective as it has been descriptive and lyrical.*

Río Duero, río Duero,
nadie a acompañarte baja,
nadie se detiene a oír
tu eterna estrofa de agua.

Indiferente o cobarde
la ciudad vuelve la espalda.
No quiere ver en tu espejo
su muralla desdentada.

Tú, viejo Duero, sonríes
entre tus barbas de plata,
moliendo con tus romances
las cosechas mal logradas.

Y entre los santos de piedra
y los álamos de magia
pasas llevando en tus ondas
palabras de amor, palabras.

Quién pudiera como tú
a la vez quieto y en marcha,
cantar siempre el mismo verso
pero con distinta agua.

Río Duero, río Duero,
nadie a estar contigo baja,
ya nadie quiere atender
tu eterna estrofa olvidada,

sino los enamorados
que preguntan por sus almas
y siembran en tus espumas
palabras de amor, palabras.

340. *El Ciprés de Silos*

A Santanderino, Diego might in another epoch have been a poet of the Montaña or the Meseta. This sonnet, from his Versos humanos *(1925), goes back to the descriptive manner of an earlier age. Unexceptionably Classical in form, it cleaves the mind with its vivid figures as cleanly as the lance-like cypress cleaves the Castilian sky.*

Enhiesto surtidor de sombra y sueño
que acongojas el cielo con tu lanza.
Chorro que a las estrellas casi alcanza
devanado a sí mismo en loco empeño.

Mástil de soledad, prodigio isleño;
flecha de fe, saeta de esperanza.
Hoy llegó a ti, riberas del Arlanza,
peregrina al azar, mi alma sin dueño.

Cuando te vi, señero, dulce, firme,
qué ansiedades sentí de diluirme
y ascender como tú, vuelto en cristales,

como tú, negra torre de arduos filos,
ejemplo de delirios verticales,
mudo ciprés en el fervor de Silos.

341. *La Giralda*

Another striking sonnet of Classical type, this time inspired by the south, with the colour and elegance that southern themes demand.

Giralda en prisma puro de Sevilla,
nivelada del plomo y de la estrella,
molde en engaste azul, torre sin mella,
palma de arquitectura sin semilla.

Si su espejo la brisa enfrente brilla,
no te contemples—ay, Narcisa—en ella;
que no se mude esa tu piel doncella,
toda naranja al sol que se te humilla.

Al contraluz de luna limonera,
tu arista es el bisel, hoja barbera,
que su más bella vertical depura.

Resbala el tacto su caricia vana.
Yo mudéjar te quiero y no cristiana.
Volumen nada más : base y altura.

342. *Guitarra*

Here is creacionismo. *At first glance the words seem meaningless, as indeed they would have been to Rivas and Núñez de Arce. Diego's images—to adapt the observation of a recent critic—are like arrows shot from the bow on a mediaeval battlefield. To one content with picking them up and curiously turning them over they seem to have no significance. But when the impression which each image conveys has sunk into the reader's mind—the " silencio verde " : contrast Juan Ramón's " silencio azul y violeta " ; the " positive " silence of the " guitarras destrenzadas " ; the conception of the guitar as a well—a new process begins in the receptive and expressive mind, and new sensations, a new picture emerge. That is the process of creation.*

Habrá un silencio verde
todo hecho de guitarras destrenzadas.

La guitarra es un pozo
con viento en vez de agua.

DÁMASO ALONSO
1898

DÁMASO ALONSO, a distinguished scholar and creative critic whose studies of Golden Age language and poetic technique have had a great influence on the younger generation of Spanish poets, is himself, too, an interesting poet showing a steady line of development from purely formal values to an ever deepening emotional content.

343. *Mañana lenta*

His first verses had the simplicity and nostalgic melancholy of the early poems of Antonio Machado. A Nature-background, sketched in with a few impressionistic strokes, a mood of resigned grief that arises out of the landscape, takes shape for a few moments and then dies away: that is " Mañana lenta ".

Mañana lenta,
cielo azul,
campo verde,
tierra vinariega.
Y tú, mañana, que me llevas.
Carreta
demasiado lenta,
carreta
demasiado llena
de mi hierba nueva,
temblorosa y fresca,
que ha de llegar—sin darme cuenta—
seca,
—sin saber cómo—
seca.

344. *Morir*

There followed a period of expressionistic imagery and Surrealist influences. "Morir" develops a theme that is to preoccupy the poet from now on: it conveys emotion, not directly, but through ase lected range of personal symbols of solitude, confusion and terror.

Por un sahara de nieblas,
caravana de la noche,
el viento dice a la noche
tu secreto.

Y el eco, buho a intervalos,
te lo trae de vuelta, ciego,
—paños de la noche—ciego.

Mundos fríos bajo lunas,
de saberlo a eternidades
y niebla, se están muriendo.

De niebla que poco a poco
te va parando a ti yertos
pies y manos, corazón
—farolillo de tu pecho,
verbena de junio, al río—.

De niebla que un hoyo negro,
engualdrapado de espantos
—¡ martillo del eco, viento !—
cuévano de claridades,
sombra, te está construyendo.

345. *Cancioncilla*

"Cancioncilla" represents another facet of Dámaso Alonso's poetic personality. Like García Lorca and Alberti, he draws on traditional folk-elements and charges their archaic simplicity with the overtones of a modern sensibility expressed with all the resources of verbal melody and skilled technique.

Otros querrán mausoleos
donde cuelguen los trofeos ;
donde nadie ha de llorar,

y yo no los quiero, no
(que lo digo en un cantar)
porque yo

morir quisiera en el viento,
como la gente de mar
en el mar.

Me podrían enterrar
en la ancha fosa del viento.

¡ Oh, qué dulce descansar,
ir sepultado en el viento,
como un capitán del viento ;
como un capitán del mar
muerto en medio de la mar !

346. *Hombre*

A typical poem of the latest period, " Hombre " produces its intense emotional effect by an accumulation of violent impressions, linked by subconscious associations and finally converging to produce the startling frisson *of the last line.*

Hombre,
gárrula tolvanera
entre la torre y el azul redondo,
vencejo de una tarde, algarabía
desierta de un verano.

Hombre, borrado en la expresión, disuelto
en ademán : sólo flautín bardaje,
sólo terca trompeta,
híspida en el solar contra las tapias.

Hombre,
melancólico grito,
¡ oh solitario y triste
garlador ! : ¿ dices algo, tienes algo
que decir a los hombres o a los cielos ?
¿ Y no es esa amargura
de tu grito, la densa pesadilla
del monólogo eterno y sin respuesta ?

Hombre,
cárabo de tu angustia,
agüero de tus días
estériles, ¿ qué aúllas, can, qué gimes ?
¿ Se te ha perdido el amo ?
No : se ha muerto.
¡ Se te ha podrido el amo en noches hondas,
y apenas sólo es ya polvo de estrellas !
Deja, deja ese grito,
ese inútil plañir, sin eco, en vaho.
Porque nadie te oirá. Solo. Estás solo.

FEDERICO GARCÍA LORCA
1899-1936

His untimely death during the Spanish Civil War—a tragedy for Spanish letters—has brought García Lorca into public notice to an extent which the quality of his work would itself fully justify. Even if we leave aside his plays, in which he touches real greatness, he stands well above most of his contemporaries. By birth a Granadino, and in character a southerner to the backbone, he devoted much of his energy to the re-creation of popular southern verse-forms; yet he excels also in the refined art of the *vanguardistas* and can be simple or cerebral at will. It is not a matter of progression, though the maturity of the later collections by comparison with the earlier is remarkable, but of the most marked versatility: so greatly does he excel in each type of poem that one would suppose he had cultivated it to the exclusion of all else.

347. *Canción de Jinete*

Here, for example, is a poem to which can be applied only one adjective—perfect. Around the objective, dramatic picture of the traveller on the black pony, the red moon, the distant towers of Córdoba and ambushed Death lies the oppressive atmosphere of suspense and mystery which all the technique of a skilled word-artist has gone to create. The tema, *for example,*

Córdoba.
Lejana y sola.

is no more than three deep notes of a bell, the echoes of the last and loudest of which are caught up faintly by the o-a *assonances, till, as the picture fades, they ring out again loudly and clearly. Again, the jogging rhythm of the second stanza gives what has been called "the nightmare sense of going on and on and yet never arriving" and the contrast between material and supernatural in the last stanza is admirably, because so subtly, hinted at. A poignancy which the author never intended is added to the piece by the reflection that he journeyed with some hesitancy from Madrid southward after the Civil War had begun, and that, as it proved, he was journeying to his death.*[1]

Córdoba.
Lejana y sola.

Jaca negra, luna grande,
y aceitunas en mi alforja.
Aunque sepa los caminos
yo nunca llegaré a Córdoba.

Por el llano, por el viento,
jaca negra, luna roja.
La muerte me está mirando
desde las torres de Córdoba.

¡ Ay qué camino tan largo !
¡ Ay mi jaca valerosa !
¡ Ay que la muerte me espera,
antes de llegar a Córdoba !

Córdoba.
Lejana y sola.

348. *Es verdad*

Some of the measure of García Lorca's versatility may be found by contrasting this poem with the last. Instead of the objective, the pictorial, the dramatic and the highly artistic we have a simple, personal, emotional ditty of a popular type rising only to the heights of a somewhat crude fantasy and not afraid to descend to bathos.

¡ Ay qué trabajo me cuesta
quererte como te quiero !

Por tu amor me duele el aire,
el corazón
y el sombrero.

[1] A critical account of this poem, by Audrey Lumsden, will be found in *B.S.S.*, 1944, XXI, 37-9.

¿ Quién me compraría a mí.
este cintillo que tengo
y esta tristeza de hilo
blanco, para hacer pañuelos ?
¡ Ay qué trabajo me cuesta
quererte como te quiero !

349. *Baladilla de los Tres Ríos*

Like Diego's " Romance del Duero ", with which it has a good deal in common, this is a modern adaptation of mediaeval balladry, with dramatic and tragic undertones and a typically mediaeval refrain.

El río Guadalquivir
va entre naranjos y olivos.
Los dos ríos de Granada
bajan de la nieve al trigo.

¡ Ay, amor
que se fué y no vino !

El río Guadalquivir
tiene las barbas granates.
Los dos ríos de Granada,
uno llanto y otro sangre.

¡ Ay, amor
que se fué por el aire !

Para los barcos de vela
Sevilla tiene un camino ;
por el agua de Granada
sólo reman los suspiros.

¡ Ay, amor
que se fué y no vino !

Guadalquivir, alta torre
y viento en los naranjales.
Dauro y Genil, torrecillas
muertas sobre los estanques.

¡ Ay, amor
que se fué por el aire !

¡ Quién dirá que el agua lleva
un fuego fatuo de gritos !

¡ Ay, amor
que se fué y no vino !

Lleva azahar, lleva olivas,
Andalucía, a tus mares.

¡ Ay, amor
que se fué por el aire !

350. *Oda al Santísimo Sacramento del Altar*

Few contemporary poets write much of religion, but García Lorca would not be a southerner if religion, of the southern type, had no place in his poetry. He was, in fact, as a child, much given to " playing at church ", saying masses and making altars, just as Santa Teresa was to playing at convents. The deeply engrained belief which inspires this poem, its sensitiveness to material impressions, the intensity of its emotion and the boldness of its language make it noteworthy. Only a southerner, however, could have written it.

EXPOSICIÓN

Pange lingua gloriosi corporis mysterium.

Cantaban las mujeres por el muro clavado
cuando te vi, Dios fuerte, vivo en el Sacramento,
palpitante y desnudo, como un niño que corre
perseguido por siete novillos capitales.

Vivo estabas, Dios mío, dentro del ostensorio.
Punzado por tu Padre con agujas de lumbre.
Latiendo como el pobre corazón de la rana
que los médicos ponen en el frasco de vidrio.

Piedra de soledad donde la hierba gime
y donde el agua oscura pierde sus tres acentos,
elevan tu columna de nardo bajo nieve
sobre el mundo de ruedas y falos que circula.

Yo miraba tu forma deliciosa flotando
en la llaga de aceites y paño de agonía,
y entornaba mis ojos para dar en el dulce
tiro al blanco de insomnio sin un pájaro negro.

Es así, Dios andado, como quiero tenerte.
Panderito de harina para el recién nacido.
Brisa y materia juntas en expresión exacta
por amor de la carne que no sabe tu nombre.

Es así, forma breve de rumor inefable,
Dios en mantillas, Cristo diminuto y eterno,
repetido mil veces, muerto, crucificado
por la impura palabra del hombre sudoroso.

Cantaban las mujeres en la arena sin norte,
cuando te vi presente sobre tu Sacramento.
Quinientos serafines de resplandor y tinta
en la cúpula neutra gustaban tu racimo.

¡ Oh, Forma sacratísima, vértice de las flores,
donde todos los ángulos toman sus luces fijas,
donde número y boca construyen un presente
cuerpo de luz humana con músculos de harina !

¡ Oh, Forma limitada para expresar concreta
muchedumbre de luces y clamor escuchado !
¡ Oh, nieve circundada por témpanos de música!
¡ Oh, llama crepitante sobre todas las venas !

MUNDO

Agnus Dei qui tollis peccata mundi. Miserere nobis.

Noche de los tejados y la planta del pie,
silbaba por los ojos secos de las palomas.
Alga y cristal en fuga ponen plata mojada
los hombros de cemento de todas las ciudades.

La gillette descansaba sobre los tocadores
con su afán impaciente de cuello seccionado.
En la casa del muerto los niños perseguían
una sierpe de arena por el rincón oscuro.

Escribientes dormidos en el piso catorce.
Ramera con los senos de cristal arañado.
Cables y media luna con temblores de insecto.
Bares sin gente. Gritos. Cabezas por el agua.

Para el asesinato del ruiseñor, venían
tres mil hombres armados de lucientes cuchillos.
Viejas y sacerdotes lloraban resistiendo
una lluvia de lenguas y hormigas voladoras.

Noche de rostro blanco. Nula noche sin rostro.
Bajo el Sol y la Luna. Triste noche del Mundo.
Dos mitades opuestas y un hombre que no sabe
cuándo su mariposa dejará los relojes.

Debajo de las alas del dragón hay un niño.
Caballitos de cardio por la estrella sin sangre.
El unicornio quiere lo que la rosa olvida,
y el pájaro pretende lo que las aguas vedan.

Sólo tu Sacramento de luz en equilibrio,
aquietaba la angustia del amor desligado.
Sólo tu Sacramento, manómetro que salva
corazones lanzados a quinientos por hora.

Porque tu signo es clave de llanura celeste
donde naipe y herida se entrelazan cantando,
donde la luz desboca su toro relumbrante
y se afirma el aroma de la rosa templada.

Porque tu signo expresa la brisa y el gusano.
Punto de unión y cita del siglo y el minuto.
Orbe claro de muertos y hormiguero de vivos
con el hombre de nieves y el negro de la llama.

Mundo, ya tienes meta para tu desamparo,
para tu honor perenne de agujero sin fondo.
¡Oh, Cordero cautivo de tres voces iguales!
¡Sacramento inmutable de amor y disciplina!

EMILIO PRADOS
1899

LIKE his younger contemporary Alberti (p. 693), Emilio Prados cultivated in his youth a simple style which many will prefer to the more involved manner of his later period when he found a part of his inspiration in politics. Though somewhat lacking in depth, he will always attract by his sincerity, imagination, and melodious language. The pieces here reprinted seem to need no commentary.

351. *Calma*

Cielo gris.
Suelo rojo.
De un olivo a otro
vuela el tordo.

En la tarde hay un sapo
de ceniza y oro.

Suelo gris.
Cielo rojo. . .

—Quedó la luna enredada
en el olivar.
Quedó la luna olvidada—.

352. *Amanecer*

¡ Qué cerca ! ¡ Desde mi ojo a tu
ojo, ni el canto de un alma !
Engarzados sobre el viento,
cómo pájaros a un mismo
cinto, prendidos al cielo
estamos los dos. ¡ Qué juntos

nuestros perfiles en medio
del día ! ¡ Qué altos van ! ¡ Qué limpios
vuelan arriba, ya sueltos,
libres del mundo, los rostros,
flotando en la luz ; abiertos
como dos flores sin tallo,
en ella, vivos, sin cuerpo
que los pueda sujetar
abajo en lo hondo, al suelo !
Juntos, por entre las nubes
están volando, altos, quietos,
parados igual que estrellas
del alba y aun más serenos
que estrellas, como dos plumas,
igual que peces del viento
suspendidos sobre él
con el sedal del silencio,
que los mantiene colgados,
por los ojos, sobre el sueño

VICENTE ALEIXANDRE

1900

THE career of the Sevilian Vicente Aleixandre has shown an interesting development from the ingenious imagery of the earliest collection through a period of Surrealist fantasy to the emotional intensity and technical achievement of his latest works. He now enjoys a position of great prestige among contemporary Spanish writers.

353. *Posesión*

Taken from his earliest collection (Ámbito, *1928*), *this is perhaps the most balanced poem which it contains, illustrating at once the poet's subtlety and simplicity, his extreme sensitiveness to exterior impressions and his bold identification of himself with the world of Nature.*

Negros de sombra. Caudales
de lentitud. Impaciente
se esfuerza en armar la luna
sobre la sombra sus puentes.

(¿ De plata ? Son levadizos
cuando, bizarro, de frente,
de sus puertos despegado
cruzar el día se siente).

Ahora los rayos desgarran
la sombra espesa. Reciente,
todo el paisaje se muestra,
abierto y mudo, evidente.

Húmedos pinceles tocan
las superficies, se mueven
ágiles, brillantes ; tensos
brotan a flor los relieves.

Extendido ya el paisaje
está. Su mantel, no breve,
flores y frutos de noche,
en dulce peso, sostiene.

La noche, madura toda,
gravita sobre la nieve
hilada. ¿ Qué zumos densos
dará en mi mano caliente ?

Su pompa rompe la cárcel
exacta, y la pulpa ardiente,
constelada de pepitas
iluminadas, se vierte.

Mis rojos labios la sorben.
Hundo en su yema mis dientes.
Toda mi boca se llena
de amor, de fuegos presentes.

Ebrio de luces, de noche,
de brillos, mi cuerpo extiende
sus miembros, ¿ pisando estrellas ? ,
temblor pisando celeste.

La noche en mí. Yo la noche.
Mis ojos ardiendo. Tenue,
sobre mi lengua naciendo
un sabor a alba creciente.

354. *La Verdad*

From Sombra del Paraíso (*1944*) *comes this splendidly impetuous evocation of former love. Typical in its fusion of the human element with Nature imagery, it gains its effect by the almost physical impact of its sensuous vitality.*

¿ Qué sonríe en la sombra sin muros que ensordece
mi corazón ? ¿ Qué soledad levanta
sus torturados brazos sin luna y grita herida
a la noche ? ¿ Quién canta sordamente en las ramas ?

Pájaros no: memoria de pájaros. Sois eco,
sólo eco, pluma vil, turbia escoria, muerta materia sorda
aquí en mis manos. Besar una ceniza
no es besar el amor. Morder una seca rama
no es poner estos labios brillantes sobre un seno
cuya turgencia tibia dé lumbre a estos marfiles
rutilantes. ¡El sol, el sol deslumbra!

Separar un vestido crujiente, resto inútil
de una ciudad. Poner desnudo
el manantial, el cuerpo luminoso, fluyente,
donde sentir la vida ferviente entre los ramos
tropicales, quemantes, que un ecuador empuja.

Bebed, bebed la rota pasión de un mediodía
que en el cenit revienta sus luces y os abrasa
volcadamente entero, y os funde. ¡Muerte hermosa vital,
ascua del día! ¡Selva virgen que en llamas te destruyes!

LUIS CERNUDA

1902

PERHAPS the most powerful of the poets born in the present century, though essentially a poet of the *tour d'ivoire*, the Andalusian Luis Cernuda began his career under the apparent influence of Guillén: compare, for example, the *décimas* of his *Primeras Poesías* with " Beato Sillón " (p. 667). But he was too original a genius not to strike out boldly for himself, and, after slowly climbing to maturity, he has remained at a consistently high level—a poet to the finger-tips, whether in the verse of *Las Nubes* (1937-40) or in the prose of *Ocnos* (1942). Never deflected by current modes from his quest for *poesía pura*, he at once delights and moves the reader by his fine and delicate treatment of lyric themes, his diaphanous images, his intricately woven network of thought. Like more than one of his predecessors, he is often difficult, but seldom obscure, and the creative energy which he releases in those who strive to know him proves an ample reward.

355. " *Se goza en sueño encantado. . . .* "

This example of Cernuda's early décimas *is a remarkable illustration of the skilful manipulation of metaphor in the service of emotion and sensation. Limpid lake and silvered mirror fuse and fade before the " inmóvil paroxismo " which is the central moment of experience re-lived (it would seem) rather than described.*

Se goza en sueño encantado.
tras espacio infranqueable,
su belleza irreparable
el Narciso enamorado.

Ya diamante azogado
o agua helada, se desata
y humanas rosas dilata
en inmóvil paroxismo,
dejando sólo en su abismo
fugaz memoria de plata.

356. "*Escondido en los muros. . . .*"

Several of the Primeras Poesías, *from which both this and the last poem are taken, seem to be attempting, with an extraordinary degree of success, to capture and record the sensations born of solitude. Here again every phrase, every word, seems to have been lived before being written, and penetrates as it touches the reader's mind.*

Escondido en los muros
este jardín me brinda
sus ramas y sus aguas
de secreta delicia.

¡ Qué silencio ! ¿ Es así
el mundo ? Cruza el cielo
desfilando paisajes,
risueño hacia lo lejos.

Tierra indolente. En vano
resplandece el destino.
Junto a las aguas quietas
sueño y pienso que vivo.

Mas el tiempo ya tasa
el poder de esta hora ;
madura su medida
escapa entre sus rosas.

Y el aire fresco vuelve
con la noche cercana,
su tersura olvidando
las ramas y las aguas.

357. *Jardín antiguo*

A not dissimilar, but maturer and more sensuous picture of what is no doubt a garden in Seville. It suggests, by its explicitness and intense clarity, a return to an earlier type of art.

Ir de nuevo al jardín cerrado,
que tras los arcos de la tapia,
entre magnolios, limoneros,
guarda el encanto de las aguas.

Oír de nuevo en el silencio,
vivo de trinos y de hojas,
el susurro tibio del aire
donde las almas viejas flotan.

Ver otra vez el cielo hondo
a lo lejos, la torre esbelta
tal flor de luz sobre las palmas :
las cosas todas siempre bellas.

Sentir otra vez, como entonces,
la espina aguda del deseo,
mientras la juventud pasada
vuelve. ¡ Sueño de un dios sin tiempo !

358. *Atardecer en la Catedral*

This longer specimen of the poet's mature art, showing the most delicate sensitiveness to every kind of impression—visual, auditory, tactile—can be trusted to make its appeal without substantial commentary. Once again we have a combination of extreme economy of expression with the utmost penetrative beauty : every nuance has significance and every word and phrase enfolds a core of experiential truth.

Por las calles desiertas, nadie. El viento
y la luz sobre las tapias
que enciende los aleros al sol último.
Tras una puerta se queja el agua oculta.
Ven a la catedral, alma de soledad temblando.

Cuando el labrador deja en esta hora,
abierta ya la tierra con los surcos,
nace de la obra hecha gozo y calma.
Cerca de Dios se halla el pensamiento.

Algunos chopos secos, llama ardida
levantan por el campo, como el humo
alegre en los tejados de las casas.
Vuelve un rebaño junto al arroyo oscuro
donde duerme la tarde entre la hierba.
El frío está naciendo y es el cielo más hondo.

Tal un sueño de piedra, de música callada,
desde la flecha erguida de la torre
hasta la lonja de anchas losas grises,
la catedral extática aparece,
toda reposo : vidrio, madera, bronce,
fervor puro a la sombra de los siglos.

Una vigilia dicen esos ángeles
y su espada desnuda sobre el pórtico,
florido con sonrisas por los santos viejos,
como huerto de otoño que brotara
musgos entre las rosas esculpidas.

Aquí encuentran la paz los hombres vivos,
paz de los odios, paz de los amores,
olvido dulce y largo, donde el cuerpo
fatigado se baña en las tinieblas.

Entra en la catedral, ve por las naves altas
de esbelta bóveda, gratas a los pasos
errantes sobre el mármol, entre columnas,
hacia el altar, ascua serena,
gloria propicia al alma solitaria.

Como el niño descansa, porque cree
en la fuerza prudente de su padre ;
con el vivir callado de las cosas
sobre el haz inmutable de la tierra,
transcurren estas horas en el templo.

No hay lucha ni temor, no hay pena ni deseo,
todo queda aceptado hasta la muerte
y olvidado tras de la muerte, contemplando,
libres del cuerpo, y adorando,
necesidad del alma exenta de deleite.

Apagándose van aquellos vidrios
del alto ventanal, y apenas si con oro
tristes se irisan débilmente. Muere el día,
pero la paz perdura postrada entre la sombra.

El suelo besan quedos unos pasos
lejanos. Alguna forma, a solas,
reza caída ante una vasta reja
donde palpita el ala de una llama amarilla.

Llanto escondido moja el alma,
sintiendo la presencia de un poder misterioso
que el consuelo creara para el hombre,
sombra divina hablando en el silencio.

Aromas, brotes vivos surgen,
afirmando la vida, tal savia de la tierra
que irrumpe en milagrosas formas verdes.
Secreto entre los muros de este templo,
el soplo animador de nuestro mundo
pasa y orea la noche de los hombres.

RAFAEL ALBERTI

1903

In the poetry of Alberti can be traced a more definite progression than in that of any of his leading contemporaries. A native of Cádiz, he first became known by poems simple in theme and texture, inspired by Gil Vicente and the *Cancioneros*—and, as one would expect in the juvenilia of a Gaditano, by the sea. After publishing three collections of this type (1925-7) he embraced the Baroque (*Cal y canto*, 1926-7), and since then has combined, or alternated, Surrealism (*Sobre los Ángeles*, 1927-8) with political verse of an advanced Socialistic nature, the latter in particular during the last years of the Second Republic and throughout the Civil War. The first three poems given here are from the earlier collections; the other three from the later.

359. *Con él*

A boyish poem, but full of charm. Young as he is, the author has caught the authentic manner of the Middle Ages. Note how he identifies himself with the sea (l. 4): "Yo marinero", he calls himself in the same collection.

Si Garcilaso volviera,
yo sería su escudero;
que buen caballero era.

Mi traje de marinero
se trocaría en guerrera
ante el brillar de su acero;
que buen caballero era.

¡ Qué dulce oírle, guerrero,
al borde de su estribera !
En la mano mi sombrero;
que buen caballero era.

360. *Sueño*

With its symmetrical quadripartite construction, its dream-like yet dynamic unreality, and its pursuit of the picturesque, this boat-song too bears the impress of youth. But it is highly evocative and holds promise of great power.

Noche.
Verde caracol, la luna.
Sobre todas las terrazas,
blancas doncellas desnudas.

¡ Remadores, a remar !
De la tierra emerge el globo
que ha de morir en el mar.

Alba.
Dormíos, blancas doncellas,
hasta que el globo no caiga
en brazos de la marea.

¡ Remadores, a remar,
hasta que el globo no duerma
entre los senos del mar !

361. *Peñaranda de Duero*

A pretty trifle, probably inspired by Encina's " No te tardes, que me muero, carcelero " (p. 160) and no less melodious than its model. Its mingling of assonance with rime riche, *its play with the sounds* r *and* rr *and the gay inconsequence of the questions which begin and end the poem give it the maximum of charm.*

¿ Por qué me miras tan serio,
carretero ?

Tienes cuatro mulas tordas,
un caballo delantero,
un carro de ruedas verdes,
y la carretera toda
para ti,
carretero.

¿ Qué más quieres ?

362. *Elegía a Garcilaso*

That Alberti's hero-worship of Garcilaso de la Vega lasted may be gathered from this elegy, which appeared in the collection Sermones y moradas *(1929-30). By comparison with most of the poems in that collection it is simple in expression and the long free lines with which the poet was experimenting at the time move along with a genuinely elegiac solemnity, set off by imagery rich as a pall of purple velvet with hangings of gold.*

. . . . antes de tiempo y casi en flor cortada.
G. de la V.

Hubierais visto llorar sangre a las yedras cuando el agua más triste se pasó toda una noche velando a un yelmo ya sin alma,
a un yelmo moribundo sobre una rosa nacida en el vaho que duerme los espejos de los castillos
a esa hora en que los nardos más secos se acuerdan de su vida
al ver que las violetas difuntas abandonan sus cajas
y los laúdes se ahogan por arrullarse a sí mismos.
Es verdad que los fosos inventaron el sueño y los fantasmas.
Yo no sé lo que mira en las almenas esa inmóvil armadura vacía.
¿ Cómo hay luces que decretan tan pronto la agonía de las espadas
si piensan en que un lirio es vigilado por hojas que duran mucho más tiempo ?
Vivir poco y llorando es el sino de la nieve que equivoca su ruta.
En el sur siempre es cortada casi en flor el ave fría.

363. *Defensa de Madrid*

At all times of national crisis, Spanish poets have been found to express their feelings in the traditional romances *(p. xxxix) and Alberti was one of the chief contributors, from the Republican side, to the Romancero of the Spanish Civil War. These noble lines, throbbing with zest and fervour, come from* El Poeta en la calle : Romances de la Guerra de España *(1936).*

Madrid, corazón de España,
late con pulsos de fiebre.
Si ayer la sangre le hervía,
hoy con más calor le hierve.
Ya nunca podrá dormirse,
porque si Madrid se duerme,
querrá despertarse un día
y el alba no vendrá a verle.
No olvides, Madrid, la guerra;
jamás olvides que enfrente
los ojos del enemigo
te echan miradas de muerte.
Rondan por tu cielo halcones
que precipitarse quieren
sobre tus rojos tejados,
tus calles, tu brava gente.
Madrid: que nunca se diga,
nunca se publique o piense
que en el corazón de España
la sangre se volvió nieve.
Fuentes de valor y hombría
las guardas tú donde siempre.
Atroces ríos de asombro
han de correr de esas fuentes.
Que cada barrio a su hora,
si esa mal hora viniere
—hora que no vendrá—, sea
más que la plaza más fuerte.
Los hombres, como castillos;
igual que almenas, sus frentes,
grandes murallas sus brazos,
puertas que nadie penetre.
Quien al corazón de España
quiera asomarse, que llegue.
¡Pronto! Madrid está lejos.
Madrid sabe defenderse
con uñas, con pies, con codos,
con empujones, con dientes,
panza arriba, arisco, recto,
duro, al pie del agua verde

del Tajo, en Navalperal,
en Sigüenza, en donde suenen
balas y balas que busquen
helar su sangre caliente.
Madrid, corazón de España,
que es de tierra, dentro tiene,
si se le escarba, un gran hoyo,
profundo, grande, imponente,
como un barranco que aguarda. . . .
Sólo en él cabe la muerte.

364. *Un Fantasma recorre Europa. . . .*

Finally, this specimen of verse from Alberti's Communistic period (De un momento a otro, *1932-8*) *illustrates his latest manner purged of its worst Surrealistic excesses and displays a flexibility of technique combining with great dignity of tone and working up to a climax of moving power.*

. . . . y las viejas familias cierran las ventanas,
afianzan las puertas,
y el padre corre a oscuras a los Bancos
y el pulso se le para en la Bolsa,
y sueña por las noches con hogueras,
con ganados ardiendo,
que en vez de trigos tiene llamas,
en vez de granos, chispas,
cajas,
cajas de hierro llenas de pavesas.

¿ Dónde estás ?
Nos persiguen a tiros.
¡ Oh !
Los campesinos pasan pisando nuestra sangre.
¿ Qué es esto ?

Cerremos,
cerremos pronto las fronteras.
Vedlo avanzar de prisa en el viento del Este,
de las estepas rojas del hambre.

Que su voz no la oigan los obreros,
que su silbido no penetre en las fábricas,
que no divisen su hoz alzada los hombres de los campos.
¡ Detenedle !

Porque salta los mares,
recorriendo toda la geografía,
porque se esconde en las bodegas de los barcos
y habla a los fogoneros
y los saca tiznados a cubierta,
y hacé que el odio y la miseria se subleven
y se levanten las tripulaciones.

¡ Cerrad,
cerrad las cárceles !
Su voz se estrellará contra los muros.
¿ Qué es esto ?

Pero nosotros lo seguimos,
lo hacemos descender del viento Este que lo trae,
le preguntamos por las estepas rojas de la paz y del triunfo,
lo sentamos a la mesa del campesino pobre,
presentándolo al dueño de la fábrica,
haciéndolo presidir las huelgas y manifestaciones,
hablar con los soldados y los marineros,
ver en las oficinas a los pequeños empleados
y alzar el puño a gritos en los Parlamentos del oro y de la sangre.

Un fantasma recorre Europa,
el mundo.
Nosotros le llamamos camarada.

MANUEL ALTOLAGUIRRE

1905

Altolaguirre, a translator and a printer of the verse of others as well as a poet in his own right, goes farther back, in spirit and manner, than Cernuda, and would often remind one of a nineteenth-century Romantic but for the greater attention which he pays to technique. Declaring at twenty-six that his favourite Spanish poets were Garcilaso de la Vega, San Juan de la Cruz and Juan Ramón Jiménez, he had already written much verse of a highly subjective type, from which, except for one transient phase, he has not notably departed. Emotion, in him, is always stronger than artistry. The two characteristic pieces which follow are self-explanatory.

365. "*Mi soledad llevo dentro. . . .*"

Mi soledad llevo dentro,
torre de ciegas ventanas.
Cuando mis brazos extiendo,
abro sus puertas de entrada
y doy camino alfombrado
al que quiera visitarla.

Pintó el recuerdo los cuadros
que decoran sus estancias.
Allí mis pasadas dichas
con mi pena de hoy contrastan.

¡ Qué juntos los dos estábamos !
¿ Quién el cuerpo ? ¿ Quién el alma ?
Nuestra separación última,
¡ qué muerte fué tan amarga

Ahora dentro de mí llevo
mi alta soledad delgada

366. *¡ Qué jardín de visiones. . . . !*

¡ Qué jardín de visiones intangibles mi cuarto !
¡ Qué delicada y fácil la imagen de tu alma !
¡ Qué parado mi cuerpo por no enturbiar el aire !
Porque mucho te quise ahora te tengo clara
entre tantos confusos sueños que te navegan.
Igual que a mi conciencia la traspasan mis actos,
te surcan los recuerdos gloriosos de tu vida.
Contigo a veces antes—¿ te acuerdas ?—admiraba
en la vida tus bellos límites exteriores.
Ahora dentro de ti como en un cielo estoy,
en un cielo infinito, con los que te quisieron.

JOSÉ GARCÍA NIETO

1914

ONE of the most interesting and significant of the younger generation of Spanish poets is José García Nieto, editor of the poetry review *Garcilaso* and co-founder of the *Juventud Creadora*, a movement which represents a return to traditional themes and forms.

367. *Madrigal a Castilla*

In the sonnet form which is his favourite poetic vehicle García Nieto conveys something of the essence of Castile, with its inviolable serenity. The verses are simple, and the emotion is intense, though restrained.

Aquélla era Castilla, mi morada,
la novia interminable del estío ;
sorprendida de verse en tanto río
tan sin querer fielmente reflejada.

La tierra roja y vuelta la mirada
—¿ por qué rubor y a qué lejano frío ?—,
llena de luz, desnuda de atavío,
castamente te he visto desposada.

¿ Y a qué varón tu limpio plenilunio ?,
¿ en qué labios el beso de tu junio ?,
¿ por qué lecho tu dura geografía ?

Estás aquí, imposible para esposa,
tan sin casar que tienes una rosa
cerrada, indescifrable, todavía.

APPENDIX

368. *Popular Songs from Castile and Andalusia*

THESE selections from Spanish verse would not be complete without some examples of popular poetry ; for " the innumerable songs or *coplas* stored in the living archives of the people's memory form in the aggregate a lyrical poem of such scope, life and beauty as to secure for the Spanish people a place among the great poets of the world."[1] These apparently slight and trivial stanzas, often of no more than three or four short lines in length, reflect all phases of life, from birth to death, and, to those who can read into them their full meaning, reveal many of the depths of the Spanish character. In form, they show the most marked divergences, and a representative, classified selection of *saetas*, *cuartetas*, *seguidillas*, *cantares de ronda* and the rest, would demand the space, not of an appendix, but of a separate volume. The few songs which follow, however, are taken from two well-known collections, and will serve to illustrate the essential virility of the genre—its sturdiness, vigour, verve, intensity, passion and dramatic power—as well as its delicate grace, its picturesqueness and its sensitive insight into the life of the spirit.

I

A todas horas del día
le estoy pidiendo a Jesús
que por su pasión y muerte
me lleve donde estás tú.

" A tomillo y romero
me hueles, niña."
" Como vengo del campo,
no es maravilla."

[1] Salvador de Madariaga : " Spanish popular poetry." In *Shelley and Calderón*, London, 1920, p. 90.

Como platillos de un peso
nuestros corazones son ;
sube el uno, baja el otro,
nunca está fiel el amor.

Creen mis padres que estoy
estudiando en Salamanca,
y estoy queriendo a una niña
como la nieve de blanca.

Cuatro velas encendidas
y un hábito franciscano
es lo que a mí me hace falta
para olvidar a quién amo.

Dicen que tú no me quieres
porque soy algo morena.
Pues morenito es el sol,
morena la gente buena.

Dices que no la quieres
    ni vas a verla,
pero la veredita
    no cría yerba.

Eché un limón a rodar,
en tu puerta se paró.
Hasta los limones saben
que nos queremos los dos.

El día que tú naciste
nacieron todas las flores,
y en la pila del bautismo
cantaban los ruiseñores.

Entre claveles y rosas
te vi asomada a la reja,
lo mismo que está la Virgen
en el altar de la iglesia.

Las golondrinas que anidan
en el hierro de tu reja,
en cuanto llega el invierno
sólo por verte se quedan.

Mi amante es un pino de oro
y una mata de romero.
La pena que a mí me mata,
que le tengo forastero.

Nace la flor en el campo,
la perla viene del mar,
y tú naciste, bien mío,
para hacerme a mí penar.

Por las estrellas del norte
se guían los marineros ;
yo me guío por tus ojos
que son dos claros luceros.

Si supiera que eras firme,
como el sol en el verano,
te entregaría las llaves
de mi pecho soberano.

Tienes en la cara, niña,
lo mejor de cielo y tierra :
dos rosas en tus mejillas,
en tus ojos dos estrellas.

Una estrella se ha perdido
y en el cielo no parece ;
en tu cuarto se ha metido,
en tu cara resplandece.

Yo te quisiera querer,
yo te quisiera adorar,
yo te quisiera poner
de Virgen en el altar.

II

A dormir va la rosa
de los rosales ;
a dormir va mi niño,
porque ya es tarde.

En la puerta del cielo
pender zapatos
para los angelitos
que están descalzos.

Duérmete, niño chiquito,
duérmete y no llores más,
que se irán los angelitos
para no verte llorar.

Quisiera ser Dios del cielo,
reina mía, para darte
la corona del Imperio
y de España el estandarte.

Tienes ojos de paloma,
mejillas de leche y sangre
y los cabellitos rubios,
como la Virgen del Carmen.

Los ojos de mi morena
ni son chicos ni son grandes ;
son como aceitunas negras
de olibaritos gordales.

Tus ojos me cautivaron,
blanca paloma sin hiel ;
tus ojos me cautivaron,
que no los moros de Argel.

Échame, niña bonita,
lágrimas en un pañuelo
y las llevaré a Granada,
que las engarce un platero.

Los colores que asoman
a tus carillos
parecen amapolas
de un verde trigo.

Yo nací en Sierra Morena,
ya una morenita quiero ;
lo moreno es de mi gusto ;
yo por lo moreno muero.

Con la luna te comparo,
con los luceros y el sol,
y, si no fuera pecado,
te comparara con Dios.

El clavel que tú me distes
el día de la Asunción
no fué clavel, sino clavo
que clavó mi corazón.

Toma, niña, esta naranja ;
te la doy porque te quiero ;
no la partas con cuchillo,
que va mi corazón dentro.

Estudiante del alma,
estudia, estudia,
que en llegando a mayores
toda soy tuya.

Dentro de mi pecho tengo
un cofre con una llave ;
muchos pretenden abrirlo
y sólo mi amante cabe.

El corazón te daré,
también te daré la vida ;
y el alma no te la doy,
porque esa prenda no es mía.

Al infierno que te vayas,
tengo que irme contigo,
porque yendo en tu compaña,
llevo la gloria conmigo.

¿ Porque un beso me has dado
riñe tu madre ?
Toma, niña, tu beso ;
dile que calle.

Me dijistes bajando
por la escalera :
" Como por ti no quede,
por mí no queda."
Yo te respondí :
" Como por ti no quede,
no queda por mí."

Tres años después de muerto
y con la tierra en la cara,
si me dieras una voz,
creo que resucitaba.

INDEX TO NAMES OF AUTHORS, WORKS AND EDITIONS IN WHICH THE EXTRACTS CAN BE FOUND

The index is arranged in alphabetical order of the authors excerpted. After each author's name come the numbers of the extracts made from his work, followed in turn by their common source (if any) and the number and source of each individual extract. The edition cited is usually, though not always, that followed in the preparation of the text. The principle adopted has been to give an edition with a good text and at the same time accessible to students.

A

B

C

D

E

F

G

H

I

J

Los nubarrones tristes
le dan sombras al mar.

El agua, férrea,
parece un duro campo llano,
de minas agotadas,
en un arruinamiento
de ruinas.

¡Nada! La palabra, aquí, encuentra
hoy, para mí, su sitio,
como un cadáver de palabra
que se tendiera en su sepulcro
natural.

¡Nada!

L

M

N

P

Q

R

S

Z

INDEX TO FIRST LINES

A

B

C

D

F

G

H

I

J

L

LL

PAGE

M

N

O

P

V

Y

GENERAL INDEX

No references are given to the Index to names of authors, works and editions. Heavy type denotes the pages on which appear the extracts from the works of the author named.

A

B

C

D

E

www.ingramcontent.com/pod-product-compliance
Lightning Source LLC
Chambersburg PA
CBHW020504110726
47899CB00004B/1053